# ANCIENT GREEK DEMOCRACY

## Interpreting Ancient History

The books in this series contain a mixture of the most important previously published articles in ancient history and primary source material upon which the secondary literature is based. The series encourages readers to reflect upon a variety of theories and methodologies, to question the arguments made by scholars, and to begin to master the primary evidence for themselves.

### Published

*Sexuality and Gender in the Classical World*
Laura K. McClure

*Ancient Greek Democracy*
Eric W. Robinson

### Forthcoming

*Roman Imperialism*
Craige Champion

# Ancient Greek Democracy

## READINGS AND SOURCES

*Edited by*
*Eric W. Robinson*

**Blackwell**
Publishing

350 Main Street, Malden, MA 02148-5018, USA
108 Cowley Road, Oxford OX4 1JF, UK
550 Swanston Street, Carlton, Victoria 3053, Australia

First published 2004 by Blackwell Publishing Ltd

*Library of Congress Cataloging-in-Publication Data*

Ancient Greek democracy: readings and sources / edited by Eric W. Robinson.
    p. cm.–(Interpreting ancient history; 2)
  Includes bibliographical references and index.
  ISBN 0-631-23393-8 (alk. paper)–ISBN 0-631-23394-6 (pbk.: alk. paper)
   1. Democracy–Greece–History. 2. Democracy–Greece–Athens–History. I. Robinson, Eric W. II. Series.

  JC75. D36 .A43 2003
  320.938′5′09014–dc21

                                  2002038286

A catalogue record for this title is available from the British Library.

Set in 10 on 12 pt Galliard
by Kolam Information Services Pvt. Ltd, Pondicherry, India
Printed and bound in the United Kingdom
by MPG Books Ltd, Bodmin, Cornwall

For further information on
Blackwell Publishing, visit our website:
http://www.blackwellpublishing.com

# Contents

| | |
|---|---|
| *Preface* | viii |
| *Acknowledgments* | x |
| *Abbreviations* | xii |
| *Map 1* | xiii |
| *Map 2* | xiv |
| Ancient Greek Democracy: A Brief Introduction | 1 |

**1 Prelude to Democracy: Political Thought in Early Greek Texts** — 7

Introduction — 7

*Sources*
Homer, *Iliad* 1.1–305, 2.1–282 — 8
Homer, *Odyssey* 2.1–259 — 21
Hesiod, *Theogony* lines 81–97; *Works and Days* lines 213–269 — 26

*Readings*
Homer and the Beginning of Political Thought in Greece — 28
*Kurt A. Raaflaub*
Commentary on Raaflaub — 41
*Lowell Edmunds*
Equality and the Origins of Greek Democracy — 45
*Ian Morris*
Further Reading — 74

**2 The Beginnings of the Athenian Democracy: Who Freed Athens?** — 76

Introduction — 76

*Sources*
Aristotle, *Constitution of the Athenians* 5–12 — 77

Herodotus, *Histories* 5.62–78                                         81
Thucydides, *History of the Peloponnesian War* 6.53–59                 86
Aristotle, *Constitution of the Athenians* 18–22                       88
Aristotle, *Politics* 1275b34–39, 1319b2–27                            92
The Athenian Archon List                                               93
Drinking Song Celebrating Harmodius and Aristogeiton                   93

*Readings*
The Athenian Revolution of 508/7 BC: Violence, Authority,
    and the Origins of Democracy                                       95
*Josiah Ober*
Revolution or Compromise?                                             113
*Loren J. Samons II*
Further Reading                                                       122

**3  Popular Politics in Fifth-century Syracuse**                     **123**
Introduction                                                          123

*Sources*
Thucydides, *History of the Peloponnesian War* 6.34–36, 38–41         123
Aristotle, *Politics* 1315b35–9, 1316a30–4, 1304a18–29                125
Diodorus, *Library of History* 11.67–68, 72–73, 76, 86–87            126
*Readings*
Sicily, 478–431 BC                                                    131
*David Asheri*
Revolution and Society in Greek Sicily and Southern Italy             135
*Shlomo Berger*
Democracy in Syracuse, 466–412 BC                                     140
*Eric W. Robinson*
Further Reading                                                       151

**4  Liberty, Equality, and the Ideals of Greek Democracy**          **152**
Introduction                                                          152

*Sources*
Herodotus, *Histories* 3.80–82                                        152
Euripides, *Suppliant Women* 346–57, 403–50                           154
Thucydides, *History of the Peloponnesian War* 2.37–42                156
Aristotle, *Politics* 1292b21–34, 1317a40–1318a10                     158

*Readings*
Shares and Rights: "Citizenship" Greek Style and American Style       159
*Martin Ostwald*
The Ancient Athenian and the Modern Liberal View of
    Liberty as a Democratic Ideal                                     171
*Mogens Herman Hansen*
Further Reading                                                       183

5   **Power and Rhetoric at Athens: Elite Leadership versus
    Popular Ideology**                                                   **185**

    Introduction                                                         185

    *Sources*
      Thucydides, *History of the Peloponnesian War* 2.65.1–11           185
      Demosthenes 21, *Against Meidias* 1–8, 12–21, 42–50, 70–87,
        95–99, 110–112, 123–131, 136–159, 193–197, 208–212,
        219–227                                                          187

    *Readings*
      Who Ran Democratic Athens?                                         201
      P. J. Rhodes
      Demosthenes 21 (*Against Meidias*): Democratic Abuse               211
      Peter J. Wilson
      Power and Oratory in Democratic Athens: Demosthenes 21,
        Against Meidias                                                  232
      Josiah Ober
      Further Reading                                                    247

6   **Limiting Democracy: The Political Exclusion of Women and Slaves**  **248**

    Introduction                                                         248

    *Sources*
      Thucydides, Pericles' Funeral Oration (*History of the Peloponnesian
        War* 2.44–6)                                                     249
      Pseudo-Xenophon, *The Constitution of the Athenians* 1; 4–8.1; 10–12   250
      Aristophanes, *The Assemblywomen*, lines 57–244, 427–476, 877–889,
        938–1056                                                         251
      Aristotle, *Politics* 1253b1–33, 54a10–24, b7–15, 59a37–b4;
        1274b32–1275a34, b19–23; 1319b2–32                               262

    *Readings*
      The Economics and Politics of Slavery at Athens                    265
      Robin Osborne
      Women and Democracy in Fourth-century Athens                       281
      Michael H. Jameson
      Women and Democracy in Ancient Greece                              292
      Marilyn Katz
      Further Reading                                                    312

*Glossary of Greek Names and Terms*                                      313

*Index*                                                                  315

# Preface

This volume is intended to provide students and other interested readers with an accessible, up-to-date survey of vital issues in ancient Greek democracy (*demokratia*). Six chapters each present a question of continuing interest matched with key ancient texts, followed by two or three recent scholarly articles on the subject. Every chapter thus invites the reader into the process of historical investigation as he or she engages the ancient testimony and sees how classical scholars analyze and gain insights from it. At the same time, the selection of topics is designed to provide an overview of the phenomenon of Greek democracy, from its earliest roots in the archaic period to its appearance and development in Athens (and, for a useful comparison, how it looked in another Greek city of the classical period). It is hoped that readers will be able to learn a great deal about *demokratia*, the present state of its study, and some of the approaches and methods of ancient historians.

An opening introduction briefly sketches the history of Greek democracy and its legacy, and also describes some of its major features. Each chapter closes with a selection of suggestions for further reading. These short bibliographies (restricted to English-language books and articles) are intended to help students researching papers or other readers interested in further exploration of that chapter's topic. A glossary at the end of the volume defines some of the more common Greek names and terms encountered in the book.

Almost all the scholarly articles included here have been previously published. Some have had sections omitted for reasons of length or focus. For easy accessibility to the Greekless reader, translations of Greek terms have been inserted and occasionally Greek phrases eliminated. Notes and bibliographies are retained to maximize the articles' usefulness to advanced students and scholars.

As for the ancient source selections in each chapter, they are for the most part given in chronological order, earliest authors to latest. Some of the older translations of the sources have had archaic terms updated for this volume. Necessarily, all the selections have been excerpted from longer original works: for context and further insights students are encouraged to seek out the unabridged text.

No attempt has been made to impose a uniform system for the spelling of transliterated Greek names and terms across the contributions in this volume: they have been
left as each author or translator chose. Readers can therefore expect to find variant
spellings (e.g., Clisthenes or Kleisthenes for Cleisthenes).

I have many people to thank for their help in bringing this project to fruition.
Working for Blackwell, Al Bertrand, Angela Cohen, and Margaret Aherne all deserve
my deepest gratitude for their roles in helping to formulate, produce, and edit the
book, and for making it all an enjoyable process. The anonymous readers provided
many useful suggestions, and I must also thank Fred Robinson, Vanessa Gorman, Phil
Kaplan, and Nino Luraghi for readings or advice at various stages along the way. Jay
Samons showed great generosity in contributing new material for the volume – and
then paid for it by (patiently) putting up with my niggles thereafter. Bryce Sady
provided invaluable help with bibliographies and proofing, all done on short notice
and with great skill. This project also benefited from funds from the Loeb Classical
Library Foundation and a research leave from Harvard University. Finally, I gratefully
thank my wife, Carwina Weng, for her proofing and especially for her love and
support.

# Acknowledgments

Aristophanes, *Assemblywomen*, lines 57–244, 427–76, 877–89, 938–1056; trans. J. Henderson, from *Three Plays by Aristophanes: Staging Women*. New York, Routledge, 1996, pp. 153–8, 164–6, 181, 183–7.

Aristotle, *The Constitution of the Athenians*, 5–12, 18–22; trans. J. M. Moore, from *Aristotle and Xenophon on Democracy and Oligarchy*. Berkeley, University of California Press, 1975, pp. 150–6, 161–6.

David Asheri, "Sicily, 478–431 BC," in *The Cambridge Ancient History*², vol. 5, eds. D. M. Lewis et al. Cambridge, Cambridge University Press, 1992, pp. 147–70.

Shlomo Berger, *Revolution and Society in Greek Sicily and Southern Italy*. Stuttgart, Franz Steiner Verlag, 1992.

Diodorus, from *Diodorus of Sicily* vol. 4; Loeb Classical Library vol. 4, trans. C. H. Oldfather. Cambridge, MA, Harvard University Press, 1946. Reprinted by permission of the publishers and the Trustees of the Loeb Classical Library. The Loeb Classical Library is a registered trademark of the President and Fellows of Harvard College.

Lowell Edmunds, "Commentary on Raaflaub," in *Proceedings of the Boston Area Colloquium Series in Ancient Philosophy* 4. Lanham, MD, University Press of America, 1988, pp. 26–33.

Euripides, *Suppliant Women*, lines 346–57, 403–50; from *Euripides: Suppliant Women, Electra, Heracles*. Loeb Classical Library, trans. D. Kovacs. Cambridge, MA, Harvard University Press, 1998. Reprinted by permission of the publishers and the Trustees of the Loeb Classical Library. The Loeb Classical Library is a registered trademark of the President and Fellows of Harvard College.

Harmodius and Aristogeiton drinking song (Athenaeus 15.50, p. 695ab, with scholion to Aristophanes *Acharnians* 980); trans. C. Fornara, from *Archaic Times to the End of the Peloponnesian War*, 2nd edn. Cambridge, Cambridge University Press, 1983, p. 39.

Mogens Herman Hansen, "The Ancient Athenian and the Modern Liberal View of Liberty as a Democratic Ideal," in J. Ober and C. Hedrick (eds.) *Demokratia*,

Princeton University Press, 1996, pp. 91–104. Reprinted by permission of Princeton University Press.

Hesiod, *Theogony*, lines 81–97 and *Works and Days*, lines 213–69; trans. A. N. Athanassakis, from *Theogony; Works and Days; Shield/Hesiod*. Baltimore, Johns Hopkins University Press, 1983, pp. 15, 72–3.

Homer, *Iliad* 1.1–305, 2.1–282; trans. R. Lattimore, from *The Iliad*. Chicago, University of Chicago Press, 1951, pp. 59–67, 76–83.

Homer, *Odyssey* 2.1–259; trans. W. Shewring, from *The Odyssey/Homer*. Oxford, Oxford University Press, 1980, pp. 12–18.

Michael H. Jameson, "Women and Democracy in Fourth-century Athens," in *Esclavage, guerre, économie en Grèce ancienne. Hommages à Yvon Garlan*, eds. P. Brulé and J. Oulhen. Rennes, Presses Universitaires de Rennes, 1997, pp. 95–107.

Marilyn Katz, "Women and Democracy in Ancient Greece," in *Contextualizing Classics: Ideology, Performance, Dialogue*, eds. Thomas M. Falkner, Nancy Felson, and David Konstan. Lanham, MD, Rowman & Littlefield, 1999, pp. 41–68.

Ian Morris, "The Strong Principle of Equality and the Archaic Origins of Greek Democracy," in J. Ober and C. Hedrick (eds.) *Demokratia*, Princeton University Press, 1996, pp. 19–48. Reprinted by permission of Princeton University Press.

Josiah Ober, "The Athenian Revolution of 508/7 BC: Violence, Authority, and the Origins of Democracy," in *The Athenian Revolution*. Princeton University Press, 1996, pp. 34–52 (originally published in *Cultural Poetics in Archaic Greece*, eds. L. Kurke and C. Dougherty. Cambridge, Cambridge University Press, 1993, pp. 215–32).

Josiah Ober, "Power and Oratory in Democratic Athens: Demosthenes 21, Against Meidias," in *Persuasion: Greek Rhetoric in Action*, ed. I. Worthington. London, Routledge, 1994, pp. 85–108.

Robin Osborne, "The Economics and Politics of Slavery at Athens," in *The Greek World*, ed. A. Powell. London, Routledge, 1995, pp. 27–43.

Martin Ostwald, "Shares and Rights: 'Citizenship' Greek Style and American Style," in J. Ober and C. Hedrick (eds.) *Demokratia*, Princeton University Press, 1996, pp. 49–61. Reprinted by permission of Princeton University Press.

Pseudo-Xenophon, *Constitution of the Athenians*, 1; 4–8.1; 10–12; trans. J. M. Moore, from *Aristotle and Xenophon on Democracy and Oligarchy*. Berkeley, University of California Press, 1975, pp. 37–9.

Kurt A. Raaflaub, "Homer and the Beginning of Political Thought in Greece," in *Proceedings of the Boston Area Colloquium Series in Ancient Philosophy* 4. Lanham, MD, University Press of America, 1988, pp. 1–25.

P. J. Rhodes, "Who Ran Democratic Athens?" in P. Flensted-Jensen et al. (eds.) *Polis and Politics*. Copenhagen, Museum Tusculanum Press, 2000, pp. 465–77.

Eric W. Robinson, "Democracy in Syracuse, 466–412 BC," in *Harvard Studies in Classical Philology* 100 (2000), pp. 189–205.

Loren J. Samons, "Mass, Elite, and Hoplite-Farmer in Greek History," in *Arion* (3rd series) 5 (1998), pp. 99–123.

Peter J. Wilson, "Demosthenes 21 (*Against Meidias*): Democratic Abuse," in *Proceedings of the Cambridge Philological Society* 37 (1991), pp. 164–95.

# Abbreviations

---

| | |
|---|---|
| *AHB* | *Ancient History Bulletin* |
| *AJA* | *American Journal of Archaeology* |
| *BCH* | *Bulletin de Correspondance Hellénique* |
| *CAH* | *Cambridge Ancient History* (Cambridge: Cambridge University Press) |
| *CJ* | *Classical Journal* |
| *C & M* | *Classica et Mediaevalia* |
| CNRS | Centre national de la recherche scientifique |
| *CP/CPH/CPh* | *Classical Philology* |
| *CQ* | *Classical Quarterly* |
| *CR* | *Classical Review* |
| *FGrH* | F. Jacoby, *Fragmente der griechischen Historiker* |
| *G & R* | *Greece & Rome* |
| *GHI* | M. N. Tod, ed., *Greek Historical Inscriptions* (1946–8) |
| *GRBS* | *Greek, Roman, and Byzantine Studies* |
| *HSCPh* | *Harvard Studies in Classical Philology* |
| *IG* | *Inscriptiones Graecae* (Berlin, 1873– ) |
| *JHS* | *Journal of Hellenic Studies* |
| *LCM* | *Liverpool Classical Monthly* |
| *ML* | R. Meiggs and D. M. Lewis, *A Selection of Greek Historical Inscriptions*, 2nd edn. (Oxford, 1988) |
| *P. Oxy.* | *Oxyrhynchus Papyri* |
| *PCPhS* | *Proceedings of the Cambridge Philological Society* |
| *QS* | *Quaderni di storia* |
| *SEG* | F. Jacoby, *Supplementum Epigraphicum Graecum* |

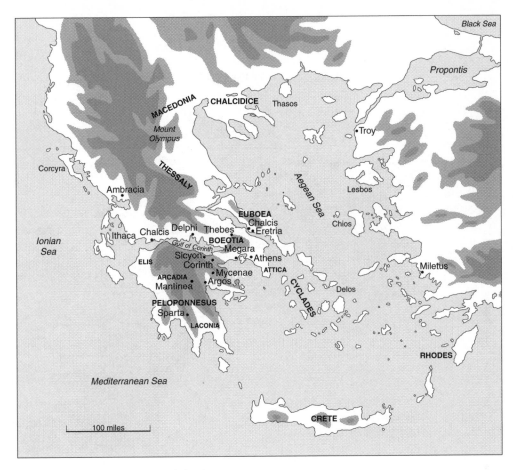

Map 1  *Mainland Greece and the Aegean*

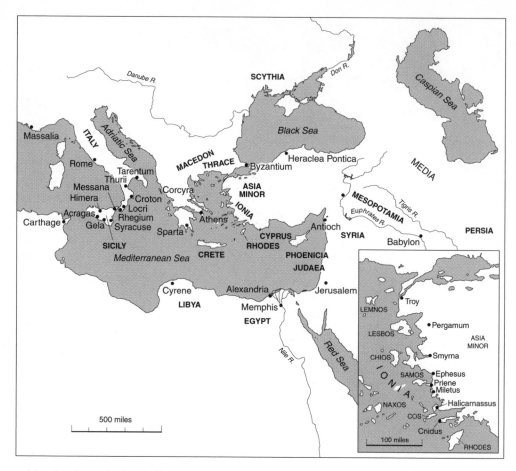

Map 2    *Greece in the Mediterranean World*

# Ancient Greek Democracy: A Brief Introduction

Democracy is one of the most astonishing and compelling inventions of the ancient Greeks. Although a few earlier civilizations might have allowed a degree of popular involvement in decision-making, and before then some primitive human societies might have been organized in roughly egalitarian fashion, the Greeks were the first people we know to have conceived and implemented the striking notion that the citizens of a community, even a large and complex one, could govern themselves. They called it *demokratia* ("people power").

The basic premise is not very different from that which still animates democracies today: that in a given community the ordinary citizens – not some king, tyrant, or clique of the especially distinguished or wealthy – should collectively hold the sovereign power to administer all public affairs for the common good. Indeed, the Greek ideal went a step farther than its typical modern counterpart in that as much as possible the people were to govern *directly*, filling offices themselves through citizen lotteries and participating in large public assemblies to debate and vote personally on most affairs of state. Elected leaders and representative bodies also played important roles but did not dominate government policy-making the way they do in the democracies of modern nations. Freedom and equality were invoked as abiding principles of democratic constitutions, then as now, though they were not always applied in the same ways.

## Historical Sketch

Traditionally, textbook accounts have turned almost exclusively to the famous case at Athens to trace the history of Greek democracy. Yet a broader view is both possible and desirable, and will be followed here.

The earliest instances of democracy arose in the sixth century BC in various city-states of the Greek world. Though reliable information for this period of Greek history is scarce, and it is not always clear how truly democratic some of the earliest were, the best candidates include Chios (in the Aegean Sea), Megara (on the mainland), Heraclea Pontica (on the coast of the Black Sea), Cyrene (on the Libyan coast), and Ambracia (in northwest Greece). By the late sixth century Athens had turned to some form of democracy (an event examined in chapter 2), as had other major states like Argos (in the Peloponnesus) and Syracuse (in Sicily) by the early fifth century. This wide geographic scattering in cities of differing types suggests that *demokratia* was not a localized phenomenon, nor the spur-of-the-moment creation of any single "inventor" (for which there is no evidence anyway), but rather grew out of attitudes and conditions widespread in the Greek world. (The first chapter of this book looks to the oldest works of Greek literature for early signs of egalitarian structures and thought that might have led to democratic innovation.) As for how popular governments took root in particular cities, existing accounts imply that, with rare exceptions, they tended to appear only after a violent revolution or military catastrophe threw the entire *polis* (city-state) into upheaval. It would seem to have taken an extraordinary political crisis, then, to allow popular governments to win through against the interests of traditional royal, tyrannical, or aristocratic authority.

Over the course of the fifth and fourth centuries BC (the Classical era) democracy became more common and continued to appear all across the Greek world. On the islands and coasts of the Aegean many of the members of Athens' vast military alliance – ultimately transformed into an empire – had been or came to be democratically governed. The long Peloponnesian War (431–404 BC) fought by the Athenian and Spartan coalitions intensified this trend within the Aegean alliance, for the Athenians favored democratic factions in their sphere of influence, in contrast to the Spartan preference for oligarchies in theirs. In fifth-century Sicily popular governments replaced tyrannical rule in most of the Greek cities starting in the 460s. (Chapter 3 investigates the case of Syracuse, the most influential *polis* in Sicily.) A number of cities in southern Italy also came to have democratic governments, as did nearby Corcyra in the Ionian Sea. The Peloponnesus on the Greek mainland had its share as well, including Argos, Elis, and Mantinea.

Sparta's defeat of Athens at the end of the fifth century led to the overthrow of many democratic regimes among its allies, and the return of tyranny to Syracuse around the same time had ramifications in that region. Nevertheless, inscriptions and literary sources make clear that democracy continued to flourish in the fourth century. Indeed, contemporary historians, orators, and philosophers speak of it as a widespread phenomenon, and inscribed state decrees indicate through their termin-ology an expansion of the institutions associated with democracy. Athens itself re-democratized after a brief interlude of autocracy following the Peloponnesian War, and many Aegean states retained their popular institutions. On the mainland, Thebes adopted democratic government, as did Sicyon, Phleious, and the Arcadian confeder-acy, at least for a time, while the Argives maintained theirs. Alexander the Great, Macedonian king and world conqueror until his death in 323, is said to have over-thrown oligarchies and established democracies among the Greek states he liberated from Persian control.

Inscriptions suggest that the spread of democratic institutions in Greek cities continued after the Classical period. But in the succeeding Hellenistic era (roughly the third through the first centuries BC) individual city-states experienced generally decreasing autonomy and influence in a Greek world now dominated by Macedonian kingdoms and large confederacies. There is also reason to believe that the increasing prevalence in this period of *demokratiai* was accompanied by a loosening of the term's meaning and a decline in actual popular participation in *polis* administration. The case of Rhodes, a vibrant, independent democracy for much of the Hellenistic period, may have been exceptional. As Roman influence grew from the second century BC on, true democracies became more rare and ultimately faded from view.

## Definition and Institutions

As it existed in the fifth and fourth centuries, democracy meant that the *demos* (the people) were sovereign in the deliberations of state. A popular assembly, to which all citizens were invited, met regularly and provided a forum for debating and voting on the most important matters. Representative councils typically prepared in advance the agenda for the assembly meetings. Popular courts, with ordinary citizens serving as jurors, tried legal cases, and administrative officials (magistrates, generals, treasurers, examiners, etc.) were either elected or chosen by lot for relatively brief terms, usually one year. Officials were held to account after their terms of office as a check on corruption. While property qualifications often applied to some of the higher offices, generally wealth requirements were minimal or non-existent for participation in the assembly, courts, and other positions.[1]

Some democracies employed more unusual institutions as well. Ostracism and analogous laws allowed the people to vote into exile for several years leaders who seemed to have grown too powerful, troublesome, or threatening to the popular order. Some states paid citizens for their service on juries or attendance at assembly meetings, encouraging active participation from all classes including the poor.

Underlying the development of these institutions were the ideals of freedom and equality. Chapter 4 examines such ideals, considering how they applied in ancient *demokratiai* and how they compare to modern uses of the terms. Chapter 5 debates the question of who really held power in ancient democracies such as Athens, the ordinary people supposedly in charge or the (typically) elite leaders who gained prominence and employed rhetoric to persuade the masses. One must also confront the fact that ancient democracies, like all other Greek constitutional forms, excluded from active citizenship women, slaves, and resident aliens. While not entirely devoid of civic rights or responsibilities, members of these groups could not join in the practice of *demokratia* in anything like the way native, freeborn males could. Chapter 6 looks at some of the reasons for and effects of these exclusions.

## The Heritage and Study of *Demokratia*

As noted earlier, there are many similarities in the basic principles of ancient and modern democracy. It would be a mistake, however, to believe that modern democracy simply evolved out of its Greek predecessor or that the legacy of *demokratia* has been cherished throughout Western history. In fact, for most of ancient and modern history Greek democracy has had anything but a good reputation or broad influence. Starting in antiquity, historians and philosophers who treated the subject often voiced grave doubts about popular government. Greek philosophers found it flawed and

ill-conceived, especially as compared to "mixed" constitutions that balanced monar-
chic, aristocratic, and democratic elements, or measured against idealized city-states
they might imagine. Roman observers often saw *demokratia* as one of those irresponsible Greek innovations to be given a wide berth or actively discouraged. Why, the
ancient critics wondered, should a city employ throngs of the poor and little-educated
to take on the complexities of public administration when the "best men," those with
elite family backgrounds and/or training, could guide the state? Would the latter not
make wiser rulers? Danger was also seen to arise from rampant demagoguery, frac-
tious and emotional assembly meetings, and the mistreatment of illustrious leaders
that could accompany rule of the "masses." Few ancient observers (whose works
survive, at least) expressed positive views.

As democratic government faded and ultimately disappeared from the cities of the
Roman Empire, *demokratia* drew less and less attention from writers, becoming little
more than a curiosity of Greek antiquity or a forgotten subject altogether, especially
as the Roman world gave way to the Middle Ages. The rediscovery of ancient history
and its political examples during the Renaissance revived the topic, but typically
"mixed" constitutions, most especially Sparta or Rome, gained the plaudits of
those looking closely at politics. Early modern writers often echoed the classical
critiques, branding democracy – particularly the famous Athenian version – as disorderly, ill-guided, and unjust to its leading figures. Even intellectuals of the French and
American revolutions found more to condemn than to embrace about it. Federalists
in America especially sought to avoid the democratic model when devising and
promoting their new constitution, preferring the perceived stability and balance of
the Roman Republic. One could occasionally find more charitable views about
democracy, but negative opinions predominated, especially among the scholarly.

Not until the nineteenth century did the tide turn. A crucial figure in this shift was
George Grote, an English banker and liberal who produced a monumental *History of
Greece* in the years between 1846 and 1856. In it he passionately defended Greek
democracy against the criticisms that had been leveled against it and praised the
Athenian state for its populist practices and its vigor. Grote's *History* proved to be
influential in Europe and in America, and classical scholars showed an increasing
willingness to consider ancient popular government in a more positive light. It did
not hurt the cause, of course, that all across the West social leveling and more liberal
thinking were transforming the political landscape and would result in a flourishing of
modern forms of democracy in the nineteenth and twentieth centuries.

Ever since this turn toward modern democracy, its ancient counterpart has been a
popular subject of classical historians, political scientists, and, to some extent, the
general public. A great many books have been published by classicists in a variety of
languages examining all aspects of *demokratia* and not infrequently making comparisons to modern versions. A sampling of English-language works will be noted here,
both to indicate the persistent, lively interest in the field and to offer suggestions for
further reading. (Readers may also look to the brief, specific bibliographies at the end
of each of this volume's chapters.)

Three of the better-known works of the last half-century have been C. Hignett's *A
History of the Athenian Constitution to the End of the Fifth Century* BC (Oxford,
1952), A. H. M. Jones' *Athenian Democracy* (Oxford, 1957), and M. I. Finley's

*Democracy Ancient and Modern* (1973; revised edition, London, 1985). Among more recent works, painstaking scholarship on the history, institutions, and practices of the Athenian democracy continues to refine and improve our knowledge of that state. Prominent examples include Mogens Hansen's volumes of collected essays on the Athenian assembly (e.g. *The Athenian Ecclesia*, Copenhagen, 1983) and his *Athenian Democracy in the Age of Demosthenes* (Oxford, 1991); Martin Ostwald's *From Popular Sovereignty to the Sovereignty of Law* (Berkeley, 1986); and P. J. Rhodes' *The Athenian Boule* (revised edition, Oxford, 1985). Focusing especially on the ideology of democracy at Athens is Josiah Ober's *Mass and Elite in Democratic Athens* (Princeton, 1989). Other important aspects are examined in Robin Osborne's *Demos: The Discovery of Classical Attika* (Cambridge, 1985); Raphael Sealey's *The Athenian Republic* (University Park, PA, 1987); R. K. Sinclair's *Democracy and Participation in Athens* (Cambridge, 1988); Philip Manville's *The Origins of Citizenship in Ancient Athens* (Princeton, 1990); and Edward Cohen's *The Athenian Nation* (Princeton, 2000).

Since the celebration of the supposed "2500th anniversary" of democracy in 1993 (counting from its advent in Athens ca. 508/7 BC), a number of notable edited volumes have appeared, including *Democracy 2500?*, eds. I. Morris and K. A. Raaflaub (Dubuque, IA, 1998); *Democracy, Empire, and the Arts in Fifth-century Athens*, eds. D. Boedeker and K. A. Raaflaub (Cambridge, MA, 1998); *Demokratia*, eds. J. Ober and C. Hedrick (Princeton, 1996); *The Good Idea: Democracy and Ancient Greece*, ed. J. A. Koumoulides (Caratzas, 1995); *Athenian Political Thought and the Reconstruction of American Democracy*, eds. P. Euben, J. R. Wallach, and J. Ober (Ithaca, NY, 1994); and *Athenian Identity and Civic Ideology*, eds. A. L. Boegehold and A. C. Scafuro (Baltimore, 1994).

Other recent works have attempted to broaden our view of ancient democracy by focusing attention on states and institutions outside Athens: see Eric W. Robinson's *The First Democracies* (Stuttgart, 1997); P. J. Rhodes' *The Decrees of the Greek States* (Oxford, 1997); and (though only partly focused on democracy) *Alternatives to Athens*, eds. R. Brock and S. Hodkinson (Oxford, 2000). James O'Neil's *The Origins and Development of Ancient Greek Democracy* (Lanham, MD, 1995) also devotes much attention outside Athens in an accessible study.

General introductions to Athenian democracy continue to appear, such as David Stockton's *The Classical Athenian Democracy* (Oxford, 1990) and Christopher Carey's *Democracy in Classical Athens* (London, 2000). The changing reputation of the Athenian democracy from antiquity through the modern era has been well presented in Jennifer Roberts' *Athens on Trial* (Princeton, 1994). John Dunn edited a very useful collection of essays tracing the evolution of democracy from antiquity to the present era in *Democracy: The Unfinished Journey 508 BC to AD 1993* (Oxford, 1992).

## NOTE

1   Broad-based oligarchies in the Greek world might employ some of the above institutions, including citizen assemblies with final authority. Sparta, for example, invited its citizens to vote on all measures put before its assembly. But other elements were decidedly less

democratic: Spartan citizens were an elite, highly regimented group kept separate from other freeborn native men of the territory and were required to make regular contributions to retain their special status. And even among this group, the ability to participate in assembl1y debates was sharply limited as compared to that of citizens in democracies.

# 1

# Prelude to Democracy: Political Thought in Early Greek Texts

---

## Introduction

The earliest democratic governments began to appear in the city-states of Greece in the sixth century BC. Where did the idea come from? Since there is no evidence that the democratic impulse came from anywhere outside Greece, scholars have looked to the texts and events of earlier Greek history for clues of its beginnings. But reliable source material is scarce for the Archaic period of Greek history (roughly the eight through sixth centuries BC). Archaeological remains can tell us a great deal about many aspects of Greek settlements and culture of the time, but are ill suited to the task of revealing specific political institutions and concepts; for these, literary evidence is essential. The first authors offering potentially relevant information are the poets Homer and Hesiod – not historians, but tellers of epic tales. The political and historical interpretation of their works is thus complicated and has engendered much debate, but still offers the best way to get a glimpse of the kind of thinking that in time led to the development of Greek democracy.

## Homer: Selections on speech and authority in assemblies

Though reliable information about Homer and his role in creating the Iliad and the Odyssey is famously lacking, most scholars believe the two great epics attributed to him date back to the second half of the eighth century BC or a little later, at least in the form we have them. The Iliad tells the story of a crucial portion of the legendary Trojan War, while the Odyssey describes the perils of the long-delayed return of the hero Odysseus to Ithaca after the end of that war. Both contain scenes where communities – either the Greek army before Troy or the people of Ithaca – gather in assemblies to hear and react to proposals made by their leaders (often called *basileis*, translated as "princes" or "kings"). While the speeches and specific events portrayed in the epics are considered fictional by modern historians, many consider them to be revealing about the attitudes of early Greeks toward power, authority, and the role of the community at large in political decisions. (*Sources*: Homer, *Iliad* 1.1–305, 2.1–282, trans. by R. Lattimore from *The Iliad* (Chicago: University of Chicago Press, 1951), pp. 59–67, 76–83; *Odyssey* 2.1–259, trans. by W. Shewring from *The Odyssey/Homer* (Oxford: Oxford University Press, 1980), pp. 12–18.)

## *Iliad* 1.1–305

Sing, goddess, the anger of Peleus' son Achilleus
and its devastation, which put pains thousandfold upon the Achaians,
hurled in their multitudes to the house of Hades strong souls
of heroes, but gave their bodies to be the delicate feasting
of dogs, of all birds, and the will of Zeus was accomplished
since that time when first there stood in division of conflict
Atreus' son the lord of men and brilliant Achilleus.

What god was it then set them together in bitter collision?
Zeus' son and Leto's, Apollo, who in anger at the king drove
the foul pestilence along the host, and the people perished,
since Atreus' son had dishonoured Chryses, priest of Apollo,
when he came beside the fast ships of the Achaians to ransom
back his daughter, carrying gifts beyond count and holding
in his hands wound on a staff of gold the ribbons of Apollo
who strikes from afar, and supplicated all the Achaians,
but above all Atreus' two sons, the marshals of the people:
'Sons of Atreus and you other strong-greaved Achaians,
to you may the gods grant who have their homes on Olympos
Priam's city to be plundered and a fair homecoming thereafter,
but may you give me back my own daughter and take the ransom,
giving honour to Zeus' son who strikes from afar, Apollo.'

Then all the rest of the Achaians cried out in favour
that the priest be respected and the shining ransom be taken;
yet this pleased not the heart of Atreus' son Agamemnon,
but harshly he drove him away with a strong order upon him:
'Never let me find you again, old sir, near our hollow
ships, neither lingering now nor coming again hereafter,
for fear your staff and the god's ribbons help you no longer.
The girl I will not give back; sooner will old age come upon her
in my own house, in Argos, far from her own land, going
up and down by the loom and being in my bed as my companion.
So go now, do not make me angry; so you will be safer.'

So he spoke, and the old man in terror obeyed him

and went silently away beside the murmuring sea beach.
Over and over the old man prayed as he walked in solitude
to King Apollo, whom Leto of the lovely hair bore: 'Hear me,
lord of the silver bow who set your power about Chryse
and Killa the sacrosanct, who are lord in strength over Tenedos,
Smintheus, if ever it pleased your heart that I built your temple,
if ever it pleased you that I burned all the rich thigh pieces
of bulls, of goats, then bring to pass this wish I pray for:
let your arrows make the Danaans pay for my tears shed.'
    So he spoke in prayer, and Phoibos Apollo heard him,
and strode down along the pinnacles of Olympos, angered
in his heart, carrying across his shoulders the bow and the hooded
quiver; and the shafts clashed on the shoulders of the god walking
angrily. He came as night comes down and knelt then
apart and opposite the ships and let go an arrow.
Terrible was the clash that rose from the bow of silver.
First he went after the mules and the circling hounds, then let go
a tearing arrow against the men themselves and struck them.
The corpse fires burned everywhere and did not stop burning.
    Nine days up and down the host ranged the god's arrows,
but on the tenth Achilleus called the people to assembly;
a thing put into his mind by the goddess of the white arms, Hera,
who had pity upon the Danaans when she saw them dying.
Now when they were all assembled in one place together,
Achilleus of the swift feet stood up among them and spoke forth:
'Son of Atreus, I believe now that straggling backwards
we must make our way home if we can even escape death,
if fighting now must crush the Achaians and the plague likewise.
No, come, let us ask some holy man, some prophet,
even an interpreter of dreams, since a dream also
comes from Zeus, who can tell why Phoibos Apollo is so angry,
if for the sake of some vow, some hecatomb he blames us,
if given the fragrant smoke of lambs, of he goats, somehow
he can be made willing to beat the bane aside from us.'
    He spoke thus and sat down again, and among them stood up
Kalchas, Thestor's son, far the best of the bird interpreters,
who knew all things that were, the things to come and the things past,
who guided into the land of Ilion the ships of the Achaians
through that seercraft of his own that Phoibos Apollo gave him.
He in kind intention toward all stood forth and addressed them:
'You have bidden me, Achilleus beloved of Zeus, to explain to
you this anger of Apollo the lord who strikes from afar. Then
I will speak; yet make me a promise and swear before me
readily by word and work of your hands to defend me,
since I believe I shall make a man angry who holds great kingship

over the men of Argos, and all the Achaians obey him.
For a king when he is angry with a man beneath him is too strong,
and suppose even for the day itself he swallow down his anger,
he still keeps bitterness that remains until its fulfilment
deep in his chest. Speak forth then, tell me if you will protect me.'
    Then in answer again spoke Achilleus of the swift feet:
'Speak, interpreting whatever you know, and fear nothing.
In the name of Apollo beloved of Zeus to whom you, Kalchas,
make your prayers when you interpret the gods' will to the Danaans,
no man so long as I am alive above earth and see daylight
shall lay the weight of his hands on you beside the hollow ships,
not one of all the Danaans, even if you mean Agamemnon,
who now claims to be far the greatest of all the Achaians.'
    At this the blameless seer took courage again and spoke forth:
'No, it is not for the sake of some vow or hecatomb he blames us,
but for the sake of his priest whom Agamemnon dishonoured
and would not give him back his daughter nor accept the ransom.
Therefore the archer sent griefs against us and will send them
still, nor sooner thrust back the shameful plague from the Danaans
until we give the glancing-eyed girl back to her father
without price, without ransom, and lead also a blessed hecatomb
to Chryse; thus we might propitiate and persuade him.'
    He spoke thus and sat down again, and among them stood up
Atreus' son the hero wide-ruling Agamemnon
raging, the heart within filled black to the brim with anger
from beneath, but his two eyes showed like fire in their blazing.
First of all he eyed Kalchas bitterly and spoke to him:
'Seer of evil: never yet have you told me a good thing.
Always the evil things are dear to your heart to prophesy,
but nothing excellent have you said nor ever accomplished.
Now once more you make divination to the Danaans, argue
forth your reason why he who strikes from afar afflicts them,
because I for the sake of the girl Chryseis would not take
the shining ransom; and indeed I wish greatly to have her
in my own house; since I like her better than Klytaimestra
my own wife, for in truth she is no way inferior,
neither in build nor stature nor wit, not in accomplishment.
Still I am willing to give her back, if such is the best way.
I myself desire that my people be safe, not perish.
Find me then some prize that shall be my own, lest I only
among the Argives go without, since that were unfitting;
you are all witnesses to this thing, that my prize goes elsewhere.'
    Then in answer again spoke brilliant swift-footed Achilleus:
'Son of Atreus, most lordly, greediest for gain of all men,
how shall the great-hearted Achaians give you a prize now?

There is no great store of things lying about I know of.
But what we took from the cities by storm has been distributed;
it is unbecoming for the people to call back things once given.
No, for the present give the girl back to the god; we Achaians
thrice and four times over will repay you, if ever Zeus gives
into our hands the strong-walled citadel of Troy to be plundered.'
    Then in answer again spoke powerful Agamemnon:
'Not that way, good fighter though you be, godlike Achilleus,
strive to cheat, for you will not deceive, you will not persuade me.
What do you want? To keep your own prize and have me sit here
lacking one? Are you ordering me to give this girl back?
Either the great-hearted Achaians shall give me a new prize
chosen according to my desire to atone for the girl lost,
or else if they will not give me one I myself shall take her,
your own prize, or that of Aias, or that of Odysseus,
going myself in person; and he whom I visit will be bitter.
Still, these are things we shall deliberate again hereafter.
Come, now, we must haul a black ship down to the bright sea,
and assemble rowers enough for it, and put on board it
the hecatomb, and the girl herself, Chryseis of the fair cheeks,
and let there be one responsible man in charge of her,
either Aias or Idomeneus or brilliant Odysseus,
or you yourself, son of Peleus, most terrifying of all men,
to reconcile by accomplishing sacrifice the archer.'
    Then looking darkly at him Achilleus of the swift feet spoke:
'O wrapped in shamelessness, with your mind forever on profit,
how shall any one of the Achaians readily obey you
either to go on a journey or to fight men strongly in battle?
I for my part did not come here for the sake of the Trojan
spearmen to fight against them, since to me they have done nothing.
Never yet have they driven away my cattle or my horses,
never in Phthia where the soil is rich and men grow great did they
spoil my harvest, since indeed there is much that lies between us,
the shadowy mountains and the echoing sea; but for your sake,
o great shamelessness, we followed, to do you favour,
you with the dog's eyes, to win your honour and Menelaos'
from the Trojans. You forget all this or else you care nothing.
And now my prize you threaten in person to strip from me,
for whom I laboured much, the gift of the sons of the Achaians.
Never, when the Achaians sack some well-founded citadel
of the Trojans, do I have a prize that is equal to your prize.
Always the greater part of the painful fighting is the work of
my hands; but when the time comes to distribute the booty
yours is far the greater reward, and I with some small thing
yet dear to me go back to my ships when I am weary with fighting.

Now I am returning to Phthia, since it is much better
to go home again with my curved ships, and I am minded no longer
to stay here dishonoured and pile up your wealth and your luxury.'
    Then answered him in turn the lord of men Agamemnon:
'Run away by all means if your heart drives you. I will not
entreat you to stay here for my sake. There are others with me
who will do me honour, and above all Zeus of the counsels.
To me you are the most hateful of all the kings whom the gods love.
Forever quarrelling is dear to your heart, and wars and battles;
and if you are very strong indeed, that is a god's gift.
Go home then with your own ships and your own companions,
be king over the Myrmidons. I care nothing about you.
I take no account of your anger. But here is my threat to you.
Even as Phoibos Apollo is taking away my Chryseis,
I shall convey her back in my own ship, with my own
followers; but I shall take the fair-cheeked Briseis,
your prize, I myself going to your shelter, that you may learn well
how much greater I am than you, and another man may shrink back
from likening himself to me and contending against me.'
    So he spoke. And the anger came on Peleus' son, and within
his shaggy breast the heart was divided two ways, pondering
whether to draw from beside his thigh the sharp sword, driving
away all those who stood between and kill the son of Atreus,
or else to check the spleen within and keep down his anger.
Now as he weighed in mind and spirit these two courses
and was drawing from its scabbard the great sword, Athene descended
from the sky. For Hera the goddess of the white arms sent her,
who loved both men equally in her heart and cared for them.
The goddess standing behind Peleus' son caught him by the fair hair,
appearing to him only, for no man of the others saw her.
Achilleus in amazement turned about, and straightway
knew Pallas Athene and the terrible eyes shining.
He uttered winged words and addressed her: 'Why have you come now,
o child of Zeus of the aegis, once more? Is it that you may see
the outrageousness of the son of Atreus Agamemnon?
Yet will I tell you this thing, and I think it shall be accomplished.
By such acts of arrogance he may even lose his own life.'
    Then in answer the goddess grey-eyed Athene spoke to him:
'I have come down to stay your anger – but will you obey me? –
from the sky; and the goddess of the white arms Hera sent me,
who loves both of you equally in her heart and cares for you.
Come then, do not take your sword in your hand, keep clear of fighting,
though indeed with words you may abuse him, and it will be that way.
And this also will I tell you and it will be a thing accomplished.
Some day three times over such shining gifts shall be given you

by reason of this outrage. Hold your hand then, and obey us.'
   Then in answer again spoke Achilleus of the swift feet:
'Goddess, it is necessary that I obey the word of you two,
angry though I am in my heart. So it will be better.
If any man obeys the gods, they listen to him also.'
   He spoke, and laid his heavy hand on the silver sword hilt
and thrust the great blade back into the scabbard nor disobeyed
the word of Athene. And she went back again to Olympos
to the house of Zeus of the aegis with the other divinities.
   But Peleus' son once again in words of derision
spoke to Atreides, and did not yet let go of his anger:
'You wine sack, with a dog's eyes, with a deer's heart. Never
once have you taken courage in your heart to arm with your people
for battle, or go into ambuscade with the best of the Achaians.
No, for in such things you see death. Far better to your mind
is it, all along the widespread host of the Achaians
to take away the gifts of any man who speaks up against you.
King who feed on your people, since you rule nonentities;
otherwise, son of Atreus, this were your last outrage.
But I will tell you this and swear a great oath upon it:
in the name of this sceptre, which never again will bear leaf nor
branch, now that it has left behind the cut stump in the mountains,
nor shall it ever blossom again, since the bronze blade stripped
bark and leafage, and now at last the sons of the Achaians
carry it in their hands in state when they administer
the justice of Zeus. And this shall be a great oath before you:
some day longing for Achilleus will come to the sons of the Achaians,
all of them. Then stricken at heart though you be, you will be able
to do nothing, when in their numbers before man-slaughtering Hektor
they drop and die. And then you will eat out the heart within you
in sorrow, that you did no honour to the best of the Achaians.'
   Thus spoke Peleus' son and dashed to the ground the sceptre
studded with golden nails, and sat down again. But Atreides
raged still on the other side, and between them Nestor
the fair-spoken rose up, the lucid speaker of Pylos,
from whose lips the streams of words ran sweeter than honey.
In his time two generations of mortal men had perished,
those who had grown up with him and they who had been born to
these in sacred Pylos, and he was king in the third age.
He in kind intention toward both stood forth and addressed them:
'Oh, for shame. Great sorrow comes on the land of Achaia.
Now might Priam and the sons of Priam in truth be happy,
and all the rest of the Trojans be visited in their hearts with gladness,
were they to hear all this wherein you two are quarrelling,
you, who surpass all Danaans in council, in fighting.

Yet be persuaded. Both of you are younger than I am.
Yes, and in my time I have dealt with better men than
you are, and never once did they disregard me. Never
yet have I seen nor shall see again such men as these were,
men like Peirithoös, and Dryas, shepherd of the people,
Kaineus and Exadios, godlike Polyphemos,
or Theseus, Aigeus' son, in the likeness of the immortals.
These were the strongest generation of earth-born mortals,
the strongest, and they fought against the strongest, the beast men
living within the mountains, and terribly they destroyed them.
I was of the company of these men, coming from Pylos,
a long way from a distant land, since they had summoned me.
And I fought single-handed, yet against such men no one
of the mortals now alive upon earth could do battle. And also
these listened to the counsels I gave and heeded my bidding.
Do you also obey, since to be persuaded is better.
You, great man that you are, yet do not take the girl away
but let her be, a prize as the sons of the Achaians gave her
first. Nor, son of Peleus, think to match your strength with
the king, since never equal with the rest is the portion of honour
of the sceptred king to whom Zeus gives magnificence. Even
though you are the stronger man, and the mother who bore you was immortal,
yet is this man greater who is lord over more than you rule.
Son of Atreus, give up your anger; even I entreat you
to give over your bitterness against Achilleus, he who
stands as a great bulwark of battle over all the Achaians.'
　　Then in answer again spoke powerful Agamemnon:
'Yes, old sir, all this you have said is fair and orderly.
Yet here is a man who wishes to be above all others,
who wishes to hold power over all, and to be lord of
all, and give them their orders, yet I think one will not obey him.
And if the everlasting gods have made him a spearman,
yet they have not given him the right to speak abusively.'
　　Then looking at him darkly brilliant Achilleus answered him:
'So must I be called of no account and a coward
if I must carry out every order you may happen to give me.
Tell other men to do these things, but give me no more
commands, since I for my part have no intention to obey you.
And put away in your thoughts this other thing I tell you.
With my hands I will not fight for the girl's sake, neither
with you nor any other man, since you take her away who gave her.
But of all the other things that are mine beside my fast black
ship, you shall take nothing away against my pleasure.
Come, then, only try it, that these others may see also;
instantly your own black blood will stain my spearpoint.'

So these two after battling in words of contention
stood up, and broke the assembly beside the ships of the Achaians. [...]

### Iliad 2.1–282

[After Achilles withdraws to his camp and re-    Zeus sends a false dream to Agamemnon
fuses to fight any longer for the Greek cause,    urging an immediate attack on the Trojans.]

Now the rest of the gods, and men who were lords of chariots,
slept night long, but the ease of sleep came not upon Zeus
who was pondering in his heart how he might bring honour
to Achilleus, and destroy many beside the ships of the Achaians.
Now to his mind this thing appeared to be the best counsel,
to send evil Dream to Atreus' son Agamemnon.
He cried out to the dream and addressed him in winged words:
'Go forth, evil Dream, beside the swift ships of the Achaians.
Make your way to the shelter of Atreus' son Agamemnon;
speak to him in words exactly as I command you.
Bid him arm the flowing-haired Achaians for battle
in all haste; since now he might take the wide-wayed city
of the Trojans. For no longer are the gods who live on Olympos
arguing the matter, since Hera forced them all over
by her supplication, and evils are in store for the Trojans.'
    So he spoke, and Dream listened to his word and descended.
Lightly he came down beside the swift ships of the Achaians
and came to Agamemnon the son of Atreus. He found him
sleeping within his shelter in a cloud of immortal slumber.
Dream stood then beside his head in the likeness of Nestor,
Neleus' son, whom Agamemnon honoured beyond all
elders beside. In Nestor's likeness the divine Dream spoke to him:
'Son of wise Atreus breaker of horses, are you sleeping?
He should not sleep night long who is a man burdened with counsels
and responsibility for a people and cares so numerous.
Listen quickly to what I say, since I am a messenger
of Zeus, who far away cares much for you and is pitiful.
Zeus bids you arm the flowing-haired Achaians for battle
in all haste; since now you might take the wide-wayed city
of the Trojans. For no longer are the gods who live on Olympos
arguing the matter, since Hera forced them all over
by her supplication, and evils are in store for the Trojans
from Zeus. Keep this thought in your heart then, let not forgetfulness
take you, after you are released from the kindly sweet slumber.'
    So he spoke and went away, and left Agamemnon

there, believing things in his heart that were not to be accomplished.
For he thought that on that very day he would take Priam's city;
fool, who knew nothing of all the things Zeus planned to accomplish,
Zeus, who yet was minded to visit tears and sufferings
on Trojans and Danaans alike in the strong encounters.
Agamemnon awoke from sleep, the divine voice drifting
around him. He sat upright and put on his tunic,
beautiful, fresh woven, and threw the great mantle over it.
Underneath his shining feet he bound the fair sandals
and across his shoulders slung the sword with the nails of silver,
and took up the sceptre of his fathers, immortal forever.
Thus he went beside the ships of the bronze-armoured Achaians.
    Now the goddess Dawn drew close to tall Olympos
with her message of light to Zeus and the other immortals.
But Agamemnon commanded his clear-voiced heralds to summon
by proclamation to assembly the flowing-haired Achaians,
and the heralds made their cry and the men were assembled swiftly.
    First he held a council session of the high-hearted princes
beside the ship of Nestor, the king of the race of Pylos.
Summoning these he compacted before them his close counsel:
'Hear me, friends: in my sleep a Dream divine came to me
through the immortal night, and in appearance and stature
and figure it most closely resembled splendid Nestor.
It came and stood above my head and spoke a word to me:
"Son of wise Atreus breaker of horses, are you sleeping?
He should not sleep night long who is a man burdened with counsels
and responsibility for a people and cares so numerous.
Now listen quickly to what I say, since I am a messenger
from Zeus, who far away cares much for you and is pitiful.
Zeus bids you arm the flowing-haired Achaians for battle
in all haste; since now you might take the wide-wayed city
of the Trojans. For no longer are the gods who live on Olympos
arguing the matter, since Hera has forced them all over
by her supplication, and evils are in store for the Trojans
by Zeus' will. Keep this within your heart." So speaking
the Dream went away on wings, and sweet sleep released me.
Come then, let us see if we can arm the sons of the Achaians.
Yet first, since it is the right way, I will make trial of them
by words, and tell them even to flee in their benched vessels.
Do you take stations here and there, to check them with orders.'
    He spoke thus, and sat down again, and among them rose up
Nestor, he who ruled as a king in sandy Pylos.
He in kind intention toward all stood forth and addressed them:
'Friends, who are leaders of the Argives and keep their counsel,
had it been any other Achaian who told of this dream

we should have called it a lie and we might rather have turned from it.
Now he who claims to be the best of the Achaians has seen it.
Come then, let us see if we can arm the sons of the Achaians.'
   So he spoke and led the way departing from the council,
and the rest rose to their feet, the sceptred kings, obeying
the shepherd of the people, and the army thronged behind them.
Like the swarms of clustering bees that issue forever
in fresh bursts from the hollow in the stone, and hang like
bunched grapes as they hover beneath the flowers in springtime
fluttering in swarms together this way and that way,
so the many nations of men from the ships and the shelters
along the front of the deep sea beach marched in order
by companies to the assembly, and Rumour walked blazing among them,
Zeus' messenger, to hasten them along. Thus they were assembled
and the place of their assembly was shaken, and the earth groaned
as the people took their positions and there was tumult. Nine heralds
shouting set about putting them in order, to make them cease their
clamour and listen to the kings beloved of Zeus. The people
took their seats in sober fashion and were marshalled in their places
and gave over their clamouring. Powerful Agamemnon
stood up holding the sceptre Hephaistos had wrought him carefully.
Hephaistos gave it to Zeus the king, the son of Kronos,
and Zeus in turn gave it to the courier Argeïphontes,
and lord Hermes gave it to Pelops, driver of horses,
and Pelops again gave it to Atreus, the shepherd of the people.
Atreus dying left it to Thyestes of the rich flocks,
and Thyestes left it in turn to Agamemnon to carry
and to be lord of many islands and over all Argos.
Leaning upon this sceptre he spoke and addressed the Argives:
'Fighting men and friends, o Danaans, henchmen of Ares:
Zeus son of Kronos has caught me fast in bitter futility.
He is hard; who before this time promised me and consented
that I might sack strong-walled Ilion and sail homeward.
Now he has devised a vile deception, and bids me go back
to Argos in dishonour having lost many of my people.
Such is the way it will be pleasing to Zeus, who is too strong,
who before now has broken the crests of many cities
and will break them again, since his power is beyond all others.
And this shall be a thing of shame for the men hereafter
to be told, that so strong, so great a host of Achaians
carried on and fought in vain a war that was useless
against men fewer than they, with no accomplishment shown for it;
since if both sides were to be willing, Achaians and Trojans,
to cut faithful oaths of truce, and both to be numbered,
and the Trojans were to be counted by those with homes in the city,

while we were to be allotted in tens, we Achaians,
and each one of our tens chose a man of Troy to pour wine for it,
still there would be many tens left without a wine steward.
By so much I claim we sons of the Achaians outnumber
the Trojans – those who live in the city; but there are companions
from other cities in their numbers, wielders of the spear, to help them,
who drive me hard back again and will not allow me,
despite my will, to sack the well-founded stronghold of Ilion.
And now nine years of mighty Zeus have gone by, and the timbers
of our ships have rotted away and the cables are broken
and far away our own wives and our young children
are sitting within our halls and wait for us, while still our work here
stays forever unfinished as it is, for whose sake we came hither.
Come then, do as I say, let us all be won over; let us
run away with our ships to the beloved land of our fathers
since no longer now shall we capture Troy of the wide ways.'
  So he spoke, and stirred up the passion in the breast of all those
who were within that multitude and listened to his counsel.
And the assembly was shaken as on the sea the big waves
in the main by Ikaria, when the south and south-east winds
driving down from the clouds of Zeus the father whip them.
As when the west wind moves across the grain deep standing,
boisterously, and shakes and sweeps it till the tassels lean, so
all of that assembly was shaken, and the men in tumult
swept to the ships, and underneath their feet the dust lifted
and rose high, and the men were all shouting to one another
to lay hold on the ships and drag them down to the bright sea.
They cleaned out the keel channels and their cries hit skyward
as they made for home and snatched the props from under the vessels.
  Then for the Argives a homecoming beyond fate might have
been accomplished, had not Hera spoken a word to Athene:
'For shame, now, Atrytone, daughter of Zeus of the aegis.
As things are, the Argives will take flight homeward over
the wide ridges of the sea to the land of their fathers,
and thus they would leave to Priam and to the Trojans Helen
of Argos, to glory over, for whose sake many Achaians
lost their lives in Troy far from their own native country.
But go now along the host of the bronze-armoured Achaians.
Speak to each man in words of gentleness and draw him backward
nor let them drag down to the salt sea their oarswept vessels.'
  So she spoke, nor did the goddess grey-eyed Athene
disobey her, but went in speed down the peaks of Olympos,
and lightly she arrived beside the fast ships of the Achaians.
There she came on Odysseus, the equal of Zeus in counsel,
standing still; he had laid no hand upon his black, strong-benched

vessel, since disappointment touched his heart and his spirit.
Athene of the grey eyes stood beside him and spoke to him:
'Son of Laertes and seed of Zeus, resourceful Odysseus:
will it be this way? Will you all hurl yourselves into your benched ships
and take flight homeward to the beloved land of your fathers,
and would you thus leave to Priam and to the Trojans Helen
of Argos, to glory over, for whose sake many Achaians
lost their lives in Troy far from their own native country?
Go now along the host of the Achaians, give way no longer,
speak to each man in words of gentleness and draw them backward,
nor let them drag down to the salt sea their oarswept vessels.'

So she spoke, and he knew the voice of the goddess speaking
and went on the run, throwing aside his cloak, which was caught up
by Eurybates the herald of Ithaka who followed him.
He came face to face with Agamemnon, son of Atreus,
and took from him the sceptre of his fathers, immortal forever.
With this he went beside the ships of the bronze-armoured Achaians.

Whenever he encountered some king, or man of influence,
he would stand beside him and with soft words try to restrain him:
'Excellency! It does not become you to be frightened like any
coward. Rather hold fast and check the rest of the people.
You do not yet clearly understand the purpose of Atreides.
Now he makes trial, but soon will bear hard on the sons of the Achaians.
Did we not all hear what he was saying in council?
May he not in anger do some harm to the sons of the Achaians!
For the anger of god-supported kings is a big matter,
to whom honour and love are given from Zeus of the counsels.'

When he saw some man of the people who was shouting,
he would strike at him with his staff, and reprove him also:
'Excellency! Sit still and listen to what others tell you,
to those who are better men than you, you skulker and coward
and thing of no account whatever in battle or council.
Surely not all of us Achaians can be as kings here.
Lordship for many is no good thing. Let there be one ruler,
one king, to whom the son of devious-devising Kronos
gives the sceptre and right of judgment, to watch over his people.'

So he went through the army marshalling it, until once more
they swept back into the assembly place from the ships and the shelters
clamorously, as when from the thunderous sea the surf-beat
crashes upon the great beach, and the whole sea is in tumult.

Now the rest had sat down, and were orderly in their places,
but one man, Thersites of the endless speech, still scolded,
who knew within his head many words, but disorderly;
vain, and without decency, to quarrel with the princes
with any word he thought might be amusing to the Argives.

This was the ugliest man who came beneath Ilion. He was
bandy-legged and went lame of one foot, with shoulders
stooped and drawn together over his chest, and above this
his skull went up to a point with the wool grown sparsely upon it.
Beyond all others Achilleus hated him, and Odysseus.
These two he was forever abusing, but now at brilliant
Agamemnon he clashed the shrill noise of his abuse. The Achaians
were furiously angry with him, their minds resentful.
But he, crying the words aloud, scolded Agamemnon:
'Son of Atreus, what thing further do you want, or find fault with
now? Your shelters are filled with bronze, there are plenty of the choicest
women for you within your shelter, whom we Achaians
give to you first of all whenever we capture some stronghold.
Or is it still more gold you will be wanting, that some son
of the Trojans, breakers of horses, brings as ransom out of Ilion,
one that I, or some other Achaian, capture and bring in?
Is it some young woman to lie with in love and keep her
all to yourself apart from the others? It is not right for
you, their leader, to lead in sorrow the sons of the Achaians.
My good fools, poor abuses, you women, not men, of Achaia,
let us go back home in our ships, and leave this man here
by himself in Troy to mull his prizes of honour
that he may find out whether or not we others are helping him.
And now he has dishonoured Achilleus, a man much better
than he is. He has taken his prize by force and keeps her.
But there is no gall in Achilleus' heart, and he is forgiving.
Otherwise, son of Atreus, this were your last outrage.'
    So he spoke, Thersites, abusing Agamemnon
the shepherd of the people. But brilliant Odysseus swiftly
came beside him scowling and laid a harsh word upon him:
'Fluent orator though you be, Thersites, your words are
ill-considered. Stop, nor stand up alone against princes.
Out of all those who came beneath Ilion with Atreides
I assert there is no worse man than you are. Therefore
you shall not lift up your mouth to argue with princes,
cast reproaches into their teeth, nor sustain the homegoing.
We do not even know clearly how these things will be accomplished,
whether we sons of the Achaians shall win home well or badly;
yet you sit here throwing abuse at Agamemnon,
Atreus' son, the shepherd of the people, because the Danaan
fighters give him much. You argue nothing but scandal.
And this also will I tell you, and it will be a thing accomplished.
If once more I find you playing the fool, as you are now,
nevermore let the head of Odysseus sit on his shoulders,
let me nevermore be called Telemachos' father,

if I do not take you and strip away your personal clothing,
your mantle and your tunic that cover over your nakedness,
and send you thus bare and howling back to the fast ships,
whipping you out of the assembly place with the strokes of indignity.'
    So he spoke and dashed the sceptre against his back and
shoulders, and he doubled over, and a round tear dropped from him,
and a bloody welt stood up between his shoulders under
the golden sceptre's stroke, and he sat down again, frightened,
in pain, and looking helplessly about wiped off the tear-drops.
Sorry though the men were they laughed over him happily,
and thus they would speak to each other, each looking at the man next
    him:
'Come now: Odysseus has done excellent things by thousands,
bringing forward good counsels and ordering armed encounters;
but now this is far the best thing he ever has accomplished
among the Argives, to keep this thrower of words, this braggart
out of assembly. Never again will his proud heart stir him
up, to wrangle with the princes in words of revilement.'
    So the multitude spoke, but Odysseus, sacker of cities,
stood up holding the staff, and beside him grey-eyed Athene
in the likeness of a herald enjoined the people to silence,
that at once the foremost and the utmost sons of the Achaians
might listen to him speaking and deliberate his counsel. [...]


## Odyssey 2.1–259

[Odysseus, ruler of Ithaca when he departed to fight at Troy, left behind an infant son, Telemachus, who comes of age toward the end of the many years of his father's absence. On the advice of the goddess Athena, Telemachus summons an assembly meeting in the hopes of doing something about the crowd of greedy suitors besieging his mother and feasting constantly at his father's household.]

Dawn comes early, with rosy fingers. When she appeared, the son that Odysseus loved sat up to put on his clothes and left his bed, then slung the keen sword about his shoulders, fastened his sandals under his glistening feet and went out from his room, like a god to look upon. At once he ordered the clear-voiced heralds to call the flowing-haired Achaeans to the assembly-place. The heralds made their proclamation and the people soon began to gather. When they were ready – when the assembly-place was filled – Telemachus also took his way there. In his hand was a spear of bronze, beside him were two swift-footed hounds, and Athene shed upon the boy a grace of presence more than human, so that as he came nearer to themselves the people all gazed at him in wonder. He took his place in his father's seat, and the elders made way for him.

The first to speak to those assembled was Lord Aegyptius, bent with age and unfathomably wise. When King Odysseus sailed with his hollow ships, bound for Troy of the noble horses, a son of Aegyptius had gone with him, and this was the spearsman Antiphus; but the savage Cyclops had killed him inside his arching cave, making a meal of him after all the rest. The old lord had three other sons; one of them – Eurynomus – was among the suitors, and the other two saw to their father's farms; but still he never forgot the first in his grief and mourning, and with a tear for him he now spoke in council:

"Men of Ithaca, listen to my words. There has been no council and no assembly here from the day when King Odysseus sailed with his hollow ships. Who has thus called us together now? On whom has there come this pressing need, among our younger men or among our elders? Has our summoner heard some news of a host of men approaching, news he would bring before us clearly as being the first to hear of it? Is there some other public matter which he would tell and apprise us of? A worthy man he must be, I think, a heaven-favoured man. May Zeus bring to accomplishment whatever good thing he has at heart!"

So he spoke, and the son of Odysseus accepted the omen joyfully, nor did he stay seated longer; eager to speak, he stood up in mid-assembly. The staff of office was put in his hands by Peisenor, a herald versed in the ways of wisdom; then he spoke thus, addressing Aegyptius first:

"Sir, the man you speak of is not far off, as you will now find. It was I who summoned the people here, because of a thing that bears hard upon me. I have heard no news of a host approaching, news I might bring before you as having myself first learned of it, nor is there any other public matter I wish to tell and apprise you of. The business is my own. Evil has fallen upon my house – a double evil. First I have lost my noble father, who once was king among all you here and ruled you as gently as a father; then something far worse has befallen me, which before long will ruin my house altogether and bring to nothing my means of living. My mother, greatly to her distress, has been beset by suitors, sons of the greatest nobles here. They dare not go to the house of Icarius her father so that he in person might receive bride-gifts for his daughter, giving her to any suitor he pleased who was acceptable to herself. Instead, they haunt my palace day in, day out; they slaughter my sheep and oxen and fatted goats; they make merry here, they selfishly drink the glowing wine, and thus abundance of things is wasted. All this is because there is no man left with the mettle of Odysseus to ward off ruin from the house, I myself am not able to ward it off; I fear I shall always be a weakling, with no skill to resist at all. Had I the strength, I would take my stand gladly enough, because these men's deeds and the havoc they make of my possessions are beyond all justice, beyond endurance. Do you feel no self-reproach yourselves, no shame for the reproach of your neighbours, of those who live all around you here? You should shrink from the anger of the gods; the gods in their indignation may bring your misdoings down on your own heads. I appeal to you by Olympian Zeus himself; I appeal by Themis, who convenes men's councils and dissolves them, cease from these ways, you men of Ithaca, and leave me unmolested to pine away in my bitter grief. Or can it be that Odysseus my noble father once did in malice some harm to the Achaeans for which in counter-malice you take your revenge on me by hounding on these men against me? Better for me that you yourselves should devour my cattle and hoarded goods. If you of Ithaca were the devourers, amends might indeed be made before long, because we of the household could accost you here and there in the town, asking aloud for our goods again till everything had been given back. Instead, you inflict upon my spirit miseries for which there is no redress."

So he spoke in his indignation, and threw down the staff upon the ground. He had burst into tears, and compassion came upon the people. They all kept silent, not having the heart to answer him unkindly; all but Antinous, who rejoined:

"What words are these, Telemachus? How arrogantly you speak, how ungovernable you are in passion! You endeavour to put us to the blush; you hope to fasten disgrace on us. Listen; it is not the Achaean suitors who are to blame; it is your own mother with her unexampled trickery. Three years have passed – and a fourth will soon be gone – since she began to baffle her suitors' hearts. She gives hope to all, she promises every man in turn, she sends out messages here and there, yet all the while her purpose is far removed. Here is one scheme that she devised. She set up in her hall an ample web, long and delicate, and began to weave. At the same time she spoke to us: 'Young men who after Odysseus' death have come here to woo me, you are eager for this marriage with me; nevertheless I ask your patience till I have finished weaving this robe, so that what I have spun may not be wasted and go for nothing; it is King Laertes' burial-robe, for the time when he is overtaken by the grim doom of distressful death. I dread reproach from Achaean women here for allowing one who had gathered great possessions to lie at his death without a shroud.' So she spoke, and our wills consented. From that time on she would weave the great web all day, but when night came she would have torches set beside her and would unravel the work. For three years on end this trickery foiled the trusting suitors; but when seasons passed and the fourth year came, one of her maids who was in the secret revealed the truth, and we came upon her undoing the glossy web; so with ill grace she finished the work perforce.

"And now, this is your answer from the suitors; take it to heart yourself, and let all the Achaeans take it to heart as well. Tell your mother to leave this place and take for husband whatever man her father bids her and she approves. Or does she mean to continue plaguing the sons of Achaeans, setting her wits to work in things where Athene has favoured her so richly? Skill in exquisite workmanship, a keen mind, subtlety – these she has, beyond anything we have heard of even in the ladies of older times – the Achaean ladies of braided tresses like Tyro and Alcmene and garlanded Mycene; not one of these had the mastery in devising things that Penelope has, yet her last device went beyond all reason. So the suitors will not cease devouring your substance and possessions as long as she keeps the frame of mind that the gods are fostering in her now. To herself she is bringing great renown, but to you the loss of wealth and substance. We will neither return to our estates nor depart elsewhere till she takes for husband whichever of us Achaeans she may choose."

Thoughtful Telemachus answered him: "Antinous, I cannot unhouse against her will the mother who bore me and who bred me. My father, alive or dead, is for certain far away from here, and it is hard that I myself should pay heavy recompense to Icarius if of my own free will I tell my mother to leave this place. I shall suffer evil from him, her father, and dark powers also will do me evil because when my mother quits this house she will call down the grim Furies on me; and with fellow-men I shall be a byword. Never then will I utter the word you ask. If your own hearts reproach you now, leave my halls and look for your feasts elsewhere, changing from house to house to consume possessions that are your own. But if to yourselves it seems a better thing, a more desirable thing, to waste one man's substance and go scot-free – so be it, waste on! I for my part will call aloud on the deathless gods, hoping that Zeus will let requital be made at last; then you will perish in these same halls and it is I who shall go scot-free."

So spoke Telemachus, and Zeus the Thunderer in response sent forth two eagles to fly down from a mountain height. For a while they flew as the wind wafted them, straining their wings side by side, but when they were right above the assembly-place with its hum of voices, they wheeled about and shook their thick feathers, sweeping low over all those there and boding death; then with their talons they tore at each other's cheeks and necks and sped away to the right, over the town and houses. The astonished people had followed the eagles with their eyes, and their hearts half guessed things that indeed were to come to pass. All this drew words from an aged lord, Halitherses the son of Mastor, who beyond the rest of his generation was versed in the lore of birds and wise in expounding it. Wishing well to all, he gave his interpretation: "Men of Ithaca, heed what I am about to say. My exposition concerns the suitors first; a great wave of trouble is rolling towards them. Odysseus will not be away from his kith and kin much longer; indeed I think he is near already, sowing seeds of death and destruction for every suitor here. As for the rest of us in Ithaca, evil will fall on many of us as well. But let us, while there is still time, consider how best to check these men, or rather, let the men check themselves – they will gain most by so doing now. I speak as no novice in prophecy; I am a master. I see fulfilment now of everything I once said to subtle-witted Odysseus himself when the Argives were embarking for Ilium and he like the rest went aboard his vessel. I told him that after many trials, after the loss of all his comrades, in the twentieth year, known by none, he would come back to Ithaca. All this is finding fulfilment now."

Eurymachus, son of Polybus, answered him: "Enough of this now, old prophesier; go home and interpret omens there; save your own children from threats of doom. This morning's omens I claim to interpret better than you. There are many birds that cross the sunlight, and not all of them have fateful meaning. No: Odysseus has perished far from here, and I wish that you had gone down to destruction with him. Then you would not have uttered these tedious soothsayings, nor would you be fanning his son's resentment in hopes of winning some gift for your own household. I will tell you plainly, and what I tell you will come to pass; if you with your store of ancient wisdom inveigle this boy into defiance, he himself will be first to suffer; and as for you, sir, we shall impose such a fine upon you as it will fret your soul to pay; you will find it very hard to bear. To Telemachus I will give this counsel publicly. Let him bid his mother go back to her father's house; her kinsmen will prepare the wedding and charge themselves with the many gifts that go with a beloved daughter. Short of that, I think that the sons of the Achaeans will never cease from the wooing that so distresses you, since, come what may, we fear nobody, not even Telemachus with his eloquence; and as for your prophecies, old babbler, we have no concern over them either; they come to nothing and only make you the more detested. And the reckless devouring of possessions will also go on just as hitherto, and recompense will never be made so long as in this matter of marriage the queen keeps her suitors in suspense. As it is, we are waiting perpetually, each of us in rivalry with his neighbour over this paragon, instead of seeking those other women whom we might well enough choose to wed."

Thoughtful Telemachus answered him: "Eurymachus, and you other overbearing suitors – on that matter I have no more to ask or to say; the gods know already where I stand, and all the Achaeans know. But now let me have a rapid ship and a crew of twenty to make the voyage out and back; I mean to go to Sparta and sandy Pylos to seek for news of my father's homecoming: he has been away from us too long. Perhaps some human witness will speak, perhaps I shall hear some rumour that comes from Zeus, a great source of tidings for mankind. If I hear that my father is alive and is on his way, I may hold my ground for a year more, despite my troubles; but if I hear he is dead and gone, then I will journey back to my own country and raise a cairn to him, then pay him in full his due of funeral honours and find a new husband for my mother."

With these words he sat down, and Mentor in turn rose to speak – a friend of his noble father in other times. When Odysseus sailed, he had left all his household in Mentor's care, bidding him guard everything securely and respect the wishes of old Laertes. His words now were of honest purpose. "Men of Ithaca, heed what I am about to say. I could wish that henceforward no sceptred king should set himself to be kind and gentle and equitable; I would have every king a tyrant and evil-doer, since King Odysseus goes utterly unremembered among the people that once he ruled with the gentleness of a father. Nor do I make it a reproach that the headstrong suitors should still do their deeds of violence in all the wickedness of their hearts, because they are staking their own lives when they grossly devour the substance of Odysseus, supposing that he will not return. It is the rest of you I am indignant with, to see how you all sit dumbly there instead of rebuking them and restraining them; you are many; the suitors are few."

Leocritus son of Euenor answered: "Mentor, what words are these? Mischief-making fool, you are urging the people to restrain us. You will find it harder than you think to fight men who in truth outnumber you, and all this for the sake of a meal. If Odysseus of Ithaca himself surprised us feasting in his palace and were bent on thrusting us out again, his wife would have little joy at his homecoming, however much she had longed for it; no, there and then he would meet an ignominious end if he took up arms against such odds; your words are folly. But come, let the people here disperse, each to his own home; and Telemachus shall be sped upon his journey by Mentor and Halitherses, who are friends of his father from long ago. But he is more likely, I surmise, to remain here a good while yet; what news he learns he will learn in Ithaca, and he will never make this journey."

So he spoke, letting the assembly break up at once. The people dispersed to their own houses; the suitors made for the palace of Odysseus. [...]

# Hesiod: Selections on rulers and justice

Hesiod was early Greece's other great epic poet. His *Theogony* and *Works and Days* were probably composed around the turn of the seventh century BC, roughly the same era as or a little later than the epics of Homer. While Hesiod's two poems are not heroic in the way of Homer's and each focuses on different themes, they nevertheless touch upon government and the proper use of power in the Greek world of Hesiod's time. The excerpt from *Theogony* lays out an idealized view of kings/lords who are blessed by the Muses; that of *Works and Days* gives a darker picture, highlighting the evil effects of rulers who have been corrupted. (*Sources:* Hesiod, *Theogony* ll. 81–97 and *Works and Days* ll. 213–269, trans. by A. N. Athanassakis from *Theogony; Works and Days; Shield/Hesiod* (Baltimore: Johns Hopkins University Press, 1983), pp. 15, 72–3.)

## *Theogony* lines 81–97

[. . .] And if the daughters of great Zeus honor a king
cherished by Zeus and look upon him when he is born,
they pour on his tongue sweet dew
and make the words that flow from his mouth honey-sweet,
and all the people look up to him as with straight justice
he gives his verdict and with unerring firmness
and wisdom brings some great strife to a swift end.
This is why kings are prudent, and when in the assembly
injustice is done, wrongs are righted
by the kings with ease and gentle persuasion.
When such a king comes to the assembly he stands out;
yes, he is revered like a god and treated with cheerful respect.
Such is the holy gift the Muses give men.
The singers and lyre players of this earth
are descended from the Muses and far-shooting Apollon,
but kings are from the line of Zeus. Blessed is the man
whom the Muses love; sweet song flows from his mouth. [. . .]

## *Works and Days* lines 213–269

[. . .] Perses, obey justice and restrain reckless wrongdoing,
for such wrongdoing harms the poor, and even the noble
find it an unwelcome burden that weighs them down
and brings them ruin. The road to fair dealings
is the better one. Justice is the winner in the race
against insolent crime. Only fools need suffer to learn.
The Oath Demon follows the trail of crooked decrees;
Justice howls when she is dragged about by bribe-devouring men
whose verdicts are crooked when they sit in judgment.
Weeping and clothed in mist, she follows through the cities
and dwellings of men, and visits ruin on those
who twist her straight ways and drive her out.
But those who give straight verdicts and follow justice,

both when fellow citizens and strangers are on trial,
live in a city that blossoms, a city that prospers.
Then youth-nurturing peace comes over the land, and Zeus
who sees afar does not decree for them the pains of war.
Men whose justice is straight know neither hunger nor ruin,
but amid feasts enjoy the yield of their labors.
For them the earth brings forth a rich harvest; and for them
the top of an oak teems with acorn and the middle with bees.
Fleecy sheep are weighed down with wool,
and women bear children who resemble their fathers.
There is an abundance of blessings and the grainland
grants such harvests that no one has to sail on the sea.
But far-seeing Zeus, son of Kronos, is the judge
of wanton wrongdoers who plot deeds of harshness.
Many times one man's wickedness ruins a whole city,
if such a man breaks the law and turns his mind to recklessness.
Then the son of Kronos sends a great bane from the sky,
hunger and plague, and the people waste away.
Women bear no children, and families dwindle
through the counsels of Zeus the Olympian,
the son of Kronos, who punishes wrong by wiping out
large armies, walls, and ships at sea.
Kings, give this verdict no little thought,
for the immortals are ever present among men,
and they see those who with crooked verdicts
spurn divine retribution and grind down one another's lives.
Upon this earth that nurtures many Zeus can levy
thirty thousand deathless guardians of mortal men,
who keep a watchful eye over verdicts and cruel acts
as they rove the whole earth, clothed in mist.
Justice is a maiden and a daughter of Zeus;
the gods of Olympos respect her noble title,
and whenever men mistreat her through false charges
she rushes to sit at the feet of Zeus Kronion
and she denounces the designs of men who are not just,
so that the people pay for the reckless deeds and evil plans
of kings whose slanted words twist her straight path.
Keep her commands, O gift-devouring kings, and let
verdicts be straight; yes, lay your crooked ways aside!
He that wrongs another man wrongs, above all, himself,
and evil schemes bring more harm on those who plot them.
The eye of Zeus sees all, notices all;
it sees all this, too, if it wishes, and knows exactly
what sort of host this town is to justice. [...]

# Homer and the Beginning of Political Thought in Greece

## Kurt A. Raaflaub

[...] To use the epics as historical evidence poses serious problems. For my present purposes it suffices simply to state my position. In the form in which they survive, the *Iliad* and *Odyssey* each are the work of one and possibly the same "monumental" poet who lived in the late eighth century in Ionia. Unlike the events and actions that are attributed to the heroes and therefore elevated into a superhuman sphere, the world in which they live and act is human, real, accessible, and understandable to the poet's audience. The practical aspects of life such as the extended household (*oikos*), the early stages of the polis, agriculture, trade, and war, assemblies and council, relationships within the community and the value system of the leading class – these practical aspects form a system that is sufficiently consistent in itself to mirror a historical society which, according to Moses Finley, is to be dated in the tenth and early ninth centuries, according to others – and more probably – a little later. However that may be, much more important is that the social, political and moral concerns we find in the epics, are the concerns of a real society and, at least in this respect, the poet's own.[1]

Nevertheless, the epics are primarily artistic masterpieces of the highest order. Equally, the poets and bards aimed primarily at entertaining their listeners and glorifying their ancestral heroes. Accordingly we should expect the epics to present, even in their more contemporary elements, a highly positive picture of the "aristocracy."[2] Over vast stretches that is indeed the case. But there are notable exceptions, and these are particularly useful for our purposes. Some of them we have already discussed; let us look at a few more.

### *Iliad* I and II

The *Iliad* begins with the quarrel between Achilles and Agamemnon which is caused by two bad mistakes on the part of the king and results in Achilles' withdrawal from the war. In its basic outline this story certainly was very old. In our poet's interpretation it is a conflict between the leader and his most eminent ally. Achilles is the better fighter and the son of a goddess but he is not equal to Agamemnon who commands the greater number of men. The stronger has to subordinate himself to the more powerful: a difficult situation which requires tact and mutual respect, qualities that are lacking in both. Achilles is perfectly justified in doing and saying what he does; he has every right to remind Agamemnon of his duties, to point out his mistakes, and to be offended by the king's decision to make another pay for his own loss. But that it is

Kurt A. Raaflaub, "Homer and the Beginning of Political Thought in Greece," in *Proceedings of the Boston Area Colloquium Series in Ancient Philosophy* 4 (Lanham, MD: University Press of America, 1988), 1–25, pp. 8–22.

Achilles, of all people, who says these things, and how he says them, is unbearable for the king who feels threatened by a conspiracy of the seer and the overbearing chieftain. In order to save his face and position, he must demonstrate his power over the rival – whatever the consequences,

> that you may learn well
> how much greater I am than you, and another man may shrink back
> from likening himself to me and contending against me.
> (I 185–187; cf. 287–291)

This is a realistic scene, probably one familiar enough to the audience. It gains an additional dimension because the poet is not satisfied with describing the quarrel between the heroes but strongly emphasizes its consequences for the community. Agamemnon is aware of his obligation as a leader: "I myself desire that my people be safe, not perish" (117). But his pride prevails and causes immense disaster for his people, so that Achilles can justly call him "devourer of his people."[3]

On the other hand, by withdrawing from the war, Achilles provides the immediate cause for the Greeks' suffering; and he knows it (240–244):

> Some day longing for Achilleus will come to the sons of the Achaians,
> all of them. Then stricken at heart though you be, you will be able
> to do nothing, when in their numbers before man-slaughtering Hektor
> they drop and die. And then you will eat out the heart within you
> in sorrow, that you did no honor to the best of the Achaians.

By sacrificing the common good to their personal feelings, both heroes, then, violate the "heroic code" and thereby threaten the very basis of their privileged position. For the hero's honor is tied to his obligation of protecting and saving his people[4] – an obligation clearly described in Sarpedon's often quoted address to Glaukos[5] and admirably met by Hector, the "Saviour of the city" par excellence, whose son Skamandrios is named Astyanax, "Lord of the city," by the Trojans in gratitude for his father's achievement.[6]

Thus both heroes are at fault, but the primary responsibility lies with the king. He therefore has to bear the brunt of popular anger, as it is expressed so vividly in the famous *Diapeira* of Book II. As a result of the king's attempt to test the resolve of his men the masses rush to the ships. No, this war is not popular, especially after Achilles' withdrawal. With great difficulty Odysseus restores order. But one man goes on ranting against the king: Thersites, full of disorderly words, "vain, and without decency, forever quarreling with the princes," the ugliest man in the camp: bandy-legged and lame on one foot, with stooped shoulders and a narrow chest, a pointed skull and almost bald (II 212–219). The poet tries hard to discredit him from the beginning, and when Thersites at the end gets his deserved beating the crowd is ecstatic: the greatest deed Odysseus has ever done (244–278). Having thus made clear that this man counts for nothing, the poet can let him say what actually is to be taken very seriously.[7] For what Thersites says not only is explicitly described as venting the anger of the masses (222 f.) but corresponds closely with Achilles' criticism of the king in Book I. He berates Agamemnon for his greed and obsession with women, and continues (233–242):

> It is not right for
> you, their leader, to lead in sorrow the sons of the Achaians.
> My good fools, poor abuses, you women, not men, of Achaia,
> let us go back home in our ships, and leave this man here
> by himself in Troy to mull his prizes of honor
> that he may find out whether or not we others are helping him.
> And now he has dishonored Achilleus, a man much better than he is . . .
> But there is no gall in Achilleus' heart, and he is forgiving.
> Otherwise, son of Atreus, this were your last outrage.

We may conclude, then, that the king's self-centered and irresponsible behavior not only threatens the well-being of the army and the success of the whole enterprise, but has caused a deep crisis of leadership. The rebellion of the most important vassal with all his followers, the enthusiastic "vote by feet" of the whole army to end the war there and then, and the tirades of the antihero par excellence are all expressions of profound dissatisfaction with the king. Odysseus' firm refutation of *polykoiraniē*, rulership by many, supports this conclusion (203 f.). Fortunately for those in power, it is still relatively easy to contain the masses. But in my view scenes such as those described in *Iliad* I and II attest an awareness that the masses fighting in the war and sitting in the assembly represent at least a potential power factor. Otherwise it would be futile for Achilles, Hector, and Thersites to decry the people's passiveness and lack of courage.

## Odyssey II

I think it can be shown that such dissatisfaction among the masses is aimed not only at the king, as in the cases of Paris/Priam and Agamemnon, but at large sections of the leading class. As is shown in the *Odyssey*, the conflict between communal and individual interests is a problem as much in peace as in war. When the survival of the community is not threatened by war the powerful nobleman with his household (*oikos*) is almost autonomous. Community and king cannot expect from him more than voluntary cooperation; there are no legal or practical possibilities short of violence to impose a superior will on an unwilling *oikos*. At the same time an individual or *oikos* that is threatened by others cannot expect help from the community; they have to help themselves or seek protection under a more powerful patron.[8]

However, Book II of the *Odyssey* shows beginnings of change in this respect as well. Odysseus has been gone for twenty years and is supposed dead. A band of suitors, sons of the best families from near and far, have occupied Odysseus' house, pressuring his wife Penelope to agree to a new marriage which would at the same time determine the succession, and threatening the king's *oikos* with economic ruin, thereby also weakening Telemachos' chances to succeed his father. Encouraged by Athena, Telemachos finally decides to fight back. He convenes an assembly. There has not been one for twenty years; the reason must be important: a threat of war or some other urgent public business (30–32). The assembly, that is, does not deal with private affairs, not even those of the *oikos* of the king. Yes, says Telemachos, I know; in fact, I have no such public business to offer for discussion (41–44) but the (private) evils that have befallen my house, caused by the suitors, are beyond all justice, beyond endurance. Do you feel no self-reproach yourselves, no shame for the reproach of your neighbors, of those who live all around you here? You should shrink from the anger of the gods; the gods in their indignation may bring your misdoings down on your own heads. I appeal to you by Olympian Zeus himself, I appeal by Themis, who convenes men's councils, cease from these ways ... [unless] my noble father once did in malice some harm to the Achaeans for which in counter-malice you take your revenge on me by hounding on these men against me? (45–79; W. Shewring's prose transl.)

So, though private business, it is of public concern, because the reputation of the community is at stake, and its safety may be in peril if indeed the gods punish injustice (143 f., cf. I 378–380). As also in the case of Hesiod, Telemachos' strongest argument is based on religious belief and hope.[9] Zeus promptly sends an omen which is interpreted by the seer Halitherses: Odysseus is close, the suitors are in mortal danger, many others in Ithaca will be hurt; let us straighten things out while there is still time (161–169). To no avail: the people, though overcome by compassion, keep silent (81–83), and the suitors are not impressed: they fear neither Telemachos nor the gods and see no reason to drop their competition for queen and kingship (85 ff., esp. 111–128; 198–201).

Then old Mentor gives a remarkable speech (229–241), insisting on three points. First, he does not reproach the suitors for their violent deeds, because they are staking their own lives in injuring the house of Odysseus (235–238, cf. 281–284). In other words: what else do you expect of young noblemen? It is their problem if in their competition for power and rank they use the most vicious methods and risk their lives. This does not seem to me to mirror a high opinion of the behavior typical of noblemen.

Second, he criticizes the people in the assembly:

It is the rest of you I am indignant with, to see how you all sit dumbly there instead of rebuking them and restraining them; you are many; the suitors are few. (239–241)

What appears a distant possibility in the *Iliad* is here turned into a direct appeal, expressed not by the despicable Thersites but by the respected Mentor. Here we grasp the very beginnings of the concept of communal responsibility.

Third, Mentor justifies the need for such communal involvement:

I could wish that henceforward no sceptered king should set himself to be kind and gentle and equitable; I would have every king a tyrant and evil-doer, since King Odysseus goes utterly unremembered among the people that once he ruled with the gentleness of a father. (230–234; cf. V 8–12)

That means: Odysseus was a good king without the faults one ordinarily expects from men in his position.[10] As Penelope says to the suitors in Book IV (687–695):

Never, in either word or deed, did he wrong any man among the people, though that is the way of heaven-protected kings; true, a king will befriend one man, but then he will persecute another. With Odysseus it was never so; he was never a tyrant to any man. But

your own...shameful actions show themselves plainly for what they are, and past
kindness leaves you ungrateful now.

For these merits, the community is obliged to Odysseus and to his family. To ignore
such obligations violates traditional rules of behavior,[11] just as the behavior of some
of the suitors is doubly objectionable because they are ignoring their personal
obligations toward their benefactor Odysseus.[12] Moreover, by showing such a lack
of gratitude, the community sets a negative example; henceforth, there will be no
incentive for a king to put the interest of the community above his own.

Telemachos appeals to the sentiments of the people and stresses moral and religious
concerns; Mentor argues politically: what appears to be a private struggle in fact is of
central importance to the community as a whole, not only because it affects its
present reputation and safety, but because it is going to determine in the future the
relationship between king and community and thereby the well-being of all. To shed
passiveness and take a stand therefore is indispensable. I think what we have here is
the earliest case in which a causal relationship is observed on a primarily political, not
moral or religious, level, and then applied to a political issue.[13]

Mentor, however, remains unsuccessful as well. Since the leading families of Ithaca
support their sons among the suitors there is no powerful leader (like Achilles in *Iliad*
I) to lend political assistance to popular sentiment. Nevertheless the suitors fear that
Telemachos might eventually succeed in arousing the people against them (IV 630–
672). Their first attempt to assassinate him fails; they meet secretly to devise a better
plan. One of them says:

> He himself is gifted in mind and counsel, and the people now by no means look kindly
> on us. We must act, then, before he summons the Achaeans to assembly....When they
> hear of our wickedness they will take it hard; I fear they will turn to violence, drive us out
> from our own country and force us to seek some foreign land. (XVI 361 ff., esp.
> 374–382)

Their plan, of course, will not be realized.

Indeed, the people and assembly are by no means negligible factors; their reactions
and sentiments are watched carefully, and in the right circumstances and with the
right leader they might suddenly play a much more significant role. We should
remember here, as Eric Havelock points out, that the assembly also has an important
function in jurisdiction and that it must witness public acts.[14] Moreover, the men it is
composed of form a decisive part of the army; as Joachim Latacz shows convincingly,
the battle scenes and parades of armies in the *Iliad* mirror the early stages of the
massive hoplite formation which could not exist without the involvement of large
segments of the non-aristocratic population.[15]

Furthermore, the *Odyssey* emphasizes the relations between upper and lower
classes, rich and poor, powerful and weak. The problems of hunger and poverty,
and the misery of the socially underprivileged are often described. Several times their
plight is connected with the vicissitudes of human fate that can turn a king into a
beggar, refugee, or slave: Odysseus and Eumaeus are obvious cases.[16] Those outsiders
are protected by Zeus. They are treated in an exemplary way by the Phaeacians,
Telemachos, Penelope, and Eumaeus. And again it is the suitors, the elite of noble

youth, who consistently and deliberately violate the norms of socially acceptable behavior. Their disaster therefore represents deserved punishment brought about by the gods and just men. Thus from its very beginning Greek social and political thought pays attention to the relationships not only between equals but also between unequals in the polis, and it does not hesitate to condemn the negative behavior of at least parts of the nobility.[17]

To sum up this part of my argument, the concerns emphasized by the epic poet in the scenes we have discussed so far all deal with basic problems of life and relationships in a community. The thought devoted to these concerns is political thought. It occupies a remarkably prominent place already in these earliest works of western literature. In keeping with the literary and poetic nature of these works, such thought is fully integrated into the narrative and expressed through action and speech. In other words, the poet uses traditional mythical narrative to discuss ethical and political problems that are important to his audience. By creating positive and negative models of social behavior, by illuminating the causes and consequences of certain actions and relating those to the well-being of the community, the poet raises the level of awareness among his listeners, he forces them to think, he educates them. Here then, to say it paradoxically, in non-political poetry in a prepolitical society, lie the roots of Greek political thought.

## Hesiod

It would be tempting to present a similar analysis of political thought in Hesiod. For reasons of space I have to limit myself to a very brief comment. While the problem of justice plays a much larger role in the Homeric epics than I was able to show in my short exposé, it is absolutely central in Hesiod's poems, particularly in the *Works and Days*. Hesiod too sees the well-being of the entire community threatened by irresponsible actions of its leaders, although the conditions in peaceful rural Boeotia lead him to concentrate not on the power struggles among the nobles and the military side of their leadership but on their role as judges.[18] Their venality and preference for crooked sentences cause him to reflect on the relationship between justice and prosperity of individual and community, and to recognize the all-important function of Zeus, the protector of justice who blesses the just and punishes the unjust. Although he cannot offer proof, his strong belief in the justice, power, and care of Zeus stimulates him to describe his insight in a series of impressive images such as the fate of the just and unjust cities (225–247) or the maltreatment of the goddess Dike, Justice, the daughter of Zeus, who howls

> when she is dragged about by bribe-devouring men
> whose verdicts are crooked when they sit in judgment . . .
> She rushes to sit at the feet of Zeus Kronion
> and she denounces the designs of men who are not just,
> so that the people pay for the reckless deeds and evil plans
> of kings whose slanted words twist her straight path.
> (220f.; 259–262; transl. A. Athanassakis)

The significance of all this for the early development of political and legal thought has
long been recognized.[19] No less significant is Hesiod's effort to complement the
negative picture of a world dominated by human injustice with the positive picture of
the just, fair, and responsible rule of Zeus among the gods. This picture is drawn in
rich detail in the *Theogony*, which has less frequently been read with careful attention
to its political aspects.[20] Like Homer, Hesiod does not argue abstractly. Rather, he
skilfully uses the possibilities offered by myth, genealogy and dramatic narrative to
develop a complex set of concepts and to present a coherent model of good leadership, thereby providing a challenging response to one of the most urgent social and
political problems of his own time.

## Conclusion: The Origin of Political Thought

Let me summarize and then explain. Already in its earliest manifestations Greek
thought dealt intensively with the following problems, among others: the detrimental
consequences of conflicts within the leading class and of irresponsible actions of kings
and noblemen; the possibilities of avoiding such conflicts and actions or controlling
and overcoming them if they occurred; the discrepancy between communal and
individual interests; the possibilities of improving and enforcing justice; the responsibility of community and nobility for the socially underprivileged and the outsiders;
the political and moral problems connected with war.

These all are political problems that were of great importance for the survival and
well-being of the community and that were to occupy Greek thought for centuries to
come. Moreover, although a decisive role as promoters and enforcers of justice is
attributed to the gods and particularly to Zeus because there is no sufficiently
powerful and just human agent to rely upon for such purposes, the problems tackled
by political thought fit into an entirely human framework of cause and effect. In other
words, the gods punish evildoers and their communities and, through seers, poets, or
leaders blessed by them, they may offer advice about salutary measures to be taken in
a crisis, but they neither cause nor solve such a crisis.[21] Rather, the crisis is caused by
specific human mistakes or irresponsible acts within a given society, and it must be
solved by that society itself. It is man's responsibility for the well-being of his
community, therefore, upon which political thought focuses its attention from the
very beginning, and that, I think, sets Greek political thought apart from any predecessors or parallels that may have existed in other civilizations, whether earlier or
contemporary; that makes it truly *political* thought.[22]

A striking example for the difference I am trying to define can be found by
comparing the Hesiodic explanation of the origin of evil in the world and its
Sumerian counterpart. In Hesiod Pandora brings all the evils into the world as
punishment for the crimes of Prometheus who tried to deceive Zeus and acted against
Zeus' strict orders. Prometheus, though divine, is the patron par excellence of man
and thereby the leader of the human community at large.[23] Therefore, just as the city
has to pay for the wrongs committed by its king or one of its citizens, so mankind has
to suffer for the injustice committed by their leader.[24] According to the Sumerian
myth, the evils came into existence when Enki, the god of sweet waters, and Ninmah,

the goddess of the earth, quarrelled at a party. In Thorkild Jacobsen's words, the evils were created, "in a moment of irresponsibility, when the gods were in their cups and succumbed momentarily to envy and a desire to show off."[25]

If this, then, is the beginning of Greek political thought, there immediately follows the question of "why then and there?" What were the causes and preconditions that made such thought possible or necessary in archaic Greece? I shall conclude by outlining a few observations that may help to answer this difficult question.[26] First, archaic Greek society was not dominated by a sacred kingship. Unlike the situation in earlier Near Eastern societies, obedience and subordination were not the principal virtues.[27] Greek religion did not demand the passive acceptance of an absolute divine will. Authority was not unassailable; criticism and independence were not principally excluded.

Second, after the turmoils of the Dark Ages Greek society was split into small and often topographically confined units in which the polis gradually became the pre-dominant form of community. There did not exist any large and centralized territorial states because, it seems, the formation of such states was required neither by major external threats nor by economic necessities. For centuries the Aegean World was pretty much left to itself. Wars mostly consisted of neighborhood conflicts that rarely threatened the existence of the community.[28] The tribal kingship inherited from the period of transition and migration was weak. The king was a *primus inter pares* whose position was based on his personal resources and qualities. The members of the "proto-aristocratic" leading class envisaged by Homer and Hesiod enjoyed basic equality. In their intensive competition for influence and power the king was vulner-able to criticism like everyone else. Eventually kingship proved unnecessary altogether and disappeared in most places.[29]

Third, the aristocracy that gradually emerged was ambitious. Their efforts to set up barriers against those not belonging to their circle[30] failed, however, because, despite their glorious self-presentation, only a relatively small gap separated them from the broad "middle" class of independent farmers. These "semi-aristocrats"[31] played an increasingly indispensable role in the hoplite army and assembly, a role that in a rudimentary form is already visible in Homer. The nobility therefore depended on that large landowning middle class, had to recognize and increasingly respect their sentiments and were in turn open to criticism. Criticism, that is, was possible, and in those small, open communities, in which everybody knew everybody, reasons for criticism were easily found. Furthermore, because of the lack of massive external pressure and the relatively harmless nature of war there was no need of a strong, disciplined, and cohesive class of leaders. Typically, the aristocracy soon sought to prove its excellence in an alternative area, that of sports. The significance of all this becomes even clearer if one compares it with the situation in early Rome.[32]

Fourth, all this happened in a period of rapid social change.[33] The population was growing. The polis developed into a tight unit in which the communal element was strengthened at the expense of the individual *oikos*, and power and political procedures were formalized and somewhat depersonalized. Colonization, seafaring, and trade offered many opportunities for success and economic gain. Social and political mobility increased. Many non-nobles acquired enough wealth and self-confidence and had proved their capabilities sufficiently to enter competition with the aristocracy which, in turn, lost much of its cohesion, exclusiveness, and unquestioned predominance.

This complex development was compounded by a deep crisis which affected large parts of Greece in the seventh century.[34] Often it resulted in violent confrontations between the mostly aristocratic wealthy landowners and large parts of the smaller landholders who were tied to the former through various forms of dependency. These conflicts usually ended in some sort of social compromise between the classes and in the possibility of increased political participation by at least those farmers who fought in the hoplite army.

Fifth, in these crises it became necessary to find new ways of solving conflicts. Each polis had its own institutions and customs; comparison with those of others must have been easy and frequent. In the course of colonization such opportunities of comparison were used more frequently and new solutions were tried out, particularly since the colonists often came from different towns and might have left home precisely because of their dissatisfaction with the existing order and the social conflicts caused by it.[35] Such violent conflicts demanded compromises and creative solutions. Often those involved agreed upon a procedure of mediation and legislation by a person or group standing above the parties. The connection between some of those mediators, belonging to the group of the "Seven Sages," and Delphi seems to indicate that such efforts were encouraged and supported by that panhellenic sanctuary. Delphi also played an important role in collecting information and giving advice in matters of colonization. All these tasks required an increasingly wide-spread, highly developed, and highly respected culture of political thought which found its expression in remarkably complex, radical, and innovative solutions. It suffices to mention the reforms introduced in Athens by Solon and Cleisthenes at the beginning and end of the sixth century.[36]

Many of these five factors existed already in the late eighth century, although they became more pronounced and significant over the next 200 years. They formed the preconditions for the emergence and further development of political thought, the framework in which such thought was not suppressed but possible and eventually even necessary. Finally, there is a sixth factor, the immediate cause that provoked the earliest manifestations of political thought and remained one of its most cogent stimuli. This is the dissatisfaction with the shortcomings of aristocratic leadership, the discrepancy between the interests of community and individual which we found at the core of Homer's and Hesiod's political concerns. By observing, criticizing and even refuting some of the values, norms, and attitudes of the aristocracy, the early thinkers were provoked to analyze and define the essential problems and needs of the community, and then to conceive and propagate alternative values and possibilities of behavior. Thus it is the long drawn-out confrontation between the claims of the community and those of an individualistic aristocracy to which the Greeks owed not only the polis in its classical form and an autonomous political sphere within the polis, but also the impetus and development of their political thought.

## NOTES

1   Finley 1977. Cf. furthermore, e.g., Gschnitzer 1981, pp. 27–47; Strasburger 1953, pp. 97–114, repr. in Strasburger 1982, I, pp. 491–518; Donlan 1981/82, pp. 137–175. The

very concept of a historical "Homeric society" has been questioned recently, e.g., by Snodgrass 1971, pp. 388–394; Snodgrass 1974, pp. 114–125; contra: Finley 1974, pp. 13–31, repr. in revised and abridged form in Finley 1977, pp. 142–158. For a critical discussion of the whole issue see now Morris 1986, pp. 81–138 (with ample bibliography).

2 That we are dealing rather with a "proto-aristocracy" has been emphasized recently, e.g., by Starr 1977, pp. 119–123; Spahn 1977, pp. 38–47; Donlan 1980, pp. 18–25.

3 *Il.* I 231: δημοβόρος βασιλεύς; cf. Theognis 1181: δημοφάγον τύραννον. It is tempting to take this as applying to the lives of the demos; the usual interpretation thinks of the people's possessions or substance and compares it with Hesiod's "gift-eating kings" (δωροφάγοι βασιλεῖς: *Works and Days* 39, 221, 264). Cf. Liddell, Scott, and Jones 1940 *s.v.* and West 1978, p. 151.

4 Cf. Redfield 1975, pp. 99–103.

5 XII 310–316: "Glaukos, why is it you and I are honored before others/with pride of place, the choice meats and the filled wine cups/in Lykia, and all men look on us as if we were immortals,/and we are appointed a great piece of land by the banks of Xanthos,/ good land, orchard and vineyard, and ploughland for the planting of wheat?/Therefore it is our duty in the forefront of the Lykians/to take our stand, and bear our part of the blazing of battle . . ."; cf. 317–321.

6 VI 402 f.: ". . . since Hector alone saved Ilion." Cf. Nagy 1979, p. 146. Phoenix's story of the siege of Kalydon and the anger of Meleagros (IX 527–599) provides another example of the conflict between the vital interests of the community and the tendency among members of its leading families to let their personal sentiments prevail.

7 Like the *Narrenfreiheit* granted to the midget or the *Hofnarr* at the courts of kings. This scene is interpreted well by Gschnitzer 1976.

8 On the nature of the polis in Homer, see the brief summary in Raaflaub 1985, pp. 43 f. In my view, in this early stage the main function of the polis was that of a "community of defense" to secure the common survival in emergencies; in times of peace, however, the private sphere of the *oikos* prevailed by far over the communal sphere with its rudimentary institutions. This problem has been discussed by many scholars; cf. Strasburger 1954, pp. 227–248 = Strasburger 1982, I, pp. 423–448 = Gschnitzer 1969, pp. 97–122; Hoffmann 1956, pp. 153–165 = Gschnitzer 1969, pp. 123–138; Starr 1957, pp. 97–108 = Starr 1979, pp. 122–133; Thomas 1966, pp. 5–14; Greenhalgh 1972, pp. 528–537; Spahn 1977, pp. 29–37; Reinau 1981, pp. 9–14; Donlan 1980, ch. 1, esp. 8 ff.; Scully 1981, pp. 1–34. See also Gschnitzer 1955, pp. 120–144 = Gschnitzer 1969, pp. 271–297, esp. 286ff.

9 Cf. Hesiod, *Works and Days*, 1–285 *passim*.

10 Cf. *Il.* I 80–83.

11 Such rules are comparable to those in the better known relationship between patron and client at Rome.

12 E.g., Antinoos in *Od.* XVI 424–432.

13 Such political causality is analyzed more incisively and with far-reaching conclusions in Solon's frag. 3 Diehl (= 4 West). For Solon's political thought, see Jaeger 1965, pp. 136–149; Jaeger 1966, pp. 75–99; Vlastos 1946, pp. 65–83; Meier 1970, pp. 19–25; Raaflaub 1981, pp. 48 f.; Havelock 1978, pp. 249–262.

14 Havelock 1978, esp. pp. 123–138.

15 Latacz 1977, esp. ch. 5 and 6 and pp. 242–244.

16 *Od.* XIII 429 ff.; XIV 191 ff.; XV 404 ff., and *passim* in XVII–XX.

17 Cf. Havelock 1978, ch. 9. The *Odyssey* is filled with positive and negative models of social behavior.

18 Cf. *Theog.* 80ff.; *Works and Days* 27ff., 219ff., 248ff., etc. Cf. on Hesiod, Burn 1936; Detienne 1963; Donlan 1980, 26ff., 48ff.; Spahn 1980, pp. 533ff.; Nagy 1982, pp. 43–73; and the lit. cited in the following notes.

19  Cf. Havelock 1978, ch. 11; Wolf 1950, pp. 120ff.; Voegelin 1957, pp. 126–164; Martin 1984, pp. 29–48; and the lit. cited in n20.

20  Cf., e.g., Solmsen 1949, pp. 3–75; Brown 1953, pp. 7–50.

21  This is expressed very clearly in *Od.* I 32–44 and Solon, fr. 3 Diehl (= 4 West), 1–16: "Never will Athens vanish away by immortal commandment,/by the Olympians' wish or by the will of Zeus . . ./Athens' own citizens, rather, astray and blinded by folly,/mad with the lust for gain, threaten their state with its end . . ." (1–6; transl. J. Willis, in Fränkel 1973, p. 220).

22  An interdisciplinary discussion of this issue among classicists and specialists on ancient Near-Eastern thought (Egypt, Mesopotamia, Israel) is a *desideratum*. Cf., e.g., Weber-Schäfer 1976, pp. 16–91 (with lit. on pp. 168f.); Frankfort et al. 1946.

23  Cf. also Aeschylus, *Prometheus Bound*, esp. 107ff., 231ff., 248ff., and 442ff.

24  City: Hesiod, *Works and Days*, 238–247. Prometheus: *ibid.*, 42–105; cf. *Theog.*, 561–564, 570–613.

25  Jacobsen 1946, p. 165.

26  I take the liberty of including in my thoughts the entire archaic period. I have learned much from Barker 1918, pp. 47–52; Vernant 1982; Meier 1980, pp. 51–90; id., Meier 1985, pp. 31–60.

27  For a society, in which these were the principal virtues, cf. Jacobsen 1946, pp. 125ff., esp. 202–207.

28  Cf. Raaflaub 1985, pp. 82–92.

29  Cf. Starr 1961, pp. 129–138 = Starr 1979, pp. 134–143; Starr 1986, pp. 64f. Drews 1983 is skeptical about the significance of archaic kingship in general.

30  Cf. Theognis 183ff., 193ff., 31f., 101ff., et al. For comments, see Donlan 1980, ch. 3; for a comparison with Rome, see Raaflaub 1986c, pp. 227–234.

31  Cf. Starr 1977, pp. 123–128.

32  Cf. Raaflaub 1984, pp. 553–563; Raaflaub 1986b, pp. 29–34.

33  For the development outlined in this section, cf., e.g., Starr 1977 and 1986; Austin and Vidal-Naquet 1977, ch. 3; Snodgrass 1980; Murray 1983.

34  The effects of this crisis are best known from Solonian Athens. Cf. Aristotle, *Ath. Pol.* 5ff. with the comm. by Rhodes 1981, pp. 90ff., 118ff.; Plut., *Solon* 13ff. with the comm. by Manfredini and Piccirilli 1977; Spahn 1977, pp. 52–59, 112–161; Gschnitzer 1981, pp. 75–84; Lintott 1982, pp. 43–47.

35  For this and the following remarks, cf. Barker 1918, pp. 3ff., 48f., and esp. Meier 1980, pp. 70–90. For the role of Delphi, see Meier 1980, 73ff.; Forrest 1957, pp. 160–175; Kiechle 1958, pp. 129–156 = Gschnitzer 1969, pp. 528–577. For the "Seven Sages," see Snell 1971; Fränkel 1973, pp. 238–240.

36  For Solon, cf. the lit. cited in n13 and n34. For Cleisthenes, see Herod. 5.66, 69f., 72f.; Aristotle, *Ath. Pol.* 20f. with Rhodes' comm. (1981) *ad loc.* (with bibl.); Lévêque and Vidal-Naquet 1964; Will 1972, pp. 63–76; Spahn 1977, pp. 161–178; Meier 1980, pp. 91–143; Siewert 1982.

## REFERENCES

Austin, M. M., and Vidal-Naquet, P., 1977: *Economic and Social History of Ancient Greece: An Introduction* (Berkeley and Los Angeles).

Barker, E., 1918: *Greek Political Theory: Plato and his Predecessors* (London and New York).

Brown, N. O., 1953: Hesiod, *Theogony* (Indianapolis).

Burn, A. R., 1936: *The World of Hesiod: A Study of the Greek Middle Ages c. 900–700* BC. (London; repr. New York, 1966).

Detienne, M., 1963: *Crise agraire et attitude religieuse chez Hésiode*, Coll. Latomus 68 (Brussels).

Donlan, W., 1980: *The Aristocratic Ideal in Ancient Greece: Attitudes of Superiority from Homer to the End of the Fifth Century* BC. (Lawrence KS).

—— 1981/82: "Reciprocities in Homer," *Classical World* 75, pp. 137–175.

Drews, R., 1983: *Basileus: The Evidence for Kingship in Geometric Greece* (New Haven).

Finley, M. I., 1974: "The World of Odysseus Revisited," *Proceedings of the Classical Association* 71, pp. 13–31; repr. in revised and abridged form in Finley 1977, pp. 142–158.

—— 1977: *The World of Odysseus*, 2nd ed. (London).

Forrest, W. G., 1957: "Colonization and the Rise of Delphi," *Historia* 6, pp. 160–175.

Fränkel, H., 1973: *Early Greek Poetry and Philosophy* (New York).

Frankfort, H., et al., edd., 1946: *The Intellectual Adventure of Ancient Man: An Essay on Speculative Thought in the Ancient Near East* (repr. Chicago, 1977).

Görgemanns, H., and Schmidt, E. A., edd., 1976: *Studien zum antiken Epos*, Beiträge zur Klass. Philologie 72 (Meisenheim/Glan).

Greenhalgh, P. A. L., 1972: "Patriotism in the Homeric World," *Historia* 21, pp. 528–537.

Gschnitzer, F., 1955: "Stammes- und Ortsgemeinden im alten Griechenland," *Wiener Studien* 68, pp. 120–144; repr. in Gschnitzer 1969, pp. 271–297.

—— ed., 1969: *Zur griechischen Staatskunde*, Wege der Forschung 96 (Darmstadt).

—— 1976: "Politische Leidenschaft im homerischen Epos," in Görgemanns and Schmidt 1976, pp. 1–21.

—— 1981: *Griechische Sozialgeschichte von der mykenischen bis zum Ausgang der klassischen Zeit* (Wiesbaden).

Havelock, E. A., 1978: *The Greek Concept of Justice from its Shadow in Homer to its Substance in Plato* (Cambridge MA).

Hoffmann, W., 1956: "Die Polis bei Homer," in *Festschrift für Bruno Snell* (Munich), pp. 153–165; repr. in Gschnitzer 1969, pp. 123–138.

Jacobsen, T., 1946: "Mesopotamia," in Frankfort et al. 1946, pp. 125–219.

Jaeger, W., 1966: "Solon's Eunomia," in *Five Essays* (Montreal), pp. 75–99.

Kiechle, F., 1958: "Zur Humanität in der Kriegführung der griechischen Staaten," *Historia* 7, pp. 129–156; repr. in Gschnitzer 1969, pp. 528–577.

Latacz, J., 1977: *Kampfparänese, Kampfdarstellung und Kampfwirklichkeit in der Ilias, bei Kallinos und Tyrtaios* Zetemata 66 (Munich).

Lévêque, P., and Vidal-Naquet, P., 1964: *Clisthène l'Athénien: Essai sur la représentation de l'espace et du temps dans la pensée politique grecque de la fin du VIe siècle à la mort de Platon* (Paris).

Liddell, H. G., Scott, R., and Jones, H. S., edd., 1940: *A Greek–English Lexicon*, 9th ed. (Oxford).

Lintott, A. W., 1982: *Violence, Civil Strife and Revolution in the Classical City: 750–330* BC. (Baltimore).

Luce, T. J., ed., 1982: *Ancient Writers* I: *Greece and Rome* (New York).

Manfredini, M., and Piccirilli, L., edd., 1977: *Plutarcho, La vita di Solone* (Milan).

Martin, R. P., 1984: "Hesiod, Odysseus, and the Instruction of Princes," *Transactions of the American Philological Association* 114, pp. 29–48.

Meier, C., 1970: *Entstehung des Begriffes 'Demokratie': Vier Prolegomena zu einer historischen Theorie* (Frankfurt).

—— 1980: *Die Entstehung des Politischen bei den Griechen* (Frankfurt).

—— 1985: *Politik und Anmut* (Berlin).

Morris, I., 1986: "The Use and Abuse of Homer," *Classical Antiquity* 5, pp. 81–138.

Murray, O., 1983: *Early Greece* (Stanford).

Nagy, G., 1979: *The Best of the Achaeans: Concepts of the Hero in Archaic Greek Poetry* (Baltimore).

——1982: "Hesiod," in Luce 1982, pp. 43–73.

Raaflaub, K., 1981: "Politisches Denken und Handeln bei den Griechen," in *Propyläen Geschichte der Literatur* I (Frankfurt), pp. 36–67.

——1984: "Freiheit in Athen und Rom: ein Beispiel divergierender politischer Begriffsentwicklung in der Antike," *Historische Zeitschrift* 238, pp. 529–567.

——1985: *Die Entdeckung der Freiheit: zur historischen Semantik und Gesellschaftsgeschichte eines politischen Grundbegriffes der Griechen*, Vestigia 37 (Munich).

——ed., 1986a: *Social Struggles in Ancient Rome: New Perspectives on the Conflict of the Orders* (Berkeley and Los Angeles).

——1986b: "The Conflict of the Orders in Archaic Rome: A Comprehensive and Comparative Approach," in Raaflaub 1986a, pp. 1–51.

——1986c: "From Protection and Defense to Offense and Participation: Stages in the Conflict of the Orders," in Raaflaub 1986a, pp. 198–243.

Redfield, J. M., 1975: *Nature and Culture in the Iliad: The Tragedy of Hector* (Chicago).

Reinau, H. J., 1981: "Die Entstehung des Bürgerbegriffs bei den Griechen" (diss., University of Basel).

Rhodes, P. J., 1981: *A Commentary on the Aristotelian* Athenaion Politeia (Oxford).

Scully, S., 1981: "The Polis in Homer: A Definition and Interpretation," *Ramus* 10, pp. 1–34.

Siewert, P., 1982: *Die Trittyen Attikas und die Heeresreform des Kleisthenes*, Vestigia 33 (Munich).

Snell, B., 1971: *Leben und Meinungen der Sieben Weisen*, 4th ed. (Munich).

Snodgrass, A. M., 1971: *The Dark Age of Greece: An Archaeological Survey of the Eleventh to the Eighth Centuries* BC. (Edinburgh).

——1974: "An Historical Homeric Society?" *Journal of Hellenic Studies* 94, pp. 114–125.

——1980: *Archaic Greece: The Age of Experiment* (Berkeley and Los Angeles).

Solmsen, F., 1949: *Hesiod and Aeschylus* (Ithaca NY).

Spahn, P., 1977: *Mittelschicht und Polisbildung* (Frankfurt).

——1980: "Oikos und Polis," *Historische Zeitschrift* 231, pp. 529–564.

Starr, C. G., 1957: "The Early Greek City State," *La Parola del Passato* 12, pp. 97–108; repr. in Starr 1979, pp. 122–133.

——1961: "The Decline of the Early Greek Kings," *Historia* 10, pp. 129–138; repr. in Starr 1979, pp. 134–143.

——1977: *The Economic and Social Growth of Early Greece, 800–500* BC. (New York).

——ed., 1979: *Essays on Ancient History: A Selection of Articles and Reviews* (Leiden).

——1986: *Individual and Community: The Rise of the Polis, 800–500* BC. (Oxford).

Strasburger, H., 1953: "Der soziologische Aspekt der homerischen Epen," *Gymnasium* 60, pp. 97–114; repr. in Strasburger 1982, vol. I, pp. 491–518.

——1954: "Der Einzelne und die Gemeinschaft im Denken der Griechen," *Historische Zeitschrift* 177, pp. 227–248; repr. in Strasburger 1982, vol. I, pp. 423–448.

——1982: *Studien zur Alten Geschichte*, 2 vols. (Hildesheim and New York).

Thomas, C., 1966: "Homer and the Polis," *La Parola del Passato* 21, pp. 5–14.

Vernant, J.-P., 1982: *Origines de la pensée grecque.* (English trans.) (Ithaca).

Vlastos, G., 1946: "Solonian Justice," *Classical Philology* 41, pp. 65–83.

Voegelin, E., 1957: *Order and History*, vol. II: *The World of the Polis* (Baton Rouge).

Weber-Schäfer, P., 1976: *Einführung in die antike politische Theorie* I (Darmstadt).

West, M. L., ed., 1978: *Hesiod: Works and Days, with Prolegomena and Commentary* (Oxford).

Will, E., 1972: *Le monde grec et l'orient* I (Paris).

Wolf, E., 1950: *Griechisches Rechtsdenken* I: *Vorsokratiker und frühe Dichter* (Frankfurt).

# Commentary on Raaflaub

## *Lowell Edmunds*

The title of Professor Raaflaub's lecture was "Homer, Hesiod, and the Beginnings of Greek Political Thought." The challenging element in this title is "Homer." Most of us do not think of Homer as a political thinker. Homeric scholarship, when it has been concerned at all with the political in Homer, has attempted to find evidence for the history of political institutions – assemblies, councils, law-courts – that might have been in existence in Homer's own time and to combine that evidence with the archaeological record, with facts from later Greek history, and with comparative evidence. The political *thought* of Homer is a paradoxical notion, and my remarks will therefore largely be concerned with what Professor Raaflaub had to say about Homer.

Almost any approach, let alone this paradoxical one, is beset with difficulties, and Raaflaub acknowledged the problems of using Homer as a historical source, addressing himself to seven preliminary questions. The fourth through the seventh of these questions were concerned with the use of poetry in general and of Homer in particular as historical evidence. He took the position that the society depicted in the Homeric epics, as distinguished from the heroes and their deeds, is historical and is that known to the poet and his audience. I am in agreement with this contention concerning the basic historicity of the material and social aspects of the epics, which do, with some notable exceptions, form a coherent picture. Certainly no one doubts that the principles of the warrior-aristocrats form a consistent code reflecting the ideology of the aristocrats of Homer's own day, in whose halls the bards sang epic song.[1]

If Homer can mirror this society and its ideology, can he also criticize them? Is Homer capable of *critical* thought about contemporary institutions? Raaflaub's answer is yes. He has enucleated a critical attitude toward the aristocratic chieftains which brings Homer unexpectedly closer to Hesiod, whose *Works and Days* reproaches the "bribe-devouring kings" he had to contend with in Boeotian Ascra. I find Raaflaub's analysis of this anti-aristocratic tendency in the *Iliad* very persuasive and, in passing, I want to add a corroborative detail. In rereading the opening books of the *Iliad* through the impulse of Raaflaub's paper, I noticed that the adjective "other," in various formulaic expressions, serves to distinguish a leader from his followers and often to express their dissension. For example, at the very beginning of the *Iliad*, Agamemnon rejects the petition of the priest Chryses, while "the other Achaeans" approve it. The result of the king's decision is the plague, sent by Chryses' patron, Apollo, which forces Agamemnon to restore Chryses' daughter, for whom he demands Briseïs as recompense – and all the rest.

I should like, however, to qualify Raaflaub's position in two respects.

Lowell Edmunds, "Commentary on Raaflaub," in *Proceedings of the Boston Area Colloquium Series in Ancient Philosophy* 4 (Lanham, MD: University Press of America, 1988), 26–33, pp. 26–31.

First, no matter what traces of political thought we find in the *Iliad*, the fact remains the fundamental situation is not a political one. A band of Achaeans from many cities is gathered in a camp on the plains of Troy. A quarrel breaks out between the leader of the Achaeans and the best warrior amongst his chieftains. Agamemnon, the leader, is *primus inter pares*; his position is based on the fact that the rules over more people than do the others. Achilles, the best warrior, like the other chieftains, is under no obligation to fight at Troy. His loyalty to Agamemnon and to his fellows is based on the principles of *philia*, a kind of friendship.[2] This *philia*, I submit, is pre-political or apolitical. The quarrel between Agamemnon and Achilles breaks out because Achilles feels that his honor has been offended. His honor is a personal matter, not a political one, and Zeus himself accords it the greatest importance. The Plan of Zeus (I 5, 498–530; XIII 345–360) provides that thousands of Achilles' fellow-Achaeans will die in order to demonstrate the need for the restoration of this honor.

The oath sworn by Achilles in Book I of the *Iliad* shows that the quarrel, which is, after all, the basis of the plot of the whole poem, is not a political matter. As he swears the oath, Achilles raises the scepter which was passed around from speaker to speaker in assemblies and courts. He says (I 234–244):

> I swear by this staff I hold – which no longer has bud
> Or leaf since it left its stump in the mountains, nor ever
> Grows green again and blooms since the sharp bronze stripped it
> Of foliage and bark, but which now the sons of Achaeans
> Bear in their hands, they who are judges among us
> And uphold the laws of Zeus – by this staff I swear
> A great oath that surely someday a desperate need
> For Achilles shall come upon all the sons of Achaeans,
> Nor will you be able to help them at all, no matter
> How grieved you are, when man-killing Hector is cutting them
> Down by the dozen. Then, I say, you'll rend
> Your heart with wrath and remorse for failing to honor
> The best Achaean of all![3]

Having finished, Achilles throws the scepter on the ground instead of handing it to someone else (245). The word for "judges" in this oath, *dikaspoloi*, is a compound noun of which the first element means "judgements," "trials," or, in the abstract, "justice." But Achilles is not in the role of a *dikaspolos*, nor are the laws sanctioned by Zeus at issue here. The scepter shows the distance that separates the quarrel of Agamemnon and Achilles from a conflict that could be adjudicated according to the norms of the polis. What would be normal in the polis is shown on the shield of Achilles in Book XVIII, on which Hephaestus represented "two beautiful cities of mortals" (490f.). In one of them, a trial is taking place in the agora before a council of elders, who sit in a circle and hold scepters in their hands. As the language of the passage makes quite clear, the issue is one of justice. The Achaeans at Troy, however, do not constitute a "beautiful city of mortals" but a band of heroes, amongst whom political justice does not operate. The quarrel between Agamemnon and Achilles concerns the institution of the *dasmos*, the division of spoils amongst warriors, and this is not an institution of the polis.

The dimension of the political is present only inferentially, as a conclusion to be drawn from the depiction, full of negative hues, as Raaflaub has rightly pointed out, of what at least some of Homer's audience might have felt was the old order, the *ancien régime*. The need for the polis, with all its problems, which are already known to Homer's audience, may be implied by the situation and still greater problems of the Achaean army. In an article published in 1963, Seth Benardete analyzed three contrasting pairs, men or mortals and heroes, Achaeans and Trojans, and Achilles and Agamemnon, and showed that, while Homer seems to give a higher ranking to heroes, Achaeans, and Achilles, the plot of the poem moves contrary to the rankings and forces us to rethink them.[4] The *Iliad* moves from the apparently higher categories to the apparently lower, with the result that the original distinctions break down and the lower categories are seen to lie beyond these distinctions. The lower, i.e. mortality as opposed to heroism, the settled life of the Trojans as opposed to the martial discipline of the Achaeans, and the vested authority of Agamemnon as opposed to the natural gifts of Achilles, might point to the polis. One recalls the myth of Er at the end of Plato's *Republic*, where Odysseus chooses the life of an ordinary citizen (620c3–d2).

There is one other way in which I would qualify Raaflaub's position. Even if we find criticism of the nobility and implicit exhortation to the masses to assume their proper role, it seems that neither Hesiod nor Homer could imagine any political order except one in which there are a number of chiefs amongst whom one is preeminent, as Agamemnon is at Troy, and as Odysseus is in Ithaca. (There are a number of "kings" in Ithaca besides Odysseus (*Od.* I 394f.) but Odysseus' family is the "most kingly" and powerful (XV 533f.).) Hesiod in the *Works and Days* addresses "kings" and tries to persuade them to give straight judgements. The *Theogony* is no less concerned with kingship and justice, and Raaflaub is right that this poem is as much political as it is theological. His insight is corroborated by a recent article by Richard Martin, who assigns the *Theogony* to a genre he calls "The Instruction of Princes."[5] Certainly, as Raaflaub has argued, the reign of Zeus is presented as a model of good government. One has only to compare the role of the Hundred-Handers in the *Theogony* with their role in the *Iliad*. In the *Theogony* Zeus (and the other gods) release the three Hundred-Handers from the Underworld to support them against the Titans (617–626). They are the "trusty guardians of Zeus" (735) and are later settled by him as his "glorious allies" at the sources of Ocean (816–817). In the *Iliad*, on the other hand, Achilles reminds Thetis that she had once summoned Briareus, one of the Hundred-Handers, to defend Zeus against the other Olympians, who intended to stage a palace revolution. Thetis can now, Achilles thinks, use this good deed as a bargaining chip to persuade Zeus to honor Achilles by disgracing Agamemnon (I 396–412). And so she uses it. Zeus' main concern, however, is what Hera will think. It is unnecessary to say more about the somewhat soap operatic results of Thetis' visit. But whatever the demerits of Zeus, whatever the demerits of Agamemnon, the *Iliad* does not seem to think beyond the institution of kingship.

Even the Thersites scene, or perhaps I could say, especially the Thersites scene, reinforces this institution. My interpretation of this scene differs somewhat from Raaflaub's. Though I agree that Thersites is able to restate the conflict between

Achilles and Agamemnon from Achilles' point of view and that Thersites expresses the resentment of the ordinary fighting man at Troy, I think that the real focus of the scene is Odysseus. Through the inspiration of Athena, he takes the scepter from Agamemnon (II 185–186) and restrains the Achaean army, which is rushing to the ships, eager to return home. He restrains kings and outstanding men with kindly words, men of the people with blows (188–206). His principle is that the rule of many is a bad thing – let there be one king, to whom Zeus has given the scepter and the laws (204–206); and the scene as a whole vindicates this principle. When the army sees Odysseus beat Thersites with the scepter and a bloody welt rises on his back and he begins to weep, they laugh with pleasure, even though they are vexed by all their cares (270). Odysseus has provided them with some comic relief, and they say that it is the best thing he has ever done. It will be a long time before Thersites dares to rebuke kings again (272–277). Odysseus then rises with the scepter to give a speech that will restore a sense of purpose. The scene as a whole has Odysseus as its protagonist and is a vindication of kingship.

I would distinguish, then, between recognition of the importance of the masses, on the one hand, and, on the other, political thought that would assign them any other role than the one they have in the *Iliad*. I agree with Raaflaub that the *Iliad* recognizes their importance, and I consider this an original and important finding. What I have to ask, however, is whether we are dealing with the mere reflex of a historical situation or with a criticism of that situation. The poem can reflect the situation without criticizing it. To return for a moment to the beginning of the scene I have just discussed, we know that in the fourth century BC Odysseus' restraint of the Achaeans was held to express an anti-democratic attitude. The speech of Polycrates against Socrates, composed as a pamphlet sometime in the 390's after Socrates' death, seems to have charged Socrates with hostility to the demos on the grounds that he often quoted this passage (II 188f.) on Odysseus' restraint of the Achaeans.[6] In other words, the actions of Odysseus, which included restraining the common soldiers with blows, are anti-democratic, and, as I have argued, Odysseus' actions in this whole episode, including his treatment of Thersites, are vindicated. The Achaeans must remain at Troy in fulfillment of their vows and promises (II 286, 339–341).

My two main criticisms or qualifications of Raaflaub's position, then, are that the situation in the *Iliad* is not fundamentally political and that neither Homer nor Hesiod can imagine any political order except one in which there are a number of "kings," i.e. noble chieftains.

I do not, however, think that this limitation on the dimension of the political, which must entail a limitation on political thought, restricts criticism of the nobility. (Such criticism is of course explicit in Hesiod's *Works and Days*.) [...]

## NOTES

1   Murray 1983, p. 49.
2   Nagy 1979, pp. 103–111.
3   Rees 1963, pp. 10–11.

4   Benardete 1963, pp. 1ff.
5   Martin 1984, pp. 29–84.
6   Xenophon, *Memorabilia* 1.2.58–59 with Libanius *Decl.* 1.121–126. Xen. defends Socrates.

## REFERENCES

Benardete, S. G., 1963: "Achilles and the *Iliad*," *Hermes* 91, pp. 1–16.
Martin, R. P., 1984: "Hesiod, Odysseus, and the Instruction of Princes," *Transactions of the American Philological Association* 114, pp. 29–48.
Murray, O., 1983: *Early Greece* (Stanford).
Nagy, G., 1979: *The Best of the Achaeans: Concepts of the Hero in Archaic Greek Poetry* (Baltimore).
Rees, E., 1963: *The Iliad of Homer* (New York).

# Equality and the Origins of Greek Democracy

## *Ian Morris*

Ian Morris seeks the origins of Greek democracy by tracing signs of egalitarian change in Greek society from the eighth through sixth centuries BC. The testimony of Homer and Hesiod is incorporated into what Morris sees as a conflict of "elite" versus "middling" ideologies detectable across the Greek literature and archaeology of the Archaic period.

## I. Introduction

Origins are out of fashion.[1] For most of [the twentieth] century, social scientists have held it as self-evident that synchronic analysis is prior to diachronic, and in the last few years many Greek historians have come to share this view, treating democracy as a static, functioning system.[2] This approach has good antecedents, most notably Aristotle's treatment of the eighty years or so from 403 to his own time as "the current constitution" (*Ath. Pol.* 42.1). But critics have always stressed that functionalism does not so much *explain* a situation as *redescribe* it in technical language – a view that Aristotle appears to have shared, prefacing his account of fourth-century institutions with a long narrative describing Athenian development since the seventh century, and beginning the *Politics* (1252a1–1253a40) with a model of the origins of the polis.

Any society can be said to function, but to understand why people live within one social system rather than another, we have to look to historical factors.[3] When the

Ian Morris, "The Strong Principle of Equality and the Archaic Origins of Greek Democracy," in J. Ober and C. Hedrick (eds.), *Demokratia* (Princeton: Princeton University Press, 1996), 19–48, pp. 19–22, 24–48.

social system in question is as unusual as that of city-state democracy, we cannot be content with showing how different institutions intersected to maintain the system, no matter how skillfully the analysis may be done. But the most influential recent treatments of Athenian democracy [...] have little to say about the Archaic social order that made democracy possible.[4]

This leaves us unable to explain why Athenians chose to organize their society in this particular way, rather than in some equally functional but quite different way. In this paper I sketch the history of what I see as some of the necessary conditions for the emergence of Greek democracy. I argue four points:

1   There was a massive social change all across central Greece in the eighth century BC, which produced a conception of the state as a community of "middling" citizens.
2   Not everyone liked this. Those who did not argued that authority lay outside these middling communities, in an inter-polis aristocracy that had privileged links to the gods, the heroes, and the East.
3   Much of the social history of the archaic period is best understood as a conflict between these two conceptions of social order.
4   At the end of the sixth century, the elitist ideology suffered major reverses. It became very difficult to claim a level of political skill denied to other citizens, and once this had happened, citizen democracy became a plausible system of government.

I suggest that we treat the origins of democracy as a process that is equally cultural and political. Mogens Hansen has recently argued that "it is the political institutions that shaped the 'democratic man' and the 'democratic life', not vice versa,"[5] but I take issue with this interpretation, arguing that a longer historical perspective shows that democratic institutions were merely one response to the emergence of broader egalitarian attitudes and ideologies. I structure my analysis around Robert Dahl's useful discussion of what he calls "the Strong Principle of Equality." Dahl suggests that "it is obvious . . . that the emergence and persistence of a democratic government among a group of people depends in some way on their *beliefs*. . . . Among a group whose members believe that they are all about equally well qualified to participate in the decisions of the group, the chances are relatively high that they will govern themselves through some sort of democratic process." This Strong Principle of Equality actually rests on two propositions:

> All members are sufficiently well qualified, taken all around, to participate in making the collective decisions binding on the association that significantly affect their good or interests. In any case, none are so definitely better qualified than the others that they should be entrusted with making the collective and binding decisions.[6]

The first of these propositions corresponds to what Dahl calls the Principle of Equal Consideration of Interests.[7] This affords to each citizen equal respect and an equal right to be heard, but reserves the possibility that some citizens may be able to decide what is in everyone's best interests and are thus qualified to make the decisions for all. I suggest that something like the Principle of Equal Consideration appeared in the eighth century, and something like the Strong Principle of Equality in the late sixth. As I imply in my title, I see the origins of democracy as a long process, spanning the whole archaic period, and a broad one, involving the whole Greek world.

The Strong Principle of Equality is not synonymous with democracy as an institutional order. But when enough people hold views of this kind, it becomes possible – and perhaps logical – to respond to the collapse of an oligarchy (whether through internal dissension or outside force) by developing new conceptions of majority rule, instead of simply finding a different group of guardians. This is what happened at Athens in 507.

A Strong Principle of Equality within a bounded citizen group crystallized over much of Greece between c. 525 and 490. As Dahl implies, in such a context the establishment of democracy is not so surprising. The remarkable thing is that such an ideology could gain the upper hand in the first place, and explaining this ought to be one of the central questions in archaic Greek history. In this paper I propose at least a partial explanation, arguing that the Strong Principle of Equality was a late-sixth-century phenomenon, which can only be explained in the light of its eighth-century roots. The core ideas were already present, and important, by 700 BC. What I offer here is a kind of social history of ideologies spanning three centuries; I pursue the longer-term history of these ideologies and their connections with broader cultural and economic processes in more detail elsewhere.[8]

I concentrate in this paper on the literary evidence from Archaic Greece. I argue that the source problems of the poetry of the period c. 700–525 are such that we must adopt a synchronic approach (section IV). Only archaeology can reveal detailed regional and chronological variations; archaic literature is too traditional to sustain a narrative history. But what we lose in detail we gain in understanding social dynamics. Historians have read this poetry too literally, systematically mistaking the elitist ideology for an objective account of social relations, characterizing the archaic poleis as "zero-sum" agonal societies dominated by aristocratic feuding over honor.[9] I dispute this. I suggest that the elitist position was a "dominant ideology" only in the sense that sociologists use that expression: it reinforced solidarity *within* a would-be elite, persuading its members of the justness of their claims, but had less influence on other groups.[10] It was not a "false consciousness," duping people into accepting aristocratic authority. On the contrary it was oppositional, working best outside the civic space, in the world of interstate aristocratic ties and closed symposia; and it was contested on all points by a rival "middling" philosophy.

I begin, though, at the end of this part of the story, with the "middling" ideology of fourth-century Athens. Such a teleological approach is perhaps an inevitable result of pursuing what Foucault castigated as the "chimera of origins." We could construct other narratives, with other beginning and end points; but if we are to understand ancient democracy, rather than redescribing it, we cannot do without such points. Chartier rightly concludes that "history stripped of all temptation to teleology would risk becoming an endless inventory of disconnected facts abandoned to their teeming incoherence for want of a hypothesis to propose a possible order among them."[11] I begin in the fourth century, then, for two reasons. First, this is where our sources are strongest; and second, I argue that this conception of equality goes back as far as we can follow the literary sources, all over the central regions of Greece.

## II. Athenian Citizen Equality

Fourth-century Athenian sources present the polis as a community of *metrioi* or *mesoi*, words that, following Walt Whitman's usage, I will translate as "middling men."[12] Like Whitman's middling man, the Athenian *metrios* was an ideological category that benefited from the vagueness of its definition. It allowed *all* Athenian citizens to think of themselves as members of a community of restrained, sensible men, characterized by "same-mindedness" (*homonoia*) and tied together by *philia*, which literally means "friendship" but carries a sense like Sahlins's category of "balanced reciprocity." The *metrios* was said to be content with "a little" money and was contrasted with both the rich and the poor. Yet even a wealthy liturgist could be called *metrios* if he lived properly. He was defined through everyday actions – providing well for his family and community, having a strong sense of shame, and above all keeping his appetites under control. Neither *mesoi* nor *metrioi* meant an economic "middle class," or a hoplite *Mittelschicht*, although membership in the phalanx was an important part of their self-imagination.[13] [...]

[Morris goes on to elaborate on the nature of Athenian citizen equality]

## III. The Eighth-century Revolution

The strong principle of equality was not peculiar to fourth-century Athens, but neither was it a timeless "Greek" *Zeitgeist*. Such beliefs were probably not important in the world of the Mycenaean palaces, and I see them beginning to take the forms we see in classical Greece in an eighth-century upheaval visible in the archaeological record.[22]

Most evidence from the Greek Dark Age (c. 1100–750) is from graves, and I have argued that in central Greece funerals drew a line within each community, between an elite group and lower, dependent groups. Most children were excluded from elite rituals. Elite funerals produced distinctive remains, which are well known to excavators, while the less formal funerals of the lower orders are only detected under favorable circumstances. The evidence for sacrifice has a similar pattern. In Dark Age central Greece, the major rites may have taken place in chiefs' houses, effectively excluding most people and defining a subgroup of full members of the community. Whitley argues that forms of rationing similarly limited other forms of symbolic behavior. All these classes of evidence, as well as house remains, suggest an elite ideology of homogeneity: rituals aggressively denied differences within the elite.[23]

There were huge changes in the eighth century. A new funerary system emerged, incorporating the whole adult and child population, often in the same cemeteries. The first signs appear at Corinth around 775, and at Argos, Athens, Megara, and many other sites by 750. Intramural burial largely ended (at Corinth by 750, elsewhere by 700), and cemeteries and settlements were now often walled. The most spectacular change was in sacrificial space. Around 750 areas for worship began to be walled, and by 700 nearly all communities had one or more substantial temples, while a few sancturaies won Panhellenic importance. Most poleis adopted a "bipolar" religious structure, with a major sanctuary in the town and another near a frontier. The Dark Age rituals in chiefs' houses died out.[24]

At first the quantity and quality of grave goods increased, presumably as some people went on differentiating status within the new ritual terrain. Spending peaked at Corinth by 750, at Athens by 725, and at Argos by 700. At most sites this phase lasted only about a generation, and a shift toward large, poor, and homogeneous citizen cemeteries followed. Around 750 the new sanctuaries began to receive huge numbers of votives, at first mainly pottery, but by 700 in many cases expensive metal items too. Snodgrass links this to the fall in grave goods: by 700 it was rarely acceptable to lavish wealth on funerals, but such offerings could be made at sanctuaries.[25] In the fourth century Aristotle (*Eth. Nic.* 1122b19–1123a4; cf. Xen., *Oec.* 2.5–7) defined spending money on sacrifices as "magnificence" (*megaloprepeia*), and concluded that "the magnificent man spends not for himself but for the common good" (*ta koina*). Historians of the eighth century often see the shift from grave goods to votives in these terms, as a victory for the community over individual families within it. However, Aristotle also observed that *megaloprepeia* must be in proportion to a man's resources, and that the poor man (*penēs*) cannot be magnificent, since if he spends lavishly he is simply foolish (*ēlithios*). Spending on the gods was ambiguous, creating both a sense of community and a hierarchical structure of honor within it. I return to this in section VI.

These changes were contested, and the archaeological record reveals varied outcomes. On Crete, despite the early appearance of "civic" forms such as agoras, temples, and lawcodes, sacrifice retained local peculiarities, and grave goods escalated until about 625; then virtually all finds except inscriptions disappear until the fourth century. In Thessaly some elements of the general pattern apply in the eighth century, but rich warrior burials continue in the seventh.[26] Athens is the most interesting case: here the eightth-century shifts are very clear, but then around 700 they were reversed. Distinct elite burials returned, while rich votives, monumental temples, and religious bipolarity are absent in the seventh century. This seems to have been a self-conscious attempt to restore the lost order of the Dark Age, and Athens remained unique in ritual terms well into the sixth century.[27]

## IV. Source Problems

Generalizations must, then, be qualified by region and period, but this is not easy to do with the written sources. Nagy argues that much of what comes down to us under the names of specific poets was in fact formed by broader processes: "The pan-Hellenic tradition of oral poetry appropriates the poet, potentially transforming even historical figures into generic ones who merely represent the traditional functions of their poetry."[28] He suggests that prior to the eighth century there was enormous regional variety in Greek oral poetry, but that by 700 some bards were traveling widely. Discrepancies between local traditions became more apparent to them, and they tried to produce poems that were relevant to all areas of Greece but specific to none, developing fixed ideas about the heroic past. It became useful for them to imagine performance as the reconstitution of a fixed text by a noncomposing rhapsode. Local mythology was marginalized in opposition to *alēthea*, "unforgotten things," known by authoritative bards. As traditions coalesced, rhapsodes retrojected into the distant past Ur-poets – first Homer, then Hesiod, Archilochus, and a range of other personas in a series of bids for Panhellenic status. This does not necessarily mean that these poets were not real people; only that they were already submerged within the genre in archaic times. Only at the end of the sixth century, Nagy suggests, did individual poets emerge as "authors."[29]

Something like this clearly happened with "Theognis." Some verses should date before 625, and others after 490; and many are also attributed to other poets. "Theognis" was a poetic persona, into which anyone could step to compose in this genre, just as "Anacreon" continued to be into the Middle Ages.[30] Ancient disputes over the poets' cities of origin might represent competing retrojections.

The problem is most acute with Archilochus. His characters' names have long aroused suspicion, and Miralles and Pòrtulas suggest that the poems resemble the worldwide "trickster" genre, in which a cunning Brer Rabbit figure with insatiable hungers for food and sex outwits opponents and unmasks their hypocrisy – he is "the outcast able to cause someone else's casting out, the figure that has been excluded but has the power to exclude." Some of his characters also appear in a third-century BC inscription, but this only adds to the problem. The text was set up by one Mnesiepes, a name meaning "he who remembers the words."[31] However we interpret him, we are dealing here with a long-term process like those that Hobsbawm and Ranger have called the invention of tradition, or perhaps better still, as Herzfeld puts it, the *negotiation* of tradition, in which actors recast one another's notions in a competitive process of literary construction.[32]

We have to recognize the continuities between certain groups of archaic poets, and the constraining powers of genre. I see three implications for historians. First, we can only approach the main body of texts synchronically. Tracing an intellectual evolution by stringing the poems together in their supposed chronological order is unwise. It finds change by ignoring continuity and explains all differences diachronically. Literary critics then step into the persona of Mnesiepes, becoming an active part of the invention of tradition.

Second, we cannot reconstruct specific events. Archilochus and Alcaeus may well have been real people, singing about other real people, but when performing they adopted poetic personas. They sang through conventional *topoi*; it was perhaps impossible for them to think constructively in any other terms. When Alcaeus called Pittacus "fatty" and "base born," we cannot assume that these charges were true, or even that the poet expected anyone to find them credible. A man singing Alcaeus took the part of the betrayed one, trying to recreate an ideal, homogeneous world by casting out the traditional enemy, just as Archilochus cast out Neoboule the "fickle one," Hipponax cast out Boupalos the "big-dick," and Demosthenes was to cast out Aeschines with accusations of servile origin. If we take anything from these stories at face value, we may be seriously misled.[33]

These are negative arguments, but the third implication is positive. The *topoi* within which events were constructed had immense cultural importance. In sections V and VI, I develop the arguments of Mazzarino and Kurke that we should divide archaic poetry into two broad traditions, which I call "elitist" and "middling." These partly correspond to formal distinctions, with lyric poetry dominating the former and elegy and iambus the latter, but the boundaries are not rigid. Hexameter was used in both traditions, with Homer in some regards standing at the head of the elitist tradition, and Hesiod of the middling; but in neither case is this a clear-cut relation-ship.[34]

For all the antagonism between the traditions (section VI), they were not rigidly separated. They should be seen as ideal types, representing the ends of a spectrum of social attitudes. Phocylides, for example, is more "middling" than Theognis, whose complex attitudes were sometimes hostile to ordinary citizens. Further, like any artists, individual poets (or traditions) were not consistent, occupying a single point on this spectrum; they rather occupied a range of positions. Thus Alcman gives us some strikingly elitist statements in his *partheneia* but in fr. 17 apparently adopts a middling, iambic persona, calling himself the eater of everything (*pamphagos*) who rejoices in common foods (*ta koina*) just like the people (*ho damos*).[35] Similarly, the same literary *topos* could be reworked in strikingly different ways within each trad-ition, as when Alcaeus reused Hesiod's image of the lustiness of women and the weakness of men in the dog days of summer.[36]

Both traditions were "elite" in the sense that most poems were produced by and for elites of birth, wealth, and education. The hostility between the extant traditions was primarily a conflict within the highest social circles over what constituted legit-imate culture. Bourdieu suggests that such struggles are common to all elites, and that very often some people will claim to monopolize a high culture that is beyond the reach of the masses, while others assert their power by deliberately transgressing, conferring high status on values and objects excluded from the privileged aesthetics. The popular aesthetic is normally not simply a failure to grasp elitist tastes, but also a conscious refusal of them, among ordinary people and among the elite. I suggest in section VI that those aristocrats who adopted the middling position deliberately assimilated themselves to the dominant civic values within archaic poleis. They were not surrendering their claims to be elite: a wealthy symposiast insisting on the excellence of *to meson* represented a situation very different from that of a poor farmer pronouncing the same words.[37] However, they claimed leadership as special members of the polis, not as a wholly distinct aristocratic community of the kind created by the elitist tradition. There is no reason to think that middling aristocrats struggled across the seventh and sixth centuries to create democracy. But the unintended consequence of their beliefs was that when the elitist ideology collapsed after 525, the general acceptance of middling values made democracy a real possibil-ity; and when a ruling elite fell apart in disorder, as at Athens in 507, democratic institutions were one obvious response.

## V. The Middling Tradition

The core features of the middling ideology go back at least to Hesiod's *Works and Days* (c. 700 BC). Like the fourth-century *metrios*, Hesiod's good man was married with children, ideally owning land, two oxen, a slave women, a hired laborer, and dependents of some kind, who received rations. He strongly endorsed the essentialist argument that the ideal community is male: women were a late addition sent to curse men. Good men knew that the gods filled the barns of those who ordered their works with due measure (*Op.* 306: *erga metria kosmein*). Hard work was the key to the gods' favor, and the only alternative was begging.[38]

Hesiod never used words such as *astoi* or *politai* for "citizens." His community consisted of neighbors (*geitones*). Possibly no concept of citizenship had yet emerged, but this may be too literal an approach. *Geitones* had a long history as a poetic *topos*, lasting into the fourth century. Hesiod advised Perses that neighbors were more important than kin, and his neighbors interacted much like fourth-century citizens. They lived in a certain tension with one another: a man had to respect his equals but also be sensitive to slights, balancing healthy rivalry and even dealings. He had to be tough but welcoming, because either too much or too little trust would ruin him.[39]

The good man's attitude toward "the poor" was also like that of the fourth-century *metrios*. They should not be mocked, but neither should they be trusted, for their empty bellies degraded them and forced them to lie.[40] The relationship with the rich was more complex. In the *Works and Days*, Hesiod said the "lords" (*basilēes*) were "gift-devouring judges" who relied on violence, not right: "The fools know neither how much greater the half is than the whole, nor what advantage there is in mallow and asphodel" (40–41) – that is, that a fair share was better than unjustly seizing everything, and that peasant foods were better than luxury. But in the *Theogony* Hesiod praised the *basilēes* to whom the Muses gave honey-sweet tongues for settling quarrels. The whole people treated them like gods when they walked through their assemblies. There is no contradiction here. The *Theogony* sets out the ideal, and the *Works and Days* shows it under attack from the unjustness endemic in the Age of Iron. When the nobles show proper respect, the city flourishes; when they do not, Shame flees to Olympus, and Zeus makes the whole community pay. Hubris – another central fourth-century concern – then destroys the city.[41]

In both poems the *basilēes* have a divine right to settle disputes, manifested in their eloquence and respect for gods and men. This is strikingly different from what we see in the fourth century, but we should hesitate before concluding that Boeotian villages around 700 really were ruled by *basilēes*. Hesiod's account parallels Homer's in *Od.* 8.166–77, and both probably drew on a tradition of advice-poetry.[42] Indeed, Ascra (and all the people in it) were probably as much a *topos* as the Thebes of tragedy: Ascra was the place where Zeus' will, personified by the good *basilēes*, was undermined by hubris.[43] Detienne suggests that in Hesiod *alēthea* was not an abstract "truth" but a form of "magico-religious" speech, available only to kings, poets, and seers, who monopolized contact with an invisible realm and drew wisdom, justice, and prophecy from it. In the *Works and Days*, Hesiod judged the *alēthea* of the *basilēes* by their behavior. It did not live up to expectations, showing that they were masters not of *alēthea* but of *apatē*.[44]

Like the *basilēes*, Hesiod appeals to outside sources of authority, casting himself as an "exterior insider" whose origin and position on the edge of the community give him privileged insights. As Nagy observes, in Ascra "the function of the *basileus* 'king' as the authority who tells what is and what is not *themis* 'divine law' by way of his *dikē* 'judgment' is taken over by the poem itself."[45] We see a similar idea of the poet absorbing external sources of legality in elegy, through identifying with semi-legendary middling lawgivers who went to Crete or Delphi to legitimate laws, which they then brought back within the community, writing them down and putting them increasingly under civic control.[46] By 500 BC the citizen body itself took authority for the laws. Ostwald argues that the sixth-century Athenian word for "law," *thesmos*, implied "something imposed by an external agency, conceived as standing apart and on a higher plane than the ordinary," while the fifth-century word, *nomos*, implied something "motivated less by the authority of the agent who imposed it than by the fact that it is regarded and accepted as valid by those who live under it."[47]

Hesiodic society has parallels in other literatures, and its mythology overlaps with Near Eastern wisdom texts. The roughly contemporary Egyptian *Instructions of Amenemopet* agrees that unrighteous profits are fleeting (9.16–10.13), but Hesiod's egalitarianism is unique. Even in the superficially similar Middle Kingdom *Protests of the Eloquent Peasant*, the good steward Rensi only believes the peasant Khun-Atep after beatings that in Ascra would have been hubristic (B. 185–190).[48] I suggest that Hesiod's egalitarianism was a peculiarly Greek product of the eighth-century trans-formation. Similarly, Nagy notes that while Greek hexameter poetry shares much with other Indo-European traditions, it also has important differences, which he also links to eighth-century changes in the archaeological record.[49]

The core of Hesiod's ideal persona recurs in elegy, despite a major change in audience. Hesiod's song was open to all, but he also knew of songs limited to those who understand (*phroneousi*). He called these *ainos* (*Op.* 202), which meant "praise" but was also the root of *ainigma*, denoting coded speech. Most elegy and iambus was *ainos* poetry, intended for a small group of "the wise" (*sophoi*). Theognis called his verses "*ainigmata* hidden by me for the good men" (681). But although they were produced by and for aristocrats, "elegiac poetics in general amount to a formal expres-sion of the ideology of the polis, in that the notion of social order is envisaged as the equitable distribution of communal property among equals."[50] In this poetry some members of the aristocracy came to terms with the polis of middling citizens while acquiring a useful weapon in intra-elite struggles. Poets and audiences could still see themselves as *sophoi* who guided the polis with special wisdom and piety, but elegists presented their own symposia as a force for moderation, not elitism. "The wise" might claim to know what was good for ordinary citizens better than the citizens did them-selves, but they did so within a Principle of Equal Consideration of Interests.[51]

To be in the middle was best. Solon called himself a shield held over rich and poor, a wolf at bay among hounds, one who made laws alike (*homoios*) for good and bad, and a boundary stone at the midpoint (*en metaichmiō*) between them (frs. 4c; 36.26–27, 18–20; 37.9–10).[52] Phocylides said simply, "*mesos* in the polis I would be" (fr. 12), and Theognis, "the middle is best in everything" (335). Restraint and moder-ation were the keys, expressed first as *aidōs*, and later as *sōphrosunē*. The middling man needed moderate wealth (as in Hesiod, *man* was the operative word: women were reviled ferociously). Phocylides, again like Hesiod, saw a fertile farm as the source of plenty, and Theognis wished only "to be rich without evil cares, unharmed, with no misfortune" (1153–54). As in Hesiod and in the fourth century, the middle was defined against the poor as well as the rich. Men were constrained (*biatai*: Solon 13.41) by poverty, and its victim "cannot say or do anything, and his tongue is tied" (Theog. 177–78). All men despised the poor, and the hungry belly was to blame for their lack of dignity and self-control. For Solon, "luxury in belly, sides, and feet" was equal (*ison*) to silver, gold, land, and horses (21.1–4).[53]

If moderate wealth was the precondition for the ideal of middling life from the seventh to the fourth century, the ogre of greed was just as consistently its enemy.

Men pursued wealth through any means, setting no limits. Wealth and hubris were inseparable. For Solon "excess breeds hubris when great wealth follows men who do not have a complete mind" (6.3–4). Hubris then destroyed the polis: "The *astoi* themselves, obsessed by greed, are prepared to ruin this great city" (4.5–6). He would check this by setting up *eunomia*, a "well-ordered world" that "makes all things wise and perfect among men" (4.39). This presumably refers to Solon's own reforms of 594, but it also continues the Hesiodic tradition of creating the ideal order by asserting it poetically, merging the lawgiver and poet.[54]

To a great extent the middle was constructed in opposition to the bogeyman of the hubristic aristocrat, defined – as in the fourth century – through his decadence and lack of control. To understand this dimension, we must now turn to the elitist tradition.

## VI. The Elitist Tradition and the Conflict of Values

In an earlier paper I argued that the *Iliad* and *Odyssey* were written down in the upheavals of the eighth century, as attempts to fix against alternative constructions an elitist view of the heroic age as a time when the community depended for its very survival on mighty individuals. The poems show us eighth-century assumptions about what a heroic age would be like, and, not surprisingly, they share some elements with the "middling" tradition. Fisher shows that hubris is the main offense of both Agamemnon in the *Iliad* and the suitors in the *Odyssey*, and that its overtones are "entirely compatible with those found in our study of *hybris* in classical Athens." There is, however, a crucial difference: the victim of hubris in each case is no middling citizen but a mighty hero, and hubris is avenged not by communal action but by individual *biē* (force) or *mētis* (cunning). Similarly, it is only partly true that Homer criticizes heroic excess in favor of polis institutions, or that the Thersites episode (*Il.* 2.270–78) undermines elitism. The main thrust of both poems was the dependence of the community on the individual hero.[55]

The heroic past assumed immense importance in the eighth century, and the variety of cults at Bronze Age tombs attests debates over its meaning. The story that Helen never went to Troy (which certainly goes back to Stesichorus, and probably to Hesiod) also suggests the scale of variations, but the Panhellenization of Homer over the next two centuries effectively silenced most alternatives.[56]

Hesiod knew there could be lying poetry and saw poets and *basilees* as competing in truth, but Homer was more aggressive, claiming to be merely the audience's point of contact with the total knowledge of the Muses. Ford notes that "by neglecting the possibility that two mortal poets might differ in their versions of a given story, [Homer] encourages us to regard the story as the enunciation of earlier deeds in their timeless structure." Homer thus naturalized a specific vision of the heroic age.[57]

Elitist sympotic poetry took for granted this appropriation of the heroic age, and the heroic warrior became a potent symbol. Some historians use references to heroic-style warfare to date the "hoplite reform,"[58] but it makes more sense to see these passages as synecdochical: the part stands for the whole, and the hero evokes a package of heroic values, loyalties, and dependencies. The "heroic" war scenes are associated with those poets who express elitist sentiments. For example, only one martial fragment (14) survives from Mimnermus, and it describes in epic tones a hero rushing forward to rout the Lydian cavalry. Alcaeus fr. 140 uses epic language for arms and armor hanging on a wall while his companions share a peaceful feast. But then the pace changes: we move to a jumbled heap of weapons on the floor, described with nonepic words such as *spathē* (sword), and to the seamy facts of the fragmented fellowship and civil war on Lesbos. The hero's weapons stand for the perfect aristocratic community, now disordered.[59]

But on the whole the world of "contemporary" nobles was a far cry from the brutal heroic age. It was a place of delicacy, elaborate manners, sweet perfumes, and wealth. Sappho's simple statement "I love luxury" (*habrosunē*: fr. 58.25) was the direct opposite of Phocylides' "*mesos* in the polis I would be." Luxury was not just a way to make life pleasant – it collapsed the distances between the aristocracy and the gods, the heroes, and the great rulers of Lydia. Even as the middling poets brought the external grounding of law under communal control, the elitists emphasized their own similarities to these three outside sources of legitimacy. They described the gods as dressed in gold and living in a golden house, pouring drinks from golden vessels, and coming to worshipers who made offerings in similar golden cups. Gentili observes that Sappho merged divine and mortal luxury in personalized epiphanies of Aphrodite, claiming to have "*privileged* religious experiences bringing closer communion with the god." Luxury bridged the gulf between mortals and gods. Sappho and her friends dwelled in a realm more like the heroic age than the seventh century. The gods moved among them, and Sappho identified as strongly with Aphrodite as Odysseus did with Athena. Lavish display made the aristocracy something more than human.[60]

Giving a golden cup or a bronze tripod to the gods was an act of *megaloprepeia* which benefited the whole community, but, as in Aristotle's account, it was open to varying interpretations. It was more than the "increasing competition for status via the conspicuous consumption of wealth" stressed by Morgan;[61] to those steeped in the elitist culture, it gave the dedicator a direct experience of the gods which was denied to ordinary mortals. These lavish dedications became common shortly before 700, and I would suggest that they, and the themes in Sappho, were reactions to the eighth-century social transformation. Assertions of elite power were generally banished from the explicit arena of funerals, but, like aristocracies in all ages, Greek nobles were adaptable. They shifted one of their primary arenas of self-definition to a more ambiguous context. At Athens, where I have suggested that a powerful elite regained control and rejected the middling ideology, rich seventh-century votives are scarce. Athenian nobles apparently did not need these new-fangled ideas and tried to recreate the simpler, ancestral rites of the Dark Age. Seventh-century Corinth and Argos, on the other hand, combined strikingly homogeneous cemeteries with fabulously wealthy rural sanctuaries of Hera.

In these dedications the worlds of nobles, gods, heroes, and Easterners intersected, most strikingly in bronze tripod-cauldrons. Catling argues that no tripods were made in Dark Age Greece, but Bronze Age Cypriot heirlooms continued to circulate; Matthäus thinks that local tripods were being made in Crete and the islands by the tenth century, in close imitation of Cypriot models. Either way, by the eighth century tripods were intimately linked with both the past and the East and were established as *the* gift of heroes. Examples dating from before c. 750 were made from almost pure copper, but in the second half of the century a new series appeared, imitating both the designs and the high tin content of Eastern (probably north Syrian) tripods. The tripod simultaneously heroized and Orientalized: all sources of external power flowed together in the act of giving a tripod to the gods. By about 650, fewer Greek-made Orientalizing tripods were being dedicated, and more hoplite arms and armor. Coming as it did at about the same time as the emergence of the phalanx as a poetic metaphor for citizen solidarity, this might represent an alternative, "middling" kind of gift to the gods; but it was paralleled by an increase in dedications of imported Oriental tripods.[62]

True aristocrats were comfortable using the East, moving within their own version of the culture of Gyges. Aristeas, significantly said to have been an ecstatic devotee of Apollo, supposedly traveled all over Asia in the seventh century, seeing mythical beasts everywhere. Elite religion adapted Eastern rites, and Carter suggests that Alcman's *partheneia* borrowed Phoenician elements.[63] The dependence on the East was just as true of the symposium, the primary context for the performance of lyric monody, as of the sanctuary. Drinking groups had probably been an important way for chiefs to gather and reward followers since at least 900, as suggested by the heavily worn krater from Koukounaries on Paros, the consistent use of ceramic kraters and amphoras to mark prestigious burials, and the burial of complete Attic drinking sets in Knossian tombs.[64] But around 700, symposia had their own Orientalizing revolution, adapting special rooms and furniture from the East. Reclining on couches of Near Eastern type and using vessels with Lydian prototypes, aristocrats sang about Lydian dress, women, and military might, judging Greek life against these standards. The new symbols justified their users' claims to superiority – they virtually mixed with the gods themselves, just like the ancient heroes, on whom society had depended for its very existence; and they felt like the kings of the East, whose power vastly exceeded that of the Greeks.[65]

The Orientalizing movement was a class phenomenon. As in many other contexts, decisions to adopt or to resist artistic innovation from overseas were political. Would-be aristocrats who felt marginalized and unfairly excluded from power welcomed new and disruptive ideas, looking outward to the past, the East, and the divine for justification. Those who believed in middling values resisted these novelties.[66]

The outcomes of these struggles varied enormously. At Athens Eastern imports and Orientalizing styles were welcomed enthusiastically in the last quarter of the eighth century but after 700 were used much more carefully by the elite. In Argos Eastern metalwork was given to Hera in large quantities,[67] but otherwise the East had a minimal impact on material culture. Only a handful of local Orientalizing potsherds are known. Corinthian aristocrats used expensive Eastern and Orientalizing objects in similar ways, but the makers of Protocorinthian pottery, probably in use across the social scale and in all contexts, debased the Eastern styles, effectively vulgarizing them. The Cretans, on the other hand, had (in Burkert's words) "been 'orientalizing' all the time." Phoenicians had been coming to Kommos since the tenth century, and there may have been a community of Levantine craftsmen at Knossos by 850. A vigorous Orientalizing pottery style, Protogeometric B, flourished in the late ninth century alongside a Middle Geometric style. The East must have meant entirely different things in Crete than in the central Aegean.[68]

In eastern Greece a handful of sanctuaries received spectacular Oriental votives in the seventh century, but few lavish Archaic burials are known, and indeed few burials of any kind before about 550.[69] Most elitist poets were placed in eastern Greece – Sappho and Alcaeus on Lesbos, Mimnermus in Colophon, Anacreon in Teos. Even Alcman of Sparta was linked with Sardis, and Ibycus of Rhegion spent much of his career on Samos. But there is no way to know whether elitist poetry really was a product of the fringes of Asia, or whether it was located there because the East was so important for it. Oriental power was more threatening for east Greeks than for mainlanders, but Nagy is surely right that these poets achieved canonical status by being generalized across Greece in a series of Panhellenic "promotions." Regardless of their ultimate origins, "eastern" poets appealed to symposiasts on the mainland and in the islands.

The elitist version of sympotic culture directly opposed the middling ideology. Murray suggests that "the *symposion* became in many respects a place apart from the normal rules of society, with its own strict code of honour in the *pistis* [trust] there created, and its own willingness to establish conventions fundamentally opposed to those within the *polis* as a whole."[70] The primary assets were beauty, eroticism, love of wine, arcane mythical knowledge, and athletic skills. The games perhaps owed as much to the East as did the symposium, and both merged with ritual friendship to form a coherent culture beyond polis morality. No rules barred ordinary citizens from entering the games, but the expense of training effectively achieved this. Stories of goat- and cowherds winning at Olympia have a mythical air, and in any case, the scale of rewards made victory an avenue of rapid promotion into elite circles. Serious competitors constituted in their own eyes an interstate elite, and it is from their literature, rather than from that of the majority of citizens, that Burckhardt created his image of Greece as an agonal society. Ordinary citizens enjoyed the spectacle of elite conflicts and honored the victors, much as fourth-century Athenian jurymen watched the struggles of wealthy litigants; but for the participants, athletic victory renewed the household's glory. The presence of a victor in one's family, like the correct use of luxury, identified a true aristocrat, someone who stood close to the gods and heroes.[71]

The middling poets resisted all these beliefs. The phalanx became the standard image for citizen solidarity and remained so until the fourth century. Archilochus mocked the heroic model by describing in lofty language how he abandoned his "blameless armament" (*entos amōmēton*) to a Thracian tribesman – but Archilochus didn't care and found the whole episode amusing (fr. 5). He preferred a short, bowlegged man with his feet on the ground to a tall, elegant, heroic officer (fr. 114). In Tyrtaeus and Callinus, the phalanx is a metaphor for the ideal citizen group. Begging is the only alternative to hard work in Hesiod (*Op.* 397–400), and to standing your ground in the ranks in Tyrtaeus (fr. 10.1–14). These are not transparent accounts of tactical changes: they are part of a series of exchanges between the two poetic traditions, what Rose calls "matters of discursive conflict."[72]

Xenophanes questioned the epic gods. Far from being companions of the elite, the gods of middling poets kept the ends of life hidden from all men.[73] But the harshest attacks were on the East. For Phocylides "an orderly polis on a rock is better than silly Nineveh" (fr. 5), and Xenophanes told how Colophon "learned useless luxuries from the Lydians while they were still free from hateful tyranny" (fr. 3.1–2). In fr. 19 Archilochus had Charon the carpenter say, "I don't care for Gyges the Golden's things, and I've never envied him. I'm not jealous of the works of gods either, and I don't lust after a magnificent tyranny. These are beyond my gaze." Aristotle describes Charon's comments as *agroikia*, "rustic" or "boorish." Fränkel suggested that "the carpenter was a stock example of the industrious man," and perhaps the audience was supposed to react to Charon as a solid, worthy citizen.[74] What he rejected was a virtual checklist of elitism – the desire to be like the king of Lydia, to rival the gods, and (at least in the eyes of critics) to be a tyrant. But perhaps the most effective attack on elite pretentions came from Hipponax, who abused the delicacy, eroticism, and Orientalism that Sappho and others saw as sources of social power. The dung-covered hero of fr. 92 found himself in a toilet with a woman who performed an obscure act on his anus while beating his genitals with a fig branch. The fragment ends with a cloud of dung beetles whirring out of the filth. The woman was *Ludizousa*, "speaking in a Lydian fashion"; perhaps the whole episode was so down-market that it did not even involve a real Lydian. This is classic iambic abuse, making it hard to take the *habrosunē* ideology seriously, and that was surely the point.[75]

There was no way to transcend the polis in the middling tradition. Not even athletic victory brought a man closer to the gods and heroes. The differences between the two poetic traditions came down to a single point: the elitists legitimated their special role from sources outside the polis; the middling poets rejected such claims. The former blurred distinctions between male and female, present and past, mortal and divine, Greek and Lydian, to reinforce a distinction between aristocrat and commoner; the latter did the opposite. Each was probably guilty of disgusting and polluting behavior in the eyes of the other. Elitist poetry was the oppositional literature of an *immanent elite*, an imagined community evoked in the interstices of the polis world – at interstate games, in the arrival of a *xenos* from a different city, or behind the closed doors of the symposium.[76]

It was opposed on all counts by beliefs that made the polis the center of the world, but that we can only see through the poetry of aristocrats who accepted it. The voices of ordinary citizens like Archilochus' Charon might express the middling ideology even more vigorously. But even as it is, we see a spectrum of opinions among the upper classes. The middle was malleable, just as "equality" and "freedom" would be in classical times. For instance, Solon and Theognis agreed that the combination of hubristic rich and desperate poor led to tyranny, but in Theognis this verged on antagonism toward the *dēmos*. "Drive the empty-headed vulgar herd with kicks," he said; "jab them with sharp goads and put a galling yoke on their neck; you will not find, among all the men the sun looks down upon, a people that loves a master more than this one" (847–50).[77]

This flexibility allowed some upper-class Greeks to accept the community of middling citizens as the source of legitimate authority, while still monopolizing political decision-making as the subcommunity of the wise. The middle was put into action in different ways in different poleis and at different times, even if the convention-bound, Panhellenic poetry does not allow us to document this.

## VII. The Emergence of Democracy

The middling tradition goes back to the eighth century, over a wide area of Greece.[78] It contained some of the key elements of the Strong Principle of Equality, but democratic institutions only emerged in the late sixth century. Herodotus mentions several experiments with popular rule around the time of Cleisthenes' reforms. About a generation earlier, Demonax of Mantineia came to Cyrene in a dynastic crisis. He divided the citizens into new tribes, set aside some land and offices for the kings, and "gave all the other things which the kings had formerly held into the midst of the people" (*es meson tōi dēmōi*: 4.161). It is hard to know exactly what Herodotus meant, or if the story is true, but he used similar language in three more passages. In 522, he says, Maiandrios wished to lay aside his tyranny over Samos. He set up a shrine of Zeus as God of Freedom and offered *isonomia*, "equality before the law," to the people (3.142). In the best-known but least plausible tale, Herodotus claims that in the very next year, the Persian noble Otanes proposed that the whole empire should be a democracy (3.80). All these plans fell through, but Herodotus mentions in passing that in 499 certain rich men were thrown out of Naxos by the *dēmos* (5.30), and that at some time around 500 Cadmus, tyrant of Cos, inspired by his sense of justice (*dikaiosynē*), "gave his rule into the midst of the Koans" (*esmeson Kōoisi*: 7.164), and moved to Sicily. He probably felt comfortable there: in 491, the Syracusan demos expelled their notables and set up their own democracy (7.155). Herodotus knew that not everyone believed his story about Otanes, so he bolstered it by emphasizing that in 492 the Persians had set up democracies all through Ionia (6.43).[79]

All these stories have well-known problems, and none can be pressed too hard,[80] but their chronological clustering is nevertheless striking. They suggest a broad trend toward granting political powers to the *dēmos* between 525 and 490. At Athens democracy was established in a violent rejection of all authority external to the polis itself, as Hippias' base in the club of tyrants and Isagoras' in Sparta were denied in favor of Cleisthenes' total commitment to the citizenry.[81] Changes in poetry and archaeology suggest that this was part of a widespread development in the last decades of the sixth century, and that with the collapse of the elitist ideology democracy became a possibility.

Around 520, aristocrats started commissioning odes in honor of returning athletic victors, to be performed by a chorus in the home city.[82] This poetry brought the victor's glory back to the community. It was an old idea: Crotty observes that in Homer "it is only by rejoining his fellows that the warrior can receive their acknowledgement and honor." The heroes had worried about what "someone" (*tis*) from the people might say, but the new epinician odes go much further, offering to incorporate everyone in the polis into a single song. The praise of other nobles was now not enough, even for such diehards as the dynasts of Thessaly. There was a crisis of praising.[83]

A group of professional poets emerged, arguing that ordinary citizens' praise was shapeless and therefore futile. It was easily misdirected, being no better than gossip. The poets' technical virtuosity, verging on incomprehensibility, marked their words as standing outside ordinary speech. They presented themselves as a neutral group, mediating between mass and elite, turning aside ordinary men's envy of those who were more successful. Pindar could describe himself at one moment as the guest-friend of Sogenes of Aegina (*Nem.* 7.61–65), and at another as an ordinary citizen (*Pyth.* 2.13), identifying with each group as the need arose.[84]

Epinician poets embraced the image of the middling citizen. Pindar agreed that the "middle rank" (*ta mesa*) had the most enduring prosperity (*Pyth.* 11.52–53), heaping praise on those who pursued the *metron*. For Bacchylides, whoever had his health and lived off his own estate rivaled "the first men" (*Ode* 1.165–68).[85] But they did not simply continue the middling tradition. They envisaged an elite distinguished from ordinary citizens by more than just greater wisdom and moderation. Pindar baldly asserted that "the piloting of poleis is passed from father to son, in the hands of the nobles" (*Pyth.* 10.71–72). Pindar divided the world into gods, extraordinary men, and ordinary men. For him, as Most puts it, "the gods are superior in that they always possess felicity, the extraordinary men in that they have, at least on one occasion and if only briefly, attained felicity." But this was not the bold elite of Sappho and Alcman. Those who won in the games attained special links with the gods and heroes (Heracles had set up and won the first Olympics), but their victories were mainly *megaloprepeia*. The elite's spending and efforts were not just for themselves or their class but were "in the common interest" (Pindar, *Pyth.* 9.93), obliging all citizens to repay it with *charis*, "gratitude," which the poet converted into praise.[86]

Like the men in Xenophanes' ideal symposia, Pindar's extraordinary men were wise enough to be pious. But Pindar also believed that in return for piety the gods granted them favor, which translated into wealth, to be spent on the games. Their wealth then became "a conspicuous star, truest light for a man" (Pindar, *Ol.* 2.55–56), illuminating the whole city. The only alternative to this public spending was to hoard wealth in the darkness, hiding the family's fame. Pindar's universe simply had no room for the Sapphic manipulation of luxury.[87]

Pindar described the nobleman with his golden cups in similar terms to the gods on Olympus, but the poets agreed that an unbridgeable gulf separated mortals from the divine. "One is the race of men, one is the race of gods," explains Pindar, "and from one mother do we both draw our breath; but a wholly sundered power has divided us, so that the one is nothing, while for the other, brazen Heaven remains secure for ever" (*Nem.* 6.1–4).[88] Aristocrats were cut off from the East just as brutally. Persia had crushed Lydia in 546, and the epinician Lydia was little more than a source of music. Luxury continued to be associated with the East, but by the time of Aeschylus' *Persians* in 472 this was entirely negative: luxury, softness, and hubris explained the Persian defeats in 490–479. It was much harder to draw on the East as a source of legitimacy after this, but the meager evidence does not allow us to say whether these changes were already underway before 500.[89]

Shorn of external sources of authority, aristocrats had to fall back on themselves and their poleis. The only alternative was to retreat to the mystery cults that flourished at this time, but as Detienne points out, "the priests and the initiates lived on the [social] margins of the city, and aspired only to a completely interior transformation." And even when transformed, the priest claimed only an inner superiority over ordinary men, rather than domination, as the archaic elitists had done.[90] For those who wished to stay in the mainstream, essentialist definitions of the aristocrat no longer held good. For Simonides there could be no "all-blameless man ... built four-square, without blame, in hand, foot, and mind" (fr. 542.24, 2–3). The best a man could hope for was to avoid doing anything disgraceful, and to be mindful of civic justice (542.27–29, 34–35). Not without cause does Gentili speak of "Simonides' deconsecration of aristocratic values," or Detienne of his demotion of *alēthea* in favor of *doxa*. Virtue became a relative matter, defined from the point of view of the polis. Simonides summed his view up in an elegiac fragment: "It is the polis that teaches the man" (fr. 15 West).[91]

The major exception perhaps proves the rule. In *Ode* 3.17–66, Bacchylides says that Hieron, tyrant of Syracuse, gave more gold to Apollo than anyone except Croesus of Lydia, and that both men had special divine favor. Burnett points out that the peculiarity of Hieron's triumph – "the victor did not drive his own team or even train his own horses, but simply paid the bills" – made the praise of his wealth most appropriate, but there is more to it.[92] Gelon had begun the Syracusan generosity to Delphi and Olympia. Herodotus (7.158–62) says that Gelon had been willing to help against Persia in 480, but only if he were made commander. His dedications perhaps continued his claims to hegemony, representing Himera as equivalent to Salamis and Plataea in preserving the freedom of the Greeks. Hieron went further, blending ritual and architecture to justify an expansionist kingship unlike anything in old Greece.[93] Likening Hieron to Croesus, as an ambitious ruler on the edge of the Greek world, with a special relationship to Apollo because of his gifts to Olympia and Delphi, fitted very well with the tyrant's program. But Bacchylides immediately undermined this message. Croesus stood for wealth and piety, but also for lack of moderation. Apollo had not saved Lydia, and Croesus despaired of the gods' *charis*, unwilling to wait any longer (3.38). Bacchylides' Apollo points out that nothing can be foreseen. Men should be cheerful, because pious deeds (*hosia*) – apparently, *any* pious deeds – bring the highest gains. "I sing clearly for the wise," explains Bacchylides (3.85). This is *ainos* poetry, giving the audience of the wise a story that ought to be chilling for a tyrant: the gods respect piety, regardless of wealth, and there is no guarantee that they will preserve the domain of any king if he forgets proper measure. McGlew concludes that "epinician seems to question, even as it proclaims, the happiness of the poet's tyrant-patron."[94]

The emergence of Athenian tragedy around 500 was part of this Panhellenic trend. The tragedians' confrontations between heroic individuals and civic-minded choruses parallel developments in non-Athenian epinician, although the tragedians found different resolutions; and the list of awards for the best tragedy is dominated by citizens of other states down to the 470s.[95] But the Panhellenic scale of changes is clearest in archaeology. Spending on aristocratic display, particularly burials, had increased slowly in many places in the sixth century, but everywhere this declined abruptly c. 500. Until about 425 burials were normally very simple, with few grave goods and no monuments. Fifth-century houses tended to be larger than those of the sixth century, but, so far as we can tell from excavation, there were hardly any differences in size and decoration between the houses at any site before the end of the fifth century. The literary sources also say that aristocrats gave up expensive clothes, fancy hairstyles, and jewelry. So little precious plate is known that some archaeologists suggest none was made during the fifth century. By 500, aristocratic efforts to differentiate themselves from other citizens in their rituals were declining. Votive offerings also declined, and the few spectacular offerings, like the temples themselves, were now normally made by the state.[96]

Dahl's Principle of Equal Consideration requires that all members of a group should agree that they are about equally well qualified to participate in making its decisions. The middling ideology was such a belief and had been important since the eighth century; but at the end of the sixth century, all viable alternatives collapsed. No doubt many nobles, whether in Thebes, Aegina, or Athens, continued to believe that they were special beings, but they increasingly conceded that they needed to be judged not just by their peers, but also by the citizens of their home communities. Many of them must also have continued to believe that aristocratic government should guide the people, just as praise and blame should be channeled through professional poets. The collapse of faith in external sources of legitimation and the establishment of the Strong Principle of Equality did not automatically produce democracy, but it made democracy a possibility. Aristocrats had to make their way within a community of men who were, after all, about equally well qualified to participate in the decisions of the group.

## VIII. Conclusion

In this paper I have tried to trace, within the archaic period, a set of ideological shifts that made Greek democracy a possibility. I have argued that the eighth century was in many ways the crucial moment. In this obscure period the polis was established as a community of *mesoi*, founded on something like what Dahl calls the Principle of Equal Consideration of Interests. *To meson* was not a class but an ideological construct, allowing *all* citizens to locate themselves in the middle. Like any construct, it was open to reinterpretation: I have suggested that Theognis appropriated it for the upper class more than he assimilated a "moderate" elite to the mass of citizens the way that Hesiod, Xenophanes, Solon, or Phocylides did. Nevertheless, I believe that it is wrong to imagine a slow evolution across the archaic period from royal to aristocratic to hoplite to thetic power. From the earliest sources, "the middle" includes all citizens: in Walzer's terms the "one good thing" was citizen birth. To call a man rich or poor, to deny his middling status, was to cast him out of the ideal polis.

But some aristocrats happily cast themselves out, forming alternative fellowships outside (and in their view above) the polis. They wanted to be a privileged supra-polis elite, dining and loving with the gods, heroes, and Lydians. The only problem was that many of their fellow citizens refused to recognize their superiority, preferring instead to mock them, and on occasion to kill them. But by 500 BC the elitist ideology was in disarray: powerless in the face of growing citizen confidence, aristocrats everywhere conceded the second proposition in Dahl's Strong Principle of Equality, that no external source of authority made them so much better qualified than other citizens that they alone should automatically be entrusted with making the collective and binding decisions.

But it required more to make a democracy. Many *poleis* entrusted themselves to the guardianship of oligarchies throughout the classical period. On the whole, it seems that democracy was only tried out when a military crisis raised the stakes and made it impossible for the guardians to claim to represent the middle. In the seventh century, the obvious response had been to find a new, better set of guardians; by the end of the sixth, it could seem sensible to do away with guardians altogether, and to find some method for the citizens to make their decisions directly.

There were many ways to do this. Democracy cannot be defined solely by a decision-making assembly. It was also possible to allow smaller bodies, such as a *boulē* (council) or a tribal assembly, to make some decisions.[97] Democracy is not something that a community either has or does not have: it consists of bundles of attitudes and institutions, and we should perhaps range the poleis along an imaginary spectrum. Some constitutions allowed citizens to make more of the binding decisions than did others, and the roles of elected representatives and other officeholders varied. Different states extended democracy into different spaces and allowed different kinds of assemblies to make the decisions. Each city-state moved around on this spectrum according to the outcome of local struggles, such as those in Athens in 510–507, 462, and 411–399.

Perhaps the best reason to seek the origins of Greek democracy is to understand its limitations. It took to an extreme the idea of a community of middling men but remained, in Dahl's terms, a guardianship of citizens over women, children, aliens, and slaves; in Held's, a "democracy of patriarchs"; and in Walzer's, "not communal freedom but oppression ... Indeed, the rule of citizens over non-citizens, members over strangers, is probably the most common form of tyranny in human history."[98] But recognizing this does not require us to reject the significance of the Greek experience. Finley rightly stressed that "moral condemnation, no matter how well-founded, is no substitute for historical or social analysis. 'Rule by the few' or 'rule by the many' was a meaningful choice, the freedom and rights that the factions claimed for themselves were worth fighting for, despite the fact that even 'the many' were a minority of the whole population."[99] These archaic origins are important, not because Greek democracy ushered in a utopia or because it began an historical trajectory leading directly to us, but because it was *different*. Wealth justified dominance over a mass of subjects in many ancient states, but the Greeks – perhaps for the first time in history – substituted for it birth within a broad male citizen body, creating new inclusions and possibilities, and new exclusions and oppressions. The consequence of this was the Strong Principle of Equality; the consequence of that, Greek democracy.

## NOTES

1   Unless otherwise indicated, I cite the fragments of the early Greek poets from the following editions (full documentation is in the References below):

Aeschylus fragments: Smyth, *Aeschylus* II.
Alcaeus, Sappho: Lobel and Page, *Poetarum Lesbiorum Fragmenta*.
Alcman, Anacreon, Simonides, Stesichorus: Page, *Poetae Melici Graeci*.
Archilochus, Callinus, Hipponax, Mimnermus, Semonides, Simonides (elegiac fragments), Solon, Tyrtaeus: West, *Iambi et Elegi Graeci*.
Bacchylides: Snell and Maehler, *Bacchylidis, Carmina cum Fragmentis*.
Hesiod fragments: Merkelbach and West, *Fragmenta Hesiodea*.
Pindar fragments: Maehler, *Pindari, Carmina cum Fragmentis*.
Xenophanes: Diels and Kranz, *Die Fragmente der Vorsokratiker*.

2   Ober, *Mass and Elite*, 36–38; Hansen, *Athenian Democracy*, 19–22; and Bleicken, *Athenische Demokratie*, 9, justify differing versions of this approach.
3   Particularly Giddens, *Central Problems*.

4   Most books review developments from Solon to Cleisthenes (e.g., Meier, *Discovery*, 29–52; Bleicken, *Athenische Demokratie*, 13–169; Ober, *Mass and Elite*, 55–75; Hansen, *Athenian Democracy*, 27–36), but very few make historical explanation of archaic social dynamics a key issue in their understandings of democracy (Manville, *Origins*, is a notable exception).

5   Hansen, *Athenian Democracy*, 320; cf. 71–72, 319.

6   Dahl, *Democracy*, 30–31, 98.

7   Ibid., 55, 85–86, 167.

8   Morris, *Darkness and Heroes*.

9   Stein-Hölkeskamp, *Adelskultur*, 86–138, is an important recent exception, providing a more nuanced account of aristocratic ideology in Theognis.

10  Abercrombie et al., *Dominant Ideology Thesis; Dominant Ideologies*.

11  Foucault, *Language*, 139–64; Chartier, *Cultural Origins*, 7.

12  Whitman, *Democratic Vistas*, 343.

13  For these features see Aesch. 1.42; 3.11, 218; Dem. 21.183; 29.24; 54.15, 17; Din. 2.8; Hyp. 4.21; Isoc. 7.40; Lys. fr. 73; see Ober, *Mass and Elite*, 257–59, 297–99. *Philia:* Arist. *Eth. Nic.* 1157b35, 1158b11–1159a5, 1171b32–1172a8, with Sahlins, *Economics*, 193–230. On the varied senses of "middle class," see Giddens, *Class Structure*, 30–32, 42–45, 61–64, 177–97. In favor of a hoplite middle class, see Spahn, *Mittelschicht*, 70–83, 174–78; Meier, *Discovery*, 29–52; on the hoplite as a model, Loraux, *Invention*, 34, 37, 98, 151; and on hoplite values, Hanson, *Western Way of War*, passim. Hanson, this volume [*Demokratia*], offers a sophisticated combination of these models.

[...]

22  In this section I summarize very briefly the arguments of Morris, *Darkness and Heroes*, chs. 5–8.

23  Morris, *Burial; Darkness and Heroes*, chs. 5–7; Whitley, *Style and Society*, 116–62, 181–83, 191–94.

24  Sanctuaries: Coldstream, *Geometric Greece*, 317–40, de Polignac, *Naissance;* and recent finds in Mazarakis-Ainian, *Rulers' Dwellings;* and Hägg et al., *Cult Practice*.

25  Snodgrass, *Archaic Greece*, 52–63, 99–100; "Economics."

26  Whitley, "Diversity;" Morris, *Darkness and Heroes*, ch. 5.

27  Morris, *Burial*, 205–10; *Darkness and Heroes*, ch. 8.

28  Nagy, *Mythology*, 48n.40.

29  Nagy, *Pindar's Homer*, 52–115, 174–98, 418–37; "Questions," 38–41. Nagy emphasizes broad evolutionary forces rather than individual rhapsodes, as I do here.

30  Chronology: Theog. 773–82, 891–94, 1103–4. Attributions, Theog. 145–48, 153–54, 227–32, 315–18, 719–28, 793–96, 1003–6, 1017–22, 1253–54. See Nagy, "Theognis," 51, but cf. West, *Studies*, 40–61. Anacreon: Rosenmeyer, *Imitation*.

31  Quotation: Miralles and Pòrtulas, *Archilochus*, 22. The names have often been discussed. See, e.g., West, *Studies*, 25–29; Burnett, *Archaic Poets*, 15–32; Nagy, *Achaeans*, 243–52; *Pindar's Homer*, 430–32.

32  Hobsbawm and Ranger, *Invention of Tradition;* Herzfeld, *Place in History*, 205.

33  Pittacus: Alc. frs. 67.4, 75.12, 106.3, 129.21, 348.1, cf. Diog. Laert. 1.81; Kurke, "Crisis," 69–75, 83–92. On the historicity of these charges, see, e.g., Page, *Sappho and Alcaeus*, 169–79; Kirkwood, *Monody*, 67–76. Compromises: Dover, "Archilochus," 199–212; Rosen, "Hipponax." Demosthenes: Ober, *Mass and Elite*, 268–79.

34  Mazzarino, *Occidente*, 191–246; Kurke, "Politics." On forms see West, *Metre*, 29–56. The choral/monodic distinction makes little difference to cultural assumptions (Davies, "Monody"). Choral context: Burnett, *Bacchylides*, 5–14. Monodic: Kirkwood, *Monody*, 1–19.

35  Cf. frs. 95, 96, 98. His "biography" is similarly ambivalent: the *Anth. Pal.* (7.18, 19, 709) calls him Lydian as well as Spartan, but the *Suda* says he was descended from slaves.

36  Alc. fr. 347; Hes., *Op.* 582–96. See Burnett, *Three Archaic Poets*, 132–34; Petropulos, *Heat and Lust*.

37  Bourdieu, *Distinction*, 40, 47–50, 88, 92–93.

38  Family: 376–80, 695–705. Bulls: 436–37. Slave: 405–6 (unless *ktētēn* is interpolated: West, *Works and Days*, 260). Laborer: 602–3. *Dmōes:* 470, 502, 559–60, 573, 597, 607–8. Women: *Op.* 58–92, 519–25, 695–705, 753–55; *Th.* 570–612. Work: *Op.* 303–14, 381–82. Begging: *Op.* 397–400. Cf. Ober, *Mass and Elite*, 220–21.

39  *Op.* 23–24, 343–45, 349–51, 370–72, 706–14. Neighbors: Alc. fr. 123; Theog. 302; Anac. fr. 354; Pindar *Nem.* 7.87–89. Fourth century: Cohen, *Law*, 85–90.

40  *Op.* 717–18; *Th.* 26–28, with Svenbro, *Parole*, 50–59; Nagy, *Mythology*, 274–75.

41  *Basilēes: Op.* 38–39, 202–12, 263–64; *Th.* 79–93. Respect, Shame, and hubris: *Op.* 174–201, 213–18, 225–64, with Fisher, *Hybris*, 185–200, 213–16.

42  Martin, "Hesiod, Odysseus"; Kurke, "Sixth *Pythian*," 104–07.

43  Griffith, "Personality"; Lamberton, *Hesiod*, 1–37; Nagy, *Mythology*, 36–82; Martin, "Metanastic Poetics," 12–16. Cf. Zeitlin, "Thebes," and Dougherty, this volume [*Demokratia*], on Delphi.

44  Detienne, *Maîtres*, 34–50, 68–78, emphasizing *Th.* 27–28.

45  Nagy, *Mythology*, 67. Exterior insider: Martin, "Metanastic Poetics," 14.

46  Szegedy-Maszak, "Legends"; Nagy, "Theognis," 31–32.

47  Ostwald, *Nomos*, 55. Arch. fr. 232 has a tantalizing reference to someone "learning the Cretan *nomoi*," apparently said in mockery.

48  Parallels: West, *Theogony*, 40–48; *Works and Days*, 3–15; Walcot, *Near East*; Millett, "Hesiod," 93–106. The Ptolemaic *Instructions of ʿOnqsheshonquy* has still more striking parallels with the *Op.*, and Walcot, "Instructions," suggests that it imitated Hesiod. However, it is in any case more hierarchical than the *Op.* (e.g., 7.12–15; 8.11; 17.17, 25; 18.7–8, 12). The Egyptian texts are translated by Pritchard, *Texts*, 407–10, 421–25, and Lichtheim, *Literature* I, 169–84; II, 146–63; III, 159–84.

49  Nagy, *Mythology*, 9–17.

50  Ibid., 270. Audience: Walsh, *Varieties*, 22–36; Nagy, "Theognis," 22–27.

51  See Xenoph. fr. 1, and Archil. fr. 124b; Xenoph. fr. 22; Theog. 469–98, 503–10, 837–44; Phoc. fr. 11; cf. Anac. fr. 356.

52  Loraux, "Solon au milieu," makes a series of excellent points about the theme of the middle in Solon's poetry.

53  Cf. Solon, fr. 5, 24.1–4; Theog. 219–20, 331–32, 401–6, 543–46, 693–94, 719–28 (= Solon fr. 24); North, *Sophrosyne*, 12–18. Moderate wealth: Phoc. fr. 7. Women: Phoc. fr. 3; Theog. 457–60; Semon. frs. 6, 7, with Loraux, *Children*, 72–110. Constraints of poverty: Theog. 173–82, 383–98, 649–52, 1062. All despise the poor: Theog. 267–70, 621–22, 699–718, 927–30; cf. Alc. fr. 360. Belly: Archil. fr. 124b; Hipp. fr. 128, with West, *Studies*, 148.

54  No limits on wealth: Solon fr. 13.71–76 = Theog. 227–32; unrighteous gain, Solon frs. 4.5–6; 13.7–11; Theog. 145–48, 465–66, 753–56. On hubris, cf. Theog. 603–4, 731–52, 833–36, 1103–04; and Archil. fr. 45, "hanging their heads they spewed up their hubris." Even if this refers to the suicide of the Lycambids (contra, West, *Studies*, 125), it is also a general comment on destructive hubris. See Fisher, *Hybris*, 201–16.

55  Morris, "Use and Abuse," 115–29. As Nagy observes ("Questions," 52), this is not inconsistent with an evolutionary model. Quotation from Fisher, *Hybris*, 176. For the other views cited, see Donlan, *Aristocratic Ideal*, 20–23; Rose, *Sons of the Gods*, 43–140; Thalmann, "Thersites"; Thornton, *Homer's Iliad*, 144–47.

56  Antonaccio, *Archaeology of Ancestors*, presents the evidence in detail, and the extensive modern literature. I set out my own views in Morris, "Tomb Cult" and develop them further in *Darkness and Heroes*, ch. 6. Helen: Hes. fr. 358; Stes. fr. 192, with Sisti, "Palinodie," 307–8; cf. Hdt. 2.112–20. Lord, *Singer*, 194, believed that there was such variety that a version of the *Iliad* existed in which the embassy in book 9 was successful.

57  Hes. *Op.* 26, 654–59; *Th.* 22–35, with Walsh, *Varieties*, 26–33. Ford, *Homer*, 92.

58  The issues remain controversial; Snodgrass, "Hoplite Reform," and van Wees, "Homeric Way of War," are the most recent discussions.

59  See Burnett, *Archaic Poets*, 123–26. Page (*Sappho and Alcaeus*, 222) makes the important point that the terminology used for these heroic arms is very like that which Herodotus (1.34) uses for Lydian armor, suggesting the kind of heroic-oriental link that I discuss below.

60  Quotation from Gentili, *Poetry*, 83–84. Delicacy: Sappho frs. 2.14; 30.4–5; 44.8–10; 46; 81; 92; 94.12–22; 98; 192; Alcm. frs. 1.64–68; 3.77; 56.3; 91; 117; Alc. fr. 130B.17–20; Anac. frs. 388.10–12; 481; Kurke, "Politics," 93–99. Divine luxury: Sappho frs. 1.7–8; 2; 33; 54; 96.27–28; 103.6, 13; 123; 127. Sappho and Aphrodite: Nagy, *Mythology*, 223–62. Burnett, *Archaic Poets*, 243–76 and 161, suggests that Alcaeus "stands in an almost priestly relation" to Zeus, Hera, and Dionysus in fr. 129. Sappho explicitly associates luxury with the heroic age in fr. 44.5–10.

61  C. Morgan, *Athletes*, 45.

62  Catling, "Workshop and Heirloom"; Matthäus, "Heirloom or Tradition?" Tin content: Filippakis et al., "Bronzes." Imports: Snodgrass, *Archaic Greece*, 105–6; Kilian-Dirlmeier, "Weihungen"; Muscarella, "Cauldrons."

63  Bolton, *Aristeas*, 134–41, 179–81. Hdt. 4.13–16 fully believed these stories. Religious borrowings: Burkert, *Revolution;* Carter, "Masks," 91, with de Polignac, "Influence," 114–17.

64  Murray, "Symposion." Koukounaries: Schilardi, "Paro," 247; Grave markers: Boardman, "Differentiation"; Catling and Lemos, *Lefkandi* II.1, 25–26. Knossos: Coldstream, "Gift Exchange," 204–6.

65  Lydian luxury: Sappho frs. 16.17–20; 39; 96.7–8; 98a.10–11; 132.3; Alcm. frs. 1.64–65; 13c; 16. Cf. Alc. frs. 49.5; 69.1–6; Anac. fr. 481; eleg. 3; Alcm. fr. 13d. Symposia: Fehr, *Gelage;* Dentzer, *Banquet;* Boardman, "Furniture."

66  Cf. Curtin, *Trade;* Appadurai, "Introduction."

67  Kyrieleis, "Babylonische Bronzen," argues that in fact most of the Oriental imports in Greek sanctuaries were given by Eastern kings, while Strøm, "Evidence from the Sanctuaries," suggests that the priests organized trade with the Near East to guarantee themselves Eastern ritual paraphernalia. Neither theory accounts very well for either the imported finds or the imitations; I assume here that most of the objects were dedicated by users of the sanctuaries, primarily Greeks (Morris, *Darkness and Heroes*, ch. 6). Borell, *Schalen*, 93–96, and Markoe, *Bowls*, 121–22, have important comments on Eastern influences.

68  Burkert, *Orientalizing*, 16. Phoenicians: Shaw, "Phoenicians"; Negbi, "Presence," 607–9. Immigrants: Boardman, *Greeks Overseas*, 56–62. Protogeometric B: Coldstream, *Geometric Greece*, 68–70, 99–102. Differences from mainland: Markoe, *Bowls*, 82–83, 110–17; Morris, *Darkness and Heroes*, chs. 5–7.

69  Simon, "Votive Offerings," 4–165, 410–21; Philipp, "Archaische Gräber."

70  Murray, "Sympotic History," 7.

71  Boutros, *Phoenician Sport*. Interstate elite: Herman, *Ritualised Friendship*, 118–65. Young, *Olympic Myth*, 107–70, argues that not all athletes were aristocrats, but also emphasizes the scale of rewards (pp. 115–33). Training: Poliakoff, *Combat Sports*, 11–19. Agonal society: Burckhardt, *Greek Culture*, 53–56, with Poliakoff, *Combat*

*Sports*, 104–15. Athenian juries: Ober, *Mass and Elite*, 144. Renewing household: Kurke, *Traffic*, 15–62.

72    Rose, *Sons of the Gods*, 160. Phalanx: Call. fr. 1; Tyrt. frs. 10; 12; Theog. 1003–6.

73    Xenoph. frs. 10–16; 2. See also Arch. frs. 16; 130; Semon. fr. 1; Solon frs. 13.65–74; 16; Theog. 133–42, 155–60, 557–60, 585–90 (=Solon fr. 13.65–74), 1075–78; Xenoph. frs. 18; 34.

74    Fränkel, *Poetry*, 138.

75    See also frs. 32; 38; 42; 72.7; 79; 125.

76    Against athletes, in favor of more useful types: Tyrt. fr. 12.1–12; Xenoph. fr. 2; Solon, in Diod. 9.2.5. On aristocrats as outsiders, see Herman, *Ritualised Friendship*; Stein-Hölkeskamp, *Adelskultur*, 233; generally, Anderson, *Imagined Communities*.

77    Classical equality, freedom: Raaflaub, *Entdeckung*, 313–27; this volume [*Demokratia*]. Rich, poor, and tyranny: Solon frs. 4.7–8, 23; 9.3–4; 33; 36.20–25; Theog. 39–52. On the *dēmos* see Donlan, "Changes," and on tyranny, McGlew, *Tyranny*, 87–123. Alcaeus and Solon both feared tyrants, but Pittacus had more in common with Solon than with Solon's tyrant: e.g., Simon. fr. 542.13; Diog. Laert. 1.77, 79; Arist. *Pol.* 1285a37–39; Strabo 13.2.3; Diod. 9.12.3. These are poor sources for a "historical" Pittacus but illustrate the negotiation of long-term traditions opposing luxury.

78    Indeed, as I argue in *Darkness and Heroes*, in certain ways it can be said to go back to the late eleventh century.

79    For further sources see Zimmermann, "Ansätze," with Ostwald, *Nomos*, 161–67. Sartori, "Verfassung," and Berger, *Revolution*, 15–56, present the western evidence.

80    Hölkeskamp, "Demonax" is the most recent skeptical discussion, with references to others.

81    Ober, "Revolution."

82    The performance context is disputed. See K. Morgan, "Pindar."

83    Crotty, *Song and Action*, 109–10; de Jong, "Voice."

84    Professionalism: Nagy, *Pindar's Homer*, 188–90; Kurke, *Traffic*, 240–50; K. Morgan, "Pindar." Defining praise: Carson, "*Protagoras*," 119–24. The power of gossip was an old theme, going back to the middling poets (e.g., Hes. *Op.* 701, 719–21; Archil. frs. 13, 14; Mimn. frs. 6 [=Theog. 793–800], 7, 15, 16; Phoc. fr. 6; Theog. 367–70), and continuing into the fourth century (Cohen, *Law*, 90–95; Hunter, *Policing Athens*, 96–119). Citizens' views: Pindar, *Ol.* 5.16; 7.89–90; 13.2–3; *Pyth.* 2.81–82; 4.295–97; 11.28–30; *Nem.* 7.65–67; 8.38–39; 11.17; *Isthm.* 1.50–51; 2.37–38; 3.1–3; fr. 109. Technique: Most, *Measures*, 23–24. Envy: Pindar *Ol.* 2.95; 11.7–8; *Pyth.* 2.89–92; 7.18–19; *Nem.* 8.21–23; *Isthm.* 2.43; Bacchyl. *Ode* 13.199–203, although cf. *Pyth.* 1.85. Kurke, *Traffic*, 86–90, 135–47, points out that by referring to *xeinoi* (e.g., *Ol.* 7.89–90; 13.3; *Pyth.* 3.69–71; *Isthm.* 1.50–51; 6.66–72) Pindar assures the victors of the existence of an elite community as well as incorporating them into the citizen community; and that when relating to a victor, even other aristocrats were "ordinary" men who might fall prey to *phthonos*. Cf. Goldhill, *Poet's Voice*, 130–32, 138–42.

85    Middle: Pindar, *Nem.* 11.47–48; *Isthm.* 6.66–72; *Paean* 1.2–5; 4.32–53. The belly theme appears at Pindar, *Isthm.* 1.49, and poverty at Pindar fr. 109; Bacchyl. *Ode* 1.168–71. Living justly, and in proportion: Pindar, *Pyth.* 2.86–88; 3.107–08; 5.14; 10.67–68; *Nem.* 7.87–89; cf. *Ol.* 7.90–92; *Pyth.* 4.284–285; 8.8–20; 11.54–56; *Nem.* 7.65–67; *Isthm.* 3.1–3; fr. 180.3; Bacchyl. *Ode* 13.44–45, against hubris.

86    Most, *Measures*, 75. Links with gods and heroes: Pindar *Ol.* 7.20–24; 10.16–19, 43–77, 102–5; *Pyth.* 4.253; 9.39–42; 10.1–3, 49–53; *Isthm.* 5.26–27; 6.19, with Nagy, *Pindar's Homer*, 116–56; Rose, *Sons of the Gods*, 160–62. *Megaloprepeia*: Kurke, *Traffic*, 163–224. Poem as recompense: Most, *Measures*, 72; Kurke, *Traffic*, 102, 116. Victory in the common interest: Pindar *Ol.* 5.4; 7.93–94; 9.19–22; *Nem.* 2.8; Bacchyl. *Ode* 6.15–16; 13.77–83.

*Charis*: MacLachlan, *Age of Grace*, 87–123, again adapting a middling theme (ibid., 73–86), which continued into fourth-century Athens (Ober, *Mass and Elite*, 226–33).

87 Wise spending: Pindar *Ol.* 2.53–56; 5.23–24; *Pyth.* 2.56; 5.1–2, 14; 6.47. Hoarding: Pindar *Ol.* 2.55–56; *Nem.* 1.31–33; *Isthm.* 1.67–68; 4.29; Bacchyl. *Ode* 3.13–14; Kurke, *Traffic*, 225–29; Most, *Measures*, 90–91.

88 Divine wealth: Pindar *Ol.* 6.39–40, 104–5; 8.51; 9.32–33; 13.65–66; *Pyth.* 1.1–2; 3.9–10, 89–90, 93–95; 4.53–54, 178; 5.9, 104; 9.6, 9, 56, 59, 109; *Nem.* 5.2–4; 6.37–38; 7.77–79; *Isthm.* 1.1; 2.1–2, 26; 4.60; 6.75; 8.6–7; *Paean* 6.1; frs. 29.1, 3; 30.1–2, 6; 75.14; 139.1, 9; 195; Bacchyl. *Ode* 9.1, 100; 11.4, 37–38, 49; 13.194–95; *Dith.* 3.34–36; 5.22; fr. 15.12; Simon. fr. 577b. Heroic wealth: Pindar *Ol.* 7.64; *Pyth.* 4.232; 10.40; *Nem.* 8.27; *Isthm.* 6.19; fr. 166.3; Bacchyl. *Dith.* 1.4. No achievement without the gods' help: Pindar *Ol.* 8.67; *Pyth.* 8.76–78; 12.29–30; *Nem.* 10.29–30; *Isthm.* 3.4–6; 5.52–53; Bacchyl. *Dith.* 3.117–118; fr. 24; Simon. fr. 526. Cannot equal the gods: Pindar *Ol.* 5.23–24; *Pyth.* 2.49–53, 88–89; 3.59–62; 10–21.29; *Nem.* 7.55–56; 11.13–16; *Isthm.* 3.17–18; 5.14–16; Bacchyl. *Ode* 5.94–96.

89 Lydia: Pindar *Ol.* 5.19; 14.17–18; *Nem.* 4.45; 8.15; fr. 125 Maehler; Bacchyl. fr. 14. Pindar *Nem.* 8.16–18 may be an exception, with Pindar offering Ajax a Lydian *mitra* (headband) decked with song, which is then linked with a mythical priest of Aphrodite. We can only speculate on what Aeschylus intended in fr. 29 (Smyth). Recent scholarship on the East as a mirror in which "Greekness" was constructed has perhaps exaggerated the role of the Persian Wars; in her excellent treatment, Hall (*Inventing the Barbarian*, 17–19) does not do justice to the archaic material, and Miller ("Parasol") shows that even after 479 a few Athenians continued to look to the East for legitimacy.

90 Detienne, *Maîtres*, 125, 137.

91 Gentili, *Poetry*, 63–71; Detienne, *Maîtres*, 105–19; Carson, "*Protagoras*"; Crotty, *Song and Action*, 33–40.

92 Burnett, *Bacchylides*, 66. See Carson, "Burners," 116–19, on 3.87.

93 Krumeich, "Dreifüsse"; Dougherty, *Poetics*, 83–102.

94 The uncertainty of life had been a popular middling theme (Archil. frs. 16, 130; Semon. fr. 1; Solon frs. 13.65–74 [=Theog. 585–90]; 16; Theog. 133–42, 155–60, 557–60, 1075–78) and was also used in Pindar *Ol.* 7.24–26; 12.10–12; *Pyth.* 3.103–6; 8.92–97; 10.63; 11.42–46; *Isthm.* 3.17–18; 4.5–6; Simon. fr. 521. McGlew, *Tyranny*, 49, although his overall argument (35–51) is rather different from mine.

95 Vernant and Vidal-Naquet, *Myth and Tragedy*, 23–48.

96 Morris, *Death-Ritual*, 118–29, 145, 151–53. Housing: Hoepfner and Schwandner, *Haus und Stadt*, 1–26, 256–67; Hoepfner, "Architekturforschung." Votives: Snodgrass, "Economics."

97 See Ruzé, "*Plethos*"; "Tribus"; Sealey, *Republic*, 91–98; Dahl, *Democracy*, 135–52.

98 Dahl, *Democracy*, 96, 97; Held, *Models*, 23; Walzer, *Spheres*, 62.

99 Finley, *Politics*, 9.

## REFERENCES

Abercrombie, Nicholas, Stephen Hill, and Bryan Turner. *The Dominant Ideology Thesis.* London: George, Allen, and Unwin, 1980.

——, eds. *Dominant Ideologies.* London: Unwin Hyman, 1990.

Anderson, Benedict. *Imagined Communities. Reflections on the Origins and Spread of Nationalism.* 2d ed. London: Verso, 1992.

Antonaccio, Carla. *An Archaeology of Ancestors*. Lanham, Md.: Rowman and Littlefield, 1995.

Appadurai, Arjun. "Introduction: Commodities and the Politics of Value." In *The Social Life of Things*. Arjun Appadurai, ed. Cambridge: Cambridge University Press, 1986, 3–63.

Berger, Shlomo. *Revolution and Society in Greek Sicily and Southern Italy. Historia* Einzelschrift 71. Stuttgart: Franz Steiner, 1992.

Boardman, John. *The Greeks Overseas*. 3d ed. London: Thames and Hudson, 1980.

——. "Sex Differentiation in Grave Vases." *Annali di Istituto Universitario Orientale, sezione di archeologia e storia antica* 10 (1988): 171–79.

——. "Symposion Furniture." In *Sympotica*. Oswyn Murray, ed. Oxford: Clarendon Press, 1990, 122–31.

Bolton, J. D. P. *Aristeas of Proconnesus*. Oxford: Clarendon Press, 1962.

Borell, Brigitte. *Attische geometrische Schalen. Eine spätgeometrische Keramikgattung und ihre Beziehung zum Orient*. Mainz: von Zabern, 1978.

Bourdieu, P. *Distinction: A Social Critique of the Judgement of Taste*. Tr. Richard Nice. Cambridge, Mass.: Harvard University Press, 1984.

Boutros, L. *Phoenician Sport: Its Influence on the Origin of the Olympic Games*. Uithoorn: Poitlarow, 1981.

Burckhardt, Jacob. *History of Greek Culture*. Tr. R. Hilty. New York: Ungar, 1963.

Burkert, Walter. *The Orientalizing Revolution*. Tr. Margaret Pinder and Walter Burkert. Cambridge, Mass.: Harvard University Press, 1992.

Burnett, Anne P. *Three Archaic Poets: Archilochus, Alcaeus, Sappho*. Cambridge, Mass.: Harvard University Press, 1983.

——. *The Art of Bacchylides*. Cambridge, Mass.: Harvard University Press, 1985.

Carson, Anne. "The Burners: A Reading of Bacchylides' Third Epinician Ode." *Phoenix* 38 (1984): 111–19.

——. "How Not to Read a Poem: Unmixing Simonides from *Protagoras*." *Classical Philology* 87 (1992): 110–30.

Carter, Jane. "Masks and Poetry in Early Sparta." In *Early Greek Cult Practice*. Robin Hägg and Nanno Marinatos, eds. Stockholm: Skrifter Utgivna i Svenska Institutet i Athen, 1988, 89–98.

Catling, Hector. "Workshop and Heirloom: Prehistoric Bronze Stands in the East Mediterranean." *Report of the Department of Antiquities, Cyprus* (1984): 69–91.

Catling, Richard W. V., and Irene S. Lemos. *Lefkandi* II. *The Protogeometric Building at Toumba*. Part 1: *The Pottery*. British School at Athens Supplementary Volume 22. London: Thames and Hudson, 1990.

Chartier, Roger. *The Cultural Origins of the French Revolution*. Tr. Lydia G. Cochrane. Durham, N.C.: Duke University Press, 1993.

Cohen, David. *Law, Sexuality, and Society: The Enforcement of Morals in Classical Athens*. Cambridge: Cambridge University Press, 1991.

Coldstream, J. Nicolas. *Geometric Greece*. London: Methuen, 1977.

——. "Gift Exchange in the Eighth Century BC." In *The Greek Renaissance of the Eighth Century* BC. Robin Hägg, ed. Stockholm: Skrifter Utgivna i Svenska Institutet i Athen, 1983, 201–7.

Crotty, Kevin. *Song and Action: The Victory Odes of Pindar*. Baltimore: Johns Hopkins University Press, 1982.

Curtin, Philip. *Cross-Cultural Trade in World History*. Cambridge: Cambridge University Press, 1984.

Dahl, Robert A. *Democracy and Its Critics*. New Haven: Yale University Press, 1989.

Davies, Malcolm. "Monody, Choral Lyric, and the Tyranny of the Handbook." *Classical Quarterly* 38 (1988): 180–95.

de Jong, Irene. "The Voice of Anonymity: Tis-Speeches in the *Iliad*." *Eranos* 85 (1987): 69–84.

Dentzer, J. -M. *Le Motif du banquet couché dans le Proche-Orient et le monde grec du VIIème au IVème siècle avant J-C.* Paris: Mélanges de l'école française à Rome, 1982.

Detienne, Marcel. *Les Maîtres de vérité dans la Grèce archaïque.* 2d ed. Paris: Maspero, 1967.

Diels, Hermann, and Walther Kranz. *Die Fragmente der Vorsokratiker.* 8th ed. Berlin: Weidmann, 1956.

Donlan, Walter. "Changes and Shifts in the Meaning of Demos in the Literature of the Archaic Period." *Parola del passato* 25 (1970): 381–95.

——. *The Aristocratic Ideal in Ancient Greece: Attitudes of Superiority from Homer to the End of the Fifth Century* BC Lawrence, Kansas: Coronado Press, 1980.

Dougherty, Carol. *The Poetics of Colonization: From City to Text in Archaic Greece.* New York: Oxford University Press, 1993.

Dover, K. J. "The Poetry of Archilochus." In *Archiloque:* Entretiens Hardt 10 (1964): 183–222.

Fehr, Burkhard. *Orientalische und griechische Gelage.* Bonn: Bouvier, 1971.

Filippakis, S., E. Photou, C. Rolley, and G. Varoufakis. "Bronzes grecs et orientaux: Influences et apprentissages." *Bulletin de correspondance hellénique* 107 (1983): 111–32.

Finley, M. I. *Politics in the Ancient World.* Cambridge: Cambridge University Press, 1983.

Fisher, N. R. E. *Hybris.* Warminster: Aris and Phillips, 1992.

Ford, Andrew. *Homer: The Poetry of the Past.* Ithaca: Cornell University Press, 1992.

Foucault, Michel. *Language, Counter-Memory, Practice.* Tr. Donald F. Bouchard and Sherry Simon. Ithaca: Cornell University Press, 1977.

Fränkel, Hermann. *Early Greek Poetry and Philosophy.* Tr. Moses Hadas and James Willis. Oxford: Blackwell, 1973.

Gentili, Bruno. *Poetry and Its Public in Ancient Greece.* Tr. Thomas Cole. Baltimore: Johns Hopkins University Press, 1988.

Giddens, Anthony. *Central Problems in Social Theory.* Berkeley: University of California Press, 1979.

——. *The Class Structure of the Advanced Societies.* 2d ed. London: Hutchinson, 1980.

Goldhill, S. *The Poet's Voice.* Cambridge: Cambridge University Press, 1991.

Griffith, Mark. "Personality in Hesiod." *Classical Antiquity* 2 (1983): 37–65.

Hägg, Robin, Nanno Marinatos, and Gullög Nordquist, eds. *Early Greek Cult Practice.* Stockholm: Skrifter Utgivna i Svenska Institutet i Athen, 1988.

Hall, Edith, *Inventing the Barbarian.* Oxford: Oxford University Press, 1989.

Hansen, Mogens Herman. *The Athenian Democracy in the Age of Demosthenes.* Oxford: Blackwell, 1991.

Hanson, Victor Davis. *The Western Way of War: Infantry Battle in Classical Greece.* New York: Oxford University Press, 1989.

Held, David. *Models of Democracy.* Stanford: Stanford University Press, 1987.

Herman, Gabriel. *Ritualised Friendship and the Greek City.* Cambridge: Cambridge University Press, 1987.

Herzfeld, Michael. *A Place in History. Social and Monumental Time in a Cretan Town.* Princeton: Princeton University Press, 1991.

Hobsbawm, Eric, and Terence Ranger, eds. *The Invention of Tradition.* Cambridge: Cambridge University Press, 1983.

Hoepfner, Wolfram. "Die frühen Demokratien und die Architekturforschung." In *Demokratie und Architektur.* W. Schuller et al., eds. Munich: Deutscher Kunstverlag, 1989, 9–16.

Hoepfner, Wolfram, and Ernst Ludwig Schwandner. *Haus und Stadt im klassischen Griechenland.* Munich: Deutscher Kunstverlag, 1986.

Hölkeskamp, Karl-Joachim. "Demonax und die Neuordnung der Bürgerschaft von Kyrene." *Hermes* 121 (1993): 404–21.

Hunter, Virginia. *Policing Athens: Social Control in the Attic Lawsuits, 420–320* BC Princeton: Princeton University Press, 1994.

Kilian-Dirlmeier, I. "Fremde Weihungen in griechischen Heiligtümern vom 8. bis zum Beginn des 7. Jhs. v. Chr." *Jahrbuch des römisch-germanischen Zentralmuseums Mainz* 32 (1985): 215–54.

Kirkwood, Gordon. *Early Greek Monody.* Ithaca: Cornell University Press, 1974.

Krumeich, Ralf. "Zu den goldenen Dreifüssen der Deinomeniden in Delphi." *Jahrbuch des deutschen archäologischen Instituts in Athen* 106 (1991): 37–62.

Kurke, Leslie. "Pindar's Sixth *Pythian* and the Tradition of Advice Poetry." *Transactions of the American Philological Association* 120 (1990): 85–107.

——. *The Traffic in Praise.* Ithaca: Cornell University Press, 1991.

——. "The Politics of *Habrosynê* in Archaic Greece." *Classical Antiquity* 11 (1992): 91–120.

——. "Crisis and Decorum in Sixth-Century Lesbos: Reading Alkaios Otherwise." *Quaderni Urbinati di Cultura Classica* n.s. 47 (1994): 67–92.

Kyrieleis, Helmut. "Babylonische Bronzen im Heraion von Samos." *Jahrbuch des deutschen archäologischen Instituts* 94 (1979): 32–48.

Lamberton, Robert. *Hesiod.* New Haven: Yale University Press, 1988.

Lichtheim, Miriam. *Ancient Egyptian Literature.* 3 vols. Berkeley: University of California Press, 1975–80.

Lobel, Edgar, and Denys Page. *Poetarum Lesbiorum Fragmenta.* Oxford: Clarendon Press, 1955.

Loraux, N. "Solon au milieu de la lice." In *Aux origines de l'hellénisme, la Crète et la Grèce. Hommages à Henri van Effenterre.* Paris: Publications de la Sorbonne, 1984, 199–214.

——. *The Invention of Athens. The Funeral Oration in the Classical City.* Tr. Alan Sheridan. Cambridge, Mass., and London, England: Harvard University Press, 1986.

——. *The Children of Athena: Athenian Ideas about Citizenship and the Division between the Sexes.* Tr. Caroline Levine. Princeton: Princeton University Press, 1993.

Lord, Albert B. *The Singer of Tales.* Cambridge, Mass.: Harvard University Press, 1960.

MacLachlan, Bonnie. *The Age of Grace: Charis in Early Greek Poetry.* Princeton: Princeton University Press, 1993.

Maehler, H., ed. *Pindari, Carmina cum Fragmentis.* Vol. 2. Leipzig: Teubner, 1989.

Manville, Philip Brook. *The Origins of Citizenship in Ancient Athens.* Princeton: Princeton University Press, 1990.

Markoe, Glenn. *Phoenician Bronze and Silver Bowls from Cyprus and the Mediterranean.* University of California Classical Studies 26. Berkeley: University of California Press, 1985.

Martin, Richard P. "Hesiod, Odysseus, and the Instruction of Princes." *Transactions of the American Philological Association* 114 (1984): 29–48.

——. "Hesiod's Metanastic Poetics." *Ramus* 21 (1992): 11–31.

Matthäus, Hartmut. "Heirloom or Tradition? Bronze Stands of the Second and First Millennium BC in Cyprus, Greece and Italy." In *Problems in Greek Prehistory.* E. B. French and K. A. Wardle, eds. Bristol: Bristol Classical Press, 1988, 285–300.

Mazarakis-Aenian, Alexandros. *From Rulers' Dwellings to Temples. Studies in Mediterranean Archaeology.* Göteborg: Paul Äströms Förlag, forthcoming.

Mazzarino, S. *Fra oriente e occidente: Ricerche di storia greca arcaica.* Firenze: Nuova Italia, 1947.

McGlew, James. *Tyranny and Political Culture in Ancient Greece.* Ithaca: Cornell University Press, 1993.

Meier, Christian. *The Greek Discovery of Politics.* Tr. David McLintock. Cambridge, Mass.: Harvard University Press, 1990.

Merkelbach, Reinhold, and Martin West. *Fragmenta Hesiodea*. Oxford: Clarendon Press, 1967.

Miller, Margaret. "The Parasol: An Oriental Status-Symbol in Late Archaic and Classical Athens." *Journal of Hellenic Studies* 112 (1992): 91–105.

Millett, Paul. "Hesiod and His World." *Proceedings of the Cambridge Philological Society* n.s. 30 (1984): 84–115.

Miralles, Carles, and Jaume Pòrtulas. *Archilochus and the Iambic Poetry.* Rome: Ateneo, 1983.

Morgan, Catherine. *Athletes and Oracles.* Cambridge: Cambridge University Press, 1990.

Morgan, Kathryn. "Pindar the Professional and the Rhetoric of the *Komos.*" *Classical Philology* 88 (1993): 1–15.

Morris, Ian. "The Use and Abuse of Homer." *Classical Antiquity* 5 (1986): 81–138.

——. *Burial and Ancient Society: The Rise of the Greek City-State.* Cambridge: Cambridge University Press, 1987.

——. "Tomb Cult and the 'Greek Renaissance': The Past in the Present in the Eighth Century BC" *Antiquity* 62 (1988): 750–61.

——. *Death-Ritual and Social Structure in Classical Antiquity.* Cambridge: Cambridge University Press, 1992.

——. *Darkness and Heroes: Manhood, Equality, and Democracy in Iron Age Greece.* Oxford: Blackwell, 1997.

——. *The Archaeology of Democracy.* In preparation.

Morris, Ian, and Kurt A. Raaflaub, eds. *Democracy 2500: Questions and Challenges.* Archaeological Institute of America Colloquium series, 1998.

Most, Glenn W. *The Measures of Praise.* Hypomnemata 83. Göttingen: Vandenhoeck and Ruprecht, 1985.

Murray, Oswyn. "The Symposion as Social Organisation." In *The Greek Renaissance of the Eighth Century* BC. Robin Hägg, ed. Stockholm: Skrifter Utgivna i Svenska Institutet i Athen, 1983, 195–99.

——. "Sympotic History." In *Sympotica.* Oswyn Murray, ed. Oxford: Clarendon Press, 1990, 3–13.

Muscarella, Oscar. "Greek and Oriental Cauldron Attachments: A Review." In *Greece Between East and West, 10th–8th Centuries* BC. Günter Kopcke and Isabelle Tokumaru, eds. Mainz: Philipp von Zabern, 1992, 16–45.

Nagy, Gregory. *The Best of the Achaeans.* Baltimore: Johns Hopkins University Press, 1979.

——. "Theognis and Megara: A Poet's Vision of His City." In *Theognis of Megara.* Thomas J. Figueira and Gregory Nagy, eds. Baltimore: Johns Hopkins University Press, 1985, 22–81.

——. *Greek Mythology and Poetics.* Ithaca: Cornell University Press, 1990.

——. *Pindar's Homer.* Baltimore: Johns Hopkins University Press, 1990.

——. "Homeric Questions." *Transactions of the American Philological Association* 122 (1992): 15–60.

Negbi, Ora. "Early Phoenician Presence in the Mediterranean Islands." *American Journal of Archaeology* 96 (1992): 599–616.

North, Helen. *Sophrosyne.* Ithaca: Cornell University Press, 1966.

Ober, Josiah. *Mass and Elite in Democratic Athens. Rhetoric, Ideology, and the Power of the People.* Princeton: Princeton University Press, 1989.

——. "The Athenian Revolution of 508/7 BC: Violence, Authority, and the Origins of Democracy." In *The Cultural Politics of Archaic Greece.* Leslie Kurke and Carol Dougherty, eds. Cambridge: Cambridge University Press, 1993, 215–32.

Ostwald, Martin. *Nomos and the Beginnings of the Athenian Democracy.* Oxford: Clarendon Press, 1969.

Page, Denys L. *Sappho and Alcaeus.* Oxford: Clarendon Press, 1955.

——. *Poetae Melici Graeci*. Oxford: Clarendon Press, 1962.

Petropulos, J. C. B. *Heat and Lust: Hesiod's Midsummer Festival Scene Revisited*. Lanham, Md.: Rowman and Littlefield, 1994.

Philipp, Hanna, "Archaische Gräber in Ostionien." *Istanbuler Mitteilungen* 31 (1981): 149–66.

Poliakoff, Michael B. *Combat Sports in the Ancient World*. New Haven, London: Yale University Press, 1987.

Polignac, François de. *La Naissance de la cité grecque*. Paris: La Découverte, 1984.

——. "Influence extérieure ou évolution interne? L'Innovation culturelle en Grèce géométrique et archaïque." In *Greece Between East and West, 10th–8th Centuries* BC Günter Kopcke and Isabelle Tokumaru, eds. Mainz: Philipp von Zabern, 1992, 114–27.

Pritchard, James B. *Ancient Near Eastern Texts Relating to the Old Testament*. 2d ed. Princeton: Princeton University Press, 1955.

Raaflaub, Kurt. *Die Entdeckung der Freiheit. Zur historischen Semantik und Gesellschaftsgeschichte eines politischen Grundbegriffes der Griechen*. Vestigia. Vol. 37. Munich: Beck, 1985.

Rose, Peter W. "Thersites and the Plural Voices of Homer." *Arethusa* 21 (1988): 5–25.

——. *Sons of the Gods, Children of the Earth: Ideology and Literary Form in Ancient Greece*. Ithaca: Cornell University Press, 1992.

Rose, V., ed. *Aristotle, Fragmenta*. Stuttgart: Teubner, 1967.

Rosen, Ralph M. "Hipponax, Boupalos, and the Conventions of the *Psogos*." *Transactions of the American Philological Association* 118 (1988): 29–41.

Rosenmeyer, Patricia. *The Poetics of Imitation: Anacreon and the Anacreontic Tradition*. Cambridge: Cambridge University Press, 1992.

Ruzé, Françoise. "Les Tribus et la décision politique dans les cités grecques archaïques et classiques." *Ktèma* 8 (1983): 299–306.

——. "*Plethos*. Aux origines de la majorité politique." In *Aux origines de l'hellénisme, la Crète et la Grèce. Hommages à Henri van Effenterre*. Paris: Publications de la Sorbonne, 1984, 247–63.

Sahlins, Marshall. *Stone Age Economics*. Chicago: University of Chicago Press, 1972.

Sartori, Franco. "Verfassung und soziale Klassen in den Griechenstädten Unteritaliens seit der Vorherrschaft Krotons bis zur Mitte des 4. Jhs. v. u. Z." In *Hellenische Poleis*. Vol. 2. Elisabeth Welskopf, ed. Berlin: Akademie-Verlag, 1974, 700–773.

Schilardi, Demetrius U. "Anaskaphi stin Paro." *Praktika tis en Athinis Arkhaiologikis Etaireias* (1979): 236–48.

Sealey, Raphael. *The Athenian Republic: Democracy or the Rule of Law?* University Park, Pa., and London: Pennsylvania State University Press, 1987.

Shaw, Joseph W. "Phoenicians in Southern Crete." *American Journal of Archaeology* 93 (1989): 165–83.

Simon, Christopher. "The Archaic Votive Offerings and Cults of Ionia." Unpublished dissertation, University of California-Berkeley, 1986.

Sisti, F. "Le due Palinodie di Stesicoro." *Quaderni Urbinati di Cultura Classica* 39 (1965): 303–13.

Smyth, Herbert Weir. *Aeschylus*. Vol. 2. *Agamemnon, Libation-Bearers, Eumenides, Fragments*. Cambridge, Mass.: Harvard University Press, 1926; revised by Hugh Lloyd-Jones, 1957.

Snell, Bruno, and Herwig Maehler. *Bacchylidis, Carmina cum Fragmentis*. Leipzig: Teubner, 1970.

Snodgrass, A. M. "The Hoplite Reform and History." *Journal of Hellenic Studies* 85 (1965): 110–22.

——. *Archaic Greece: The Age of Experiment*. Berkeley and Los Angeles: University of California, 1980.

——. "The Economics of Dedication at Greek Sanctuaries." *Scienze dell' antichità* 3–4 (1989–90): 287–94.

Spahn, Peter. *Mittelschicht und Polisbildung.* Frankfurt am Main, Bern, and Las Vegas: Peter Lang, 1977.

Stein-Hölkeskamp, Elke. *Adelskultur und Polisgesellschaft.* Stuttgart: Steiner, 1989.

Strøm, Ingrid. "Evidence from the Sanctuaries." In *Greece Between East and West, 10th–8th Centuries* BC. Günter Kopcke and Isabelle Tokumaru, eds. Mainz: Philipp von Zabern, 1992, 46–60.

Svenbro, Jesper. *La Parole et le marbre.* Lund: Lund University Press, 1976.

Szegedy-Maszak, Andrew. "Legends of the Greek Law-Givers." *Greek, Roman and Byzantine Studies* 19 (1978): 199–209.

Thalmann, William G. "Thersites: Comedy, Scapegoats, and Heroic Ideology in the *Iliad.*" *Transactions of the American Philological Association* 118 (1988): 1–28.

Thornton, Agathe. *Homer's "Iliad." Its Composition and the Motif of Supplication. Hypomnemata* 81. Göttingen: Vandenhoeck and Ruprecht, 1984.

Vernant, Jean-Pierre, and Pierre Vidal-Naquet. *Myth and Tragedy in Ancient Greece.* New York: Zone, 1988.

Walcot, Peter. "Hesiod and the Instructions of 'Onchsheshonqy.'" *Journal of Near Eastern Studies* 21 (1962): 215–19.

——. *Hesiod and the Near East.* Cardiff: Cardiff University Press, 1966.

Walsh, George B. *The Varieties of Enchantment.* Chapel Hill: University of North Carolina Press, 1984.

Walzer, Michael. *Spheres of Justice.* New York: Basic Books, 1983.

Wees, Hans van. "The Homeric Way of War: The *Iliad* and the Hoplite Phalanx." *Greece and Rome* 41 (1994): 1–18, 131–55.

West, Martin L. *Hesiod. Theogony.* Oxford: Oxford University Press, 1966.

——. *Studies in Greek Elegy and Iambus.* Berlin: de Gruyter, 1974.

——. *Hesiod. Works and Days.* Oxford: Oxford University Press, 1978.

——. *Greek Metre.* Oxford: Oxford University Press, 1982.

——. *Iambi et Elegi Graeci.* 2d ed. 2 vols. Oxford: Clarendon Press, 1991–1992.

Whitley, James. "Social Diversity in Dark Age Greece." *Annual of the British School at Athens* 86 (1991): 341–65.

——. *Style and Society in Dark Age Greece.* Cambridge: Cambridge University Press, 1991.

Whitman, Walt. *Democratic Vistas.* 1871. Rept. in *The Portable Walt Whitman.* James van Doren, ed. New York: Viking, 1974, 317–82.

Young, David C. *The Olympic Myth of Greek Amateur Athletics.* Chicago: Ares Press, 1984.

Zeitlin, Froma I. "Thebes: Theater of Self and Society." In *Nothing to Do with Dionysos? Athenian Drama in Its Social Context,* J. Winkler and F. Zeitlin, eds. Princeton: Princeton University Press, 1990, 130–67.

Zimmermann, Hans-Dieter. "Frühe Ansätze der Demokratie in den griechischen Poleis." *Klio* 57 (1975): 293–99.

# Further reading

Finley, M. I., *The World of Odysseus,* 2nd edn. (London, 1977). (*A pioneering work, now somewhat dated.*)

Gagarin, Michael and Paul Woodruff (eds.) *Early Greek Political Thought from Homer to the Sophists* (Cambridge, 1995).

Hammer, Dean, *The Iliad as Politics: The Performance of Political Thought* (Norman, 2002).

Hanson, Victor D., *The Other Greeks* (Berkeley, 1999), chapters 2–5.

Morris, Ian and Barry Powell (eds.), *A New Companion to Homer* (Leiden, 1997).

Murray, Oswyn, *Early Greece*, 2nd edn. (Oxford, 1993).

Osborne, Robin, *Greece in the Making 1200–479* (London, 1996).

Raaflaub, Kurt A., "Poets, Lawgivers, and the Beginnings of Political Reflection in Archaic Greece," in *The Cambridge History of Greek and Roman Political Thought*, eds. C. J. Rowe and M. Schofield (Cambridge, 2000), 23–59.

Robinson, Eric W., *The First Democracies: Early Popular Government outside Athens* (Stuttgart, 1997).

Wees, Hans van, *Status Warriors* (Amsterdam, 1992).

# 2

# The Beginnings of the Athenian Democracy: Who Freed Athens?

## Introduction

Though the very earliest democracies likely took shape elsewhere in Greece, Athens embraced it relatively early and would ultimately become the most famous and powerful democracy the ancient world ever knew. Democracy is usually thought to have taken hold among the Athenians with the constitutional reforms of Cleisthenes, ca. 508/7 BC. The tyrant Peisistratus and later his sons had ruled Athens for decades before they were overthrown; Cleisthenes, rallying the people to his cause, made sweeping changes. These included the creation of a representative council (*boule*) chosen from among the citizens, new public organizations that more closely tied citizens throughout Attica to the Athenian state, and the populist ostracism law that enabled citizens to exile dangerous or undesirable politicians by vote. Beginning with these measures, and for the next two centuries or so with only the briefest of interruptions, democracy held sway at Athens.

Such is the most common interpretation. But there is, in fact, much room for disagreement about when and how democracy came to Athens. Ancient authors sometimes refer to Solon, a lawgiver and mediator of the early sixth century, as the founder of the Athenian constitution. It was also a popular belief among the Athenians that two famous "tyrant-slayers," Harmodius and Aristogeiton, inaugurated Athenian freedom by assassinating one of the sons of Peisistratus a few years before Cleisthenes' reforms – though ancient writers take pains to point out that only the military intervention of Sparta truly ended the tyranny. The vague, conflicting, or scanty testimony of the ancients has led modern scholars to clash over the question of exactly when Athens democratized, with some arguing that the most crucial steps took place not under Cleisthenes but decades earlier under Solon, or decades later in the time of the popular politicians Ephialtes or Pericles, or (more rarely) later still in the aftermath of the lost Peloponnesian War at the end of the fifth century.

The following selections begin with an ancient account of Solon's reforms, usually dated to ca. 594 BC, and then provide varying perspectives on the later events which brought down the tyranny of Peisistratus' sons and enabled Cleisthenes to enact his far-reaching reforms (ca. 514–507 BC). Two modern scholars then offer contrasting analyses and conclusions regarding how truly democratic these later events were.

# Aristotle, *Constitution of the Athenians* (5–12)

Aristotle was one of the greatest philosophers of ancient Greece. He lived in the fourth century BC and was not a native of Athens, though he spent much time there. He wrote on a vast array of subjects, from physics to biology to ethics and politics. This treatise (authored either by Aristotle himself or by one of his students) begins with a history of Athens' political development and ends with a detailed analysis of features of the constitution in the fourth century.

The selection below recounts the efforts of Solon to reform the Athenian state in the early sixth century. It is valuable not just for Aristotle's description of events, but for the inclusion of fragments of Solon's own political poetry, which is available to us only in quoted passages such as these. (*Source*: Aristotle, *Ath. Pol.* 5–12, trans. J. M. Moore, from *Aristotle and Xenophon on Democracy and Oligarchy* (Berkeley: University of California Press, 1975), pp. 150–6.)

## Solon

V   In this political situation, when the majority were the slaves of the few, the people opposed the leaders of the state. When the strife was severe, and the opposition of long standing, both sides agreed to give power to Solon as mediator, and entrusted the state to him; at that time he had written the poem which begins:

> Grief lies deep in my heart when I see the oldest of the Ionian states being murdered. . . .

In this poem he champions both sides against the other, and argues their position, and then recommends an end to the prevailing rivalry.

Solon was one of the leading men by birth and reputation, but "middle class" in wealth and position; this is agreed from other evidence, and Solon himself makes it clear in the following poem, where he advises the rich not to be greedy:

> Restrain in your breasts your mighty hearts; you have taken too much of the good things of life;
> satisfy your pride with what is moderate, for we shall not tolerate excess, nor will everything turn out as you wish.

He always attaches the over-all blame for the strife to the rich; this is why he says at the opening of the poem that he is afraid of their "avarice and overbearing pride", since this was the cause of the conflict.

VI   When he had taken power, Solon freed the people both then and for the future by making loans on the security of a person's freedom illegal; he passed laws, and instituted a cancellation of debts both private and public which men call the *seisachtheia*, for they shook off their burdens. Some try to attack him in this context; it happened that when Solon was about to introduce his *seisachtheia* he told some of the leading citizens, and then (according to the democratic version of the story) he was outmanoeuvred by his friends, while those who wish to blacken his reputation say that he was a party to fraud. These men borrowed money and bought large areas of land; shortly afterwards, when debts were cancelled, they were rich. This is alleged to be the origin of those who later appeared to have been wealthy for generations. However, the democratic account is more convincing. It is unlikely that Solon would have been so moderate and public-spirited in other respects, that, when he had it in his power to subject the other group and become tyrant of the city, he chose to incur the hostility of both sides, and preferred what was right and the salvation of the city to his own advantage, but yet would have sullied himself with such a trivial and manifest fraud. That he had power to become tyrant is demonstrated by the perilous state of the city's affairs at the time; he himself mentions it frequently in his poems, and all other sources agree. One must therefore conclude that this charge is false.

VII   Solon established a constitution and enacted other laws; the Athenians ceased to use Draco's code except for his homicide laws. Solon's laws were inscribed on *kurbeis* set up in the portico of the King Archon, and all swore to observe them. The nine Archons used to take their oath on the Stone, and undertook to set up a golden statue if they broke one of the laws; hence the oath which they still take now. Solon made his laws binding for a hundred years and arranged the constitution in the following way. He divided the people into four property classes according to wealth, as had been done before; the four classes were: *pentakosiomedimnoi, hippeis, zeugitai* and *thetes*. He distributed the other magistracies to be held by the *pentakosiomedimnoi, hippeis* and *zeugitai*, allotting the nine Archons, the Treasurers, the *poletai*, the Eleven and the *kolakretai* to various classes in accordance with their property qualification. The *thetes* received only the right to sit in the *ekklesia* and the *dikasteria*. The property qualification for a *pentakosiomedimnos* was a minimum yearly return from his own property of 500 measures, dry or liquid. The *hippeis* had a minimum of 300, and some say that the class was also restricted to those able to maintain a horse; they deduce this from early dedications, for there is a statue of Diphilos on the Acropolis with the following inscription:

> Anthemion, the son of Diphilos, made this dedication to the gods, having risen from the *thetes* to the class of the *hippeis*.

A horse stands by, showing the connection between the *hippeis* and being able to maintain a horse. None the less, it is more plausible that this class should have been defined by measures of produce like the *pentakosiomedimnoi*. The minimum qualification for the *zeugitai* was 200 measures, wet and dry combined, while the remainder of the population formed the *thetes* and were not entitled to hold office. This is why even now, when they are about to cast lots for a magistracy and a man is asked what his class is, nobody would say that he was one of the *thetes*.

VIII   Magistracies were selected by lot from a group previously elected by each tribe. For the nine Archons, each tribe made a preliminary selection of ten men, and they cast lots among them; this is the origin of the practice which survives today by which each tribe picks ten men by lot, and then lots are cast again among them. Evidence that Solon instituted selection by lot in accordance with property classes is the law about the Treasurers which is still in force; this lays down that the Treasurers shall be selected by lot from the *pentakosiomedimnoi*. These were Solon's provisions about the nine Archons. In early times, the Areopagus had summoned the candidates and selected the man it judged suitable for each office itself and installed him for the year. Solon retained the four tribes which already existed and the four tribal Kings; within each tribe there were three *trittues* and twelve *naukrariai*. The officers in charge of the *naukrariai* were called *naukraroi*, and they controlled contributions and expenditure; this is why many of the laws of Solon which are no longer in force contain the phrases "the *naukraroi* shall collect" and "shall be spent from the funds of the *naukrariai*". Solon instituted a *Boule* of 400 members, 100 from each tribe, and he gave the Areopagus the duty of watching over the laws, analogous to its earlier position of guardian of the constitution. It had extensive supervisory powers over the important aspects of political life, and punished wrongdoers with full powers to inflict fines or other penalties; fines were deposited in the treasury, and there was no obligation to state the reason for the fine. The Areopagus tried those who conspired to overthrow the constitution under a law of impeachment which Solon introduced.

Solon realised that the city was often split by factional disputes but some citizens were content because of idleness to accept whatever the outcome might be; he therefore produced a specific law against them, laying down that anyone who did not choose one side or the other in such a dispute should lose his citizen rights.

IX  The magistracies were reformed in this way. The following seem to be the three most [populist] features of Solon's constitution: first and most important, that nobody might borrow money on the security of anyone's freedom; secondly, that anyone might seek redress on behalf of those who were wronged; thirdly, the feature which is said to have contributed most to the strength of the [multitude], the right of appeal to the *dikasterion*, for when the people have the right to vote in the courts they control the constitution. The fact that the laws have not been drafted simply or clearly, but are like the provisions controlling inheritances and heirs, inevitably leads to disputes; hence the courts have to decide everything, public and private. Some think that Solon made his laws obscure deliberately to give the people the power of decision. This is not likely; the obscurity arises rather from the impossibility of including the best solution for every instance in a general provision. It is not right to judge his intentions from what happens now but by analogy with the rest of his provisions.

X  Those were the [populist] aspects of his legislation; before introducing his laws, he carried out the cancellation of debts, and after that the increase of the measures, weights and coinage. For it was under Solon that the measures were made larger than the Pheidonian standard, and the mina, which formerly had a weight of seventy drachmae was increased to the hundred it now contains. The old coin was the two-drachma piece. He established weights for coinage purposes in which the talent was divided into sixty-three minae, and the three added minae were divided proportionately for the stater and the other weights.

XI   After the reform of the constitution which has been described above, Solon was annoyed by people approaching him criticising some parts of his legislation and questioning others. He did not wish to make alterations or to incur unpopularity while in Athens, and so went abroad to Egypt for trading purposes and also to see the country, saying he would not return for ten years; he said it was not right for him to stay to interpret the laws but that everyone should follow them as they were drafted. He had incurred the hostility of many of the leading men because of the cancellation of debts, and both sides had changed their attitude to him because his legislation had been different from what they had expected. The common people had expected him to redivide all property, while the wealthy had expected him to restore them to their traditional position, or at most only to make minor alterations to it. Solon had resisted them both, and, when he could have made himself tyrant by joining which-ever side he chose, had preferred to be hated by both while saving his country and giving it the best constitution possible.

XII   That this was Solon's attitude is agreed by all authorities, and he himself comments on it in his poems in the following terms:

> To the people I gave as much privilege as was sufficient for them, neither reducing nor exceeding what was their due. Those who had power and were enviable for their wealth I took good care not to injure. I stood casting my strong shield around both parties, and allowed neither to triumph unjustly.

In another passage he describes how the ordinary people should be handled:

> The people will follow their leaders best if they are neither too free nor too much restrained, for excess produces insolent behaviour when great wealth falls to men who lack sound judgement.

In another passage he discusses those who wish for a redistribution of land:

> They came to plunder with hopes of riches, and each of them expected to find great wealth; they thought that although I spoke soothingly I would reveal stern determin-ation. Their expectation was vain, and now they are angry and look askance at me like an enemy. This is wrong, for with the gods I carried out what I said, and did nothing else foolishly; it does not please me to act with the violence of a tyrant nor to give equal shares of our rich country to worthless and noble alike.

He discusses the cancellation of debts and those who had previously been enslaved but were freed through the *seisachtheia* in the following passage:

> Which of my aims did I abandon unattained, the aims for which I had assembled the people? My witness to this before the judgement of the future will be the great mother of the Olympian gods, dark Earth; I took up the markers fixed in many places – previously she was enslaved, but now is free. Many I brought back to Athens, their divinely founded city, who had been sold abroad, one unjustly, another justly, and others who had fled under compulsion of debt, men who no longer spoke the Attic tongue, so wide had their wanderings been. Those at home, suffering here the outrages of slavery and trembling at

the whims of their masters, I freed. This I achieved by the might of law, combining force and justice; I carried it out as I promised. I drafted ordinances equally for bad and good, with upright justice for each. Another man holding the spur that I held, a man of evil counsel and greed, would not have restrained the people. Had I been willing to indulge the enemies of the people or do to them what the people wished to do, the city would have lost many men. That is why I set up a strong defence all round, turning like a wolf at bay among the hounds.

Again, of the later attacks of both parties he says reproachfully:

If I must express my reproach of the people in clear terms, they would never otherwise even have dreamed of what they now possess. The greater and more powerful also should praise me and make me their friend,

for, he says, if anyone else had held his position,

he would not have restrained the people nor checked them before they squeezed all the cream from the milk. But I stood, as it were in no man's land, a barrier between them.

# Herodotus, *Histories* (5.62–78)

The reforms of Solon (described above in the Aristotle selection) did not in the end save Athens from civil strife, and after years of disturbances Peisistratus established a tyranny. After his death, his sons Hippias and Hipparchus took up the reins of power. In ca. 514 an assassination attempt (described by other sources below) resulted in the death of Hipparchus. In the following selection, the historian Herodotus chooses this point in time to begin his account of the liberation of Athens, which resulted, he says, in democracy.

Herodotus of Halicarnassus, renowned as the earliest of the Greek historians, lived and traveled in many parts of Greece, including Athens. His *Histories* (produced in the last third of the fifth century) centers on the great struggle between the Greeks and the Persians of the early fifth century, but ranges broadly over many other topics in Greek and non-Greek history and ethnography. (*Source*: Herodotus, *Histories* 5.62–78, trans. G. Rawlinson).

62. Having thus related the dream which Hipparchus saw, and traced the descent of the Gephyræans, the family [to which] his murderers belonged, I must proceed with the matter whereof I was intending before to speak: the way in which the Athenians got quit of their tyrants. Upon the death of Hipparchus, Hippias, who was king, grew harsh towards the Athenians; and the Alemæonidæ, an Athenian family which had been banished by the Pisistratidæ, joined the other exiles, and endeavoured to procure their own return, and to free Athens, by force. They seized and fortified Leipsydrium above Pæonia, and tried to gain their object by arms; but great disasters befell them, and their purpose remained unaccomplished. They therefore resolved to shrink from no contrivance that might bring them success; and accordingly they contracted with the Amphictyons to build the temple which now

stands at Delphi, but which in those days did not exist. Having done this, they proceeded, being men of great wealth, and members of an ancient and distinguished family, to build the temple much more magnificently than the plan obliged them. Besides other improvements, instead of the coarse stone whereof by the contract the temple was to have been constructed, they made the facings of Parian marble.

63.  These same men, if we may believe the Athenians, during their stay at Delphi persuaded the Pythoness [the Priestess] by a bribe to tell the Spartans, whenever any of them came to consult the oracle, either on their own private affairs or on the business of the state, that they must free Athens. So the Lacedæmonians [= the Spartans], when they found no answer ever returned to them but this, sent at last Anchimolius, the son of Aster – a man of note among their citizens – at the head of an army against Athens, with orders to drive out the Pisistratidæ, albeit they were bound to them by the closest ties of friendship. For they esteemed the things of heaven more highly than the things of men. The troops went by sea and were conveyed in transports. Anchimolius brought them to an anchorage at Phalerum; and there the men disembarked. But the Pisistratidæ, who had previous knowledge of their intentions, had sent to Thessaly, between which country and Athens there was an alliance, with a request for aid. The Thessalians, in reply to their entreaties, sent them by a public vote 1000 horsemen, under the command of their king, Cineas, who was a Coniæan. When this help came, the Pisistratidæ, laid their plan accordingly: they cleared the whole plain about Phalerum, so as to make it fit for the movements of cavalry, and then charged the enemy's camp with their horse, which fell with such fury upon the Lacedæmonians as to kill numbers, among the rest Anchimolius, the general, and to drive the remainder to their ships. Such was the fate of the first army sent from Lacedæmon, and the tomb of Anchimolius may be seen to this day in Attica; it is at Alopecæ (Foxtown), near the temple of Hercules in Cynosargos.

64.  Afterwards, the Lacedæmonians despatched a larger force against Athens, which they put under the command of Cleomenes, son of Anaxandridas, one of their kings. These troops were not sent by sea, but marched by the mainland. When they were come into Attica, their first encounter was with the Thessalian horse, which they shortly put to flight, killing above forty men; the remainder made good their escape, and fled straight to Thessaly. Cleomenes proceeded to the city, and, with the aid of such of the Athenians as wished for freedom, besieged the tyrants, who had shut themselves up in the Pelasgic fortress.

65.  And now there had been small chance of the Pisistratidæ falling into the hands of the Spartans, who did not even design to [besiege] the place, which had moreover been well provisioned beforehand with stores both of meat and drink, – nay, it is likely that after a few days' blockade the Lacedæmonians would have quitted Attica altogether, and gone back to Sparta, – had not an event occurred most unlucky for the besieged, and most advantageous for the besiegers. The children of the Pisistratidæ were made prisoners, as they were being removed out of the country. By this calamity all their plans were deranged, and – as the ransom of their children – they consented to the demands of the Athenians, and agreed within five days' time to quit Attica. Accordingly they soon afterwards left the country, and withdrew to Sigeum on the Scamander, after reigning thirty-six years over the Athenians. By descent they were Pylians, of the family of the Neleids, to which Codrus and Melanthus likewise belonged, men who in former times from foreign settlers became kings of Athens.

And hence it was that Hippocrates came to think of calling his son Pisistratus: he named him after the Pisistratus who was a son of Nestor. Such then was the mode in which the Athenians got quit of their tyrants. What they did and suffered worthy of note from the time when they gained their freedom until the revolt of Ionia from King Darius, and the coming of Aristagoras to Athens with a request that the Athenians would lend the Ionians aid, I shall now proceed to relate.

66. The power of Athens had been great before; but, now that the tyrants were gone, it became greater than ever. The chief authority was lodged with two persons, Clisthenes, of the family of the Alcmæonids, who is said to have been the persuader of the Pythoness, and Isagoras, the son of Tisander, who belonged to a noble house, but whose pedigree I am not able to trace further. Howbeit his kinsmen offer sacrifice to the Carian Jupiter. These two men strove together for the mastery; and Clisthenes, finding himself the weaker, called to his aid the common people. Hereupon, instead of the four tribes among which the Athenians had been divided hitherto, Clisthenes made ten tribes, and parcelled out the Athenians among them. He likewise changed the names of the tribes; for whereas they had till now been called after Geleon, Ægicores, Argades, and Hoples, the four sons of Ion, Clisthenes set these names aside, and called his tribes after certain other heroes, all of whom were native, except Ajax. Ajax was associated because, although a foreigner, he was a neighbour and an ally of Athens.

67. My belief is that in acting thus he did but imitate his maternal grandfather, Clisthenes, king of Sicyon. [...]

[68. ...] With respect to the Dorian tribes, not choosing the Sicyonians to have the same tribes as the Argives, he changed all the old names for new ones; and here he took special occasion to mock the Sicyonians, for he drew his new names from the words "pig," and "ass," adding thereto the usual tribe-endings; only in the case of his own tribe he did nothing of the sort, but gave them a name drawn from his own kingly office. For he called his own tribe the Archelaï, or Rulers, while the others he named Hyatæ, or Pig-folk, Oneatæ, or Ass-folk, and Chœreatæ, or Swine-folk. The Sicyonians kept these names, not only during the reign of Clisthenes, but even after his death, by the space of sixty years; then, however, they took counsel together, and changed to the well-known names of Hyllæans, Pamphylians, and Dymanatæ, taking at the same time, as a fourth name, the title of Ægialeans, from Ægialeus, the son of Adrastus.

69. Thus had Clisthenes the Sicyonian done. The Athenian Clisthenes, who was grandson by the mother's side of the other, and had been named after him, resolved, from contempt (as I believe) of the Ionians, that his tribes should not be the same as theirs; and so followed the pattern set him by his namesake of Sicyon. Having brought entirely over to his own side the common people of Athens, whom he had before disdained, he gave all the tribes new names, and made the number greater than formerly; instead of the four phylarchs he established ten; he likewise placed ten demes in each of the tribes; and he was, now that the common people took his part, very much more powerful than his adversaries.

70. Isagoras in his turn lost ground; and therefore, to counterplot his enemy, he called in Cleomenes, the Lacedæmonian, who had already, at the time when he was besieging the Pisistratidæ, made a contract of friendship with him. A charge is even brought against Cleomenes that he was on terms of too great familiarity with

Isagoras's wife. At this time the first thing that he did, was to send a herald and require that Clisthenes, and a large number of Athenians besides, whom he called "The Accursed," should leave Athens. This message he sent at the suggestion of Isagoras: for in the affair referred to, the blood-guiltiness lay on the Alcmæonidæ and their partisans, while he and his friends were quite clear of it.

71. The way in which "The Accursed" at Athens got their name, was the following. There was a certain Athenian, called Cylon, a victor at the Olympic games, who aspired to the sovereignty, and aided by a number of his companions, who were of the same age with himself, made an attempt to seize the citadel. But the attack failed; and Cylon became a suppliant at the image. Hereupon the Heads of the Naucraries, who at that time [held sway] in Athens, induced the fugitives [to leave] by a promise to spare their lives. Nevertheless they were all slain; and the blame was laid on the Alcmæonidæ. All this happened before the time of Pisistratus.

72. When the message of Cleomenes arrived, requiring Clisthenes and "The Accursed" to quit the city, Clisthenes departed of his own accord. Cleomenes, however, notwithstanding his departure, came to Athens, with a small band of followers; and on his arrival sent into banishment seven hundred Athenian families, which were pointed out to him by Isagoras. Succeeding here, he next endeavoured to dissolve the council, and to put the government into the hands of three hundred of the partisans of that leader. But the council resisted, and refused to obey his orders; whereupon Cleomenes, Isagoras, and their followers took possession of the citadel. Here they were attacked by the rest of the Athenians, who took the side of the council, and were besieged for the space of two days; on the third day they accepted terms, being allowed – at least such of them as were Lacedæmonians – to quit the country. And so the word which came to Cleomenes received its fulfilment. For when he first went up into the citadel, meaning to seize it, just as he was entering the sanctuary of the goddess, in order to question her, the priestess arose from her throne, before he had passed the doors, and said – "Stranger from Lacedæmon, depart hence, and presume not to enter the holy place – it is not lawful for a Dorian to set foot there." But he answered, "Oh! woman, I am not a Dorian, but an Achæan." Slighting this warning, Cleomenes made his attempt, and so he was forced to retire, together with his Lacedæmonians. The rest were cast into prison by the Athenians, and condemned to die, – among them Timasitheüs the Delphian, of whose prowess and courage I have great things which I could tell.

73. So these men died in prison. The Athenians directly afterwards recalled Clisthenes, and the seven hundred families which Cleomenes had driven out; and, further, they sent envoys to Sardis, to make an alliance with the Persians, for they knew that war would follow with Cleomenes and the Lacedæmonians. When the ambassadors reached Sardis and delivered their message, Artaphernes, son of Hystaspes, who was at that time governor of the place, inquired of them "who they were, and in what part of the world they dwelt, that they wanted to become allies of the Persians?" The messengers told him; upon which he answered them shortly – that "if the Athenians chose to give earth and water to King Darius, he would conclude an alliance with them; but if not, they might go home again." After consulting together, the envoys, anxious to form the alliance, accepted the terms; but on their return to Athens, they fell into deep disgrace on account of their compliance.

74. Meanwhile Cleomenes, who considered himself to have been insulted by the Athenians both in word and deed, was drawing a force together from all parts of the Peloponnese, without informing any one of his [intent]; which was to revenge himself on the Athenians, and to establish Isagoras, who had escaped with him from the citadel, as despot of Athens. Accordingly, with a large army, he invaded the district of Eleusis, while the Bœotians, who had concerted measures with him, took Œnoë and Hysiæ, two country-towns upon the frontier; and at the same time the Chalcideans, on another side, plundered divers places in Attica. The Athenians, notwithstanding that danger threatened them from every quarter, put off all thought of the Bœotians and Chalcideans till a future time, and marched against the Peloponnesians, who were at Eleusis.

75. As the two hosts were about to engage, first of all the Corinthians, bethinking themselves that they were perpetrating a wrong, changed their minds, and drew off from the main army. Then Demaratus, son of Ariston who was himself king of Sparta and joint-leader of the expedition, and who till now had had no sort of quarrel with Cleomenes, followed their example. On account of this rupture between the kings, a law was passed at Sparta, forbidding both monarchs to go out together with the army, as had been the custom hitherto. The law also provided that, as one of the kings was to be left behind, one of the Tyndaridæ should also remain at home; whereas hitherto both had accompanied the expeditions, as auxiliaries. So when the rest of the allies saw that the Lacedæmonian kings were not of one mind, and that the Corinthian troops had quitted their post, they likewise drew off and departed.

76. This was the fourth time that the Dorians had invaded Attica: twice they came as enemies, and twice they came to do good service to the Athenian people. Their first invasion took place at the period when they founded Megara, and is rightly placed in the reign of Codrus at Athens; the second and third occasions were when they came from Sparta to drive out the Pisistratidæ; the fourth was the present attack, when Cleomenes, at the head of a Peloponnesian army, entered at Eleusis. Thus the Dorians had now four times invaded Attica.

77. So when the Spartan army had broken up from its quarters thus ingloriously, the Athenians, wishing to revenge themselves, marched first against the Chalcideans. The Bœotians, however, advancing to the aid of the latter as far as the Euripus, the Athenians thought it best to attack them first. A battle was fought accordingly; and the Athenians gained a very complete victory, killing a vast number of the enemy, and taking seven hundred of them alive. After this, on the very same day, they crossed into Eubœa, and engaged the Chalcideans with the like success; whereupon they left four thousand settlers upon the lands of the Hippobotæ, – which is the name the Chalcideans give to their rich men. All the Chalcidean prisoners whom they took were put in irons, and kept for a long time in close confinement, as likewise were the Bœotians, until the ransom asked for them was paid; and this the Athenians fixed at two minæ the man. The chains wherewith they were fettered the Athenians suspended in their citadel; where they were still to be seen in my day, hanging against the wall scorched by the Median flames, opposite the chapel which faces the west. The Athenians made an offering of the tenth part of the ransom-money: and expended it on the brazen chariot drawn by four steeds, which stands on the left hand immediately that one enters the gateway of the citadel. The inscription runs as follows: –

> "When Chalcis and Bœotia dared her might,
> Athens subdued their pride in valorous fight;
> Gave bonds for insults; and, the ransom paid,
> From the full tenths these steeds for Pallas made."

78. Thus did the Athenians increase in strength. And it is plain enough, not from this instance only, but from many everywhere, that freedom is an excellent thing; since even the Athenians, who, while they continued under the rule of tyrants, were not [at all] more valiant than any of their neighbours, no sooner shook off the yoke than they became decidedly the first of all. These things show that, while undergoing oppression, they let themselves be beaten, since then they worked for a master; but so soon as they got their freedom, each man was eager to do the best he could for himself. So fared it now with the Athenians.

# Thucydides, *History of the Peloponnesian War* (6.53–59)

An Athenian who fought in the war about which he wrote his brilliant history, Thucydides lived in the mid-to-late fifth century, a later contemporary of Herodotus. In his writing Thucydides demonstrates keen political insight, a great concern for precise reporting of events, and, in contrast to Herodotus, a tight focus on his main subject, which is the Peloponnesian War (431–404 BC) with its causes and conse- quences. Nevertheless, on rare occasion Thucydides will digress, as he does in the selection below. Interrupting his account of the year 415 and Athenian fears of political conspiracies, he goes back a hundred years to recall the Peisistratid tyranny and the would-be tyrant-slayers Harmodius and Aristogeiton. (*Source*: Thucydides, *History of the Peloponnesian War* 6.53–59, trans. R. Crawley.)

[...] The commons had heard how oppressive the tyranny of Pisistratus and his sons had become before it ended, and further that that tyranny had been put down at last, not by themselves and Harmodius, but by the Lacedaemonians, and so were always in fear and took everything suspiciously.

Indeed, the daring action of Aristogiton and Harmodius was undertaken in conse- quence of a love affair, which I shall relate at some length, to show that the Athenians are not more accurate than the rest of the world in their accounts of their own tyrants and of the facts of their own history. Pisistratus dying at an advanced age in possession of the tyranny, was succeeded by his eldest son, Hippias, and not Hipparchus, as is vulgarly believed. Harmodius was then in the flower of youthful beauty, and Aris- togiton, a citizen in the middle rank of life, was his lover and possessed him. Solicited without success by Hipparchus, son of Pisistratus, Harmodius told Aristogiton, and the enraged lover, afraid that the powerful Hipparchus might take Harmodius by force, immediately formed a design, such as his condition in life permitted, for overthrowing the tyranny. In the meantime Hipparchus, after a second solicitation of Harmodius, attended with no better success, unwilling to use violence, arranged to insult him in some covert way. Indeed, generally their government was not grievous to the multitude, or in any way odious in practice; and these tyrants cultivated wisdom and virtue as much as any, and without exacting from the Athenians more than a twentieth of their income, splendidly adorned their city, and carried on their wars, and provided sacrifices for the temples. For the rest, the city was left in full enjoyment of its existing laws, except that care was always taken to have the offices in the hands of some one of the family. Among those of them that held the yearly archonship at Athens was Pisistratus, son of the tyrant Hippias, and named after his grandfather, who dedicated during his term of office the altar to the twelve gods in the market-place, and that of Apollo in the Pythian precinct. The Athenian people afterwards built on to and lengthened the altar in the market-place, and obliterated the inscription; but that in the Pythian precinct can still be seen, though in faded letters, and is to the following effect:

> Pisistratus, the son of Hippias,
> Set up this record of his archonship
> In precinct of Apollo Pythias.

That Hippias was the eldest son and succeeded to the government, is what I positively assert as a fact upon which I have had more exact accounts than others, and may be also ascertained by the following circumstance. He is the only one of the legitimate brothers that appears to have had children; as the altar shows, and the pillar placed in the Athenian Acropolis, commemorating the crime of the tyrants, which mentions no child of Thessalus or of Hipparchus, but five of Hippias, which he had by Myrrhine, daughter of Callias, son of Hyperechides; and naturally the eldest would have married first. Again, his name comes first on the pillar after that of his father; and this too is quite natural, as he was the eldest after him, and the reigning tyrant. Nor can I ever believe that Hippias would have obtained the tyranny so easily, if Hipparchus had been in power when he was killed, and he, Hippias, had had to establish himself upon the same day; but he had no doubt been long accustomed to overawe the citizens, and to be obeyed by his mercenaries, and thus not only conquered, but conquered with ease, without experiencing any of the embarrassment of a younger brother unused to the exercise of authority. It was the sad fate which made Hipparchus famous that got him also the credit with posterity of having been tyrant.

To return to Harmodius; Hipparchus having been repulsed in his solicitations insulted him as he had resolved, by first inviting a sister of his, a young girl, to come and bear a basket in a certain procession, and then rejecting her, on the plea that she had never been invited at all owing to her unworthiness. If Harmodius was indignant at this, Aristogiton for his sake now became more exasperated than ever; and having arranged everything with those who were to join them in the enterprise, they only waited for the great feast of the Panathenaea, the sole day upon which the citizens forming part of the procession could meet together in arms without suspicion. Aristogiton and Harmodius were to begin, but were to be supported immediately by their accomplices against the bodyguard. The conspirators were not many, for better security, besides which they hoped that those not in the plot would be carried away by the example of a few daring spirits, and use the arms in their hands to recover their liberty.

At last the festival arrived; and Hippias with his bodyguard was outside the city in the Ceramicus, arranging how the different parts of the procession were to proceed. Harmodius and Aristogiton had already their daggers and were getting ready to act, when seeing one of their accomplices talking familiarly with Hippias, who was easy of access to every one, they took fright, and concluded that they were discovered and on the point of being taken; and eager if possible to be revenged first upon the man who had wronged them and for whom they had undertaken all this risk, they rushed, as they were, within the gates, and meeting with Hipparchus by the Leocorium recklessly fell upon him at once, infuriated, Aristogiton by love, and Harmodius by insult, and smote him and slew him. Aristogiton escaped the guards at the moment, through the crowd running up, but was afterwards taken and dispatched in no merciful way: Harmodius was killed on the spot.

When the news was brought to Hippias in the Ceramicus, he at once proceeded not to the scene of action, but to the armed men in the procession, before they, being some distance away, knew anything of the matter, and composing his features for the occasion, so as not to betray himself, pointed to a certain spot, and bade them repair thither without their arms. They withdrew accordingly, fancying he had something to say; upon which he told the mercenaries to remove the arms, and there and then picked out the men he thought guilty and all found with daggers, the shield and spear being the usual weapons for a procession.

In this way offended love first led Harmodius and Aristogiton to conspire, and the alarm of the moment to commit the rash action recounted. After this the tyranny pressed harder on the Athenians, and Hippias, now grown more fearful, put to death many of the citizens, and at the same time began to turn his eyes abroad for a refuge in case of revolution. Thus, although an Athenian, he gave his daughter, Archedice, to a Lampsacene, Aeantides, son of the tyrant of Lampsacus, seeing that they had great influence with Darius. And there is her tomb in Lampsacus with this inscription:

> Archedice lies buried in this earth,
> Hippias her sire, and Athens gave her birth;
> Unto her bosom pride was never known,
> Though daughter, wife, and sister to the throne.

Hippias, after reigning three years longer over the Athenians, was deposed in the fourth by the Lacedaemonians and the banished Alcmaeonidae, and went with a safe conduct to Sigeum, and to Aeantides at Lampsacus, and from thence to King Darius; from whose court he set out twenty years after, in his old age, and came with the Medes to Marathon. [ . . . ]

# Aristotle, *Constitution of the Athenians* (18–22)

Aristotle's account here of the fall of the tyranny and Cleisthenes' reforms owes much to Herodotus, but also adds important details not found in the earlier histor-

ian's work. (*Source*: Aristotle, *Ath. Pol.*     (Berkeley: University of California Press,
18–22, trans. J. M. Moore, from *Aristotle*     1975), pp. 161–6.)
*and Xenophon on Democracy and Oligarchy*

XVIII   Their position and age meant that the state was run by Hipparchus and
Hippias; Hippias was the older, a natural politician and a wise man, and he presided
over the government. Hipparchus was fond of amusements, and interested in love
affairs and the arts – he was the man who sent for Anacreon and Simonides and
their associates and the other poets. Thettalos was much younger, and violent and
outrageous in his behaviour, which was the cause of all their troubles. He fell in
love with Harmodius, and when his love was not returned; far from restraining his
anger, he gave vent to it viciously; finally, when Harmodius' sister was to carry a
basket in the procession at the Panathenaia, he stopped her, and insulted Harmodius as effeminate. Hence Harmodius and Aristogeiton were provoked to their plot,
in which many took part. At the time of the Panathenaia, when they were watching
for Hippias on the Acropolis (for it so happened that he was receiving the procession while Hipparchus despatched it), they saw one of the conspirators greet
Hippias in a friendly way. They thought that they were betrayed. Wishing to achieve
something before they were arrested, they went down into the city, and, not
waiting for their fellow conspirators, killed Hipparchus as he was organising the
procession by the Leokoreion; thus they spoiled the whole attempt. Harmodius was
killed immediately by the guards, but Aristogeiton was captured later, and tortured
for a long time. Under torture he accused many nobles who were friends of the
tyrants of complicity. At first enquiries had been unable to find any trace of the
plot, for the story that Hippias had disarmed those in the procession and searched
them for daggers is not true, for they did not carry weapons in the procession at
that time – it was a later innovation of the democracy. The democrats say that
Aristogeiton accused the friends of the tyrants deliberately in order to involve them
in impiety and weaken their faction if they killed their friends who were innocent;
others say that he was not making it up, but did reveal those who were in the
plot. Finally, when, despite all his efforts, death eluded him, he promised that he
would implicate many others; having persuaded Hippias to give him his hand as a
pledge, he reviled him for giving his hand to the murderer of his brother. This
angered Hippias so much that his fury overcame him, and he drew his dagger and
killed him.

XIX   After this the tyranny became much more severe; in avenging his brother,
Hippias had killed or exiled many people, and was distrusted and hated by all.
About three years after the death of Hipparchus, Hippias tried to fortify Munichia
because of his unpopularity in the city of Athens; he intended to move his residence
there, but while this was going on he was expelled by Cleomenes, the Spartan king,
because the Spartans were repeatedly receiving oracles instructing them to end the
tyranny at Athens. The reason was this. The Athenian exiles, who were led by the
Alcmeonids, could not bring about their return unaided; a number of attempts failed.
One of these unsuccessful attempts involved the fortification of Leipsudrion, a point

over Mt. Parnes; there they were joined by some supporters from the city, but the place was besieged and taken by the tyrants. This was the origin of the well-known drinking song about the disaster which ran:

> Alas, Leipsudrion, betrayer of friends, what heroes you destroyed, men brave in battle and of noble blood; then they showed the quality of their families.

Having failed, then, in all other attempts, the Alcmeonids contracted to rebuild the temple at Delphi, and in this way they obtained plenty of money to secure the support of the Spartans. Whenever the Spartans consulted the oracle, the priestess instructed them to free Athens; finally she persuaded them, although they had ties of hospitality with the Peisistratids. The Spartans were swayed no less by the friendship between the Peisistratids and the Argives. First, they sent Anchimolos with an army by sea. He was defeated and killed because Kineas the Thessalian came to the help of the Athenians with a thousand cavalry. The Spartans were angered by this, and sent their king, Cleomenes, with a larger force by land; he defeated an attempt by the Thessalian cavalry to prevent his entry into Attica, shut up Hippias inside the so-called Pelargic wall, and besieged him with Athenian help. While he was conducting the siege, it happened that the sons of the Peisistratids were captured as they attempted to slip out of the city secretly. After their capture, the Peisistratids agreed, in return for the children's safety, to hand over the Acropolis and leave with their own property within a period of five days. This was in the Archonship of Harpaktides when they had held the tyranny for about seventeen years after the death of their father; the whole period including their father's reign had lasted forty-nine years.

## Cleisthenes

xx   After the fall of the tyranny, there was a struggle between Isagoras the son of Teisander, who was a supporter of the tyrants, and Cleisthenes, who was of the family of the Alcmeonids. When Cleisthenes lost power in the political clubs, he won the support of the people by promising them control of the state. The power of Isagoras waned in turn, and he called in Cleomenes again, for he had ties of friendship with him. He persuaded him to "expel the curse", for the Alcmeonids were thought to be amongst those accursed. Cleisthenes retired into exile, and Cleomenes arrived with a few men and expelled seven hundred Athenian families as being under the curse. Having done this, he tried to dissolve the *Boule* [council] and to put Isagoras and three hundred of his friends in control of the city. The *Boule* resisted and the people gathered; the supporters of Cleomenes and Isagoras fled to the Acropolis. The people surrounded them and besieged them for two days; on the third they let Cleomenes and all those with him go under a truce, and recalled Cleisthenes and the other exiles. The people had taken control of affairs, and Cleisthenes was their leader and champion of the people, for the Alcmeonids had been the group probably most responsible for the expulsion of the tyrants and had stirred up trouble for them for much of the time. Even before the Alcmeonids, Kedon had attacked the tyrants, and therefore his name also figures in the drinking songs:

Pour a draught also for Kedon, boy, and do not forget him, if it is right to pour wine for brave men.

XXI   The people trusted Cleisthenes for these reasons. At that time, as their leader, in the fourth year after the overthrow of the tyranny which was the Archonship of Isagoras, he first divided all the citizens into ten tribes instead of the earlier four, with the aim of mixing them together so that more might share control of the state. From this arose the saying "No investigation of tribes" as an answer to those wishing to inquire into ancestry. Then he established a *Boule* of 500 instead of 400, fifty from each tribe; previously there had been 100 from each. His purpose in not splitting the people into twelve tribes was to avoid dividing them according to the *trittues* [thirds] which already existed; there were twelve *trittues* in the four old tribes, and the result would not have been a mixing. He divided Attica into thirty sections, using the demes as the basic unit; ten of the sections were in the city area, ten around the coast and ten inland. He called these sections *trittues*, and placed three into each tribe by lot, one from each geographical area. He made fellow demesmen of those living in each deme so that they would not reveal the new citizens by using a man's father's name, but would use his deme in addressing him. Hence the Athenians use their demes as part of their names. He set up demarchs with the same functions as the previous *naukraroi*, for the demes took the place of the *naukrariai*. Some of the demes he named after their position, others after their founders, for not all were still connected with a particular locality. He left the citizens free to belong to clan groups, and phratries, and hold priesthoods in the traditional way. He gave the tribes ten eponymous heroes selected by the Delphic oracle from a preliminary list of a hundred.

XXII   These changes made the constitution much more democratic than it had been under Solon. A contributory factor was that Solon's laws had fallen into disuse under the tyranny, and Cleisthenes replaced them with others with the aim of winning the people's support; these included the law about ostracism. It was in the fifth year after this constitution was established in the Archonship of Hermokreon, that they formulated the oath which the *Boule* of 500 still take today. At that time they selected the *strategoi* [generals] by tribes, one from each; the Polemarch was the overall commander of the army. Eleven years later, in the Archonship of Phainippos, the Athenians won the battle of Marathon. This made the democracy so confident that after a further two years had passed they first used the law of ostracism; it had been passed from a suspicion of those in power, because Peisistratus had started as leader of the people and *strategos*, and become tyrant. The first to be ostracised was one of his relations, Hipparchus, the son of Charmus, of Kollytos; it was the desire to expel him which was the primary motive of Cleisthenes in proposing the law. With the customary forbearance of the democracy, the people had allowed the friends of the tyrants to continue to live in Athens with the exception of those who had committed crimes in the civil disorders; their leader and champion was Hipparchus. In the year immediately following, the Archonship of Telesinos, they cast lots for the nine Archons by tribes from the five hundred previously elected by the demesmen; this first happened then after the tyranny; all their predecessors were elected. In the same year, Megacles, the son of Hippocrates, from Alopeke was ostracised. For three years they ostracised the friends of the tyrants, the original purpose of ostracism, but in the fourth year they also removed anyone else who seemed to be too powerful. The first man to be ostracised who was not connected with the tyranny was Xanthippus, the son of Ariphron.[...]

# Aristotle, *Politics* (1275b34–39 and 1319b2–27)

The *Politics* is a more abstract work on Greek political theory and practice than the *Constitution of the Athenians*, though it occasionally mentions in passing useful historical detail. The two passages below preserve important information about the expansion and reorganization of the citizen body under Cleisthenes. (*Source*: Aristotle, *Politics* 1275b34–39 and 1319b2–27, trans. B. Jowett.)

## 1275b34–39

[...] There is a greater difficulty in the case of those who have been made citizens after a revolution, as by Cleisthenes at Athens after the expulsion of the tyrants, for he enrolled in tribes many metics [resident aliens], both strangers and slaves. The doubt in these cases is, not who is, but whether he who is ought to be a citizen [...]

## 1319b2–27

The last form of democracy, that in which all share alike, is one which cannot be borne by all states, and will not last long unless well regulated by laws and customs. The more general causes which tend to destroy this or other kinds of government have been pretty fully considered. In order to constitute such a democracy and strengthen the people, the leaders have been in the habit of including as many as they can, and making citizens not only of those who are legitimate, but even of the illegitimate, and of those who have only one parent a citizen, whether father or mother; for nothing of this sort comes amiss to such a democracy. This is the way in which demagogues proceed. Whereas the right thing would be to make no more additions when the number of the commonalty exceeds that of the notables and of the middle class – beyond this not to go. When in excess of this point, the constitution becomes disorderly, and the notables grow excited and impatient of the democracy, as in the insurrection at Cyrene; for no notice is taken of a little evil, but when it increases it strikes the eye. Measures like those which Cleisthenes passed when he wanted to increase the power of the democracy at Athens, or such as were taken by the founders of popular government at Cyrene, are useful in the extreme form of democracy. Fresh tribes and brotherhoods should be established; the private rites of families should be restricted and converted into public ones; in short, every contrivance should be adopted which will mingle the citizens with one another and get rid of old connections. [...]

# The Athenian Archon List

Archons were the highest-ranking officials in Athens; nine men were chosen to serve every year. Texts and documents sometimes provide us with the name of the "eponymous" archon, the archon whose name was used to date the year. One fragment of an inscribed stone block, transliterated below, gives the names of several such archons datable to the years 527/6 to 522/1, years in which the Peisistratid tyrants still controlled Athens. (The Athenian calendar year ran roughly from July to June as we would reckon it, and is thus often represented as a combination of two of our years: 527/6, 526/5, etc.)

Cleisthenes' name is on this list (though a few letters must be restored to read it). This would seem to undermine Herodotus' statements that Cleisthenes' family, the Alcmaeonids, lived in exile throughout the tyranny of the Peisistratids, and raises the possibility that Cleisthenes the reformer had, at least early on, much closer relations to the tyrants than the literary traditions about him suggest. (*Source*: translation by Eric W. Robinson, based on the Greek text of R. Meiggs and D. M. Lewis, *A Selection of Greek Historical Inscriptions* (revised edn, Oxford, 1988), #6.)

**Fragment C**

| | |
|---|---|
| [On]eto[rides] | (527/6) |
| [H]ippia[s] | (526/5) |
| [C]leisthen[es] | (525/4) |
| [M]iltiades | (524/3) |
| [C]alliades | (523/2) |
| [.....]strat[os] | (522/1) |

# Drinking Song Celebrating Harmodius and Aristogeiton

Literary sources from the fifth century and later refer to or quote from a drinking song probably originating in the late sixth century, which celebrated the heroism of the "tyrant slayers", Harmodius and Aristogeiton (on whom see the selections in this chapter above). Such material is especially valuable since it may hint at what everyday, contemporary Athenians (i.e., not later historians or philosophers) thought about the liberation of their homeland in the late sixth century. (*Source*: Athenaeus 15.50, p. 695ab, with scholion to Aristophanes, *Acharnians* 980, trans. C. Fornara, from *Archaic Times to the End of the Peloponnesian War*, 2nd edn (Cambridge: Cambridge University Press, 1983), p. 39.)

## (1) Athenaeus 15.50, p. 695ab

I shall bear my sword in a branch of myrtle/like Harmodios and Aristogeiton/when they killed the tyrant/and made Athens a place of isonomia [equality under law].

Dearest Harmodios, you are surely not dead/but are in the Islands of the Blest, they say,/where fleet-footed Achilleus is/and, they say, good Diomedes the son of Tydeus.

I shall bear my sword in a branch of myrtle/like Harmodios and Aristogeiton/when at the festival of Athena/they killed the tyrant Hipparchos.

Figure   *The Tyrant Slayers. Sources tell us that as early as 510 BC the Athenians erected a statue group commemorating the tyrannicides Harmodius and Aristogeiton. The originals were lost during the Persian invasion of 480–479, though the Roman-era copies portrayed here probably accurately represent replacements made not long afterwards. (From the Archaeological Museum (Museo Archeologico Nazionale), Naples, Italy.)*

Your fame shall be throughout the world forever,/dearest Harmodios and Aristogeiton,/because you killed the tyrant/and made Athens a place of isonomia.

### (2) Scholiast to Aristophanes, *Acharnians* 980 (426/5)

Aristoph. *Acharnians* 980: Nor shall he (War) sing the Harmodios (song) in my
company.

    *Scholion*: In their drinking gatherings (the Athenians) sang a certain song called
that of Harmodios, the beginning of which was "Dearest Harmodios, you are surely
not dead." They sang it for Harmodios and Aristogeiton because they destroyed the
tyranny of the Peisistratidai . . .

# The Athenian Revolution of 508/7 BC: Violence, Authority, and the Origins of Democracy

## *Josiah Ober*

In this influential but controversial article
Ober argues that mass action by the Athenian populace was essential in enabling
Cleisthenes to bring forth a democratic
new order.

The periodization of history is, of course, a product of hindsight, and most historians
realize that any past era can accurately be described as an "age of transition." Fixing
the end of the archaic period and the transition to the classical is thus a historiographic problem, one that reflects contemporary scholarly inclinations more than it
does ancient realities. Nevertheless, since historians cannot work without periodization, and since English-language historiography seems to be entering a post-Annales
phase characterized by a renewed interest in the significance – especially the symbolic
and cultural significance – of events,[1] it may be worthwhile to look at a series of events
that can be taken as the beginning of a new phase of Greek history. The events we
choose to mark the transition will be different for any given region or polis, but for
those interested in Athenian political history, the end of the archaic and the beginning
of something new may reasonably be said to have come about in the period around
510 to 506 B.C., with the revolutionary events that established the form of government that would soon come to be called *dēmokratia*.[2]

    If the "Athenian Revolution" is a historically important event (or series of events),
it is often described in what seem to me to be misleading terms. Historians typically

Josiah Ober, "The Athenian Revolution of 508/7 BC: Violence, Authority, and the Origins of Democracy," in *The Athenian Revolution* (Princeton: Princeton University Press, 1996), 34–52; originally
published in *Cultural Poetics in Archaic Greece*, eds. L. Kurke and C. Dougherty (Cambridge: Cambridge
University Press, 1993), pp. 215–32.

discuss the revolution in the antiseptic terminology of "constitutional development," and their narrative accounts tend to be narrowly centered on the person and intentions of Cleisthenes himself. Putting Cleisthenes at the center of the revolution as a whole entails slighting a significant part of the source tradition. And that tradition, which consists almost entirely of brief discussions in Herodotus (5.66, 69–78) and the *Athēnaiōn Politeia* [Aristotle's *Constitution of the Athenians*] (20–21), is scanty enough as it is. The reconstruction of the events of 508/7 offered here is simultaneously quite conservative in its approach and quite radical in its implications. I hope to show that by sticking very closely to the primary sources, it is possible to derive a plausible and internally coherent narrative that revolves around the Athenian people rather than their leaders. A close reading of the sources shows that the dominant role ascribed to elite leaders in modern accounts of a key point in the revolution is supplementary to the ancient evidence. All historians supplement their narratives with assumptions, models, and theories; supplementation of the source material, in order to fill in apparent gaps and silences, is an inevitable part of the process of even the most self-consciously narrative (rather than analytical) forms of historical writing. But such supplements (especially those that are widely accepted) must be challenged from time to time, lest they become so deeply entrenched as to block the development of alternative readings that may explain the source tradition as well or better.

Both of our two main sources state that during a key period of the revolution, Cleisthenes and his closest supporters were in exile. They imply that the main Athenian players in the revolt were corporate entities: the *boulē* and the demos. The ascription of authoritative leadership in all phases of the revolution to Cleisthenes may, I think, be attributed to the uncritical (and indeed unconscious) acceptance of a view of history that supposes that all advance in human affairs comes through the consciously willed actions of individual members of an elite.[3] In the case of other historical figures, for example Solon, proponents of this elite-centered Great Man approach to history can at least claim support in the primary sources. But although he *is* regarded by the sources as the driving force behind important political reforms, Cleisthenes is not described in our sources as a Solon-style lawgiver (*nomothetēs*). The *Athēnaiōn Politeia* (20.4) calls him *tou dēmou prostatēs* (the leader who stands up before the people) and, though the label is anachronistic for the late sixth century, it seems to me a pretty reasonable description of Cleisthenes' historical role: like later Athenian politicians, Cleisthenes' leadership was not dependent on constitutional authority, but rather upon his ability to persuade the Athenian people to adopt and to act on the proposals he advocated. In sum, I will attempt to show that though Cleisthenes is indeed a very important player in Athens' revolutionary drama, the key role was played by the demos. And thus, *dēmokratia* was not a gift from a benevolent elite to a passive demos, but was the product of collective decision, action, and self-definition on the part of the demos itself.

Having advocated the study of historical events, and having simultaneously rejected the individual intentions of the elite leader as the motor that necessarily drives events, I shall go one step further out on the limb by suggesting that *the* moment of the revolution, the end of the archaic phase of Athenian political history, the point at which Athenian democracy was born, was a violent, leaderless event: a three-day riot in 508/7 that resulted in the removal of King Cleomenes I and his Spartan troops from the soil of Attica.

In order to explain the events of 508/7, we need to review the revolutionary period that began in 510 BC – a fascinating few years characterized by a remarkable series of expulsions from the territory of Attica and returns to it. The series opened with the ouster of Hippias, son of Peisistratos. In 510 the Spartans, urged on by multiple oracles from Delphic Apollo, decided to liberate Athens from the rule of the Peisistratid tyrant. A preliminary seaborne invasion of Attica was repulsed by the tyrant's forces. King Cleomenes I then raised a second army, which he marched across the Isthmus into Athenian territory. This time Hippias' forces failed to stop the invasion. With the Spartans in control of Attica, the tyrant and his family were forced to retreat to their stronghold on the Acropolis. The Acropolis was a formidable obstacle, the defenders were well supplied with food and drink, and the Spartan besiegers were initially stymied. Indeed, it looked as if they might abandon the attempt after a few days (Hdt. 5.64–65). But then Hippias made the mistake of trying to smuggle his sons past the besiegers and out of Athens. They were caught by the Spartans and held hostage. Hippias then surrendered on terms, and was allowed to leave Athens with his family. Thus ended the tyranny.[4]

But the liberation raised more questions than it answered. Who would now rule Athens? One might suppose that the spoils of political authority would end up going to the victors. But as Thucydides (6.53.3; cf. Aristophanes *Lysistrata* 1150–56) pointed out, few Athenians had played much part in the expulsion. The victorious Spartans, for their part, had no interest in progressive political innovation. They surely intended Athens to become a client-state, with a status similar to that of their allies in the Peloponnesian League. This would presumably mean that Athens would be governed by a rather narrow oligarchy, the form of government that (at least in the mid-fifth century: Thuc. 1.19) Sparta mandated as standard for all members of the league.[5] The Spartans did not permanently garrison Athens (this was not their style), but after withdrawing their forces they remained very interested in Athenian politics. In the aftermath of the "liberation," King Cleomenes, the dominant figure in late-sixth-century Sparta, encouraged attempts by Isagoras and other Athenian aristocrats to establish a government that would exclude most Athenians from active political participation.

In the period 510–507 the political battlefield of Athens was disputed not between men who called themselves or thought of themselves as oligarchs and democrats, but rather between rival aristocrats. We cannot say exactly what sort of government Isagoras envisioned, but in light of subsequent developments it seems safe to assume that he intended to place effective control of affairs into the hands of a small, pro-Spartan elite. Isagoras' main opponent was Cleisthenes the Alcmaeonid. Despite the fact that Cleisthenes himself had been willing to accept the high office of archon under the Tyranny, some elements of the Alcmaeonid family had probably been active in resistance to the Tyrants.[6] Cleisthenes, obviously a leading figure among the Alcmaeonids by 508/7, may have felt that his family's antityrannical activity had earned him a prominent position in the political order that would replace the Tyranny. But that position did not come automatically. Indeed, Isagoras, with his Spartan connections, was gaining in influence and was elected archon for 508/7 BC[7] Thus, as Herodotus (5.66.2) tells us, Cleisthenes was getting the worst of it. In response, Cleisthenes did a remarkable thing: *ton dēmon prosetairizetai*. I will leave this phrase untranslated for the time being, for reasons that will become clear later. At.

any rate, because he had in some way allied himself with the demos, Cleisthenes now began to overshadow his opponents in the contest for political influence in Athens (Hdt. 5.69.2).

It is worth pausing at this point in the narrative to ask what the social and institutional context of the struggle between Isagoras and Cleisthenes would have been. Herodotus and the author of the *Athēnaiōn Politeia* employ the political vocabularies of the mid-fifth and late fourth centuries, respectively. But we must not apply the model of politics in Periclean or Demosthenic Athens to the late sixth century. Isagoras and Cleisthenes had recourse to few if any of the weapons familiar to us from the political struggles of those later periods – ideologically motivated *hetaireiai* (aristocratic clubs), ostracism, the *graphē paranomōn* (a legal procedure for use against those proposing illegal decrees) and other public actions in people's courts, finely honed orations by orators trained in the art of rhetoric. What shall we imagine in their place?

Late-archaic Athens was surely more dominated by the great families than was Athens of the fifth and fourth centuries. On the other hand, it would be a serious mistake to suppose that the scion-of-a-great-family/ordinary-citizen relationship can be seen in fully developed patron/client terms – for late-archaic Athens, the model of Roman republican politics is as anachronistic as is that of democratic politics. The reforms of Solon had undercut the traditional authority associated with birth. The policies of the Tyrants themselves had gone a long way in breaking down the traditional ties of dependence and obedience between upper- and lower-class Athenians. Moreover, Solon's creation of the formal status of citizen – a result of prohibiting debt slavery and of legal reforms that made Athenians potentially responsible for one another's welfare – had initiated a process whereby the demos became conscious of itself in forthrightly political terms. The Tyrants had encouraged political self-consciousness on the part of the masses of ordinary citizens by the sponsorship of festivals and building programs. The upshot was that by 510–508 BC the ordinary Athenian male had come a long way from the status of politically passive client of a great house. He saw himself as a citizen rather than as a subject, and at least some part of his loyalty was owed to the abstraction "Athens."[8]

And yet, the political institutions in which an Athenian man could express his developing sense of citizenship were, in early 508, still quite rudimentary and were still dominated by the elite. We may suppose that the traditional "constitution," as revised by Solon, still pertained. Thus there were occasional meetings of a political Assembly that all citizens had the right to attend. But it is unlikely that those outside the elite had the right or power to speak in that Assembly; nor could they hope to serve on the probouleutic council of 400, as a magistrate, or on the Areopagus council.[9] Cleisthenes, as a leading member of a prominent family and as an Areopagite, surely did have both the right and the power to address the Assembly. It seems a reasonable guess that it was in the Assembly (although not necessarily uniquely here) that he allied himself to the demos, by proposing (and perhaps actually passing) constitutional reforms. The masses saw that these reforms would provide them with the institutional means to express more fully their growing sense of themselves as citizens. By these propositions and/or enactments Cleisthenes gained political influence, and so Isagoras began to get the worst of it (Hdt. 5.69.2–70.1).[10]

But if Cleisthenes now had the people on his side, Isagoras was still archon, and moreover he could call in outside forces. No matter what measures Cleisthenes had managed to propose or pass in the Assembly, a new constitutional order could become a practical political reality only if the Assembly's will were allowed to decide the course of events. Isagoras, determined that this would not be allowed, sent word of the unsettling developments to Cleomenes in Sparta. Cleomenes responded by sending a herald to the Athenians, informing them that, ostensibly because of the old Cylonian curse, they were to expel (*exeballe*) Cleisthenes and many others from the city (Hdt. 5.70.2). Cleisthenes himself duly left (*autos upexesche*: Hdt. 5.72.1).

Even after Cleisthenes' departure, Isagoras and/or Cleomenes must still have felt uneasy about the Athenian situation. A smallish (*ou . . . megalēi cheiri*) mixed-nationality military force, featuring a core of Spartans and led by Cleomenes, soon arrived in the city (*parēn es tas Athēnas*: Hdt. 5.72.1). Cleomenes now, on Isagoras' recommendation, ordered further expulsions; Herodotus (5.72.1) claims that a total of 700 families were driven out (*agēlateei*). The archon Isagoras and his Spartan allies were clearly in control of Athens. That could have been the end of what we might call the progressive movement in Athenian politics. Athens might well have become another Argos – an occasionally restive but ultimately impotent client-state of Sparta. After all, the Spartans were the dominant military power in late-sixth-century Greece, whereas Cleisthenes and the other leading Athenians who opposed Isagoras were now powerless exiles.

But, of course, that was not the end of it. What happened next is the moment of revolution I alluded to earlier. According to Herodotus, Isagoras and Cleomenes next (*deutera*)

> attempted to abolish the *boulē* (*tēn boulēn kataluein epeirato*),[11] and to transfer political authority to a body of 300 supporters of Isagoras. But when the *boulē* resisted and refused to obey (*antistatheisēs de tēs boulēs kai ou boulomenēs peithesthai*), Cleomenes, together with Isagoras and his supporters, occupied the Acropolis (*katalambanousi tēn akropolin*). However, the rest of the Athenians (*Athēnaiōn de hoi loipoi*), who were of one mind (*ta auta phronēsantes*) [regarding these affairs], besieged them [on the Acropolis] for two days. But on the third day a truce was struck and the Lacedaemonians among them were allowed to leave the territory [of Attica]. (Hdt. 5.72.1–2)

In the aftermath of the expulsion of the Spartans, at least some of the non-Spartan members of Cleomenes' army (perhaps including Athenian supporters of Isagoras, although not Isagoras himself), who had been detained in Athens, were summarily executed (Hdt. 5.72.4–73.1). After these events (*meta tauta*) the Athenians recalled (*metapempsamenoi*) Cleisthenes and the 700 families (Hdt. 5.73.1). A new constitutional order (presumably resembling the order proposed by Cleisthenes or enacted on his motion before he was expelled) was soon put into place.[12]

Meanwhile, Cleomenes felt that the Athenians had "outraged" him "with both words and deeds" (*periubristhai epesi kai ergoisi*: Hdt. 5.74.1). I would gloss Herodotus' statement as follows: Cleomenes had been outraged by "the words" (of the *bouleutai* when they refused the dissolution order) and "the deeds" (of the demos in its uprising against the Spartans and the Athenian quislings). The Spartan king wanted revenge. He still planned to put Isagoras into power in Athens, but his counterattack of 506 fizzled due to a lack of solidarity in the Peloponnesian ranks on the one side and Athenian unity and military discipline on the other (Hdt. 5.74–77). Within just a few years, Athens had moved from the position of Spartan client-to-be to that of a powerful, independent polis. Athens twice had been occupied by an outside power, and the Athenians had rejected the rule of a narrow elite in favor of a radical program of political reforms, risen up successfully against their occupiers when the reform program was threatened, institutionalized the reforms, defended the new political order against external aggression, and begun on the road that would soon lead to democracy. It is an amazing story, and Herodotus (5.78) points out to his readers just how remarkable was the Athenian achievement. This, then, was the Athenian Revolution.

Herodotus' account is quite closely followed, and perhaps in a few places amplified, by the account of the Aristotelian *Athēnaiōn Politeia*. I will focus on three aspects of the story that seem to me particularly notable. Two are familiar topoi of Cleisthenes scholarship; the third is not.

The first peculiarity is that Cleisthenes, an Areopagite and a leading member of a fine old family, was willing in the first place to turn to the demos – the ordinary people, who, as Herodotus points out, "formerly had been held in contempt" (*proteron apōsmenon*: Hdt. 5.69.2). The second striking thing is that after his recall from exile, Cleisthenes *fulfilled* the promises he had made to the demos (in the form of proposals or enactments of the Assembly). He fully earned the trust they placed in him by establishing a form of government that, at least in the long run, doomed aristocratic political dominance in Athens. Much ink has been spilled over Cleisthenes' apparently peculiar behavior. Since Cleisthenes' actions seem to fly in the face of the aristocratic ethos ("Thou shalt not mix with the lower sort") and to contradict a common assumption about human nature itself ("Thou shalt always act in self-interest"), sophisticated explanations have been devised to explain what he was up to. Among views of Cleisthenes in the scholarly literature, two dominate the field, at least in the English-speaking world. One, well represented by David M. Lewis' influential article in *Historia*, is what we might call the "cynical realist" view, which holds that Cleisthenes was no true friend of the Athenian demos, but instead he benefited (or at least intended to benefit) the Alcmaeonids by extraordinarily clever gerrymandering in his establishment of the demes.[13] Lewis' "realist" view was advanced to counter the other dominant view: the "idealist" view of an altruistic Cleisthenes. This second viewpoint is perhaps best exemplified by the work of Victor Ehrenberg, who saw Cleisthenes as a selfless democratic visionary.[14]

I would not want to deny that Cleisthenes embraced a vision of a new society (see below) or that he hoped for a privileged place for his own family in that society. Yet neither the "realist" view of Cleisthenes the diabolically clever factional politician, nor the "idealist" view of Cleisthenes the self-consciously altruistic Father of Democracy, adequately accounts for the third peculiarity in Herodotus' story – the uprising that doomed Isagoras and his partisans by forcing the surrender and withdrawal from Attica of the Spartans. Although the sparing accounts of Herodotus and the *Athēnaiōn Politeia* do not give us a great deal to work with, it appears that a spontaneous insurrection against Isagoras and the Spartans followed in the wake of Cleomenes' attempt to abolish the *boulē* and his occupation of the Acropolis. Without the uprising, the Cleisthenic reforms would have remained empty words: proposals or enactments voided by the efficient use of force by an outside power.

We will probably never know the details of what actually happened between Cleomenes' attempt to dissolve the *boulē* and his surrender on terms, but we can at least say what did *not* happen, and this may be useful in itself. First, and perhaps foremost, we should not imagine the siege of the Spartans on the Acropolis as an organized military campaign. Whatever may have been the form of the pre-Cleisthenic Athenian military forces, there is no mention in Herodotus or the *Athēnaiōn Politeia* at the siege of military leaders, or of any other sort of formal leadership – no reference to a polemarch or to *stratēgoi*, no *naukraroi* calling in their clients from the fields. Now, the silence of our sources is a notoriously slippery ground for argument, but (as demonstrated by their accounts of, e.g., Cylon and the *naukraroi*, Solon and the Eupatrids, and Peisistratos and the Alcmaeonids) both Herodotus and the author of the *Athēnaiōn Politeia* were very interested in aristocratic leadership – whether it was individual or collective and institutional. I find it hard to believe that the presence of aristocratic leaders at the insurrection could have been forgotten or their identity fully suppressed in the sixty years or so between the revolution and Herodotus' arrival in Athens. Surely this brave resistance to the Spartan occupiers of the Acropolis is just the sort of thing that aristocratic families would remember for several generations. And it was just this sort of family tradition that formed the basis of much of Herodotus' Athenian narrative. One cannot, of course, exclude the possibility that Herodotus intentionally covered up the role played by leaders. But why would he want to do so? To further glorify the Alcmaeonid Cleisthenes? Yet even if Herodotus did favor the Alcmaeonids (which is far from certain), the hypothetical leaders would have been Alcmaeonid allies, since Cleisthenes was immediately recalled and his constitutional reforms enacted.[15] In the end, positing aristocratic leadership for the action that expelled the Spartans is an *ignotus per ignotum* argument, a modern supplement that relies for its credibility entirely on the unprovable (and elitist) assumption that aristocratic leadership in such matters would have been *sine qua non*. It is preferable in this case to trust our only sources and suppose that Herodotus and the *Athēnaiōn Politeia* mention no leaders because Athenian tradition recorded none, and that Athenian tradition recorded none because there were none – or at least none from the ranks of the leading aristocratic families.

Moreover, there is no mention in Herodotus or the *Athēnaiōn Politeia* of Athenian hoplites at the siege of the Acropolis: according to Herodotus, it is *Athēnaiōn hoi loipoi* (the rest of the Athenians) who, united in their view of the situation, do the besieging. *Athēnaiōn Politeia* (20.3) mentions *to plēthos* and *ho dēmos*. This does not, of course, mean that no men wearing hoplite armor took part in the siege – but it is noteworthy that there is no suggestion in either source that anything resembling a "regular" army formation was called up. This might best be explained by the hypothesis that no "national" army existed in the era before the carrying out of Cleisthenes' constitutional reforms. If there was no national army properly speaking, then archaic Athenian military actions were ordinarily carried out by aristocratic leaders (presumably often acting in cooperation with one another): men who were able to muster bodies of armed followers.[16] If this is right, the mass expulsion recommended by Isagoras and carried out by Cleomenes (which no doubt focused on aristocratic houses) would have completely disrupted the traditional means of mustering the Athenian army – and this may well have been among their motives for the expulsion. It is not modern scholars alone who doubt the ability of masses to act without orders from their superiors.

The action that forced the surrender of the Spartans was evidently carried out in the absence of traditional military leaders and without a regular army. How then are we to visualize this action? The Athenian siege of the Acropolis in 508/7 is best understood as a riot – a violent and more or less spontaneous uprising by a large number of Athenian citizens. In order to explain Cleomenes' actions, we must assume that the riot broke out very suddenly and was of relatively great size, intensity, and duration.[17]

After their occupation of the Acropolis, Cleomenes and his warriors were barricaded on a natural fortress, one that had frustrated the regular Spartan army during the siege of Hippias only a couple of years earlier. Yet on the third day of the siege the royal Spartan commander agreed to a humiliating conditional surrender – a surrender that left his erstwhile non-Lacedaemonian comrades to the untender mercies of the rioters. Cleomenes' precipitous agreement to these harsh terms must mean that he regarded the forces arrayed against him as too numerous (throughout the period of the siege) to contemplate a sortie. Why could the Spartans not simply have waited out the siege, as Hippias had been prepared to do? Given the undeveloped state of archaic Greek siegecraft, it is unlikely that the Spartans feared a successful assault on the stronghold. It is much more likely that (unlike Hippias) they had not had time to lay in adequate supplies. This suggests that Cleomenes had occupied the Acropolis very quickly, which in turn probably means that he was caught off guard by the uprising. This inferential sequence supports a presumption that the uprising occurred quite suddenly. What, then, was the precipitating factor?

Herodotus' account, cited above, describes the action in the following stages:

1 Isagoras/Cleomenes attempts to dissolve the *boulē*.
2 The *boulē* resists.
3 Cleomenes and Isagoras occupy the Acropolis.
4 The rest of the Athenians are united in their views.
5 They besiege the Spartan force.
6 Cleomenes surrenders on the third day of the siege.

If we are to follow Herodotus, we must suppose that steps 1, 2, 3, 5, and 6 are chronologically discrete and sequential events. Step 4 cannot, on the other hand, be regarded as a chronological moment; word of events 1–3 would have spread around Athens through the piecemeal word-of-mouth operations typical of an oral society. Presumably those living in the city would have learned what was going on first, and the news would have spread (probably very quickly, but not instantaneously) to the rural citizenry.[18] Herodotus' language (*ta auta phronēsantes* – "all of one mind") supports the idea of a generalized and quite highly developed civic consciousness among the Athenian masses – an ability to form and act on strong and communal views on political affairs.

If we take our lead from Herodotus' account, two precipitating factors can be adduced to explain the crystallization of opinion and the outbreak of violent anti-Spartan action on the part of the Athenian demos. First, the riot may have been sparked by the Spartan attempt to dissolve the *boulē* and the *boulē*'s resistance (thus the demos' action would commence as a consequence of steps 1 and 2, but before step 3). According to this scenario, Cleomenes and Isagoras will have been frightened by the sudden uprising into a precipitous defensive retreat to the nearby stronghold of the Acropolis. Alternatively, the riot might have broken out only after the Spartan occupation of the Acropolis (thus after step 3). On this reading of the evidence, the riot would be precipitated by the Spartan's offensive (in both senses of the term) takeover of the sacred Acropolis. This second hypothesis would certainly fit in with Herodotus' (5.72.3–4, cf. 5.90.2) story of Cleomenes' sacrilegious behavior and disrespect to the priestess of Athena. Yet this scenario is not, to my mind, fully satisfactory. It does not explain why Cleomenes felt it necessary to bring his entire force up to the Acropolis. Why did Isagoras and his partisans (*ho te Kleomenēs kai ho Isagorēs kai hoi stasiōtai autou*: Hdt. 5.72.2) go up to the Acropolis with Cleomenes? And if the occupation of the Acropolis by Spartan forces was a deliberate and unhurried act of aggression, how are we to explain the failure to bring up enough supplies to last even three days?[19]

It is certain that *Athēnaiōn Politeia* (20.3) saw Cleomenes' move to the Acropolis as a defensive response to a riot: when "the *boulē* resisted (*tēs de boulēs antistasēs*) and the mob gathered itself together (*kai sunathroisthentos tou plēthous*), the supporters of Cleomenes and Isagoras fled for refuge (*katephugon*) to the Acropolis."[20] Here the move to the Acropolis is specifically described as a defensive reaction to the council's resistance and the gathering of the people. *Athēnaiōn Politeia*'s statement has independent evidentiary value only if its author had access to evidence (whether in the form of written or oral traditions) other than Herodotus' account – on which he obviously leaned heavily. This issue of Quellenforschung cannot be resolved in any definitive way here, but it is not de facto unlikely that the author of *Athēnaiōn Politeia*, who certainly had independent information on Cleisthenes' actual reforms, could have read or heard that Cleomenes and Isagoras fled to the Acropolis when a mob formed subsequent to the unsuccessful attempt to dissolve the *boulē*. At the very least, we must suppose that *Athēnaiōn Politeia* interpreted Herodotus' account of the move to the Acropolis as describing a flight rather than a planned act of aggression.[21]

Finally, let us consider the only other classical source for these events: Aristophanes' *Lysistrata* (lines 273–82). Here the chorus of Old Athenian Men, girding themselves for an assault on the Acropolis (held by a mixed-nationality force of women), urge each other on "since when Cleomenes seized it previously, he did not get away unpunished, for despite his Laconian spirit he departed giving over to me his arms, wearing only a little cloak, hungry, dirty, hairy-faced...that's how ferociously I besieged that man, keeping constant guard, drawn up seventeen ranks deep at the gates." This is not, of course, history, but a poetic and comic description. Cleomenes' surrender of arms and his hunger are plausible enough, but the overly precise reference to "seventeen ranks" is unlikely to reflect historical reality. Nevertheless, as Rosalind Thomas points out, the Aristophanes passage probably does represent a living popular tradition about the siege.[22] And that tradition evidently focused on the military action of the people rather than on any doings of their leaders.

Although certainty cannot be achieved in the face of our limited sources, I think it is easiest to suppose that a spontaneous riot broke out when the *boulē* resisted. Caught off guard, Cleomenes and Isagoras retreated with their forces to the Acropolis stronghold to regroup. Rapidly spreading news of the occupation of the

Acropolis further inflamed the Athenians, and so the ranks of the rioters were continually augmented as rural residents took up arms and streamed into the city. From Cleomenes' perspective, the bad situation, which had begun with the resistance of the *boulē*, only got worse as time went on. Stranded on the barren hill without adequate food or water, and with the ranks of his opponents increasing hourly, Cleomenes saw that his position was hopeless and negotiated a surrender. This scenario has the virtue of incorporating all major elements of Herodotus' account and the two other classical sources for the events, explaining Cleomenes' behavior in rational terms, and accommodating the means of news transmittal in an oral society.

If, as I have argued above, the Athenian military action that led to the liberation of Athens from Spartan control was a riot, precipitated by the refusal of the *bouleutai* to obey Isagoras' or Cleomenes' direct order that the *boulē* dissolve itself in favor of the 300 Isagoreans, how are we to explain the relationship between the *boulē's* act of defiance and the uprising itself? In the absence of direct textual evidence for either the motives of the *bouleutai* or their relationship to the demos, I offer, for comparative purposes, the example of another famous revolutionary refusal by a political body to dissolve when confronted with authority backed by force. Although such comparisons are supplementary, and not evidentiary in a formal sense, they are useful if they expand common assumptions about the limits of the possible, in this case by showing that an act of disobedience could indeed precipitate a revolution.

On June 17, 1789, the representatives of the Third Estate of the Kingdom of France, a body originally called together by the king, declared themselves to be the National Assembly of France. This act of self-redefinition was not accepted as valid by the existing, and heretofore sovereign, authority of the kingdom. Six days later, on June 23, King Louis XVI surrounded the assembly hall with some 4,000 troops and read a royal proclamation to the self-proclaimed Assemblymen in which he stated that the Third Estate's act in taking the name "The National Assembly" was voided; all enactments of the so-called National Assembly were nullified. Louis concluded his speech with the words, "I order you, gentlemen, to disperse at once." But the National Assembly refused either to disperse or to renounce its act of self-naming.[23]

According to the brilliant interpretation of these events by Sandy Petrey, the Third Estate's renaming of itself, and Louis' declaration that the renaming was void, set up a confrontation between speech acts – both the Third Estate and Louis made statements that were intended to have material effects in the real world of French society; both sides were attempting to *enact* a political reality through the speech act of naming (or, in Louis' case, "unnaming"). In the normal environment of prerevolutionary France, the king's statement would have been (in the terminology of J. L. Austin's speech-act theory, on which Petrey's interpretation is based) "felicitous" or efficacious – the Assembly would *be* dissolved because a sovereign authority had stated that it was dissolved. Yet, as Petrey points out, in a revolutionary situation, speech acts are not, at the moment of their enunciation, either felicitous or infelicitous *ipso facto*. Rather, their felicity or efficacy is demonstrated only in retrospect. In this case, the National Assembly did not dissolve when so ordered. By refusing to acknowledge the power of the king's speech to create real effects in the world, the Assembly contested the legitimacy of the king's authority.[24]

The confrontation of speech acts was not the end of the story. Louis subsequently attempted to enforce his will through the deployment of military force. This attempt was frustrated by the outbreak of riots in the streets of Paris. In the words of W. Doyle, in the weeks after the confrontation of June 23, "nobody doubted that the King was still prepared to use force to bring the Revolution to an end. The only thing that could prevent him was counterforce, and as yet the Assembly had none at its disposal. It was saved only by the people of Paris."[25] And thus the French Revolution was launched. Because the revolution succeeded, it turned out that the Third Estate's act of renaming had been felicitous and Louis' proclamation of nullification infelicitous; if the proof of the pudding is in the eating, the proof of the revolutionary speech act is in the rebellion.

Although the efficacy of its speech acts were as yet undemonstrated, the self-redefinition of the Third Estate as the National Assembly on June 17 and the refusal of the Assemblymen of France to acknowledge the force of the king's proclamation of dissolution on June 23 helped to precipitate a revolution because they contested the "inevitability" or "naturalness" of the power of the king's speech to create political realities. Once the king's official proclamations were no longer regarded as expressions of sovereign authority, political discourse ceased to be a realm of orderly enactment and became a realm of contested interpretations. The success of any given interpretation was no longer based on its grounding in eternal and universally accepted truths about power and legitimacy; rather, success in interpretation was now contingent upon the subsequent actions of the French people acting en masse – in this case, by rioting and besieging the Bastille.

The parallels between the early stages of the French and the Athenian revolutions are certainly not exact, but both similarities and differences may be instructive. First, it is much less clear in the Athenian case where, at any point in the story, sovereign authority lay – or indeed, if we should be talking about sovereignty at all. Isagoras was archon in 508/7, and so the dissolution order issued to the *boulē* could be seen as carrying the weight of legitimately sanctioned authority. But the archon of Athens did not (I suppose) command the absolute sovereignty claimed by Louis XVI, and the perceived legitimacy of Isagoras' authority was probably not enhanced by his employment of foreign military support. What of the comparison of the Athenian *boulē* to the National Assembly? This will depend on what body Herodotus meant by the word *boulē*. There are three choices (and all have had supporters among modern scholars) – the Areopagus Council, the Solonian Council of 400, or a newly established Council of 500. The parallel to the National Assembly is closest if we follow the hypothesis, recently revived by Mortimer Chambers, that the *boulē* in question was (perhaps a pro tem version of) the Council of 500, set up according to Cleisthenes' proposals and the Assembly's enactment before the arrival of the Spartans. This hypothesis would go far in explaining both Cleomenes' interest in eliminating the council and the brave determination of the councilmen to resist. But Chambers' argument, based in part on his rejection of the existence of a Solonian Council of 400, must remain for the time being an attractive speculation.[26] In any event, we cannot be sure exactly what powers the *boulē* claimed or its constitutional relationship to the archon.

Yet despite these caveats and uncertainties, several relevant factors in the French and Athenian cases seem quite similar. Herodotus' revealing comment that a king was "outraged by both words and deeds" (5.74.1) fits the French Revolution as well as the Athenian. In both cases, because of a verbal act of defiance by a political body, "official" political discourse – previously regarded by all concerned as authoritative and stable, as productive of acts of establishment, as a *thesmos* – became a battle-ground contested by two mutually exclusive interpretations regarding the source of legitimate public authority. Isagoras (or Cleomenes) said the *boulē* was dissolved. The *bouleutai* denied, by their resistance, the validity of this statement. As in the case of the French Revolution, it would be the actions of the ordinary people in the streets that would determine which of the opposed interpretations was felicitous and effica-cious – rapidly evolving realities would decide whether the statement of Isagoras or of the *bouleutai* conformed to reality. In both revolutions, the official authority's recourse to military force was stymied by superior unofficial force in the form of mass riots. Both revolutions featured short but decisive sieges (the Acropolis and the Bastille) by leaderless crowds of citizens; both sieges ended in a negotiated surrender by the besieged leaders of organized military forces.[27] Furthermore, both uprisings featured summary (and, I would add, morally reprehensible) killings of individuals identified as enemies of the revolution. The Athenian Revolution, no less than the French, was baptized in the blood of "counter-revolutionaries."[28] Yet the difference between Athens and France in this regard is also salient: the decade after 507 saw no equivalent to either Jacobinite Terror or Thermidorian reaction.

In terms of assigning credit (or blame) for the uprising and its aftermath, it is important to note that though the brave action of the bourgeois gentlemen of the Third Estate in naming themselves the National Assembly helped to foment the French Revolution, those gentlemen did not take the lead in storming the Bastille,[29] and they were not able subsequently to control the direction of the revolution. Nor were the *bouleutai* in control of the Athenian Revolution. Neither Herodotus nor *Athēnaiōn Politeia* assigns the *boulē* a leadership role in the insurrection after its refusal to disperse: according to Herodotus, after the *boulē* refused to obey the dissolution order, Cleomenes and Isagoras occupied the Acropolis, and *ta auta phronēsantes, Athēnaiōn hoi loipoi* besieged the Acropolis – taken literally, this com-ment would seem to exclude the *bouleutai* from any role at all. For *Athēnaiōn Politeia* (20.3), it was when "the *boulē* resisted and the mob gathered itself together" that "the supporters of Cleomenes and Isagoras fled to the Acropolis," and subsequently it was *ho dēmos* that besieged them. Both authors seem to agree on the importance of the *boulē*'s act of defiance, but both also agree in seeing the key event as the uprising of the Athenian masses.[30]

Finally, how are we to interpret the political implications of this riotous uprising and its relationship to the subsequent Athenian political order – to the "constitution of Cleisthenes"? Once again, a comparative approach may offer some clues. The highly influential work of E. P. Thompson on food riots in eighteenth-century England, and that of Natalie Z. Davis on religious riots in sixteenth-century France, has led to the development of a useful approach to the historical assessment of rioting. This model is discussed in some detail in a recent article by Suzanne Desan, who points out that, according to Thompson and Davis, violent collective actions in early-modern England and France were not merely random outbreaks indicative of generalized popular dissatisfaction. Rather, these riots are best read as acts of collective self-definition, or redefinition. The English peasants were, for example, rioting in support of the reenactment of what Thompson described as a "moral economy" – a view of the world that was actually quite conservative in that it assumed the legitimacy of paternalistic (or at least clientistic) relations between peasantry and local aristocracy.[31]

The riot of 508/7 can thus be read as a collective act of political self-definition in which the demos rejected the archon Isagoras as the legitimate public authority. As Herodotus' account suggests, the riot was the physical, active manifestation of the Athenians having come to be "of one mind" about civic affairs. This reading clarifies the general role of Cleisthenes in the Athenian Revolution and the scope of his accomplishments. More specifically, it helps to explain the relationship between Cleisthenes and the demos in the months before and after the definitive moment of the riot.

Let us return to the problems of the context and meaning of Herodotus' famous and problematic comment (5.66.2) that *Kleisthenēs ton dēmon prosetairizetai*. This phrase is often taken to be a description of a straightforward event with a straightforward subject and object. A. de Sélincourt's Penguin translation is typical: "Cleisthenes...took the people into his party." But we need not give the middle form *prosetairizetai* quite such a clearly active force, nor need we imagine it as describing an event that occured in a single moment. I would suggest as an alternate (if inelegant) translation: "Cleisthenes embarked on the process of becoming the demos' trusted comrade."[32] Herodotus' account certainly implies that Cleisthenes had developed a special relationship with the demos *before* his expulsion from Athens. That relationship, which I have suggested above was characterized by proposals or enactments in the Assembly, was evidently the proximate cause of Isagoras' calling in of Cleomenes. But there is no reason to suppose that the process referred to by the verb *prosetairizetai* was completed before Cleisthenes was expelled. In short, I would suggest that Cleisthenes did not so much absorb the demos into his *hetaireia*, as he *himself* was absorbed into an evolving, and no doubt somewhat inchoate, demotic vision of a new society, a society in which distinctions between social statuses would remain but in which there would be no narrow clique of rulers.

The sea change in Athenian political practice implied by Cleisthenes' new relationship with the demos was not signaled by an act of noblesse oblige – opening the doors of the exclusive, aristocratic *hetaireia* to the masses. Rather, it was a revolution in the demos' perception of itself and in an aristocrat's perceptions regarding his own relationship, and that of all men of his class, to the demos. Cleisthenes acknowledged the citizens of Athens as equal sharers in regard to the *nomoi* (laws), and under the banner of *isonomia* the men of the demos became, in effect if not in contemporary nomenclature, Cleisthenes' *hetairoi*.[33] We must remember that Herodotus' terminology is that of the mid-fifth rather than the late sixth century. But in the fifth century, when Herodotus was writing his *Histories*, Athenian *hetairoi* were expected to help one another, and to seek to harm their common enemies. The demos looked out for Cleisthenes' interests by attacking the Spartans and by recalling him immediately upon their departure. Political friendship is a two-way street, and Cleisthenes had no real option other than to look after the interests of the demos by devising and working to implement (through enactments of the Assembly) an institutional framework that would consolidate and stabilize the new demotic vision of politics. That vision had grown up among the Athenian citizen masses in the course of the sixth century and had found an active, physical manifestation in the riot that occurred during Cleisthenes' enforced absence from the scene. The "constitution of Cleisthenes" channeled the energy of the demos' self-defining riot into a stable and workable form of government.

In sum, Cleisthenes was not so much the authoritative leader of the revolution as he was a highly skilled interpreter of statements made in a revolutionary context and of revolutionary action itself. This is not to deny any of his brilliance, or even his genius. But it is to see his genius *not* in an ability to formulate a prescient vision of a future democratic utopia, *nor* in an ability to hide a selfish dynastic scheme behind a constitutional façade, but rather in his ability to "read" – in a sensitive and perceptive way – the text of Athenian discourse in a revolutionary age, and to recognize that Athenian mass action had created new political facts. Cleisthenes saw that the revolutionary action of the Athenian demos had permanently changed the environment of politics and political discourse. After the revolution there could be no secure recourse to extra-demotic authority. If Athens were to survive as a polis, there would have to be a new basis for politically authoritative speech, but that basis must find its ground in the will of the demos itself. Having read and understood his complex text, Cleisthenes knew that there could be no turning back to rule by aristocratic faction – or at least he saw that any attempt to turn back the clock would bring on a bloodbath and make effective resistance to Sparta impossible. And so, acting as a good *hetairos*, well deserving of the *pistis* (good faith) placed in him (*Athēnaiōn Politeia* 21.1) by his mass *hetaireia*, Cleisthenes came up with a constitutional order that both framed and built upon the revolution that had started without him.

# NOTES

1  See the introduction to Hunt 1989.
2  This is a traditional breaking point: Burn (1960, 324), for example, ends his narrative of archaic Athenian history with the expulsion of Hippias. Hansen (1986) argues that *dēmokratia* was the name Cleisthenes used from the beginning. The relevant ancient sources are conveniently collected, translated, and annotated in Stanton 1990, 130–67.
3  For representative statements of the centrality of Cleisthenes' role, see Zimmern 1961, 143–44: "Cleisthenes the Alcmaeonid, the leader of the popular party,... made a bid for power. [After the Spartan intervention and the occupation of the Acropolis,] *Cleisthenes and the councillors* [my emphasis] called the people to arms and blockaded the rock ... [upon the surrender of the Spartans] Cleisthenes was now master of the situation." Murray 1980, 254: "Kleisthenes 'took the people into his party'... proposed major reforms, *expelled Isagoras* [my emphasis], and in the next few years held off the attempts of the Spartans and their allies to intervene." Forrest 1966, 194: "Finally, with the *demos*' firm support, *he was able to rout Isagoras* [my emphasis] together with a Spartan force." Other textbooks do point out that Cleisthenes was in exile, e.g., Sealey 1976, 147; Bury and Meiggs 1975, 36; and especially M. Ostwald in *The Cambridge Ancient History*, 2d ed. (1988), 4:305–7. The modern account of the revolution closest in spirit to the one I offer here is perhaps Meier 1990, 64–66.
4  For the tyranny and its end, see D. M. Lewis in *The Cambridge Ancient History*, 2d ed. (1988), 4:287–302, with sources cited.
5  The government would not have been called an oligarchy because the word had not yet been invented; for the history of the term, see Raaflaub 1983.

6   Accommodation and resistance of Alcmaeonids to the tyranny: Lewis in *The Cambridge Ancient History*, 2d ed. (1988), 4:288, 299–301. But cf. the skepticism of Thomas (1989, 263–64), who argues that the Alcmaeonids may have made up the tradition of their antityrannical activity and the story of their exile under the Peisistratids from whole cloth.

7   Isagoras as archon: *Ath. Pol.* 21.1. The attempt by McCargar (1974) to separate Isagoras, opponent-of-Cleisthenes, from the archon of 508/7 on the grounds that *some* archons in this period were evidently relatively young (perhaps not much over thirty) and Isagoras *may* have been relatively mature seems to me chimerical, especially in light of the extreme rarity of the name. *Ath. Pol.* 22.5 claims that after the institution of the tyranny, and until 487/6, all archons were elected (*hairetoi*). The Tyrants had manipulated the elections to ensure that their own supporters were in office (see Rhodes 1981, 272–73); exactly how the elections would have been carried out in 509/8 (and thus what Isagoras' support consisted of) is unclear. We need not, anyway, suppose that Isagoras' election was indicative of a broad base of popular support; more likely his support was centered in the (non-Alcmaeonid) nobility. On the power of the archaic archon, see *Ath. Pol.* 3.3, 13.2 with the comments of Rhodes 1981, ad locc.

8   See Ober 1989, 60–68; Manville 1990, 124–209; Meier 1990, 53–81. On the lack of formal patronage structures in classical Athens, see Millett 1989.

9   Solonian constitution: Ober 1989, 60–65, with references cited. For the Areopagus from the time of Solon to Cleisthenes, see Wallace 1989, 48–76.

10  Cleisthenes' connection with the demos is underlined by Hdt. 5.69.2 and by *Ath. Pol.* 20.1. Since Wade-Gery's seminal article (1933, 19–25), it has been widely accepted that the Assembly was the arena in which Cleisthenes won the favor of the people; cf. discussion by Ostwald 1969, 149–60.

11  The implied subject of the verb *epeirato* is either Cleomenes or Isagoras. The grammar seems to point to Cleomenes, although presumably it was Isagoras (as archon) who gave the official order to the *boulē*. The point is in any case merely procedural: Herodotus' narrative demonstrates that Cleomenes and Isagoras were working hand in glove throughout.

12  Herodotus (5.66.2) implies that at least some of the reforms were put into place before Cleomenes' arrival; *Ath. Pol.* (20–21) discusses the reforms after giving the history of the revolution proper. I think it is most likely that some reforms were proposed and perhaps actually enacted by the Assembly before Cleomenes' arrival, but presumably there would not have been time for all the details of the new constitution to have been put into place. See below for the question of when the Council of 500 was established. For a review of the chronological issue, see Hignett 1952, 331–36; Rhodes 1981, 244–45, 249; Chambers 1990, 221–22.

13  Lewis 1963.

14  Ehrenberg 1973, 89–103: In 510 Cleisthenes was "a man of new and radical ideas" (89); in 508 he gained support "by revealing plans of a new democratic order" (90); "his reforms were... the first examples of democratic methods" (91). Cleisthenes was not primarily interested in personal power, rather "power was to him a means of creating the constitutional framework for a society on the verge of becoming democratic" (91). For Ehrenberg, then, Cleisthenes is both selfless and a strong leader whose place is "at the helm" (102). Cf. Ehrenberg 1950.

15  For a detailed discussion of the role of oral traditions (of family and polis) in Herodotus' construction of his account of the revolution, and a vigorous attack on the hypothesis that Herodotus was an Alcmaeonid apologist, see Thomas 1989, 144–54, 238–82.

16  Frost 1984.

17  I am assuming throughout that Cleomenes was an experienced and sane military commander, and that his decisions were made accordingly. On the dubious tradition of the

madness of Cleomenes, see Griffiths 1989. It is interesting to note how the demos' action simply disappears in some respectable scholarly accounts, e.g., Ehrenberg 1973, 90: "Cleomenes and Isagoras met, however, with the resistance of the council...which they had tried to disband and which was most likely the Areopagus....The Spartans withdrew, Isagoras was powerless, and many of his followers were executed."

18   On how information was disseminated in Athens, see Hunter 1990.

19   Herodotus' statement that Cleomenes seized the Acropolis and was subsequently thrown out along with the Lacedaemonians (ἐπεχείρησέ τε καὶ τότε πάλιν ἐξέπιπ τε μετὰ τῶν Λακεδαιμονίων: 5.72.4) makes it appear likely that the whole force had gone up to the Acropolis together, had been besieged together, and had surrendered together. It is unlikely that a significant part of Cleomenes' forces joined him on the hill after the commencement of the siege, and Herodotus says nothing about any of his men being captured in the lower city before the surrender. It is worth noting that Cylon (Hdt. 5.71; Thuc. 1.126.5–11) and Peisistratos (twice: Hdt. 1.59.6, 60.5) had earlier seized the Acropolis, each time as the first stage in an attempt to establish a tyranny. Cleomenes' case is different in that his move came *after* he had established control of the city.

20   Stanton (1990, 142, 144 n. 6) translates *sunathroisthentos tou plēthous* as "the common people had been assembled," on the grounds that "the verb 'had been assembled' is definitely passive." But I take the (morphologically) passive participle *sunathroisthentos* as having a reflexive rather than a passive meaning; on the distinction, see Rijksbaron 1984, 126–48. For a reflexive meaning for the passive participle of *sunathroizō*: Xen. *Anabasis* 6.5.30; of *athroizō*: Thuc. 1.50.4, 6.70.4; and especially Aristotle *Pol.* 1304b33.

21   For a discussion of the relationship between Herodotus' narrative and *Ath. Pol.* 20–21, see Wade-Gery 1933, 17–19; and Rhodes (1981, 240–41, 244), who argues that Herodotus was *Ath Pol.*'s sole authority for 20.1–3. For general discussions of *Ath. Pol.*'s use of sources, see Chambers 1990, 84–91.

22   Thomas 1989, 245–47.

23   "Je vous ordonne, Messieurs, de vous séparer toute de suite." For the resolution of the Abbé de Sieyès renaming the Assembly, and the response of Louis at the "Royal Session" of June 23, see Wickham Legg 1905, 18–20, 22–33. For a narrative account of this stage of the revolution, see Doyle 1980, 172–77.

24   Petrey 1988, esp. 17–51. Petrey's work is based on the ground-breaking linguistic theory of Austin 1975.

25   Doyle 1980, 177.

26   Chambers 1990, 222–23.

27   For the siege of the Bastille, see Godechot 1970, 218–46. The Bastille was a formidable, if dilapidated, fortress, guarded by a small force of eighty-four pensioners and thirty-two Swiss mercenaries. For the week before the assault of July 14, its commander, Governor de Launey, had refurbished the defenses to withstand an assault. Yet "he had only one day's supply of meat and two days' supply of bread, and moreover there was no drinking water inside the fortress...de Launey may...have thought that if he were attacked by an unarmed or ill-armed crowd the assault would not last longer than one day and that at nightfall the rioters would disperse" (219). It is tempting to suppose that Cleomenes thought along similar lines.

28   On the killing of Governor de Launey and seven other defenders of the Bastille on July 14, and of other agents of the Old Regime in the days thereafter, see Godechot 1970, 243–46. The Athenian killings have been questioned on the grounds of the wording of *Ath. Pol.* 20.3 (Κλεομένην μὲν καὶ τοὺς μετ᾽ αὐτοῦ πάντας ἀφεῖσαν ὑποσπόνδους), but

as Ostwald (1969, 144 with n. 6) points out, this need only refer to the Lacedaemonian troops; cf. Rhodes 1981, 246–47.

29  For the composition of the crowd (mostly artisans from Paris) that stormed the Bastille, and the absence of Assemblymen or any other formal leaders, see Godechot 1970, 211, 221–26, 230, 237–39.

30  Cf., for example, Hammond 1959, 185–86: "The Council resisted. It raised the people against Cleomenes and Isagoras, who seized the Acropolis and found themselves besieged"; Ostwald 1969, 144: "The Council refused to be intimidated and, with the support of the common people, besieged the acropolis"; Stanton 1990, 144 n. 6: the council in question must have been the Areopagus, since unlike the councils of 400 or 500, it "would have been sufficiently permanent and would have contained a sufficient accumulation of politically experienced men to organize resistance to a military force. A major thrust was the assembling of the common people . . . and this could have been achieved by the influence which ex-arkhon clan leaders in the Areopagos held over their retainers." The Areopagus leadership theory would need to explain how Cleomenes' force could be strong and decisive enough to "drive out" 700 families dispersed through Attica (cf. Stanton [1990, 141 n. 14], who questions the number 700), but too weak to stop at most 100–200 men (numbers of Areopagites: Wallace 1989, 97 with n. 23; Hansen 1990 – from which we must deduct those expelled with the 700), who were presumably gathered in one place to hear the dissolution order, from organizing a resistance.

31  Desan 1989.

32  It is important to keep in mind that the terminology is in any event Herodotus', not Cleisthenes'. It was probably not in use in Cleisthenes' day, and reflects rather the political vocabulary of the mid-fifth century: Chambers 1990, 221.

33  On *isonomia* and its meaning, see Ober 1989, 74–75, with literature cited.

# REFERENCES

Austin, J. L. 1975. *How to Do Things with Words.* Ed. J. O. Urmson and Marina Sbisà. 2d ed. Cambridge, Mass.: Harvard University Press.

Burn, A. R. 1960. *The Lyric Age of Greece.* London: Edward Arnold.

Bury, J. B., and R. Meiggs. 1975. *History of Greece to the Death of Alexander the Great.* 4th ed. London and New York: Macmillan.

Chambers, Mortimer, ed. and comm. 1990. *Aristoteles, Staat der Athener.* Aristotles Werke in deutscher Übersetzung, vol. 10.1. Berlin: Akademie-Verlag.

Desan, Suzanne. 1989. "Crowds, Community, and Ritual in the Work of E. P. Thompson and Natalie Davis." In Hunt 1989, 47–71.

Doyle, William. 1980. *Origins of the French Revolution.* New York: Oxford University Press.

Ehrenberg, Victor. 1950. "Origins of Democracy." *Historia* 1:515–48.

——. 1973. *From Solon to Socrates.* 2d ed. London: Methuen.

Forrest, W. G. 1966. *The Emergence of Greek Democracy: The Character of Greek Politics, 800–400 B.C.* London: Weidenfeld and Nicolson.

Frost, F. J. 1984. "The Athenian Military Before Cleisthenes." *Historia* 33:283–94.

Godechot, J. 1970. *The Taking of the Bastille, July 14, 1789.* Trans. J. Stewart. London: Faber and Faber.

Griffiths, Alan. 1989. "Was Kleomenes Mad?" In *Classical Sparta: Techniques Behind Her Success,* ed. A. Powell, 51–78. London: Routledge.

Hammond, N. G. L. 1959. *A History of Greece to 322 B.C.* Oxford: Clarendon.

Hansen, M. H. 1986. "The Origin of the Term *demokratia.*" *Liverpool Classical Monthly* 11 (March): 35–36.

———. 1990. "The Size of the Council of the Areopagos and Its Social Composition in the Fourth Century B.C." *Classica et Mediaevalia* 41:55–61.

Hignett, C. 1952. *A History of the Athenian Constitution to the End of the Fifth Century B.C.* Oxford: Clarendon.

Hunt, Lynn, ed. 1989. *The New Cultural History.* Berkeley and Los Angeles: University of California Press.

Hunter, Virginia. 1990. "Gossip and the Politics of Reputation in Classical Athens." *Phoenix* 44:299–325.

Lewis, D. M. 1963. "Cleisthenes and Attica." *Historia* 12:22–40.

McCargar, David J. 1974. "Isagoras, Son of Teisandros, and Isagoras, Eponymous Archon of 508/7: A Case of Mistaken Identity." *Phoenix* 28:275–81.

Manville, P. B. 1990. *The Origins of Citizenship in Ancient Athens.* Princeton: Princeton University Press.

Meier, C. 1990. *The Greek Discovery of Politics.* Trans. David McLintock. Cambridge, Mass.: Harvard University Press.

Millett, Paul. 1989. "Patronage and Its Avoidance in Classical Athens." In Wallace-Hadrill 1989, 15–47.

Murray, Oswyn, 1980. *Early Greece.* London: Fontana.

Ober, Josiah. 1989. *Mass and Elite in Democratic Athens: Rhetoric, Ideology, and the Power of the People.* Princeton: Princeton University Press.

Ostwald, Martin, 1969. *Nomos and the Beginnings of the Athenian Democracy.* Oxford: Clarendon.

Petrey, Sandy. 1988. *Realism and Revolution: Balzac, Stendahl, Zola and the Performances of History.* Ithaca, N.Y.: Cornell University Press.

Raaflaub, Kurt A. 1983. "Democracy, Oligarchy, and the Concept of the "Free Citizen" in Late Fifth-Century Athens." *Political Theory* 11:517–44.

Rhodes, P. J. 1981. *A Commentary on the Aristotelian "Athenaion Politeia."* Oxford: Clarendon.

Rijksbaron, Albert. 1984. *The Syntax and Semantics of the Verb in Classical Greek.* Amsterdam: J. C. Gieben.

Sealey, Raphael. 1976. *A History of the Greek City States, ca. 700–300 B.C.* Berkeley and Los Angeles: University of California Press.

Stanton, G. R. 1990. *Athenian Politics c. 800–500 B.C.: A Sourcebook.* London and New York: Routledge.

Thomas, Rosalind. 1989. *Oral Tradition and Written Record in Classical Athens.* Cambridge: Cambridge University Press.

Wade-Gery, H. T. 1933. "Studies in the Structure of Athenian Society: II. The Laws of Kleisthenes." *Classical Quarterly* 27:17–29.

Wallace, Robert W. 1989. *The Areopagos Council, to 307 B.C.* Baltimore and London: The Johns Hopkins University Press.

Wallace-Hadrill, Andrew, ed. 1989. *Patronage in Ancient Society.* New York and London: Routledge.

Wickham Legg, L. G., ed. 1905. *Select Documents Illustrative of the French Revolution.* Oxford: Clarendon.

Zimmern, Alfred. 1961. *The Greek Commonwealth.* 5th ed., rev. Oxford: Oxford University Press.

# Revolution or Compromise?

## *Loren J. Samons II*

Samons criticizes Ober's approach and the democratic nature of Cleisthenes' offers a more skeptical interpretation of reforms.

[...] Reaction to the so-called elitist theory stimulates much of Ober's work in these essays [in *The Athenian Revolution*] and (along with "naive positivism") brings forth his most polemical passages. The study of Athenian democracy, in Ober's view, has been dominated by an (often unspoken) adoption of Robert Michels's "Iron Law of Oligarchy," as reflected by Ronald Syme in *The Roman Revolution* and transmitted through Syme's immense *auctoritas* to scholars of Greek history.[1] Syme asserted (for Ober infamously) that "in all ages, whatever the form and name of government, be it monarchy republic, or democracy, an oligarchy lurks behind the façade," and Ober repeatedly complains that Greek historians, imbibing Syme's dictum with their mother's milk, have allowed a kind of Romanized vision of *clientela*, great houses, and *factiones paucorum* to cloud the picture of Athenian democracy.[2] Thus proponents of the "elitist theory" seek to study the relatively small group of leaders who in their view are necessary for the function of any government and the real power active in any "democracy." "*In place of* an analysis of institutions and prosopography" (emphasis added) Ober prefers an "ideological" approach that "demands close study of political language, in order to show what it was that constituted the will of the demos, and in order to trace how the popular will was translated into individual and collective action within the evolving framework of institutionalized political structure" (133–34 with n. 21). Moreover, this method is distrustful of "common sense" arguments, which assume "that the Athenians tended to think pretty much like us" (134), replacing these with admittedly ideological models "not native" to the ancient world (14), but which if handled self-consciously (we are told) will be able to provide a "meaningful and useful" representation of the past (15; cf. 6, 13).

Ober draws on such models freely, noting the influences of the "Cambridge school" of intellectual history (123), "revisionist Marxism" (141), and "game theory" (163), but especially acknowledging debts to Foucault's treatment of power as "discursive" (8, 10, 88–90) and to J. L. Austin's "speech-act" theory, which treats speech as "performative" (that is, capable of bringing something into being: 151): "The felicity [i.e., success] of the speech act is demonstrated by perlocutionary effects: the subsequent behavior of the relevant members of a society" (152).

Models may perhaps be helpful in the study of ancient societies when crucial evidence is lacking or ancient practices appear alien to modern eyes. But models are themselves the creations of modern scholars (and are often developed for analysis of post-ancient societies), and their use clearly implies a belief that in fact the ancient

Loren J. Samons, "Mass, Elite, and Hoplite-Farmer in Greek History," *Arion* (3rd series) 5 (1998), 99–123, pp. 107–15, 121–2, excerpted by the editor and with text at the end provided by the author.

Athenians *did* tend to think and act in ways similar to those for whom (and by whom) the models were originally developed. Thus naiveté attributed to those who do not employ models often is most evident in those who adopt them readily and then defend them on the grounds of some putative superiority to "source-based" analysis. Such a fundamental objection may serve as an appropriate introduction to several problematic areas noted in Ober's methods and conclusions. [...]

At times Ober's method does not appear so foreign to the eyes of the naive positivist, for he sometimes provides the reader with a glimpse into the results his preferred approaches might offer for the study of an actual historical event, and the case of Cleisthenes' role in the foundation of Athenian *demokratia* serves (from this perspective) both as the eponymous paper and centerpiece of the volume. Moreover, here we have the Oberian method in panoply: the shield of the straw man to be demolished is introduced at the outset ("the Great Man as the motor driving Athenian history," a model "employed by Greek historians since the early 1960s to explain the behavior of Cleisthenes the Alcmaeonid, the figure often credited with 'founding' Athenian democracy," 32), followed by the actual weapon of the more or less conventional argument itself, which is then crested with a methodological flourish – here the "speech-act" model of J. L. Austin. Let us take each piece of equipment in turn.

Ironically, among the few scholars who employ a kind of "Great Man" approach to Cleisthenes' reforms are P. Lévêque and P. Vidal-Naquet, who focus on the reformer's Alcmeonid heritage and supposed geometric and mathematical principles, but whose work is nonetheless praised by Ober as a "classic" (33).[3] Perhaps, therefore, he means Herodotus himself, who wrote that it was Cleisthenes who "established the tribes and *demokratia* for the Athenians" (6.131.1). Many scholars since the 1960s have hardly seen Cleisthenes as a "Great Man," unless we mean by that simply a member of one of the most important families in Athens who in some way introduced major political reform to the Athenian polis. Some have seen this as a (partially) self-interested attempt at gerrymandering and an attack on local cult ties (Lewis), an effort to smash the regional power of other aristocrats and ensure dominance of the city-aristocracy (Sealey), an attempt to grant all citizens the right of equal political participation in order to end previous aristocratic feuds and utilizing the banner of *isonomia* (Ostwald) which represented a real movement toward democracy (Ehrenberg), or as a way to defeat political rivals by (in part) uniting Attica and reuniting the supporters of the Peisistratids, but which had unforeseen consequences (including the fall of Cleisthenes himself: Fornara and Samons).[4] Any living proponents of the "Great Man" theory need not fret, however, for one finds in Ober's own analysis that such men apparently did exist and play important historical roles *before* the creation of democracy. Thus Solon and the tyrants, we are told, were responsible for the creation of a politically self-conscious citizenry (38), while their actions would seem to have robbed Cleisthenes of any but superficial credit for the regime associated with his name.[5]

Ober's analysis of the ancient evidence for the reforms of Cleisthenes advances along very conventional lines.[6] In fact, Ober himself claims "that by sticking very closely to the primary sources it is possible to derive a plausible and internally coherent narrative that revolves around the Athenian people rather than their leaders" (34). The generous reader of this sentence will not conclude that Ober's goal was merely to establish if such a "plausible" interpretation was "possible" given the evidence, but rather that an honest attempt was made to evaluate the evidence before any conclusions were drawn. However, these conclusions may give this reader pause: Ober maintains that "the point at which Athenian democracy was born, was a violent, leaderless event: a three-day riot in 508/7 that resulted in the removal of King Cleomenes I and his Spartan troops from the soil of Attica" (36).

To arrive at this conclusion difficult and important historical questions are simply neglected. Thus Cleisthenes' Alcmeonid background and his clan's problematic relationship to the Peisistratid tyrants is swept away in two sentences and a footnote (37 with n. 6). The family's connection rested on more than Cleisthenes' archonship in 525 during the tyranny: Cleisthenes, after all, was the homonymous grandson of the tyrant of Sicyon, and his sister had been married to Peisistratus himself; moreover, after the revolution of 508/7 Cleisthenes' government sought some kind of arrangement with Persia (Hdt. 5.73)[7] and years later the Alcmeonids were accused of plotting to help the Persians (with whom Peisistratus' son Hippias had taken refuge). Now Ober recognizes that the model of democratic politics from the Periclean or Demosthenic age will not apply to the late sixth century (37–38). And yet the *ideology* that developed during those ages was apparently already a historical factor to be reckoned with: thus Cleisthenes' proposed reforms were enacted (probably through the Assembly) because "[t]he masses saw that these reforms would provide them with the institutional means to express more fully their growing sense of themselves as citizens" (38). Here the model of mass self-consciousness and unity calls forth the evidence of its own existence.[8] The only other evidence Ober musters is Herodotus' statement that the Athenians were all "thinking the same things" after the Spartans under Cleomenes seized the acropolis (see below).

Ober argues for contextualization elsewhere (see Chapter 10), and it may be well to consider the context of Greece in the late sixth century and the Alcmeonids' arguably unique position in Athenian society and politics.[9] The Athenians of 508/7 lived in a world where two kinds of poleis predominated: those ruled by more or less broad timocratic oligarchies (see Hanson) and those ruled by tyrannies. *Demokratia* was not part of the political landscape, thus when Cleisthenes "took the *demos* into partnership" after the experience of three or four years of narrow oligarchic rule and factional fighting (Hdt. 5.66.2), how were the people of Athens to interpret his action? Many, undoubtedly, described the movement in the only terms they possessed: Cleisthenes, the erstwhile ally (but late enemy) of the Peisistratids, will now likewise champion us (the people) against the aristocrats.[10] To the Spartans, moreover, this new regime will have resembled nothing so much as a reinstitution of a Peisistratid-style tyranny by one of the clan's former compatriots, and probably this is how Isagoras sold Cleomenes on another expedition to the north. The innovation of Cleisthenes (on this view) was his ability to combine an existing tyrannic tactic (championship of the *demos* against the aristocrats) with the basic structure of timocratic polis government (including property qualifications for office, and working council/assembly/magistrates), while making residence in Attic demes (as opposed to membership in clan-controlled phratries) the deciding criterion for citizenship.

The chronological issues of precisely when Cleisthenes actually made his proposals, and whether they were partially or fully enacted before the Athenian resistance to

Cleomenes and the Spartans, are brushed aside (40–1 with n. 12; 48), but only an answer to these questions will assure us of what the resisting Athenian *boule* and *demos* believed they may have been fighting to protect – leaving aside the very obvious possibility that they had *no* positive program in mind, but rather simply sought a removal of the particular aristocrats led by Isagoras (his *stasiotai*: Hdt.) and the invading force of their Spartan allies. The same can be said for the putative name of Cleisthenes' regime (a very vexed question): since Ober utilizes democratic "ideology" in his explanation, he presumably assumes that the name *demokratia* existed in 507, or that it was created shortly thereafter by this act of "self-definition on the part of the demos itself" (35).[11]

Perhaps most troubling is the view of the Athenian resistance to the Spartans' attempt to overthrow the *boule* (probably Cleisthenes' new *boule* of five hundred, although Ober is agnostic: 48). For Ober this was a leaderless and spontaneous "riot" of Athenian citizens after the Spartans under Cleomenes failed to dismantle the *boule* and seized the acropolis (43–46). Herodotus' report that the Athenians were "all thinking the same things" for Ober "supports the idea of a generalized and quite highly developed civic consciousness among the Athenian masses – an ability to form and act on strong and communal views on political affairs" (44). But even if this ambitious exegesis were accepted it could not obscure the fact that there is absolutely no suggestion (much less an indication) of a mob or a riot in the accounts of Herodotus and Aristotle. Herodotus' account (upon which Aristotle relied)[12] is never presented as a whole by Ober, and it taken together suggests conclusions very different from those he draws.

> ...Cleomenes having arrived in Athens with a small force banished seven hundred families of the Athenians, which Isagoras had suggested to him. And having done these things, next he tried to dissolve the *boule*, and he was placing the official powers (*archai*) in the hands of three hundred partisans (*stasiotai*) of Isagoras. (2) But after the *boule* resisted and did not wish to obey, both Cleomenes and Isagoras and his partisans seized the acropolis. The remaining Athenians, having the same things in mind (*ta auta phronesantes*), besieged them for two days. On the third day, however many were Lacedaemonians departed from the country under treaty. (Hdt. 5.72.1–2)

In Aristotle the *plethos* is said to have been "collected together," and the Spartans besieged and then allowed to leave the Athenian stronghold after three days under truce (*Ath. Pol.* 20.3).[13] Now since Greek has perfectly good words for "mob" and "violent uprisings," and since Herodotus and Aristotle did not use those terms, why should we infer their existence? Surely not even the "speech-act" theory requires the assumption of phantom mobs and riots?

It will perhaps be best to leave aside the issue of whether a "riot" (never testified to have occurred) of a "mob" (never testified to have existed) could have been "leaderless" (36). Yet one may note that Ober here relies on an argument from silence (Herodotus does not name any leaders: 42) buttressed by a historical example of another putative leaderless mob action: the French Revolution (48–50). The facts that the Athenian *boule* resisted the Spartans before the people expelled them and that the Third Estate/National Assembly refused to be disbanded by Louis XVI before the Bastille was stormed, are stripped of their causal significance.

In all this the effect of Austin's speech-act theory is hardly palpable (cf. 47). But it perhaps reappears in the conclusion, where Cleisthenes is described as "not so much the authoritative leader of the revolution as ... a highly skilled interpreter of statements made in a revolutionary context and of revolutionary action itself," whose effectiveness rested "in his ability to 'read' – in a sensitive and perceptive way – the text of Athenian discourse in a revolutionary age, and to recognize that Athenian mass action had created new political facts" (52). Enough has been said about the evidence to show that this formulation bears it no resemblance, whatever its relationship to the "speech-act" model. [ ... ]

In the end, the precise nature of Cleisthenes' reforms and the reasons behind them may resist any compelling reconstruction, whether model-driven or not. Our sources simply do not provide enough information to paint a clear picture of the events. As much as it may surprise moderns steeped in the tradition of democracy, the Athenians apparently evinced very little interest in Cleisthenes and his reforms in the century or so after they occurred.[14] As we have seen, Herodotus tells us little more than that Cleisthenes reformed the Athenian tribes and gave Athens *demokratia* – a term he uses rarely and in problematic ways.[15] By the time fourth-century authorities like Aristotle became interested in Athens' constitutional history and Athenian democracy *per se*, most important facts about Cleisthenes and the later reformer Ephialtes – the individuals moderns usually consider *the* crucial actors in the creation of Athenian democracy – simply could not be recovered. (Compare the fulsome traditions surrounding the tyrant Peisistratus and the lawgiver Solon.) The virtual vacuum of information about Cleisthenes that existed in antiquity suggests that extreme caution must be exercised in attempting to reconstruct the events of ca. 507 (much less the motives behind them).

Confronted with this situation, scholars attempting to analyze Cleisthenes' reforms have tended to adopt one of two lines of inquiry. Either they have endeavored to infer the nature of the reforms from the name or banner ostensibly attached to them (*isonomia* or *demokratia*), or they have attempted to characterize Cleisthenes' or the Athenians' actions by pulling apart the ancient descriptions of the political reforms themselves.

Analysis of the possible name of the Cleisthenic regime for some time centered on the theory that Cleisthenes or his supporters put forward his reforms under the banner *isonomia*, and that this term reflected a putatively democratic concept (on this view) of something like "equality of the law." Yet recent scholarship has suggested that we cannot confidently associate the term *isonomia* with Cleisthenes' regime, nor, even if we knew Cleisthenes had employed this term, could we conclude that the polyvalent slogan tells us anything significant about the reforms. A term that sounded well in many contexts, *isonomia* could describe an aristocratic regime with "equal distribution of privileges" as well as serve as an epithet for *demokratia*.[16]

The term *demokratia*, which the Athenians used regularly after the mid-fifth century to describe their regime, has the best *a priori* support as the name Cleisthenes gave to his new government (assuming for the moment that he attached *any* banner to the reforms). However, we have no direct testimony to the existence of this term before about the 470s–460s, and the partisan or pejorative connotations of the term well into the second half of the fifth century make its adoption by Cleisthenes or his supporters less than attractive.[17]

In light of these facts, analysis of the reforms themselves would seem to offer the most potentially fruitful method for approaching the events of ca. 507. P. J. Rhodes, the foremost student of the Aristotelian *Constitution of the Athenians* (our best source for the reforms), provides a useful summary of such work:

> There have been many attempts to make political sense of Cleisthenes' reforms by explaining why his tribal system should have been constructed as it was: the most fruitful are those which are based firmly on detailed knowledge of that construction...
> Cleisthenes will at least have "mixed up" the people, and have encouraged the unification of the state, by combining in one tribe men from different parts of Attica (it may be significant that the *astu* [= "city center"], where most of the families active in politics must have lived, was distributed through all ten tribes)... The old network of influences was one in which the Alcmaeonids were not well placed, and Cleisthenes could claim that he was doing away with unfair channels of influence..., while doing his own family a good turn; since their homes to the south of the city were assigned to three tribes, and the coastal strip towards Sunium, where they may have had land and dependants... was assigned to the same three tribes, it seems that in addition they were well placed in the new system and could count on seeing familiar faces in the meetings of their tribes.[18]

Such a view of the reforms provides some explanation for them without exceeding the meager testimony of our sources. In attempting to draw any further conclusions about the events ca. 508/7, one must be wary of allowing knowledge of Athens' later democratic government to influence interpretations of the reforms' motivations in the late sixth century: one cannot simply *assume* that Cleisthenes could have foreseen (much less that he would have approved of) the later changes that would give Athens a radically democratic regime. It is questionable whether Cleisthenes' Hellas knew anything of state payment for public service or full citizenship without property qualifications, elements that would become virtually synonymous with Athenian *demokratia* after the mid-fifth century. As already noted, late sixth-century Greece offered only two basic alternatives for the organization of polis government: (1) a regime based on a more or less sovereign body of citizens (at least usually restricted to those holding some amount of property) and governed by magistrates selected from the more wealthy or aristocratic elements in the society,[19] or (2) the repression of these traditional polis powers (elite magistrates and an assembly of citizens) via the rule of a tyrant or a narrow clique (*dynesteia*). Such tyrants could often rely on the support of the poorer elements of the commons (*demos*) to the extent that they protected or championed them in the face of aristocratic domination, a technique clearly employed (for example) by the Peisistratids in Athens.[20]

When viewed within their context and not through the distorting lens of what Athens would become after 462/1, Cleisthenes' reforms resemble nothing so much as an attempt to combine elements of tyrannic championship of the *demos* with traditional polis government. For the Athenian *demos* now gained power through Cleisthenes' new *boule* of 500 (who would be chosen by lot from all citizens and who would prepare the business for the sovereign assembly) and perhaps through the ten new tribal assemblies. As Rhodes notes, the tribes themselves were microcosms of Attica since they comprised "thirds" (*trittyes*) drawn from three areas of Attica, and they served as the organizing force for much of the new Athenian regime, including the military and the selection of important officials like archons. Since the new tribes were created out of whole cloth, they bypassed existing social and religious structures, and perhaps thereby offered more political scope to individuals inhibited by those structures.[21]

Yet Cleisthenes' reforms also ensured that wealthier Athenians continued to enjoy important political privileges through the retention of Solon's system of property qualifications for major magistracies (if not for service on the *boule* itself).[22] Moreover, although aristocratic power at the local level may have been weakened through the Cleisthenic regime's "mixing" of different regional elements and its emphasis on the common demesmen's role in determining citizenship (as opposed to its control by the presumably aristocratically dominated phratries), the aristocrats retained their property and their control of important cults.[23] Elite Athenians would therefore continue to wield significant influence in the regions where they held property as well as in the central government in Athens.

After the expulsion of the Peisistratids in 511/10, Athens had swung from a tyrannic regime based on championship of the *demos* and repression of (certain) aristocrats to an elite regime seemingly dominated by a few aristocratic clans. Cleisthenes arguably "split the difference" between these two political forms, offering something both to the common members of the *demos* and to wealthier Athenians, while avoiding what either group feared most: domination by certain elites in the absence of a champion to defend them (in the case of the *demos*) or domination by a tyrant who usurped aristocratic authority and prestige (in the case of the elites).

To the extent that Cleisthenes offered institutional power to a *demos* that previously had looked to the Peisistratid tyrants as defenders, one might conclude that his reforms had characteristics that (in retrospect) could be described as "democratic." To the extent that he made no effort at massive economic or social reforms (especially the cancellation of debts or redistribution of land) and in fact retained a system of property qualifications that assured elite control of important offices, he might be seen as a more conservative reformer than Solon. For despite its popularity in ancient (and modern) accounts of Athens' constitutional history, Solon's radical cancellation of all debt had risked an elite revolt as well as an economic catastrophe, and ultimately had created (or at best not alleviated) the conditions that the Peisistratids exploited.

Cleisthenes sought a solution to Athens' political problems and his own failure to dominate the current aristocratic environment by combining existing political principles and institutions in novel ways. That he ultimately intended for these reforms to improve the position of his own clan, in part by making the Alcmeonid family the obvious patrons of the newly empowered *demos*, is a reasonable if not provable assumption.[24] If so, he apparently failed in his attempt, for the credited founder of *demokratia* disappears from history soon after his reforms, and the Alcmeonid clan suffered a series of political setbacks until Cleisthenes' nephew Pericles found a new way to champion the *demos*.[25]

## NOTES

1 R. Michels, *Political Parties: A Sociological Study of the Oligarchical Tendencies of Modern Democracy*, trans. E. and C. Paul (New York 1962 [orig. ed. 1915]), and R. Syme, *The Roman Revolution* (Oxford 1939).

2  Syme (note 1), 7. Throughout Ober argues against the propriety of using Roman
    comparanda for Greece: see *The Athenian Revolution* (Princeton 1996), especially 18–
    26, 53, 182; cf. Victor D. Hanson, *The Other Greeks* (Berkeley, 1999), 214.

3  Vidal-Naquet modifies this position slightly in the preface to the new English edition of
    the work, but the text remains unaltered: *Cleisthenes the Athenian*, trans. D. A. Curtis
    (New Jersey 1996), xxxiv–xxxv.

4  D. M. Lewis, "Cleisthenes and Attica," *Historia* 12 (1963), 22–40; R. Sealey, "Regional-
    ism in Archaic Athens," *Historia* 9 (1960), 155–80 = *Essays in Greek Politics* (New York
    1967), 9–38; M. Ostwald, *Nomos and the Beginnings of Athenian Democracy* (Oxford
    1969), 149–158 and *From Popular Sovereignty to the Sovereignty of the Law* (Berkeley
    1986), 15–28; V. Ehrenberg, "The Origins of Demokratia," *Historia* 1 (1950), 515–48
    and *From Solon to Socrates* 2nd ed. (London 1973), 90–103; C. W. Fornara and
    L. J. Samons II, *Athens from Cleisthenes to Pericles* (Berkeley 1991), 37–58.

5  Other "Great Men" appear elsewhere in Ober's work, including Themistocles (64) and
    even Pericles (65–66, but cf. 54). Pericles' insights are nonetheless limited to the military
    sphere and the invention of "grand strategy" – no such credit is given to him in the arena
    of politics. Athenian leaders are elsewhere allowed to create military strategies while "the
    polis of Athens" is credited with discovering "in democratic politics a way to broaden
    the base of the social order" (70).

6  This is true elsewhere as well. In Chapter 8 Ober writes as if he finds the *method* of
    M. H. Hansen objectionable (109), but in fact his substantive criticisms often involve
    *practice* (115–117), i.e., what conclusion *should* be drawn from a given piece of evidence.
    In Chapter 7 (93–94) he engages in conventional analysis to show that Demosthenes 21
    *Against Meidias* was actually delivered. Here, however, he never treats the possibility that
    Demosthenes might have finished the speech without ever delivering (or even intending
    to deliver) it publicly. (Such an act would be understandable if he actually took a bribe not
    *to prosecute* Meidias, as Aeschines 3.51–52 implies (cf. Plut. *Dem.* 12).) We are instead
    presented in the text with the false alternatives of an unfinished and unpublished speech,
    or a finished and delivered speech (but cf. his notes 16 and 17).

7  This initiative cannot be attributed to "the people," since they seem to have rejected such
    a Persian connection when it was put before them (Hdt. 5.73.3).

8  Ober's confidence in the existence of this ideology also provides a unique solution to the
    problem of the lack of extant texts describing democratic theory from ancient Athens.
    Ober opines that "the simplest hypothesis is . . . [that] few such texts ever existed," and
    that such texts were unnecessary in Athens because "democratic ideology so dominated
    the political landscape that formal democratic theory was otiose" (147–48). The "simplest
    hypothesis" is of course that *no* such texts existed, though it is ingenious to argue from the
    *absence* of evidence for a given ideology's theoretical support that the ideology pervaded
    the "political landscape." Can we, after all, complain about the scanty evidence for
    Cleisthenes' reforms (34) only to postulate a "growing sense of themselves as citizens"
    among the Athenians?

9  Instead, they are treated as just another "fine old family" (40). But the Alcmeonids
    apparently stood outside the narrow Eupatridai who controlled cults (among other
    things), and moreover are the only Athenian family known to have suffered from a
    curse. See Fornara and Samons (note 4), 1–24.

10  For tyrants (including Peisistratus) as champions of the farming class, see Hanson, 114–
    15, 471–72 (n. 21), with literature.

11  For the problems surrounding the origins and original meanings of the term, see Fornara
    and Samons (note 4), 48–56, with literature cited, R. Sealey, *The Athenian Republic*
    (University Park 1987), 91–102, and M. H. Hansen, *The Athenian Democracy in the
    Age of Demosthenes* (Oxford 1991), 69–71.

12   For the reliance of the *Athenaion Politeia* on Herodotus here, see P. J. Rhodes, *A Commentary on the Aristotelian Athenaion Politeia* (Oxford 1981), 240–46.

13   The passage perhaps deserves quotation: "With the *boule* having offered resistance and the people having been collected together (*sunathroisthentos*), those around Cleomenes and Isagoras fled into the acropolis, and the *demos* sitting down (*proskathezomenos*, i.e., in before the acropolis) besieged (*epoliorkei*) them for two days. On the third day they released Cleomenes and all those with him under treaty (*hupospondous*)." The military flavor of this passage suggests a picture far different from a riot. Ober wishes to read the passive participle *sunathroisthentos* reflexively, i.e., the "mob gathered itself together": 45 with n. 20.

14   See Samons, *Arion* 8.3 (2001), 152 n. 4.

15   Hdt. 5.69, 6.131.1 (*demokratia*). Herodotus employs the noun *demokratia* in only one other passage (6.43.3); there he describes Persian-imposed regimes that replaced tyrannies in Asia Minor that can hardly have been "democracies" in the Athenian sense. These passages, Herodotus' failure to use *demokratia* in his famous debate on forms of government (3.80–82), and his rare use of the verbal form of the term (4.137.2, 6.43.3) suggest that the meaning of *demokratia* had yet to crystallize (at least outside Athens) by the time of Herodotus' composition.

16   See Fornara and Samons (note 4), 41–8, 166–7 with bibliography.

17   For the term's problematic development, meaning, and connotations, see Sealey (note 11), 91–102. For its relatively late appearance, see K. A. Raaflaub, "Power in the Hands of the People: Foundations of Athenian Democracy," in I. Morris and K. A. Raaflaub, eds., *Democracy 2500? Questions and Challenges* (Dubuque, IA 1997), 31–66.

18   P. J. Rhodes, *A Commentary on the Aristotelian Athenaion Politeia* (revised ed.; Oxford 1993), 254–55, which see for the scholarship Rhodes cites in support of this summary.

19   Such regimes are sometimes referred to as "democracies," since they accepted the principle of popular control of the state (via the vote in citizen assemblies) and *may* have had relatively low property qualifications: cf. E. Robinson, *The First Democracies: Early Popular Government outside Athens*, Historia Einz. 107 (Stuttgart 1997). However, no evidence suggests that the term *demokratia* developed elsewhere before its emergence in (early fifth-century?) Athens, and Athenian *demokratia* eventually possessed a combination of specific qualities (the absence of a property qualification for citizenship, heavy reliance on the lottery for selecting officials, and extensive use of payment for public service) that would help define *demokratia* and would distinguish Athens' classical regime from other popular governments.

20   The Peisistratids apparently enjoyed popular support throughout their reign, a fact that deserves emphasis since it illustrates the difference between the political environments of sixth- and fifth-century Hellas. Opposition to the Peisistratid tyrants came from (some) Athenian aristocrats and the Spartans, while the Athenian *demos* failed to rise up against the family even after Hippias became "harsh" (one may infer that only the aristocrats felt the severity of his rule after his brother's assassination in 514). The association of "tyrants" with aristocratic/oligarchic forces or political ideals developed later (in the fifth century), when *demokratia* could be characterized as a force opposing both tyranny and oligarchy.

21   However, one must remember that the tribal assemblies met in the city of Athens itself, and families with strong city-center connections (including the Alcmeonids) probably benefited from this arrangement.

22   For the qualifications for service on the *boule* and the possibility of property qualifications for service before ca. 462/1, see P. J. Rhodes, *The Athenian Boule* (revised ed.; Oxford 1985), 1–16.

23   In fact, the major religious structures in Athens (including the four old Ionian tribes) remained in place after Cleisthenes' reforms.

24  Cf. Lewis, "Cleisthenes and Attica" (note 4), 22–40.
25  For the Alcmeonid family's subsequent history, see Fornara and Samons (note 4), esp. 17–36.


# Further reading

The articles by Robert Wallace, Kurt Raaflaub, Josiah Ober, Walter Eder, and David Castriota in *Democracy 2500? Questions and Challenges*, eds. I. Morris and K. A. Raaflaub (Dubuque, IA, 1998).

Badian, Ernst, "Back to Kleisthenic Chronology," in *Polis and Politics*, eds. P. Flensted-Jensen et al. (Copenhagen, 2000), 447–64.

Develin, Robert and Martin Kilmer, "What Kleisthenes Did," *Historia* 46 (1997), 3–18.

Fornara, Charles and Loren J. Samons II, *Athens from Cleisthenes to Pericles* (Berkeley, 1991).

Hölscher, Tonio, "Images and Political Identity: The Case of Athens," in *Democracy, Empire, and the Arts in Fifth-century Athens*, eds. D. Boedeker and K. A. Raaflaub (Cambridge, MA, 1998), 153–84.

Karpyuk, Sergei, "Crowd in Archaic and Classical Greece," *Hyperboreus* 6 (2000), 79–102, esp. 93–6.

Ostwald, Martin, *Nomos and the Beginnings of the Athenian Democracy* (Oxford, 1969).

—— "The Reform of the Athenian State," in *The Cambridge Ancient History* vol. 4, 2nd edn. (Cambridge, 1988), 306–46.

Rhodes, Peter J., *A Commentary on the Aristotelian Athenaion Politeia*, revised edn. (Oxford, 1993).

# 3

# Popular Politics in Fifth-century Syracuse

---

## Introduction

In the course of the fifth century BC democracy became increasingly common in various parts of the Greek world. Syracuse, a large and prosperous city in eastern Sicily, represents an interesting case given the city's importance and the available source material. In the mid-460s the people of Syracuse overthrew the tyrant dynasty established by Gelon that had ruled it and surrounding territories for nearly two decades, and, according to ancient authors, adopted a democratic government that lasted almost sixty years. But the testimony on the subject is not without its difficulties and contradictions, and modern scholars have disagreed about the nature of the Syracusan government: was it a radical democracy like Athens of the mid- to late fifth century, a more moderate form of popular government, or something else entirely?

## Thucydides, *History of the Peloponnesian War* (6.34–36, 38–41)

Thucydides alone of the writers included in this section was alive during the period of Syracuse's democracy, and here purports to describe a meeting of the popular assembly at Syracuse in 415 – potentially very valuable testimony. However, one must always be cautious about the speeches ancient historians include in their accounts: even with authors as painstaking as Thucydides, the speeches we read likely owe at least as much to the writer of the history as to the original words that may have been spoken. This is especially so when, as here, there is no reason to believe that the author himself could have attended the meeting in question.

Context: Thucydides has just finished describing the launching of a massive Athenian attack force headed for Sicily when he turns to an assembly meeting held in

Syracuse not long afterwards. Several men have already spoken about rumors of a coming assault, we are told. Then the distinguished leader Hermocrates offers his thoughts. We begin with the very last words of his speech. (*Source*: Thucydides, *History of the Peloponnesian War* 6.34–36, 38–41, trans. R. Crawley.)

"[...] That the Athenians are coming to attack us, and are already upon the voyage, and all but here – this is what I am sure of."

[35] Thus far spoke Hermocrates. Meanwhile the people of Syracuse were at great strife among themselves: some contended that the Athenians had no idea of coming and that there was no truth in what he said; some asked if they did come what harm they could do that would not be repaid them tenfold in return; and others made light of the whole affair and turned it into ridicule. In short, there were few that believed Hermocrates and feared for the future. Meanwhile Athenagoras, the leader of the people and very powerful at that time with the masses, came forward and spoke as follows:

[36] "For the Athenians, he who does not wish that they may be as misguided as they are supposed to be, and that they may come here to become our subjects, is either a coward or a traitor to his country; and as for those who carry such tidings and fill you with so much alarm, I wonder less at their audacity than at their folly if they flatter themselves that we do not see through them. The fact is that they have their private reasons to be afraid, and wish to throw the city into consternation to have their own terrors cast into the shade by the public alarm. In short, this is what these reports are worth; they do not arise of themselves, but are concocted by men who are always causing agitation here in Sicily.[...]

[38] [...] Persons here invent stories that neither are true nor ever will be. Nor is this the first time that I see these persons, when they cannot resort to deeds, trying by such stories and by others even more abominable to frighten your people and get into their hands the government: it is what I see always. And I cannot help fearing that trying so often they may one day succeed, and that we, as long as we do not feel the smart, may prove too weak for the task of prevention, or, when the offenders are known, of pursuit. The result is that our city is rarely at rest, but is subject to constant troubles and to contests as frequent against herself as against the enemy, not to speak of occasional tyrannies and infamous cabals. However, I will try, if you will support me, to let nothing of this happen in our time, by gaining you, the many, and by chastising the authors of such machinations, not merely when they are caught in the act – a difficult feat to accomplish – but also for what they have the wish though not the power to do; as it is necessary to punish an enemy not only for what he does, but also beforehand for what he intends to do, if the first to relax precaution would not be also the first to suffer. I shall also reprove, watch, and on occasion warn the few – the most effectual way, in my opinion, of turning them from their evil courses. And after all, as I have often asked, what would you have, young men? Would you hold office at once? The law forbids it, a law enacted rather because you are not competent than to disgrace you when competent. Meanwhile you would not be on a legal equality with the many! But how can it be right that citizens of the same state should be held unworthy of the same privileges?

[39] "It will be said, perhaps, that democracy is neither wise nor equitable, but that the holders of property are also the best fitted to rule. I say, on the contrary, first, that

the word *demos,* or people, includes the whole state, oligarchy only a part; next, that if the best guardians of property are the rich, and the best counsellors the wise, none can hear and decide so well as the many; and that all these talents, severally and collectively, have their just place in a democracy. But an oligarchy gives the many their share of the danger, and not content with the largest part takes and keeps the whole of the profit; and this is what the powerful and young among you aspire to, but in a great city cannot possibly obtain."

[40] "But even now, foolish men, most senseless of all the Hellenes that I know, if you have no sense of the wickedness of your designs, or most criminal if you have that sense and still dare to pursue them – even now, if it is not a case for repentance, you may still learn wisdom, and thus advance the interest of the country, the common interest of us all. Reflect that in the country's prosperity the men of merit in your ranks will have a share and a larger share than the great mass of your fellow country-men, but that if you have other designs you run a risk of being deprived of all; and desist from reports like these, as the people know your object and will not put up with it. If the Athenians arrive, this city will repulse them in a manner worthy of itself; we have, moreover, generals who will see to this matter. And if nothing of this be true, as I incline to believe, the city will not be thrown into a panic by your intelligence, or impose upon itself a self-chosen servitude by choosing you for its rulers; the city itself will look into the matter, and will judge your words as if they were acts, and instead of allowing itself to be deprived of its liberty by listening to you, will strive to preserve that liberty, by taking care to have always at hand the means of making itself respected."

[41] Such were the words of Athenagoras. One of the generals now stood up and stopped any other speakers coming forward, adding these words of his own with reference to the matter in hand: "It is not well for speakers to utter calumnies against one another, or for their hearers to entertain them; we ought rather to look to the intelligence that we have received, and see how each man by himself and the city as a whole may best prepare to repel the invaders. Even if there be no need, there is no harm in the state being furnished with horses and arms and all other insignia of war; and we will undertake to see to and order this, and to send round to the cities to reconnoitre and do all else that may appear desirable. Part of this we have seen to already, and whatever we discover shall be laid before you." After these words from the general, the Syracusans departed from the assembly. [...]

# Aristotle, *Politics*

Aristotle's testimony in the *Politics* seems at one point to confirm that democracy followed the fall of tyranny at Syracuse, but at another to suggest that something more moderate, a *politeia* ("polity" – a constitution mixing democratic and oli-garchic elements), had been in place down to 412 BC, just after the defeat of the Athen-ian expedition. (*Source*: Aristotle, *Politics* 1315b35–9, 1316a30–4, and 1304a 18–29, trans. B. Jowett.)

## 1315b35–9

[...] Of other tyrannies, that of Hiero and Gelo at Syracuse was the most lasting. Even this, however, was short, not more than eighteen years in all; for Gelo continued tyrant for seven years, and died in the eighth; Hiero reigned for ten years, and Thrasybulus was driven out in the eleventh month. In fact, tyrannies generally have been of quite short duration. [...]

## 1316a30–4

[...] [A] tyranny often changes into a tyranny, as that at Sicyon changed from the tyranny of Myron into that of Cleisthenes; into oligarchy, as the tyranny of Antileon did at Chalcis; into democracy, as that of Gelo's family did at Syracuse; into aristocracy, as at Carthage, and the tyranny of Charilaus at Lacedaemon. [...]

## 1304a18–29

[...] Governments also change into oligarchy or into democracy or into a constitutional government because the magistrates, or some other section of the state, increase in power or renown. Thus at Athens the reputation gained by the court of the Areopagus, in the Persian War, seemed to tighten the reins of government. On the other hand, the victory of Salamis, which was gained by the common people who served in the fleet, and won for the Athenians the empire due to command of the sea, strengthened the democracy. At Argos, the notables, having distinguished themselves against the Lacedaemonians in the battle of Mantinea, attempted to put down the democracy. At Syracuse, the people, having been the chief authors of the victory in the war with the Athenians, changed the constitutional government into democracy. [...]

# Diodorus of Sicily, *Library of History*

Diodorus was a native of Sicily who lived centuries later than the events under discussion but who composed an expansive history of the world based on the accounts of earlier historians, most of whose works are now lost to us. His narratives of Sicilian history are especially valuable for the gaps in our knowledge that they help to fill. However, Diodorus' work is not infrequently marred by inaccuracy or faulty chronology. (*Source*: Diodorus 11.67–68, 72–73, 76, 86–87, trans. C. H. Oldfather, from *Diodorus of Sicily* vol. 4 (Cambridge, MA: Harvard University Press, 1946), pp. 299, 301, 303, 305, 313, 315, 319, 321, 323, 347, 349, 351.)

## 11.67–68

[...] Gelon, the son of Deinomenes, who far excelled all other men in valour and strategy and out-generalled the Carthaginians, defeated these barbarians in a great battle, as has been told; and since he treated the peoples whom he had subdued with fairness and, in general, conducted himself humanely toward all his immediate neighbours, he enjoyed high favour among the Sicilian Greeks. Thus Gelon, being beloved by all because of his mild rule, lived in uninterrupted peace until his death. But Hieron, the next oldest among the brothers,[1] who succeeded to the throne, did not rule over his subjects in the same manner; for he was avaricious and violent and, speaking generally, an utter stranger to sincerity and nobility of character. Consequently there were a good many who wished to revolt, but they restrained their inclinations because of Gelon's reputation and the goodwill he had shown towards all the Sicilian Greeks. After the death of Hieron, however, his brother Thrasybulus, who succeeded to the throne, surpassed in wickedness his predecessor in the kingship. For being a violent man and murderous by nature, he put to death many citizens unjustly and drove not a few into exile on false charges, confiscating their possessions into the royal treasury; and since, speaking generally, he hated those he had wronged and was hated by them, he enlisted a large body of mercenaries, preparing in this way a legion with which to oppose the citizen soldiery. And since he kept incurring more and more the hatred of the citizens by outraging many and executing others, he compelled the victims to revolt. Consequently the Syracusans, choosing men who would take the lead, set about as one man to destroy the tyranny, and once they had been organized by their leaders they clung stubbornly to their freedom. When Thrasybulus saw that the whole city was in arms against him, he at first attempted to stop the revolt by persuasion; but after he observed that the movement of the Syracusans could not be halted, he gathered together both the colonists whom Hieron had settled in Catana and his other allies, as well as a multitude of mercenaries, so that his army numbered all told almost fifteen thousand men. Then, seizing Achradinê, as it is called, and the Island, which was fortified, and using them as bases, he began a war upon the revolting citizens.

68. The Syracusans at the outset seized a part of the city which is called Tychê, and operating from there they dispatched ambassadors to Gela, Acragas, and Selinus, and also to Himera and the cities of the Siceli in the interior of the island, asking them to come together with all speed and join with them in liberating Syracuse. And since all these cities acceded to this request eagerly and hurriedly dispatched aid, some of them infantry and cavalry and others warships fully equipped for action, in a brief time there was collected a considerable armament with which to aid the Syracusans. Consequently the Syracusans, having made ready their ships and drawn up their army for battle, demonstrated that they were ready to fight to a finish both on land and on sea. Now Thrasybulus, abandoned as he was by his allies and basing his hopes only upon the mercenaries, was master only of Achradinê and the Island, whereas the rest of the city was in the hands of the Syracusans. And after this Thrasybulus sailed forth with his ships against the enemy, and after suffering defeat in the battle with the loss of numerous triremes, he withdrew with the remaining ships to the Island. Similarly he

led forth his army also from Achradinê and drew them up for battle in the suburbs, but he suffered defeat and was forced to retire with heavy losses back to Achradinê. In the end, giving up hope of maintaining the tyranny, he opened negotiations with the Syracusans, came to an understanding with them, and retired under a truce to Locri. The Syracusans, having liberated their native city in this manner, gave permission to the mercenaries to withdraw from Syracuse, and they liberated the other cities, which were either in the hands of tyrants or had garrisons, and re-established democracies in them. From this time the city enjoyed peace and increased greatly in prosperity, and it maintained its democracy for almost sixty years, until the tyranny which was established by Dionysius. But Thrasybulus, who had taken over a kingship which had been established on so fair a foundation, disgracefully lost his kingdom through his own wickedness, and fleeing to Locri he spent the rest of his life there in private station. [...]

## 11.72–73, 76

72. In Sicily, as soon as the tyranny of Syracuse had been overthrown and all the cities of the island had been liberated, the whole of Sicily was making great strides toward prosperity. For the Sicilian Greeks were at peace, and the land they cultivated was fertile, so that the abundance of their harvests enabled them soon to increase their estates and to fill the land with slaves and domestic animals and every other accompaniment of prosperity, taking in great revenues on the one hand and spending nothing upon the wars to which they had been accustomed. But later on they were again plunged into wars and civil strife for the following reasons. After the Syracusans had overthrown the tyranny of Thrasybulus, they held a meeting of the Assembly, and after deliberating on forming a democracy of their own they all voted unanimously to make a colossal statue of Zeus the Liberator and each year to celebrate with sacrifices the Festival of Liberation and hold games of distinction on the day on which they had overthrown the tyrant and liberated their native city; and they also voted to sacrifice to the gods, in connection with the games, four hundred and fifty bulls and to use them for the citizens' feast. As for all the magistracies, they proposed to assign them to the original citizens, but the aliens who had been admitted to citizenship under Gelon they did not see fit to allow to share in this dignity, either because they judged them to be unworthy or because they were suspicious lest men who had been brought up in the way of tyranny and had served in war under a monarch might attempt a revolution. And that is what actually happened. For Gelon had enrolled as citizens more than ten thousand foreign mercenaries, and of these there were left at the time in question more than seven thousand.

73. These aliens resented their being excluded from the dignity attending magistracies and with one accord revolted from the Syracusans, and they seized in the city both Achradinê and the Island, both these places having their own well-built fortifications. The Syracusans, who were again plunged into disorder, held possession of the rest of the city; and that part of it which faced Epipolae they blocked off by a wall and made their own position very secure; for they at once easily cut off the rebels from access to the countryside and soon caused them to be in want of provisions. But

though in number the mercenaries were inferior to the Syracusans, yet in experience of warfare they were far superior [...]

76. In Sicily the Syracusans, in their war upon the mercenaries who had revolted, kept launching attack after attack upon both Achradinê and the Island, and they defeated the rebels in a sea-battle, but on land they were unable to expel them from the city because of the strength of these two places. Later, however, after an open battle had been fought on land, the soldiers engaged on both sides fighting spiritedly, finally, although both armies suffered not a few casualties, victory lay with the Syracusans. And after the battle the Syracusans honoured with the prize of valour the elite troops, six hundred in number, who were responsible for the victory, giving them each a mina of silver.

While these events were taking place, Ducetius, the leader of the Siceli, harbouring a grudge against the inhabitants of Catana because they had robbed the Siceli of their land, led an army against them. And since the Syracusans had likewise sent an army against Catana, they and the Siceli joined in portioning out the land in allotments among themselves and made war upon the settlers who had been sent by Hieron when he was ruler of Syracuse. The Catanians opposed them with arms, but were defeated in a number of engagements and were expelled from Catana, and they took possession of what is now Aetna, which was formerly called Inessa; and the original inhabitants of Catana, after a long period, got back their native city.

After these events the peoples who had been expelled from their own cities while Hieron was king, now that they had assistance in the struggle, returned to their fatherlands and expelled from their cities the men who had wrongfully seized for themselves the habitations of others; among these were inhabitants of Gela, Acragas, and Himera. In like manner Rhegians along with Zanclians expelled the sons of Anaxilas, who were ruling over them, and liberated their fatherlands. Later on Geloans, who had been the original settlers of Camarina, portioned that land out in allotments. And practically all the cities, being eager to make an end of the wars, came to a common decision, whereby they made terms with the mercenaries in their midst; they then received back the exiles and restored the cities to the original citizens, but to the mercenaries who because of the former tyrannical governments were in possession of the cities belonging to others, they gave permission to take with them their own goods and to settle one and all in Messenia. In this manner, then, an end was put to the civil wars and disorders which had prevailed throughout the cities of Sicily, and the cities, after driving out the forms of government which aliens had introduced, with almost no exceptions portioned out their lands in allotments among all their citizens.

## 11.86–87

[...] And after the enrolment of citizens which had taken place in the cities and the redistribution of the lands, since many had been added to the roll of citizens without plan and in a haphazard fashion, the cities were in an unhealthy state and falling back again into civil strife and disorders; and it was especially in Syracuse that this malady prevailed. For a man by the name of Tyndarides, a rash fellow full of effrontery, began by gathering about him many of the poor, and organizing them into an armed unit he proceeded to make of them a personal bodyguard ready for an attempt to set up a tyranny. But after this, when it was evident that he was grasping after supreme power, he was brought to trial and condemned to death. But while he was being led off to prison, the men upon whom he had lavished his favours rushed together and laid hands upon those who were arresting him. And in the confusion which arose throughout the city the most respectable citizens, who had organized themselves, seized the revolutionists and put them to death along with Tyndarides. And since this sort of thing kept happening time and again and there were men whose hearts were set on a tyranny, the people were led to imitate the Athenians and to establish a law very similar to the one they had passed on ostracism.

87. Now among the Athenians each citizen was required to write on a potsherd (*ostracon*) the name of the man who, in his opinion, was most able through his influence to tyrannize over his fellow citizens; but among the Syracusans the name of the most influential citizen had to be written on a olive leaf, and when the leaves were counted, the man who received the largest number of leaves had to go into exile for five years. For by this means they thought that they would humble the arrogance of the most powerful men in these two cities; for, speaking generally, they were not exacting from violators of the law a punishment for a crime committed, but were effecting a diminution of the influence and growing power of the men in question. Now while the Athenians called this kind of legislation ostracism, from the way it was done, the Syracusans used the name petalism. This law remained in force among the Athenians for a long time, but among the Syracusans it was soon repealed for the following reasons. Since the most influential men were being sent into exile, the most respectable citizens and such as had it in their power, by reason of their personal high character, to effect many reforms in the affairs of the commonwealth were taking no part in public affairs, but consistently remained in private life because of their fear of the law, attending to their personal fortunes and leaning towards a life of luxury; whereas it was the basest citizens and such as excelled in effrontery who were giving their attention to public affairs and inciting the masses to disorder and revolution. Consequently, since factional quarrels were again arising and the masses were turning to wrangling, the city fell back into continuous and serious disorders. For a multitude of demagogues and sycophants was arising, the youth were cultivating cleverness in oratory, and, in a word, many were exchanging the ancient and sober way of life for the ignoble pursuits; wealth was increasing because of the peace, but there was little if any concern for concord and honest conduct. As a result the Syracusans changed their minds and repealed the law of petalism, having used it only a short while. [...]

## NOTE

1   Deinomenes had four sons, Gelon, Hieron, Polyzelus, and Thrasybulus.

# Sicily, 478–431 BC

## *David Asheri*

[...] The liberation of Syracuse, like that of Acragas, had to await the death of her established tyrant and the revolt which his harsh successor provoked. When Hiero died in 467 his brother Thrasybulus seized power; Polyzalos must have been dead at that time. But Gelon had a son, next in line to the throne after Thrasybulus, who had to be awarded some governorship or command. His disappointment gave rise to a dynastic crisis. Wider discontent at Syracuse is ascribed to Thrasybulus' violent character and to his execution or exiling of many citizens in order to confiscate their property. At last the Syracusans revolted, chose their own leaders and seized the suburbs outside the walls of Achradina. Military aid, infantry, cavalry and even ships promptly arrived from the free cities of Acragas, Gela and Himera, as well as from pro-Punic Selinus and the Sicels. Basing himself on the fortified island of Ortygia and in the walled quarter of Achradina, Thrasybulus tried to resist with an army of mercenaries and a force of colonists from Aitna, but after his defeat on land and sea he was forced to leave with his garrison. He was given permission to retire to the friendly town of Epizephyrian Locri in southern Italy, there to spend the rest of his life as a private citizen (Diod. xi.67–8).

The end of tyranny at Syracuse precipitated the immediate dissolution of the Deinomenid epicracy [area of control] in eastern Sicily. Again, as in the case of Acragas, it was not out of the love of liberty for all that the nascent republic of Syracuse assisted in the break-up of its own dominions, but out of the imperative need for loyal allies in the fierce fight for its own liberty. A general autonomistic movement spread from city to city, calling for liberty (rather than "democracy"), repatriation of the deported or exiled "Old Citizens", enlistment of "New Citizens" to swell the popular ranks, and redistribution of land. This programme appears to be a restoration of the *status quo ante* rather than an innovative plan. At first, armed violence raged everywhere; the garrisons and governors found themselves besieged in their own quarters and acropolis by the rebellious citizenries. Later, a "Common Resolution" (*koinon dogma*) was endorsed by most cities, according to which the "Old Citizens" were entitled to return and partial rights were conferred upon veterans and immigrants who had been naturalized in their respective cities by the tyrants. The garrisons on active service were required to leave the cities and settle in the territory of Messana, the only city in Sicily still governed by tyrants (Diod. xi.72–3, 76).

Five autonomous, republican city states grew up within a few years on the ruins of the Syracusan epicracy: Syracuse itself, Catana, Naxus, Leontini and Camarina. All started new issues of coins, usually rejecting types associated with tyranny (with the exception of the Syracusan quadriga, which gradually lost its former political mean-

David Asheri, "Sicily, 478–431 BC," in *The Cambridge Ancient History*² vol. 5, eds. D. M. Lewis et al. (Cambridge: Cambridge University Press, 1992), 147–70, pp. 156–9, 165–8.

ing) and adopting new types with gods or local river-deities. The republic of Syracuse was left with her own city territory on the south eastern corner of the island and with her colonial outposts at Acrae and Casmenae. The Dorian colony of Aitna was attacked by a host of armed Sicels under the leadership of Ducetius [...] in co-operation with a republican army from Syracuse. The Aitnaeans were ejected, and the original Catanaeans came back from Leontini, where they had been confined since 476. Aitna again became Catana, a Chalcidian city; the territory was delimited anew, with the Sicels recovering their confiscated lands while the returning Catanaeans redistributed their own portion among themselves. Clearly, free Syracuse preferred an anti-Deinomenid Chalcidian–Sicel population on the banks of the Simeto to a Dorian base of potential followers of a new tyrant. The ejected Aitnaeans removed to Inessa, a Sicel township on the slopes of Etna west of Catana (it is variously located in the area of Civiti or Paternò), taking with them the bones of Founder Hiero from his desecrated tomb. At Inessa a new Aitna grew up near the Sicel township, and some form of coexistence had to be worked out by both communities, possibly more along the lines of the peaceful Chalcidian model than on the coercive Syracusan one. A coin of Aitna with the head of Selinus replacing the Syracusan quadriga on the obverse has been hesitantly attributed to the new Dorian settlement at Inessa.

Naxus too must have been restored by its original population returning from Leontini. At any rate, Thucydides mentions that the town existed in 425. A new urban plan, consisting of straight streets and long rectangular blocks with boundary stones at the crossroads, can plausibly be attributed to the resettlement at this time, since nothing about a Deinomenid foundation at Naxus is known from extant sources. Leontini, relieved at last of its surplus population of deportees, now looked forward to a new era of prosperity. On the southern coast, Camarina was soon restored. After standing deserted since Gelon deported the population to Syracuse in about 485, the deportees and their descendants came back to their former houses and lands. A number of additional colonists joined the resettlement, and two new quarters, unearthed by recent excavations, had to be erected to the east and west of the original town to house the enlarged population. In 456 (or 452) this "newly peopled seat" had already become a town that "nourishes the people" (Pindar's words), boasting of an Olympic victor of its own, the first since 528 BC.[1] After a period of twenty-five years without any coinage, Camarina now started minting silver *litrae*, showing on the reverse Athena, the chief goddess of the city (a temple of Athena is among the excavated remains). [...]

## Democracy and Culture at Syracuse and Acragas

The three decades following the fall of the tyrannies were crucial to Syracuse's constitutional and socio-economic development and its rise to the rank of a major hegemonic power in the West. After Thrasybulus and his garrison left Syracuse in 466, there was protracted strife between two classes of citizens, whom Diodorus (presumably following Timaeus) termed the "Old" and the "New". The "Old" were the victims of tyranny, excluded and dispossessed, mostly living in the suburbs outside the walls of Achradina, and some returning exiles. The "New" were the élite which had been created under tyranny – veteran soldiers, 7,000 of them still left in town, immigrants from the Peloponnese, wealthy people who had been deported to Syracuse from towns razed to the ground (such as Megara Hyblaea and Euboea) and could not be repatriated. The "New" had been installed by the tyrants in the walled quarters of Ortygia and Achradina and presumably assigned land in the countryside. The restoration of the *ancien régime* as conceived by the "Old" citizens implied a thorough reversal of the situation, including the exchange of quarters, properties and political rights, a programme evidently unacceptable to the "New". Entrenched in their respective quarters, "Old" and "New" citizens started a war of nerves and attrition that went on for years. In 463 an assembly of the "Old" deliberated on the establishment of "democracy" and a cult of Zeus the Liberator, with an annual festival of Liberty. They also voted to reserve all magistracies for themselves to the exclusion of the "New" citizens. A true civil war ensued, with blockades and attacks on land and sea. It was finally won by the "Old" in 461, thanks mainly to an élite corps of 600 *epilektoi*.[2] At this stage some compromise must have been made, the "Old" probably agreeing that the restoration of property be made by legal means and that the "New" be assigned other land and houses in compensation. In fact, Syracusan courts became so busy with claims to confiscated property that the belief that Greek forensic oratory was actually born of such trials was seriously credited in antiquity.

It was out of these changes that the new institutions of republican Syracuse – the General Assembly, the Council, the board of *strategoi* – took shape. Typical elements of radical democracy, such as sortition and payment for office, were never introduced at Syracuse, but a variant of Athenian ostracism, called *petalismos*, came into use for a short while, allegedly after a certain Tyndarides made an abortive attempt at tyranny in 454. Imperial ambitions were aroused along with the rise of democracy, as usually occurred in ancient maritime city states. In 453 two admirals, first Phayllus then Apelles, were sent with a fleet to the Tyrrhenian Sea to ravage the Etruscan coast and the islands of Elba and Corsica,[3] a reminder to all concerned that the new democracy was not loath to adopt Hiero's Tyrrhenian policy. Then, in 440, Ducetius' death gave Syracuse a golden opportunity to re-establish its epicracy on land. The next year the Syracusans were capable of building one hundred triremes, besides doubling their cavalry and increasing their infantry. Democratic Syracuse was rapidly becoming a major power in the West, as it had been under its great tyrants, an achievement that, at this point, did not even cost it very much, for Syracuse was now simply taking advantage of Etruscan decline, Sicel disorientation, and Carthaginian self-imposed isolation.

Under democracy, Syracuse was on the verge of becoming the greatest city state in the Greek world and a centre of Hellenic culture. With some 20,000 citizens and a total population of a quarter of a million, Syracuse was a "megalopolis" (Pindar's term) by fifth-century Greek standards, "in no way smaller than Athens" (as Thucydides put it), including a prosperous community of Phoenician merchants with vessels in port and houses in town, and a growing number of Etruscan and Sicel slaves. The four quarters of Syracuse – Ortygia on the island with its archaic temples, Achradina on the mainland opposite with its large and regular streets, Temenites outside the walls with its old theatre, probably built up under Hiero, and a fourth suburb, later named Tyche – were densely populated. The famous quarries north of the unwalled suburbs, on the still empty plateau of Epipolae, were in full use both for building stone and as prisons.

Summing up the general situation at Syracuse at mid-century, Diodorus writes that "a multitude of demagogues and sycophants was arising, the youth were cultivating cleverness in oratory, and, in a word, many were exchanging the ancient and sober way of life for the ignoble pursuits; wealth was increasing because of the peace, but there was little if any concern for concord and honest conduct".[4] In this moralistic vein later Greek historians perceived the changes from Deinomenid culture, with its ostentatious architecture, court poetry and the politically innocuous comedies of Epicharmus, to a democratic, written and more sophisticated culture. With the remarkable exception of the choral lyric, an import from mainland and Aegean Greece, and comic theatre, literature and science made their first appearance in Syracuse after the fall of its tyranny. The mime of Sophron gradually evolved from Epicharmus' comedy as a genuine creation of Doric Sicily. The art of persuasion and the theoretical study of rhetoric, traditionally "first invented" by Corax and Tisias of Syracuse, attained a high level of excellence thanks to the genius of Gorgias, a recognized master of his art before he visited Athens in 427 BC. Finally, in the field of historiography, Sicily did not lag far behind Ionia. Antiochus of Syracuse, a younger contemporary of Herodotus active in the third quarter of the fifth century, was the author of the first continuous *History of Sicily*, beginning with the mythical king Kokalos and ending with the year of the Congress of Gela (424/3 BC), and of a great treatise *On Italy*. Writing in Ionic, the dialect of historiography at that time, his wide interest lay in the history of the Greek as well as the non-Greek West. Yet this new written culture did not oust fine arts. It was the Syracusan engravers working at the mint under democracy who achieved an unsurpassed mastery of sculptural design. The best known example is the first issue of a bullion silver decadrachm, once wrongly identified with the gold "Damareteion" struck, according to Diodorus, immediately after the battle of Himera (see *CAH* IV[2] 775), but now connected by most numismatists with the final liberation of Syracuse in 461 BC.

Acragas, the second greatest city in Sicily, continued to be the major rival of Syracuse. Its new regime after 472/1 was at first an oligarchy of wealthy citizens. An Assembly of the "Thousand" was established and then abolished by Empedocles (by what authority we do not know) just three years after it had been set up. A less narrow oligarchy developed. Anecdotes about Empedocles, deriving in part from Timaeus, imply the functioning at his time of a Council and magistrates, the existence of factions, the plundering of public funds alongside the use of judicial means to prevent illegalities of any kind. But Acragas never became a "democracy" of the Syracusan, let alone the Athenian, type. [...]

## NOTES

1   Praxiteles of Mantinea, who calls himself "Syracusan and Camarinean" on an inscription from Olympia (Hill, *Sources*[2]), vaguely datable in the second quarter of the fifth century, was possibly an Arcadian who settled first at Syracuse under the Deinomenids and then joined the colony of Camarina. For a different, and widely accepted, view of this inscription, see Jeffery 1961, 160–1, 211.

2   Theories that this élite corps became later an oligarchic "council" or vigilante cabal (see especially Diod. XI.86.5 on Tyndarides, 454 BC.); a picked body of six hundred in summer 414 (Thuc. VI.96.3, 97.3); *epilektoi* under Hermocrates in 413 (Diod. XIII.11.4); oligarchic *synedrion* of Six Hundred in 317 (Diod. XIX.4.3, etc.) are largely unwarranted. For a battle between Syracusans and mercenaries in the (otherwise unknown) "plain of Glaukoi" (?) see *P. Oxy.* IV 665 (*FGrH* 557).

3   Whether Phayllus' name should be read on an inscription from Selinus (*SEG* XII 411) and identified with the Syracusan admiral is still a matter of dispute; see now Giuffrida Ientile 1983, 68–9 with n. 33.

4   XI.87.5 (tr. Oldfather).

## REFERENCES

Giuffrida Ientile, M. *La pirateria tirrenica. Momenti e fortuna* (Suppl. to *Kokalos* 6). Rome, 1983.

Hill, G. F. *Sources for Greek History Between the Persian and Peloponnesian Wars* (2nd edn ed. R. Meiggs and A. Andrewes). Oxford, 1951.

Jeffery, L. H. *The Local Scripts of Archaic Greece.* Oxford, 1961 (2nd edn ed. A. W. Johnston, Oxford, 1989).

# Revolution and Society in Greek Sicily and Southern Italy

## Shlomo Berger

[. . .] (43) Thrasybulus had replaced his brother, Hieron, as tyrant in 467. His policies were harsh: he executed many citizens, banished others (confiscating their property) and employed a growing army of mercenaries against the alienated citizenry.

As Thrasybulus rose to power,[1] he also had to come to terms with problems created during the reigns of previous tyrants: the enfranchisement of foreigners in general and mercenaries in particular, relations with the "empire" in Sicily and the overthrow of the tyranny in Acragas in 472/1, which had been preceded by a war between the cities.[2] His reliance on mercenaries generated civic opposition, which included aristocrats who had until then supported the tyranny. In due course a stasis [factional conflict] broke out.[3] The tyrant attempted to quell the struggle but his efforts were rebuffed by an angry crowd and he was forced to take refuge in his citadel in Ortygia. The two opposing sides sought all possible aid. Thrasybulus called on his Sicilian allies as well as mercenaries who had been settled by Hieron in Catane. The Syracusans,

Shlomo Berger, *Revolution and Society in Greek Sicily and Southern Italy* (Stuttgart: Franz Steiner Verlag, 1992), pp. 36–40.

who controlled the other neighborhoods in the city, courted the Geloans, Acragan-tines, Selinuntines and the Himeraeians. In addition, they sent emissaries to Sicel towns in the hinterland to seek aid, which they in fact received. Thus, a localized stasis developed into a broad struggle against tyranny. In the ensuing battle, Thrasybulus had to admit defeat, but was permitted to leave the city with his mercenaries for Locri on the Italian mainland.

Aristotle mentions, furthermore, that the tyrant's own family participated in the coup, evincing their displeasure with Thrasybulus who had corrupted Hieron's son, the legitimate heir, in order to seize power for himself. After his removal, it was decided to eliminate tyranny altogether.

The interference of other Sicilians in the affair attests to a movement away from tyranny on the island. This movement eventually became more powerful than the network of intermarriages among the tyrants' dynasties.[4] The cooperation of the Sicels is of particular importance. Their willingness to assist marks the beginning of a local movement of Sicels under the leadership of Ducetius.[5]

The tactical component of the stasis is also of interest. The tyrant was entrenched in Ortygia from which he ruled the city; the citizens were in control of other parts of the city. It was very difficult to penetrate the fortified citadel, but from within it the tyrant could easily influence the life of the Syracusan citizens. This explains the willingness of the citizens to allow Thrasybulus to pass freely to Italy,[6] a pattern which re-emerges in local history.

The new regime was democratic and a new cult to Zeus Eleutherios, Zeus the Liberator, was established. Diodorus styles it a democracy, although Aristotle defines it as a *politeia* ["polity"] (*Pol.* 1304a27). In any case, the basic character of the regime was considered anti-tyrannical. The act of establishing a democracy, however, initi-ated a contest over the establishment of the new arrangements in the city, rather than mitigating their difficulties.

(44) Although the chronology[7] is not clear it may be supposed that the democracy was established over the course of several years (466–461).[8] After the festivities were over, the Syracusan assembly convened to discuss the nature of the new body-politic and the public offices. It was decided to give access to public office only to "old citizens". "New citizens", enrolled under Gelon and Hieron, were considered un-worthy and their loyalty to Syracuse was questioned. It is not surprising that the "new citizens" revolted; many were enfranchised mercenaries and they led the struggle against the "old citizens". They occupied the citadel, Ortygia, and neighboring Achradina. In contrast to Thrasybulus, however, they had no external support, and were forced to surrender to the new civic body. An elite corps – the "Six Hundred" – won praise for the victory, as well as a large sum of money. The same technique employed by both Thrasybulus and the mercenaries led to different consequences.

Events also show that the overthrow of the tyranny had a social as well as a political context which engendered a response to the "social revolution" forced by the Deinomenids.[9] The basic dichotomy lay between the "old" and "new" citizens. This is not to say that individually they were homogeneous groups. The "old" comprised all citizens before Gelon's rise to power. It was a bizarre coalition of ex-Gamoroi [landowner],[10] demos and ex-Kyllirioi who fought against the "new" citizens which included enfranchised aristocrats from Euboea, Megara Hyblaea and Camarina, as well as enfranchised mercenaries, some of whom were non-Greek.

The express aim of the "old citizens" to reduce the civic rights of the "new" was in fundamental contradiction to the principles of a democratic regime and serves to illustrate the extent of aristocratic influence in the post-tyrannical polis. In fact, the definition of "old" citizens smacks of aristocracy itself. It is also possible that the "old" wanted to expel the "new" from the city altogether but, fearing the strength of the ex-mercenaries, they decided to behave more moderately. The struggle which ensued after the assembly's decision attests to the ex-mercenaries' power.[11]

The conflict and decisions made in Syracuse are all connected with the *Koinon Dogma* or "General Settlement" of the Greek cities on the island in 461. The agreement called for the banishment of all mercenaries from the cities, their relocation in Messana, the recall of all exiled "old" citizens, and the return of all their property. The agreement was not implemented easily due to conflicting interests which existed in nearly every city, and in this respect Syracuse was no exception.

(45) In 454/3[12] a "violent and insolent" citizen named Tyndarides organized many of the local poor, gave them money and employed them as his personal guards in an effort to become tyrant. After his plot was uncovered, he was put on trial and sentenced to death. While he was imprisoned, the poor attacked his guards and in the midst of the turmoil, the *chariestatoi*, the "best of the citizens", who appeared on the scene to defend the guards, slew Tyndarides as well as his bodyguards.[13]

This event is also related to the results of the "General Settlement". Many people who were enrolled in the registers of citizens (*politographia*) demanded land or other property, but the rights of some claims were disputed.[14] Tyndarides made overtures to the dissatisfied (referred to in Diodorus as "the poor") while the aristocracy, owners of the property, stood in opposition. The rift between the groups resulted in the introduction of *petalismos*, a short-lived local brand of ostracism,[15] in which ballots were drawn up on olive leaves; exile was for five years. The aristocracy decided to retire from public life so as not to expose themselves to the threat of exile. Consequently, according to Diodorus, the city was mismanaged and the demos had to repeal the law and recall the aristocracy. This case demonstrates the pervasive power of the aristocracy and its effect on the "democratic" regime in Syracuse. Although democratic institutions probably were introduced, they were nevertheless overrun by aristocratic influence.

After these events there is a lapse in the accounts of staseis in Syracuse for a forty year period. During this time Syracuse continued to expand its dominion over new areas of Sicily, combating Greeks and Sicels alike; democratic Syracuse adopted the policies of Deinomenid Syracuse. Syracuse eventually achieved pre-eminence among the Greeks in the West.[16] Moreover, the war forced upon her by the Athenians exhibited her standing among the Greeks in general. Polyaenus describes a slave revolt in the city during the Athenian expedition which is not mentioned by Thucydides. In any case, it is doubtful whether it had any connection with the civic body and the citizens. Hermocrates is again portrayed as the great savior of the city.[17]

(46) The triumph over the Athenians, however, resulted in stasis in the city. Aristotle recounts that the demos, who had contributed to the victory, demanded a share in the governance of the polis. It was they who had succeeded in transforming the regime from a *politeia* to a democracy.[18] Diodorus relates how Diocles, leader of the demos, persuaded them to alter the constitution; *nomothetai* were to be elected,

charged with the composition of a new constitution, and public offices were to be filled by lot. The new regime became a "radical" democracy.[19]

Hermocrates, the war hero, had been sent to assist the Spartans in the Aegean.[20] The local aristocracy[21] which appeared euphoric, did not notice that a large portion of the demos had been politicized while serving in the military. At the end of the war, they demanded a reward. Election by lot, because of its immediate effects, must have wounded the aristocracy severely. Little is known about other enactments,[22] but it can be assumed that they followed the Athenian model,[23] even though Athens itself was on its way to an oligarchic coup. [...]

## NOTES

1   Arist. *Pol.* 1315b38; Thrasybulus ruled for eleven months altogether. Thus the stasis broke out in 466/5 (Diod. 11.67.1). See also the discussion in Barrett (1973) 29–31.
2   Compare with events in Acragas, 472/1.
3   Arist. *Pol.* 1312b9; Diod. 11.67.5–68.7.
4   Finley (1979) 47.
5   On the Sicels in the Syracusan *chora*: Di Vita (1956); Adamesteanu (1962).
6   Hüttl (1929) 65f.
7   Diodorus dates the beginning of the events to 463 (11.71.1) and their conclusion to 461 (11.75.1). From his narrative, however, we may infer that the events took place at a former date, a short while after the overthrow of the tyranny in 466. In fact, one can detect a change in the sources he used between 11.72.1 and 72.2, and this may explain the change of the dates as well. If we date the events to 466 or immediately afterwards, there is too long a gap before concluding the stasis in 461. But it is hopeless to redate the events; exact Sicilian datings for the period in Diodorus are not available. Any reader can detect the pattern of subsuming events in Sicily from several years within a given year, as in the years 466/5, 463, 461, 459/8, 454/3. As to the sixties, one should note also that prolonged wars ensued between Greeks and local non-Greeks: *FGrH* 577 F1. See also Barrett (1973) 30–1.
8   Sources: Arist. *Pol.* 1303a–b2; Diod. 11.72.2–73, 76.1–2.
9   Diod. 11.86.3; see also Arist. F 137R; Strabo 6.17.8.
10  Wentker (1956) 51–3, claims that the Gamoroi returned to power. Rizzo (1970) ch. 1, suggests the elite corps (the "Six Hundred") was the nucleus of the new aristocracy, the *chariestatoi.* See also Lintott (1982) 189–90.
11  Diodorus mentions seven thousand mercenaries, who remained in the city after the coup. Together with the rest of the civic population it must have been one of the largest cities of the Greek world at that time. Compare with the figures in Ruschenbusch (1979) 1–17.
12  The chronological problem discussed in n. 7, is relevant to this case as well. It is likely that the events mentioned under 454/3 were in fact spread over several years. However, the date of the stasis itself can be fixed to this particular year.
13  Diod. 11.86.4–5.
14  Arist. F 137R; Pausanias 6.17.8; Asheri (1980) 155.
15  Diod. 11.87; see also Hesychios s.v. *Petalismos*; Pollux 8.19; Berve (1967) 188–9; Berger (1989).
16  See Finley (1979) 58–74; Asheri, *CAH* V² (1992).
17  Polyaenus 1.43.1.

18 Arist. *Pol.* 1304a27.

19 Diod. 13.35; on Diocles, Manni (1979) 220–30.

20 Thuc. 8.26.1; on Hermocrates: *FGrH* 566 F102a; Westlake (1958); Grosso (1966); Hinrichs (1981); Sordi (1981).

21 The growth in aristocratic power can be shown in the reduction in the number of generals from fifteen to three during the Athenian expedition: Thuc. 6.72.9–73.1–2. See also Lintott (1982) 189–90.

22 Two more reforms are attached to Diocles' new regime: one concerned the transfer from generals to archons of the right to preside over an assembly. It is based on a difference between Thuc. 6.41.1 (who says that the generals presided over the assembly) and Diod. 13.92 (which recounts the archons who fined Dionysius the Elder for illegal proposals in 406). See Hüttl (1929) 86. The second reform was the increase of the number of generals from three to ten. Thucydides (n.21) mentions the reduction to three generals; Plat. *Ep.* 8.354d, mentions the dismissal of ten generals just before Dionysius' rise to power. See Hüttl (1929) 77. We may also conclude, in the same way, that the generals were still elected and not selected by lot, as can be deduced from Diod. 13.11.5. All these examples are nevertheless circumstantial.

23 See Berger (1989).

## REFERENCES

Adamesteanu, D. (1962): "L'ellenizzazione della Sicilia ed il momento di Ducezio", *Kokalos* 8, 167–198.

Asheri, D. (1980): "Rimpatrio di esuli e ridistribuzione di terre nelle città siciliote ca. 466–461 a.C.", in *Philias Charin. Studies in Honor of E. Manni.* Rome 1, 143–158.

Asheri, D. (1992): "Sicily, 478–431 BC", *CAH* V², eds. D. M. Lewis et al. Cambridge.

Barrett, W. S. (1973): "Pindar's Twelfth *Olympian* and the Fall of the Deinomenidai", *JHS* 93, 23–35.

Berger, S. (1989): "Democracy in the Greek West and the Athenian Example", *Hermes* 117, 303–314.

Berve, H. (1967): *Die Tyrannis bei den Griechen.* Munich.

Finley, M. I. (1979): *Ancient Sicily.* London.

Grosso, F. (1966): "Ermocrate di Siracusa", *Kokalos* 12, 102–143.

Hinrichs, F. T. (1981): "Hermokrates bei Thukydides", *Hermes* 109, 46–59.

Hüttl, W. (1929): *Verfassungsgeschichte von Syrakus.* Prague.

Lintott, A. (1982): *Violence, Civil Strife and Revolution in the Classical City.* London.

Manni, E. (1979): "Diocle di Siracusa fra Ermocrate e Dionisio", *Kokalos* 25, 220–231.

Rizzo, F. R. (1970): *La republica di Siracusa nel momento di Dudezio.* Palermo.

Ruschenbusch, E. (1979): *Untersuchungen zu Staat und Politik in Griechenland vom 7.–4. Jh. v. Chr.* Bamberg.

Sordi, M. (1981): "Ermocrate di Siracusa, demagogo e tiranno mancato", *Scritti in onore di F. Grosso.* Rome, 595–600.

Vita, A. di (1956): "La penetrazione siracusana nella Sicilia sudorientale alla luce delle più recenti scoperte archeologiche", *Kokalos* 2, 177–205.

Wentker, H. (1956): *Sizilien und Athen.* Heidelberg.

Westlake, H. D. (1958): "Hermocrates the Syracusan", in (1969): *Essays on the Greek Historians and Greek History.* Manchester, 174–202.

# Democracy in Syracuse, 466–412 BC

## Eric W. Robinson

Scholars have reached conflicting conclusions about the nature of the Syracusan constitution in the years between 466 and 412 BC. Some consider that a democracy existed, while others would deny that title. Even those who accept the ancient testimony for *demokratia* sometimes assert that the popular government was of a moderate or even aristocratic kind, and was certainly not as radical as the contemporary Athenian variety.

In terms of the history of ancient democracy, this issue is an important one to settle. Syracuse is one of the few classical poleis other than Athens both to have a fair amount of narrative extant about its political history and to have been labeled a *demokratia*. If modern scholars are to understand the phenomenon of ancient democracy beyond the well-known Athenian example, then it is essential to clarify how places like Syracuse fit into the picture.

The present study will examine the case of Syracusan democracy in the second half of the fifth century from two different perspectives. First we will look at the direct constitutional evidence, statements by ancient historians and others that one constitution or other came into being by revolution or legislation. Scholars have naturally looked primarily to this kind of testimony to sort out the issue. The evidence is not unequivocal: while it seems to support the contention that democracy held sway, there are elements which prompt some commentators to question the popular nature of the government. That Syracuse possessed a vigorous *demokratia* at this time emerges most clearly only after considering more indirect evidence as well, to include the attitude displayed by the ruling *demos*, demagoguery in the assembly, and the fostering of political rhetoric. Exploration of these topics suggests the existence of a vibrant democratic ideology comparable in some ways to that of fifth- and fourth-century Athens.

Before examining the testimony, let us briefly review the definition of democracy. Among historians, philosophers, and other authors of fifth- and fourth-century Greece there seems to have been a rough consensus about the character of *demokratia*. Fundamentally, in the governing of the state the *demos* must be sovereign (*kyrios*, Aristotle *Pol.* 1278b8–13). This sovereignty was most directly accomplished through the ruling assembly which met to legislate and to decide important matters of state policy. The assembly was composed of all the citizens, who included all or most of the freeborn native males within the community. Property qualifications for participation in the assembly were minimal or nonexistent, though more substantial ones could obtain for higher magistracies. Magistrates, whether elected or allotted, served for brief terms and were held accountable to the *demos*. Ostracism or similar measures enabling a voting majority to temporarily banish threatening individuals were some-

Eric W. Robinson, "Democracy in Syracuse, 466–412 BC," *Harvard Studies in Classical Philology* 100 (2000), pp. 189–205.

times enacted, as was state pay for service on juries or other public bodies, though such practices were far from universal in democracies. Freedom (*eleutheria*) and equality were motivating ideals of the body politic whatever the particular institutions.[1]

## Constitutional Testimony

The most important accounts concerning the new Syracusan government of 466[2] come in Diodorus' *Bibliotheke*, Aristotle's *Politics*, and Thucydides' history. At 11.67–68 Diodorus, who likely drew on Timaeus for this portion of his narrative,[3] states that when the Deinomenid tyrant Thrasybulus came to power he showed himself to be an even crueler ruler than his brother Hieron had been, murdering and exiling many Syracusans while bringing in numerous mercenaries to maintain his control. The citizens soon banded together to oust him: the entire polis was united in the effort, and Thrasybulus was forced to gather an army of allies and mercenaries to fight the Syracusans. He seized parts of the city and waged war until, defeated in battles on land and sea, he negotiated his withdrawal to Locri. Diodorus states that from this time the city enjoyed peace and prosperity and "guarded its democracy for almost sixty years, until the tyranny of Dionysius" (11.68.6).

At this point the Syracusans made a number of key decisions. They liberated and restored democracies to other Sicilian cities which had also been under tyranny (11.68.5). They also held an assembly meeting (*ekklesia*) in Syracuse at which the citizens took counsel about their own democracy (11.72). Ceremonial matters were voted on, including the commissioning of a colossal statue to Zeus Eleutherios (the Liberator) and the institution of annual games and sacrifices in honor of Eleutheria.[4] The assembly also decided to restrict office-holding to those who had been citizens before the Deinomenid tyranny – for during his reign Gelon had made 10,000 foreign mercenaries citizens, and the original Syracusans did not trust the 7000 or so mercenary-citizens who were still around (11.72.3). The denial of access to office sparked a nasty rebellion; the foreigners (*xenoi*, as Diodorus calls them) were defeated only after a difficult fight.[5]

Diodorus describes another significant episode for the new democracy, this in his account for the year 454 (11.86–87). After a man named Tyndarides attempted a coup, and other would-be tyrants threatened now and again, the Syracusans instituted the practice of petalism, a sort of Syracusan ostracism. The goal was to protect against tyranny by countering the presumption and influence of the most powerful.[6] Leaders could now be exiled by a simple popular vote; the exile was for a period of five years (instead of Athens' ten), and votes were recorded on olive leaves rather than ostraka. However, after a short period of time the Syracusans discontinued the practice. According to Diodorus, the best and most prominent men were avoiding public affairs for fear of petalism, leaving matters in the hands of less capable, troublesome leaders, which resulted in factional conflict (*stasis*). So the Syracusans repealed the law.[7] (The Athenians eventually stopped their practice as well, though only after several decades of occasional use.)

Aristotle in the *Politics* seems to confirm Diodorus' assertion of democratic revolution in 466: at 1316a32–33 the philosopher lists the end of the tyranny of Gelon's family in Syracuse as an example of transition from tyranny to *demokratia*.[8] But this testimony is confused by his assertion at 1304a27–29 that after the victory over the Athenians in 413, a triumphant Syracusan *demos* changed the government from a *politeia* to a *demokratia*.[9] This assertion implies that the government down to 413 had been a *politeia* or polity, a system which the philosopher says mixes oligarchic and democratic elements (*Pol.* 1293b33–34). Aristotle certainly seems to contradict himself with these statements – did he consider Syracuse a polity or a democracy? One cannot get around the problem by supposing that sometime between 466 and 413 there was another constitutional revolution, omitted in all our sources, in which the post-Deinomenid democracy became a polity. There is simply no evidence for this; moreover, Thucydides, our only contemporary source for these events, clearly identifies Syracuse as a *demokratia* during Athens' Sicilian expedition of 415–413.[10] This testimony is crucial. On the one hand, it rules out a shadowy prior revolution from *demokratia* to *politeia* (unless we want to imagine a *second* unattested revolution back to *demokratia* before 415), thus retaining the contradiction in Aristotle. On the other hand, and more importantly, it offers powerful evidence that Syracuse was indeed democratic during the period claimed by Diodorus.

## Interpretations

It is perhaps surprising, then, that a number of scholars confidently conclude from the testimony described above that the Syracusan state was not democratic after the fall of the Deinomenid tyranny, at least not until the reforms of Diocles many decades later in 412. Wentker in his 1956 book *Sizilien und Athen* asserted that a polity was installed, one dominated by wealthy landowners. Despite a scathing rebuttal by Brunt in a review of Wentker's book, others have since voiced similar interpretations. Lintott, for example, claims that a "broad oligarchy" took over affairs after the tyrants fell, with an aristocratic elite retaining substantial control thereafter. Caven makes similar statements. And in a recent book on Syracusan imperialism and government, Consolo Langher maintains that power was in the hands of the knightly and hoplite classes: polity, not full democracy, held sway in Syracuse after the revolution.[11] At least one non-classicist has used such views to fuel sweeping conclusions: Spencer Weart declares in his new book *Never at War* that no well-established democracy, ancient or modern, has *ever* made war on another one. He can make this startling argument only because of the occasionally voiced notion that Syracuse, before and during the time of its war with Athens, was not really a democracy.[12]

To reach such conclusions scholars primarily rely upon Aristotle's passage stating that Syracuse went from polity to democracy in 412. No other direct evidence is available. But as we have seen, Aristotle compromises his statement by later describing the revolution against Thrasybulus as resulting precisely in democracy. The contradiction renders his testimony a dubious basis for assertions of an undemocratic Syracuse, while Diodorus' and Thucydides' statements that *demokratia* existed are unambiguous. If but one of the Aristotle passages is to be plucked out and given credence, it ought to be the one confirmed by the other sources.

Though the *Politics* does not lack for contradictions within its pages, it might be possible to save Aristotle in this instance to the following degree: in the *Politics* and the *Nicomachean Ethics* when comparing correct (*orthai*) and deviant (*parekbaseis*) forms of constitutions, he refers to *politeia* and *demokratia* as counterparts, the good and bad versions of rule by the mass (*plethos*) of the citizens.[13] Perhaps in using *politeia* at *Pol.* 1304a27–29 Aristotle merely meant that in 412 the legislation pushed through by the demagogue Diocles[14] turned a relatively responsible popular government into an irresponsible one – not that it became popular for the first time. Such a reading would elide the apparent contradiction and accord more neatly with the other sources.[15] Furthermore, Aristotle's use of *politeia* in this sense could have been contextually determined: since Diocles had convinced the people to adopt another trademark democratic institution, sortition for officials, Aristotle naturally labeled the post-412 government *demokratia*. He then needed, however, another term to describe the earlier democracy. In the philosopher's vocabulary of constitutional types, *politeia* came the closest.

Another modern scholar analyzing post-Deinomenid Syracuse takes a somewhat more careful path than the commentators mentioned above. Berger does not deny the title democracy to the Syracusan government, but contends that aristocratic elements remained highly influential. This conclusion, while still open to debate, at least does not fly in the face of the majority of the testimony. Berger points to two incidents from the period as particularly revealing: the *demos'* denial of full participation to the mercenary-citizens of Gelon, and the brief duration of petalism at Syracuse. These events Berger declares to be fundamentally undemocratic and to demonstrate the "pervasive power of the aristocracy."[16] Regarding the first incident, one might point out that there is nothing inherently undemocratic about restricting citizenship: famous democracies ancient and modern have done it frequently. The United States, although priding itself on its immigrant heritage, has at times placed the severest limitations on which people from which countries might immigrate or be naturalized (consider the Chinese Exclusion Act of 1882, enforced well into the twentieth century); and in the great Athenian democracy the very restrictive Periclean law of 451/450 tightly controlled access to citizenship.[17] Moreover, the original Syracusan citizens had good reason to be suspicious of foreign mercenaries brought into the city for the purpose of assuring a tyrant's power over them – why should the newly empowered *demos* respect such citizenship? That the people refused to do so should not be interpreted as the mark of political elitism. Secondly, regarding the duration of petalism, the fact that such a forceful populist tool was employed at all is a strong indicator of thorough-going democracy, even if after a time the citizens discontinued its use. Aristocratic power could not have been as dominant as Berger supposes for such a popular weapon to have been enacted and used with terrific effect against the elite of the city.

In sum, the *prima facie* case for the existence of democracy in Syracuse from 466–412 is more formidable than some commentators are willing to believe, and the available ancient testimony hardly seems to warrant reading aristocracy into the picture. However, one must concede that Aristotle's inconsistency opens the door for speculation about its nature, and the direct constitutional testimony is sparse enough to leave room for debate. Let us consider, then, other evidence which is not so much constitutional as ideological. Through more than one study Josiah Ober has established that a coherent popular ideology existed in Athens during its democracy, an ideology which successfully challenged the aristocratic values of the elites.[18] It is possible to identify a similar ideology at work in Syracuse, albeit from a much smaller store of available evidence. Peripheral passages not often taken into account show the Syracusan *demos* behaving in archetypically "democratic" ways between 466 and 412, bolstering the case for a radically popular government.

## Generals, Demagogues, and the Use of Rhetoric

One of the reasons Diodorus gives for the enacting of petalism in Syracuse was to check the pride of the powerful ( . . . ταπεινώσειν τὰ φρονήματα τῶν πλεῖστον ἰσχυόντων ἐν ταῖς πατρίσι, 11.87.2). Another sign of a populist sentiment to bring the mighty low can be seen in the pattern of arbitrary and/or harsh punishment of generals which emerges in this period. Throughout antiquity, of course, states of varying governments have at times accused failed generals of malfeasance; nevertheless, democracies seem to have been particularly enamored of this activity,[19] and Syracuse in our period shows a healthy number of incidents relative to the available testimony. Diodorus records for the year 453 that a man named Phayllus was elected navarch to lead an expedition against Tyrrhenian pirates. He took his forces as far as an island in the enemy sphere and ravaged it but did not seem to do anything else of significance. Upon his return, the citizens (*hoi Syrakosioi*) convicted him of treachery and sent him into exile. A replacement was selected, who, not surprisingly, campaigned against the pirates much more aggressively (11.88). Though Diodorus accepts the verdict of the people, briefly stating that Phayllus did secretly (*lathrai*) take a bribe from the enemy, one cannot help wonder how he or his source knew the truth of the matter. Was clear proof of the "secret" bribery at hand, or was this just a case of public frustration with a dilatory commander inspiring charges from opponents? Two years later another unsuccessful general suffered the wrath of the people. Bolkon, acting in cooperation with allied forces, attempted to come to the aid of a city besieged by Ducetius and the Sicels. Bolkon was defeated and driven out of his camp by the enemy; with the onset of winter, he withdrew homeward as did his opponent. Once again the Syracusans read foul play into events: the general was accused of secretly acting in concert with Ducetius, convicted of treason – and executed. (Diodorus makes no comment as to the truth of the charges this time.) As one might expect, the next summer Bolkon's successor, acting under clear orders to take the war to Ducetius, attacked straightaway (11.91).[20] Finally, Thucydides reports a similar episode. In 414, during the early stages of the Athenian siege against the city, the Syracusans sustained a number of defeats. They could not match the Athenian ground or sea forces, lost important skirmishes for control of the territory around the city, and seemed unable to stop the progress of the Athenian siege works (6.96–102). Their generals soon came under fire and were stripped of their office; new ones were elected. The reasoning, reported by Thucydides, is telling: the Syracusans considered that their recent woes resulted from the generals' bad luck *or* from their treachery ( . . ὡς ἢ δυστυχίᾳ ἢ προδοσίᾳ τῇ ἐκείνων βλαπτόμενοι . . . , 6.103.4). Apparently it was unclear which was the cause, or the cause simply did not matter. The people were upset at the results of the campaign and took it out on the generals.[21]

Syracuse's harsh or vengeful behavior toward its generals does not in itself prove the existence of democracy, but it is suggestive of a populist attitude very much in line with the ancient stereotype – and sometimes the reality – of *demokratia*. Critics of democracy such as the "Old Oligarch" in his *Constitution of the Athenians* and Aristotle in the *Politics* take it as an established fact that in democracy the poor majority rule in their own interest and against the interest of the aristocrats. Elites suffer in public arenas like the courts, where (lower) class interest overwhelms justice; their political influence is often eclipsed by demagogues; and the assembled people blame leaders personally for failures of state policy.[22] To modern, democratically inclined ears this sort of whining from aristocratic circles may not arouse the intended sympathy. Nevertheless, occasions of victimization matching the accusations do occur. Consider the Old Oligarch's complaint, "If anything bad results from a decision taken by the *demos*, the *demos* charges that a few men acting against them corrupted things."[23] This allegation matches what we have seen happening in Syracuse, where unsuccessful generals were not merely disregarded but were assumed to have committed treason and were punished on that basis. Democratic Athens, the target of the Old Oligarch's observations, also provides plentiful examples of generals finding themselves on trial or in flight from an angry *demos* after military debacles. Thucydides himself, forced into exile after the fall of Amphipolis, makes an obvious case. Even more notable is Nicias' dread of slanderous political attack should he dare to give up the siege of Syracuse in 413 – indeed, what Nicias fears most of all is the accusation that he was bribed to betray his men and withdraw.[24] The most infamous Athenian example comes with the actual execution, decreed by an overwrought assembly, of the generals in command at the battle of the Arginusae Islands in 406.[25] The Athenians later recognized the error of their rash act, but of course could not put things right. One can only conclude that military leaders at Athens and Syracuse, usually members of the elite classes, served the demos at some personal risk: glory and popular influence could be theirs with success, but failure not uncommonly brought angry accusations of betrayal followed by dismissal, exile, or even execution. Ancient critics saw this as class-based injustice and – more importantly for our purposes – typical of democracy.

High-handed treatment of generals was not an anomalous populist feature within the broader picture of Syracusan politics. One finds further indications of typical democratic behavior in emotional or rash decision-making in the public assembly.[26] Some of the punitive actions already discussed resulted from demotic over-excitement, and other reports are worth nothing, most particularly those indicating loud and boisterous *ekklesia* meetings at Syracuse. Diodorus describes a meeting that took place just after the final defeat of the Athenians in which a popular demagogue spoke in favor of harsh punishment for captured Athenians. The proposal was well received; in fact, when Hermokrates took the floor and began to speak in opposition, "the *demos* made an uproar (*thorubountos*) and cut off his speech." The multitude only quieted itself down and allowed another person to present his views because it expected a more congenial opinion from him.[27] After listening to all the speeches the crowd (*to plethos*) approved the severe punishments which the first demagogue had recommended (13.33). Plutarch also mentions this event, emphasizing the immoderate tumult and insolence (*hubris*) of the crowd (*Nic.* 28). We might imagine similar behavior at another *ekklesia* from a couple of years earlier.

Thucydides in a brief account informs us that the Athenians, having arrived in Sicily, did not invade at once but kept their distance. This delay led the Syracusans to "despise their foe and order their generals to lead them out against" the enemy, "as the rabble (*ochlos*) tends to do when swelled with confidence" (6.63.2). Of course, marching out for battle played into Athenian hands and resulted in a major defeat. The use of *ochlos* here recalls Alcibiades' earlier sweeping characterization of the Sicilian population (surely aimed at the Syracusans most of all) as a mixed collection of mobs (*ochloi*) prone to disorder and disunity (Thuc. 6.17).[28]

The reported activities of demagogues at Syracuse further suggest a vibrant democracy, not only because they accord with Aristotle's comments on the subject (*Politics* 1292a4–30), but also because potent demagoguery can exist only if the mass of ordinary people to whom demagogues make their appeals wield real power in the state. Diodorus says that starting in the 450s when petalism was employed, there arose a multitude of demagogues and sykophants (*demagogon plethos kai sukophanton*), and the young began to practice slick oratory (*logou deinotes*) (11.87). We have seen one case already of demagogues at work among the people in the debate over Athenian prisoners reported in Diodorus and Plutarch. There are other notable instances, including the inspiring of new popular legislation in 412. Diodorus describes Diocles, the prime mover, as a demagogue who "persuaded the *demos*" to make the reforms.[29] Then there was the famous assembly debate of 415, just before the Athenian expedition, featuring Hermocrates and a very shrill *prostates tou demou*, Athenagoras. The latter's speech, as reported by Thucydides (6.35–40), is remarkable for its fierce defense of popular rule and its vision of young oligarchic revolutionaries lurking in the shadows, waiting for an excuse to seize power. But most of all what strikes the reader is the speech's colossal wrong-headedness: Thucydides locates it, with its denial of a coming Athenian attack, right after his description of preparations for the very attack. The speech inevitably strikes the reader as a blatant piece of demagoguery, a rant which spews groundless accusations and potentially endangers the state. It may be that Thucydides intended this episode as a commentary on the (mal)functioning of the democracy at Athens, and various theories have been proposed about which Syracusan speaker was meant to mirror whom at Athens.[30] But unless one is willing to take the extreme step of claiming Thucydides invented the entire incident – particularly unlikely given Thucydides' obvious interest in and knowledge of Sicilian affairs – the debate adds further color to the picture presented in Diodorus of a Syracusan politics aflame with populist rhetoric and demagogic appeals.

That political rhetoric should be widely practiced in a democracy is natural, for sovereign assemblies and popular courts provide numerous occasions for its use. It was certainly a fixture in fifth- and fourth-century Athens, which became a center for sophistic and rhetorical training. But according to the ancient writers, Athens was not the first home of political oratory. In fact, it was generally agreed that the art of rhetoric arose in *Syracuse* at precisely the time under discussion. The sources are late but quite clear. Late antique rhetorical introductions called *Prolegomena* explain that a man named Corax invented rhetoric to help gain control over a disorderly *demos* after the fall of the Deinomenid tyranny. "Corax, having demonstrated the works of rhetoric, was able to persuade the Syracusan *demos*."[31] Some of these traditions suggest that Corax made his mark in the assembly; others say his activity focused on the courtroom. But all agree that the transition to democracy enabled, or indeed necessitated, the development of such arts. Corax spread his knowledge to students, including a certain Tisias, famous for initiating a lawsuit against his teacher and also authoring what may have been the first treatise devoted to rhetoric.[32]

Recent commentators have questioned the veracity of these traditions in terms of details about the earliest rhetoricians and the content of their works. One scholar, Thomas Cole, argues that the late traditions attributed theoretical advances to Tisias and Corax simply because it was assumed Aristotle and other commentators *must* have been building on previous masters; in all likelihood the Syracusans' works were not nearly so extensive or fundamental. Cole even suggests that Corax and Tisias might have been the same person.[33] The state of the evidence makes such assertions difficult to prove: nothing directly contradicts the late testimonia, but neither is there any corroboration beyond the most elementary facts. However, for our purposes questions about precisely which theories Tisias and Corax developed and with what influence, or even whether they were one or two people, are not important. No one has questioned their existence in and association with Syracuse, nor is there any reason to do so. That the ancient traditions place the pioneers of rhetorical theory in Syracuse (whatever the content of their treatises or their actual impact on later theorists) and tie their activities to the democracy developing there remains very significant.

## Conclusion

Democracy certainly existed in Syracuse from 466 until Dionysius' rise to power in 406. The evidence presented above shows that the *demos* not only controlled the state – choosing and controlling their leaders, passing and revoking laws, and deciding the highest matters of state policy – but did so in a willful manner consistent with a deeply-rooted populist ideology, one fitting the criticisms of aristocratic detractors of democracy. The people often treated their generals harshly or arbitrarily, seeing betrayal in every dilatory move or military setback; they let their passions spill over in raucous public assemblies, sometimes to the detriment of good policy; they raised to prominence demagogues whose influence depended on their oratorical gifts or the fears they could stir up about oligarchic enemies of democracy; and in doing all this they inspired the first works of rhetorical theory. It seems entirely appropriate that all the ancient observers used the word *demokratia* in describing the government.

How then might we compare the Syracusan democracy of 466–412 to other democracies of the Greek world? Strauss has argued that it is best not to use adjectives such as "radical," "extreme," or "moderate" to describe the Athenian democracy because of the inaccuracy and inherent aristocratic bias of the terms.[34] Adopting a similar caution for Syracuse, we may conclude the following. In purely institutional terms, Diocles' reforms of 412 may have rendered the state more democratic than it had been before, given the general ancient (though not modern) assumption that increased use of the lot is a democratic trait. Yet to describe the aftermath as being a different constitution, as does Aristotle and some modern scholars, invites error. Across several decades down to the time when Diocles incited the assembly to pass his laws, Syracuse had been functioning institutionally and ideologically as a thorough-going democracy, one to all appearances as forceful as contemporary Athens. To call one state "radical" and the other "moderate" (let alone to call one democratic and the other not) obscures this fundamental reality.

## NOTES

1 I have discussed classical definitions of *demokratia* at some length in *The First Democracies: Early Popular Government Outside Athens* (Stuttgart 1997) ch. 2.

2 Diodorus 11.38.7, 11.86.6 and Aristotle *Pol.* 1315b34–38 combine to suggest a date for the overthrow of Thrasybulus in 466 or 465. W. S. Barrett argues convincingly that it must have been 466 in "Pindar's Twelfth *Olympian* and the Fall of the Deinomenidai," *JHS* 93 (1973) 23–35.

3 K. Meister, *Die sizilische Geschichte bei Diodor von den Anfängen bis zum Tod des Agathokles* (diss. Ludwig-Maximilians-Universität, Munich 1967) 47; D. Asheri, "Sicily, 478–431 BC," in the *CAH*² 5, ed. D. M. Lewis et al. (Cambridge 1992) 147–170, at 165.
K. Sacks, in the course of his argument for a more independently minded Diodorus than hitherto accepted, notes that the Sicilian historian did not always despise democracy even though he seems to have considered the system vulnerable to demagoguery. *Diodorus Siculus and the First Century* (Princeton 1990) 167. There is no reason to think Diodorus' lateness has impaired his understanding of *demokratia*: other portions of his history seem to show a clear enough understanding of the government involved, and in any case fifth- and fourth-century sources corroborate his use of the term here (see below). On the sometimes slippery nature of the term in the Hellenistic period and beyond, see J. A. O. Larsen, "Representation and Democracy in Hellenistic Federalism," *CP* 40 (1945) 65–97, esp. 88–91, and G. E. M. de Ste. Croix, *The Class Struggle in the Ancient Greek World* (Ithaca 1981) 321–326.

4 "Liberty" (11.72.2).

5 11.73. Aristotle *Pol.* 1303b1–2 apparently refers to the same incident but with a notable discrepancy. During his discussion of how faction can be caused in cities by the admission of additional citizens, he states that "the Syracusans after the tyrannical period, having made citizens of foreigners and mercenaries, fell into stasis and battle." This summary version implies that the outsiders were made citizens *after* the fall of the Deinomenids, not by them. No explanation is offered as to why faction then broke out (denial of offices? Perhaps the new *demos* voted to confirm only partially a previous grant of citizenship, prohibiting them from office, which sparked the fighting). On the whole the much fuller Diodoran account is to be preferred, though one is left to wonder whether Aristotle made an error in his rush to offer a condensed example of stasis-by-citizenship or was working from a slightly different tradition. See also D. Keyt, *Aristotle Politics Books V and VI* (Oxford 1999) 91–92.

6 "For by this means they thought that they would humble the arrogance of the most powerful men in these two cities" (Oldfather) τούτῳ γὰρ τῷ τρόπῳ διελάμβανον ταπ εινώσειν τὰ φρονήματα τῶν πλεῖστον ἰσχυόντων ἐν ταῖς πατρίσι (11.87.2). Tyndarides had collected a sizable bodyguard from among the poorest (τῶν πενήτων), a common practice for seekers of tyranny. It is risky to read a genuine political program into this power play: Diodorus does not describe Tyndarides as leader of the people or demagogue, only as a person of presumptuous daring. No aristocratic crackdown results from his defeat, but rather petalism, specifically aimed at the high and mighty of the city.

7 Diodorus does not tell us whether another marker of *demokratia*, pay for public service, was enacted at Syracuse in addition to petalism. It may or may not have been: given the meager

evidence for Syracusan history in this era, the negative *argumentum e silentio* is particularly weak. Sortition for offices other than the generalship apparently begins only in 412 after Diocles' legislation (Diod. 13.34).

8   Cf. *Pol.* 1312b10–16.

9   Cf. W. L. Newman, *The Politics of Aristotle*, vol. 4 (Oxford 1902) 328–329; J. Aubonnet, *Aristote Politique*, vol. 2 (Paris 1973) 168, 233.

Diodorus also mentions important political changes at Syracuse soon after the Athenian expedition, changes instituted by Diocles and including the choosing of offices by lot. He does not, however, apply a label either to the old or the new political order (13.33–35), leaving us with his earlier statement that the *demokratia* in Syracuse continued for sixty years.

10  (Describing Athenian despair after a Syracusan naval victory in 413:) "These were the only cities that they had yet encountered, similar to their own in character, under democracies (*dēmokratoumenais*) like themselves, which had ships and horses, and were of considerable magnitude" (Crawley) (7.55.2). See also 6.39, where two years earlier Athenagoras uses the name *demokratia* in his defense of the government at Syracuse.

11  H. Wentker, *Sizilien und Athen. Die Begegnung der attischen Macht mit den Westgriechen* (Heidelberg 1956) 52–53; P. A. Brunt, review of Wentker in *Classical Review* 7 (1957) 243–245; A. Lintott, *Violence, Civil Strife, and Revolution in the Classical City* (London 1972) 187–191; B. Caven, *Dionysius I, Warlord of Syracuse* (New Haven 1990) 15; S. N. Consolo Langher, *Un imperialismo tra democrazia e tirannide. Siracusa nei secoli V e IV a.C.* (Rome 1997) 51–53. Earlier standard works such as W. Hüttl's *Verfassungsgeschichte von Syrakus* (Prague 1929) accept the ancient testimony for democracy in Syracuse during this time (65–99). More recent authors who concur, though not all to the same degree, include: M. Giangiulio, "Gli equilibri difficili della democrazia in Sicilia: il caso di Siracusa," in *Venticinque secoli dopo l'invenzione della Democrazia*, L. Canfora et al. (Paestum 1998) 107–123; J. L. O'Neil, *The Origins and Development of Ancient Greek Democracy* (Lanham 1995) 43–44, 73–75; Asheri (as above, n. 3) 165–170; D. M. Lewis, "Sicily, 413–368 BC," in the *CAH²* 6, ed. D. M. Lewis et al. (Cambridge 1992) 120–155, esp. 125–126; M. I. Finley, *Ancient Sicily²* (Totowa, NJ 1979) 58–73; Brunt, review cited above.

12  S. Weart, *Never at War: Why Democracies Will Not Fight One Another* (New Haven 1998) esp. 1–37, 298–299.

13  *Pol.* 1279a22–b19, esp. a37–39; *Nic. Eth.* 8.10–11 (1160a31–1161b11), esp. 10.3.

14  See note 9.

15  Attractive as it is, this interpretation must remain uncertain because of the multivalent nature of the term for Aristotle. For example, in some places *politeia* denotes a government in which the hoplite class rules (*Pol.* 1265b26–29; 1279b2–4; 1288a6–15), a definition which sounds too restrictive even for Aristotle's favored, conservative forms of democracy (*Pol.* 1291b30–39, 1292b22–34, and 1318b6–1319a6). On the awkward double duty polity performs in the middle books of the *Politics*, caught between two conflicting analytical schemata, see R. Mulgan, "Aristotle's Analysis of Oligarchy and Democracy," in *A Companion to Aristotle's* Politics, ed. D. Keyt and F. D. Miller, Jr. (Oxford 1991) 307–322, esp. 309–312.

Keyt (as above in n.5) 99–100 tentatively offers a different solution to the apparent contradiction: he points to Aristotle's statement at *Pol.* 1297b24–25 that in former times *politeiai* were called democracies. But the context of this statement, 1297b16–28, hardly suits Keyt's suggestion, for Aristotle is discussing times far earlier than fifth-century Syracuse: he mentions the *first* Greek constitutions (after the fall of the primeval kings) and their development with the growth of cities and the emergence of heavily armed soldiers. Even if the statement could be taken to apply to our period, one would expect it to refer to writers other than Aristotle himself – would he not wish to correct source anachronisms in his own treatises, aware of the problem as he is?

16  S. Berger, *Revolution and Society in Greek Sicily and Southern Italy* (Stuttgart 1992) 37–39; "Democracy in the Greek West and the Athenian Example," *Hermes* 117 (1989) 303–314.

17  On U.S. immigration law and the Chinese, L. E. Sayer, *Laws Harsh as Tigers: Chinese Immigrants and the Shaping of Modern Immigration Law* (Chapel Hill 1995) and E. P. Hutchinson, *Legislative History of American Immigration Policy, 1798–1965* (Philadelphia 1981).

Concerning the Periclean law, see generally C. Patterson, *Pericles' Citizenship Law of 451/0 BC.* (New York 1981). A. L. Boegehold offers some informed speculation about the popular politics behind the measure in "Pericles' Citizenship Law of 451/0 BC," in *Athenian Identity and Civic Ideology*, ed. A. L. Boegehold and A. C. Scafuro (Baltimore 1994) 57–66.

18  *Mass and Elite in Democratic Athens* (Princeton 1989); *The Athenian Revolution* (Princeton 1996). For ideas on the shifting equilibrium in democratic Syracuse, cf. Giangiulio (as above, n. 11) 110–119.

19  M. H. Hansen, *The Athenian Democracy in the Age of Demosthenes* (Oxford 1991) 215–218.

20  The tendency of the replacements to fall right into line with the popular will is understandable, and it further indicates a *demos* fully in charge: consider Thucydides' praise of Pericles for bucking the trend of *demokratia* by actually daring to stand up to the whims of the people, something the ordinary democratic politician fails to do (2.65.8–10).

21  Actual treason seems particularly unlikely here: Thucydides, fascinated by the manner of warfare and the shifting tides of the battle for Syracuse, provides a detailed description of the fighting which led up to these events, yet at no point gives any hint of collusion or betrayal by Syracusan leaders.

22  *Pol.* 1279b8–10, 1292a4–30, 1304b20–35, 1318b16–17; Ps-Xen. *Ath. Pol.* 1.3–9, 13–14, 2.9–10, 17–20. On these and other critics of democratic rule, see J. Ober, *Political Dissent in Democratic Athens* (Princeton 1998). Affirming the truth of ancient assertions that the *demos* mistreated leaders at Athens is R. A. Knox, "'So Mischievous a Beaste'? The Athenian *Demos* and Its Treatment of Its Politicians," *G&R* 32 (1985) 132–161. On generals as especially abused (two out of every board of ten may have faced prosecution during their careers), see Hansen, *Athenian Democracy*, 215–218.

23  Ps-Xen. *Ath. Pol.* 2.17.

24  ...ὡς ὑπὸ χρημάτων καταπροδόντες οἱ στρατηγοὶ ἀπῆλθον (7.48.4). See also the incident in 424 in which three Athenian generals were exiled or fined for alleged bribery after departing Sicily with their forces when peace broke out, Thuc. 4.65.

25  Diod. 13.100–103; Xen. *Hell.* 1.6.33–1.7.35.

26  Aristotle considers it the hallmark of the most radical kind of democracy when, as he puts it, "the multitude rule, and not the law." *Pol.* 1292a5; the irresponsibility of the *demos* in Athens (and Syracuse) is one of Thucydides' featured subjects. Cf. Ober, *Political Dissent* ch. 2 (see n. 22).

27  "Now at this time the whole city of Syracuse offered sacrifices to the gods, and on the next day, after the Assembly had gathered, they considered what disposition they should make of the captives. A man named Diocles, who was a most notable leader of the populace, declared his opinion [*to punish the Athenian captives harshly*].....When this motion had been read, Hermocrates took the floor and endeavored to show that a fairer thing than victory is to bear the victory with moderation. But when the people shouted their disapproval and would not allow him to continue, a man named Nicolaüs, who had lost two sons in the war, made his way, supported by his slaves because of his age, to the

platform. When the people saw him, they stopped shouting, believing that he would denounce the prisoners" (Oldfather) (13.19.4–6).

28   Alcibiades was doubtless exaggerating for political purposes, and Thucydides may have been trying to make subtle criticisms of Athenian democracy by highlighting Syracusan misadventures (cf. J. Ober, "Civic Ideology and Counterhegemonic Discourse: Thucydides on the Sicilian Debate," in *Athenian Identity and Civic Ideology*, ed. A. L. Boegehold and A. C. Scafuro [Baltimore 1994] 102–126). But such agendas are not important for the present argument: neither Thucydides nor Alcibiades could have been at all persuasive in making these statements if Syracuse was not generally known to be a democracy.

29   13.34.6; cf. 13.19.4. As Diodorus continues on with his account in 13.35 he seems to confuse the person and actions of the popular politician Diocles with an earlier, legendary Syracusan lawgiver. E. Manni, "Diocles di Siracusa fra Ermocrate e Dionisio," *Kokalos* 25 (1979) 220–231.

30   E.g., E. F. Bloedow, "The Speeches of Hermocrates and Athenagoras at Syracuse in 415 BC: Difficulties in Syracuse and in Thucydides," *Historia* 45 (1996) 141–158; G. Mader, "Strong Points, Weak Argument: Athenagoras on the Sicilian Expedition (Thucydides 6.36–8)," *Hermes* 121 (1993) 433–440; F. T. Hinrichs, "Hermokrates bei Thukydides," *Hermes* 109 (1981) 46–59.

31   Anonymous *prolegomena artis rhetoricae*, no. 4 in H. Rabe, ed. *Prolegomenon Sylloge* (Leipzig 1931).

32   Rabe nos. 5, 7, 13, 17; Cic. *Brutus* 46. The last citation goes back to Aristotle, showing that at least some elements of the Tisias and Corax traditions described above were current in the Classical period. Other early references to the men or their work can be found in Plato, *Phaedrus* 267A, 273B, and Aristotle *Rhet.* 1402a17, *Soph. el.* 183b29–34.

33   T. Cole, *The Origins of Rhetoric in Ancient Greece* (Baltimore 1991) 22–29, 53–54, 82–83, and "Who was Corax?" *Illinois Classical Studies* 16 (1991) 65–84. In a similarly revisionist vein see now E. Schiappa, *The Beginnings of Rhetorical Theory in Classical Greece* (New Haven 1999). For more conservative views see G. Kennedy, *The Art of Persuasion in Greece* (Princeton 1963) 58–61 (slightly modified in *A New History of Classical Rhetoric* [Princeton 1994] 11, 33–34); D. A. G. Hinks, "Tisias and Corax and the Invention of Rhetoric," *Classical Quarterly* 40 (1934) 61–69. Leery of the contributions of Tisias and Corax but convinced that the circumstances of democracy powerfully encouraged the development of rhetorical art (at least in Athens) is H. Yunis, "The Constraints of Democracy and the Rise of the Art of Rhetoric," in *Democracy, Empire, and the Arts in Fifth-Century Athens*, ed. D. Boedeker and K. A. Raaflaub (Cambridge, MA 1998) 223–240.

34   B. S. Strauss, "Athenian Democracy: Neither Radical, Extreme, Nor Moderate," *AHB* 1 (1987) 127–129.

# Further reading

Bloedow, Edmund F., "The Speeches of Hermocrates and Athenagoras at Syracuse in 415 BC: Difficulties in Syracuse and in Thucydides," *Historia* 45 (1996), 141–58.

Lewis, David M., "Sicily, 413–368 BC," in *The Cambridge Ancient History*, vol. 6, 2nd edn., eds. D. M. Lewis et al. (Cambridge, 1992), 120–55.

Mader, Gottfried, "Strong Points, Weak Argument: Athenagoras on the Sicilian Expedition (Thucydides 6.36–8)," *Hermes* 121 (1993), 433–40.

Rutter, N. Keith, "Syracusan Democracy: 'Most Like the Athenian?'," in *Alternatives to Athens*, eds. R. Brock and S. Hodkinson (Oxford, 2000), 137–51.

# 4

# Liberty, Equality, and the Ideals of Greek Democracy

## Introduction

It is a curious fact that substantive theoretical discussions of democracy are rare among classical writers – most, it seems, had little interest in the subject, and when their works do mention it one often detects a clear anti-democratic bias. Nevertheless, there do exist helpful treatments of it and occasional comparisons with its conceptual rivals, monarchy (one-man rule) and oligarchy (rule by a few or by an elite class). The following selections from ancient historians, a dramatist, and a philosopher describe in different ways the ideals of *demokratia*, those which were thought to distinguish it from the alternatives. Two modern scholars then discuss these ideals, comparing them to the way modern democratic societies view themselves, with particular attention to ancient and modern conceptions of liberty and "rights."

## Herodotus, *Histories* (3.80–82)

Herodotus portrays here a meeting among plotting Persian noblemen that supposedly took place after the death of the Persian king Cambyses (522 BC). They debate what sort of government they should establish in their country: democracy, oligarchy, or continued monarchy. Despite Herodotus' insistence on the historicity of this exchange, modern scholars generally consider that the arguments used here reflect Greek political thinking during Herodotus' time, and not an actual discussion among Persians from the previous century. The word *demokratia*, interestingly, does not appear here, though clearly that is the government type in question (cf. Herodotus 6.43); rather, its proponent in the debate chooses to use the term *isonomia* ("equality under law"), suggesting that this word had a more congenial ring to it at the time than *demokratia*. (*Source*: Herodotus, *Histories* 3.80–82, trans. G. Rawlinson.)

[. . .] [T]he conspirators met together to consult about the situation of affairs. At this meeting speeches were made, to which many of the Greeks give no credence, but they were made nevertheless. Otanes recommended that the management of public affairs should be entrusted to the whole nation. "To me," he said, "it seems advisable, that we should no longer have a single man to rule over us – the rule of one is neither good nor pleasant. You cannot have forgotten to what lengths Cambyses went in his haughty tyranny, and the haughtiness of the Magi you have yourselves experienced. How indeed is it possible that monarchy should be a well-adjusted thing, when it allows a man to do as he likes without being answerable? Such licence is enough to stir strange and unwonted thoughts in the heart of the worthiest of men. Give a person this power, and straightway his manifold good things puff him up with pride, while envy is so natural to human kind that it cannot but arise in him. But pride and envy together include all wickedness – both of them leading on to deeds of savage violence. True it is that kings, possessing as they do all that heart can desire, ought to be void of envy; but the contrary is seen in their conduct towards the citizens. They are jealous of the most virtuous among their subjects, and wish their death; while they take delight in the meanest and basest, being ever ready to listen to the tales of slanderers. A king, besides, is beyond all other men inconsistent with himself. Pay him court in moderation, and he is angry because you do not show him more profound respect – show him profound respect, and he is offended again, because (as he says) you fawn on him. But the worst of all is, that he sets aside the laws of the land, puts men to death without trial, and subjects women to violence. The rule of the many, on the other hand, has, in the first place, the fairest of names, [*isonomia*]; and further it is free from all those outrages which a king is wont to commit. There, offices are decided by lot, the magistrate is answerable for what he does, and measures rest with the commonalty. I vote, therefore, that we do away with monarchy, and raise the people to power. For the people are all in all."

81. Such were the sentiments of Otanes. Megabyzus spoke next, and advised the setting up of an oligarchy: – "In all that Otanes has said to persuade you to put down monarchy," he observed, "I fully concur; but his recommendation that we should call the people to power seems to me not the best advice. For there is nothing so void of understanding, nothing so full of [insolence] as the unwieldy rabble. It were folly not to be borne, for men, while seeking to escape the [insolence] of a tyrant, to give themselves up to the [insolence] of a rude unbridled mob. The tyrant, in all his doings, at least knows what he is about, but a mob is altogether devoid of knowledge; for how should there be any knowledge in a rabble, untaught, and with no natural sense of what is right and fit? It rushes wildly into state affairs with all the fury of a stream swollen in the winter, and confuses everything. Let the enemies of the Persians be ruled by democracies; but let us choose out from the citizens a certain number of the worthiest, and put the government into their hands. For thus both we ourselves shall be among the governors, and power being entrusted to the best men, it is likely that the best counsels will prevail in the state."

82. This was the advice which Megabyzus gave, and after him Darius came forward, and spoke as follows: – "All that Megabyzus said against [the multitude] was well said, I think; but about oligarchy he did not speak advisedly; for take these three forms of government – democracy, oligarchy, and monarchy – and let them

each be at their best, I maintain that monarchy far surpasses the other two. What government can possibly be better than that of the very best man in the whole state? The counsels of such a man are like himself, and so he governs the mass of the people to their heart's content; while at the same time his measures against evil-doers are kept more secret than in other states. Contrariwise, in oligarchies, where men vie with each other in the service of the commonwealth, fierce enmities are apt to arise between man and man, each wishing to be leader, and to carry his own measures; whence violent quarrels come, which lead to open strife, often ending in bloodshed. Then monarchy is sure to follow; and this too shows how far that rule surpasses all others. Again, in a democracy, it is impossible but that there will be malpractices: these malpractices, however, do not lead to enmities, but to close friendships, which are formed among those engaged in them, who must hold well together to carry on their villanies. And so things go on until a man stands forth as champion of the commonalty, and puts down the evil-doers. Straightway the author of so great a service is admired by all, and from being admired soon comes to be appointed king; so that here too it is plain that monarchy is the best government. Lastly, to sum up all in a word, whence, I ask, was it that we got the freedom which we enjoy? – did democracy give it us, or oligarchy, or a monarch? As a single man recovered our freedom for us, my sentence is that we keep to the rule of one. Even apart from this, we ought not to change the laws of our forefathers when they work fairly; for to do so, is not well."

# Euripides, *Suppliant Women* (lines 346–57, 403–50)

Euripides was one of the three great Athenian tragedians of the fifth century BC. He produced the *Suppliant Women* probably around 422. As in other Greek tragedies, the action of this play is set in the mythological past, and yet political conditions point to the contemporary world. Here, the legendary Theseus, king of Athens, sometimes acts and speaks as if he were the popular leader of a democratic city. In the course of a dispute with Thebes over the burial of Argive champions who died attacking the city (the "Seven Against Thebes"), Theseus decides on a plan and argues with a foreign herald over the virtues of popular government as against one-man rule. (*Source:* Euripides, *Suppliant Women* 346–57, 403–50, trans. D. Kovacs, from *Euripides: Suppliant Women, Electra, Heracles* Cambridge, MA: Harvard University Press, 1998, pp. 49, 55, 57, 59.) (Note: bracketed text indicates questionable authenticity.)

*Theseus:*   [...] Here is what I shall do: I shall go and win release of the bodies, persuading the Thebans with my words. If that fails, then it shall be done by force, and the gods will not begrudge it. I want the city too to ratify this decision, and ratify it they will since that is what I wish. But if I add my reasons I will have more of the people's good will. And in fact I have made the people sovereign by freeing this city and giving them equal votes. I shall take Adrastus along as the proof of what I am saying and appear before the citizen assembly. When I have won them over on this point, I shall gather a picked band of Athenian youth and return here. [...]

*Herald*:   Who is the land's master? To whom shall I bring a message from Creon, who controls Cadmus' land since Eteocles was killed near the seven gates in fraternal bloodshed by Polynices?

*Theseus*:   To begin with, stranger, you started your speech on a false note by asking for the master here. The city is not ruled by a single man but is free. The people rule, and offices are held by yearly turns: they do not assign the highest honors to the rich, but the poor also have an equal share.

*Herald*:   Your words put me one point ahead, as in a game of draughts. The city I have come from is ruled by one man and not by a rabble. There is no one to fool the city with flattering speech and lead it this way and that to suit his own advantage. [At first he is welcome and gives much pleasure, but later he causes harm, and then, by the further expedient of slander, he conceals his earlier misdeeds and slips out of the reach of justice.] And anyway how can the common people, if they cannot even make a speech properly, know the right way to guide a city? It is time, not haste, that gives superior learning. Now the poor farmer, even if he is no fool, has no chance, because of his labor, to attend to the city's business. What is more, the better sort find it a sorry business when a man of low birth, a former nonentity, achieves prominence by entrancing the common people with his glib tongue.

*Theseus*:   This herald is a clever talker and loves to speak elaborately on what is no part of his errand! Well, since you have begun this contest, hear me out: for it was you who proposed this debate.
    There is nothing more hostile to a city than a tyrant. In the first place, there are no common laws in such a city, and one man, keeping the law in his own hands, holds sway. This is unjust. When the laws are written, both the powerless and the rich have equal access to justice, [and it is possible for the weaker man to address the same words to the fortunate man whenever he is badly spoken of,] and the little man, if he has right on his side, defeats the big man. Freedom consists in this: "Who has a good proposal and wants to set it before the city?" He who wants to enjoys fame, while he who does not holds his peace. What is fairer for a city than this?
    [Wherever the people rule the land, they take pleasure in the young citizens that are its strength. But a king thinks this hateful, and he kills the nobles <and> all he regards as proud, fearing for his power. How then could a city be strong in the future when someone culls and cuts away the boldest of the young as one does the towering stalk in a springtime meadow? And why should one acquire wealth and a livelihood for one's children merely to produce greater livelihood for the tyrant? And why gently raise girls in the house only to be a sweet pleasure for the ruler when he wants them and a source of tears for those who raised them? Better to die than see one's children forcibly molested!] [...]

# Thucydides, *History of the Peloponnesian War* (2.37–42)

After the first year of Athens' war with Sparta and the Peloponnesian League, the Athenian popular leader Pericles spoke at a burial ceremony to honor those who died fighting that year (431). This Funeral Oration, recounted by Thucydides and excerpted below, is perhaps the most famous speech to survive from antiquity, and its patriotic praise tells us much about the ideals of the Athenian democracy. (*Source*: Thucydides, *History of the Peloponnesian War* 2.37–42, trans. R. Crawley.)

[...] But what was the road by which we reached our position, what the form of government under which our greatness grew, what the national habits out of which it sprang; these are questions which I may try to solve before I proceed to my panegyric upon these men; since I think this to be a subject upon which on the present occasion a speaker may properly dwell, and to which the whole assemblage, whether citizens or foreigners, may listen with advantage.

"Our constitution does not copy the laws of neighbouring states; we are rather a pattern to others than imitators ourselves. Its administration [is in the hands of] the many instead of the few; this is why it is called a democracy, If we look to the laws, they afford equal justice to all in their private differences; if to social standing, advancement in public life falls to reputation for capacity, class considerations not being allowed to interfere with merit; nor again does poverty bar the way, if a man is able to serve the state, he is not hindered by the obscurity of his condition. The freedom which we enjoy in our government extends also to our ordinary life. There, far from exercising a jealous surveillance over each other, we do not feel called upon to be angry with our neighbour for doing what he likes, or even to indulge in those injurious looks which cannot fail to be offensive, although they inflict no positive penalty. But all this ease in our private relations does not make us lawless as citizens. Against this fear is our chief safeguard, teaching us to obey the magistrates and the laws, particularly such as regard the protection of the injured, whether they are actually on the statute book, or belong to that code which, although unwritten, yet cannot be broken without acknowledged disgrace.

"Further, we provide plenty of means for the mind to refresh itself from business. We celebrate games and sacrifices all the year round, and the elegance of our private establishments forms a daily source of pleasure and helps to banish the spleen; while the magnitude of our city draws the produce of the world into our harbour, so that to the Athenian the fruits of other countries are as familiar a luxury as those of his own.

"If we turn to our military policy, there also we differ from our antagonists. We throw open our city to the world, and never by alien acts exclude foreigners from any opportunity of learning or observing, although the eyes of an enemy may occasionally profit by our liberality; trusting less in system and policy than to the native spirit of our citizens; while in education, where our rivals from their very cradles by a painful discipline seek after manliness, at Athens we live exactly as we please, and yet are just as ready to encounter every legitimate danger. In proof of this it may be noticed that the Lacedæmonians do not invade our country alone, but bring with them all their confederates; while we Athenians advance unsupported into the territory of a neighbour, and fighting upon a foreign soil usually vanquish with ease men who are defending their homes. Our united force was never yet encountered by any enemy, because we have at once to attend to our marine and to dispatch our citizens by land upon a hundred different services; so that, wherever they engage with some such fraction of our strength, a success against a detachment is magnified into a victory over the nation, and a defeat into a reverse suffered at the hands of our entire people. And yet if with habits not of labour but of ease, and courage not of art but of nature, we are still willing to encounter danger, we have the double advantage of escaping the experience of hardships in anticipation and of facing them in the hour of need as fearlessly as those who are never free from them.

"Nor are these the only points in which our city is worthy of admiration. We cultivate refinement without extravagance and knowledge without effeminacy; wealth we employ more for use than for show, and place the real disgrace of poverty not in owning to the fact but in declining the struggle against it. Our public men have, besides politics, their private affairs to attend to, and our ordinary citizens, though occupied with the pursuits of industry, are still fair judges of public matters; for, unlike any other nation, regarding him who takes no part in these duties not as unambitious but as useless, we Athenians are able to judge at all events if we cannot originate, and instead of looking on discussion as a stumbling-block in the way of action, we think it an indispensable preliminary to any wise action at all. Again, in our enterprises we present the singular spectacle of daring and deliberation, each carried to its highest point, and both united in the same persons; although usually decision is the fruit of ignorance, hesitation of reflection. But the palm of courage will surely be adjudged most justly to those, who best know the difference between hardship and pleasure and yet are never tempted to shrink from danger. In generosity we are equally singular, acquiring our friends by conferring, not by receiving, favours. Yet, of course, the doer of the favour is the firmer friend of the two, in order by continued kindness to keep the recipient in his debt; while the debtor feels less keenly from the very consciousness that the return he makes will be a payment, not a free gift. And it is only the Athenians who, fearless of consequences, confer their benefits not from calculations of expediency, but in the confidence of liberality.

"In short, I say that as a city we are the school of Hellas; while I doubt if the world can produce a man, who where he has only himself to depend upon, is equal to so many emergencies, and graced by so happy a versatility, as the Athenian. And that this is no mere boast thrown out for the occasion, but plain matter of fact, the power of the state acquired by these habits proves. For Athens alone of her contemporaries is found when tested to be greater than her reputation, and alone gives no occasion to her assailants to blush at the antagonist by whom they have been worsted, or to her subjects to question her title by merit to rule. Rather, the admiration of the present and succeeding ages will be ours, since we have not left our power without witness, but have shown it by mighty proofs; and far from needing a Homer for your panegyrist, or other of his craft whose verses might charm for the moment only for the impression which they gave to melt at the touch of fact, we have forced every sea and land to be the highway of our daring, and everywhere, whether for evil or for good, have left imperishable monuments behind us. Such is the Athens for which these men, in the assertion of their resolve not to lose her, nobly fought and died; and well may every one of their survivors be ready to suffer in her cause. [...]

# Aristotle, *Politics* (trans. B. Jowett)

## 1292b21–34

From what has been already said we may safely infer that there are so many different kinds of democracies and of oligarchies. For it is evident that either all the classes whom we mentioned must share in the government, or some only and not others. When the class of [farmers] and of those who posses moderate fortunes have the supreme power, the government is administered according to law. For the citizens being compelled to live by their labour have no leisure; and so they set up the authority of the law, and attend assemblies only when necessary. They all obtain a share in the government when they have acquired the qualification which is fixed by the law – the absolute exclusion of any class would be a step towards oligarchy; hence all who have acquired the property qualification are admitted to a share in the constitution. But leisure cannot be provided for them unless there are revenues to support them. This is one sort of democracy, and these are the causes which give birth to it. [...]

## 1317a40–1318a10

The basis of a democratic state is liberty; which, according to the common opinion of men, can only be enjoyed in such a state; – this they affirm to be the great end of every democracy. One principle of liberty is for all to rule and be ruled in turn, and indeed democratic justice is the application of numerical not proportionate equality; whence it follows that the majority must be supreme, and that whatever the majority approve must be the end and the just. Every citizen, it is said, must have equality, and therefore in a democracy the poor have more power than the rich, because there are more of them, and the will of the majority is supreme. This, then, is one note of liberty which all democrats affirm to be the principle of their state. Another is that a man should live as he likes. This, they say, is the privilege of a freeman, since, on the other hand, not to live as a man likes is the mark of a slave. This is the second characteristic of democracy, whence has arisen the claim of men to be ruled and be ruled by none, if possible, or, if this is impossible, to rule and be ruled in turns; and so it contributes to the freedom based upon equality.

Such being our foundation and such the principle from which we start, the characteristics of democracy are as follows: – the election of officers by all out of all; and that all should rule over each, and each in his turn over all; that the appointment to all offices, or to all but those which require experience and skill, should be made by lot; that no property qualification should be required for offices, or only a very low one; that a man should not hold the same office twice, or not often, or in the case of few except military offices: that the tenure of all offices, or of as many as possible, should be brief; that all men should sit in judgement, or that judges selected out of all should judge, in all matters, or in most and in the greatest and most important – such as the scrutiny of accounts, the constitution, and private contracts; that the assembly should be supreme over all causes, or at any rate over the most important, and the magistrates over none or only over a very few. Of all magistracies, a council is the most democratic when there is not the means of paying all the citizens, but when they are paid even this is robbed of its power; for the people then draw all cases to themselves, as I said in the previous discussion. The next characteristic of democracy is payment for services; assembly, law-courts, magistrates, everybody receives pay, when it is to be had; or when it is not to be had for all, then it is given to the law-courts and to the stated assemblies, to the council and to the magistrates, or at least to any of them who are compelled to have their meals together. And whereas oligarchy is characterized by birth, wealth, and education, the notes of democracy appear to be the opposite of these – low birth, poverty, mean employment. Another note is that no magistracy is perpetual, but if any such have survived some ancient change in the constitution it should be stripped of its power, and the holders should be elected by lot and no longer by vote. These are the points common to all democracies; but democracy and demos in their truest form are based upon the recognized principle of democratic justice, that all should count equally; for equality implies that the poor should have no more share in the government than the rich, and should not be the only rulers, but that all should rule equally according to their numbers. And in this way men think that they will secure equality and freedom in their state.

# Shares and Rights: "Citizenship" Greek Style and American Style

## Martin Ostwald

The celebration of the anniversaries of three revolutionary events that have shaped the social and political outlook of our world affords a welcome excuse to take a close look at some of the assumptions on which our social and political system is based. Two of these events mark the triumph over an internal tyrannical regime: the reforms of Cleisthenes of about 508 BC, which laid the groundwork for Athenian democracy, and the *Déclaration des droits de l'homme et du citoyen*, adopted by the French Assembly in 1789. The American Declaration of Independence of 1776, followed in 1789 by the Constitution of the United States and two years later by the Bill of Rights, constitutes the liberation from an oppressive external colonial rule. What can these three events teach us in an age that is trying to find multicultural values beyond those of the

Martin Ostwald, "Shares and Rights: 'Citizenship' Greek Style and American Style," in J. Ober and C. Hedrick (eds.), *Demokratia* (Princeton: Princeton University Press, 1996), pp. 49–61.

Western world? I believe that the multiculturalism we seek is best approached through exploring the multiculturalism that is already part of our tradition, and I propose to deal with one of its features in this paper.

Citizenship, as the late Charles Norris Cochrane observed, is one of the two fundamental concepts that Hellenism bequeathed to Western civilization.[1] But concepts of citizenship also differentiate basic American attitudes so fundamentally from those of the ancient Greeks that a comparison of the two will, I hope, lead to a deeper understanding of the foundations on which our own social and political culture rests as well as of the structure we have erected on those foundations.

My primary purpose here is not to explore certain formal or legal requirements of citizenship in ancient Greece and the United States, respectively, and then compare one with the other. I propose, rather, to treat citizenship as reflecting different sets of social values, which can be dubbed "individualistic" on the American side and "communal" on the Greek. I hope to show that what Americans tend to see in terms of the "rights" of the individual, the Greeks tended to see in the more comprehensive context of sharing in and being part of a community on which the individual depends for his or her sense of identity.

There are pitfalls along the way: while my aim is to compare basic assumptions underlying views of citizenship in two different cultures, citizenship itself is not an unchanging unitary concept, frozen within each of the two cultures that concern us here; on the Greek side there is the difficulty of trying to derive one general notion of "citizenship" from the multiplicity of Greek city-states over the many centuries of their development; on the American side, there are problems of growth and shifts of meaning of what constitutes a "citizen" even within the short span of American history: to be a "citizen" did not mean the same in 1775 as it meant in 1777; it did not mean the same before as after Reconstruction, or before and after the Civil Rights legislation of the 1960s.[2] And yet I believe that within each culture certain basic values did not change: on the Greek side, Aristotle, one of the greatest social theorists of all time, managed to distill in his *Politics* social and political beliefs and principles that can be accepted as characterizing all Greek states at most stages in their development, and that will, therefore, give us a valid insight into a general Greek view of citizenship. There is no comparable theoretical work on the American side; but an examination of great public documents such as the Declaration of Independence and the Fourteenth Amendment reveals a striking consistency in the delineation of what characterizes a person as a citizen, that is, as a person acknowledged by the community as its member. This makes it possible to recognize salient differences among the many similarities between Greek and American political culture. We are helped by the fact that "equality" and "freedom" (or "liberty")[3] are key words in defining the society and the individual who is part of it in both Aristotle's *Politics* and in the American documents; if this indicates a close relation of modern political principles with those of the ancients, an examination of the differences between Greek and American *equality* and Greek and American *freedom* will reveal to us two dissimilar kinds of social perspective that are equally part of the foundations of Western culture.

The Declaration of Independence does not speak of citizenship, but it lays the groundwork for it in proclaiming as a self-evident truth "that all Men are created equal, that they are endowed by their Creator with certain unalienable Rights, that among these are Life, Liberty, and the Pursuit of Happiness" and "that to secure these Rights, Governments are instituted among Men." What is revolutionary about this is, first, that it applies ideas generated by the English Enlightenment[4] to give moral impetus and support to the political measures that brought about the American Revolution. Second, in doing so it justifies the institution of government on the grounds that government secures and guarantees as rights for each individual certain gifts granted equally to every Man[5] by whoever created him or her – be it God or nature or none of the above. With the benefit of hindsight, we know that some crucial terms in the Declaration were left for later generations to define, or rather refine, in a principled way,[6] especially as it became necessary to translate its general moral principles into legal principles: the question whether slaves and women are to be included among "all Men"; the question of what is meant by *happiness* and what are the parameters within which an individual is free to pursue it, and so forth. Important though these later developments are, they are less germane to the issue under consideration than the more fundamental article of faith here enunciated, namely that the individual, insignificant though he or she may be, has the right to assert his/her share of life, liberty, and the pursuit of happiness even against the powers of the state, and that the state, in its turn, is powerless to deprive him/her of these rights. We shall look in vain for any Greek text before or after Aristotle for a similar recognition of individual rights.

The Declaration of Independence predicates these rights as self-evident truths applicable to all, that is, even those over whom our Founding Fathers had no political authority. It does not speak of "citizens," because the regulation of citizenship was in 1776 a matter for each state to decide. In other words, it is a statement of general principles that, at the time, were moral but not legal, because they could not be enforced by a court of law.

It is the Fourteenth Amendment to the Constitution, ratified on July 28, 1868, as part and parcel of the Reconstruction, that legally confirmed the end of a process that had transformed a moral into a legal principle and at the same time made the regulation of citizenship a federal matter. Its first section reads, "All persons born or naturalized in the United States, and subject to the jurisdiction thereof, are citizens of the United States, nor shall any State deprive any person of life, liberty, or property, without due process of law, nor deny to any person within its jurisdiction the equal protection of the laws."

Unlike the Declaration of Independence, the Fourteenth Amendment claims applicability not to all men, but to "all persons [now explicitly gender-free] born or naturalized in the United States, and subject to the jurisdiction thereof," and it calls these persons "citizens" both of the United States and of the several states in which they reside. In enjoining the several states from making or enforcing "any law which shall abridge the privileges and immunities of citizens of the United States," the framers of the Fourteenth Amendment not only clearly established federal citizenship as a legal right but also reserved to the federal government the eminent protection of this right: the federal judiciary guarantees that this right shall not be abridged by a particular state. That the federal judiciary did not always conscientiously implement this injunction is immaterial to the present point; what matters is that it establishes certain legal rights to protect the individuals who are recognized as members of the community, the citizens. The moral "rights" affirmed by the

Declaration of Independence are translated into legal language as "privileges and immunities" guaranteeing "life, liberty, and property" to the citizen.[7]

In the same spirit, the "equality" with which the Declaration of Independence distributed "unalienable Rights" is now reflected in the equal protection of the laws. The federal government extends this protection – not to "all Men," over whom no single government can claim jurisdiction – but to all citizens over whom it has jurisdiction and for whom it can legislate. Thus the "equality," predicated of "all Men" as a birthright ("are created"), which had still been denied to slaves as late as the Dred Scott case of 1857, came closer to realization. Nevertheless, women had to wait until the Nineteenth Amendment was passed in 1920 before they were recognized as full citizens.

In differentiating a "human being" from a "citizen," the Fourteenth Amendment gave an answer to a problem harder to deal with in terms of Aristotelian principles: if man is "by nature" – a reasonable facsimile of the faceless "Creator" of the Declaration of Independence – a "social and political being," a *zōion politikon*,[8] it becomes tricky to make precise distinctions between the two. The repercussions of this difficulty can be seen in Aristotle's treatment of kingship in Book 3 of the *Politics*: absolute kingship (*pambasileia*) is said to be viewed by some as not being a "constitution" (*politeia*) at all, "because it is not in accordance with nature that one person should have authority over all citizens, wherever a state consists of equals."[9]

The question of who these "equals" (*homoioi*) are, is unequivocally answered in one sense: they are the "free" (*eleutheroi*).[10] This not only denies equality to slaves but excludes from the political community also a number of free persons, such as resident aliens and foreign visitors (Arist. *Pol.* 3.1, 1275a7–14), to whom the United States extends at least some equality in the form of equal protection of the law, trial by jury, etc. At the same time, the "freedom" on which this "equality" rests has only a limited application to women, children, and, surprisingly enough, to old men: while Aristotle concedes that women "constitute half of the free population," children are "incomplete citizens" (*politai ateleis*, 3.5, 1278a4–6), who "by reason of their age have not yet been registered" and only "develop into partners of the political community."[11] Old men are not citizens in an unqualified sense, because they are "superannuated."[12] Complete equality as citizens, then, is extended in the Greek sense only to free males who are still in their prime. Citizenship has, accordingly, a much narrower compass than it has in the United States. The Fourteenth Amendment recognizes no disabilities of women and children. But that such disabilities actually existed is shown by the fact that the Twenty-Sixth Amendment, ratified on July 1, 1971, extended the franchise to eighteen year olds. This implies a partial disability of the young until the end of their seventeenth year. The Nineteenth Amendment, ratified August 26, 1920, likewise implies an earlier disability of women in that it gave them the suffrage for the first time in the United States.

We might here note another aspect of the narrow confines of citizenship in Aristotle: whereas the Fourteenth Amendment explicitly puts born and naturalized citizens on the same level,[13] Aristotle dismisses the problem of naturalization as marginal (*Pol.* 3.1, 1275a2–6), though he concedes a minimal share in the community also to free noncitizens.[14] Birth, when accepted by the relevant social institutions as legitimate, was the universal criterion for citizenship among the Greeks;[15] naturalization was rare, exceptional, and usually honorific.[16]

The difference between American and Aristotelian "equality" goes considerably further. The high value attached to equality in both cultures does not mean that either the Americans or the Greeks claim that all men are "equal" in all respects. The equality the Declaration of Independence attributes to all men as a birthright is "unalienable," because no human power can remove it – the Greeks would say that it exists "by nature." It entitles all "equally" to enjoy life, liberty, and the pursuit of happiness. But we are far from "equal" in the way we each exercise that equality: what I do with my life is different from what you do with yours, my "liberty" or right to privacy is likely to result in different activities from the way you use yours, and we are not equal in the way we severally pursue happiness. Equality of rights also constitutes practical limits on each individual's freedom of action. In saying that no citizen shall be deprived of life, liberty, and property without due process of law, the Fourteenth Amendment establishes legal limits on what we are naturally equally entitled to do: the statement that no person shall be denied the "equal" protection of the laws means that the same laws protect all citizens equally.

The differences between this approach to "equality" and the corresponding Greek view of *isotēs* or *to ison* are more glaring than their similarities. Equality derived from the enjoyment of freedom by all citizens makes its only appearance in Aristotle in his criticism of democrats for mistakenly believing that equal enjoyment of freedom makes them equal in every respect.[17] Note that no rights are involved: although Aristotle shares with the Declaration of Independence the belief that all men are "by nature" equal,[18] the conclusion he draws from that is radically different: since natural equality makes the rule of one man unjust, "all men should have a share in ruling" by taking turns in ruling and being ruled.[19] Eligibility to hold office is not seen as something a citizen is entitled to as a right; eligibility is merely the logical corollary of natural equality. Office holding is part of the condition of being a citizen, and status as a free man makes one equal to all other citizens.[20] Equality of citizens exists negatively in that neither the affluent nor the indigent dominate society, and positively in that freedom gives the same political weight to all.[21] The nature of this equality, its relation to freedom, and its implications are most clearly set forth in the second chapter of *Politics* 6:

> The idea underlying a democratic form of government is freedom .... The populist notion of justice is that no citizen is better than any other[22] in a quantitative and not in a qualitative sense. In the light of this notion of justice, the common people are necessarily sovereign, and what the majority decides is final and is just. For they maintain that each citizen must have an equal share;[23] as a consequence those without means enjoy greater authority in democracies than the affluent, for their number is greater and authority goes with majority decisions.[24]

Aristotle's idea of equality seems to me to go beyond anything stated in the American documents in two respects. While in American theory the equality derived from our Creator gives us a common moral sense from which the Declaration of Independence derives our title to liberty, the relationship is reversed in Aristotle: freedom, in the sense of already "having the status of free men," is the basis on which citizens can be regarded as equals. Freedom is the precondition for equality, not equality for freedom. Further, the equality guaranteed by the Fourteenth

Amendment entitles all citizens equally to the protection of the laws; Aristotle, on the other hand, says very little about the relation of equality to the laws, except that, taking advantage of the double meaning of *isos* as both "equal" and "equitable," he calls *equality* a notion of justice valid only for "equals";[25] to the first kind of democracy he attributes an equality embodied in law (*nomos*), which demands that neither the affluent nor the indigent should dominate society.[26] In his view the equal status of all citizens as free men entails equality in appointments to office, and he believes that this is realized by the rota of taking turns at ruling and being ruled. The right of each citizen to equal treatment under the law[27] is of less interest to him as a manifestation of equality than the question of access to the various magistracies, which, in a *politeia* worthy of its name and especially in a democracy, is open to any free citizen on the rota principle. We have seen that this access is not envisaged in terms of a right but follows logically from the status of a citizen as a free man.[28]

The divergence of Greek from American thinking is even more glaring when it comes to defining "free" and "freedom." Greek uses *eleutheria* and *eleutheros* both in a social sense of individuals who are not slaves as well as in a political sense of states: the political meaning comes to the fore most prominently in Herodotus, according to whom the issue in the Persian Wars was the Greeks' defense of their *eleutheriē* against the Persians;[29] Aristotle, however, tends to give only a social sense to both adjective and noun in the *Politics* to contrast the status of a "free" man with that of a slave. Like Aristotle, both the Declaration of Independence and the Fourteenth Amendment predicate "freedom" of an individual. But the liberty they promise entitles a person to privacy by marking off an aspect of life in which the state cannot interfere; and, as a corollary, it extends the protection of the rights of the individual also to the protection of the rights of minorities. Aristotle, on the other hand, looks on freedom as the individual's membership card in society. There is, to the best of my knowledge, neither in Aristotle nor anywhere else in Greek thought any reference to the rights of minorities, simply because there were no minority groups recognized among the citizens.

Unlike "liberty," *eleutheria* is not expressed in terms of the "privileges or immunities" that the Fourteenth Amendment guarantees to the citizen; rather, all citizens, regardless of the kind of constitution under which they live, and regardless of economic condition, enjoy the status of free men which differentiates them from slaves.[30] The only "privilege" a free citizen can be said to enjoy is the *timē* (honor) of holding office.[31] But how much of a "privilege" can that be in a state, such as a democracy, where it is shared by all citizens? One of the essential definitions of *politeia*, a term that connotes both "citizenship" and "statehood," includes the way in which public offices are distributed;[32] and the art of citizenship (*politikē*) is the rule of and over persons who are equal in that they are all free.[33] In praising the principle of reciprocity, Aristotle says that

> since it is not possible for all to hold office at once, they do so either on an annual basis or on the basis of some other kind of term. . . . The better course would be to have always the same persons [*sc.*, seasoned professionals] as rulers, if possible; but where that is impossible because all are equal in nature, and where it is regarded as right that . . . all should have a share in ruling . . . those who are equal yield their office to one another in turn, and retain their equality even outside their term of office: some rule and others are ruled as if having changed their personality.[34]

In short, all citizens are equally privileged: the "privilege" is a privilege only to the extent that slaves and foreigners are excluded from it.

It is time to take stock of our inquiry so far: while the Declaration of Independence and the Fourteenth Amendment treat "citizenship" and the two notions of "equality" and "liberty" as rights, Aristotle sees none of the three Greek equivalents – *politēs*, *isotēs*, and *eleutheria* – as a "right" or a "title," although certain rights are implied when we try to translate these terms into our conceptual framework. How did Aristotle think of them?

To try to answer this question, we must begin with the linguistic evidence. Where we would use the word *right* to express the most important aspects of citizenship, Aristotle works with a number of expressions that, though they may incidentally connote "rights," primarily denote "sharing," "participation" (*metechein*), or "being in a position to do something" (*exeinai*). There is in his vocabulary nothing that corresponds exactly to our concept of "right" in the sense of "claim" or "entitlement."[35] To understand this way of thinking, we have to remember that for Aristotle the state is a compound entity, all of whose constituent parts "participate in" or "share in" it.[36] The standard way of describing the status of citizenship is "having a share in the social and political community" (*metechein tēs politeias* [or *tēs poleōs*]).[37] The norm of this status is found in a democracy, where all citizens have an equal share, based on freedom and equality.[38] For Greeks freedom and equality, as well as the state itself, are entities that citizens share through the community to which they belong; they do not possess them as rights to which they feel individually entitled.

There is, however, a term that, at first glance, seems to come closer to describing what we understand by "rights." When we read, for example, that a specified amount of property determines eligibility for office in oligarchies and in some democracies, "eligibility," that is, the "right" to hold office, is expressed by the phrase *exousian einai metechein* (to have the possibility to share).[39] However, a closer look reveals that it is not a "right" that is expressed. Since we are told in the immediate sequel that without an income it is impossible to enjoy the leisure necessary to devote oneself to public affairs,[40] the key verb *exeinai* clearly refers to leisure not as a "right," but as a precondition for public service; it describes something "permissible," "allowable," that is open to a person, not something to which a person is "entitled."[41]

What applies to property qualifications applies to eligibility to office in general: it is not a "right" but a "sharing in office" or "sharing in honors" (*metechein archēs* [or *timēs*], *meteinai archēs*).[42] Like citizenship, public offices are thought of as forming a kind of pool owned by the political community to which those who are full members of the community have access, but to which they do not necessarily have a "claim." The political community as a whole, the *politeia*, assigns offices,[43] and the verb used for the distribution of this share is commonly a form of the verb "to give" (*didonai*) either in its simple form or in the compounds "to give away" or "to give a share in" (*apodidonai* or *metadidonai*).[44]

This "assignment" does not involve the granting of rights: the essential thing for the Greeks is that the corporate entity makes accessible to its members something it owns and controls: it opens to the citizen in actuality the enjoyment of a share in the corporation, which he already possesses potentially. R. K. Sinclair has examined some central aspects of this "sharing" in a work he entitled *Democracy and Participation in*

*Athens.*[45] "Participation" is indeed the most suitable term in English, but it does not go quite far enough to capture what is involved in *methexis* and *meteinai*. To understand what is involved, we have to think of a "share" not in terms of the stock market, in which shares can be disposed of at will, but in the terms in which each limb has a share in the human body: my leg "shares" or "participates" in my body in the sense that whatever affects it affects my body, and whatever affects my body affects it.

"Rights" constitute for us only one aspect of citizenship, namely political and legal entitlements that are based on the fact of recognized membership in the corporation that is society and/or the state. They have a positive as well as a negative aspect: my rights define the space in which I can freely move without threat of outside interference; but they are also limited by your rights, which prevent me from encroaching on your territory. "Rights" are guaranteed by laws and are determined and enforced by a court of law. "Rights" need to be claimed or exercised in order to be valid: my "right" to vote makes me only a potential and passive citizen; while I do not lose my citizenship by failing to exercise it, I am not an active participant in the political process if I fail to vote.

*Methexis*, on the other hand, gives a citizen a full share in the society in which he lives. No act of his can make him an active member of the community: the degree to which he is a citizen is not determined by himself, but by the expectations of the community of which he is a part in terms of the contribution he can make to its functioning. When Solon divided the citizen-body into the so-called four "property-classes,"[46] he did not set up a system of graduated entitlements: his purpose was to determine the degree of service the state could expect of each group of citizens, since there was no public pay for public service: only the highest class, the *pentakosiome-dimnoi*, whose estates had an annual production rate of five hundred bushels, could be expected to serve as treasurers and in other high offices; cavalry service, based on the ability to keep horses, was expected of the second highest class; ownership of a team of oxen was deemed a sign of the ability to provide one's own armor and thus to serve as a hoplite in the heavy infantry; and the unpropertied, the lowest class, could be called on only for attendance and voting at assembly and at jury meetings. Membership in each of these classes was not a precondition for graduated rights: the Athenian name for "property-class" was *telos*, derived from the verb *teleō*, which denotes the fulfilment of a public obligation, such as the payment of a tax. Thus, belonging to a given class did not describe a "right" ("what your country can do for you") but the expectation the community had of a member ("what you can do for your country").[47]

While "rights" describe only the political aspect of citizenship, "sharing" has facets that the term *rights* does not express. A citizen also "shares" in the social, economic, and religious life of his community not as an "entitlement" but by virtue of belonging to a group that recognizes him as its member. It is taken for granted and expected of him that he will participate in its life; it is not viewed as a "right" that outsiders do not possess. By sharing in the *politeia*, a citizen is part of the corporation that is the state: the "right" to participate and its implementation inhere inseparably in citizenship.

The meaning of this is perhaps best driven home by an observation on the place of religion in the modern American and classical Greek civic communities, respectively.

By introducing the principle of separation of church and state, Americans banish religion from the political sphere and relegate it to an area that guarantees the individual his "liberty" of conscience against state interference. Greek religion is not a matter of conscience: it consists only in "doing the conventional thing by the gods" (*theous nomizein*). The "conventional thing" is, significantly, the verbal expression of *nomos*, the norms accepted by the state, including its statutes. This indicates concretely that religion is part of the civic order, that citizenship does not involve what we understand as "religious freedom" or "religious belief," even if, to the best of our knowledge, an individual was in the Greek world "free" from public constraints (other than social pressure) in his/her participation in divine worship. Tolerance of the religious convictions of others, which is for us part and parcel of the liberty a citizen enjoys, was not part of the freedom enjoyed by the citizen of an ancient Greek state.

I have chosen religion as an extreme example of what citizenship meant to the Greeks, bound inextricably to their individual communities and sharing with those communities every aspect of their lives. Citizenship was neither a right nor a matter of participation, but a matter of belonging, of knowing one's identity not in terms of one's own personal values but in terms of the community that was both one's possession and possessor. When he defined the human individual as a *zōion politikon*, Aristotle stated a profound reality of Greek society.

## NOTES

1  Cochrane, *Christianity and Classical Culture*, 86–87.
2  For an excellent account of the problems involved, see Kettner, *Citizenship*.
3  A few words ought to be said about the possibility of differentiating *liberty* from *freedom*. None of the many attempts to distinguish between them has won universal acceptance. The Declaration of Independence speaks of "liberty" in detailing the rights with which we are said to be endowed but proclaims at the end that "these United Colonies are, and of Right ought to be, *Free* and Independent States," perhaps because "liberty" has no cognate adjective in English, so that the adjective derived from *freedom* has to be borrowed to express it. Even if that be the reason, it is true that the noun *freedom* occurs neither in the Declaration of Independence nor in the Fourteenth Amendment. Modern English translations of Aristotle's *Politics* use *liberty* or *freedom* indifferently as translations of *eleutheria*, presumably in order to express its relation to the adjectival *eleutheros*, "free." The only firm distinction between *liberty* and *freedom* I can think of in English is that *freedom* may be followed by either *to* or *from*, whereas *liberty* may be followed only by *to*.
4  The attempt of Wills, *Inventing America*, to see the Scottish Enlightenment rather than Locke and the English Enlightenment as the chief philosophical source of the Declaration (for which see Becker, *Declaration of Independence*, ch. 2) has been decisively refuted by Hamowy, "Jefferson and the Scottish Enlightenment."
5  For Jefferson's meaning, see the pertinent remarks of Wood, *Radicalism*, 178–79. For the status of women, children, and slaves, see Kettner, *Citizenship*, 197–98, 311–12.
6  Some aspects of this problem have been discussed by Rodgers, *Contested Truths*; on problems left unanswered even after the Constitution, see Kettner, *Citizenship*, 231.

7   For the transformation of the "pursuit of happiness" in the Declaration into "property" in the Fourteenth Amendment, see the remarks of Wills, *Inventing America*, 240–55, with the critique of Hamowy, "Jefferson and the Scottish Enlightenment," 516–19.

8   Arist., *Pol.* 1.2, 1253a1–3: ἐκ τούτων οὖν φανερὸν ὅτι τῶν φύσει ἡ πόλις ἐστί, καὶ ὅτι ὁ ἄνθρωπος φύσει πολιτικὸν ζῷον (These considerations make it evident that the city-state belongs to the group of things that exist by nature, and that man is by nature a social and political being). Cf. also *Eth. Nic.* 1.7, 1097b11 and 9.9, 1169b18–19. Note also the phrase διὰ τὸ τὴν φύσιν ἴσους εἶναι πάντας (because all are by nature equal) at *Pol.* 2.2, 1261a39–b2.

9   Arist. *Pol.* 3.16, 1287a10–18.

10  Ibid. 3.6, 1279a21; 3.8, 1280a5.

11  Ibid. 1.13, 1260b15–20, esp. 18–20.

12  Ibid. 3.1, 1275a12–18.

13  This is already the case in the Declaration of Independence, which complains that the King "has endeavoured to prevent the Population of these States; for that Purpose obstructing the Laws for Naturalization of Foreigners. . . . "

14  Arist. *Pol.* 3.1, 1275a13–14: ἀτελῶς μετέχουσι τῆς τοιαύτης κοινωνίας (They share in a community of this sort in an incomplete sense).

15  See γένος ἴσοις ἢ μείζοσι (than their equals or superiors in birth) at 3.9, 1281a6; and at 1277b8–9 the definition of πολιτικὴ ἀρχή as τῶν ὁμοίων τῷ γένει καὶ τῶν ἐλευθέρων (rule over persons of a similar rank in birth and the free).

16  See Osborne, *Naturalization*, vol. I, 5–8.

17  Arist. *Pol.* 5.1, 1301a28–31.

18  See above, p. 162 with n. 8, and especially *Pol.* 2.2, 1261a39–b2: διὰ τὸ τὴν φύσιν ἴσους εἶναι πάντας. Here and in the following, I use "man" in its generic sense (= "mankind") and use the masculine to include both male and, where appropriate, female. It must not be forgotten that for the Greeks only the male can be a "citizen" in the full sense of the word.

19  Arist. *Pol.* 2.2, 1261a39–b5. The text is full of difficulties. I have adopted the version of W. D. Ross. The point made here is again made at 3.16, 1287a10–18, cf. n. 3 above.

20  Arist. *Pol.* 1.7, 1255b20: ἡ δὲ πολιτικὴ ἐλευθέρων καὶ ἴσων ἀρχή (rule of citizens is over persons equal and free).

21  Ibid. 4.4, 1291b31–37. "Political weight" seems to be an appropriate equivalent to κυρίους in this context.

22  I believe this to be the most accurate rendering of the idea underlying τὸ ἴσον ἔχειν, which literally means "to have the equal thing." Since, as I hope to show in the sequel, membership in the community is invariably described in terms of "sharing," "participating in" (μετέχειν, μετεῖναι), the only "thing" all citizens have equally is a share in the community.

23  See n. 21 above.

24  Arist. *Pol.* 6.2, 1317a40–b10.

25  Ibid. 3.9, 1280a11–12: οἷον δοκεῖ ἴσον τὸ δίκαιον εἶναι καὶ ἔστιν, ἀλλ᾽ οὐ πᾶσιν ἀλλὰ τοῖς ἴσοις (what is just is held to be and is equitable, not for all but for those who are equal).

26  Ibid. 4.4, 1291b30–34. Cf. n. 21 above.

27  The idea is partially expressed in the Greek concept *isonomia*. See Ostwald, *Nomos*, 96–136.

28  For a different approach to "equality," see Ian Morris's essay [this volume]; for a different approach to the relation of "freedom" to "equality," see Mogens H. Hansen's essay [this volume].

29 See von Fritz, "Die griechische ΕΛΕΥΘΕΡΙΑ." But even here Demaratus' famous remark to Xerxes (Hdt. 7.104), ἐλεύθεροι γὰρ ἐόντες οὐ πάντα ἐλεύθεροί εἰσι· ἔπεστι γάρ σφι νόμος, τὸν ὑποδειμαίνουσι πολλῷ, ἔτι μᾶλλον ἢ οἱ σοὶ σέ (for though they are free, they are not free in all respects: law is above them, and they fear it much more than your men fear you), seems to apply more to the Lacedaemonians as individuals than to the Greeks in a collective sense.

30 Arist. Pol. 3.8, 1279b39–1280a5.

31 Ibid. 3.10, 1281a31: τιμὰς γὰρ λέγομεν εἶναι τὰς ἀρχάς (for we say that "offices" are "honors"); cf. also 3.16, 1287a11–18, where the point is made that those who are equal by nature must necessarily have the same standard of right and wrong and naturally accept the same values (τὸ αὐτὸ δίκαιον ἀναγκαῖον καὶ τὴν αὐτὴν ἀξίαν καταφύσιν εἶναι), which are said to include also their attitude to τιμαί: consequently, they do not regard either ruling or being ruled as right, and take their turns (ἀνὰ μέρος) at both. See also the expression ἐν ταῖς τιμαῖς εἶναι as a synonym for τῶν ἀρχῶν μετέχειν at 4.4, 1290b12 and 5.6, 1305b4.

32 See ibid. 4.3, 1290a7–8: πολιτεία μὲν γὰρ ἡ τῶν ἀρχῶν τάξις ἐστί (for a régime is the ordering of public offices). Cf. also 3.4, 1277b7–16.

33 Ibid. 1.7, 1255b20: ἡ δὲ πολιτικὴ ἐλευθέρων καὶ ἴσων ἀρχή.

34 Ibid. 2.2, 1261a32–b5.

35 I owe to Mordechai E. Ostwald the observation that what I am trying to describe here comes very close to Leo Strauss's description of Greek society in his Natural Right, 129–32. My fundamental disagreement with Strauss concerns his inclusion of citizenship among "classic natural rights."

36 Arist. Pol. 1.13, 1260b13–14. Cf. also 4.3, 1290a2–5.

37 E.g., ibid. 2.8, 1268a24, 27–28; also 10, 1272a16. Cf. 4.6, 1293a3–4; 8, 1294a12–14; 4.13, 1297b4–6; 5.3, 1302b26–27; 6, 1306b10–11, 13–14; 6.13, 1332a32–35; 7.10, 1329b37. It is not uncommon to find κοινωνεῖν, "associate in," in place of the relevant forms of μετέχειν, e.g., 2.1, 1260b38–42 and 2.8, 1268a18: κοινωνεῖν < τῆς πολιτείας >; cf. τὴν πολιτικὴν κοινωνίαν (to participate in the social and political community/in the community of the city-state) at 2.10, 1272b14–15; 4.5, 1292b23–25: ἀνάγκη γὰρ ἢ πάντα τὰ εἰρημένα μέρη τοῦ δήμου κοινωνεῖν τῆς πολιτείας, ἢ τὰ μὲν τὰ δὲ μή (for either all the aforementioned parts of the people must participate in the social and political community or some do and others do not). For both expressions together, see 4.11, 1295a29–31: ἀλλὰ βίον τε τὸν τοῖς πλείστοις κοινωνῆσαι δυνατὸν καὶ πολιτείαν ἧς τὰς πλείστας πόλεις ἐνδέχεται μετασχεῖν (but a way of life that is possible for the majority to participate in and a social and political community that it is possible for most cities to share in). Occasionally, μέτεστι τῆς πόλεώς τινι is used in place of μετέχειν; see, e.g., 3.9, 1281a4–7. On the whole question, see Manville, Origins, 7–11.

38 Ibid., 4.4, 1291b34–37.

39 Ibid., 4.4, 1291b40–1292a4; cf. also 3.5, 1277b34–35. For oligarchies, see ibid. 4.5, 1292a39; cf. 6, 1292b29–32. So also at 4.6, 1292b35–41, 1293a14–15; 6.6, 1320b25–26. Similarly, 3.1, 1275b18–20.

40 Ibid., 4.6, 1292b32–33: τὸ δὲ δὴ ἐξεῖναι σχολάζειν ἀδύνατον μὴ προσόδων οὐσῶν (The possibility of enjoying leisure does not exist in the absence of income). The textual problem seen here by Ross is not apparent to me.

41 So also exousia in Aristotle's discussion of Plato's restriction of the amount of property a person can own cannot possibly refer to the "right" of a citizen to own no more than five times the amount of the smallest property; see ibid. 2.6, 1266b5–7: Πλάτων δὲ τοὺς Νόμους γράφων μέχρι μέν τινος ᾤετο δεῖν ἐᾶν, πλεῖον δὲ τοῦ πενταπλασίαν εἶναι τῆς 'ελαχίστης μηδενὶ τῶν πολιτῶν ἐξουσίαν εἶναι κτήσασθαι

(When he wrote the *Laws,* Plato believed that increase should be permitted up to a certain point, but that no citizen should be allowed to acquire more than five times the amount of the smallest property).

42    Ibid. 2.11, 1273b12–13; 3.1, 1275a22–23, 28, 32–33; 10, 1281b25–26; cf. 2.11, 1274a21; 3.5, 1277b36. For τιμῶν μετέχειν, see 3.4, 1278a35–38; 4.11, 1296a15; 13, 1297b6–11; 5.7, 1306b23; 12, 1316b21.

43    Ibid., 5.3, 1302b6–9: ὑβριζόντων τε γὰρ τῶν ἐν ταῖς ἀρχαῖς καὶ πλεονεκτούντων στασιάζουσι καὶ πρὸς ἀλλήλους καὶ πρὸς τὰς πολιτείας τὰς διδούσας τὴν ἐξουσίαν (Offensive behavior and graft on the part of those in office give rise to conflicts among them and against the regimes that give them license). The ἐξουσία here referred to is presumably the possibility the political system gives to officials to enrich themselves and act arrogantly. Cf. also 7.9, 1329a13–16: λείπεται τοίνυν τοῖς αὐτοῖς μὲν ἀμφότερα (*sc.,* military duty and deliberation) ἀποδιδόναι τὴν πολιτείαν ταῦτα, μὴ ἅμα δέ, ἀλλ' ὥσπερ πέφυκεν ἡμὲν δύναμις ἐν νεωτέροις, ἡ δὲ φρόνησις ἐν πρεσβυτέροις εἶναι (what is left for the state is to grant both functions to the same persons, but not simultaneously, but, as nature wants it, strength is found in younger, and good sense in older men).

44    In addition to the preceding note, see 4.13, 1298a6–9. Also 5.6, 1306a25–26. Cf. also 6.7, 1321a26–29.

45    See the References below.

46    For the role these property-classes played in shaping the Athenian democracy, see V. D. Hanson's essay in [*Demokratia*].

47    I discuss this problem in greater detail in "Public Expense: Whose Obligation?"

# REFERENCES

Becker, Carl. *The Declaration of Independence: A Study in the History of Political Ideas.* New York: Harcourt, Brace, 1922.

Cochrane, C. N. *Christianity and Classical Culture: A Study of Thought and Action from Augustus to Augustine.* Rev. ed. London, New York, and Toronto: Oxford University Press, 1944.

Fritz, Kurt von. "Die griechische ELEUTHERIA bei Herodot." *Wiener Studien* 78 (1965): 5–31.

Hamowy, R. "Jefferson and the Scottish Enlightenment: A Critique of Garry Wills's 'Inventing America: Jefferson's Declaration of Independence'." *William and Mary Quarterly* 36 (1979): 503–23.

Kettner, James H. *The Development of American Citizenship, 1608–1870.* Chapel Hill: University of North Carolina Press, 1978.

Manville, Philip Brook. *The Origins of Citizenship in Ancient Athens.* Princeton: Princeton University Press, 1990.

Osborne, Michael J. *Naturalization in Athens.* 4 vols. Brussels: Academie voor Wetenschapen, Letteren en Schone Kunsten (WLSK), 1981–83.

Ostwald, Martin. *Nomos and the Beginnings of the Athenian Democracy.* Oxford: Clarendon Press, 1969.

——"Public Expense: Whose Obligation? Athens 600–454 B.C.E." In *Proceedings of the American Philosophical Society* 139 (1995): 368–79.

Rodgers, Daniel T. *Contested Truths: Keywords in American Politics since Independence.* New York: Basic Books, 1987.

Sinclair, R. K. *Democracy and Participation in Athens.* Cambridge: Cambridge University Press, 1988.

Strauss, Leo. *Natural Right and History.* Chicago: University of Chicago Press, 1953.

Wills, Garry. *Inventing America: Jefferson's Declaration of Independence.* Garden City, N.Y.: Doubleday, 1978.

Wood, Gordon S. *The Radicalism of the American Revolution.* New York: Alfred A. Knopf, 1992.

# The Ancient Athenian and the Modern Liberal View of Liberty as a Democratic Ideal

## Mogens Herman Hansen

As the title of my paper suggests, my intention is to compare Athenian *eleutheria* with political freedom in Western democracies, and to discuss differences and similarities between the ancient and the modern concept of liberty. For many years the fashion has been to emphasize the differences. The purpose of my paper is to advocate a swing of the pendulum and argue that the undeniable differences are overshadowed by the striking similarities. My paper must therefore be read as a plea, not as an attempt to present a so-called "objective" or "balanced" view of the problem.

Today the term *democracy* denotes both a set of political institutions and a set of political ideals[1] – ideals that are believed to be furthered by democratic political institutions more than by any other form of government.[2] As a set of political institutions, democracy is commonly defined as a political system in which power – directly or indirectly – rests with the whole of the people.[3] As a set of political ideals, democracy is connected first of all with liberty, next with equality.[4] It is remarkable how, in this respect, modern democracy resembles ancient Athenian *dēmokratia*.

In liberal democratic thought democracy, liberty, and equality form a triad and are often described as the three points of a triangle.[5] As for the ancient view, I will restrict myself to quoting two passages, one from a champion and one from an opponent of popular government. Let me begin with three lines from Aristotle's *Politics* which in one sentence condense what he repeats throughout this part of his treatise:

> For if liberty (*eleutheria*) and equality (*isotēs*), as is thought by some, are chiefly to be found in democracy (*dēmokratia*), they will be best attained when all persons alike share in the government to the utmost. And since the people are in the majority, and the opinion of the majority is decisive, such a government must necessarily be a democracy.[6]

Here we learn that *dēmokratia* was both a political system and a set of political ideals, that the two central ideals were *eleutheria*, "liberty," and *isotēs*, "equality," and that

Mogens Herman Hansen, "The Ancient Athenian and the Modern Liberal View of Liberty as a Democratic Ideal," in J. Ober and C. Hedrick (eds.), *Demokratia* (Princeton: Princeton University Press, 1996), pp. 91–104.

the concepts of *dēmokratia-eleutheria-isotēs* were commonly juxtaposed so as to form a triad.[7]

Now Aristotle disliked democracy, but his critical account of the democratic principles is confirmed, for example, by Pericles' praise of popular rule in the funeral oration as reported by Thucydides:[8]

> It has the name democracy (*dēmokratia*) because government is in the hands not of the few but of the majority (*es tous pleionas oikein*).[9] In private disputes all are equal (*pasi to ison*) before the law; and when it comes to esteem in public affairs, a man is preferred according to his own reputation for something, not, on the whole, just turn and turn about,[10] but for excellence, and even in poverty no man is debarred by obscurity of reputation so long as he has it in him to do some good service to the State. Freedom is a feature of our public life (*eleutherōs politeuomen*); and as for suspicion of one another in our daily private pursuits, we do not frown on our neighbor if he behaves to please himself or set our faces in those expressions of disapproval that are so disagreeable, however harmless.

In this famous passage we are supposed to be persuaded that Athens is a *dēmokratia*, that its political system is based on the principle *es tous pleionas oikein* [administration in the hands of the majority], and that the basic ideals of democracy are *pasi to ison* [all are equal] and *eleutherōs politeuomen* [freedom is a feature of public life].

It is important to keep in mind that the concepts of freedom and equality overlap – both in modern political thought and in ancient Athenian democratic ideology. Freedom of speech, for example, is seen sometimes as a kind of equality, but sometimes as a kind of liberty protected by the democratic constitution.[11] In Athens every citizen's right to address his fellow citizens is commonly called *isēgoria*, and the term indicates that the ideal is viewed as a kind of equality.[12] It is every citizen's *equal* right to speak that is stressed. But in Euripides' *Supplices*, for example, the same right is also described as a kind of liberty.[13] The situation is similar in modern liberal democracy. Discussions of equality invariably lead to the question, Equality of what? and to many liberal democrats the obvious answer has been, Equality of liberty![14] Thus liberty and equality tend to coalesce precisely as *eleutheria* and *isotēs* tended to coalesce in ancient Athens.

There is yet another similarity between modern and ancient democratic ideology that concerns the relation between liberty and equality: To modern champions of participatory or radical democracy, equality is more important than liberty, but to liberal democrats liberty matters more than equality.[15] The Athenians held similar views: In classical Athens – and as far back as the sources go – *eleutheria* eclipsed *isotēs*.

Many historians hold that the central aspect of democratic equality and of democratic ideology altogether was *isonomia*.[16] But the term *isonomia* is poorly attested in classical Athens.[17] First, it is not found in symbouleutic and forensic speeches, whereas the terms *eleutheria* and *eleutheros* are commonly used. Next, the names a state gives its warships often reflect its slogans and political values. In the Athenian navy several triremes were called *Dēmokratia* and *Eleutheria*;[18] one was called *Parrhēsia*,[19] but there is no sign of any trireme ever being called *Isonomia*.[20] Third, the political cults did not include *isonomia*: both *dēmokratia* and *eleutheria* were made divine and worshiped by the Athenians, *Dēmokratia* in its own right as a separate goddess,[21] *Eleutheria* in connection with the cult of Zeus Eleutherios;[22] but *isonomia* was never represented as a goddess and never connected with any form of worship. All three observations indicate that the key concept of Athenian democratic ideology was *eleutheria*, not *isonomia*.

So much for the close connection between *eleutheria* and *isotēs* and the similar connection between liberty and equality in liberal democratic theory. I now turn to the main question and ask, What is political liberty? and what was *eleutheria* in ancient Athenian democratic thought?

By way of introduction I will briefly point out that in sources describing classical Athens we can detect at least seven different uses of the noun *eleutheria* and the adjective *eleutheros*.

1   The most common use of *eleutheros* is in the sense of "free" as opposed to being a slave (*doulos*).[23] This sense of *eleutheria*, however, is not particularly democratic since slaves existed in all poleis independent of their constitutions.
2   *Eleutheria* was regularly invoked as a basic democratic ideal in debates that contrasted democracy and tyranny, cf. the famous dictum of Democritus: "Poverty under democracy is as much to be preferred to so-called prosperity under an autocracy as freedom to slavery."[24] The opposite of this form of *eleutheria* was being enslaved in a metaphorical sense, i.e., being subjected to a despotic ruler. Note that in Democritus *dēmokratia* is linked with poverty, *penia*, just as it is in the next case.
3   When status was at stake, *eleutheros* often had the meaning of being freeborn in the sense of being a born citizen.[25] In such a context one would expect *eleutheros* to denote both citizens and free foreigners as opposed to slaves (see 1 above), but there can be no denying that *eleutheria* used in a democratic polis about descent was restricted to citizens and excluded both free foreigners and slaves.[26] This type of *eleutheria* was a specific democratic value and formed the basis of one view of democratic equality: according to Aristotle democrats believed that since they were all *eleutheroi* (by descent) they ought to be equal in everything.[27] In Aristotle *aporos* is used synonymously with *eleutheros*[28] and the antonyms are *plousios* or *euporos*.[29] So in this case democracy is opposed to oligarchy, not tyranny.
4   In classical Athens all citizens were both entitled and expected to participate in the running of the democratic institutions – not, as one might have expected, as voters in the Assembly, but rather by taking turns in filling all the magistracies. "To rule and be ruled in turns" was described as *eleutheria* and conceived of as a kind of freedom to be found in democracies only.[30]
5   The most controversial form of democratic liberty, however, was the ideal that everybody had a right to live as he pleased (*zēn hōs bouletai tis*) without being oppressed by other persons or by the authorities.[31] It is sometimes stressed that a person's *eleutheria* in this sense was restricted by the (democratic) laws;[32] other sources emphasize that the principle *zēn hōs bouletai tis* applied to the private and not to the public sphere of life.[33]
6   Next, *eleutheros* is often used in the sense of *autonomos* as against being dominated by others (*hypēkoos*).[34] But again, *eleutheria* in the sense of *autonomia* applied to oligarchies – and sometimes even to monarchies – as well as to democracies. It was

the freedom *of* the polis, whereas democratic liberty was freedom *within* the polis.[35]

7    Finally, *eleutheros* is sometimes taken by the philosophers to denote a person who is self-restrained.[36] *Eleutheria* in the sense of "self-control" is not far from some modern philosophers' view of positive freedom (cf. *infra*); but though often focusing on self-control, Plato and Aristotle hardly ever take it to be a kind of *eleutheria*,[37] and furthermore, *eleutheria* in this sense has no bearing on political and especially on democratic freedom.[38]

Only four of these seven uses are specifically connected with democracy, namely: *eleutheros* (a) in the sense of being a free-born citizen, (b) in the sense of being entitled to participate in the running of the political institutions, (c) in the sense of living as one pleases, and (d) in the sense of not being subjected to a despotic ruler. The four uses can in fact be reduced to two: the right to participate in political decision-making is inextricably bound up with being a full citizen by birth (a + b);[39] and the right to live as one pleases is often opposed to being ruled, especially by a monarch, and any kind of interference by others in one's private life is rejected as illegitimate and undemocratic (c + d).[40]

Now, how are these two types of freedom related to the notion of liberty advocated in Western democracies in the twentieth century? In contemporary liberal democratic theory liberty is commonly subdivided into negative freedom and positive freedom.[41] Negative freedom is freedom from oppression by the state or by other individuals. Positive freedom is harder to define in one sentence. Following Kant, Hegel, and Isaiah Berlin, philosophers take positive freedom to be some form of self-government or self-mastery, a notion that implies that one is divided into two selves, and that "positive freedom" consists in allowing one's true self to dominate one's other self.[42] Students of political theory take a somewhat different view: they interpret self-determination as an entitlement to participate in collective decision-making, i.e., in a democracy, to be politically active in a free society.[43] Since it is *political* liberty that interests us in our context, I will concentrate on the second line of thought and subscribe to the following description of positive freedom: "There is a link between liberty and democracy through the connection between self-government and self-determination: the self-determined – the free – individual is the self-governing individual. Here individual liberty is seen to involve participation in, rather than the absence of, government."[44] The negative and the positive aspects of freedom are essentially opposed: if we suppose that every aspect of life can be regulated by political decision-making, there is, in principle, no guaranteed freedom from political oppression, but if, on the other hand, we maximize freedom from public interference with the different ways citizens live, there is no political decision-making left in which citizens can participate. The negative and the positive aspects of freedom can only be reconciled if combined with a distinction between a public sphere, in which positive political freedom operates, and a private sphere, in which negative individual freedom is protected against interference from the state.[45] Freedom in the private sphere is connected with the concept of fundamental rights that protect one's person and property and guarantee that one can live as one pleases, as long as he or she respects the laws. Freedom in the public sphere is connected with free elections and with every citizen's right to participate in politics.

Like its modern counterpart, ancient democratic *eleutheria* had two aspects: freedom to participate in the democratic institutions and freedom to live as one pleased. The dual nature of *eleutheria* is most clearly described by Aristotle in the *Politics:*

> A basic principle of the democratic constitution is liberty. That is commonly said, and those who say it imply that only in this constitution do men share in liberty; for that, they say, is what every democracy aims at. Now one aspect of liberty is being ruled and ruling in turn. . . . Another element is to live as you like. For this, they say, is what being free is about, since its opposite, living not as you like, is the condition of a slave. So this is the second defining principle of democracy, and from it has come the ideal of not being ruled, not by anybody at all if possible, or at least only in turn.[46]

According to Aristotle liberty is partly political participation by ruling in turn, partly freedom from political oppression by not being ruled but by living as one pleases. A positive political freedom is contrasted with an individual negative freedom. Aristotle's description of democratic liberty is stated in general terms and there is no explicit reference to Athens, but all the sources show that in this respect the Athenians conformed to the norm.[47] The ideal "to live as one pleases" is praised as a fundamental democratic value by Otanes in the Constitutional Debate in Herodotus,[48] by Athenian statesmen in Thucydides' speeches,[49] and by the Orators in the speeches they delivered before the People's Court.[50] And to rule in turn is singled out by King Theseus in Euripides' play as an essential feature of Athenian democracy.[51]

The view I have presented here is one I have developed and advocated in two recent publications,[52] but it is not the prevailing view among students of ancient history and philosophy. The fashion today is to emphasize the differences between ancient Athenian *eleutheria* and modern democratic liberty: the Athenians, it is said, had no notion of individual rights; the polis was a type of society that permeated all aspects of life; consequently there was no "private sphere" out of reach of the polis, and no notion of what we call negative freedom, i.e., freedom from oppression by the state and its government. Furthermore, "positive freedom" in modern thought is far from the ancient notion of freedom as political participation. And, to top it all, an insuperable difference is that ancient *eleutheria* was intimately related to the opposition between the free and the slave, whereas, in the modern world, the absence of slavery places the concept of liberty in a very different setting.[53] I respond with five points.

1   The view of Isaiah Berlin and many philosophers that positive freedom is self-determination in the sense of self-control, is far from the Athenian view of political freedom as citizen participation in running the democratic institutions. But, as I noted above, political scientists prefer to see this aspect of freedom as individual self-determination *through participating in the creation of the social order.* When political freedom is connected with political participation, the similarity between ancient Athenian and modern political freedom becomes apparent.

2   To illustrate the gulf between modern negative freedom and ancient *eleutheria,* some scholars adduce Benjamin Constant's illuminating essay *De la liberté des anciens comparée à celle des modernes.* Here ancient *political* liberty is taken to consist of collective decision-making by all citizens in assembly, whereas modern liberty is *individual* and consists in guarantees against infringements of every

person's right to live as he or she pleases. This type of freedom is, according to Constant, unknown in ancient Greece and Rome.[54] But those who adduce Constant usually forget to add that he explicitly excepts classical Athens from his general analysis of ancient liberty. In Athens, he says, the concept of freedom was very similar to the modern concept, allegedly because commerce was an important factor in the Athenian economy.[55] Whether Constant's explanation is right or wrong is debatable. The important point is that he detected the obvious similarity between ancient Athenian *eleutheria* and the "modern" type of liberty he experienced in his own age. What separates him from us is that he took Sparta and not Athens to be the model of a Greek polis and thus based his analysis of ancient liberty on Sparta and on the philosophers (who admired Sparta more than Athens), whereas he took Athens to be the exception. One of the first to take the opposite stand was George Grote, who maintained that in most respects Athens was the rule and Sparta the exception. Consequently he believed that the democratic ideal of every man's right to live as he pleased was typical of classical Greece.[56] I prefer to avoid generalizations, but following Constant and Grote, I would like to stress the similarity between the Athenian and the liberal notion of personal freedom.

3     The alleged difference between individual liberty in ancient Athens and in modern liberal thought lies in the principles and arguments used to justify it. In modern democratic thought liberty is about the protection of individual rights against infringements by the state or by other people, whereas, it is held, in Athens "the authority of the community over individuals was relatively unrestricted." As Martin Ostwald has pointed out,[57] it is certainly true that the Athenians had no developed concept of "rights" as we have it today. But in practice they certainly knew about the privileges and liberties connected with their democratic constitution, and these rights were highly valued and crucial for their belief that democracy was the best constitution.

Several of the Attic Orators state with approval the rule that no citizen could be executed without due process of law.[58] Admittedly thieves and robbers were not included: they could be put to death immediately if they were caught in the act and had to confess.[59] But that limitation, though important, does not seriously alter the fact that "no execution without a trial" (*mēdena akriton apokteinai*) was felt to be a right that all citizens enjoyed.[60]

Another rule forbade torture of Athenian citizens.[61] It was warranted by a decree (*psēphisma*) probably passed immediately after the expulsion of the tyrants in 510–509 before the introduction of the democracy.[62] It was nevertheless adopted by the democrats and, like the expulsion of the tyrants, was later associated with democracy. The principle that free men are exempt from corporal punishment is closely connected with democracy in Demosthenes' speech against Androtion.[63]

The Athenian democracy further provided some protection of a citizen's home. Demosthenes was severely criticized by Aeschines for breaking into a house and arresting the alleged traitor, Antiphon, without a warrant, i.e., a *psēphisma* of the People,[64] and in the Assembly Aeschines got his way and secured the man's release. Demosthenes, in his turn, accuses Androtion of having surpassed the Thirty in brutality: they had people arrested in the marketplace, but, when exacting arrears of *eisphora*, Androtion conducted the Eleven to the debtors' houses and had them arrested there.[65]

Finally, in Aristotle's *Constitution of Athens*, we are told that "as soon as the Archon enters upon his office, he proclaims through the public herald that whatever a person possessed before he entered upon his Archonship he will have and possess until the end of his term."[66] Like the ban on torture of citizens, this is probably a survival from the sixth century. It may even go back to Solon, a measure to reassure the Athenians that, after the *seisachtheia* (shaking off of burdens), no further infringements of private property would take place.[67] But even if the origin and original purpose of the proclamation are obscure, what we know for sure is that it was still valid in the fourth century and understood as a guarantee that no redistribution of property would take place in Athens, as happened in other Greek poleis.

In addition to the protection of person, home, and property, the most treasured of individual rights is freedom of speech, cherished by democrats but suppressed by supporters of authoritarian rule.[68] Once more we find the same ideal in democratic Athens,[69] as in Demosthenes' remark that a basic difference between Spartan oligarchy and Athenian democracy is that in Athens you are free to praise the Spartan constitution and way of life, if you so wish, whereas in Sparta it is prohibited to praise any other constitution than the Spartan.[70]

It is not enough, however, to have laws and regulations protecting the citizens: there must also be ways of enforcing them if they are infringed by the democratic polis itself and its officials. Consequently the Athenians provided for both public and private prosecution of magistrates and connected the democracy with the rule of law and the protection of citizens against their rulers. An obvious example is Aeschines' praise of the rule of law in democratic Athens: "As you are well aware, Athenians, in a democracy it is the laws that protect the individual and the *politeia*, whereas the tyrant and the oligarch are protected by mistrust and armed body-guards. Oligarchs, and those who run the unequal states, have to guard them-selves against those who would overthrow the state by force; you who have an equal state based on the laws have to punish those who speak or have led their lives contrary to the laws."[71] Here legal protection of the citizens is singled out as the hallmark of democracy. The comparison between the three constitutions in that passage leaves no doubt that the laws Aeschines has in mind are laws binding the rulers, not the ruled. In oligarchies and tyrannies citizens are exposed to the whims of their rulers, in democracies the laws protect the citizens. Against whom? Obviously against the political leaders and the magistrates, who must respect the democratic laws in their dealings with the citizens.

4    It is often said that *eleutheria* was basically different from modern liberty because the connotation of being free in the sense of not being a slave lay behind any use of *eleutheria*.[72] It is true that *eleutheria* in the sense of self-determination was rooted in the opposition free/slave,[73] whereas the modern concept of liberty does not have slavery as its antonym (except in a metaphorical sense). But two consid-erations will suffice to show that *eleutheria* as a democratic ideal was viewed differently from *eleutheria* in its social sense (free *versus* slave). First, as a consti-tutional ideal *eleutheria* was specifically democratic and not a value praised in oligarchies or monarchies; the oligarchs[74] (and the philosophers[75]) did not have

an alternative interpretation of *eleutheria*, as we shall see they had of equality; they simply rejected *eleutheria* as a mistaken ideal,[76] and that would not have been possible if the critics of democracy had felt that "not being a slave" was an important aspect of the democratic ideal. Second, as a democratic ideal *eleutheria* (in the sense of personal freedom) applied not only to citizens but also to metics and sometimes even to slaves. Thus, a slave, who in the social sphere was deprived of *eleutheria*, might well, in a democratic polis, be allowed a share in, for example, freedom of speech, though only privately and of course not in the political assemblies.[77]

To sum up, the idea of self-determination may well be behind all uses of *eleutheria*,[78] but the sources show that Greek democrats distinguished constitutional liberty from liberty in the social sense, and imposed the distinction on the rest, by inducing aristocrats and oligarchs to hate *eleutheria* as a mistaken democratic value and, in this context, to ignore (or suppress) the notion of *eleutheria* as being opposed to *douleia* [slavery].

5   That the Athenians did distinguish a public sphere from a private sphere is now, I think, acknowledged by most scholars and to refute the opposite view would be to flog a dead horse. But a note of warning is in order: the Athenian distinction is between the private (*to idion*) and the public (*to koinon* or *dēmosion*), which is not quite the same as our opposition between the individual and the state. First, in many modern discussions, e.g., of democratic freedom, the contrast individual/ state is itself somewhat twisted: the opposite of individual freedom is not state authority but public control.[79] Next, in the Greek sources, the public sphere is mostly identified with the polis,[80] whereas the private sphere is sometimes a social sphere without any emphasis on the individual: family life, business, industry, and many types of religious association belonged in the private and not in the public sphere. The Athenians distinguished between the individual as a private person and as a citizen rather than between the individual and the state. Thus, instead of *individual* freedom, it is preferable to speak about *personal* or *private* freedom, which was often individual in character, but not invariably so.

I conclude that Athenian democratic *eleutheria* in several important respects was strikingly similar to the concept of freedom in modern liberal democracies. As a democratic ideal *eleutheria* had two aspects: it was both freedom to participate in political decision-making (positive freedom) and freedom from political oppression (negative freedom). It was linked with the distinction between a public sphere (in which political freedom applied) and a private sphere (in which each individual was allowed to live as he pleased). Freedom of speech was perhaps the right most cherished by the Athenian democrats, as it is in liberal democracies. Together with *dēmokratia* and *isotēs*, *eleutheria* formed a triad, just as liberty, equality, and democracy form a triad in liberal democratic thought.

But why this similarity? It cannot be the classical influence on European political thought during the Enlightenment. Admittedly, the modern concepts of democracy, liberty, and equality have sprung from three sources: the American Revolution, the French Revolution, and the English utilitarians. But the positive view of democracy, and the triangle democracy-liberty-equality did not emerge until the mid-nineteenth century. And George Grote was one of the first to link it with the classical tradition. If we look for the influence of classical tradition on the modern concepts of democracy, liberty, and equality, we should probably shift the focus of interest from the American and French Revolutions to the mid-nineteenth century and on. But let me end with another warning: Tradition must not be overrated (it sometimes is, especially by classicists), and correspondingly we must not underrate our capacity in similar circumstances to develop strikingly similar but basically unrelated institutions and ideals. I am inclined to believe that liberty, equality, separation of the public from the private, and protection of personal rights are ideals fostered in the ancient Greek world by the development from tyranny over oligarchy to democracy, and, independently, in modern Europe by a somewhat similar development, from monarchy over republic to democracy. In my view the Athenian example was of little or no importance for those who in the nineteenth century developed the liberal view of democratic freedom, and there is no evidence of any *direct* tradition transmitted from Athens to Western Europe and America in the eighteenth century.[81]

# NOTES

1  Sartori, "Democracy," 112; Hättich, *Begriff,* 10, 17; Burdeau, *Démocratie*, 10; Pennock, *Democratic Political Theory*, 14.

2  Dahl, *Democracy*, 88–89.

3  Pennock, *Democratic Political Theory*, 7; Holden, *Understanding Liberal Democracy*, 5; Naess, *Democracy, Ideology, and Objectivity*, 276–329.

4  Sartori, "Democracy," 116–177; Pennock, *Democratic Political Theory*, 16.

5  E. Vacherot, *La Démocratie* (Paris: F. Chamerot, 1860) 7: "Démocratie, en bon langage, a toujours signifié le peuple se gouvernant lui-même; c'est l'égalité dans la liberté" [Democracy, properly speaking, has always signified the self-government of the people; it is the equality contained in liberty] = Tocqueville 2.2.1, but without his modifications. B. Holden, *Understanding Liberal Democracy*, 28: "Democracy, liberty and equality form, as it were, the three points or angles of a triangle."

6  Arist. *Pol.* 1291b34–38.

7  Cf. also Plato *Rep.* 563b; Isoc. 7.20; Dem. 10.4; Arist. *Pol.* 1310a28–33.

8  Thuc. 2.37.1–3.

9  For this interpretation of *es tous pleionas oikein*, cf. Thuc. 5.81.2, 8.38.3, 8.53.3, 8.89.2. Raaflaub, "Perceptions of Democracy," 60 and especially Harris, "Pericles' Praise of Athenian Democracy," 163–66.

10  Gomme, *HCT*, II, 108; Hornblower, *Commentary*, 300.

11  Rawls, "Basic Liberties," 55–57.

12  Wood, *Peasant-Citizen and Slave*, 130.

13  Eur. *Supp.* 438–41.

14  Plamenatz, "Equality of Opportunity," 84; Berlin, *Four Essays on Liberty*, 125; Sartori, *Democratic Theory*, 348.

15  Liberal democrats "put liberty at the top of their value hierarchy, above equality" (Pennock, *Democratic Political Theory*, 16).

16  Finley, "Freedom of the Citizen," 10; Mulgan, "Liberty in Ancient Greece," 12; Bleicken, *Die athenische Demokratie*, 32, 191, 263, 312. Meier, *Greek Discovery*, 55, 66–68, 162.

17    Hansen, *Was Athens a Democracy?* 42n.140.

18    Triremes called *Dēmokratia: IG* II² 1604, line 24; 1606, line 59; 1620, line 32; 1623, line 326. Called *Eleutheria: IG* II², 1604, line 49; 1607, line 85; 1627, line 202; 1631, line 488.

19    *IG* II² 1624, line 81.

20    Hansen, *Was Athens a Democracy?* 42n.142.

21    *IG* II² 1496, lines 131–32; 2791, cf. Raubitschek, "Demokratia."

22    Agora I 2483 = Wycherley, *Agora*, no. 39; Xen. *Oec.* 7.1; Hdt. 3.142.4. Raaflaub, *Entdeckung der Freiheit*, 132–35.

23    Xen. *Hell.* 1.6.24; Arist. *Pol.* 1253b3–4.

24    Democr. fr. 251.

25    Dem. 57.69; Aeschin. 3.169; Arist. *Ath. Pol.* 42.1. Cf. *Pol.* 1281a6; 1283a33; 1290b9; 1291b26; 1301a28–35. I follow Wyse, *Speeches of Isaeus*, 281 *pace* Rhodes, *Commentary*, 499.

26    Arist. *Pol.* 1281b22–23.

27    Ibid., 1301a28–35.

28    Ibid., 1290b18.

29    Ibid., 1280a4–5; 1290b1–3.

30    Ibid., 1317b2–3; Eur. *Supp.* 406–8; cf. Isoc. 20.20.

31    Hdt. 3.83.3; Thuc. 2.37.2; 7.69.2; Lys. 26.5; Plato *Rep.* 557b; Isoc. 7.20.

32    E.g., Hdt. 3.83.3.

33    E.g., Thuc. 2.37.3.

34    Xen. *Hell.* 3.1.20; *IG* II² 126, line 16.

35    Cf. Raaflaub, *Entdeckung der Freiheit*, on *Polisfreiheit* (148), and *das innenpolitische Freiheitsbegriff* (258).

36    Cf., e.g., Plato *Tht.* 172c; *Phdr.* 256b; *Def.* 412d, 415a; Xen. *Mem.* 1.2.5.

37    In Arist. *Eth. Nic.* there is no discussion of *eleutheria* and *eleutheros*, and only *eleutheriotēs* and *eleutherios*, "generous" and "generosity," are concepts of any consequence.

38    Arist. *Pol.* 1325a19, referring to the philosopher who is *apolis*.

39    Dem. 9.3.

40    Hdt. 3.83.

41    Sartori, *Democratic Theory*, 282–87; Berlin, *Four Essays on Liberty*, 118–72; Taylor, "What's Wrong with Negative Liberty?" Gray, "On Negative and Positive Liberty," 321–48; Ryan, "Freedom," 163–66.

42    Berlin, *Four Essays on Liberty*, 131–34.

43    Kelsen, *General Theory*, 284–85: "Freedom is self-determination and political freedom is self-determination of the individual by participating in the creation of the social order." Sartori, *Democratic Theory*, 286: "It can be argued that political freedom has also a positive aspect. . . . Now, there is no doubt that political freedom cannot be inert, that it postulates some activity; in other words that it is not freedom *from*, but also *participation in*. No one denies this. But we must not overstress this latter aspect." J. Plamenatz, response to UNESCO's questionaire about democracy (1949): "Representative democracy is government by persons freely chosen by the great majority of the governed," in Naess, *Democracy, Ideology, and Objectivity*, 329. Cf. also Gray, *Liberalism*, 57; Dahl, *Democracy*, 89.

44    Holden, *Understanding Liberal Democracy*, 21. Cf. also Lucas, *Democracy and Participation*, 134: "Political freedom requires not only that a subject may hold opinions of his own and express them, but that he should have some real opportunity to ventilate his views, make common cause with those that are like-minded, and persuade others, who in turn may be able to persuade those to whom the decision is entrusted. Freedom of speech and the right of association are a beginning, but they need to be supplemented by some

duty on rulers to listen, and some further provision that arguments and pleas are not only heard but sometimes heeded." Gray, "On Negative and Positive Liberty," 327: "Now both the understanding of freedom as consisting in the entitlement to a voice in political decision-making and the understanding of freedom as rational choice in accordance with standards that are one's own and which accord with a natural moral order are present in the modern liberal tradition but, as Berlin has emphasized, neither is distinctive of it." Dahl, *Democracy*, 311: "The democratic process…promotes freedom as no feasible alternative can: freedom in the form of individual and collective self-determination."

45   Berlin, *Four Essays on Liberty*, 124, 126; Holden, *Understanding Liberal Democracy*, 12–13, 140–41.

46   Arist. *Pol.* 1317a40–b17.

47   Plato *Rep.* 557b; *Def.* 412d; Isoc. 7.20.

48   Hdt. 3.83.2–3.

49   Thuc. 2.37.2; 7.69.2.

50   Lys. 26.5.

51   Eur. *Supp.* 406–8; cf. Isoc. 20.20.

52   Hansen, *Was Athens a Democracy?* 8–21, 25–28; *The Athenian Democracy*, 74–85.

53   Sartori, *Democratic Theory*, 292; Berlin, *Four Essays*, xl–xli; Gray, *Liberalism*, 1; Mulgan, "Liberty in Ancient Greece"; Bleicken, *Die athenische Demokratie*, 313.

54   B. Constant, *De la Liberté des anciens comparée à celle des modernes* (1819) reprinted in M. Gauchet, *De la liberté chez les modernes: Écrits politiques* (Paris: Livre de Poche, 1980), 491–515.

55   Constant, *Liberté*, 500: "Athènes était de toutes les républiques grecques la plus commerçante, aussi accordait-elle à ces citoyens infiniment plus de liberté individuelle que Rome et que Sparte" [of all the Greek republics Athens was the most commercial, and furthermore it granted its citizens infinitely more individual liberty than did Rome or Sparta]; cf. ibid., note 14: "Si le caractère tout à fait moderne des Athéniens n'a pas été suffisament remarqué, c'est que l'esprit général de l'époque influait sur les philosophes, et qu'ils écrivaient toujours en sens inverse des moeurs nationales" [If the Athenians' altogether modern disposition has not been sufficiently noticed, the reason is that the spirit of the time influenced the philosophers and that they always wrote placing themselves in opposition to the various national mores].

56   G. Grote, *History of Greece*, vol. 6, 180: "This portion of the speech of Perikles [§ 37] deserves peculiar attention, because it serves to correct an assertion, often far too indiscriminately made, respecting antiquity as contrasted with modern societies – an assertion that the ancient societies sacrificed the individual to the state, and that only in modern times has individual agency been left free to the proper extent. This is preeminently true of Sparta: – it is also true in a great degree of the ideal societies depicted by Plato and Aristotle: but it is pointedly not true of the Athenian democracy, nor can we with any confidence predicate it of the major part of the Grecian cities."

57   [This volume.]

58   Isoc. 15.22; Lys. 22.2; Hansen, *Was Athens a Democracy?* 13.

59   Arist. *Ath. Pol.* 52.1.

60   Lys. 19.7; Dem. 25.87.

61   Andoc. 1.43.

62   MacDowell, *Andocides*, 92–93.

63   Dem. 22.55.

64   Ibid., 18.132.

65   Ibid., 22.51–52.

66   Arist. *Ath. Pol.* 56.2. Mossé, "La Démocratie athénienne."

67   Rhodes, *Commentary*, 622.

68    Rawls, "The Basic Liberties," 55–79.
69    Eur. *Hipp.* 421–23; Dem. 45.79 and *Ep.* 3.13. Raaflaub, "Des Freien Bürgers Recht."
70    Dem. 20. 105–8.
71    Aeschin. 1.4–5.
72    Mulgan, "Liberty in Ancient Greece," 8–9.
73    Meier, "Freiheit," 426; Raaflaub, *Die Entdeckung der Freiheit,* 29–70, 160–88.
74    Ps. Xen. *Ath. Pol.* 1.8; Theophr. 28.6.
75    Plato *Rep.* 557b–58c, 562b–64a; Arist. *Pol.* 1310a26–33; 1318b39–41.
76    Hansen, *Was Athens a Democracy?* 12, cf. Raaflaub, "Democracy, Oligarchy," 525–56
      *pace* Mulgan, "Liberty in Ancient Greece," 18–20.
77    Dem. 9.3; Ps. Xen. *Ath. Pol.* 1.12.
78    Democ. fr. 251.
79    Taylor, "What's Wrong with Negative Liberty?" 175–77.
80    Isoc. 7.30; Dem. 20.57.
81    Hansen, *Was Athens a Democracy?* 26–28; "The Tradition of the Athenian Democracy,"
      passim.

## REFERENCES

Berlin, I. *Four Essays on Liberty.* London and New York: Oxford University Press, 1969.

Bleicken, Jochen. *Die athenische Demokratie.* 2d ed. Paderborn: Schöningh, 1994.

Burdeau, G. *La Démocratie.* Paris: Editions de Seuil, 1956.

Constant de Rebecque, Henri Benjamin. *De la Liberté des anciens comparée à celle des modernes* (1819). In *Cours de politique constitutionelle ou Collection des ouvrages publiés sur le gouvernement représentatif.* Edouard Laboulaye, ed. Paris, 1861.

Dahl, Robert A. *Democracy and Its Critics.* New Haven: Yale University Press, 1989.

Finely, M. I. "The Freedom of the Citizen in the Greek World." *Talanta* 7 (1976): 1–23.

Gomme, A. W. (with Antony Andrewes and Kenneth J. Dover). *A Historical Commentary on Thucydides.* 5 vols. Oxford: Clarendon Press, 1945–81.

Gray, J. 1984. "On Negative and Positive Liberty." In *Conceptions of Liberty in Political Philosophy.* Z. Pelzcynski and J. Gray, eds. New York: St. Martin's Press, 1984, 321–48.

—— 1986: *Liberalism: Milton Keynes.* Minneapolis: University of Minnesota Press, 1986.

Grote, George. *A History of Greece: From the Earliest Period to the Close of the Generation Contemporary with Alexander the Great.* 12 vols. 1859–65. Rept. London: Dent; New York: Dutton, 1907.

Hansen, M. H. *Was Athens a Democracy? Popular Rule, Liberty and Equality in Ancient and Modern Political Thought.* Historisk-filosofiske Meddelelser 59. Copenhagen: The Royal Danish Academy of Sciences and Letters, 1989.

——. *The Athenian Democracy in the Age of Demosthenes.* Oxford: Blackwell, 1991.

——. "The Tradition of the Athenian Democracy A.D. 1750–1990." *Greece and Rome* 39 (1992): 14–30.

Harris, E. "Pericles' Praise of Athenian Democracy. Thucydides 2.37.1." *Harvard Studies in Classical Philology* 94 (1992): 157–67.

Hättich, M. *Begriff und Formen der Demokratie.* Mainz: Hase and Koehler, 1966.

Holden, B. *Understanding Liberal Democracy.* Oxford: Philip Allan, 1988.

Hornblower, Simon. *A Commentary on Thucydides.* Volume I: *Books I–III.* Oxford: Clarendon Press, 1991.

Kelsen, H. *General Theory of Law and State*. Cambridge, Mass.: Harvard University Press, 1946.

Lucas, J. R. *Democracy and Participation*. Harmondsworth and Baltimore: Penguin, 1976.

MacDowell, Douglas M., ed. *Andocides. On the Mysteries*. Oxford: Clarendon Press, 1962.

Meier, C. "Freiheit." In *Geschichtliche Grundbegriffe*, II. Otto Brunner et al., eds. Stuttgart: Klett, 1975, 426–29.

——. *The Greek Discovery of Politics*. Tr. David McLintock. Cambridge, Mass.: Harvard University Press, 1990.

Mossé, C. "La Démocratie athénienne et la protection de la propriété." *Symposion* 4 (1981): 263–71.

Mulgan, R. G. "Liberty in Ancient Greece." In *Conceptions of Liberty in Political Philosophy*. Z. Pelczynski, ed. New York: St. Martin's Press, 1984, 7–26.

Naess, A., et al. *Democracy, Ideology, and Objectivity: Studies in the Semantics and Cognitive Analysis of Ideological Controversies*. Oslo: Oslo University Press, 1956.

Pennock, J. R. *Democratic Political Theory*. Princeton: Princeton University Press, 1979.

Plamenatz, J. "Equality of Opportunity." In *Aspects of Human Equality*. L. Bryson et al., eds. New York: [distributed by] Harper, 1956.

Raaflaub, Kurt. "Des Freien Bürgers Recht der freien Rede." In *Studien zur antiken Sozialgeschichte: Festschrift Friedrich Vittinghoff*. Werner Eck, Hartmut Galsterer, and Hartmut Wolff, eds. Cologne/Vienna: Böhlau, 1980, 7–57.

——. "Democracy, Oligarchy and the Concept of the 'Free Citizen' in Late Fifth-Century Athens." *Political Theory* 11 (1983): 517–44.

——. *Die Entdeckung der Freiheit. Zur historischen Semantik und Gesellschaftsgeschichte eines politischen Grundbegriffes der Griechen*. Vestigia, Vol. 37. Munich: Beck, 1985.

——. "Contemporary Perceptions of Democracy in Fifth-Century Athens." *Classica et Mediaevalia* 40 (1989): 33–70.

Raubitschek, A. E. "Greek Inscriptions." *Hesperia* 12 (1943): 12–88.

Rawls, J. "The Basic Liberties and Their Priority." In *Liberty, Equality and Law: Selected Tanner Lectures on Moral Philosophy*. Sterling M. McMurrin, ed. Cambridge: Cambridge University Press, 1987, 1–87.

Rhodes, P. J. *A Commentary on the Aristotelian Athēnatiōn Politeia*. Oxford: Clarendon Press, 1981.

Ryan, A. "Freedom." In *The Blackwell Encyclopaedia of Political Thought*. David Miller, ed. Oxford and New York: Basil Blackwell, 1987, 163–66.

Sartori, G. *Democratic Theory*. Detroit: Wayne State University Press, 1962.

——. "Democracy." In *International Encyclopaedia of the Social Sciences*, 112–21.

Taylor, Charles. "What's Wrong with Negative Liberty?" In *The Idea of Freedom: Essays in Honour of Isaiah Berlin*. A. Ryan, ed. Oxford and New York: Oxford University Press, 1979.

Wood, Ellen Meiksins. *Peasant-Citizen and Slave: The Foundations of Athenian Democracy*. London: Routledge; New York: Verso, 1988.

Wycherley, R. E. *The Athenian Agora*, III. *Literary and Epigraphical Testimonia*. Princeton: Princeton University Press, 1957.

Wyse, W. *The Speeches of Isaeus*. Cambridge: Cambridge University Press, 1904.

# Further reading

Hansen, Mogens, *Was Athens a Democracy? Popular Rule, Liberty, and Equality in Ancient and Modern Political Thought* (Copenhagen, 1989).

Henderson, Jeffrey, "Attic Old Comedy, Frank Speech, and Democracy," in *Democracy, Empire, and the Arts in Fifth-century Athens*, eds. D. Boedeker and K. A. Raaflaub (Cambridge, MA, 1998), 255–74.

Mulgan, R., "Aristotle's Analysis of Oligarchy and Democracy," in *A Companion to Aristotle's Politics*, eds. D. Keyt and F. D. Miller, Jr. (Oxford, 1991), 307–22.

Murray, Oswyn, "Liberty and the Ancient Greeks," in *The Good Idea: Democracy and Ancient Greece*, ed. J. A. Koumoulides (Caratzas, 1995), 33–55.

Raaflaub, Kurt A., "Equalities and Inequalities in Athenian Democracy," in *Demokratia*, eds. J. Ober and C. Hedrick (Princeton, 1996), 139–74.

Wallace, Robert W., "Private Lives and Public Enemies: Freedom of Thought in Classical Athens," in *Athenian Identity and Civic Ideology*, eds. A. L. Boegehold and A. C. Scafuro (Baltimore, 1994), 127–55.

—— "Law, Freedom, and the Concept of Citizens' Rights in Democratic Athens," in *Demokratia*, eds. J. Ober and C. Hedrick (Princeton, 1996), 105–37.

# 5

# Power and Rhetoric at Athens: Elite Leadership versus Popular Ideology

## Introduction

As compared to oligarchies or monarchies in which relatively few made the crucial policy decisions, *demokratiai* gave extraordinary authority to the everyday citizens who packed the assemblies and manned the juries; indeed, judged against modern representative democracies, where "the people" turn over governmental control to distant, periodically elected representatives, citizens of ancient democracies directly wielded astonishing power over their own laws and fate. Nevertheless, leaders did emerge who, by dint of their ambition, elite background, speaking ability, wealth, or other factors, achieved prominence and disproportionate influence. At Athens, for example, several of the most important state offices, including archons, required occupants to be men of property; and not everybody would have the training, talent, or opportunity to influence assemblies and law courts on a regular basis with the force of their speech.

So where did the balance of political power lie – with a wealthy elite of orators and office-holders or the voting masses who listened to and judged their words? The following selections explore this question with regard to the Athenian democracy of the fifth and fourth centuries.

## Thucydides, *History of the Peloponnesian War* (2.65.1–11)

In the second year of the Peloponnesian War (430 BC) Pericles, a popular and influential politician from one of Athens' elite families, makes a speech urging the Athenians to persevere in the war despite their current difficulties. Thucydides then offers this commentary, in which he claims that such was Pericles' influence that he turned what was in name a democracy into a verit- able "rule by the first citizen." (*Source*: Thucydides, *History of the Peloponnesian War* 2.65.1–11, trans. R. Crawley.)

[...] Such were the arguments by which Pericles tried to cure the Athenians of their anger against him and to divert their thoughts from their immediate afflictions. As a community he succeeded in convincing them; they not only gave up all idea of sending to Lacedaemon, but applied themselves with increased energy to the war; still as private individuals they could not help smarting under their sufferings, the common people having been deprived of the little that they were possessed, while the higher orders had lost fine properties with costly establishments and buildings in the country, and worst of all, had war instead of peace. In fact, the public feeling against him did not subside until he had been fined. Not long afterwards, however, according to the way of the multitude, they again elected him general and committed all their affairs to his hands, having now become less sensitive to their private and domestic afflictions, and understanding that he was the best man of all for the public necessities. For as long as he was at the head of the state during the peace, he pursued a moderate and conservative policy; and in his time its greatness was at its height. When the war broke out, here also he seems to have rightly gauged the power of his country. He outlived its commencement two years and six months, and the correctness of his previsions respecting it became better known by his death. He told them to wait quietly, to pay attention to their [navy,] to attempt no new conquests, and to expose the city to no hazards during the war, and doing this, promised them a favourable result. What they did was the very contrary, allowing private ambitions and private interests, in matters apparently quite foreign to the war, to lead them into projects unjust both to themselves and to their allies – projects whose success would only conduce to the honour and advantage of private persons, and whose failure entailed certain disaster on the country in the war. The causes of this are not far to seek. Pericles, indeed, by his rank, ability, and known integrity, was enabled to exercise an independent control over the multitude – in short, to lead them instead of being led by them; for as he never sought power by improper means, he was never compelled to flatter them, but, on the contrary, enjoyed so high an estimation that he could afford to anger them by contradiction. Whenever he saw them unseasonably and insolently elated, he would with a word reduce them to alarm; on the other hand, if they fell victims to a panic, he could at once restore them to confidence. In short, what was nominally a democracy became in his hands government by the first citizen. With his successors it was different. More on a level with one another, and each grasping at supremacy, they ended by committing even the conduct of state affairs to the whims of the multitude. This, as might have been expected in a great and sovereign state, produced a host of blunders, and amongst them the Sicilian exped-ition; though this failed not so much through a miscalculation of the power of those against whom it was sent, as through a fault in the senders in not taking the best measures afterwards to assist those who had gone out, but choosing rather to occupy themselves with private cabals for the leadership of the commons, by which they not only paralysed operations in the field, but also first introduced civil discord at home. [...]

# Demosthenes 21, *Against Meidias* (1–8, 12–21, 42–50, 70–87, 95–99, 110–112, 123–131, 136–159, 193–197, 208–212, 219–227)

Demosthenes, born into a wealthy though not distinguished family, became a prominent Athenian politician in the fourth century and one of the greatest orators of classical antiquity. Many of his speeches survive. They are models of ancient rhetoric and also valuable sources of information about the laws, politics, and attitudes of contemporary Athens.

The following extensive excerpts come from a courtroom speech written as part of Demosthenes' prosecution of a personal and political enemy who allegedly punched him in the face at one of Athens' annual religious festivals. (*Source*: Demosthenes 21, *Against Meidias* 1–8, 12–21, 42–50, 70–87, 95–99, 110–112, 123–131, 136–159, 193–197, 208–212, 219–227, trans. C. R. Kennedy, from *The Orations of Demosthenes*.)

The rudeness and the insolence [*hubris*], men of the jury, with which Midias uniformly behaves to all, are pretty well known, I imagine, both to you and the rest of my fellow countrymen. The course which any one of you would have taken upon being grossly assaulted [*hubristheis*] I took myself: I arraigned this man before the people for committing a contempt of the festival, having not only received blows from him at the Dionysia, but suffered many other outrages during the whole of my choragic service. [2] The assembly, taking a just and proper view, were so incensed and exasperated, so warmly sympathised with the wrongs which they knew I had sustained, that, notwithstanding all the efforts of the defendant and others in his behalf, they would not listen to them nor pay any respect to their wealth or their promises, but passed sentence against him unanimously: upon which, men of the jury, many of you who are now in court and many other citizens came up to me, urging and entreating that I would proceed with the case, and deliver the defendant over to you: for two reasons assuredly, as it seems to me, O Athenians; both considering that I had been shamefully treated, and wishing at the same time to punish him for what they had observed of his conduct upon other occasions, as an audacious ruffian who was beyond all control.

[3] Under these circumstances, whatever care had to be taken by me has been duly observed on your behalf; and now that the case is brought into court, I am here, as you see, to accuse, having rejected, O Athenians, large sums of money which I might have had for not accusing, and withstood many prayers and solicitations, aye, and menaces too. [4] For the rest, which depends on you – the more persons he has annoyed by his canvassing, (I saw what he was doing just before the courts opened,) the more confident am I that I shall obtain justice. I cannot think so ill of any juror as to suppose, that you will be indifferent to a cause in which you yourselves warmly took my part before; or that any one of you, in order to enable Midias hereafter to commit assaults with impunity, will give a verdict upon oath for aught but what he considers just.

[5] If, men of Athens, I were about to accuse him of an unconstitutional measure, or of misconduct upon an embassy, or anything else of the like description, I should not have thought of making any request to you, considering that on the trial of such matters the accuser has only to prove his case, the defendant has to beg for mercy as well. But since, my adversary having corrupted the umpires, and my tribe having on that account been unjustly deprived of the tripod, [6] and I myself having received blows and been insulted in a way that scarcely any choir-master ever was insulted before, I am now prosecuting that judgment which the people indignant and sympa-thising with my wrongs pronounced against him, I will not hesitate even to be a suppliant. For, if such an expression be admissible, I am now a defendant, inasmuch as to obtain no redress for an insult is a sort of calamity. [7] I therefore pray and beseech you all, men of the jury, in the first place to give me a favourable hearing; and in the next place, if I prove that Midias the defendant has insulted not only me, but you and the laws and all other people, to avenge both me and yourselves. For thus the case stands, men of Athens. I have been insulted, and my person has been outraged on that occasion: but the point now to be tried and decided is, whether or no it should be lawful to commit such acts and to insult the first Athenian one meets with impunity. [8] Therefore, if any of you supposed before, that this trial was got up for a private purpose, let them now consider, it is for the public good that no one be permitted so to behave; and thus assuring themselves that the case is one of general interest, let them give it their attentive consideration, and pronounce such verdict as appears most conformable to justice. [...]

[13] The Pandionian tribe had not had a choir-master for two years: and the assembly having met, at which the Archon is required by law to allot the flute-players for each chorus, there was a discussion and a wrangling, the Archon blaming the Superintendents of the tribe, and the Superintendents the Archon; whereupon I came forward and volunteered to take the office of choir-master, and on the drawing of lots I got the first choice of flute-player. [14] You, men of Athens, expressed all of you the utmost satisfaction, both at my offer and the chance that turned up; and you applauded and clapped your hands in token of approbation and pleasure: Midias the defendant (he alone, as it appears) took umbrage, and he never ceased persecuting me with annoyances (great and small) during the whole period of my office. [15] What trouble he caused me by opposing the discharge of my choristers from military duty, or by offering himself as Superintendent for the Dionysia and requiring you to elect him, or in other ways of that sort, I shall pass by: for I am aware that, although to me, who was then annoyed and insulted, every one of these affronts caused as much irritation as the gravest injury could have done, to you who are out of the affair they would hardly appear worth going to trial about. I will mention that only, the hearing of which will excite equal indignation in you all. [16] Indeed the next proceeding, of which I am about to speak, passes common bounds: and I would not have attempted to accuse him now, had I not instantly at the time convicted him before the assembly. My sacred apparel – (all I consider sacred which a man provides himself with for the festival, so long as he uses it) – and the golden crowns, which I ordered for an ornament to my chorus, he sought, men of Athens, clandestinely to destroy, going by night to the house of the goldsmith; and he effected their destruction, but not entirely; for he was not able. Has any one ever heard of so daring an act planned or perpetrated in the city? [17] Yet he was not satisfied with this: he even corrupted the teacher of my chorus,

O Athenians; and had not Telephanes the flute-player behaved in the kindest manner to me, and determined, on seeing the trick, to drive this fellow away, and to form and instruct my choristers himself, we should have taken no part in the contest, men of Athens, but my chorus would have come in untrained, and we should have fallen into the utmost disgrace. Nor did his insolence stop here: it was so exuberant, that he offered to corrupt the crowned Archon; he incited the choir-masters to conspire against me; bawling, threatening, standing by the umpires while they took their oath, blocking, nailing up the side-scenes, (the public property! and he a private person!) he continued giving me unspeakable trouble and annoyance. [18] For all that has taken place in the assembly, or before the umpires in the theatre, you, men of the jury, are my witnesses; and of all statements those are most to be relied on, to the truth of which the hearers bear witness for the speaker. Having then previously corrupted the umpires for the contest of men, he put two crowning points as it were to all his pranks: – he made a gross assault upon my person; and to him it was mainly owing that my tribe, which did best in the contest, failed to get the prize.

[19] The indignities which he has offered to me and my fellow-tribesmen, and the contempts which he has committed of the festival, for which I preferred my plaint, are these, men of Athens, and many more, of which I will give you as full a detail as I can presently. I have other villanies of his to tell you, a large number of them, insults to a good many Athenians, many daring atrocities of this miscreant. [20] Some of the aggrieved parties, men of the jury, dreading the defendant and his audacity, his associates, his wealth, and what else he has about him, kept silence under their wrongs; some attempted to get redress and failed; others made up the quarrel, thinking it perhaps to their advantage. Well: they who accepted his terms have satisfaction on their private account: satisfaction for the laws, which Midias violated both in ill-using those persons and lastly in ill-using me and all the rest, it is for you to demand. [21] For all together make one penal reckoning, whatever you deem just. I will first prove the outrages which I have suffered myself, then what you have suffered; after which I will review all the rest of his life, men of Athens, and show that he deserves not one death but a thousand. [...]

[42] Since it appears therefore that he has done what I accuse him of, and has done it to insult me, the next thing is to consider the laws, men of the jury: for according to them you are sworn to decide. And observe how much heavier wrath and punishment is due in their estimation to wilful and wanton trespassers, than to people offending in any other way. [43] In the first place, all these laws concerning damage, (that I may begin with them,) if a man does a wilful injury, require him to pay double damages, if an involuntary one, single only: and with reason. For the injured party is in any case entitled to redress; but the injurer is not by the law pronounced equally culpable, whether he acts intentionally or unintentionally. Again, the laws of homicide punish wilful murderers with death and perpetual exile and confiscation of property, but to those who kill accidentally they extend compassion and mercy. [44] And not only in these instances are the laws found to be severe to the perpetrators of malicious outrage, but in every instance. How comes it that, if a man does not satisfy a judgment, the law has not left the ejectment-suit to be a private matter, but ordered the imposition of a fine to the treasury? And again, how comes it that, if a man gets from another by mutual consent either one talent or two talents or ten, and fraudulently keeps them, he has no affair with the state; but, if a man obtains a thing of small

value, which he has forcibly taken from another, the laws require a further penalty to be given, as much to the treasury as to the individual? Wherefore so? [45] Because the legislator considered that all crimes committed with violence are common injuries, even to those not immediately concerned; for strength belongs to a few, but the laws to all, and one acting under persuasion requires only private redress, but one suffering violence requires public. Therefore he gave the indictments even for personal outrage to any one that likes to prosecute, but the penalty he made entirely public: for he considered that the aggressor injured the state as well as the insulted party, and that the punishment was a sufficient compensation to the sufferer, and it was not meet that for such injuries he should get money for himself. [46] And to such a length did he go, that, if an outrage be done even to a slave, he allows an indictment for it just the same: for he thought the question was, not, who is the sufferer, but what is the character of the action; and finding it to be unjustifiable, he forbade the thing to be done either to a slave or at all. For there is nothing, men of Athens, nothing in the world more intolerable than a personal outrage, or which you ought more deeply to resent. Take and read me the law concerning personal outrage. There is nothing like hearing the law itself.

## The Law

[47] "If any one commit a personal outrage upon man, woman, or child, whether free-born or slave, or commit any illegal act against any such person, let any Athenian that chooses (not being under disability) indict him before the Judges; and let the Judges bring the case into the court of Heliæa in thirty days from the date of the indictment, if no public business prevent it, otherwise, as soon as possible. And whomsoever the court shall find guilty, let the court forthwith award him such penalty, either corporal or pecuniary, as he shall appear to deserve. But if any person preferring an indictment on his own account according to the law shall fail to prosecute, or having prosecuted shall not obtain a fifth part of the votes, let him pay a thousand drachms to the treasury. And if a fine be awarded for the outrage, let the party, in case of an outrage upon a freeman, be imprisoned until he has paid it."

[48] You hear, O Athenians, the humanity of the law, which allows not even slaves to be insulted in their persons. By the Gods, let me ask – Suppose a man carried this law to the barbarians, from whom slaves are brought to Greece, and praising you and discoursing of Athens, addressed them thus – [49] "There are certain people in Greece so mild and humane in their disposition, that, although they have suffered from you many injuries, and enmity with you is their natural inheritance, they permit not even those whom they have paid a price for and purchased for slaves to be abused, but have passed this law of state to prevent it, and have punished many already with death for transgressing this law." [50] If this were told and explained to the barbarians, would they not all with one voice (think ye) adopt you for their state-friends? He that transgresses such a law – not only esteemed among the Greeks, but which even the barbarians would admire – judge what punishment can be adequate to his deserts. [...]
[70] If there be any of you, O Athenians, whose wrath against Midias does not incline him to pass sentence of death, he takes not the proper view: for it is not right or just, that the forbearance of the sufferer should help to save a man whose insolence

was unbounded. The one you should punish as if he had gone to extremities; the other you should requite in avenging him.

[71] It cannot be said that no dreadful consequence has ever resulted from such acts, and that I am magnifying the thing in speech and making it terrible. The case is very different. All, or at least many, know Euthynus, the young man that wrestled formerly, and took such a revenge on Sophilus the Pancratiast; (he was a robust swarthy man; I am sure some of you know whom I mean:) on him at a party of pleasure quite private in Samos, because the striker thought to insult him, he avenged himself by taking his life. Many know that Euæon, the brother of Leodamas, killed Bœotus at a public supper and entertainment on account of a single blow. [72] For it is not the blow that causes anger, but the disgrace: it is not the beating that is so grievous to freemen, grievous though it is, but the insult. For the striker, O Athenians, may do many things (some of which the sufferer cannot even describe to another) by his gesture, by his look, by his voice; when he strikes to insult, when as an enemy, when with his fist, when on the cheek. These things excite, these things put men beside themselves, when they are unused to indignities. No one, O Athenians, by a report can present the grievance so vividly to his hearers, as in truth and in fact the insult appears to the sufferer and the bystanders.

[73] By Jupiter and the Gods! Only think, men of Athens, and consider among yourselves, how much more reason had I to be angry, when Midias so treated me, than Euæon who killed Bœotus had then. He was struck by an acquaintance, who was drunk, in the presence of six or seven persons, also acquaintances, who were sure afterwards to rebuke the one party for his conduct, and to commend the other for having been patient and restrained himself: and besides, he had gone to supper in a house where he was not obliged to go. [74] I was insulted by an enemy, sober and in the morning, who did it purposely and not under the excitement of wine, in the presence of many persons both aliens and citizens, and that too in a temple, and where, being choir-master, I was compelled to go. And I think, men of Athens, I have been prudent, or rather fortunate, in having then restrained myself and not been led on to do anything fatal: though I look with great indulgence upon Euæon or any person who has defended himself from insult; [75] and so, I think, did many who sat in judgment upon that case; for I am told he was convicted only by a single vote, although he neither shed tears nor petitioned any of the jurors, nor did any act, great or small, to conciliate the panel. Let me assume, that the adverse voters condemned him not because he retaliated, but because he went so far as to take life; while those who acquitted him had allowed even this excess of vengeance to a man outraged in his person. [76] How say you then? I, that never retaliated at all – so careful have I been to prevent anything fatal occurring – from whom should I obtain redress for my injuries? From you, I conceive, and from the laws: and other people should be warned by example, that one is not to revenge oneself in a passion upon bullies and blackguards, but to bring them before you, and you will maintain and enforce the remedies provided by law for the injured against their oppressors.

[77] Some of you, I dare say, men of the jury, expect to hear what was the quarrel existing between us; for you must imagine that no person could treat a fellow-citizen with such brutal violence without some strong provocation. I will give you then a full explanation of it from the beginning, to convince you that even for what then

occurred he deserves most clearly to be punished. The tale will be brief, though I may appear to begin far back.

[78] When I brought actions against my guardians for my paternal inheritance, being quite a stripling, ignorant even of this man's existence, and having no knowledge of him, (would I had not any now!), when the cause was coming on to be tried in about three or four days, he and his brother rushed into my house, and tendered me the trierarchy. It was the brother who gave his name and made the tender, Thrasylochus; but all the acts and proceedings were by Midias. [79] And first they broke open the doors of the apartments, as if they became theirs at once by the exchange: then in the presence of my sister, who was still in the house and was a young maiden, they uttered obscene language, such as only people like them would utter; (for I could not be induced to repeat to you any of the words then spoken;) and on my mother and me and all of us they poured every possible kind of abuse. But the most shameful part of all – beyond mere words – was this: they gave my guardians a release of the actions, as if they belonged to them. [80] Old matters are these certainly, yet I think some of you remember them; for the whole city at the time heard of the exchange, and the plot which they laid, and their brutal behaviour. I being then quite friendless and very young, that I might not be deprived of the property in the hands of my guardians, expecting to recover not merely what I actually obtained, but all that I knew I had been deprived of, gave to these men twenty minas, the sum for which they had provided a deputy trierarch.

Such is the foul usage which I then received from these men. [81] Having afterwards brought an action against Midias for abusive language, I obtained judgment by default; for he did not appear. The judgment was not paid, and I became entitled to execution; yet I never touched any of his effects, but again brought an action of ejectment, and down to the present day I have not been able to try it: such tricks and pretences does he find to baffle me with. And whilst I deem it my duty to do everything cautiously and by process of law and justice, the defendant, as you hear, thought proper to offer shameful affronts, not only to me and mine, but to my fellow-tribesmen on my account. [82] Call me the witnesses to prove the truth of these statements, to show you that, before I have obtained satisfaction for my former wrongs, I have again suffered the outrages which you have heard.


## Witnesses

"We, Callisthenes of Sphettus, Diognetus of Thoricus, Mnesitheus of Alopece, know that Demosthenes, for whom we are witnesses, has brought an action of ejectment against Midias, who is now publicly prosecuted by him, and that eight years have already elapsed since that action was commenced, and that Midias has been the cause of all the delay by continually making excuses and postponing the cause."

[83] Let me tell you, men of Athens, what a base thing he has done in the affair of the suit; and mark his insolent and overbearing behaviour on every occasion. In the suit – I mean that in which I obtained judgment against him – I got for arbitrator Straton of Phalerum, a man of humble means and no lawyer, but of unexceptionable character and thoroughly honest; which indeed not properly or justly, but most shamefully, has been

the ruin of the poor fellow. [84] This Straton, acting in the arbitration for us, when the day of hearing had at last come, and all the tricks of the law, affidavits and pleas, had been gone through, and nothing further remained, at first requested me to defer the arbitration, then to adjourn it till the following day; at length, as I would not consent, and the defendant did not appear, and it was getting late, he made an award against him. [85] In the evening after dusk Midias the defendant comes to the office of the Archons, and finds the Archons going out, and Straton just going away after giving the judgment by default, as I learned from one of the persons present. At first he actually pressed Straton to return the award which he had given against him as an award in his favour, and the Archons to alter the record; and he offered them fifty drachms: [86] finding that they resented the thing, and that neither of the parties could be prevailed upon, after threatening and abusing them, he goes away, and does what? – Only observe his malignity! Having moved for a new trial, he never took the oath, but allowed the award to become absolute against him, and was returned as unsworn. Wishing his design to remain a secret, he waited for the last day of the arbitrators, which falls in Thargelion or Scirophorion, on which some of the arbitrators come and some do not, [87] and having persuaded the chairman to put the vote contrary to all the laws, without superscribing the name of any witness to the summons, laying a charge in the defendant's absence, no one appearing, he disfranchises and outlaws the arbitrator. And now an Athenian citizen, because Midias suffered a judgment by default, has been deprived of all his civic rights and been completely disfranchised: and it is not safe, as it appears, either to bring an action against Midias for an injury, or to be an arbitrator for him, or even to walk on the same road. [. . .]

[95] Now call me Straton himself, who has undergone this misfortune. I suppose he will be allowed to stand. There he is, O Athenians; a poor man perhaps, but not a bad one; a citizen, who has served in every campaign during his age of service, and committed no crime; yet there he stands in silence, deprived not only of all other common privileges, but of the power to speak and to complain: and it is not lawful for him even to tell you whether he has been treated justly or unjustly. [96] And such treatment he has suffered from Midias, from the wealth and insolence of Midias, because he is poor and without friends and one of the many. And had he accepted the fifty drachms from him in contempt of the laws, and declared the award which he pronounced against him to be in his favour, he would have been in possession of his franchise, free from all harm, and sharing equal privileges with the rest of us: but since he regarded Midias less than justice, and feared the laws more than his threats, he has fallen into the dreadful calamity which you see by this person's contrivance.

[97] And will you let a man so cruel, so unfeeling – who takes such vengeance for injuries which he himself only says he has sustained, for he never had sustained any – will you let him escape, when you have caught him inflicting an outrage on a fellow-citizen? And if he pays no regard either to the festival or to religion or anything else, won't you convict him? – won't you make him an example? [98] And what will you say, men of the jury? In Heaven's name, what fair or honourable excuse will you have to allege? Peradventure, that he is an odious blackguard; for that is the truth. But surely, O Athenians, you ought to detest such people rather than to pardon them. Or because he is rich? But this you will find is pretty much the cause of his insolence: therefore you should rather take away the means which enable him to be insolent, than pardon him in consideration of them. To allow an audacious blackguard like

him to have wealth at his command, is to have put arms in his hands against yourselves.

[99] What then remains? To pity him, I suppose. He will have his children by him and weep, and beg for mercy on their account: that resource is left him. But you are surely aware, that pity is due to men who suffer something unjustly which they cannot bear, not to men who are punished for their crimes. And who can justly pity the defendant's children, seeing that he pitied not the children of this man, who (besides other causes of distress) see no possible remedy for their father's calamity; for there is no debt by paying which this man can recover his position: he is just absolutely disfranchised by the fury and ruffianism of Midias. [...]

[110] Such, men of Athens, have been the practices of Midias against myself. He accused me falsely of a murder, with which I was in no way concerned, as the event proved; he indicted me for desertion of post, having himself deserted his post thrice; and the troubles in Eubœa, which were caused by his friend Plutarch – (I had nearly forgotten this) – he attempted to lay them to my charge, before it became evident to all that the thing had been contrived by Plutarch. [111] And lastly, when the lot had fallen on me to be councillor, he accused me on my probation; and the thing came to a terrible pass for me; for, instead of obtaining satisfaction for my wrongs, I was in danger of being punished for things with which I had no concern. And thus ill-used as I am, persecuted in the manner that I describe to you, though not a person wholly friendless or without means, I know not, O Athenians, what course to take. [112] For – if I may say a word upon such topics now – the bulk of us, O Athenians, have no share of common or equal rights, like the wealthy; we have not indeed. They have what time they please allowed them for answering complaints, and their offences come before you stale and cold; whereas, if anything happen to one of us, he is tried fresh after the act. And there are witnesses ready for them, and advocates all prepared against us; but for me, as you perceive, some persons are unwilling even to give evidence of the truth. [...]

[123] A practice such as this, a contrivance, O Athenians, to involve people who seek just redress in still further calamities, is not a thing for me to be vexed and indignant at, and for the rest of you to disregard. Far otherwise. You should all equally resent it, considering and observing, O Athenians, that the poorest and weakest among us are most exposed to oppression; while ruffians that have money can most readily commit outrages, and, instead of being punished for their misdeeds, hire persons to embarrass their accusers. [124] You must not overlook these things: you should consider that a man, who by fear and intimidation prevents our obtaining satisfaction of him for our wrongs, in effect deprives us of the common rights of speech and liberty. I perhaps have repelled (another may repel) a false and malignant calumny, and I have not been destroyed; but what will you the many do, unless by public example you make it dreadful to all to abuse their riches in such a way? [125] When a man has answered and stood his trial upon the charges against him, then may he avenge himself on those who attacked him wrongfully; and even then, when he sees them committing wrong, he is not to snatch them out of the way beforehand, not seek by false accusations to escape from his own trial; nor ought he to be vexed at suffering punishment, but careful from the beginning not to misbehave himself.

[126] What insults I have sustained in my official character and in my person, and how I have escaped through snares and ill-usage of every kind, you have heard,

O Athenians: and a good deal I pass by, for it would not be very easy to tell all; but thus the matter stands. In none of these proceedings have I alone been wronged: but by the offences touching the chorus my tribe, a tenth part of you, has been wronged as well as myself; by his outrages to my person, and by his machinations against me, the laws are wronged, to which every one of you is indebted for security; and by all these things the God, whose choir-master I was, is wronged, and the essence of holiness, whatever it be, the venerable and the divine. [127] Those then, who would punish the defendant as fully as his deeds deserve, should not feel as if the question concerned me alone, but considering that the laws, the God, the state, are all included in the same injury, they should take vengeance accordingly, and regard any persons who support and stand by the defendant not merely as advocates, but as approvers of what he has done.

[128] If Midias, O Athenians, had behaved himself on other occasions with discretion and decency, if he had wronged no other citizen, and been thus intemperate and violent with me alone, I should have looked upon it as my peculiar misfortune, and been afraid that, by showing the moderation and mildness of his general conduct, he might evade punishment for his outrage on me. [129] As it is however, the wrongs which divers of you have sustained from him are so many in number and of such a character, that I am relieved from this apprehension, and have now a different fear, that, when you hear of so many cruel injuries done by him to other men, it may occur to you to reason in this sort of way: "How have you been worse injured than any one of the rest, that you take it thus to heart?" It would be impossible for me to tell you of all his doings, nor could you endure to listen to them: indeed, if both our measures of water, all mine and all his, were added to what is left, it would not be sufficient. [130] However I will mention the most striking and flagrant; or rather I will do this – read to you all the memoranda, as I have set them down for myself; and I will begin with whichever you would like to hear first, then go to another, and so on with the remainder, as long as you choose to listen. There is a vast variety of them, a multitude of outrages, tricks upon relations, impieties to the gods; and there is hardly a place in which you will not find many acts worthy of death to have been committed by him.

*[Memoranda of the misdeeds of Midias are read to the jury.]*

[131] These are the things that he has done to every man that came across him, O Athenians: and I have omitted others; for no one could recount all at once the long series of outrages which Midias during his whole life has been guilty of. It is curious however to see what a pitch of arrogance he has reached by never having been punished for any of them. Nothing that could be done between man and man was brilliant or brave or desperate enough for him, as I imagine: unless he could affront a whole tribe and council and class, and bully a large number of you in a body, he considered his life would be insupportable. [...]

[136] I observe, men of the jury, in the case of other people who are brought to trial, that the offences laid to their charge are one or two, while they have arguments of this sort in abundance – "What man here knows anything of the kind against me? Who has ever seen me doing such a thing? No one has. These men calumniate me out of spite: I am oppressed by false testimony" – and the like. With Midias however it is just the reverse. [137] I take it, you all know his disposition, his offensive and overbearing behaviour; and some of you, I dare say, have been wondering about things which they know themselves, but have not heard from me now. Many of the injured parties

don't even like to tell all that they have suffered, dreading this man's violence and litigiousness, and the fortune which makes such a despicable fellow strong and terrible: [138] for where a rogue and a bully is supported by wealth and power, it is a wall of defence against any attack. Let Midias be stripped of his possessions, and most likely he will not play the bully: if he should, he will be less regarded than the humblest man among you; he will rail and bawl to no purpose then, and be punished for any misbehaviour, like the rest of us. [139] Now, it seems, Polyeuctus and Timocrates and the ragamuffin Euctemon are his body-guard: these are a sort of mercenaries he keeps about him, and others also besides them, a confederate band of witnesses, who never trouble you openly, but by simply nodding their heads affirm any lie with perfect ease. By the Powers, I don't believe they get any good from him; but they are wonderful people, O Athenians, for making up to the rich, and attending on them and giving evidence. [140] All this, I take it, is formidable to any of you that live by yourselves as well as you can; and therefore it is you assemble together, that, where taken separately you are overmatched by any one, either in friends or riches or anything else, you may collectively be more than a match for him, and put a stop to his insolence.

[141] Possibly however an argument of this sort will be addressed to you: "Why did such a person, after sustaining such and such an injury, never demand satisfaction of me? or why" – naming perhaps some other aggrieved party. I imagine you all know the reasons why people forbear to seek redress: there is want of leisure, love of quiet, inability to speak, lack of means, and a thousand other causes. [142] Yet I conceive, it does not become the defendant to allege this now, but to show that he is not guilty of what I charge him with: if he cannot show it, he deserves to perish all the more; for if he is so mighty a person as to be able to do these things, and prevent each of us in turn from calling him to account, you ought all, now you have him in your power, to take common vengeance upon him, as a common enemy of the state.

[143] Alcibiades, we know, lived in Athens in the days of her ancient prosperity. How many and how important were the services he had rendered to the people; yet see how your ancestors dealt with him, when he thought proper to be offensive and insolent. It is assuredly from no wish to liken Midias to Alcibiades that I mention the case; I am not so silly or so stupid; but to make you see and understand, men of Athens, that there is nothing, there can be nothing, neither birth nor riches nor power, which the mass of the people ought to tolerate, if accompanied with insolence. [144] Alcibiades, O Athenians, is said to have been by his father's side of the race of the Alcmæonids; who, as we are told, were driven into exile by the tyrants for espousing the democratic party, and, having borrowed money from Delphi, liberated the commonwealth and expelled the sons of Pisistratus. By his mother's side he came from Hipponicus and that house which boasts of many signal obligations conferred upon the people. [145] And, besides having these things in his favour, he himself took arms for the people, twice in Samos and a third time in Athens, displaying loyalty to his country not by gifts of money or words, but by hazarding his life. Nay more; he had been competitor in the chariot-race at Olympia, and had won victories and garlands; and he was considered (as they tell us) to be of all men the ablest general and most eloquent speaker. [146] Nevertheless your ancestors, his contemporaries, did not for any of these reasons allow him to insult them, but banished and exiled him from the city; and the Lacedæmonians being then powerful, they submitted to have Decelea fortified against them, and to have their ships taken, and to the last extrem-

ities, deeming it more honourable to suffer anything by compulsion than consent to be treated with indignity. [147] Yet what outrage did Alcibiades ever commit equal to that which Midias is now proved to be guilty of? He slapped Taureas on the cheek, while discharging the choragic office. Granted. But it was an act done by one choir-master to another; and he was not then violating the present law, for it had not then been enacted. He imprisoned Agatharchus the painter, so they say; but he had caught him in a trespass, we are told; and it is not fair even to mention it to his reproach. He mutilated the busts of Hermes. All acts of impiety, I conceive, should be visited with the same anger; and can the total destruction of a sacred robe differ from the mutilation of Hermes' busts? Of that offence however Midias stands convicted. [148] Let us compare the cases. Who is Midias, and who are they to whom he so demeans himself? Rest assured, men of the jury, that (besides being dishonourable) it would be unlawful and unrighteous in you, the descendants of such a people, when you have got in your power a rascally and outrageous bully, a mere nobody and the son of nobody, to accord him either mercy or pity or favour. Why should you? For his services as general? Why, even as an individual soldier he is not good for anything, much less as a leader of others. But for his speeches? In none did he ever utter a word for the public good, but he abuses every one's private character. [149] For his family's sake [perhaps]. And which of you is ignorant of his mysterious birth, resembling what one sees in a tragedy? Two of the most opposite things have befallen him. His real mother who brought him forth was the most sensible of human beings, while she that passed for his mother, she that took him supposititiously, was the most foolish of all women. Why? Because the one sold him as soon as he was born; the other, when she might have purchased a better for the same price, bought Midias. And hence it is, that having obtained advantages to which he was not entitled, [150] having found a country which of all states is reputed to be the most constitutionally governed, he is able in no way, as it seems, to bear his fortune or to make use of it. His nature, essentially barbarous and hateful to the Gods, drags him violently on, and makes it evident that he treats his present privileges as if they were not his own; which indeed is the case.

[151] The performance of this odious wretch having been such as I have enumerated, some of his intimate friends, men of the jury, came advising me to withdraw and compromise the cause; not succeeding with me, they never dared to say that he had not committed gross offences and merited the heaviest punishment, but took this ground, that he had already been found guilty and condemned. "What penalty," said they, "do you expect the court will inflict upon him? Don't you see that he is wealthy, and will speak of trierarchies and official services? Mind that he doesn't beg himself off by it and laugh at you, paying much less to the state than what he offers you." [152] Now, in the first place, I don't believe an Athenian jury capable of anything mean, nor imagine they will sentence him to any lighter penalty than one by which his insolence will be checked; that is, either death, or at least, confiscation of his property. In the next place, as to his [liturgies] (official services), his trierarchies and such matters. I will tell you what I think. [153] If this be to serve liturgies, to say before you in all the assemblies and on every occasion, "We are the people who serve liturgies, we are the men who advance the taxes, we are the wealthy class" – if to talk in this style is to serve liturgies, I acknowledge that Midias is the most magnificent person in the state; for surely his harsh and unfeeling way of talking about these

things grates upon our ears in every assembly. [154] But if you want to know what liturgies he really performs, I will tell you; and mark how fair a test I will bring him to, comparing him with myself.

The defendant, O Athenians, being about fifty years of age or somewhat less, has served no more liturgies than I have, who am thirty-two. And I served the trierarchy, immediately after quitting boy's estate, at that period when we were two together in command, and when we defrayed the whole cost out of our private purses, and manned the ships ourselves. [155] The defendant, when he was at the age which I am now, had not begun to serve offices; he has only entered upon the duty since you have established the company of twelve hundred, from whom these men collect a talent, and for that sum procure a deputy-captain; then the state finds the crews and provides tackle; so the result is, that some of them really spend nothing, and, while they appear to have served an office, have enjoyed exemption from all other services.

[156] Well, but what else? He has once furnished a tragic chorus; I have furnished a chorus of flute-players: and that the expense of this greatly exceeds the cost of the other, every one must be aware. And my service now was voluntary; his then was forced upon him by a tender of exchange, for which surely he can deserve no thanks. What besides? I have feasted my tribe, and furnished a chorus at the Panathenæa: he has done neither. [157] I was ten years director of one of your tax-boards, paying as much as Phormio and Lysithides and Callæschrus and the wealthiest people, not from property in my possession, (for I had been robbed by my guardians,) but from the reputation of what my father left me and what I ought to have obtained on coming of age. Thus have I dealt by the people: how has Midias? Not even to this day has he been director of a board of taxes, though he never was deprived by any one of the least part of his inheritance, but received from his father a large estate. [158] Where then are his grand doings? Where are his liturgies and magnificent outlays? I cannot see, unless one looks at these things – he has built a house at Eleusis so large as to darken all in the place; and he carries his wife to the mysteries, or anywhere else that she likes, with his white pair from Sicyon; and he himself pushes through the market-place with three or four attendants, talking of beakers and drinking-horns and saucers loud enough for the passers-by to hear. [159] I know not how the mass of the people are benefited by what Midias purchases for his luxury and pride; but I see that the insolence which they encourage in him reaches a good many of you, and some of the humblest too. Then don't honour and admire things of this kind always; don't judge of liberality by these tests, whether a man builds splendid houses, or has many female servants or handsome furniture; but look who is spirited and liberal in those things which the bulk of you share the enjoyment of Midias, you will find, has nothing of that kind about him. [...]

[193] I fancy he will not scruple to accuse even the people and the assembly, but will repeat now what he ventured to say on his first arraignment; namely, that all who stayed at home when they should have been on military service, and all who had deserted the garrisons, took part in the assembly, and those that voted against him were choristers and aliens and persons of that sort. [194] For he had reached such a pitch of impudence, men of the jury, as all you that were present know, that by railing and threatening, and looking at whatever part of the assembly was clamorous for the moment, he thought to strike the whole people with terror. I should think therefore his tears now would look somewhat ridiculous. [195] How? you pestilent creature!

Can you ask these men to pity your children or yourself, or to take an interest about you – these men whom you have cast public shame upon? Are you to be a singular instance of a man, who in his life is so conspicuous for overweening arrogance and pride, that even strangers are offended when they observe his audacity, his voice and gestures, his attendants, wealth, and insolence – but on his being brought to trial is immediately an object of compassion? [196] You would indeed be a person of wonderful fortune, or rather talent, if in so short a time you could attract to yourself two things of the most opposite natures, disgust at your conduct, and pity for your artifices. Not a particle of compassion on any account do you deserve, but on the contrary, hatred and ill-will and indignation: that is due to you for your conduct. But I revert to what I said, that he will accuse the people and the assembly. [197] When he does this, bethink you, men of the jury, that he came to you in the assembly and accused the horsemen who had served with him, when they crossed over to Olynthus. Now again, having stayed at home, he will accuse the people to those who were out on service. Will you agree then, that, whether you stay at home or go out, you are such as Midias pronounces you to be, or rather that Midias is at all times and places execrable and abominable? I think you will characterise him thus! What can be said of a person, whom neither cavalry soldiers nor colleagues in command nor friends can endure? [...]

[208] I have head that Philippides and Mnesarchides and Diotimus of Euonymia and others like them, rich men and trierarchs, will earnestly entreat you to pardon him, and ask it as a favour to themselves. I would not say a word to you in disparagement of those persons; I should be mad to do so: but I will mention what, when they prefer this request, ought to be passing in your minds. [209] Consider, men of the jury: should these persons – (Heaven forbid it should occur, nor ever will it!) – but should they become masters of the government with Midias and the like of him, and should any one of you, you the commons and people's men, offend any of these persons, (not as grossly as Midias has me, but in some other way,) and be brought into a court composed of them, what pity or mercy would he obtain, think ye? They'd be likely to show him favour, wouldn't they? – or to listen to a petition from one of the multitude, and not say at once, "The scurvy rascal! he to insult one! he to be independent! a fellow that should be content if one lets him live!" [210] Towards people who would thus treat you, O Athenians, let not your own feelings be any different: have respect, not for their riches and reputation, but for yourselves. These men have many good things, which no one prevents their enjoying; then don't let them deprive us of that security, which the laws give us for a common property. [211] It will be no injustice or hardship to Midias, to possess as much as the bulk of you whom he insults and calls beggars, and to be stripped of that superfluity which excites him to be insolent. And surely these persons are not justified in asking such things of you – "Do not decide according to the laws, men of the jury: do not give redress to a party who has been deeply injured: do not regard your oaths: grant this as a favour to us." Such, if they ask anything for the defendant, will be the substance of what they ask, though not precisely in those words. [212] However, if they are friends, and think it hard that Midias should not be rich, they are exceedingly rich themselves, I am happy to say; let them give him money of their own, that you may vote conscientiously, as you were sworn to do when you entered the jury-box, and that they may oblige their friend at their own cost, not at the expense of your honour. If they have money and will not sacrifice it, how can it be proper for you to sacrifice your oath? [...]

[219] [...] It was not me alone, men of Athens, that he meant to beat or insult in doing what he did then, but all who may be supposed less able than I am to obtain satisfaction for their wrongs. If you did not all receive blows or affronts in the performance of choragic duties, you must be aware that you were not all choir-masters together, and that no man single-handed ever could bully you all at once. [220] But when any injured party fails to obtain satisfaction, each of you should expect that he will be the next to suffer wrong; nor should you be indifferent to such things, nor wait till they fall upon yourselves, but take the earliest possible precaution against them. Midias hates me perhaps, and some one else hates each of you. Would you allow those who hate you to have the power of doing, each to the object of his hatred, what Midias has done to me? I should imagine not. Then don't leave me, O Athenians, to the defendant's mercy. Only see. [221] Presently, when the court rises, every one of you sooner or later will return home, not heeding nor caring nor troubling himself in the least, whether a friend or an enemy will cross his path, whether a big or a little man, a strong or a weak, or anything of the kind. Wherefore so? Because he is sure in his mind of this, having a firm reliance upon the constitution, that no one will lay hands upon him or assault or strike him. [222] Thus walking in security yourselves, will you leave me not equally secured? And what can induce me to survive such treatment, if you refuse to assist me? "Oh, never fear," it may be said; "you'll not be insulted again." But suppose I am: will you punish then, after acquitting now? Do not abandon me or yourselves or the laws, O Athenians. [223] If you will only look and consider, by what it is that you the jurors of the day are powerful and masters of everything in the state, whether the state empanels two hundred jurors or a thousand or any number whatsoever, you will find it is not by your being the only citizens arrayed in arms, nor because the jurors are the most able-bodied and robust men, nor by your being the youngest in age or anything of that sort, but because the laws are powerful. [224] And what is the power of the laws? If any of you is injured and cries out, will they run up and assist him? No; they are but written words, and cannot do this. In what then consists their strength? In your enforcing, in your making them effectual always for the benefit of those who need them. Thus are the laws powerful by you, and you by the laws: [225] you should defend them therefore just the same as you would defend yourselves against injustice, and regard the wrongs of the laws, by whomsoever they are found to be committed, as matters of public concern; and there should be no services, no compassion, no influence, no contrivance, nothing whatsoever by which a man who has transgressed the laws can escape the penalty.

[226] You that were spectators at the Dionysia hissed and hooted the defendant when he entered the theatre; so that you gave tokens of abhorrence before you had heard a syllable about him from me. Were you angry then before the thing was proved? – did you invite the aggrieved party to seek justice? – did you clap your hands when I arraigned him in the assembly? – [227] yet, when the case against him is established, and the people sitting in a temple have precondemned him, and all the other performances of the miscreant have been brought under review, and you are appointed to be his judges, and it rests with you to settle everything by a single verdict, will you now hesitate to give me redress, to satisfy the people, to admonish other men, and, that you may live yourselves in perfect safety for the future, to make this man an example to all?

For all the reasons which have been urged, and especially for the sake of the God, whose festival he is convicted of profaning, give that verdict which is just and righteous, and punish the defendant.

The final disposition of this case is not known for certain, though there is some evidence that Meidias made a substantial payment to Demosthenes either as a fine after conviction or in a pre-trial settlement (Aeschines 3.51–52). It is therefore possible that Demosthenes' speech was never actually delivered before a jury.

# Who Ran Democratic Athens?

## P. J. Rhodes

I start from Thucydides, 2.65: in 430, after deposing Perikles from his generalship of 431/0 (which is mentioned by Diodorus 12.45.4 and Plutarch *Per.* 35.4–5 but not by Thucydides), the Athenians again "elected him general and entrusted the whole conduct of affairs to him" (2.65.4); he "held the masses on a light rein, and led them rather than let them lead him" (2.65.8); "the result was in theory democracy but in fact rule by the first man" (2.65.9). Elsewhere in Book 2 we read that at the time of the Peloponnesian invasion in 431 Perikles "refused to call an assembly or any kind of meeting, fearing that the people might make a mistake if they met in a spirit of passion rather than judgment" (2.22.1); but at the time of the second invasion in 430, when the Athenians' commitment to the war was wavering, "he called a meeting (since he was still in office as general)" (2.59.3).

My concern in this paper is not with Thucydides' representation of Perikles but with the system in which Perikles and the other Athenian politicians had to work. If it is wrong to talk of Perikles as "prime minister of Athens", and of such entities as the "moderate democratic party" or the "war party", as people used to talk, how ought we to talk? Did the Athenians, could the Athenians, "entrust the whole conduct of affairs" to Perikles? What formal powers could a Perikles or a Kleon possess? What further means of exercising influence did they have, in addition to their formal powers? How far was anybody able to work out a policy for Athens and to see that Athens followed that policy? If there was not anything like a "moderate democratic party" or a "war party", what groups of like-minded citizens were there?

Let us begin with formal powers. In the two middle quarters of the fifth century the ten generals (*strategoi*) were not only military commanders but political leaders. They were elected annually and could be re-elected. Originally one had to be from each of the ten tribes; but by the 430s the system had been modified so that at any rate one tribe could supply no general and one other could supply two. It used to be thought that the purpose of the modification was to make one man general-in-chief, or to

P. J. Rhodes, "Who Ran Democratic Athens?" in P. Flensted-Jensen et al. (eds.), *Polis and Politics* (Copenhagen: Museum Tusculanum Press, 2000), pp. 465–77.

recognise Perikles' special position and provide an opportunity for other men in his tribe; but it has now been established that (with the exception of Alkibiades in 407/6)[1] Classical Athens never had a general-in-chief, superior to the other nine;[2] and it seems likely that the modification of the system of electing generals was intended to provide not for any kind of superior general but for cases in which one or more tribes did not have any strong candidate of their own for the generalship.[3]

Plutarch tells us that Perikles was elected general for each of the last fifteen years of his life (*Per.* 16.3). The fifteen may not be precisely right, and I should not be happy with the assumption that Perikles must not have been general in 444/3,[4] but we have independent evidence that he was general in most of the years from 441/0 onwards, and I see no reason to doubt it for the years for which we lack evidence. This repeated election of Perikles was at the same time a recognition of his standing in Athens and a means of conferring formal power on him.

But what power? The generals commanded expeditions which they were appointed by the assembly to command, and presumably they had on-going duties in connection with the army and navy. On campaign, they might have to take various decisions which could not wait for consultation of the assembly, but they risked trouble if they took decisions which the assembly disapproved of, as the generals who acquiesced in the treaty of Gela in Sicily in 424 found out when they returned to Athens (Thuc. 4.65) – though as far as we can tell they really had no choice in that matter.

In the political realm in Athens itself the generals had very little constitutional power. Two passages from Thucydides Book 2 which I cited at the beginning of this paper suggest that during the Peloponnesian War they had some power in connection with decisions to summon or not to summon meetings of the assembly, decisions which normally rested with the council of five hundred and its standing committee, the *prytaneis*; and, whereas nearly every surviving decree of the assembly has as its proposer an individual identified by name, among the few exceptions there are two from the time of the Peloponnesian War which are recorded as *gnome strategon*, a proposal of the generals (*IG* I[3] 89.55sqq.; 92). As we shall see, any Athenian citizen in full possession of his rights could make a proposal in the assembly; I am sure there were many occasions when one of the generals made a proposal and the proposal was recorded in his own name, without any indication of the fact that he was a general; in proposing these two decrees as a body the generals were not exercising any special power, but these two decrees do suggest that during the Peloponnesian War the generals had a slightly higher political profile than at other times – but only slightly. Formal constitutional power will not have taken Perikles very far towards one-man rule in Athens: he was not superior to his fellow generals, and the power of the generals was limited; despite Thucydides, the Athenians in 430 did not "entrust the whole conduct of affairs to him".

So, if Perikles or anybody else enjoyed a dominant position in Athens, this was not through formal political power.[5] Where did formal power lie, and in what ways could a dominant figure dominate?

In Classical Athens all important decisions and many comparatively unimportant ones were taken by an assembly which was open to all adult male citizens, and normally attended by about 6,000 of them (between 10 and 20 per cent of those eligible). In Athens as in other Greek states the making of the decision in the assembly had to be preceded by a discussion in a smaller body, the council of five hundred

([Arist.] *Ath. Pol.* 45.4); but the Athenian interpretation of that rule required only that the council should agree to put an item on the assembly's agenda: the council could make a positive recommendation but it did not have to do so; and once the item reached the assembly any citizen was free to make a speech, and any citizen was free to put forward a fresh proposal or an amendment to a proposal already made.

A man who wanted to direct Athenian policy had to persuade the citizens to vote for his proposals and the proposals of men who thought on the same lines as he did; and if he held office as general that might make it easier for him to catch the chairmen's eyes and be invited to speak, and it might add weight to what he said, but it gave him no advantage beyond that. I shall consider the organisation of support below, but the debates in the assembly were not a sham: some at least of the citizens will have gone with a relatively open mind, intending to decide how to vote after they had listened to the speeches – some of them, I dare say, taking the arguments seriously and deciding on the basis of the arguments, others being more like the "spectators of speeches" referred to by Kleon in the Mytilene debate (Thuc. 3.38.4), swayed more by the performances as performances than by the content of the speeches. I imagine there were more floating voters in the Athenian assembly than there are in a modern parliament, and a successful politician had to be a successful speaker, who could persuade those floating voters.

Kleon is often referred to as one of the first examples of a new kind of politician,[6] and one of the ways in which he differed from men like Perikles is that he did not hold the generalship, or any other office, year after year. Indeed, it may never have occurred to him that a man like himself could be general until in the debate on Pylos in 425 Nikias invited Kleon to take over his generalship and, if we can believe Thucydides' narrative, Kleon was distinctly reluctant to do so (Thuc. 4.27.5–28.4).[7] The basis of Kleon's position in Athens was not that he had been appointed to a major office but simply that he was τῷ πλήθει πιθανώτατος, the man whom the masses found most persuasive (Thuc. 4.21.3). The "new politicians" were primarily speakers; the arts of argument and public speaking were among those taught by the sophists to men who wanted to succeed in public life; and *rhetor*, "speaker", was one of the words which came to be used in the fourth century to denote a politician.

Making good speeches was important, but of course it was not the only thing that mattered. I agree with Finley that it would be naïve to think that "Pericles came to a vital assembly meeting armed with nothing but his intelligence, his knowledge, his charisma and his oratorical skill, essential as all four attributes were".[8]

Since every decision in the assembly was preceded by a discussion in the council, access to the council was useful. Every citizen – whether general, or holder of some other office, or lay citizen not holding any office – had the right to apply to the *prytaneis* for permission to address the council, and I am sure this was a right which the leading politicians exercised. But it was helpful to be a member of the council, or else to have one or more friends who were members of the council, who could ensure that the leader's approaches met with a favourable response, and could make proposals which embodied the leader's suggestions or which referred the leader and his suggestions to the assembly. Members of the council were appointed by lot, as representatives of their demes, for one year at a time, and nobody could serve more than twice in his life. Probably there was not a great deal of competition for appointment, and a man who wanted a place for himself in a particular year would be able to get it without too much difficulty; but a leader who wanted support in the council year after year would need a fair number of friends to represent his interests. In the mid fourth century, it was probably not just accidental that Demosthenes was himself a member of the council in 347/6, the year in which Athens made a peace treaty with Philip of Macedon: his opponent Aischines alleges that he obtained his place by bribery (*In Ctes.* 62), but we need not take that seriously. In a later year Aischines refers to Demosthenes' getting one of the members to make a proposal on his behalf, and this time the accusation is that the innocent proposer did not understand the effects of the proposal he was induced to make (*In Ctes.* 125). In the late fifth century, Kleon himself was a member of the council either in 428/7 (appointed just after Perikles' death) or more probably in 427/6 (the year in which the fate of Mytilene was decided); Hyperbolos was a member in 421/0 (appointed just after the death of Kleon at Amphipolis).[9]

Athens certainly did not have political parties of the modern kind, with a policy on a range of issues, an organisation, signed-up members and discipline to keep the members on the right lines. It came nearer to that in the 340s and the 330s than at other times, when for Demosthenes resistance to Philip of Macedon was all-import-ant, whatever its effect on Athens' finances, while for Euboulos, Aischines and their supporters the restoration of Athens' finances was all-important, even if it meant collaborating with Philip, and Demosthenes could complain that Philip required his supporters to be friendly with supporters of Philip and not with opponents of Philip (Dem. 19.225–226). At that time, electing Demosthenes to a major office did mean voting for resistance to Philip.[10] At other times, some men would inevitably be known as pro-Spartan and so on – when Kimon was ostracised in 461 his opponents objected to him as pro-Spartan and anti-democratic, *philolakon* and *misodemos* (Plut. *Per.* 9.5) – but when they stood for office they stood primarily as individuals, and if they were associated with a particular policy that was only one of the relevant facts about them.

Various other facts might be relevant. After Solon had liberated the dependent peasants known as *hektemoroi*, Athens no longer had a class of men who were formally dependent on others, but for a long time after that many ordinary citizens may still have been informally dependent on one of the greater families. Most citizens cer-tainly, and probably all, belonged to one of the quasi-kinship organisations known as phratries; the old view that a typical phratry had at its core an aristocratic *genos* ("clan") which enjoyed a privileged position in the phratry has come under attack,[11] but I think it is still possible that the phratries began as organisations which linked a major family with its dependants, and it is certainly true that the same families belonged to the same phratries for generations and that these were units through which patterns of informal influence could be built up and maintained.[12]

Since the reforms of Kleisthenes, every citizen had also belonged to a deme, and to the *trittys* and the tribe of which his deme formed a part. Deme membership like phratry membership was hereditary. When this structure was first set up, each citizen lived in or at any rate owned some property in the deme to which he belonged; Thucydides tells us that there was not much geographical mobility before the Pelo-ponnesian War (2.14.2); during and after the war the proportion of citizens living in the deme they belonged to is likely to have declined, though we do not know to what extent. The demes, *trittyes* and tribes were units through which the leading men could exercise influence. Kimon offered daily supplies to all his fellow-demesmen ([Arist.] *Ath. Pol.* 27.3);[13] in speeches attributed to Lysias we find references to men's giving help to their fellow-demesmen at the time of a military expedition (Lys. 16.14, 31.15–16).

The institution of liturgies is important here – the institution by which rich men, instead of having their money taken from them in taxation by state officials and then spent by state officials, were called on to spend their money directly for some public purpose, maintaining and commanding one of the navy's ships for a year, or paying for and training a group of people giving a performance in a festival. The liturgies we hear most about were liturgies of the Athenian state, but there were also some local liturgies in individual demes. Through this system of liturgies rich men were forced into the public eye, but there was more to it than that.

Many of the liturgies were competitive. Sometimes prizes were offered for the trierarchs whose ships were the first to be ready to sail; and in any case a trierarch would naturally want his ship to be smarter and better equipped than his rivals' ships.[14] There were competitions in connection with many of the festival perform-ances which were supported by liturgies – tragedies, comedies, dithyrambs for boys' choruses, dithyrambs for men's choruses, and so on – and to win the prize you needed not only a good text to perform but also well costumed and well trained performers. In some of the competitions, the rival groups of performers were repre-sentatives of their tribes: they were not for the tragedies and comedies, but they were (for instance) for the dithyrambs.

It was regarded as a sign of a patriotic citizen to perform more liturgies, and to devote more money and effort to them, than the minimum that could be required of him, and in law-court speeches men boast of the liturgies they have undertaken (§§ 1–10 of Lys. 21 [*Defence on a Charge of Taking Bribes*], provide a good example). A lavish and successful performance would bring a man distinction: Nikias was a great performer of liturgies, and he was particularly renowned for the delegation which he led to the great festival of Apollo on Delos in 417 (Plut. *Nic.* 3–4.1); the next year, 416, Alkibiades entered seven teams in the chariot race at Olympia, a more blatantly self-centred form of festival expenditure, but he is represented by Thucydides as justifying that on the grounds that it was not simply selfish indulgence but it as well as his performance of liturgies brought glory to Athens (Thuc. 6.16.2–3, replying to the accusation of Nikias, 6.12.2). In addition to the general distinction which could be earned through a successful liturgy, there was also the particular pride and gratitude of those associated with the success: the men who had rowed in the trierarch's ship or who had performed in the *choregos'* chorus, and to a lesser extent all the members of the tribe whose chorus had won this year's dithyrambic competi-tion. Liturgies provided the leading men with an opportunity to win distinction in general and to win the support of some men in particular.

If we slice Athenian society in another direction, we can find another way in which men who wanted to acquire supporters could find them. Athens did not have the elaborate system of age classes for which Sparta is famous, but we do often find Athenians referring not only to their fellow-demesmen and -tribesmen but also to their contemporaries, their *helikiotai*. For two years between the ages of eighteen and twenty an Athenian was in a special intermediate category as an *ephebos*, "on the verge of adulthood". In the 330s a regular system of military and patriotic training was instituted for the *epheboi*,[15] but we know that before then the word was already in use and there were training opportunities for those who wanted to take advantage of them, and this will have thrown together men born in the same year. By the second half of the fourth century, but apparently not earlier, a selective call-up of hoplites to fight in the army was made by summoning the men of specified age-groups.[16] Men of more or less the same age will have exercised together in the *gymnasion*, and will have drunk together in the *symposion; hetaireiai*, groups of men who shared a social and sometimes a political purpose, will have been groups of contemporaries. A man who wanted to become a political leader would have various opportunities to make himself known to and to win the support of his contemporaries, and he could be expected to make the most of them. In the debate on the Sicilian expedition, Nikias, himself about twenty years older than Alkibiades,[17] refers to the younger men who have been summoned to the assembly to support Alkibiades, and urges the older men not to be ashamed to oppose them (Thuc. 6. [12.2–] 13.1).

One particular kind of supporter we should look out for is the man who attaches himself to one of the political leaders and becomes as it were an agent of that leader, a man who perhaps hopes that he will himself be one of the leaders of the next generation: the word *hetairos*, "companion", is often used to refer specifically to agents of this kind. So Perikles is said to have reserved himself for the great occasions, and otherwise to have had "friends and other speakers" active in the assembly on his behalf; Metiochos, described as "one of the *hetairoi* of Perikles", was mocked by a comedian as a Jack-of-all-trades who held every kind of office (Plut. *Per.* 7.7–8, *Prae. ger. reip.* 811c–813a).[18]

Agents could do more than make speeches in the council and assembly on a leader's behalf and hold offices in which they would cooperate with their leader. There is the notorious hoard of 190 ostraca prepared in the 480s for use against Themistokles, the work of just fourteen hands;[19] and the story of Athens' last ostracism, in which Alkibiades and Nikias colluded to secure the removal of Hyperbolos, implies that Alkibiades and Nikias had supporters whose votes they could to some extent control.[20] Otherwise our best evidence for the work of political agents comes from the run-up to the oligarchic revolutions of 411 and 404 (Thuc. 8.54.4, 66.1; Lys. 12.43–47); but the kind of activity which was mentioned there must also have been engaged in by loyal democrats in more normal times, and indeed Thucydides refers to the *hetaireiai* as "the conspiracies which already happened to exist in the city with a view to lawsuits and offices".

The mention of lawsuits brings me to another area in which a man could draw attention to himself and win supporters (but also make enemies). The Athenians' reputation for being addicted to litigation seems to have been well deserved: what we know of the arrangements for trials suggests that a fairly large number of Athenians went to law fairly often. Trials were very personal affairs. Even on charges of offences against the state, it was nearly always left to one or more individuals to prosecute on their own initiative, and, although the prosecutors and defendants could enlist friends to speak on their behalf, and could employ experts to write their own speeches for them, they were expected to stand up in court and deliver their speeches themselves. And sometimes in the speeches delivered in trials men did not keep narrowly to the subject of the charge, but reviewed their own and their opponents' careers and tried to demonstrate that they were more satisfactory citizens than their opponents.[21]

The Athenians did not distinguish as we should like between unlawful behaviour and politically unwise or unsuccessful behaviour, so there were many prosecutions of politicians for advising a course of action that had turned out badly or of generals for failing to win a battle – often with an allegation of bribery thrown in – and there were many more cases where the formal charge was not overtly political but the background information reveals a political motive. Juries were large – always hundreds and sometimes thousands – so a good speech in court would impress almost as large an audience as a good speech in the assembly. The lawcourts gave the politicians the opportunity not only to attack their opponents but to keep themselves in the public eye, to remind people of their liturgies and other achievements, and to support their *hetairoi*, their fellow-demesmen and their other friends and dependants, and to earn their gratitude and their support in turn.

Let us return to the running of Athens. When generals were elected, some men would vote for a candidate because of his reputation as a commander; some would vote because of a personal connection, through a phratry or a deme to which they both belonged, or because the candidate was a contemporary whom the voter had known for many years; and indeed some might vote for him because they approved of what he stood for. Some candidates would have little trouble in getting themselves elected, because they were lucky and had no serious rival in their own tribe; another tribe might have three or four serious candidates, of whom one would be elected as general from his own tribe and another might fill a place left vacant by a tribe with no strong candidate of its own. Sometimes a man would be elected in a particular year because he had connections with a particular area and it looked as if those connections were going to be useful in the year in question: Thucydides, with his connections in Thrace, elected for 424/3, may be an example of this.[22] It really does not make sense to do as people did in the first half of the twentieth century, to analyse the list of generals as far as we know it (and even for the time of the Peloponnesian War we do not know all the generals of every year) and to argue that in one year the war party was in the ascendant but in the next year the moderate conservatives regained the upper hand.[23]

Men with different views could be elected in the same year, if each of them had enough supporters, and even appointed to command the same expedition. I imagine that this is how we should explain the appointment of both Alkibiades and Nikias to command the Sicilian expedition in 415, rather than supposing that "the Athenians" – meaning the electorate as a whole – deliberately chose to appoint both men in the hope that each would counteract the excesses of the other.[24] In 433 Kimon's son Lakedaimonios was one of the three generals given the command of Athens' first squadron of ships sent to support Kerkyra against Korinth: Thucydides gives the names of the generals without any comment (1.45.3); Plutarch thinks that Perikles contrived this in order to humiliate Lakedaimonios (*Per.* 29.1–2), but there are other, more likely possibilities. The decision to support Kerkyra had been a close thing (Thuc. 1.44.1), and it may be that Lakedaimonios owed his appointment not to Perikles but to Athenians who were unhappy with Perikles' willingness to risk a confrontation with the Peloponnesians, and who were numerous enough to get one of their men appointed.

This brings us back to the making of policy and the passing of decrees through the assembly. There were not political parties with programmes and disciplines, but leading politicians did have agents, and had supporters of various kinds. Perikles will have had a hard core of men who normally voted for proposals which he made or was known to approve of – because of a family or personal connection with Perikles, or because they thought he was a good leader, or because they wanted the same things for Athens as he did. There will also have been a large outer layer of men who would sometimes vote as Perikles wanted on some issues, but whose support had to be won again and again, and could not be counted on. Other politicians will have fancied themselves as leaders too – Perikles was never the unchallenged leader Thucydides wants us to believe – and sometimes they and their supporters will have backed Perikles and sometimes they will have not.

Perikles was not a prime minister who had to have a policy on every issue that arose in the assembly: there may well have been some questions on which he was happy to accept whatever the outcome was. And, on questions on which he did have a policy, he could usually ensure that proposals he wanted were made, but he could not ensure that other proposals were not made. Thanks to the evidence of texts inscribed on stone, we know a fair number of decrees and their proposers from the fifth and fourth centuries. A few men turn up as proposers several times; a few more three or four times; and a great many just once or twice.[25] The decrees we have are only a small fraction of the total that were enacted: if we had more, we should have more from the men whose names already turn up frequently, but we should also find many more turning up just once or twice. Athens' democratic machinery encouraged, and indeed required, participation by the ordinary citizens, and the result was that some men devoted a large amount of time and effort to public affairs, while many more were not active in that way regularly but were occasionally – perhaps in the year in which they served in the council, or, like some members of the British House of Lords, when a subject in which they had a particular interest came up. Some of the men who proposed decrees occasionally may have been acting on behalf of one of the leading politicians – as one of Perikles' men in the council this year, for instance. Others, pretty certainly, will not have been anybody's agent but will have proposed their one decree because they wanted to do so.

I believe that Perikles and other leading politicians did have a policy for Athens, a general direction in which they wanted Athens to move. But I do not believe that they felt obliged to have a strong opinion and to influence the decision on every question that came before the assembly; and even when they did have a strong opinion and did want to influence the decision they could not be sure of getting the decision they wanted every time. The assembly was perfectly capable of taking one decision at one meeting, and then at its next meeting (or even at the same meeting) taking another decision which would hamper the carrying-out of the first – not because the mob was fickle, as Thucydides and other critics of democracy would have us think (e.g. Thuc. 2.65.3–4), but simply because different proposals attracted the support of different collections of men within an unregulated body of voters. I believe that Perikles could count on getting decisions that he was happy with most of the time, on most of the issues he felt strongly about, and that to that extent the policies which Athens followed between about 460 and 430 were on the whole Perikles' policies, but that he could never be sure of getting the decision that he wanted on a particular issue on a particular occasion. I believe that the decision to support Kerkyra in 433 was the decision which Perikles wanted, which Thucydides does not state but Plutarch does (*Per.* 29.1); but what Thucydides does state is that on the first day in the assembly opinion tended to favour Korinth against Kerkyra (1.44.1).

Athens was not anarchic: in practice, most of the time there was enough agreement on ends and means for the separate decisions of the assembly to take Athens reasonably consistently in one direction. But the potential for anarchy was always there, and sometimes two steps forwards were followed by one step backwards. No one man, however influential, was ever entirely in control: if we want a parallel from the modern world we should think of the shifting coalitions of a country like Italy rather than the entrenched majority parties of the United Kingdom or the United States.

## NOTES

1   Xen. *Hell.* 1.4.20; *strategos autokrator* in Diod. 13.69.3, Plut. *Alc.* 33.2. Xenophon and Diodorus are independent of each other, and I know of no one who has doubted the special nature of this appointment.
2   Dover (1960) = (1988) 159–180. This is not undermined by Bloedow (1981), or Bloedow (1987).
3   Piérart (1974); refined by Mitchell (2000). (See also *eadem* [1997] 96 n. 35.)
4   An assumption made by Wade-Gery (1932) 206 = (1958) 240–241.
5   Compare the view of democratic Athens advanced by Ober (1980). Athens did not have what he would call a "ruling" élite (p.11).
6   See especially Connor (1971).
7   See Lewis (1992) 417.
8   Finley (1983) 76(–84).
9   See Rhodes (1972) 4, 57 n. 3. Gomme in Gomme *et al.* (1945–81) III. 718, 721, dates the debate on Mytilene to the Athenian year 427/6 and the battle at Amphipolis to 422/1; both possibilities for Kleon's year in the council are discussed by Atkinson (1992) 57–58, who like me prefers 427/6.
10   Cf. Rhodes (1978). On political leaders and their followers my views differ, I think in emphasis rather than fundamentally, from those expressed by Hansen (1983) 220–222; cf. *idem* (1987) 72–86; *idem* (1991) 280–287: see Rhodes (1986) 139; *idem* (1994) 93–94.
11   Bourriot (1976); Roussel (1976); cf. Lambert (1993) 59–77. Their views are rejected by Ito (1997) – in Japanese, with a short English summary.
12   Millett (1989) argues that democratic Athens deliberately minimised the scope for patronage: I accept that it attempted to do this, but do not believe that the possibilities of patronage were eliminated.
13   Better than texts which make this an offer to all the citizens: see Rhodes (1981) *ad loc.*
14   Prizes: e.g. *IG* II$^2$ 1629 = Tod, *GHI* 200 (trans. Harding 121) 190–204. Thuc. 6.31.3, in connection with the Sicilian expedition, writes in general terms of each trierarch's determination that his ship should be the best.
15   [Arist.] *Ath. Pol.* 42.2–5 gives an account of the system: see Rhodes (1981) *ad loc.*
16   [Arist.] *Ath. Pol.* 53.7. For earlier practice see *ibidem* 26.1 with Rhodes (1981) *ad loc.* and Andrewes (1981).
17   Nikias was older than Sokrates (Pl. *Lach.* 186C), so born before 469 (Davies [1971] 404); Alkibiades is first attested as a hoplite in 433/2 or 432/1 (Pl. *Symp.* 219E–220E, *Chrm.* 153A–B) and as a general in 420/19 (Plut. *Alc.* 15.1), so he was born not later than 452/1 or 451/0 but probably not much earlier than that (Andrews, in Gomme *et al.*

[1945–81] IV. 48–49; Davies [1971] 18; and on the chronology of 432 Ste. Croix [1972] 319–320).

18   However, he is not attested at all except in *Prae. ger. reip.* and the fragment which it quotes. For another such agent see [Dem.] 59.43: Stephanos was "one of those who shout beside the platform, who make prosecutions and denunciations for pay, and who are written on to other men's motions".

19   Broneer (1938); cf. Lang (1990) 142–161.

20   Cf. Rhodes (1994) 93–94.

21   In my contribution to a book edited by E. M. Harris & L. Rubinstein I shall demonstrate that this, which is currently regarded as regular practice, did indeed happen sometimes but not regularly.

22   Cf. Mitchell (n. 4, above).

23   E.g. West (1924).

24   E.g. Bury & Meiggs (1975) 294. Kagan (1981) 170–171 is not far from this.

25   Hansen (1984) = *idem* (1989) 93–125 with *addenda* 126–127.

## BIBLIOGRAPHY

Andrewes, A. 1981. "The Hoplite *Katalogos*," *Classical Contributions Presented to M.F. McGregor* (Locust Valley) 1–3.

Atkinson, J. E. 1992. "Curbing the Comedians: Cleon Versus Aristophanes and Syracosius' Decree," *CQ*² 42: 56–64.

Bloedow, E. F. 1981. "Hipponicus and Euthydemus (Euthynus)," *Chiron* 11: 65–72.

Bloedow, E. F. 1987. "Pericles' Powers in the Counter-Strategy of 431," *Historia* 36: 9–22.

Bourriot, F. 1976. *Recherches sur la nature du génos*, Champion for U. de Lille III (Paris).

Broneer, O. 1938. "Excavations on the North Slope of the Acropolis, 1937: Ostraka," *Hesperia* 7: 228–243.

Bury, J. B., & Meiggs, R. 1975. *A History of Greece to the Death of Alexander the Great* (4th edn. London).

Connor, W. R. 1971. *The New Politicians of Fifth-Century Athens* (Princeton).

Davies, J. K. 1971. *Athenian Propertied Families, 600–300 B.C.* (Oxford).

Dover, K. J. 1960. "δέκατος αὐτός," *JHS* 80: 61–77.

Dover, K. J. 1988. *The Greeks and their Legacy, Collected Papers* II (Oxford).

Finley, M. I. 1983. *Politics in the Ancient World* (Cambridge).

Gomme, A. W. *et al.* 1945–81. *A Historical Commentary on Thucydides* (Oxford).

Hansen, M. H. 1983. *The Athenian Ecclesia* (Copenhagen).

Hansen, M. H. 1984. "The Number of *Rhetores* in the Athenian *Ecclesia*, 355–322 B.C.," *GRBS* 25: 123–155.

Hansen, M. H. 1987. *The Athenian Assembly in the Age of Demosthenes* (Oxford).

Hansen, M. H. 1989. *The Athenian Ecclesia* II (Copenhagen).

Hansen, M. H. 1991. *The Athenian Democracy in the Age of Demosthenes* (Oxford).

Ito, S. 1997. "'Genos' in Ancient Athens: Bourriot's Theory Re-examined," *Shigaku-Zasshi* 106.11.

Kagan, D. 1981. *The Peace of Nicias and the Sicilian Expedition* (Ithaca).

Lambert, S. D. 1993. *The Phratries of Attica* (Ann Arbor).

Lang, M. 1990. *The Athenian Agora* xxv. *Ostraka* (Princeton).

Lewis, D. M. 1992. "The Archidamian War," *CAH*² V: 370–432.

Millett, P. C. 1989. "Patronage and Its Avoidance in Classical Athens," in A. Wallace-Hadrill (ed.), *Patronage in Ancient Society* (London) 15–47.

Mitchell, L. G. 1997. *Greeks Bearing Gifts: The Public Use of Private Relationships in the Greek World, 432–323 B.C.* (Cambridge).

Mitchell, L. G. 2000. "A New Look at the Election of Generals at Athens," *Klio* 82: 344–60.

Ober, J. 1989. *Mass and Elite in Democratic Athens* (Princeton).

Piérart, M. 1974. "À propos de l'élection des stratèges athéniens," *BCH* 98: 125–146.

Rhodes, P. J. 1972. *The Athenian Boule* (Oxford).

Rhodes, P. J. 1978. "On Labelling Fourth-Century < Athenian > Politicians," *LCM* 3: 207–211.

Rhodes, P. J. 1981. *A Commentary on the Aristotelian* Athenaion Politeia (Oxford).

Rhodes, P. J. 1986. "Political Activity in Classical Athens," *JHS* 106: 132–144.

Rhodes, P. J. 1994. "The Ostracism of Hyperbolus," in R. Osborne & S. Hornblower (eds.), *Ritual, Finance, Politics: Athenian Democratic Accounts Presented to David Lewis* (Oxford) 85–98.

Roussel, D. 1976. *Tribu et cité*, Annales Littéraires de l'université de Besançon cxciii (Paris).

Ste. Croix, G. E. M. de. 1972. *The Origins of the Peloponnesian War* (London).

Wade-Gery, H. T. 1932. "Thucydides the Son of Melesias," *JHS* 52: 205–227.

Wade-Gery, H. T. 1958. *Essays in Greek History* (Oxford).

West, A. B. 1924. "Pericles' Political Heirs," *CP* 19: 124–146, 201–228.

# Demosthenes 21 (*Against Meidias*): Democratic Abuse[1]

## Peter J. Wilson

Wilson illuminates the tensions in the Greek concept of *hubris* and the rhetorical ploys on display in Demosthenes' speech, in part showing how elements in the oration can be seen as undermining the democratic ideology to which Demosthenes blatantly appeals.

The title given to speech number twenty-one of Demosthenes at some time in antiquity, although surely not by Demosthenes himself,[2] is *KATA MEIΔIOΥ ΠEPI TOΥ KONΔΥΛOΥ* – "*Against Meidias, concerning the punch*". This refers of course to the punch on the cheek which Demosthenes received from Meidias in the very orchestra of the theatre of Dionysos at Athens on the day of the competition in the men's dithyramb, in which Demosthenes was *chorēgos* [producer of a chorus] for his *phylē* [tribe], Pandionis, at the Great Dionysia of 348 B.C. – an act of physical abuse perpetrated under the gaze of "more than 30,000 Greeks" – (that is the Platonic Sokrates' exaggeration, not mine)[3] – in that place and at that time of

Peter J. Wilson, "Demosthenes 21 (*Against Meidias*): Democratic Abuse," *Proceedings of the Cambridge Philological Society* 37 (1991), 164–195, pp. 164–175, 180–195.

maximum Athenian self-regard. The act which forms the ostensible basis of Demosthenes' case is thus self-evident: for by the powerful trope of the homogeneity across time and place of the Athenian *dēmos* [people], the spectators who were in the theatre on that day are identical to those citizens at the subsequent *ekklēsia* [public assembly] which met (also in the theatre) to hear complaints arising from the conduct of individuals at the festival, and they are the same men empanelling the court today.[4] They booed and hissed Meidias in the theatre, passed a preliminary motion against him in the *ekklēsia* and so, today, their course of action is clear.[5]

However, there are problems with this (Demosthenic) simplification of the case. For it is not for assault that Demosthenes is prosecuting or (with a qualification whose importance will become clearer), *purporting* to prosecute Meidias [...] nor, incidentally, is it for verbal abuse or slander [...] though both of these variations on the theme of abuse do play a part in the complex plan of his speech.[6] Rather, the abuse of which Demosthenes speaks at such length is gathered somewhat elusively under the rubric of *hubris*, and any discussion of Dem. 21 needs to come to terms with the issues raised by its representation of *hubris*.

## The Rhetoric of Hubris

In their recent work on Athenian conceptions of the citizen body, Winkler and Halperin, developing studies by MacDowell, Fisher and others, have traced what could be termed a democratic ideology of *hubris*.[7] Or rather, the particular manifestation of democratic ideology so well analysed by Winkler and Halperin is that of the equality and inviolability of every citizen's body, and this is policed by the concept of *hubris*.

> At the boundaries of a citizen's body the operation of almost all social and economic power halted ... To violate the bodily sanctity of a citizen by treating him as one would a slave, by manhandling him, or even by placing a hand on his body without his consent was not only to insult him personally but to insult the corporate integrity of the citizen body as a whole and to offend its fiercely egalitarian spirit. It was an act of *hybris* ... which signified the violation of a status distinction, the attempted reduction of a person to a status below the one he actually occupied ... *Hybris* was thus the anti-democratic crime *par excellence*, and it called down upon the offender the full wrath of the democratic judicial system.[8]

Halperin and others have considered the way such a notion of *hubris* was functionally crucial to the operation of democratic egalitarian ideology, and this speech is a central text for any such analysis. However, by looking more closely at the contexts in which this text must be located, at its own special aims within a specific socio-legal conflict and at its complex rhetorical manoeuvres, it is perhaps possible to get further behind this ideological strategy to see how it is being promoted, and by whom.[9] This speech represents a particularly important moment (for us) in the construction of this ideology, and in its (purported) operation and testing. The paradox that although *hubris* figures so prominently in our democratic sources yet we know of very few secure cases of prosecution for *hubris*[10] is not alleviated by the fact that, if we are to accept MacDowell's arguments, Demosthenes is not here writing a prosecution for a technical γραφὴ ὕβρεως [indictment for hubris].[11] Moreover, the issue is further complicated by the likelihood that this speech which talks at such length *about hubris* was not risked in the public domain of the courts.[12] Further, the previous supposedly parallel cases of *hubris* which Demesthenes cites in this speech are on the whole not from especially democratic public contexts, but rather from the narrower private sphere of the *symposion*, private conflicts between individuals and so on. The point may turn out to be that, despite the egalitarian ideology discussed by Halperin and Winkler, some bodies were more equal than others.

What interests me most about the representation of *hubris* in Dem. 21 in this light is a disparity which is constantly (un)covered. On the one hand there is the ideological and legal function of *hubris* in establishing the absolute equality of τιμή [honor] among citizens (where τιμή denotes the status and rights of the citizen as such) and, on the other hand, there is the unavoidable fact that in the zero-sum game of the pursuit of τιμή (in a more developed and pre-democratic sense) in Athens, those who care most are those who *have* – or think they can get – most: like Meidias, but also, like Demosthenes.[13]

To put this another way, *hubris* in Dem. 21 seems to me a way of assimilating two important aspects of democratic abuse, aspects which turn upon reading "the abuse of democracy" with both a subjective and an objective sense for the genitive. On the one hand, there are the forms of abuse which are current in democratic contexts, and which are the ostensible subject and content of Demosthenes' speech; while on the other hand, there is the abuse which is perpetrated *on* democratic ideology itself, and which seems to me to be a constitutive aspect of the ambivalent nature of Athenian democracy, what might be called the refusal, or the inability, of democracy to operate in accordance with its own ideology.[14] A precise legal definition of *hubris* of a kind we might recognise seems to be lacking in the fifth- and fourth-century context. Moreover "abuse" seems an altogether appropriate term more generally for many of the charges made in Athenian courts, where the establishment of fact often plays a secondary rôle to the construction and destruction of character-types of one's opponents.[15] An illuminating example of the very different line the Athenians drew between accusation and abuse is provided by the fact that in Athenian law a sufficient defence for a person accused of verbal abuse – κακηγορία – was to show that what he had said was *true*.[16] As Todd writes:[17]

> On the point of law, we should always remember that an Athenian trial is an adversarial and not an inquisitional procedure: the jury are not there to find out the truth, but to decide which of two theses they find preferable . . .

In the wider project of attempting to understand the operation of Athenian law on its own terms, within its dynamic social context, it is becoming more generally accepted that "Athenian courts were more concerned with dispute-settlement than with the enactment of justice in our objective sense".[18] Here the work of Humphreys is also instructive. She argues, for example, that witnesses in Athenian courts are not called for the specific testimony they offer (which frequently evaded the central point at issue) so much as to give the dikasts the impression that the litigant had solid support from those best acquainted with the case and from markedly "solid" citizens.[19]

Hence Demosthenes' thorough attack on Meidias' witnesses, including Polyeuktos, Timokrates and "dusty" Euktemon – Εὐκτήμων ὁ κονιορτός – who are called paid henchmen, sycophants, perjurers and parasites on the rich (§§103, 139) [. . .]

In §§45–50 Demosthenes provides an exposition of the law which is also a clearly democratic ideological interpretation. He explains why in the case of a violent crime the laws insist that an equal amount be paid to the treasury and to the person directly affected:

> Because the legislator considered all violent actions to be offences against the community and harmful even to those not involved. (§45)

The idea that the civic body consists of the aggregate bodies of all citizens lies behind this, and as Demosthenes goes on to explain, this public nature of the crime is the reason it is prosecuted by ὁ βουλόμενος [any willing citizen] and *graphē* [public indictment], and the reason too why the penalty goes entirely to the *polis*. The term ὁ βουλόμενος thus inscribes an ideology of the collective in accordance with which desire and duty coincide. Yet in the move from this ideology to its practical instantiation a gulf appears. For insofar as there is any intimation of disinterestedness in the notion of ὁ βουλόμενος, or at least of action in the common as opposed to purely personal interest, in practice there is no known case of ὁ βουλόμενος being anything other than ὁ παθών [the victim].[24]

Demosthenes' interpretation of the purpose and character of the law is an illuminating explanatory fiction. The law, the actual words of which he is eager to hear – "for there's nothing like hearing the law itself" (§46) – is apparently another glory of which the Athenians can proudly boast. They are to be praised before the barbarians – "from whom slaves are imported to Greece" (§48) – for being Greeks of such civilised and humane ways that this law forbids the commission of *hubris* even against slaves. This is in spite of the wrongs the Athenians have suffered at the hands of the barbarians and despite their natural hatred for them (§§48–9). Because of the projected admiration the barbarians will have of this, "if they understand it" (§50 – is this feigned realism?), the transgressor *a fortiori* must by Greek, or rather, by *Athenian* standards, pay a massive penalty. Athenian practice is here not simply defined and extolled in opposition to that of a projected barbarian Other; rather, Demosthenes' not particularly sensitive story plays with that paradigmatic opposition and momentarily reverses the polarity in such a way that the projected audience of the Other is to regulate the behavior of his audience of Athenian dikasts.

## The Good Fight

The law, and Demosthenes' exegesis, end up telling us little or nothing about what constitutes an act of *hubris*. Another direction to pursue is provided by Murray's work on *hubris* in the archaic period, particularly its connection with the world of the aristocratic *symposion*.[25] Murray explains the emphasis on injured *timē* [honor] in the law as it is known from the classical period by referring its introduction to a time when formal distinctions between grades of citizens were vitally important – that is, to the time of Solon. Yet one might wonder whether in the process of its transformation to a democratic complexion the law of *hubris* did not retain, beneath its new ideological identity, traces of this aristocratic heritage.[26] Such an uneasy democratisation of *hubris* seems to explain the hints which emerge to the effect that *hubris* in the democracy was still doing essentially the same work, but according to a standard of *timē* which had officially been banished from the city. At the same time, those who *did* go some or all of the way in prosecuting for *hubris* must have done so only from a position of considerable individual strength.

It may at first seem paradoxical that there was evidently so much at stake for Demosthenes in *not* appearing the passive or acquiescent victim of Meidias' violence. Yet there may be here another clue to the puzzle of why so few cases of prosecution for *hubris* are known to have been undertaken – the alleged victims would be slow to make public knowledge the fact that they felt they had suffered the huge loss of personal status which it implied. If so, the sense of security and protection offered by this part of democratic law and ideology must be regarded as insufficient to counterbalance the sense of shame in not being able to defend one's own σῶμα [body] and τιμή.

In this light it is instructive to look at the passage in the speech in which Demosthenes produces what sounds very much like a justification – (a defence?) – for his non-retaliation against Meidias' assault in the theatre. He presents his behaviour rather as an indication of his εὐλάβεια [discretion] and σωφροσύνη [prudence] in the face of hubristic provocation. In §§70–6 Demosthenes sets about this by citing two cases in which a perceived affront to one man's honour through *hubris* was followed by violent retaliation: in both cases, the alleged *hubristai* [violators] ended up dead. From these parallels Demosthenes wants his audience to appreciate the saving extent of his own restraint, the seriousness of the potential disaster which he forestalled. Yet for all that, σωφροσύνη (and εὐλάβεια) are not especially heroic virtues of the man of action. σωφροσύνη in particular is often construed as a virtue of women and it has been described by Dover, on the basis of a wide sample of occurrences in inscriptions and literature, as primarily a " 'negative' virtue, which restraints one from doing wrong", as opposed to "the 'positive' virtue [especially ἀρετή, excellence] shown in achievement".[27] In trying to make a virtue of his inaction, Demosthenes momentarily sets at risk his own individualistic self-image as an autonomous, dynamic agent able to defend himself and others.

The examples Demosthenes cites here are both unambiguously, and emphatically, from the private sphere. In the first, which seems to have happened some considerable time ago, Euthynos the famous wrestler – a young fellow (τὸν νεάνισκον §71) – and Sophilos the pankratiast [fighter] – "a mighty man, dark-skinned, I'm sure some of you know whom I mean" (§71) – were at a private party with some friends on Samos. Euthynos (it seems)[28] "thought he was showing *hubris*", and so "defended himself so vigorously that he actually killed him" (§71). This anecdote depends in part for its point, as MacDowell notes,[29] on registering surprise that the young wrestler managed to fell the seasoned pankratiast: a surprise tainted by no small amount of admiration. Yet the admiration is for a course of action which is exemplary of the path Demosthenes himself did *not* follow. The same applies to the second example, in which Euaion killed Boiotos "at a private party with a shared meal because of a single blow" (§71).[30] Demosthenes expresses his sympathy for Euaion "and anyone else who has helped himself when dishonoured" (§74), and he goes on to interpret the verdict of the court in that instance – where Euaion was convicted by only a single vote – as showing, on the side of the convictors, not a condemnation of the self-defence, only of its extent, and on the side of the acquitters, the concession of even that excessive degree of revenge "to one whose body had been subjected to *hubris*" (§75).

Demosthenes goes on to employ *a fortiori* arguments which ostensibly explain his emphasis on the *differences* between these cases and his own – the absolute publicity of Meidias' actions demands all the greater anger and his own restraint requires the dikasts and the laws to provide a more powerful revenge than was meted out against Euaion. These arguments are evidently meant to transcend the problems of the residual admiration for the individuals' actions by referring the decision to the civic collective and its laws, thereby negotiating the move from potentially explosive self-help to the impersonal sovereignty of the law. Yet at the same time the very *oppositions* elaborated by Demosthenes which make these arguments possible proceed in his narrative from an original posited *similarity*. The movement to the *a fortiori* argument attempts to distance the similarities which draw the conflict between Demosthenes and Meidias into the (private) sphere of in-fighting among the rich.[31] It is this continuity, at once required and suppressed by Demosthenes, which in escaping his rhetorical control reveals once again the essentially individualistic standards of *timē* at stake.

It is little surprise that Demosthenes' leading example sets two famous athletic combatants against one another; while in the second instance the men are simply named – Euaion, the brother of Leodamas, and Boiotos – in the first case the two are actually defined by their athletic capacities: wrestler and pankratiast. Demosthenes has evidently gone to rather more trouble to select this parallel, which took place some time ago, far from Athens and at a private occasion. Given his tempering of the trope "You all know about . . ." with "well, if not all, many at least . . ." (§71), it is quite clear that the incident was far from well known. Demosthenes makes no explicit comment on the relevance or otherwise of these men's pursuits. Although they were evidently not active politically (as Euaion and Boiotos were), their case offers the perfect literalisation of the latently violent, competitive and combative ethos which lay at the base of Athenian politics. The completely physical conflict of these athletes in a struggle for manly honour is, as it were, one extreme on a continuous scale on which the fisticuff of Meidias is also to be placed.[32] Sophokles could, through the distanciated screen of tragic representation, write of "the wrestling beneficial for the *polis*", but not everyone regarded the literal παλαισμοσύνη [wrestler's art] as beneficial for the collective good.[33] The combat sports in particular, including wrestling and the pankration, were entirely oriented towards *individual* achievement and their practitioners were obsessed with personal victory. Poliakoff has argued that these archaic sports acted as a safety-valve for those competitive impulses which, while fitting for heroes, were less suitable for citizens of the *polis*, and he explains the increase in their popularity under democratic conditions in these terms, especially given the reduction of the military sphere as an arena for potential displays of individual prowess.

The persistence – indeed, the increased prominence – of these "aristocratic" activities in the democratic context mirrors the increased importance of competitive events such as were institutionalised in the *chorēgia* [provision of a public chorus] and other competitive liturgies as sites for public display and the fight for *timē* among the élite. Much of what Demosthenes says about *hubris* in this speech, in his generalisations, his citation of other cases and his caricature of Meidias as the *hubristēs*, attracts attention to a split in the ideology of *hubris*.[34] The examples of Euthynos and Euaion reveal a kind of *hubris* where there is simply no question of raising the claim to be protecting the corporate integrity of the civic body; while Demosthenes' own urgent desire to dissociate the *hubris* he ascribes to Meidias from this other form betrays much more than an oppositional relationship between the two.

In a passage of the *Rhetoric* in which Aristotle proclaims the need for precise definitions of crimes, including *hubris*, he draws attention to the important aspect of motivation in defining what constitutes *hubris*:

> For *hubris* is not committed on any occasion when a man strikes, but if it is for some reason, such as inflicting dishonour on another or to please himself. (*Rh.* 1.1374a)

The statement that *pleasure* might be a possible motive behind *hubris* is very suggestive – it is an illicit, stolen and therefore all the more intense pleasure. Towards the end of the speech (§§170 ff.), after demolishing Meidias' record of service to the city, Demosthenes is quick to add that there are many who *have* done good service:

> Nevertheless you've never given to any of them, nor would you give, the reward of permitting each of them to inflict *hubris* on his personal enemies, wherever he wishes and in whatever way he can. (§170)

Demosthenes is here evidently to some extent exposing the logic of how the system *does* work, or else it would not be necessary to argue against it, and claim that the reverse is normative, at such great length. Not even the favourite mythic heroes of the radical democrats, Harmodios and Aristogeiton, were granted this "gift" of committing *hubris* on whomever they wished – and they, significantly, were tyrant-slayers.[35]

In the texts of Aischines one often, unsurprisingly, finds tropes which reverse much of what Demosthenes says about himself. When he turns in the speech against Ktesiphon to attack the public record of his real opponent, Demosthenes, Aischines accuses him of embezzlement and adds: "You are a rich man and serve as *chorēgos* to your own pleasures" (3.240). In the Athenian public sphere the pursuance of pleasure often implies some infringement against the collective, just as *hubris* places individualistic desires above the interests of wider collectives.[36] A *chorēgia* "ἐφ' ἡδονῆι" [for pleasure] is one like the classic case of Alkibiades, abusing his fellow-*chorēgos* Taureas, the laws, the gods, the democracy.[37] There is a pleasure too, though it is heavily shielded and protected by an arsenal of civic tropes, in Demosthenes' own *chorēgia* which is the starting-point of Dem. 21, a pleasure of which Meidias deprived Demosthenes to a certain extent. "You are *chorēgos* to your own pleasures . . ."[38] – at the very upper tier of Athenian wealth and status *hubris* and pleasure no doubt often went together in self-presentation and performance before the *dēmos*.

## Demosthenes and His Audience

The *kondulos* [punch] of the title, the punch in the face, is the pre-textual act of physical abuse to the body of Demosthenes and, so we are asked to believe, thus to the body politic. A pretext it certainly is for a vast torrent of verbal abuse against Meidias. The narrative strategies which are so central to virtually all the forensic texts which survive from the Attic courts produce highly complex forms of representation. Humphreys has pointed out the way in which in urban courts the results of the process of crystallisation of local opinion had to be artifically recreated, and this act of imaginative and dramatic recreation in narrative from the βῆμα [speaker's platform] is indeed very theatrical itself.[39] It is to be seen at work in the lengthy account of Meidias' assault on Demosthenes' house some sixteen years earlier, when his young sister, his mother and himself were subjected to verbal abuse, "abuse some of which can and some of which cannot be repeated" (§79). Demosthenes restages this abuse in the civic centre, τὸ κοινόν, and this transference to the civic centre is part of the democracy's neutralisation of the dangers of disruption and conflict at the peripheries. By describing some of Meidias' abuse in that local context as ἄρρητα – "unutterable" – in its restaging before the whole *polis*, Demosthenes deploys a powerful trope of tabooed language. By concealing, or rather by *gesturing* to conceal, Demosthenes endows these "unutterable obscenities" with a greater power than any direct repetition could give them (ἄρρητα, after all, is a word used of the Mysteries, whose power of silence is well known).[40]

Dem. 21 creates and manipulates relations between Demosthenes and his audience with great complexity and subtlety. Perhaps the most pervasive strategy is the repeated claim to normative behaviour, behaviour which is at every point valuable to the social order. Thus in the opening paragraph of the speech he says

> My own reaction was just what the reaction of any of you to *hubris* would have been, . . . (§1)

A crucial aspect of this attempt to establish an agreed account of normative behaviour is here the assimilation in social terms between Demosthenes and his audience – he in fact ascribes to *them* the prescriptive course of action to follow when subjected to *hubris*, which happens to be the course which he followed. Yet whatever the socio-economic composition of the dikasts was in reality,[41] they are certainly *not leitourgoi* [performers of liturgies] and so in other words they are incapable (except hypothetically or imaginatively, which is perhaps crucial)[42] of fulfilling the norm outlined by Demosthenes in this sentence.[43]

Another striking example is in §§111–12 where, after describing himself as "neither one of the most friendless nor one of the completely poor" (an understatement, surely, if not intended as such), Demosthenes goes on to position himself among "us, the rest of the people" in opposition to the rich in terms of the inequalities between the two groups in practical legal powers:

> We, the rest of the population, men of Athens, do not share equality nor legal protection before the rich, no, not at all. (§112)

Yet when it suits his argument, Demosthenes can shift the dividing-line from "us/the filthy rich" to "me/you, the helpless many". §124 provides a good example. Pointing out that he has been able to repel the lies and sycophancy launched against him by Meidias, he asks his audience:

> But what will you the many do, unless you publicly make everyone afraid of the misuse of wealth for this purpose? (§124)

In all of these manoeuvres, the homogeneity of the *dēmos* which I mentioned above is a crucial postulated constant. Demosthenes' audience must always be the same, and to reinforce this impression Demosthenes deploys a powerful rhetoric of the collective in which the wishes and thoughts of the *dēmos* remain open to continual reinterpretation and construction. §2 is a paradigmatic instance. ὁ δῆμος is the subject of the lengthy single sentence of this paragraph, and in his report of the decision of the people at the *ekklēsia* in the theatre, Demosthenes construes it as a statement of unequivocal unanimous will. "The entire *dēmos*... with one judgment voted against him..." *Dēmos* can stand at the head of a string of singular verbs for actions, desires, thoughts (unlike its translations which shift into plurals[44]). As an "impersonal" subject ("*dēmos*" has recently been well described by Ober as an ideological, imaginative construct),[45] it is a very useful way of eliding real difference, and of mediating his position with that of his immediate dikastic audience.

## The Theatre of Conflict

In the case of the *kondulos*, the events were scarcely peripheral, but absolutely central, to the civic gaze.[46] Their theatricality consists rather in the place and occasion of their performance, and in that their actors were two of the brightest stars on the civic stage. Demosthenes' narrative of the events in the theatre (§§13ff.) underscores their theatricality – here abuse makes better theatre than theatre, and it is the highlight of social drama. This narrative is also a narrative of the self-construction of Demosthenes and a highly dramatic account of his performance before another ekklesiastic audience of the *dēmos*, the meeting of the *ekklēsia* at which the archon allotted pipers to the *chorēgoi*. Demosthenes saves the honour of his *phylē*, Pandionis, by his voluntary assumption of the dithyrambic *chorēgia* after a lapse of two years. "I came forward and volunteered to serve as *chorēgos*";[47] he received by lot the first choice of *aulētēs* [flute payer] (hinting perhaps at a suggestion of divine favour), and his audience (again identified with the current panel of dikasts) cheered and applauded him, "and your cheering and applause were such as to show both approval and pleasure" (§14). This narrative of individualistic action has almost heroic overtones,[48] and testifies to the desire of members of the élite to (re)create their glorious deeds before large audiences.[49] Similarly, Demosthenes claims later in the speech that in the conduct of his public life Meidias characteristically needs a large audience to insult:

> I suppose he considered any transaction between single individuals not distinguished or macho or worthy of regard; but unless he abused a whole *phylē* or *boulē* [council] or class, and harassed large numbers of you at once, he thought his life would not be worth living. (§131)

This desire to be *regarded*, in both senses (to be an object of θαῦμα, wonder[50]), by a large public audience is one which Demosthenes can easily attribute pejoratively to his opponent, linking it to an allegation that Meidias sought to achieve this end through manipulation of the relations of power inherent in his position as a preeminent πλούσιος [rich man] before the collective civic audience.[51] Yet it is evidently a desire which also motivates Demosthenes himself, whose tendentious arguments to the effect that the *chorēgia* is a religious or properly civic office do not mask the fact that it was one of the most privileged sites in Athenian public life for the ostentatious display of wealth and power by élite individuals.[52] [...]

[The author goes on to describe a general interrelation in fourth-century Athens between theater and politics, oratory and acting (here excised) before turning to the speech as abuse of democratic ideology.]

## The Abuse of Democracy

Leaving the theatre for a moment, I want to look further at the way a speech of abuse composed for an institutionalised site of civic *logos* [discourse] in democratic Athens perpetrates abuse of its own on the very ideology it at times so effusively espouses. To do this I shall select two passages in which Demosthenes cites and evaluates the actions of individual Athenian citizens – one the "ordinary" democratic citizen, in the person of Straton the arbitrator, the other Alkibiades, the vertiginous *enfant terrible* of the fifth-century democracy who proved most difficult and in the end impossible to accommodate within its structures.

Straton of Phaleron was the unlucky citizen to whom the lot assigned the arbitration of an earlier case of slander initiated by Demosthenes against Meidias.[71] Demosthenes' apparently casual description of him as

> ...a poor man, not involved in politics, but otherwise not bad, in fact very respectable (§83)

is an illuminating vignette. The association between being poor (πένης, as various writers have pointed out, signifies "one who has to work for a living" rather than "destitute")[72] and being base is implicit but clear.[73] As MacDowell notes,[74] ἀπράγμων is here used in a sense not quite typical in speeches of the period, since by this time it had predominantly come to imply "reluctant to litigate", antonym of the pejorative φιλοπράγμων. MacDowell thinks that ἀπράγμων here carries the negative connotation of "ignorant of the law", but I would suggest that in keeping with Demosthenes' strong, and somewhat nostalgic, democratic tone throughout much of his speech, he is perhaps to be seen to be reactivating the older notion whereby the citizen who is "uninvolved politically" is regarded as worthless[75] – that is ἄχρειος, to use another term from the Periklean Funeral Oration.[76]

At any rate, the trope is here deployed in such a way as to point unavoidably to the correlation between wealth (and thus leisure) and political eminence. Todd uses this and other passages to argue for a "real" jury composed mainly of farmers who were neither particularly rich nor poor.[77] However, whatever this may be interpreted to say about their real socio-economic status, by associating political inactivity with poverty, this description provides itself with a safety-valve – *these* dikasts, after all, are not altogether politically inactive and so, hearing this, they are free to delude themselves, just for the moment, that they have something in common with the rich, the leisured and the good.[78] A democratic discourse in which basic pejorative value-terms such as κακός [bad] or πονηρός [base] are regularly used simply to denote the lower socio-economic groups must surely be a discourse established and operated by an élite. Demosthenes' description of Straton seems rather less casual when he repeats it in the silent presence of Straton himself before the court (§95). Because he gave a verdict against him, Meidias manoeuvred to have Straton disenfranchised, and so Demosthenes must adduce him as a *silent* witness to Meidias' arrogance and hubristic use of his wealth. The fact that he is allowed to appear in court at all has puzzled commentators ancient and modern, since as an *atimos* [one deprived of civil rights] he was technically excluded from the *agorā* [civic center].[79] Hansen takes this to mean that such exclusion was not always enforced,[80] MacDowell sees it as evidence that the courts were not strictly part of the *agorā* – but I think the question of his *silence* must be a clue to the issue. For no doubt it is exclusion from *logoi* in these arenas of civic *logos* which rendered most effective the penalty of *atimiā* on the citizen – as Demosthenes says, Straton has even been deprived of τὸ φθέγξασθαι [speaking aloud].[81] Demosthenes here uses the opposition between the ordinary citizen and the rich and powerful greatly to his own advantage. Straton suffered because of "the fact of being one of the many" (§96), and by merging this very old case with the current one, Demosthenes uses this concrete instance of Meidias' treatment of one individual citizen (cf. also §87, §88, §90, §95) to typify his alleged abuse of all citizens, a movement from the particular to the general which is a crucial strategy for the whole speech.[82]

From the ordinary citizen cited patronisingly to the extraordinary citizen cited with a nostalgic wistfulness: but if Straton can stand as an exemplary ordinary citizen suffering at the hands of an enemy of the people, what does it mean to cite *Alkibiades* as an example in a context such as this? He is introduced at a new turn in the speech at §143, after Demosthenes has just built up to labelling Meidias "a common enemy to the state" (§142). The logical point of the comparison would be that Alkibiades, despite his enormous benefactions to the city, was driven into exile by the people for his insolence, his *hubris*. But Demosthenes is at pains to emphasise that he doesn't want to liken Meidias to Alkibiades – "I'm not that mad or out of my head!" (§143) No indeed, for the figure of Alkibiades is shrouded in the golden glow of nostalgia [...] The aura of λαμπρότης [brilliance] which hangs about his memory, his unabashed pursuance of aristocratic goals which were an abuse of democratic egalitarianism and which could easily be interpreted as a prelude to tyranny – all of these make him a very ambivalent figure for democratic ideology. Or rather, the contradictions inherent in his actions seem to exemplify the contraditions within democracy itself. To the faded Athens of the fourth century Alkibiades can be presented as a glorious instance of aristocratic birth, wealth and power combined, at least for a time, with goodwill for the *dēmos*. Alkibiades is thus virtually cited for praise in Demosthenes' speech, and Nouhaud has shown how details of his career are favourably distorted by Demosthenes.[83] One clear advantage in mentioning Alkibiades at all is that his aggressive outburst in the theatre when *chorēgos* against Taureas, also *chorēgos*, was a useful and famous parallel. Yet Demosthenes underplays the transgressive and hubristic aspects of Alkibiades' behaviour then, pointing out that both men were *chorēgoi* and that "this law" (§147) was not then in existence. Yet all that can be gleaned of the fifth-century context of this incident suggests that it was perceived as a flagrant demonstration of Alkibiades' imagined superiority over the laws, the people and the democracy.[84] Demosthenes even makes the extremely tendentious claim that the destruction by Meidias of the costumes and crowns of his *choreutai* was more serious than was the mutilation of the *hermai* [statue busts], an act depicted as "an oligarchical and tyrannical conspiracy" (Thuc. 6.60–1).[85]

This mention of the tyrant brings me back to the theatre, which was certainly a privileged place in the city for the representation and negotiation of the problematic relations between *hubris*, the figure of the tyrant and democracy – "*hubris* begets a tyrant" unless of course "a tyrant begets *hubris*" (Soph. *O.T.* 873).[86] Near the end of the speech, Demosthenes accentuates the democratic coordinates of his attack on Meidias as he polarises the political scene into an opposition between Meidias and everyone else. This polarisation isolates Meidias as the virtual embodiment of all that is wrong in the city, and as a structure of thought it is reminiscent of the objectification of a community's ills which is the rationale behind the *pharmakos* [scapegoat]-complex.[87] Perhaps the passage which comes nearest to deploying this notion in the civic sphere is the rhetorical climax of §§140–2. Demosthenes, who never takes the position of wanting Meidias punished only for the single, discrete crime committed in the theatre, turns the full force of an ideology of the collective against an individual, and calls on the masses, weak as individuals, to band together and assert their collective superiority over Meidias.

> For if someone is so mighty that, when he behaves in this way, he can prevent each of us individually from getting justice from him, now, since he is in our grasp, he must be punished jointly by all for all, as a common enemy of the state. (§142)

Later he raises the spectre of an anti-democratic coup when he imagines for his audience what the fate of a *dēmotikos* [populist] would be if Meidias and his supporters became "in control of the state" (§209). In an Athens which had undergone two oligarchic coups and whose abhorrence of internal conflict or *stasis* was highly marked, this rhetoric may have had a cutting edge.[88] However, that the fear of tyranny was often not so much a fear of the real potential for an individual to seize total power in the *polis* as a conceptual representation which helped to shape images of political excess and opposition for the citizens has been well argued by various writers.[89] The most sophisticated of these imaginary constructions were those which played so large a part in tragic representation, but political oratory shares much of this conceptual idiom.[90] It is striking, however, that the terminology which is normally used for tyranny in tragedy and comedy is *extremely* rare in connection with the historical so-called "thirty tyrants".[91] There are a few noteworthy occasions when Demosthenes uses terms with strong tragic overtones – such as when he calls Meidias his αὐτόχειρ or "slayer" (§106); or speaks of "lamenting" – θρηνῶν (§113) – his problems in organising his case against Meidias, or when in a rhetorical climax at §198 he declares by Zeus and Apollo and Athena that he must let the truth be known, with the expression εἰρήσεται γάρ, "for it shall be said", whether for good or ill – εἴτ ἄμεινον εἴτε μή. MacDowell notes that this is an iambic trimeter and perhaps a quotation from some lost tragedy.[92]

Although there are no explicit comparisons of Meidias to the figure of the tyrant, he is certainly given many of the characteristic signs of the tyrant, particularly in the portrayal of his wealth and his hubristic attitude to and use of it. Like many tragic tyrants, he is portrayed as a boundary-breaker, a transgressor of the supporting poles of free Greek/barbarian, man/woman, god/mortal. For example, in his account of the disenfranchisement of Straton, Demosthenes portrays Meidias as wilfully wielding the ultimate weapon in the civic arena – *atimiā* [loss of civic rights] – which in some contexts is equated with death.[93] When he says that it isn't even safe to walk along the same street as Meidias (§87) and that he displays ὠμότης [savagery] (§88), he is evoking familiar tropes of tyrannical behaviour.[94] Demosthenes adumbrates rhetoric-ally what the consequences will be if Meidias is allowed to continue his hubristic career:

> If anyone who tries to help himself when subjected in contravention of all the laws to *hubris* by Meidias is going to suffer this and similar treatment, it will be best to kowtow to those who commit *hubris*, as they do in foreign parts, not to resist them. (§106)

Imagined oriental practice again offers a mirror in which to see proper Greek practice: Demosthenes mobilises one of the most deeply-rooted tropes in Athenian rhetoric – the barbarian versus Greek opposition which in its specifically political complexion is often the opposition of free self-ruling citizen to tyrant and subjects. Other hints that such a model is at work are the allegation that Meidias would want to nail his enemies to a board (§105) – a punishment construed as typically oriental, which here raises the spectre of the threat to violate the bodily integrity of the citizen;[96] and the description of Meidias at various points as "abominable" (§§ 137, 167, 171), a word known previously only from tragedy or paratragic passages of comedy.[97]

These hints of tyrannical attributes translate in the "real" world into allegations of various forms of transgressive abuse in the form of personal conspicuous consumption – for example, Meidias has a house at Eleusis which is so huge that it overshadows the entire neighbourhood (§ 158); Demosthenes says he takes his wife around in a carriage drawn by a pair of white horses from Sikyon, "and he clears a way for himself through the *agorā* with an escort of three or four slaves, talking about 'goblets' and 'drinking-horns' and 'chalices' loudly enough for passers-by to hear" (§158). Elsewhere Demosthenes alleges effeminacy and perhaps a touch of orientalising luxury when he says that, when Meidias could no longer avoid going out on the military expedition to Euboia, he never put on his breastplate, but rode on a silver mule-chair and carried with him fine cloaks and goblets and flagons of wine (§133). This sort of abuse depends for its effect on democracy's much-vaunted egalitarianism, a deeply, and perhaps predominantly, symbolic egalitarianism which is prone to be particularly sensitive to such flagrant, public displays of wealth and power.

Meidias' abuse of democratic ideology (as presented by Demosthenes) authorises Demosthenes to employ in turn some of the most fundamentally emotive tropes of abusive civic rhetoric. The citation of Alkibiades and the comparison of his career to Meidias' lead Demosthenes to raise the issue of the rôle of *genos* in the political sphere. Just as with *timē*, *genos* has a double evaluation here – suggesting both high, aristocratic, birth and also status as a true-born Athenian citizen. Demosthenes rhetorically proposes, and then rejects, grounds on which Meidias might be shown συγγνώμη [mercy], φιλανθρωπία [pity] or χάρις [favor] (§§148–50). After dismissing his career as general and public speaker, Demosthenes proceeds to *genos*, and thereby explicitly shows that aristocratic birth *could* be proffered in a democratic context as a ground for indulgent consideration.

> His high birth, by Zeus! Well, every one of you knows the secret; it's like something in a tragedy, this man's origins. Two complete opposites are involved in his case: his real mother, the one who gave birth to him, was the most sensible person in the world, while his supposed mother, who took him as her child, was the stupidest of all women. The evidence: the former sold him as soon as he was born; the latter could have bought a better one at the price, and this is the one she purchased! (§150) And so for this reason he has got possession of wealth which doesn't belong to him, and has become a citizen of a city where the rule of law probably prevails more than in any other; and I suppose he's completely unable to tolerate or make use of these circumstances, but the truly barbarian and god-loathed part of his nature is overwhelming and violent, and makes it obvious that he uses what he has as though it belonged to others – as indeed is the case. (§§149–50)

This explicit, if somewhat comic, depiction of Meidias' origins as reminiscent of something from a tragedy forges an overt link between the social drama of this conflict and the foremost civic forum for the representation of social conflict and disorder, tragedy. This topos from the tragic stage, a place from which Athenian citizens (as characters) are markedly absent but where issues of origins, birth and status are paramount, becomes in the arena of the courts a topos of abuse.[98] The abominable Meidias – and I mentioned above the use of the tragic κατάπτυστος of him – is the abominable Other within the civic scene: changeling, tyrant, barbarian slave. As Todd points out, this is a form of abuse which is unlikely to have irritated the poor men among the dikasts since, whatever else they may not have been, they were certainly not slaves from abroad, but *autochthones* [native born].[99] Quasi-comic abuse here combines pungently with the final horizon of all abusive attacks in Athenian civic fora – the claim that one's opponent isn't a member of the "men's club" of citizenship,[100] and so shouldn't properly even be allowed to play the game.[101] Meidias is (§148) a nobody and son of a nobody; "nobody" in this context quite clearly means a "not-one-of-*Us*". The rhetorical movement in this passage from denial of high birth to the denial of civic status is reminiscent of the Oidipal shift from god-like king to what is worse than a slave; while the powerful climax of §150 with its implication that he is an impostor, a counterfeit citizen who has utterly overturned the stabilising hierarchies, also evokes the reversals of Oidipous (Soph. *O. T.* 1187–8).[102] This abuse lends itself to being read as yet another insight into a now familiar aspect of Athenian "civic psychology", if it is possible to speak of the psychology of an ideological and political construct. The many exclusions which operated in fifth- and fourth-century democracy – particularly of slaves, women and foreigners – produced powerful and potentially destructive social tensions. With this came an intense fear in the Athenian imagination of what would happen if such outsiders somehow penetrated into the inner circle of citizenship. Demosthenes is perhaps at his most successful here in harnessing this fear in extended abuse of Meidias, in alleging his actual transgression of these boundaries, and the convergence in Meidias of virtually every non- or anti-civic type. Yet the rapidity with which Demosthenes passes from these tropes to a scrutiny of Meidias' record of services to the city – clear markers, that is, of his *acknowledged* civic status – must raise the question of the status of such abuse, its anticipated effect. Davies has written of this practice as "no more than a game ... but the underlay is a lot more serious than that".[103] Game and underlay, I would suggest, are scarcely distinguishable, and "serious game" might be a better formulation.

## Demosthenes 21: Money for Old Tropes?

Dem. 21 is an invaluable text for the historian interested in *hubris* in Athenian democracy, in the dynamic operation of the *chorēgia* and in the place of the theatre in fourth-century Attic society. I have also attempted to demonstrate its exemplary quality as an exercise in the rhetorical negotiation of individual and collective, private and public interests in fourth-century Athens. In conclusion I want to draw attention briefly to some ambiguities regarding the status of Dem. 21 as a text.

In the attempt to do away with Meidias which Dem. 21 dramatises, Demosthenes constructs a civic scenario in which his body is cast as the exemplary object of anti-democratic violence, of *hubris*.

> I was subjected to *hubris* and my body abused that day, but now the question will be contested and decided as to whether it should be permitted to do this sort of thing and to commit *hubris* upon any one of you with impunity. (§7)

In this scenario all other difference is elided so that Demosthenes' body can stand for that of each and any citizen. Yet Demosthenes relinquished his rôle as the testing-point of this sensitive ideological negotiation.[104] Having missed the specific institutional occasion for which it was composed, Dem. 21 continues to present itself as the performance text of that event. With its repeated self-referentiality to that absent context – cf. §3 "... I am present, as you see ..." – its studied affectation of *ex tempore*[105] and its constant self-authorisation predicated on the physical presence of Demosthenes in the court,[106] Dem. 21 is a particularly edifying example of the non-transparency of classical texts, since it is not what it insistently proclaims itself to be.[107] The affectation of an institutional form by a classical text not intended for such a destination is familiar from the *Tetralogies* of Antiphon and much of the Isokratean corpus. In this regard the consignment of Dem. 21 to an audience of readers (and perhaps "hearers" too)[108] may well have multiple determinations: as part of a continued campaign against Meidias outside the court system, as a statement of political alignment, but certainly also as a central text in the projection and perpetuation of a self-image by Demosthenes.[109] The perils of a public confrontation over *hubris* are thereby avoided and the advantages from the circulation of a flattering self-portrait as civic benefactor and heroic democrat retained.

## NOTES

1   I would like to thank Richard Hunter, Paul Cartledge and Simon Goldhill very warmly for their generous criticism and encouragement. An earlier version of this paper was delivered to the Cambridge Ancient Literature seminar; my thanks also to all who participated there.

2   It appears in *Parisinus Graecus* 2934, ix–x saec. (S). Cf. L. Canfora, *Discorsi e lettere di Demostene* (1974) 31–3, who notes that the most usual ancient scholarly practice in citing a work is to quote the opening words of the work.

3   Pl. *Smp.* 175e; see A. Pickard-Cambridge, *The dramatic festivals of Athens* ed. 2 rev. J. Gould and D. M. Lewis (1988) 263.

4   The clearest instance of this equation is in §18 – καὶ τούτων, ὅσα γε ἐν τῶι δήμωι γέγονεν ἢ πρὸς τοῖς κριταῖς ἐν τῶι θεάτρωι, ὑμεῖς ἐστέ μοι μάρτυρες πάντες, ἄνδρες δικασταί. "And as far as concerns the incidents at the meeting of the *dēmos* or before the judges in the theatre, you are all my witnesses, dikasts." (All translations of Dem. 21 are adapted from D. M. MacDowell, *Demosthenes: Against Meidias (Oration 21)* (1990).) According to a passage late in the speech – §§193–4 – Meidias contested this equation by claiming its inaccuracy in fact for the particular instance at the *probolē*, when the meeting of the *ekklēsia* was allegedly full of those who should have gone out on campaign, those who left the garrison-forts unmanned, καὶ χορευταὶ καὶ ξένοι καὶ τοιοῦτοί τινες (§193). Such explicit "analysis" of the *actual* composition of an *ekklēsia* is extremely rare and Demosthenes can call it τοῦ δήμου κατηγορεῖν... [καὶ] τῆς ἐκκλησίας... (§193) – "accusation of the *dēmos* [and] the *ekklēsia*..." This whole question is a subject of current debate between Hansen, Ostwald and Ober; in regard to the relation between *dēmos* and *dikastērion*, Hansen adopts a concept of representation, which implies a *distinction*, not identity – see M. H. Hansen, "*Demos, ekklesia*, and *dikasterion*. A reply to Martin Ostwald and Josiah Ober", *C & M* 40 (1989) 103–4; while Ober has employed the term "synecdoche," by which the part symbolically stands for the whole – see J. Ober, "The nature of Athenian democracy", *CPH* 84 (1989) 322–34. From my reading of Dem. 21 I find Ober's the more attractive position, but the way even within this single speech the issue is contested should alert one to the dangers of fixing on too narrow an interpretation of a complex rhetorical trope manipulated to suit different aims: cf. R. K. Sinclair, "Lysias' speeches and the debate about participation in Athenian public life", *Antichthon* 22 (1988) 62.

5   See esp. §§226–7.

6   R. Osborne, "Law in action in classical Athens", *JHS* 105 (1985) 50 points out that victims of violence had a choice of procedure open to them, as there was considerable overlap between βλάβη and αἰκεία, prosecuted by *dikai*, and ὕβρις, prosecuted by *graphē*. Demosthenes himself goes to great length to counter an imagined objection of Meidias that he has brought an inappropriate suit – see esp. §§25–8; cf. P. J. Rhodes, *A commentary on the Aristotelian* Athenaion Politeia (1981) 659–60.

7   J. J. Winkler, *The constraints of desire: the anthropology of sex and gender in ancient Greece* (1990) ch. 2: "*Phallos politikos*: representing the body politic in Athens", *Differences* 2 (1990) 29–45; D. M. Halperin, *One hundred years of homosexuality and other essays on Greek love* (1990) ch. 5; D. M. MacDowell, "*Hybris* in Athens", *G & R* 23 (1976) 14–31; N. R. E. Fisher, "*Hybris* and dishonour", *G & R* 23 (1976) 177–93, 26 (1979) 32–47.

8   Halperin (1990) 96.

9   In my attempt to do this I have benefited from some of the insights of the so-called critical legal studies movement, with its understanding of rhetoric not simply as the neutral codification of forms of argument but as a contribution to the critique of ideology – see esp. J. B. White, *Heracles' bow: essays on the rhetoric and poetics of the law* (1985); R. M. Unger, *The critical legal studies movement* (1986); V. Kahn, "Rhetoric and the law", *Diacritics* 19.2 (1989) 21–34; Kahn (1989) 34 – "Precisely because rhetoric teaches argument on both sides of a question, it does not simply codify the ideological assumptions of a given culture but also shows that forms of argument can be unmoored from a given ideology, thus allowing for the articulation of conflicting interests. In the

same way, the law is a formal structure that articulates both the dominant ideology and the grounds of contradiction and disagreement in a given society."

10   Osborne (1985) 50 lists that mentioned in Isaios 8.41 against Diokles and that brought by Apollodoros against Phormio which was "adjourned" – [Dem.] 45.4. Cf. N. R. E. Fisher, "The law of *hybris* in Athens", ch. 6a of P. Cartledge, P. Millett and S. Todd (edd.), *Nomos: essays in Athenian law, politics and society* (1990) 123–5, 133–4; he considers the fragmentary evidence for other cases.

11   MacDowell (1990) 16, against the dominant view represented e.g. by A. R. W. Harrison, *The law of Athens* II (1968–71) 62–3; however that the case was not a *graphē hubreōs* was recognised long ago by L. Gernet, *Recherches sur le dévelopement de la pensée juridique et morale en Grèce* (1917) 193. Fisher (1990) 134 suggests that the introduction of the *probolē* procedure may imply that some of the difficulties in the operation of the *hubris* law were recognised.

12   The crucial text is Aischin. 3.52, which speaks of Demosthenes "selling" (ἀπέδετο) the *hubris* against him and the preliminary vote of the *dēmos* for 30 mnai; cf. K. J. Dover, *Lysias and the* Corpus Lysiacum (1968) 172; Osborne (1985) 50–1; Canfora (1974) 44–5; H. Erbse, "Über die Midiana des Demosthenes", 412–31 of *Ausgewählte Schriften zur klassischen Philologie* (1979 [orig. 1956]) is the most prominent dissenter, believing that Dem. 21 or something very like it was delivered. J. Ober, *Mass and elite in democratic Athens: rhetoric, ideology, and the power of the people* (1989) 207 n. 28 seems to agree with Erbse, but his lack of clarity and detailed argument precisely at this point are consonant with his evident desire that this prize piece of "democratic discourse" should have reached its "proper" audience. Ober's somewhat idealised image of the workings of Athenian democracy relies heavily on those intensely "democratic" passages in Demosthenes of which Dem. 21 provides some of the best examples. See below.

13   Osborne (1985) 50 writes that a *graphē hubreōs* would in practice inevitably become an "open trial of strength"; cf. Gernet (1917) 292–301; Fisher (1976) 181–2; on the concept of the "zero-sum" competition see A. W. Gouldner, *Enter Plato: classical Greece and the origins of social theory* (1965) 49–51; Winkler, *Constraints* 47.

14   See C. Mossé, "Égalité démocratique et inégalités sociales: le débat à Athènes au IVème siècle", *Metis* 2 (1987) 165–76, 195–206 for a good discussion, on the basis of a comparison between Dem. 20 and Dem. 21, of the way in which political equality was coming to seem more and more compromised by social inequalities.

15   See K. J. Dover, *Greek popular morality in the time of Plato and Aristotle* (1974) 5–6.

16   Dem. 23.50; Lys. 10.30; see D. M. MacDowell, *The law in classical Athens* (1978) 126–9.

17   S. Todd, "The use and abuse of the Attic orators", *G & R* 37 (1990) 172.

18   S. Todd and P. Millett, "Law, society and Athens", ch. 1 of Cartledge, Millett, Todd (1990) 14, referring in particular to the pioneering work of L. Gernet, *Droit et société dans la Grèce ancienne* (1955 [orig. 1937]) 67 and U. E. Paoli, *Studi sul processo attico* (1933) 66–72; cf. Osborne (1985).

19   S. Humphreys, "Social relations on stage: witnesses in classical Athens", *History and Anthropology* I (1985) 313–69.

[...]

24   In the two cases cited by Osborne (above n. 10) the men who bring them "are not simply men who *happen* to volunteer, they are men with a very distinct interest in the outcome of the cases": Osborne (1985) 50.

25   O. Murray, "The Solonian law of *hubris*", ch. 6b of Cartledge, Millett, Todd (1990).

26   When Murray writes – Murray (1990) 144 – that the activity of the violent *kōmos* "provides a historical background to the deliberately 'hybristic' pattern of behaviour which Demosthenes attributes to Meidias" it is not entirely clear who we are to imagine as *perceiving* this pattern of behaviour, and what that might imply. Was Demosthenes

activating an anti-aristocratic bias, or is the "historical background" visible only to the historian?

27 Dover (1974) 67.

28 See MacDowell (1990) 288–9 for a discussion of some of the difficulties in this passage.

29 MacDowell (1990) 288.

30 Note that in §73 Euaion and Boiotos are described as γνώριμοι, as are those at their dinner-party. The word has a marked social register, suggesting "notable" as well as "known (to one-another)". Cf. Dem. 19. 259.

31 Cf. his attempts to head this off elsewhere in the speech – e.g. §§126, 128–37. These arguments are sufficiently extended and overwrought to suggest that they are being put forward with the likelihood that the opposite position is more likely to have been regarded as normative.

32 The conflict between Paphlagon and the Sausage-seller in Aristoph. *Knights* often deploys metaphors from wrestling – e.g. 262 ff., 490 ff., 711.

33 See esp. Xenophanes 2 (West); M. B. Poliakoff, *Combat sports in the ancient world: competition, violence, and culture* (1987) 92– 4, 99–107.

34 Cf. here the fundamental work of Gernet (1917) 1–31, 183–9, 389–424.

35 See M. W. Taylor, *The tyrant slayers: the heroic image in fifth-century B.C. Athenian art and politics* (1981).

36 MacDowell (1978) 129.

37 [And.] 4. 20–1. See below.

38 By the date of Aischin. 3 (330 B.C.), χορηγεῖν may have already developed its common later sense of simply "provide for", and I believe there may be a play on this sense in this passage. J. Taillardat, *Les images d' Aristophane: études de langue et de style* (1965) 146 cites Aristophanes fr. 564 (K.-A.), of c.411, as the first extant example of such a use.

39 Humphreys, "The evolution of legal process in ancient Attica", 229–56 of E. Gabba (ed.), *Tria Corda: Scritti in onore di Arnaldo Momigliano* (1983) 248 writes of the way the speech-writer, "like a playwright or a post-classical novelist, constructs a social milieu in which the audience can believe . . . an artistic representation of the community before an audience of city jurors". Cf. also Humphreys (1985); J. Ober and B. Strauss, "Drama, political rhetoric, and the discourse of Athenian democracy", 237–70 of J. J. Winkler and F. I. Zeitlin (edd.), *Nothing to do with Dionysos?: Athenian drama in its social context* (1990).

40 Used of Persephone – Eur. fr. 63 (Nauck); cf. *Hel.* 1307; *I.G.* 3.713. Cf. W. Burkert, *Greek religion* (1985 [orig. 1977]) 161, 276, 455 n. 3; P. Scarpi, "The eloquence of silence. Aspects of a power without words", 19– 40 of M. G. Ciani (ed.), *The regions of silence: studies on the difficulty of communicating* (1987).

41 See Todd's good reassessment of the evidence, S. C. Todd, "*Lady Chatterley's Lover* and the Attic orators: the social composition of the Athenian jury", *JHS* 110 (1990) 146–73; also Sinclair (1988).

42 Cf. §219: εἰ δὲ μὴ πάντες ἐπαίεσθε μηδὲ πάντες ἐπηρεάζεσθε χορηγοῦντες, ἴστε δήπου τοῦθ', ὅτι οὐδὲ ἐχορηγεῖθ' ἅμα πάντες, οὐδὲ δύναιτ' ἄν ποθ' ὑμᾶς οὐδεὶς ἅπαντας μιᾶι χειρὶ προπηλακίσαι. "If you were not all struck and not all treated outrageously in service as *chorēgoi*, you know of course that neither were you all *chorēgoi* at once, and no one could ever abuse you all with a single hand."

43 Ober, *Mass and elite* 224–6 discusses the "dramatic fiction, which was based upon flattering the members of the audience by treating them if [sic] they were all well off and hence confronted by the problems associated with meeting financial obligations to the state".

44 Cf. MacDowell (1990) 89 – "The people acted in the right and proper way: they were all so angry and incensed . . . "

45 Ober, "Athenian democracy" 329–32.

46   The deeply ideological and rhetorical activities of constructing what *is* central to the civic gaze should not be overlooked. The orchestra of the theatre of Dionysos no doubt was the privileged focus of civic attention during the days of the city's premier festival, but there is still an important elision between a recognition of this fact and a statement such as that with which Demosthenes opens his speech: τὴν μὲν ἀσέλγειαν, ὦ ἄνδρες δικασταί, καὶ τὴν ὕβριν, ἧι πρὸς ἅπαντας ἀεὶ χρῆται Μειδίας, οὐδένα οὔθ᾽ ὑμῶν οὔτε τῶν ἄλλων πολιτῶν ἀγνοεῖν οἴομαι – "The bullying, dikasts, and the *hubris*, with which Meidias constantly treats everyone, are known to all of you and to the rest of the citizens, I suppose." The image of Attic society as a whole as a "face-to-face" society is, as Osborne and others have noted, indeed a myth, but it is a myth propagated in the first instance by the Athenians themselves in certain contexts. See R. Osborne, *Demos: the discovery of classical Attika* (1985) 64–5; Ober, *Mass and elite* 31–3.

47   παρέρχομαι is a word used in the various civic contexts of the individuals who come forward to speak before mass audiences, including in the theatre – cf. §7 and see e.g. Plut. *Nik.* 3.4; Aristoph. *Th.* 443; W. J. Slater, "The epiphany of Demosthenes", *Phoenix* 42 (1988) 127–8 and n. 7 points to the importance of the word in statements of epiphany – see esp. Eur. *Ba.* 5.

48   See Slater's interesting article (1988), dealing with Dem. 18 (*On the crown*), one of the few to discuss the dramatic qualities of Demosthenean narrative. Slater (1988) 126: "The soteriology of the dramatic self-presentation is contrasted with Aeschines' efforts at heroic appearance on the stage; the stage of life is contrasted with the theatre; the allegedly comic Demosthenes triumphs over the ineptly heroic Aeschines. Throughout runs the motif of heroic epiphany." I would argue that a similar motif of heroic intervention, if not quite epiphany, runs through Demosthenes' account here in Dem. 21.

49   Cf. Z. Petre, "Quelques problèmes concernant l'élaboration de la pensée démocratique athénienne entre 510 et 460 av. N.E.", *StudClas* 11 (1969) 44: "...les aristocrates athéniens semblent s'être accommodés des nouveaux cadres de la cité qui, s'ils ne reconnaissaient plus leur domination comme groupe, offraient un terrain beacoup plus vaste aux exploits et aux ambitions d'une gloire individuelle". Ober, *Mass and elite* 155.

50   θαῦμα and cognates have a predominantly visual reference, denoting the effect of amazement, awe, wonder produced in the *viewer*. P. Chantraine, *Dictionnaire étymologique de la langue grecque* II (1968) 424–5 accepts its relation to the θεά-group.

51   The climax of this sentence, ἀβίωτον ὤιετ᾽ ἔσεσθαι τὸν βίον αὐτῶι – "he thought his life would not be worth living", has something of a tragic ring to it, perhaps a particularly Euripidean one, given the use of ἀβίωτος in *Ion* 670 and *Alk.* 242, and the typically Euripidean polyptoton in ἀβίωτον... βίον, with which cf. the passage from *Alk*. The rare ἀβίωτος is confined mainly to drama and Plato. See below on other tragic colour in Demosthenes' representation of Meidias.

52   Note the way in which Demosthenes manages to convert Meidias' offer to be elected ἐπιμελητής, or superintendent for the Dionysia (§15), to abuse. Although of lower public profile than the *chorēgia*, this was an important office involving great expense for, among other things, the organisation of the procession – πομπή. As MacDowell (1990) 238 remarks with characteristic dryness, "Although D. disparages it, it may have been no more selfish than D.'s own offer to be a khoregos"; cf. Pickard-Cambridge, *Dramatic festivals* 91 and n. 7; "Suidas" s.v. ἐπιμεληταί: ἐπιμεληταὶ ἐχειροτονοῦντο τῶν χορῶν, ὡς μὴ ἀτακτεῖν τοὺς χορευτὰς ἐν τοῖς θεάτροις. "Superintendents of the *choroi* were elected, so that the *choreutai* were not disorderly in the theatres." This suggests that they had some duties concerning the discipline of *choroi* in the theatre, a position Meidias may have exploited.

[...]

71   See Ober, *Mass and elite* 210–11 for a discussion of this passage.

72    See M. M. Markle, "Jury pay and assembly pay at Athens", 265–97 of P. Cartledge and F. Harvey (edd.), *Crux: Essays in Greek history presented to G. E. M. de Ste. Croix on his 75th birthday* (1985) 267–71, developing P. Vidal-Naquet and M. M. Austin, *Economic and social history of Greece: an introduction* (1977 [orig. 1972]) 16; G. E. M. de Ste. Croix, *The class struggle in the ancient Greek world* (1981) 431. Ober, *Mass and elite* 210 translates as "a labouring man".

73    Markle (1985) 287–8 n. 40 thinks Demosthenes wants to stress that Straton *had formerly had sufficient* property to serve as a hoplite, before he became an enemy of Meidias.

74    MacDowell (1990) 304.

75    This is in keeping with the way Demosthenes uses a public/private opposition throughout to characterise his activities and attitudes in contrast to Meidias'; cf. e.g. §§ 17, 25, 35, 61.

76    See Thuc. 2.40.2; Loraux, *Invention* 178–9 [n. 87 below].

77    Todd, "Social composition"; see above.

78    Cf. Dover (1974) 34–5. See § 218: Demosthenes says that if they convict Meidias the jurors will be regarded as καλοὶ κἀγαθοὶ καὶ μισοπόνηροι, another appropriation of aristocratic terminology.

79    See MacDowell (1990) 318–19.

80    M. H. Hansen, Apagoge, endeixis *and* ephegesis *against* kakourgoi, atimoi *and* pheugontes (1976) 62.

81    §95; cf. §90:... ἄτιμον Ἀθηναίων ἕνα εἶναι δεῖ καὶ μήτε συγγνώμης μήτε λόγου μήτε ἐπιεικείας μηδεμιᾶς τυχεῖν...

82    From §§99–100 it might almost seem as if Meidias were on trial for committing *hubris* to Straton.

83    M. Nouhaud, *L'Utilisation de l'histoire par les orateurs attiques* (1982) 296.

84    See esp. [And.] 4. 20–1; M. Ostwald, *From popular sovereignty to the sovereignty of law: law, society, and politics in fifth-century Athens* (1986) 120–1 discusses some of the problems in this passage. See above.

85    However, as Dover (1974) 12 and MacDowell (1990) point out, Alkibiades' alleged involvement in the mutilation of the *hermai* is "a piece of popular tradition" (Dover) and he seems not even to have been accused of it in 415 B.C.; cf. also C. Tuplin, "Imperial tyranny: some reflections on a classical Greek political metaphor", 348–75 of Cartledge and Harvey (edd.), *Crux* (1985) 368; Nouhaud (1982) 296 writes of "l'aspect étrange et excessif de la comparaison".

86    On *hubris* in this passage see Fisher (1979) 41–2. Fisher's article offers a good corrective to "the frequent assumption that *hubris* is a moral term that particularly suggests 'tragedy', an explanation of men's falls in terms of divine punishment for human offences that arouse the appropriate 'tragic' emotions": Fisher (1979) 45.

87    On which see most recently and conveniently L. J. Bennett and W. B. Tyrrell, "Making sense of Aristophanes' *Knights*", *Arethusa* 23 (1990) 235–54. See also J.-P. Vernant in J.-P. Vernant and P. Vidal-Naquet, *Myth and tragedy in ancient Greece* (1988 [orig. 1972]) 128–35. This model was used in political rhetoric by [Lysias] against Andokides: 6.53. Its usefulness for eliding political conflict and disorder is clear – cf. N. Loraux, "L'oubli dans la cité", *Le temps de la réflexion* 1 (1980) 223; *The invention of Athens: the funeral oration in the classical city* (1986 [orig. 1981]) 198; "Repolitiser la cité", *L'homme* 26 (1986) 239–55.

88    Cf. Isok. 20.9–11.

89    See Aristoph. *Wasps* 486–507; D. Lanza, *Il tiranno e il suo pubblico* (1977); P. E. Easterling, "Kings in Greek tragedy", 33–45 of J. Coy and J. de Hoz (edd.), *Estudios sobre los géneros literarios* II (1984); Loraux, *Invention* 208–9, 215–16 discusses a certain association in political rhetoric between *oligarchiā* and *tyrannis*. Demosthenes can, for example,

represent the struggle with Philip as one of free city-state against a tyrant. See J. W. Leopold, "Demosthenes on distrust of tyrants", *GRBS* 22 (1981) 227–46; E. Lévy, *Athènes devant la défaite de 404: histoire d'une crise idéologique* (1976) 137–42.

90   However, cf. E. Hall, *Inventing the barbarian: Greek self-definition through tragedy* (1989) esp. 13–17.

91   See Tuplin (1985) 368–9; Lévy (1976) 142–4.

92   MacDowell (1990) 406; see also above.

93   Cf. §§100, 106.

94   Cf. also the opening description of Meidias in §2 as ... θρασὺν ὄντα καὶ βδελυρὸν καὶ οὐδὲ καθεκτὸν ἔτι. See MacDowell (1990) 156 on οὐδὲ καθεκτὸν as "out of control".

[...]

96   Cf. F. Hartog, *The mirror of Herodotus: the representation of the other in the writing of history* (1988 [orig. 1980]) 142–3; Hall (1989) 158.

97   See MacDowell (1990) 355.

98   Cf. J. K. Davies, "Athenian citizenship: the descent group and the alternatives", *CJ* 73 (1978) 111–14; MacDowell (1990) 365 cites as a parallel Andok. 1.129, referring to the matrimonial affairs of his opponent Kallias: τίς ἂν εἴη οὗτος; Οἰδίπους, ἢ Αἴγισθος; ἢ τί χρὴ αὐτὸν ὀνομάσαι; another "tragic" topos of abuse in civic rhetoric is seen in the attacks on Aischines as τριταγωνιστής, player of slave-rôles and so on. The point of such attacks, as P. Ghiron-Bistagne has well noted – *Recherches sur les acteurs dans la Grèce ancienne* (1976) 160 – is not that the played "bit parts", but that the parts of the τριταγωνιστής were generally the extremely antipathetic rôles of tyrants and the like. There is an interesting parallel between these attacks made in the fourth century and those of the fifth directed against the likes of Kleon, Hyperbolos and Kleophon. Cf. Ostwald (1986) 214–29. It is particularly striking that Kleon's alleged maltreatment of and antagonism towards the *hippeis* find a close parallel in Meidias' alleged activities in §§ 132–5.

99   Todd, "Social composition" 164, cf. N. Loraux, *Les enfants d'Athéna: idées athéniennes sur la citoyenneté et la division des sexes* (1981) 35–73; 36: "Au regard du narcissisme officiel, il n'est en effet de citoyen qu' autochthone."

100  An expression of P. Vidal-Naquet, *The black hunter: forms of thought and forms of society in the Greek world* (1986 [orig. 1981]) 5 and Loraux, *Invention* 24.

101  Cf. Dover (1974) 32; Winkler, *Constraints* 46.

102  Cf. Vernant and Vidal-Naquet (1988 [1972]) ch. 5.

103  Davies (1978) 112.

104  On the issue of the non-delivery of Dem. 21 see above n. 12.

105  Cf. e.g. §130. With this rehearsed spontaneity goes too Demosthenes' attempt to attach any opprobrium involved in the idea and activity of writing up a speech to Meidias, by claiming a transparent identity between Meidias' ἔργα and his own λόγοι – §§191–2. It may be possible to detect here a general, "popular" attitude of ambivalence or suspicion towards the written speech in contrast to the attitude of the élite (of wealth, social standing and education) who were presumably the recipients of Dem. 21. See W. V. Harris, *Ancient literacy* (1989) 104. His general conclusion at 115 is that literacy "becomes at least in Athens, a mark in theory of a proper citizen and in practice of the urban citizen with property".

106  See e.g. §§3, 40, 151–2, 215–16.

107  See the excellent article of N. Loraux, "Thucydide n'est pas un collègue", *QS* 12 (1980) 55–81.

108  Cf. J. Svenbro, *Phrasikleia: anthropologie de la lecture en Grèce ancienne* (1988).

109  Cf. here J.-P. Vernant, *L'individu, la mort, l'amour: soi-même et l'autre en Grèce ancienne* (1989), ch. 10 "L'individu dans la cité" esp. 224–7.

# Power and Oratory in Democratic Athens: Demosthenes 21, Against Meidias

## *Josiah Ober*

Ober uses Demosthenes' speech to demon-   Athens, one with the power to transform
strate the triumph of popular ideology at   aristocratic ideals.

To study politics and political life is to study power and the play of power. But what is power? A simple definition of a powerful entity might be "one with the ability to satisfy its own desires by instrumentally affecting the behaviour of others".[1] This simple definition leaves a lot undecided: what sorts of entities are we talking about (individuals? corporate groups?), and what are their desires? These questions can be answered (at least in a preliminary way) by applying the definition to a concrete historical situation. In the case of fourth-century Athens, it is clear enough that there were powerful individuals within society – most obviously wealthy men capable of affecting the behaviour of workers (whether slave or free) and of satisfying their desires for material goods by appropriating the surplus generated by the labour of others. On the other hand, it is equally obvious that the fourth-century Athenian demos, as a collective entity, was powerful in that it was often able to satisfy its desires for (*inter alia*) autarchy (in the Aristotelian sense) and autonomy by affecting the behaviour of both Athenian citizens and others in a variety of ways (for example, by levying taxes and paying soldiers to protect state interests and assets). In Athens, as in other societies, the spheres dominated by different powerful entities sometimes came into conflict; notable among these conflicts was the clash between public and private interests. There was a high potential for discord between powerful Athenian individuals (for example, rich men who wished to retain the use of their wealth to satisfy their private desires) and the demos (which was determined to put some part of that wealth to public use in ensuring autarchy and autonomy). A good number of "individual vs. community" conflicts were eventually adjudicated in the lawcourts of Athens. And hence dicanic oratory was among the primary instruments whereby the power of the individual Athenian was tested against the power of the demos. The study of oratory in Athens should, therefore, be able to tell us something about how power worked in democratic Athens – and vice versa. But before we can hope to understand the instrumental role of oratory in negotiating the play of power in Athenian society, we will have to refine and expand our definition of power.

There is a large modern literature on the subject of power; here I will focus on two major paradigms. The first and more traditional approach to power, which we may call the "coercion" paradigm, sees power as centred in the state and fundamentally based on force or the threat of force; that is, the ability to deploy violent physical

Josiah Ober, "Power and Oratory in Democratic Athens: Demosthenes 21, Against Meidias," in I. Worthington (ed.), *Persuasion: Greek Rhetoric in Action* (London: Routledge, 1994), pp. 85–108.

coercion.[2] The state, as sovereign authority, attempts to monopolise the right to use force legitimately within society (for example, by police actions) and to deploy force externally (by making war). The state is the primary locus of power in that all holders of legitimate protections and privileges within society (for example, property-owners and citizens) look to the state to exert force when necessary to enforce those protections and privileges. Thus, for example, if my brother is murdered or my house is robbed, I must expect agents of the state to apprehend and punish the perpetrator, rather than taking vengeance myself. And, on the other hand, as long as I obey the laws and fulfil my various duties and responsibilities as a member of society, I can expect to remain free from the operations of power. This model sees power as essentially juridical and repressive. Both those who approve of and those who oppose the state and its ideals can agree that, according to the coercion paradigm, power is exerted in order to repress behaviour that is deemed likely to threaten the sovereign authority of the state and which contravenes its laws.

The second approach to power, which we may call the "discourse" paradigm, is less interested in overt coercion, sovereignty, state apparatuses, and law as such. It focuses instead on how social and political knowledge is produced and disseminated throughout society.[3] According to this second paradigm, power is not centralised anywhere, and is neither "legitimate" nor "illegitimate". Thus sovereignty is not at issue and a study of formal juridical institutions alone will not reveal the fundamental workings of power. Rather than seeing power as repressive, the discourse paradigm sees power as productive: it emerges through the production of social understandings regarding what is true and what behaviours are right, proper, even conceivable. As a consequence, the concept of freedom becomes problematic. Since power is productive and omnipresent (rather than repressive and located in the state) it is not simply a matter of my being free to do whatever is not prohibited. Rather, all of my social interactions, including my speech, are (at least potentially) bound up with a regime of power that is also a regime of truth. It is not easy to get outside power, since all forms of social communication (including speech) will depend upon generally agreed-upon truths (for example, schemes of social categorisation) as the fundamental premises of meaningful interchange. Coercive violence itself is thus part of discourse: the regime of knowledge will prescribe under what conditions one category of person may or may not perpetrate violence upon another and what constitutes violence (for example, whether a free man may strike a slave or whether it is meaningful to speak of a husband raping his wife). The regime of knowledge/truth/power is thus maintained through discourse. A key question that faces the student of power working within the discourse paradigm is how, and by whom, social understandings are produced and reproduced – or challenged and overthrown.

Which of these two approaches is most useful in assessing the *dunamis* [power] of the individual, the *kratos* [might] of the Athenian demos and their relationship to public oratory in the fourth century? The applicability of a coercion paradigm of power to the Athenian polis, is, I believe, necessarily limited by its dependence on the notion of the sovereign state – a concept that seems to have been foreign to the demotic Athenian understanding of state and society.[4] There are, on the other hand, obvious affinities (some of which were discussed by Plato and Aristotle) between formal rhetoric and the broader realm of social and political discourse.[5] Thus, I will argue here that focusing on power as discourse will explain more about how persuasive public speech functioned in classical *demokratia* than would an exclusive focus on power as overt coercion.

If we describe the set of assumptions employed in decision-making by most Athenians as a "regime of truth", it becomes apparent that one of the key "truths" upon which democratic Athenian society depended was that citizens were simultaneously equals and unequals. Citizens were equals in the public realm of political (including judicial) decision-making. In the public sphere every citizen's vote had (in principle anyway) identical weight. The introduction of pay for public service and the use of the lot ensured that every citizen (at least those over thirty) had equal access to the perquisites and the risks associated with most forms of government activity (for example, magistracies).[6] In the fourth century most Athenians, including the elite, seemed willing to live with public, political equality – in any event there was no systematic effort to challenge it between 403 and 322. Yet citizens remained unequal in private life. Despite the fears of elite critics of democracy, the Athenian demos never consistently employed its collective power to equalise access to desirable material goods.[7] In so far as happiness is measured by ease of access to material goods, the rich Athenian lived a happier life than his poor neighbour. All Athenians knew that and most seemed to be quite willing to live with it. Why were elite Athenians willing to tolerate public equality and why did ordinary Athenians, for their part, willingly countenance private inequality? Opacity is not an adequate answer; the Athenian regime of truth was unable to obscure fully the contradiction or the complexity of the balancing act: Theophrastus' "Oligarchic Man", who expresses his anti-democratic ideas in the Assembly (*Characters* 26.2) as well as to strangers (*xenoi*) and like-minded associates (26.7) and complains that it is shaming to have to sit next to his social inferiors in the Assembly (26.5), expresses in comic terms what we may guess was a fairly widespread sense of unease among the elite.[8] Aristotle (*Politics* 1301a25–39 and 1302a24–31) believed that the tendency of democrats was to generalise equality (and so to oppress superior members of society) while that of oligarchs was to generalise inequality (and so to oppress the poor); both tendencies, to Aristotle, were unjust and led to instability. In the *Politics* he unsuccessfully attempted a solution to the problem of balancing equalities by devising a system of mathematical proportions.[9] How did the Athenian regime finesse the problem?

In *Mass and Elite in Democratic Athens* I argued that powerful elite individuals and the mass of ordinary citizens who composed the demos struck and maintained a viable social contract in part through the discursive operations of public oratory. In the Assembly and especially in the lawcourts, individual speakers employed the power of speech (sharpened in some cases by formal training in the arts of rhetoric) in an attempt to explain themselves – their lives, their needs, their current circumstances, and their relationship to the demos – to mass audiences. The audience in turn assessed the form and the content of the speaker's address, sometimes responding vocally to specific comments. After the speeches had been delivered, the members of the audience exerted power through their collective judgement. In the ongoing dialectical give and take of public oratory, audience response, and demotic judgement, a set of common attitudes and social rules was hammered out. Thus Athenian ideology, the discursive basis of Athenian society, was not given from on high and was not a unique product of elite culture, but rather it was established and constantly revised in the practice of public debate. The matrix of power within which oratory

was practised in democratic Athens made the *techne* of public speaking both dangerous and exciting. The Athenians were well aware of both the speaker's power – his
desire and ability to sway his audience; and the power of the audience – its willingness
and ability to punish the speaker for rhetorical missteps. Furthermore, the content of
many speeches was overtly concerned with issues of power. In the Assembly, the
question was often how Athenian military strength could be increased and how it
should be deployed. In the lawcourts, the issue was frequently whether or not a
display of personal power by an individual Athenian had abrogated Athenian rules
regarding appropriate social behaviour.

The theme of "personal power vs. social rules" was especially to the fore in cases
involving charges of *hubris*. "Insolent outrage" is a reasonable enough translation for
the term as it was used in Attic oratory, but Athenian law never spelled out exactly
what behaviours constituted acts of *hubris*.[10] Because the law did not explain to him
what *hubris* was, the juryman in a *graphe hubreos* [indictment for *hubris*] (or other
action in which the law against *hubris* was invoked) had to judge the entire social
context: the social and political statuses of litigant and defendant; their families,
friends, and past behaviour; the location and timing of the incident; and its ramifications for the whole of the demos.[11] This lack of nomothetic specificity is a problem
for the coercion paradigm with its concern for "rule of law", but it makes perfect
sense within the discursive paradigm of power. The Athenian juror did not judge
litigants according to an externalised, juridicially "given" model of appropriate
behaviour. Rather, he judged within and through a regime of social knowledge and
truth, a regime which his decision would participate in articulating – whether by
strengthening existing assumptions about social categories and behaviour or by
revising them.

For the historian, the proof of any analytic pardigm lies in its practical explanatory
usefulness. In *Mass and Elite in Democratic Athens* I applied discourse analysis to the
corpus of Attic oratory; here (belatedly responding to a suggestion by Daniel Tomp-
kins) I propose to focus on a single oration. Demosthenes 21 (*Against Meidias*) is a
particularly good example of the relationship between oratory and power that I have
sketched out in abstract terms above. Whether or not it was formally a *graphe hubreos*,
the case did centre on a charge of *hubris*. Demosthenes' speech is openly concerned
with defining the limits of behaviour appropriate to the most powerful individuals in
Athenian society, and with the public consequences of allowing those limits to be
breached (8). Moreover, after years of neglect, a new critical edition of the speech has
appeared, as have significant interpretive articles. This new scholarship has clarified
(even where it has not resolved) issues of chronology, law, composition, and deliv-
ery.[12]

The specific incidents that led Demosthenes to bring charges against Meidias are
laid out clearly in the speech's narrative (13–19): in the spring of 348 Demosthenes
was *choregos* [chorus producer] for his tribe Pandionis. His preparations for the
presentation of his tribal chorus at the Festival of Dionysus were hampered in
various ways by Meidias, a well-known wealthy politician who had an old personal
quarrel with Demosthenes. Demosthenes persevered and presented the chorus, but
at the Dionysia itself, in the orchestra of the theatre, Meidias punched Demosthenes
in the face. At the Assembly meeting held in the theatre following the Dionysia,
Demosthenes brought a *probole* [vote for prosecution] against Meidias, charging

him with misconduct during the festival. The vote of the Assembly went against Meidias (6). This prejudicial judgement in a *probole* did not entail punishment of the miscreant,[13] but gave Demosthenes a boost in their future dealings by demonstrating that public opinion was behind him: the demos agreed that Meidias' behaviour had been out of line. If Demosthenes wanted more than a moral victory, however, it was up to him to bring formal charges in a *dikasterion* [jury court]. For whatever reason, Demosthenes did not immediately do so. Here certainty about the course of events ends.

Demosthenes 21, as we have it, purports to be a prosecutor's speech, delivered in a public lawsuit (not a private action: 25, 28) before an Athenian *dikasterion* by Demosthenes in 347/6. Yet since antiquity (Plut. *Demosthenes* 12; Dion. Hal. *First Letter to Ammaeus* 4), readers of the speech have expressed doubts about whether it was actually delivered. [ . . . ]

[The author discusses ancient and modern    gave this speech at a trial.] arguments about whether Demosthenes

[ . . . ] In sum, the case for supposing that *Against Meidias* was never delivered is no more compelling than one that might be made against other major public speeches in the Demosthenic corpus (for example, 20, 22 or 23). I will proceed on the assumption that we are dealing with a speech that was delivered in a *dikasterion* in more or less the form we have it, and was subsequently published by its author.

The internal evidence of the speech indicates that the trial of Meidias took place about two years after the incident in the theatre.

[ . . . ] At the trial itself, Demosthenes and Meidias each used the power of oratory in attempting to persuade the jury to vote in his favour. But that power depended on a close "fit" with audience expectations and presuppositions. This meant adapting form and content of the rhetorical performance to the ideological context determined by an audience representing a cross-section of the mature (over thirty) citizen male population of Athens – over whelmingly men who were not members of a social elite.[20] The two litigants, on the other hand, were both celebrities, members of the same elite social category: both were very wealthy, both highly skilled speakers, both *rhetores*, that is, members of Athens' small cadre of expert politicians.[21] Thus, from the point of view of a juror whose judgement was based on established social categories, there might be little to choose between the two contestants. But social categorisation would not be the sole basis of his judgement. Both men would probably be known to him, at least by reputation – and he might well have heard them speak in Assembly or at previous trials.[22] The architectonics of each contestant's rhetorical self-presentation therefore consisted of building upon the audience's existing opinion of himself, using his rhetorical skills as his tools. The building materials included the facts of the case, the life histories of the litigants and the audience's social presuppositions.

Among Demosthenes' problems in constructing a persuasive case against Meidias was the relative slightness of the offence, a problem that was exacerbated by the passage of time. The positive vote at the initial *probole* in the Assembly was certainly in his favour, but two years later who really cared if one rich politician had bopped another in the nose? Given the existence of a strongly anti-elitist streak in Athenian popular ideology, Demosthenes must have worried that many jurors would see the incident as a silly intra-elite spat, and one that could have been solved quickly enough if Demosthenes had just been man enough to hit back. Demosthenes' central problem, then, was the tendency of the jurors to lump himself and Meidias into a single social category ("over-powerful elite politicians"). If that category were distinct from the one in which the jurors placed themselves ("regular guys"), there was a dreadful likelihood that the jurors would take on the role of spectators of a rather foolish tiff among people for whom they felt no inherent sympathy. They might simply laugh the case out of court. Thus, among Demosthenes' rhetorical goals was to draw a crystal clear set of distinctions between himself and his adversary. Meidias is to be stranded beyond an unbridgeable gulf constructed by Demosthenes' oration; on the near side stands the prosecutor, shoulder-to-shoulder with the demos. But it was more complex than that; Demosthenes must also remind the audience of his own continued possession of elite characteristics, since on these characteristics rested his claim to the privileged political position accorded the *rhetor*.[23] In sum, since the construction of social categories was a key part of Athens' truth regime (that is, the understandings the jury would use in their judgement), Demosthenes must work with a set of assumptions about the category to which both he and Meidias belonged. At the same time he must confound assumptions about the homogeneity of the category. He must explain to the audience that "we are indeed both elite and both powerful, but we are very different sorts of men in terms of our worth to the demos".

The actual speech negotiates these difficulties with great finesse. The unbridgeable gulf between Demosthenes/demos and Meidias is brilliantly sketched. In a number of passages Meidias is shown to be vastly wealthy and, as a direct result of that wealth, arrogant (66–67, 96, 98, 100, 194) and scornful of the demos and those he regards as his inferiors (132, 134, 185, 193–195, 198, 203–204, 211). Worse yet, his wealth gave him considerable power within the society, power which he wilfully used to destroy those ordinary citizens who stood in the way of fulfilling his desires (20, 98, 106, 109, 123–124, 137). In sum, Meidias was "rich, bold, with a big head and a big voice, violent, [and] shameless" (201). Meidias could be depicted as *sui generis*, isolated within society in wilful self-exile (198). But elsewhere Demosthenes locates the entire class of the excessively wealthy across the gulf with Meidias. Here he suggests that Meidias' behaviour is indicative of the anti-democratic attitudes harboured by the wealthy elite: they longed to gain control of the state and if they ever did come to power, they would be merciless to the ordinary working man (208–210). In contrast to rich Meidias and his rich cronies, Demosthenes paints a picture of himself as a middling sort of man: a hoplite (not a cavalryman, like Meidias) who, along with his fellow soldiers, was shocked by lurid tales of Meidias' combined cowardice and grotesque extravagance during the Euboean campaign (133; cf. 1 and 112).

In other passages Demosthenes presents himself rather differently: not among those who are weak or friendless, but indeed as a member of the Athenian elite, able and willing to use his elite attributes – wealth, speaking ability, standing in the community – to help defend the rest of the citizens against the likes of Meidias (111, 189, 192 and 219). And thus he reveals himself as a powerful figure in his own right. Demosthenes must, of course, sidestep the appearance of arrogance. He avoids contradicting Athenian assumptions regarding the reality of popular control of affairs by pointing out that he is not alone in his heroic resistance to Meidias. Time and again, Demosthenes claims allegiance to and alliance with the laws – in one dramatic passage he literally takes the reified laws of Athens as his kin, asking the jury to contrast him, surrounded by the laws, with Meidias, surrounded by weepy relatives.[24] This striking image reveals a vital distinction Demosthenes establishes between himself and his rival. Whereas Meidias depends on his family for support, Demosthenes is a public figure, devoted to the public good. He is, at least by implication, a powerful man only through the backing of the actively expressed will of the people – just as the laws themselves are just inscribed letters unless the people are willing to act boldly in their defence (223–225; cf. 37 ff., 57, and see below). Demosthenes' wealth is meaningful to him only because it allows him to face down bullies like Meidias and to give generously to the public weal (156–157 and 189). Meidias, on the other hand, is selfish with his money: he uses it in vulgar and offensive displays calculated to humiliate ordinary citizens (133, 158–159 and 195–196). He never willingly contributes to public projects and arrogantly believes that the special tax (*proeisphora*) he is forced to pay gives him the right to harangue and berate the rest of the citizenry in the Assembly (151–169).

So far we have touched on two of the rhetorical strategies Demosthenes employed in *Against Meidias* in order to distinguish himself from his rival. First he draws a line between the elite cavalryman and the ordinary hoplite. Next, he contrasts styles of elite behaviour: the selfish, anti-democratic man interested in his private goods versus the selfless public man who takes the laws as his kin. A third, more subtle, tactic may have helped Demosthenes distinguish between the nature and function of his powers and those of his rival. At section 154 Demosthenes specifically points out the differences in their ages: he claims to be thirty-two, while his opponent is "about fifty or a little less". The jury might suppose that there was an eighteen-year gap in their ages, but Harris ("Demosthenes' Speech", pp. 121–5) argues convincingly that Demosthenes was lying about his own age. He suggests, no doubt rightly, that Demosthenes' primary motive here was to emphasise the disparity between the two men's liturgical records: Demosthenes' generous record looked even better if compressed into a shorter lifespan. There was, however, a pointed subtext: overstating the age difference helps Demosthenes to depict himself as a young man confronting a man considerably his senior in both years and political strength. This contrast would have considerable resonance for Athenians, raised on stories of the youthful exploits of Theseus, mythical founder of the democracy.[25]

Demosthenes had previously "reminded" his listeners of a story, one which he claimed many of them would know well, of a youth's successful confrontation with an older, stronger, insolent man.[26] At sections 71–72, to illustrate the serious consequences that could result from acts of *hubris*, Demosthenes tells two brief tales of men who killed other men who dared offer them *hubris*. The first concerns Euthynus and Sophilus (71):

> Everyone knows – or if not everyone, many people – that on one occasion Euthynus the famous wrestler, the young man (*neaniskos*), defended himself even against Sophilus the pancratist. The latter was a strong man, dark – I'm sure certain ones of you know the man I mean. They were in Samos, just passing the time privately (*idiai*) with some

friends; and because he [Euthynus] thought him insolent (*auton hubrizein*), he defended himself so vigorously that he actually killed him.

The implied parallel to young, vigorous Demosthenes and older, stronger Meidias is quite clear in the context of the oration.[27] The second tale is equally instructive (71–72):

> Many people (*polloi*) know that Euaion, the brother of Leodamas, killed Boeotus at a dinner party (ἐν δείπνῳ καὶ συνόδῳ κοινῇ) because of one blow. It was not the blow that made him angry, but the dishonour (*atimia*); nor is being hit such a serious matter (*deinon*) to free men (*eleutherois*), though it is serious, but rather being hit with *hubris*.

As in the case of the Euthynus *logos* [story], that of Euaion is one of revenge for insolence offered in a specifically private context (see MacDowell, *ad loc.*). But with Euaion – to whom Demosthenes pointedly compares himself (73–76) – the speaker adds that hubristic assault brings with it the threat of *atimia*, and points to the psychological effect of insolent assault on *eleutheroi*. Demosthenes' follow-up to the double story is to point out that in his own case the context of the insult was not private but public: he was *choregos*, the assault occurred in the theatre at a public festival and was witnessed by citizens and foreigners alike (74; cf. 31 ff.). It is in the transposition of what might well have remained a private affair between rival aristo-crats to the public realm dominated by the demos that the stakes involved in the play of power and ideology are most clearly exposed.

After relating the early history of his conflict with Meidias – a tale that enables Demosthenes to emphasise his extreme youth (78) – the prosecutor introduces the poignant figure of Strato the arbitrator. With the Strato *logos*, the speaker confronts his audience with the implications of private-realm aristocratic arrogance spilling over into the public realm. When we combine the salient points of the Euthynus and Euaion stories, we get a tale of justifiable revenge executed by a brave young man against an older, stronger man in order to redress the *atimia* associated with an act of *hubris*. Strato, by contrast, is far from an aristocratic youth in the first flush of his strength: an older man (as an arbitrator (*diaitetes*) he was, by definition, sixty years old), he was a worker and inexperienced in public affairs (*penes, apragmon*: 83). Moreover, says Demosthenes, Strato was no rascal (*poneros*), indeed he was a useful citizen (*chrestos*: 83; cf. 95): the exemplary ordinary Athenian who did his mandatory year's public service as arbitrator not because he was ambitious but because it was his duty.[28] Strato was assigned by lot to Demosthenes and Meidias when the former indicted the latter for slander (foul language used in the presence of Demosthenes' sister and mother, when Meidias and his brother broke into Demosthenes' home (*oikia*) demanding a property-exchange (*antidosis*): 78–80). On the day of the arbitration, Meidias did not (at first) show up and so Strato reluctantly gave a default verdict against him. After Demosthenes had gone home in triumph, Meidias arrived at the arbitrators' offices and tried to bribe Strato to reverse his judgement. Strato refused and Meidias later vindictively and manipulatively gained a judgement against Strato and so "he expelled and disenfranchised (ἐκβάλλει καὶ ἀτιμοῖ) the arbitra-tor" (87). Strato, like Euaion, thus suffered *atimia* (cf. 92) at the hands of a hubristic man – and yet the meaning of *atimia* has shifted dramatically with the move from the private to the public sphere, as has the victim's power to defend himself.

The *atimia* which Euaion suffered when punched by Boeotus was personal and social dishonour: his worth was compromised in his own eyes and those of his fellows. This loss of honour (*time*) carried with it no formal political disabilities and was evidently wiped clean by Euaion's vigorous self-defence. The meaning of *atimia* for Strato was quite different: rather than being stripped of private honour, the arbitrator lost his status as a citizen. Moreover, since Meidias had secured the judgement through the legal system, there was no recourse for Strato as there had been for Euthynus and Euaion – as an *atimos*, Strato became utterly powerless (92 and 95). Having lost even the right to speak in public fora, he is put on display by Demosthenes as a mute example of the ghastly effects on an ordinary Athenian of hubristic power exercised in the public realm. Fisher (see n. 10) has emphasised the linkage of *hubris* with dishonour; indeed, what we might call the "economy of *time* [honor]" provides the appropriate context for private acts of *hubris* and revenge for those acts. But the fate of Strato – the exemplary ordinary Athenian (*aner polites*: 88; *Athenaion hena*: 90; *ton pollon heis*: 96) who became *atimos* in the process of doing his public duty – suggests that the wilful exertion of personal power in the public realm has as its target not private or family honour, but the quality of citizenship itself. Although there is talk of *philotimia* [love of honor, ambition] in the speech (67, 159, 162), this attribute is associated specifically with the elite. The speech thus underlines a crucial difference between elite and demotic strata of Athenian society. The most precious possession of the elite individual was his honour. The most precious possession of the ordinary Athenian was the dignity he enjoyed because he was a citizen: the "basket" of privileges, immunities, duties and responsibilities he enjoyed by the simple fact of his citizen status. Citizen-dignity may most readily be defined by the intersection of individual freedom (*eleutheria*: 124, 180), political equality (*isotes*: 67, 111) and security (*bebaiotes*: 222; *asphaleia*: 227).

Honour and dignity had much in common: both implied a rejection of self-abasement and an immunity from degrading violations of the body's physical integrity (179 and 180).[29] But in Greek aristocratic society, honour (as has often been pointed out) was a scarce resource in an endless zero-sum game. In the simplest two-player simulation, Player A gains in honour only at the expense of the honour of Player B.[30] Although Athenian citizenship was highly exclusivist by modern standards, dignity was not in the same sense a scarce commodity within the community of citizens. The dignity of Citizen A was not ordinarily enhanced at the expense of his fellows. In the course of the fifth and fourth centuries, the Athenian citizenry radically augmented the material and psychic value of citizenship.[31] Thus, while the total number of players did not expand much, the total "quantity" of dignity available to the players was expansive. Dignity was a citizen's personal possession in the sense that it could be lost through individual acts (for example, engaging in prostitution) or removed by legal judgement. Yet it was simultaneously a collective possession of the demos. The downside of this collective ownership was that the total sum of dignity could be reduced (and thus each individual's immunities and so forth lessened) if the citizenry failed to act to guard its possession. It was the power of collective action that had created citizen dignity in the first place;[32] a lack of collective defence in the face of threats offered by powerful individuals could result in its loss (45, 57, 124, 140 and 142).

The chain of reasoning developed above helps to explain the argument that underlies Demosthenes' speech. It was one thing for powerful honour-driven aristocrats to attack one another and to defend themselves in private. It was quite another thing when an aristocrat began to bring his *hubris* to bear on ordinary citizens. At this point, and especially when attacks were upon citizens acting in formal public capacities (as *choregoi* or *diaitetai*: 31–34, 87), it was incumbent upon the collectivity to resist staunchly the deployment of individual power. Nothing less than the individual and collective dignity of the citizen was at stake: "If anyone who tries to stand up for himself when quite illegally assaulted by Meidias is going to suffer this [court-mandated expulsion and disenfranchisement] and similar treatment, it will be best just to offer *proskunesis* [bow down] to hubristic men, as they do in barbarian lands, rather than try to resist them" (106). If the citizenry will not stand up to Meidias, they will cease to be dignified citizens and will devolve into salaaming subjects of the powerful few.[33]

In order to avoid this nauseating outcome, the jurors must see the situation clearly: Meidias is an exemplar (*paradeigma*: 76, 97, 227) of the powerful rich. The individual rich man, and the rich as a class, are desirous of forcing their hierarchical approach to private life and their hierarchical system of social categorisation upon the whole of Athenian political society. Intolerant of equality and freedom, they long to humiliate and subjugate all ordinary persons, whom they regard not as dignified citizens but as subhuman (185 and 208–209). Individually, ordinary Athenians were much too weak to stand up against the violence of the powerful elite. And the laws alone had no force capable of preventing their misuse by the elite. But acting collectively, in defence of the laws and customs of the democratic order, the demos was indeed powerful enough to force the elite to recognise the dignity of each citizen, and powerful enough to discipline any of those who dared to step out of line (140–142):

> All this [the tale of Meidias and his toadies], I suppose, is frightening to each one of the rest of you, living individually as best you can. That's why you should unite: individually each of you is weaker than they [the rich] are, either in friends or resources or something else; but united you'll be stronger than each of them and you will put a stop to their *hubris*... If a man is so powerful (*dunasthai*) that he can prevent each of us singly from getting justice from him, now, since he is in our grasp, he must be punished jointly by all for all, as a common enemy of the state.

A desirable outcome was thus possible: mass strength could trump individual strength. Yet for this desirable outcome to be realised, given the structure of Athenian legal procedure, it was necessary that a brave and resourceful individual citizen be willing to stand up to the exemplary hubristic malefactor by dragging him into court. Enter Demosthenes, the man who (as he explains in detail) has what it takes to confront the monster and bring him to justice: the necessary elite attributes of wealth and rhetorical skill and allegiance to the public good.

Yet Demosthenes makes clear that prosecuting Meidias with the support of laws and demos and in defence of the dignity of the citizenry required more than just personal strength and bravery in the face of superior strength. It also entailed a willingness to sacrifice individual honour since it meant that Demosthenes had to forgo deadly private vengeance. This "sacrifice" meant, however, that he could have his cake and eat it too. By constructing an image of himself as a bold young elite,

Demosthenes shows that he is the sort of man who *could* successfully have defended his *time*, just as Euthynus and Euaion had defended theirs. But, happily for the demos, Demosthenes is also the moderate, middling citizen who sees clearly that the interest of the state (avoiding bloodshed while simultaneously making a public example of Meidias and thus curbing the insolence of the rich as a class) must override his natural urge to dispatch his rival on the spot (74–76; cf. 219):

> I think my decision [not to retaliate physically] was prudent (*sophronos*), or rather it was providential (*eutuchos*), when I acquiesced at the time and was not induced to do anything disastrous – though I fully sympathise with Euaion and anyone else who has defended himself when dishonoured (*atimazomenos*)... When I exercised so much care to prevent any disastrous result that I did not defend myself at all, from whom ought I to obtain atonement for what was done to me? From you and the laws, I think; and an example (*paradeigma*) ought to be set, to show everyone else that all hubristic men should not be fought off at the moment of anger, but referred to you, in the knowledge that you are the guarantors and guardians of legal protection for victims.

Later in the speech Demosthenes underlines his selflessness by pointing out that it is not he who is most in danger from Meidias (123–124; cf. 221–222):

> You should all be equally angry, in view of the fact that the likeliest of you to suffer easy maltreatment are the poorest and weakest (*penestatoi, asthenestatoi*)... In my own case, no doubt, I repulsed lies and accusations... I haven't been annihilated. But what will you, *hoi polloi*, do, unless you publicly frighten everyone away from the misuse of wealth for this purpose [*hubris*]?

We can now grasp the import of the peroration and see how it relates to the proem of the speech: Demosthenes, the elite *rhetor* (cf. 189), had done his part by dragging Meidias, master of legal evasion, into court. The demos in Assembly had done its part by condemning Meidias in the initial *probole* (2–3). Now it was up to the jurors to be as true to their own interests and to the common ideals on which Athenian political life was predicated. They must use their collective power of judgement to destroy the dangerous individual and re-establish the authority of the demotic regime of truth (227):

> Before the case was proved you showed your anger, you called on the victim [Demosthenes] to take revenge, you applauded when I brought a *probole* against him in the Assembly; yet now that the case has been demonstrated, and the demos sitting in a sacred precinct has given a preliminary condemnation of him ... when it is in your power to deal with it all by a single vote, will you now fail to support me, to offer *charis* [favor] to the demos, to teach everyone a lesson (τοὺς ἄλλους σωφρονίσαι), and to secure a safe life for yourselves in future by making of him an example (*paradeigma*) to everyone?

Finally we need to consider the issue of to what degree Demosthenes' oratory was, and could have been, independent of the discursive regime that forms its deep context. In a recent article on *Against Meidias*, Peter Wilson argues that in several key passages Demosthenes loses rhetorical control of his own text: although he hoped to depict himself as a loyal democrat, his speech is hopelessly subverted by established and elitist aristocratic norms.[34] And thus (in the terminology adopted above) social power in the form of a truth regime wins out in the end – and that regime was ultimately a product of elite, not demotic, ideals and discourse. Is this actually the case? While conforming in obvious ways to demotic ideals, does Demosthenes' oratory finally and helplessly serve to subvert them? Is the democratic ideology which is so prominent in much of the speech actually twisted against itself by the irresistible power of an overarching aristocratic value system? I do not think so. Rather, it seems to me that Demosthenes' speech shows us how a central aristocratic ideal (*time*) is at once transformed by and delimited within the public democratic environment. Demosthenes tells his audience an interesting and complex story about honour and its relationship to *hubris*. By invoking the examples of Euthynus and Euaion he shows the enduring importance of honour within the "realm of inequality" that characterised the sub-society of the elite. By exploring the two senses of *atimia* he shows how personal honour is transubstantiated into citizen dignity in the realm of equality that characterises citizen society. The example of Strato, by demonstrating the danger that "a Meidias" represents to the individual dignity of the ordinary citizen, shows why a democracy must isolate and regulate elite behaviour patterns. And his speech itself is an example of how the democratic regime can and should use the skills and attributes of the "good elite" speaker in reasserting order.

Demosthenes' speech participates actively in democratic ideals. Its persuasive power is overtly intended to allow the power of the people to find its target; that is, the powerful individual who embodies the continuing threat of "non-transformed" aspects of aristocratic culture to spill over into the public realm. Oratory is thus a lens which focuses the great but diffuse power of the Athenian truth regime upon appropriate objects. The pre-trial lack of focus is symbolised by the avid but inchoate hissing and shouting against Meidias in the theatre, by the many who approached Demosthenes to urge him to follow through on the prosecution (2, 23, 198, 216, 226), and perhaps even by the overwhelming but forceless initial vote at the *probole*. Demosthenes implies that if the regime had been working smoothly, and Meidias had been a proper citizen, the latter would have listened carefully to these expressions of demotic dissatisfaction and would have conformed to the spirit of the laws without the need of a trial (61 and 63). But Meidias is a rogue-elite, who thinks he can ignore or override all signs of popular disfavour. In this situation, discourse must be translated into overt action (30). It is through the speech of the prosecutor and the subsequent vote of the people gathered as *dikastai* [jurors], that the regime is reified. At this point speech and judgement become concrete forces for action, in a way that a general regime of thought or law, that remains both everywhere and nowhere, never could. *Logos* [word] becomes *ergon* [deed] and thus the power of the people is manifested in the life of the citizen (223–225):

> For in fact, if you cared to consider and investigate the question of what it is that gives power and control (ἰσχυροὶ καὶ κύριοι) over everything in the polis to those of you who are jurors at any given time ... you would find that the reason is not that you alone of the citizens are armed and mobilised in ranks, nor that you are physically the best and strongest, nor that you are youngest (*neotatoi*) in age, nor anything of the sort, but rather you'd find that you are powerful (*ischuein*) through the laws. And what is the power (*ischus*) of the laws? Is it that, if any of you is attacked and gives a shout, they'll

come running to your aid? No, they are just inscribed letters and have no ability to do that. What then is their motive power (*dunamis*)? You are, if you secure them and make them authoritative (*kurioi*) whenever anyone asks for aid. So the laws are powerful (*ischuroi*) through you and you through the laws. You must therefore stand up for them in just the same way as any individual would stand up for himself if attacked; you must take the view that offences against the law are common concerns (*koina*).

Here, several of the key themes I have attempted to elucidate are set out clearly: the power of the collectivity, the association of individual powerfulness with youthfulness, the relationship between the individual acting in defence of his own person and honour, and the need for common action in defence of common dignity.

The movement from inanimate law to political action through the medium of speech that is at the heart of the passage quoted above suggests that Athenian oratory, while deeply enmeshed in common assumptions about social categories and proper behaviour, is more than a ventriloquisation of a truth regime. The individual speaker, with his individual attributes and perspective, was indispensable as the spark that fired the system. It was in this dynamic relationship between truth regime and individual initiator/orator that Athenian democracy existed. Without the common assumptions I have dubbed the "regime of truth", Athens would have been no more than a mob of self-interested individuals – and thus certainly would have fallen prey to the endless round of debilitating *stasis* [factional conflict] that characterised the histories of so many Greek poleis in the fourth century.[35] Without the intervention of distinct voices and individual histories into the matrix of social assumptions, Athenian society would have been static and nightmarish, an Orwellian *1984* with the demos as Big Brother. The balance of individual and social power was always uneasy; a good part of the enduring fascination of Attic oratory is its depiction – at the level of both form and content – of a highwire act with no net.

# NOTES

1   Cf. R. Dahl, "The Concept of Power", *Behavioral Science* 2 (1957), p. 202: "A has power over B to the extent that he can get B to do something that B would not otherwise do." All unattributed single number citations are from Demosthenes 21, *Against Meidias*; translations are adapted from D. M. MacDowell, *Demosthenes, Against Meidias* (Oxford: 1990), hereafter cited only as MacDowell.

2   Definition of "paradigm": J. Ober, "Models and Paradigms in Ancient History", *AHB* 3 (1989), pp. 134–7. What I am calling the coercion paradigm finds its philosophical underpinnings in seventeenth-century social contract theory, notably T. Hobbes' *Leviathan* of 1651 (New York: 1950), and J. Locke's *Two Treatises of Government* of 1689 (Cambridge: 1970). Contract theory explains the ultimate basis of legitimate authority by positing an exchange of complete individual freedom for the security offered by voluntary submission to a political sovereign. Locke's definition of power (*Second Treatise*, sec. 3, p. 268) is succinct: "Political power I take to be a right of making laws with penalties of death, and consequently all less[er] penalties for the regulating and preserving [of] property, and of employing the force of the community, in execution of such laws, and in defence of the commonwealth from foreign injury; and all this only for the public good."

3   The discourse paradigm, developed in the 1960s and 1970s, finds its most complete expression in the work of Michel Foucault; for example, *Discipline and Punish: The Birth of the Prison*, trans. A. Sheridan (New York: 1979); *The History of Sexuality*, I, trans. R. Hurley (New York: 1980); and *Power/Knowledge: Selected Writings and Other Interviews 1972–1977*, ed. Colin Gordon, trans. C. Gordon *et al.* (New York: 1980).

4   J. Ober, "The Nature of Athenian Democracy", *CPh* 84 (1989), pp. 322–4.

5   For Plato and Aristotle on oratory and discourse see S. Halliwell, "Philosophy and Rhetoric", in I. Worthington (ed.), *Persuasion: Greek Rhetoric in Action* (London: 1994), pp. 222–43. Cf. G. Kennedy, *Aristotle, On Rhetoric: A Theory of Civic Discourse* (New York: 1991), pp. 309–12, and B. Vickers, *In Defence of Rhetoric* (Oxford: 1988), pp. 83–147.

6   The few exceptions (for example, the Treasurers of Athena, limited to the highest wealth class: [Arist.] *Athenaion Politeia* 47.1) are to be explained in terms of the demos' concern with maintaining fiscal accountability. General accounts of the opportunities and responsibilities of the Athenian citizen: R. K. Sinclair, *Democracy and Participation in Athens* (Cambridge: 1988); M. H. Hansen, *The Athenian Democracy in the Age of Demosthenes: Structure, Principles and Ideology* (Oxford: 1991).

7   Elite fears: for example, Arist. *Politics* 1318a24–26; cf. J. Ober, *Mass and Elite in Democratic Athens: Rhetoric, Ideology, and the Power of the People* (Princeton: 1989), pp. 197–8. There probably were cases in which juries convicted rich men out of greed, but no evidence that this was done consistently: see ibid., pp. 200–1.

8   For an earlier (second half of the fifth century) manifestation of anti-democratic sentiment, see [Xenophon], *Constitution of the Athenians*. Plato, *Republic* 553a–c, suggests that oligarchic attitudes were stimulated by witnessing one's distinguished father punished by death, exile or disenfranchisement in the people's court (*dikasterion*).

9   Arist. *Politics* 1280a22–24, 1282b14–84a3, 1287a13–17, 1296b15–34, 1301a25–1302a15; cf. F. D. Harvey, "Two Kinds of Equality", *C & M* 26 (1965), pp. 101–46 and "Corrigenda", *C & M* 27 (1966), pp. 99–100, and J. Ober, "Aristotle's Political Sociology: Class Status and Order in the 'Politics'", in C. Lord and D. K. O'Connor (eds), *Essays on the Foundations of Aristotelian Political Science* (Berkeley and Los Angeles: 1991), pp. 120–30.

10  Definition of *hubris*: MacDowell, pp. 17–23, concluding that "[*hubris*] essence consists of having energy or power and misusing it self-indulgently" (p. 19). See too N. R. E. Fisher, "*Hybris* and Dishonour I", *G & R*[2] 23 (1976), pp. 177–93; "*Hybris* and Dishonour II", *G&R*[2] 26 (1979), pp. 32–47; and "The Law of *Hubris* in Athens", in P. Cartledge, P. Millett and S. Todd (eds), *Nomos: Essays in Athenian Law, Politics and Society* (Cambridge: 1990), pp. 123–38. On the "open texture" of Athenian law and the social significance of an avoidance of strict definition: R. Osborne, "Law in Action in Classical Athens", *JHS* 105 (1985), pp. 40–58; S. C. Humphreys, "Law as Discourse", *History and Anthropology* 1 (1985), pp. 241–64; S. Todd and P. Millett, "Law, Society and Athens", in P. Cartledge, P. Millett and S. Todd (eds), *Nomos*, pp. 1–18.

11  The seriousness with which the juror would have undertaken his task is underlined by Aristotle, *Politics* 1311a1–2, who notes that the demos feared the *hubris* of the powerful just as the *oligoi* feared property confiscation.

12  Edition: MacDowell; articles: E. M. Harris, "Demosthenes' Speech Against Meidias", *HSCPh* 92 (1989), pp. 117–36 and P. Wilson, "Demosthenes 21 (*Against Meidias*): Democratic Abuse", *PCPhS* 37 (1991), pp. 164–95.

13  *Probole* procedure: A. R. W. Harrison, *The Law of Athens*, I (Oxford: 1968), pp. 59–64; D. M. MacDowell, *The Law in Classical Athens* (London: 1975), pp. 194–7; and MacDowell, pp. 13–17.

[…]

20 Social composition of Athenian juries: M. M. Markle, "Jury Pay and Assembly Pay at Athens", in P. A. Cartledge and F. D. Harvey (eds), *Crux. Essays Presented to G. E. M. de Ste. Croix* (London: 1985), pp. 265–97; Ober, *Mass and Elite*, pp. 142–4; and S. Todd, "*Lady Chatterley's Lover* and the Attic Orators: The Social Composition of the Athenian Jury", *JHS* 110 (1990), pp. 146–73.

21 Definition of *rhetor*: Ober, *Mass and Elite*, pp. 105–12 and Hansen, *Athenian Democracy*, pp. 143–5.

22 Function of gossip in the making of a man's reputation: K. J. Dover, "Anecdotes, Gossip and Scandal", in *The Greeks and Their Legacy: Collected Papers*, II. *Prose Literature, History, Society, Transmission, Influence* (Oxford: 1988), pp. 45–52; V. Hunter, "Gossip and the Politics of Reputation in Classical Athens", *Phoenix* 44 (1990), pp. 299–325; and D. Cohen, *Law, Sexuality, and Society: The Enforcement of Morals in Classical Athens* (Cambridge: 1992), pp. 89–97.

23 On the balance between elite and demotic claims on the parts of *rhetores*: Ober, *Mass and Elite, passim*.

24 Sections 186–188. I am indebted to Danielle Allen for drawing my attention to the key importance of this passage; see also section 7.

25 The ideological underpinnings of the Theseus myth are discussed in detail in a forthcoming book by B. Strauss on fathers and sons in Athenian political ideology. On the social and political significance of acting out a culture's central myths see J. Ober and B. Strauss, "Drama, Political Rhetoric, and the Discourse of Athenian Democracy", in J. J. Winkler and F. I. Zeitlin (eds), *Nothing to Do with Dionysos? Athenian Drama in Its Social Context* (Princeton: 1990), pp. 245–6, with literature cited. Cf. also section 69: Meidias' failure to demonstrate "youthful enterprise" (*eneanieusato*). Demosthenes pointedly mocks Meidias' pretensions to youthful machismo at section 131: Meidias no longer thinks it *neanikos* to insult individuals, so he insults whole groups; and section 201: Meidias falsely thinks it *neanikos* to ignore "you", the people. The root meaning of *neanikos* is "youthful", and MacDowell's translation of *neanikos* as "macho" is on the mark.

26 This is an example of the "everybody knows" topos: Ober, *Mass and Elite*, pp. 149–50 and 163. This is used elsewhere in the speech (for example, 1, 16, 137, 149, 167) and helps to establish Demosthenes' solidarity with popular knowledge and wisdom.

27 At section 78 Demosthenes moves immediately to the story of his early problems with Meidias, describing himself then as a "very young lad" (*meirakullion*) who was confronted by a violent and profane break-in by Meidias and his brother.

28 Interpretation of this passage: Ober, *Mass and Elite*, pp. 209–11. I follow Goodwin (cf. MacDowell, *ad loc.*) in translating ἄλλως δ' οὐ πονηρὸς as "moreover not bad" rather than (per MacDowell and others) "but in other ways not bad". MacDowell (loc. cit.) and Wilson ("Demosthenes 21", pp. 180–1, citing Thuc. 2.40.2) seem to me to get the force of *apragmon* wrong. There is certainly an echo here of Pericles' Funeral Oration (Thuc. 2.40.1–2); both Pericles/Thucydides and Demosthenes are manipulating traditional sentiments about the link between wealth, public activity and usefulness to the community (cf., for example, the Solonian *tele*). But the point of the Strato story is that this ordinary man became Meidias' victim through no fault of his own. Strato's *apragmosyne* is his lack of overt political ambition, not an unwillingness to do his public duty. Since the Athenian laws require certain public duties, every Athenian (not just those who are ambitious) is at risk from the Meidas-type. Note too, that *chrestos*, which in elite discourse could mean "elite", here clearly means "a man who is a positive asset to the state" in contrast to the *poneros* who is a public liability.

29 On bodily integrity see J. J. Winkler, *The Constraints of Desire: The Anthropology of Sex and Gender in Ancient Greece* (New York: 1990), pp. 54–64; D. M. Halperin, *One Hundred*

*Years of Homosexuality and Other Essays on Greek Love* (New York: 1990), p. 96; and Wilson, "Demosthenes 21", pp. 164–5.

30  Zero-sum, honour/shame-based competition and its links to a "Mediterranean society" model: Winkler, *Constraints of Desire*, pp. 45–70 and Cohen, *Law, Sexuality, and Society*, pp. 35–69.

31  For the origins of this process see P. B. Manville, *The Origins of Citizenship in Ancient Athens* (Princeton: 1990); for its development in the fifth and fourth centuries: Ober, *Mass and Elite*, pp. 53–103.

32  J. Ober, "The Athenian Revolution of 508/7 BC: Violence, Authority, and the Origins of Democracy", in L. Kurke and C. Dougherty (eds), *Cultural Poetics in Archaic Greece: Tyranny, Cult and Civic Ideology* (Cambridge: 1993), pp. 215–32.

33  Cf. section 124: anyone who stands in the way of convicting Meidias "is simply taking away our enjoyment of free speech (*isegoria*) and freedom (*eleutheria*)".

34  Wilson, "Demosthenes 21", pp. 170–1, 181–2, 186–7. In arguing that aristocratic norms subverted what was ostensibly democratic discourse Wilson follows N. Loraux, *The Invention of Athens: The Funeral Oration in the Classical City*, trans. A. Sheridan (Cambridge: 1986).

35  Cf. Arist. *Politics* 1302a31–b3 (recalling much of the language of Dem. 21): men fight *staseis* in order to gain *time* and material goods (*kerdos*), and to avoid *atimia* and punishments. What stirs them up in the first place is either seeing others increasing their share of *time* and *kerdos*, or *hubris*, fear (*phobos*), pre-eminence (*hyperoche*), contempt (*kataphronesis*), or disproportionate self-aggrandisement (*auxesis*).

## Further reading

Bers, Victor, "Dikastic *Thorubos*," in *Crux*, eds. P. A. Cartledge and F. D. Harvey (London, 1985), 1–15.
Brock, Roger, "The Emergence of Democratic Ideology," *Historia* 40 (1991), 160–9.
Connor, W. R., *The New Politicans of Fifth-century Athens* (Princeton, 1971).
Hansen, Mogens, "The Number of Rhetores in the Athenian Ecclesia, 355–322," *Greek, Roman, and Byzantine Studies* 25 (1984), 123–55 = *The Athenian Ecclesia* II (Copenhagen, 1989), 93–125, with addenda.
Knox, R. A., " 'So Mischievous a Beaste'? The Athenian *Demos* and Its Treatment of Its Politicians," *Greece and Rome* 32 (1985), 132–61.
MacDowell, Douglas, *Demosthenes: Against Meidias* (Oxford, 1990).
Ober, Josiah, *Mass and Elite in Democratic Athens* (Princeton, 1989).
—— *Political Dissent in Democratic Athens* (Princeton, 1998).
Ostwald, Martin, *From Popular Sovereignty to the Sovereignty of Law* (Berkeley, 1986).
Tacon, Judith, "Ecclesiastic *Thorubos*: Interventions, Interruptions, and Popular Involvement in the Athenian Assembly," *Greece and Rome* 48 (2001), 173–92.
Yunis, Harvey, *Taming Democracy: Models of Political Rhetoric in Classical Athens* (Ithaca, NY, 1996).

# 6

# Limiting Democracy: The Political Exclusion of Women and Slaves

---

## Introduction

Women and slaves, though as a group far outnumbering the free-born male population in Greece, experienced complete exclusion from the political arena of the democratic polis. How this can be explained, and with what ramifications for our understanding of the nature of Greek democracy, is the subject of this chapter.

At Athens, which once again provides far and away the most testimony, women and slaves were, among other restrictions, barred from attending meetings of the assembly, holding annual public offices, serving as jurors, independently initiating legal proceedings, or even owning property outright. In these and other respects they were, in effect, non-citizens. And yet the story is more complicated than this. The citizenship status of Athenian women was meaningful and carefully tracked, for a law of ca. 451 decreed that only children with *two* Athenian parents could be counted as citizens. Furthermore, citizen women had public religious duties that held great importance for the city as a whole. Slaves were not citizens in any legal respect, and yet male slaves who were freed became metics (resident aliens) and in rare circumstances a metic might attain citizenship upon decree of the assembly – so, at least theoretically, enslaved men could rise higher in terms of participation in the democracy than free-born women ever could.

Why did the Greeks view women and slaves in the terms they did? What role did each group really play in a democratic city? The ancient sources selected below range from the rhetorical to the comical to the philosophical, but all concern themselves in one way or another with the place of women and slaves in the polis, especially a democratic one. The modern analyses use these and other sources in varying ways to address the questions posed.

# Thucydides, Pericles' Funeral Oration (*History of the Peloponnesian War* 2.44–6)

For most of Pericles' famous speech, as portrayed by Thucydides in his history, the Athenian leader praises the character and achievements of Athens, its government, and its people (see selection in chapter 4). Toward the end he addresses the families of those who died gloriously in battle. His exhortations afford a revealing look at ideas of gender and family roles in a Greek democracy at war. (*Source*: Thucydides, *History of the Peloponnesian War* 2.44–6, trans. R. Crawley.)

[. . .] "Comfort, therefore, not condolence, is what I have to offer to the parents of the dead who may be here. Numberless are the chances to which, as they know, the life of man is subject; but fortunate indeed are they who draw for their lot a death so glorious as that which has caused your mourning, and to whom life has been so exactly measured as to terminate in the happiness in which it has been passed. Still I know that this is a hard saying, especially when those in question of whom you will constantly be reminded by seeing in the homes of others blessings of which once you also boasted: for grief is felt not so much for the want of what we have never known, as for the loss of that to which we have been long accustomed. Yet you who are still of an age to beget children must bear up in the hope of having others in their stead; not only will they help you to forget those whom you have lost, but will be to the state at once a reinforcement and a security; for never can a fair or just policy be expected of the citizen who does not, like his fellows, bring to the decision the interests and apprehensions of a father. While those of you who have passed your prime must congratulate yourselves with the thought that the best part of your life was fortunate, and that the brief span that remains will be cheered by the fame of the departed. For it is only the love of honour that never grows old; and honour it is, not gain, as some would have it, that rejoices the heart of age and helplessness.

"Turning to the sons or brothers of the dead, I see an arduous struggle before you. When a man is gone, all are wont to praise him, and should your merit be ever so transcendent, you will still find it difficult not merely to overtake, but even to approach their renown. The living have envy to contend with, while those who are no longer in our path are honoured with a goodwill into which rivalry does not enter. On the other hand, if I must say anything on the subject of female excellence to those of you who will now be in widowhood, it will be all comprised in this brief exhortation. Great will be your glory in not falling short of your natural character; and greatest will be hers who is least talked of among the men whether for good or for bad.

"My task is now finished. I have performed it to the best of my ability, and in word, at least, the requirements of the law are now satisfied. If deeds be in question, those who are here interred have received part of their honours already, and for the rest, their children will be brought up till manhood at the public expense: the state thus offers a valuable prize, as the garland of victory in this race of valour, for the reward both of those who have fallen and their survivors. And where the rewards for merit are greatest, there are found the best citizens.

"And now that you have brought to a close your lamentations for your relatives, you may depart."

# Pseudo-Xenophon, *The Constitution of the Athenians* (1; 4–8.1; 10–12)

Sometimes called "The Old Oligarch" by modern scholars for the views he expresses, the author of this text is in fact unknown. The treatise was preserved among the works of Xenophon and is dated to the last third of the fifth century. The author criticizes the Athenian democracy for its domination by the ordinary masses of citizens and makes some interesting comments about the treatment of resident aliens (metics) and slaves. (*Source*: Pseudo-Xenophon, *Constitution of the Athenians* 1; 4–8.1; 10–12, trans. J. M. Moore, from *Aristotle and Xenophon on Democracy and Oligarchy* (Berkeley: University of California Press, 1975), pp. 37–9.)

[1] Now, in discussing the Athenian constitution, I cannot commend their present method of running the state, because in choosing it they preferred that the masses should do better than the respectable citizens; this, then, is my reason for not commending it. Since, however, they have made this choice, I will demonstrate how well they preserve their constitution and handle the other affairs for which the rest of the Greeks criticise them. [...]

[4] Again, some people are surprised at the fact that in all fields they give more power to the masses, the poor and the common people than they do to the respectable elements of society, but it will become clear that they preserve the democracy by doing precisely this. When the poor, the ordinary people and the lower classes flourish and increase in numbers, then the power of the democracy will be increased; if, however, the rich and the respectable flourish, the democrats increase the strength of their opponents. [5] Throughout the world the aristocracy are opposed to democracy, for they are naturally least liable to loss of self control and injustice and most meticulous in their regard for what is respectable, whereas the masses display extreme ignorance, indiscipline and wickedness, for poverty gives them a tendency towards the ignoble, and in some cases lack of money leads to their being uneducated and ignorant.

[6] It may be objected that they ought not to grant each and every man the right of speaking in the *Ekklesia* [assembly] and serving on the *Boule* [council], but only the ablest and best of them; however, in this also they are acting in their own best interests by allowing the mob also a voice. If none but the respectable spoke in the *Ekklesia* and the *Boule*, the result would benefit that class and harm the masses; as it is, anyone who wishes rises and speaks, and as a member of the mob he discovers what is to his own advantage and that of those like him.

[7] But someone may say: "How could such a man find out what was advantageous to himself and the common people?" The Athenians realise that this man, despite his

ignorance and badness, brings them more advantage because he is well disposed to them than the ill-disposed respectable man would, despite his virtue and wisdom. [8] Such practices do not produce the best city, but they are the best way of preserving democracy. [ . . . ]

[10] Slaves and metics at Athens lead a singularly undisciplined life; one may not strike them there, nor will a slave step aside for you. Let me explain the reason for this situation: if it were legal for a free man to strike a slave, a metic or a freedman, an Athenian would often have been struck under the mistaken impression that he was a slave, for the clothing of the common people there is in no way superior to that of the slaves and metics, nor is their appearance. [11] There is also good sense behind the apparently suprising fact that they allow slaves there to live in luxury, and some of them in considerable magnificence. In a state relying on naval power it is inevitable that slaves must work for hire so that we may take profits from what they earn, and they must be allowed to go free. Where there are rich slaves it is no longer profitable for my slave to be afraid of you; in Sparta my slave would be afraid of you, but there, if your slave is afraid of me, he will probably spend some of his own money to free himself from the danger. [12] This, then, is why in the matter of free speech we have put slaves and free men on equal terms; we have also done the same for metics and citizens because the city needs metics because of the multiplicity of her industries and for her fleet; that is why we were right to establish freedom of speech for metics as well.

## Aristophanes, *The Assemblywomen*

Aristophanes, a famous writer of comic plays at Athens, composed *The Assembly-women* ca. 392 BC. His comedies – outrageous, witty, satirical, often obscene – can be very enlightening about contemporary Athenian attitudes, but care must be taken in their interpretation because of the difficulty in judging from our distant vantage point exactly what was intended as a joke and why. One must also always keep in mind that female characters were written and performed by men. In this fanciful play, a group of women plan to sneak into an assembly meeting and pass a motion to hand over control of the state to women, with humorous consequences. (*Source*: Aristophanes, *Assemblywomen*, lines 57–244, 427–476, 877–889, 938–1056: trans. J. Henderson, from *Three Plays by Aristophanes: Staging Women* (New York: Routledge, 1996), pp. 153–8, 164–6, 181, 183–7.)

*Praxagora*:  Well, now that you're all here, please sit down. [*The women except Praxagora sit in the chairs.*] I want to ask you if you've done everything we agreed.

*First Woman*:  I have! First, I've let my armpits get nice and bushy, just as we agreed; then, whenever my husband goes off to the agora, I oil myself and spend the whole day in the sun trying to get a tan.

*Second Woman*:  Me too! I threw my razor out of the house so I'd get all hairy and not look female at all!

*Praxagora*:   Have you all got your beards – the ones you were told to bring with you when next we met?

*[The women onstage produce false beards.]*

*First Woman*:   Sure, by Hekate! I've got this nice one here!

*Second Woman*:   And mine's far nicer than Epikrates'!

*Praxagora [to the Chorus]*:   And what about all of *you*?

*First Woman*:   They've got them; look, they're nodding yes.

*Praxagora*:   All right, I see you've taken care of the preliminaries: and you've got your men's boots and walking-sticks and suits, just as instructed?

*First Woman [producing a huge shillelagh]*:   Look, I've brought Lamios' shillelagh; I took it while he was asleep!

*Second Woman*:   Must be the shillelagh he carries when he farts!

*Praxagora*:   Yes, by Zeus the Savior, and perfectly suited to the very man who dresses in Argos' goat-leather jacket and shepherds the public – executioner! But let's get on with the next items of business, while the stars are still in the sky. The Assembly we're prepared to attend begins at dawn.

*First Woman*:   By Zeus, we've got to leave time to get seats right under the Chairman's dais.

*Second Woman [taking a knitting-basket out of her bundle]*:   I brought this along, just for something to do while the men are filing into Assembly.

*Praxagora*:   While the *men* are filing in, stupid?

*Second Woman*:   Sure, by Artemis! I can hear just as well when I'm knitting. My kids haven't got anything to wear!

*Praxagora*:   Listen to you! Knitting? You mustn't risk showing *any* part of your body to the men. Wouldn't we be in fine shape, if the assemblymen are all there and then some woman has to climb over them, hitching up her clothes, and flashes her, her – Phormisios! If we're the *first* to get to our seats, no one will notice that we're keeping our clothes wrapped tight around us. And when we unfurl the beards that we're going to stick on our chins, who would suspect that we're not men? Take Agyrrhios: now that he's wearing Pronomos' beard he passes for a man; and yet this very man used to be a woman! And now, you see, he's the most powerful figure in the polis. And it's because of *him*, I swear by this all-important day, that we must dare such an act of daring, hopeful of somehow being able to take over the government and do something good for the polis! As it is, our polis is oarless and becalmed.

*First Woman*:   But how can a congregation of women, with women's minds, expect to address the people?

*Praxagora*:   Much better than anybody, that's how! They say that the young men who've been reamed the most are also the most effective orators! And as luck would have it, that's exactly what nature suits *us* for!

*First Woman*:   I'm not so sure: inexperience is a dangerous thing.

*Praxagora*:   Well, isn't that why we've gathered *here*, to practice what we're going to say *there*? Come on, attach your beard; [*to the other women*] and that goes for everyone else who's been practicing how to gab.

*First Woman*:   Is there anyone here, friend, who doesn't know how to *gab*?

*Praxagora*:   All right then, *you* put on your beard and become a man; I'll set out these garlands and put on *my* beard too, just in case I decide to make a comment. [*They attach their beards.*]

*Second Woman*:   Face this way, darling Praxagora. My dear, what a ridiculous sight this is!

*Praxagora*:   Ridiculous?

*Second Woman*:   Looks like somebody bearded a grilled squid!

*Praxagora*   [*moving behind the lectern and speaking in the voice of a Herald*]: Purifier, please make your rounds with the sacrificial cat. Assemblymen, come forward into the sanctified area. Ariphrades, stop chattering! You there, come forward and take a seat! Who wishes to address the Assembly?

*First Woman*:   I do!

*Praxagora* [*indicating the pile of garlands*]:   Then put on the garland and may your speech be propitious.

*First Woman* [*putting on the garland*]:   There we are.

*Praxagora*:   You may speak.

*First Woman*:   Don't I get a drink first?

*Praxagora*:   Drink?

*First Woman*:   Well, sir, what did I put on a garland for, then?

*Praxagora*:   Get out of here! You would have done the same thing to us in the *real* Assembly!

*First Woman* [*flaring*]:   What? They drink in the real Assembly, don't they?

*Praxagora*:   Listen to *you* – "drink"!

*First Woman*:   Sure, by Artemis, and they drink it *straight!* Their decrees, when you think about the reasoning behind them, are like the ravings of drunkards! By god, and they pour libations too: why else would they make those long prayers, if they didn't have wine? And they *yell* at each other like drinkers, and the police drag away the guy who's had too much and gets out of hand.

*Praxagora*:   Well, *you* may get back to your seat and sit down! You're worthless!

*First Woman* [*returning to her seat*]:   By Zeus, I would have been better off without this beard – I'm absolutely *parched* with thirst!

*Praxagora* [*to the seated women*]:   Is there another candidate orator among us?

*Second Woman [rising]:*   Me!

*Praxagora [motioning her forward and extending another garland]:*   Put this on then. We can't stop now, after all our planning. Now, carry on like a man and speak cogently; lean on your stick like this [*she adopts an oratorical posture*].

*Second Woman:*   I would have preferred to yield the floor to one of the usual speakers, sitting quietly and listening to a very good speech. But as far as my own vote goes, I say we outlaw the use of kegs in barrooms – to hold water! It is a bad policy, by the Twain Goddesses.

*Praxagora:*   By the Twain Goddesses, you bungler? Where is your *mind?*

*Second Woman:*   What's the matter? I didn't ask for a drink!

*Praxagora:*   God no, but you *did* swear by the Twain when you're supposed to be a man! [*Dejectedly*] And the rest was so *good*, too.

*Second Woman:*   Oh! [*Resuming a manly voice*] By Apollo . . .

*Praxagora:*   No, stop. [*She plucks the garland from Second Woman's head.*] I won't take another step on the road to being an assembly woman until everything's exactly right.

*Second Woman [snatching back the garland]:*   Give me the garland. I want to try my speech again; I think I've got it down nicely now. [*She assumes the rhetorical posture.*] In my view, ladies . . .

*Praxagora:*   You loser! You're calling men *women!*

*Second Woman [pointing to the audience]:*   It's that Epigonos over there:   I caught sight of him and thought I was addressing women!

*Praxagora [pointing her away from the lectern]:*   Shoo. You go back to your seat over there too. [*To the seated women*] To judge from what I've seen of *your* abilities it seems best that I put on this garland and make the speech *myself.* [*Taking the lectern*] I beseech the gods to grant success to today's deliberations. My own stake in this country is equal to your own, and I am annoyed and depressed at all the polis' conduct of affairs. For I see her constantly employing leaders who are scoundrels. If one of them turns virtuous for one day, he makes up for it by being wicked for ten. You turn to another one, and he causes even worse trouble. I realize how difficult it is to talk sense to men as cantankerous as you, who fear those who want to befriend you and consistently court those who do not. There was a time when we convened no assemblies at all, but at least we knew that Agyrrhios was a scoundrel. Nowadays we do convene them, and the people who attend and draw pay for it praise him to the skies, while those who cannot attend say that the people who attend for the money deserve the death-penalty.

*First Woman:*   Well said, by Aphrodite!

*Praxagora:*   Pitiful! You swore by Aphrodite! Wouldn't it be charming if you spoke that way in the Assembly?

*First Woman:*   But I wouldn't have!

*Praxagora*:   Well, don't get into the habit now. [*Resuming her speech*] And about this alliance:   when we were examining the issue, the people insisted that the polis would perish if we did not ratify it. But when it finally *was* ratified, the people were unhappy, and the alliance's staunchest supporter had to leave town in a hurry. When it's a question of building up our navy, the poor are all for it, while the rich and the farmers are against it. First you are angry with the Korinthians, and they with you; then they're fine people, so you have to be fine as well. The Argives are morons, but Hieronymos is a sage. And occasionally we get a fleeting glimpse of salvation, but Thrasyboulos gets angry that you're not begging *him* to help you.

*First Woman*:   This man's intelligent!

*Praxagora*:   That's the way to applaud! [*Resuming her speech*] And *you*, the sovereign people, are responsible for this mess! For while you're drawing your civic pay from public funds, each of you is figuring how you can personally profit. Meanwhile the state staggers around like Aisimos. But listen to my advice and you shall escape from your muddle. I propose that we turn over governance of the polis to the women, since they are so competent as stewards and treasurers in our households.

*All the Women*:   Hear hear! Well said! Pray continue, sir!

*Praxagora*:   That their character is superior to ours I will demonstrate. First of all, they dye their wool in hot water according to their ancient custom, each and every one of them. You'll never see them trying anything new. Contrast the Athenian polis:   we are never content to do well with a tried and true method but are always fiddling around with something novel. Meanwhile the women settle down to their cooking, as they always have. They carry burdens on their heads, as they always have. They celebrate the Thesmophoria, as they always have. They bake cookies, as they always have. They drive their husbands nuts, as they always have. They hide their lovers in the house, as they always have. They buy themselves little extras, as they always have. They like their wine neat, as they always have. They like to get fucked, as they always have. And so, gentlemen, let us hand over governance of the polis to the women, and let's not beat around the bush about it or ask what they plan to accomplish. Let's simply let them govern. You need consider only two points:   first, as mothers they'll want to protect the soldiers; and second, who could be quicker at sending rations to soldiers than the mothers who bore them? No one is more inventive at getting funds than a woman. Nor would a woman ruler ever get cheated, since women themselves are past masters at cheating. I'll pass over the other arguments. Adopt my resolution and you'll lead happy lives.

*First Woman*:   Well said, dearest Praxagora! What skill! You rascal, how did you learn all this so well?

*Praxagora*:   I lived with my husband on the Pnyx [hill where the assembly met], with the refugees, and learned everything by listening to the orators there. [...]

[After the meeting took place, a man who attended tells what happened to Praxagora's husband, Blepyros, who missed it.]

*Chremes:*  Well, after that a pale, good-looking young man sprang to his feet to address the people – looked very much like Nikias. He made a case for handing the polis over to the women! And they all cheered and yelled their approval, this mass of cobblers, while the people from the country made deep rumbles.

*Blepyros:*  They had sense, by god!

*Chremes:*  But they were the minority, and the speaker drowned them out. In his view, women could do no wrong, and you no right.

*Blepyros:*  What were his arguments?

*Chremes:*  First, he called you a criminal.

*Blepyros:*  And what did he call *you?*

*Chremes:*  I'll get to that. Then he called you a crook.

*Blepyros:*  Only me?

*Chremes:*  That's right, and an informer too.

*Blepyros:*  Only me?

*Chremes:*  That's right, you and [*indicating the spectators*] this crowd here as well!

*Blepyros:*  Well, that's a different story – who'd deny *that?*

*Chremes:*  He went on to say that a woman is a creature bursting with brains and productive of profit, and furthermore that women never divulge the secrets of the Thesmophoria, by contrast with you and me, who leak what we say in Council all the time.

*Blepyros:*  By Hermes, that last point's fair enough.

*Chremes:*  Then he said that women lend each other dresses, jewelry, money, drinking cups, one to another without witnesses, and always return everything with nothing held back; while most of us men, he said, cheat.

*Blepyros:*  By Poseidon, we do it even when there *are* witnesses!

*Chremes:*  He included other items in his eulogy of the women:  that they don't inform on people, don't sue them, don't try to overthrow the democracy, but instead do it lots of good.

*Blepyros:*  And what was voted?

*Chremes:*  To turn the polis over to *them*. That seemed to be the only thing that hasn't been tried.

*Blepyros:*  And this passed?

*Chremes:*  That's what I'm telling you.

*Blepyros:*  They've been put in charge of everything that used to be the business of the citizens?

*Chremes:*   That's the way it is.

*Blepyros:*   So *I* won't be going to court anymore, but my *wife* will?

*Chremes:*   And you won't be taking care of your dependents anymore – your wife will.

*Blepyros:*   And I won't have to groan myself awake at dawn anymore?

*Chremes:*   God no, all that's the women's concern now; you can stop groaning and stay at home farting all day!

*Blepyros:*   But there lies the danger for men our age: once they've taken the reins of power they'll force us against our will to –

*Chremes:*   To what?

*Blepyros:*   To screw them!

*Chremes:*   And what if we can't?

*Blepyros:*   They won't make us breakfast!

*Chremes:*   By Zeus you'd better do it then: you can eat breakfast and screw at the same time.

*Blepyros:*   But it's absolutely terrible when you're forced!

*Chremes:*   But if this is the policy of the polis, every true man's got to do his part!

*Blepyros:*   Well, there *is* that traditional saying: however brainless and foolish our policies may be, all our affairs will turn out for the best.

*Chremes:*   And I hope they *do* turn out for the best, Lady Pallas [Athena] and all the Gods! [. . .]

[Later, some consequences are portrayed.]

[*In the doorway of one of the stage houses is an old woman, and at the upper window of the house next door is a young girl; both look anxiously up and down the street.*]

*First Old Woman:*   Where in the world are the men? Dinner must be over by now! Here I am, thoroughly plastered with makeup and wearing my party dress, just standing around, whistling myself a song, with my trap all set to catch one of the men who walk by. Ye Muses, descend to these my lips with some spicy Ionian tune!

*Girl:*   This time you've got downstairs ahead of me, old hag. You thought you'd strip the vines when I wasn't looking and entice some guy with your singing! If you try it, I'll sing a song of my own. And if the audience expects this to be boring, I trust they'll find something sweet and comic in it anyway.

[. . .]

*Epigenes:*

> How I wish I could sleep with the girl
> and not have to bang a pug-nosed crone first!
> That doesn't sit well with a free man!

*First Old Woman [unheard by Epigenes]:*

> You'll bang to your sorrow then, by Zeus;
> the days of Charixene are past!
> If this is still a democracy,
> we've got to do it legal and proper!

But I'll go inside to see what he's going to do. [*She ducks inside again, but leaves the door slightly ajar.*]

*Epigenes:*   Ye gods, just let me get the pretty girl alone! It's *her* I got drunk to visit and *her* I've so long been longing for!

*Girl [appearing in her window]:*   I've completely fooled the damnable old thing; she's gone inside, thinking that I'm going to stay inside. But here's the very boy we were talking about!

> Hither now, hither now,
> my dear one,
> come to me and be
> my bedmate tonight!
> A powerful passion
> sets me awhirl
> for your curly hair!
> What is this strange longing
> that attacks me and holds me
> in its grinding grip?
> Release me, Eros, I beg you!
> Please make this boy
> come to my very own bed!

*Epigenes:*

> Hither now, hither now,
> my dear one,
> run to the door for me
> and open it wide!
> If you don't I'll fall down
> and die!
> I want to lie in your lap
> and play see-saw with your butt!
> Aphrodite, why have you driven
> me mad for this girl?
> Release me, Eros, I beg you!
> Please make this girl
> come to my very own bed!

And yet nothing I've said
comes near to matching my need!
I beg you, dearest,
open the door for me,
throw your arms around me;
I'm hurting for you!
Oh my gold-bauble delight,
flower of Aphrodite,
honeybee of the Muses,
child of the Graces,
personification of utter
voluptuousness,
open the door for me,
throw your arms around me;
I'm hurting for you!

[*He knocks at the Girl's door, but before she can come down to him the First Old Woman bursts from her doorway and accosts him.*]

*First Old Woman*:   Hey you, what's this knocking? Looking for *me*, are you?

*Epigenes [recoiling]*:   Surely you jest!

*First Old Woman*:   Yes you are; you were banging on my door!

*Epigenes*:   I'll be damned if I was!

*First Old Woman*:   Well, what *is* your business, then, with the torch and all?

*Epigenes*:   I'm looking for a fellow from Wankton.

*First Old Woman*:   Which one?

*Epigenes*:   Not Mr. Balling, whom *you're* perhaps expecting.

*First Old Woman [seizing him by the arm]*:   By Aphrodite, whether you like it or not –

*Epigenes [shaking her off]*:   Wait, I'm not in your jurisdiction; the statute of limitations is sixty years! You're tabled. I'm involved only in cases under twenty!

*First Old Woman*:   That might have been true under the old system, my sweet; but according to current law you've got to deal with *me* first.

*Epigenes*:   When gambling it's legal to pass the deal.

*First Old Woman*:   You didn't obey that law when you had your dinner.

*Epigenes*:   I don't know what you're talking about. I've got to bang on *this* door.

*First Old Woman [pointing to her crotch]*:   Not until you bang *this* one first!

*Epigenes*:   No thanks, I don't need a bucket just now.

*First Old Woman*:   I know you like me; you were just surprised to see me here. Come on, give us a kiss.

*Epigenes [retreating]*:    No! I'm, ah, terrified of your lover!

*First Old Woman*:    Who?

*Epigenes*:    The finest of painters.

*First Old Woman*:    Who are you talking about?

*Epigenes*:    The one who decorates funeral urns. Better get out of here before he spots you in the doorway!

*First Old Woman*:    I know what you want, I know!

*Epigenes*:    And I know what *you* want, by Zeus!

*First Old Woman*:    By Aphrodite, who gave me the luck of the draw, I'm not giving you up!

*Epigenes*:    You're a crazy little old lady!

*First Old Woman [waggling her fingers at him]*:    Nonsense! I'm personally going to escort you to my bed!

*Epigenes*:    Why do we need tongs for our buckets, when we could run a crone like this down the well and use *her* to haul them up?

*First Old Woman*:    Very funny, sir! But you just get over here to *my* house!

*Epigenes*:    No! I don't have to obey you unless you've paid the polis the 2% tax on me.

*First Old Woman*:    By Aphrodite, you do too! I just *love* sleeping with boys your age!

*Epigenes*:    And I just *hate* sleeping with women *your* age! I'll never consent.

*First Old Woman [producing a piece of paper]*:    *This* will make you, by Zeus!

*Epigenes*:    What is it?

*First Old Woman*:    The regulation that says you've got to come to *me*.

*Epigenes*:    Tell me what in the world it says.

*First Old Woman*:    All right, I shall. [*Reading*] The women have decreed: if a young man desires a young woman he may not hump her until he first bangs an old woman. Should he in his desire for the young woman refuse to do this preliminary banging, the older women shall be entitled with impunity to drag off the young man by the pecker.

*Epigenes*:    Dear me, this very day I'm to be Prokrustes!

*First Old Woman*:    Our laws must be obeyed!

*Epigenes*:    What if one of my fellow demesmen or friends comes and goes bail for me?

*First Old Woman*:    No man is any longer permitted to transact business over the one-medimnos limit!

*Epigenes*:    Can't I swear off my duty?

*First Old Woman*:   You can't squirm out of *this* duty!

*Epigenes*:   I'll get myself exempted as a merchant.

*First Old Woman*:   You'll be sorry if you do!

*Epigenes*:   So what am I to do?

*First Old Woman*:   Follow me into my house.

*Epigenes*:   Is it a necessity?

*First Old Woman*:   Diomedes' necessity!

*Epigenes*:   In that case, begin by strewing the bier with dittany and four broken vine-branches as kindling, and deck it with ribbons, and put the urn beside it, and place the water-jug outside the door.

*First Old Woman*:   Surely you're going to buy me a wedding garland too.

*Epigenes*:   Yes, by Zeus, provided I can find one made of wax somewhere, because I think you're going to disintegrate pretty quick in there!

*[As the First Old Woman draws Epigenes into her house, the Girl emerges from her doorway.]*

*Girl*:   Where are you dragging him off to?

*First Old Woman*:   I'm bringing my own man home!

*Girl*:   That's not very prudent. He's the wrong age to be sleeping with you – you're more his mother than his wife! If you old women start enforcing a law like this, you'll fill the whole country up with Oedipuses! [*She steps between Epigenes and the First Old Woman.*]

*First Old Woman*:   You dirty slut, you've thought up this objection out of pure envy. But I'll make you pay for it. [*She goes into her house*].

*Epigenes [embracing the Girl]*:   By Zeus the Savior, sweetest, you've done me a favor by getting that crone off my back! When the lights are out I'll give you a big, juicy token of my gratitude! [*The Girl leads him toward her door.*]

*[Enter a Second Old Woman, older and uglier than the First.]*

*Second Old Woman [to the Girl]*:   Hey you! Where are you taking *him*, in violation of the law? It's clearly stated that he's got to sleep with me first.

*Epigenes*:   Oh no! Where did *you* pop out of? What an apparition of damnation! This one's even more revolting than the last one!

*Second Old Woman*:   Get over here!

*Epigenes [to the Girl, who runs in terror back to her own house]*:   Don't let *her* drag me away, I beg you!

*Second Old Woman*:   Not I but the law drags you away! [. . .]

# Aristotle, *Politics*

In the following selections Aristotle offers his views about the natural condition of men, women, and slaves, and about citizenship in a Greek state, including democra- cies. (*Source*: Aristotle, *Politics* 1253b1– 33, 54a10–24, b7–15, 59a37–b4; 1274b32–75a34, b19–23; 1319b2–32: trans. B. Jowett.)

On the natural rule of men over slaves and women:

## 1253b1–34, 54a10–24, b7–15, 59a37–b4

Seeing then that the state is made up of households, before speaking of the state we must speak of the management of the household. The parts of household manage- ment correspond to the persons who compose the household, and a complete household consists of slaves and freemen. Now we should begin by examining everything in its fewest possible elements; and the first and fewest possible parts of a family are master and slave, husband and wife, father and children. We have therefore to consider what each of these three relations is and ought to be: – I mean the relation of master and servant, the marriage relation (the conjunction of man and wife has no name of its own), and thirdly, the procreative relation (this also has no proper name). And there is another element of a household, the so-called art of getting wealth, which, according to some, is identical with household manage- ment, according to others, a principal part of it; the nature of this art will also have to be considered by us.

   Let us first speak of master and slave, looking to the needs of practical life and also seeking to attain some better theory of their relation than exists at present. For some are of opinion that the rule of a master is a science, and that the management of a household, and the mastership of slaves, and the political and royal rule, as I was saying at the outset, are all the same. Others affirm that the rule of a master over slaves is contrary to nature, and that the distinction between slave and freeman exists by law only, and not by nature; and being an interference with nature is therefore unjust.

   Property is a part of the household, and the art of acquiring property is a part of the art of managing the household; for no man can live well, or indeed live at all, unless he be provided with necessaries. And as in the arts which have a definite sphere the workers must have their own proper instruments for the accomplishment of their work, so it is in the management of a household. Now instruments are of various sorts; some are living, others lifeless; in the rudder, the pilot of a ship has a lifeless, in the look-out man, a living instrument; for in the arts the servant is a kind of instrument. Thus, too, a possession is an instrument for maintaining life. And so, in the arrangement of the family, a slave is a living possession, and property a number of such instruments; and the servant is himself an instrument which takes precedence of all other instruments.[...] The master is only the master of the slave; he does not belong to him, whereas the slave is not only the slave of his master, but wholly belongs to him. Hence we see what is the nature and office of a slave; he who is by nature not his own but another's man, is by nature a slave; and he may be said to be another's man who, being a human being, is also a possession. And a possession may be defined as an instrument of action, separable from the possessor.

But is there any one thus intended by nature to be a slave, and for whom such a condition is expedient and right, or rather is not all slavery a violation of nature?

There is no difficulty in answering this question, on grounds both of reason and of fact. For that some should rule and others be ruled is a thing not only necessary, but expedient; from the hour of their birth, some are marked out for subjection, others for rule.

[...] And it is clear that the rule of the soul over the body, and of the mind and the rational element over the passionate, is natural and expedient; whereas the equality of the two or the rule of the inferior is always hurtful. The same holds good of animals in relation to men; for tame animals have a better nature than wild, and all tame animals are better off when they are ruled by man; for then they are preserved. Again, the male is by nature superior, and the female inferior; and the one rules, and the other is ruled; this principle, of necessity, extends to all mankind. [...]

Of household management we have seen that there are three parts – one is the rule of a master over slaves, which has been discussed already, another of a father, and the third of a husband. A husband and father, we saw, rules over wife and children, both free, but the rule differs, the rule over his children being a royal, over his wife a constitutional rule. For although there may be exceptions to the order of nature, the male is by nature fitter for command than the female, just as the elder and full-grown is superior to the younger and more immature. [...]

On citizenship in a state:

## 1274b32–75a34, b19–23

He who would inquire into the essence and attributes of various kinds of govern-ments must first of all determine "What is a state?" At present this is a disputed question. Some say that the state has done a certain act; others, no, not the state, but the oligarchy or the tyrant. And the legislator or statesman is concerned entirely with the state; a constitution or government being an arrangement of the inhabitants of a state. But a state is composite, like any other whole made up of many parts; – these are the citizens, who compose it. It is evident, therefore, that we must begin by asking, Who is the citizen, and what is the meaning of the term? For here again there may be a difference of opinion. He who is a citizen in a democracy will often not be a citizen in an oligarchy. Leaving out of consideration those who have been made citizens, or who have obtained the name of citizen in any other accidental manner, we may say, first, that a citizen is not a citizen because he lives in a certain place, for resident aliens and slaves share in the place; nor is he a citizen who has no legal right except that of suing and being sued; for this right may be enjoyed under the provisions of a treaty. Nay, resident aliens in many places do not possess even such rights completely, for they are obliged to have a patron, so that they do but imper-fectly participate in citizenship, and we call them citizens only in a qualified sense, as we might apply the term to children who are too young to be on the register, or to old men who have been relieved from state duties. Of these we do not say quite simply that they are citizens, but add in the one case that they are not of age, and in the other, that they are past the age, or something of that sort; the precise expression is immaterial, for our meaning is clear. Similar difficulties to those which I have mentioned may be raised and answered about deprived citizens and about exiles. But the citizen whom we are seeking to define is a citizen in the strictest sense, against whom no such exception can be taken, and his special characteristic is that he shares in the administration of justice, and in offices. Now of offices some are discontinuous, and the same persons are not allowed to hold them twice, or can only hold them after a fixed interval; others have no limit of time – for example, the office of dicast [juror] or ecclesiast [assembly-goer]. It may, indeed, be argued that these are not magistrates at all, and that their functions give them no share in the government. But surely it is ridiculous to say that those who have the supreme power do not govern. Let us not dwell further upon this, which is a purely verbal question; what we want is a common term including both dicast and ecclesiast. Let us, for the sake of distinction, call it "indefinite office", and we will assume that those who share in such office are citizens. This is the most comprehensive definition of a citizen, and best suits all those who are generally so called. [...]

He who has the power to take part in the deliberative or judicial administration of any state is said by us to be a citizen of that state; and, speaking generally, a state is a body of citizens sufficing for the purposes of life.

But in practice a citizen is defined to be one of whom both the parents are citizens [...]

On citizen license in extreme democracies:

## 1319b2–32

[...] The last form of democracy, that in which all share alike, is one which cannot be borne by all states, and will not last long unless well regulated by laws and customs. The more general causes which tend to destroy this or other kinds of government have been pretty fully considered. In order to constitute such a democracy and strengthen the people, the leaders have been in the habit of including as many as they can, and making citizens not only of those who are legitimate, but even of the illegitimate, and of those who have only one parent a citizen, whether father or mother; for nothing of this sort comes amiss to such a democracy. This is the way in which demagogues proceed. Whereas the right thing would be to make no more additions when the number of the commonalty exceeds that of the notables and of the middle class – beyond this not to go. When in excess of this point, the constitution becomes disorderly, and the notables grow excited and impatient of the democracy, as in the insurrection at Cyrene; for no notice is taken of a little evil, but when it increases it strikes the eye. Measures like those which Cleisthenes passed when he wanted to increase the power of the democracy at Athens, or such as were taken by the founders of popular government at Cyrene, are useful in the extreme form of democracy. Fresh tribes and brotherhoods should be established; the private rites of families should be restricted and converted into public ones; in short, every contrivance should be adopted which will mingle the citizens with one another and get rid of old connections. Again, the measures which are taken by tyrants appear all of them to be democratic; such, for instance, as the licence permitted to slaves (which may be to a certain extent advantageous) and also that of women and children, and the allowing everybody to live as he likes. Such a government will have many supporters, for most persons would rather live in a disorderly than in a sober manner. [...]

# The Economics and Politics of Slavery at Athens

## *Robin Osborne*

Robin Osborne reviews the extent and ramifications of slavery at Athens, and attempts to show that slavery, a seemingly undemocratic institution, in fact reinforced the reigning democratic ideology at Athens.

Xenophon in the *Memorabilia* (2.7) tells the following story. Socrates one day met Aristarkhos looking miserable. Aristarkhos explained that he was at a loss what to do, since the end of the Peloponnesian War and the subsequent civil strife at Athens had given him a household full of fourteen female relatives and at the same time cut him off from all his usual sources of income (agriculture, renting out urban property, selling furniture). Socrates pointed out that others managed to feed large households, but Aristarkhos remarked that their households were made up of slaves. Socrates got Aristarkhos to agree that his free-born relatives were better than slaves and that they possessed many craft skills (cooking, making clothes), and suggested that it was preposterous to take the attitude that because the women were free and relatives they should only eat and sleep; rather they should be put to work. Aristarkhos was persuaded, the women were put to work, the household became profitable and all the members of it more happy.

This (rather improbable) story sums up Athenian slavery for many. Slavery was an institution, they think, which the Athenians maintained through prejudice alone: it was purely because they did not like the idea of devoting their lives, and the lives of their women, to production that slavery was so dominant. Not only did slavery go against what should have been their democratic principles of treating all alike, but it was also economically irrational, both in the short term, in that individuals would have been more prosperous without slaves, and in the longer term, in that slavery prevented technological development. What is more, the prejudice which fostered slavery was an aristocratic prejudice and it worked only in the interests of the rich: as long as commercial exploitation of craft activity remained the preserve of slaves, the

Robin Osborne, "The Economics and Politics of Slavery at Athens," in *The Greek World*, ed. A. Powell (London: Routledge, 1995), pp. 27–43.

profits of craft activity remained confined to those with enough capital to purchase slaves, and those short of resources were compelled to remain in the ideologically approved agricultural sphere, despite the hazards involved there and the very limited scope for betterment which fixed resources of land offered. Both economically and politically the ordinary Athenian citizen would have been better off if there had been no slaves.[1] This chapter looks at the ways in which slaves were used at Athens, and attempts to assess the economic and political impact of slavery.

There is no doubt that the number of slaves at Athens was large, although it is impossible to determine exact numbers. A variety of ancient figures survive: Hypereides suggested that his proposal after the battle of Khaironeia (338/7) to enfranchise slaves and others who had lost civic rights would enfranchise "more than 15 myriads [150,000]" of slaves from the silver mines and the rest of the land;[2] Athenaios quotes Ktesikles as saying that Demetrios' census in c. 317 recorded 21,000 citizens, 10,000 metics and 400,000 slaves. Thucydides records that during the Dekeleian war the Athenians "were deprived of the whole territory and more than two myriads of slaves deserted and the greater part of these were *kheirotekhnai* (skilled manual labourers), and all the sheep and yoke beasts were lost". None of these figures is unproblematic in itself, and together they make an even more problematic set. Both Hypereides and Thucydides are simply guessing, Hypereides presumably guessing the total number of slaves, Thucydides a significant proportion (but what proportion?). Ktesikles' figures for metics and citizens are credible, but it is very unlikely that the census counted slaves and the slave figure must be a guess: given the other high figures also quoted in this passage for slaves in other Greek cities (including Aigina where, since we are dealing with a small island, the absurdity of the resulting population density is clear), this guess seems to be based on a particular conception of classical Greek society as dominated by slaves.[3]

Arguably, the absolute number of slaves is actually less significant for any assessment of the place of slavery than the question of just how slaves were distributed across society. And here we do have some evidence to play with. In the first place, there is evidence from the orators about the numbers of slaves in craft workshops: Lysias records 120 slaves in his family's possession in 403, of whom it seems certain that the majority were employed in manufacturing shields; Demosthenes records that his father had two workshops, one with 32 or 33 knifemakers and the other with 20 couchmakers; Aeschines alleges that Timarkhos had 10 or 11 slaves working, making leather goods; Demosthenes records that Pantainetos in the mines had a workshop with 30 slaves; Demosthenes records the income from Pasion's shield factory as 1 talent a year, which may imply that it employed about 60 slaves.[4]

Second, there are literary sources which make assumptions about the limits to ownership of domestic slaves. Orators occasionally expect, or pretend to expect, the dikasts to own slaves: thus Lysias in the defence of Kallias on an impiety charge argues that:

> The contest here seems to me not to concern just these men, but involves all the city. For *therapontes* (servants) do not belong to these men alone, but to all the others who, once they have cast an eye upon the fortune of these, will no longer have in mind what good they can do to their masters in order to become free, but what falsity they can plant on them in an information.[5]

Similarly, Demosthenes in the speech for Apollodoros' prosecution of Stephanos writes:

> I have a lot to say about how I have been a victim of *hubris*, but I see that there is not enough water left in the clock. So I will say something which will make you all recognize that the behaviour of which I have been a victim has been excessive – if each of you were to consider to himself what slave he left at home, and were then to picture himself as having suffered from that slave what I have suffered from this one. It is not as if your slave is Syros or Manes or whatever his name is, while this is Phormio, for the deed is the same. Those are slaves and this is a slave; I am a master and you are masters.[6]

If the implication in these passages is that any Athenian citizen over thirty with enough free time to appear in the courts could reasonably be expected to own a slave,[7] then the implication of Plato's throw-away remark in *Republic* 578d–579a ("Suppose a very rich man with fifty or more slaves...") suggests an upper limit on normal domestic holdings.

These literary testimonies can be finessed with evidence from inscriptions. The two most important sources here are the Attic stelai and a late fifth-century list of sailors.[8] When the property of those found guilty of mutilating the Hermai and profaning the Mysteries was sold off in 414/13 their slaves were also sold. The lists of property sold do not survive complete, and the way in which the sales proceeded means that any individual's slaves were not necessarily all sold on a single occasion,[9] but we can trace 16 slaves from the property of Kephisodoros (a metic [resident alien], who could not own land in Attica), 9 slaves from that of Adeimantos (in 4 different lots), 7 (or possibly 8) from that of Axiokhos (sold in 2 different lots),[10] 4 and 6 slaves from properties whose owners' names do not survive, and lots of just 1 slave from the property of Polystratos and of an unknown owner. Kephisodoros' slaves may have worked in a single unit: they comprise three Thracian women, two Thracian men, two Syrian men, a Karian man, a Karian youth and a Karian child, two Illyrian men, a Skythian man, a Kolkhian man, a man perhaps from Malta and a Lydian woman with equally various prices ranging (for the adults) from somewhere between 85 and 88 dr. for the Lydian woman to 301 dr. for one of the Syrian men. The others' slaves, sold in separate lots, most probably were attached to distinct units of property. Whether they were bought by one or more than one purchaser we cannot know.[11]

While those whose property was confiscated in 414/13 were almost certainly wealthy men, the list of sailors from the last years of the Peloponnesian War gives us a glimpse of rather more humble classes. The exact context for this unique inscription is not known, but it is almost certainly related to the Athenian decision to honour those who fought in the sea battle at Aigospotamoi. The list (which again, is only partly preserved) distinguishes between the ships' officers, marines (*epibatai*), citizen rowers, archers and slave rowers, and gives citizen names by first name and demotic, slave names by first name and owner's name. Ninety-five more or less certainly different owners' names appear with the slaves, and of these ninety-five, four certainly owned three slaves and three more possibly did; ten certainly (and two more possibly) owned two slaves. In nine of the 95 cases, the owner himself figures among the citizens on the lists, in one case as an officer (*pentekontarkhos*), in six cases as *epibatai* (marines), in one case as an ordinary citizen rower and in one case as trierarch. The contrast between the hoplite *epibatai* and the ordinary citizen rowers is particularly marked in that one group of ten *epibatai* includes six slave owners (lines 83–93) while in another group of 23 citizen sailors none are attested as slave owners.[12]

The combined testimony of the literary texts and the inscriptions suggests that Athenians of the hoplite class and above would regularly be slave owners, indeed owners of enough slaves to have disposable slaves to put into triremes. Athenians of less than the hoplite census would seem regularly not to have had disposable slaves, but may only rarely have had no slave at all. Slaves might be employed in workshops, either directly under the eye of the owner or working independently, but were also part of any household group and could be expected to be found on any of the properties of a rich man. Only, it would appear, in the context of craft production were large numbers of slaves found in a single group.[13]

We know of no large-scale craft unit which employed Athenian citizens. Citizens certainly were skilled in certain craft activities: the records of the building work on the Erekhtheion [a large temple] in the last decade of the fifth century show citizens, metics and slaves working side by side.

> In the eighth prytany of the tribe Pandionis. Received from the Treasurers of the Goddess, Aresekhmos of Agryle and his colleagues, 1239 dr. [drachmas] 1 ob. [obols]. Expenditure: purchases: 2 boards on which we inscribe the accounts, at 1 dr. each: 2 dr. Total purchases: 2 dr. Stonework: for channelling the columns at the east end opposite the altar. The third column from the altar of Dione: Ameiniades who lives in Koile, 18 dr.; Lysanias, 18 dr.; Somenes slave of Ameiniades, 18 dr.; Timokrates, 18 dr. The next column: Simias who lives in Alopeke, 13 dr.; Kerdon, 12 dr. 5 obols; Sindron slave of Simias, 12 dr. 5 obols; Sokles slave of Axiopeithes, 12 dr. 5 obols; Sannion slave of Simias, 12 dr. 5 obols; Epiekes slave of Simias, 12 dr. 5 obols; Sosandros slave of Simias, 12 dr. 5 obols. The next column: Onesimos slave of Nikostratos, 16 dr. 4 obols; Eudoxos who lives in Alopeke, 16 dr. 4 obols; Kleon, 16 dr. 4 obols; Simon who lives in Agryle, 16 dr. 4 obols. Antidotos slave of Glaukos, 16 dr. 4 obols; Eudikos, 16 dr. 4 obols. The next column: Theugenes of Peiraieus, 15 dr.; Kephisogenes of Peiraieus, 15 dr.; Teukros who lives in Kydathenaion, 15 dr.; Kephisodoros who lives in Skambonidai, 15 dr.; Theugeiton of Peiraieus, 15 dr.[14]

In so far as there is a distinction between free and slave labour it is that the more highly skilled jobs are performed by free labour, the more basic jobs by slaves: only three citizens and five metics are sculptors, only one citizen and five metics woodcarvers whereas sixteen slaves are found beside twelve metics and nine citizens as masons.

Although the Erekhtheion is clearly a major project, the epigraphic records show that it did not employ labour in large groups but established individual contracts. In this respect, working on the Erekhtheion was more akin to being independently employed in one's own workshop than to being part of a large enterprise. It is clear that there were citizens who worked as craftsmen on their own, although they make little impact on either literary or epigraphic records: thus the shoes for the public slaves at Eleusis are made by a citizen cobbler.[15]

Most craft activities could equally reasonably be pursued by individuals or by groups, with only limited advantages in group activity. But the mining of silver only made sense as a group activity, because of the amount of mining that had to be done before either the "washing" process or the refinement and smelting of the silver became worthwhile. And it is in the mining of silver that there is almost no trace of citizen labour,[16] and plentiful indication that the labour force was servile. The issue in Xenophon's treatment of the mines and how they could be made more profitable for Athens is not the status of the work-force in them but who should own the slaves that work there. Xenophon records that:

> Nikias son of Nikeratos owned 1,000 slaves in the silver mines, which he let out to Sosias the Thracian on condition that he would pay him an obol a day net per man and that he would always keep the number constant. Hipponikos had 600 slaves hired out in the same way, who brought in a mna (60 dr.) a day net. Philemonides had 300 bringing in 30 dr. And others as they were able, I think. But why talk about the past? There are still many men in the silver mines nowadays who are let out on the same conditions. If my suggestions were to be carried out, the only innovation would be that, just as private individuals who have acquired slaves have provided themselves with a permanent source of revenue, so the city would acquire public slaves up to a ratio of three slaves for each citizen . . .[17]

Xenophon goes on to imagine the total number of publicly owned slaves in the mines rising to 10,000. We have no direct evidence for the numbers of slaves actually employed in the mines, but modern scholars have made calculations which suggest that the actual numbers at any one time were probably something above 10,000 during the fourth-century height of the workings, and perhaps as many as 22,000 or even 30,000.[18] Conditions in the mines were reputed to be poor,[19] but we cannot assess the effects of this on shortening the lives of those employed there. It is to be noted, however, that no slave identifiable as a mine worker is to be found among those who figure in the manumission lists from the third quarter of the fourth century.[20]

Just as mines and craft workshops of any size may have employed almost exclusively slaves, so slaves may also have dominated domestic work. When we are told in court about a free Athenian woman who was employed as a wet-nurse, the speaker feels obliged to explain that this occurred in circumstances of peculiar poverty,[21] and although we might have expected that the physical participation in the nourishment of a potential citizen would make that a special case, other evidence suggests that even a wet-nurse might be a slave.[22] For Theophrastos it is the mark of the stingy man that he does not buy a slave girl for his wife, and in comedy and the orators whenever we are given a glimpse inside a household there are slaves there. So, the "two-up, two-down" town household pictured in Lysias 1 includes a slave (girl), as does the propertied household of [Demosthenes] 47, and the country household that forms the focus of Menander's *Georgos* (which uses hired labour for agricultural work). In [Demosthenes] 47 not only is the speaker's household well provided with slaves, but the alarm is raised by the domestic slaves (*therapontes*) from neighbouring houses.[23]

The free women of a household might work alongside the female slaves in some domestic tasks, as Iskhomakhos' wife is portrayed as doing in Xenophon's *Oikono-mikos* (7.6), and domestic servants might come to enjoy a special place in the affections of their owners,[24] and even to exploit that special place (as Moskhion does in [Demosthenes] 48.14). The manumission lists include fifty female wool spinners (*talasiourgoi*), and these seem best interpreted as general domestic servants rather than as workshop workers. There is no sign that free domestic labour was an alternative to slave domestic labour. There were a number of terms in use to describe personal servants, terms such as *therapon* (manservant), *therapaina* (maidservant), and *oiketes* (household servant), and none of these terms is ever used to refer to a free person: it is clear that the expectation is that such a person will always be a slave. The clearest text of all on this is perhaps Plato. *Laws* 776e–777a:

> [Some people tell good stories about faithful slaves but] other people say the opposite –
> that there is no health in the soul of a slave, and that the sensible man must never trust
> slaves an inch. The wisest of all our poets even gives the opinion, speaking for Zeus, that
> "Zeus who sounds afar takes away half a man's wits when they are taken into slavery."
> Everyone takes a different understanding of these things, and some do not trust the pack
> of servants (*oiketai*) at all, and like those of the nature of beasts, with goads and whips
> make the souls of servants (*oiketai*) not just thrice but many times as slavish as they were,
> while others do the opposite of all this.[25]

The area where there is most debate about the extent to which slaves were employed is agriculture.[26] No one doubts that slaves were extensively used in agricultural operations on the estates of some rich men: Xenophon's *Oikonomikos* makes that clear beyond all reasonable doubt, especially in the section dealing with the qualities required in the (slave) bailiff who controls the workforce.[27] What is more, eleven *georgoi* [farmers] along with two vinedressers appear among the manumitted slaves on the fourth-century manumission lists. But the question that is far less tractable is of the extent to which slave labour was an integral part of the agricultural operations of the peasant farm. Literary evidence is never going to give a clear answer to this, partly because of its inherent bias towards the wealthy and partly because of the difficulty of demonstrating a negative from literary evidence. We can perhaps do better by assessing whether there was a structural necessity for slave labour in peasant agriculture.

I offer the following as a possible working hypothesis. It is dependent on a number of estimates of quantities, all of which might be questioned but all of which seem to me, on the basis of current understanding, to be of the right order of magnitude. Modern assessments of the area of Attica which can be exploited by agriculture have varied considerably. If we allow for tree crops and pastoral exploitation, it may not be unreasonable to reckon half or more of Attica to have been exploited in antiquity,[28] but the amount of land which could be cropped with cereals was somewhat less. Just how much less it is difficult to determine, but there can be little doubt that Jardé's figure of 20 per cent arable, only half of which was cropped each year, is too small, and that a figure of around one third, or even a little more, is more reasonable.[29] If we assume that around one third of the 2,400 square kilometres of Attica was cultivated with cereals annually, then, allowing for some biennial fallow (more universal on the estates of the rich, perhaps), we might assume that just over one fifth of Attica (say 50,000 ha.) was sown with cereals each year.[30] I have estimated elsewhere, using liturgical and eisphora [tax] demands as my baseline, that perhaps between a quarter and a third of the agricultural land of Attica was in the hands of the 2,000 richest families comprising perhaps approaching 3,000 citizens.[31] This suggests perhaps 15,000 ha. of cereals cultivated by the richest 3,000 citizens each year, 35,000 ha. cultivated by the other 25,000 citizens.

There are two great labour crises during the agricultural year: ploughing and sowing, and harvesting. For both these operations the "window" is relatively short and the labour demand high. Just how much pressure there is over ploughing and sowing is very dependent on when the autumn rains come, and no good modern comparative figures seem to exist from which any calculation can be made. But recent work by Paul Halstead and Glynis Jones has given some excellent modern compara- tive data for the reaping of cereals.[32] Halstead and Jones suggest that reaping barley requires 1.5–4.5 man-days per stremma, 15–45 man days per hectare. This gives a labour demand of between 225,000 and 675,000 man-days to reap the harvest from the estates of the rich, 525,000 to 1,575,000 man-days to reap that from the estates of the peasant farmers. If we reckon on a harvest period of three weeks,[33] and on a lowish figure of two man-days a hectare,[34] getting in the harvest of the rich would need just under 15,000 men's labour, getting in the harvest from peasant estates something around 35,000 men's labour. This suggests that it may have been possible for peasant farmers to reap their own cereal harvest with the aid of labour from the rest of the family (women and juveniles) and from any normally domestic slaves.[35] The area where there would be a massive need for additional labour would be on the estates of the rich, where we have other reasons to believe that slave labour was employed. But it is worth noting that what those practising extensive agriculture for the market, who have plenty of land but need to keep costs down and therefore labour down, need, even more than those practising intensive agriculture primarily for subsistence, is a source of *additional* labour for use during the peak periods, that is labour, whether free or slave, which is either not employed at all, or not employed in agricultural tasks, during the rest of the year.[36] Thus, even on the estates of the rich, any slave labour force employed will need some non-agricultural occupation for much of the year.[37]

Can we make sense of this pattern of slave employment? Is there any economic reason for the exclusive employment of slaves in mines and in domestic labour, and for their rather more limited employment in agriculture? To take agriculture first, the demand for agricultural labour on any farm is far from even. Even the most careful planning of crops will still leave some times of the year when there is little agricultural work to be done, and other times when the labour demand is very great.[38] But additionally, on a family farm the labour available varies considerably at different stages of the family's own history, depending on the amount of female and juvenile labour available, a variation emphasized by the normally late age of male marriage.[39] Any increase in the size of the household not only gave additional labour, it also created additional demand, and so might provoke the purchase or leasing of further land. Thus in the case of any individual household, the demand for labour in excess of that which could be provided from its own resources would vary both annually and over a whole life-cycle, and the calculation of whether it would be worth employing slave labour specifically for agricultural tasks might be a delicate one which depended on changes foreseeable in the household itself during the potential working life of the slave. Aristotle claims that a poor man has an ox instead of a slave.[40] It is very difficult to believe that the poor would regard the ox, useful for ploughing and carting but useless for other agricultural tasks, as a higher priority than additional human labour, and if we are to make any sense of Aristotle's claim at all, it would be to suggest that there is a stage in the life-cycle of the household when the traction of the ox for ploughing and sowing might seem a higher priority than additional human labour in gathering and processing the harvest.[41]

By contrast with agriculture, craft activities have a much less complex cycle. While there doubtless was a delicate relationship between supply and demand (as indeed part of the opening story of Aristarkhos suggests), this will not have been something easy to judge in advance, affected as it would be by political events (such as the loss of the Peloponnesian War). In general, additional hands could be put to productive use throughout the year, and the presence or absence of a labour input by the family would not necessarily play a crucial role. Demosthenes' father had all his money invested in non-agricultural activities, and Timarkhos had slaves working independently as leather-workers: it is clear that for these men ownership of slaves engaged in craft activity was a source of income not closely tied to the household at all. But if this explains why use of slaves is more convenient in craft production than in agriculture, it will not explain why citizens should not themselves labour at these activities in groups.

We get some idea of the economics of the ownership of slaves engaged in craft activity from Demosthenes' account of his own father's workshops. Demosthenes reports that his father's knife-makers had a capital value of around two talents and yielded half a talent a year net, while his couch factory had a value of something over 4,000 dr. and yielded 1,200 dr. a year net. In the former, slaves worth on average just under 450dr. would yield just over 90 dr. net profit per head; in the latter, slaves worth on average something over 200 dr. would yield 60 dr. per slave per head. These figures suggest that slaves might realize their own capital value in around four or five years. The figures which we have for slaves hired out to work in the mines suggest a slightly more profitable situation: Nikias' slaves in the fifth century, hired out at an obol a day with the lessee replacing any losses, would yield 60 dr. a year to him, and clearly enough to their lessee for him to be able to write off losses. Calculating *just* how much profit in all might come from slave labour in the mines depends on making a series of guesses. If about 1,000 talents a year of silver was extracted from the mines, by, say, 10,000 slaves who cost ½ dr. a day to keep (300 talents a year) then the total net income per slave would be something over 400 dr. a year – from which capital costs (including the purchase of replacement slaves) have to be subtracted. Silver mining may have been extremely profitable for those who hit rich, but also a rather risky business, since the lessee of a dud concession faced high capital costs for little return.

How would this compare with the profitability of such labour for a citizen? If the profits of craft labour were such that one who practised it would earn enough to buy a slave every four years, why did citizens not practise crafts more? Two considerations are important here: the length of the working year, and the question of dependents.

The relationship between man-days and production is clearly much more direct in craft production than in agricultural production. In agriculture, man-days of sowing not done or reaping not done have a drastic effect on production, but man-days of weeding not done have a minor effect. In craft production, any man-day lost has much the same effect on lost production. The farmer could, arguably, afford, at many times of the year, to spend whole days taking part in festivals or attending political meetings or the courts, in a way that the man working at a craft could not.[42] If the citizen craftsman took 25 per cent of his time off doing other things (and the number of festivals means that he could easily have taken even more time off than that), then he loses 25 per cent of his income. Gaining payment for attending the assembly, serving as a dikast, or serving in some magistracy might help make up for this for such a man, but for the farmer such payments, and any craft work he might find available during the slack seasons, were virtually pure gain. Slaves, notoriously, had no leisure.[43]

As to dependents, unlike the slave, the citizen craftsman is unlikely to be a single man: the obol or two a day sheer profit per slave that these craft units bring in would actually be insufficient to support a household, even without the distractions of religious and political life.

It seems unlikely, therefore, on the basis of these rough and ready hypothetical calculations, that citizens could actually have supported their households, let alone continued to take any part in public life, had they taken employment doing the tasks that slaves did. The special situation of Aristarkhos' household now becomes apparent: Aristarkhos is able to put his household to work because it includes so many female relatives. His is not the normal family unit at all, but a quite extraordinary unit which is the product of extraordinary political circumstances. The female relatives, unencumbered by menfolk or, apparently, young children, supply him with an abundance of labour, well in excess of the daily labour demand of the household. Surely no normal household could offer such a labour surplus, for while we should not underrate the labour input of women into the normal Athenian household, much of that labour would have been directly spent on the subsistence of that household, and only in abnormal circumstances did the supply of free female labour approximate in any way to the deliberate accumulation of slaves without subsistence duties such as made up the craft workshops.

If the division between use of slave labour in craft production and use of free labour in agriculture was not economically irrational, that is not to deny that it was compassed about with prejudices. Socrates, not entirely without irony, sums these up well in Xenophon's *Oikonomikos*:

> The trades known as the trades of artisans (*banausikai*) are decried with good reason and held in low esteem in the cities. They disfigure the body of those who practise and pursue them, by compelling them to remain seated and in the shade, and some even cause you to spend the whole day sitting by the fire. When the bodies get softened in this way the souls lose a great deal of their strength, and especially artisans' trades leave one very little time for friends and for the city, and the result is that men like these seem very inadequate in their relations with friends and when it comes to defending the city. Hence in some cities, especially those which have a military reputation, no citizen may pursue an artisan's trade (*banausikai tekhnai*).[44]

The political aspect of this prejudice similarly exercises Aristotle in his discussion of citizenship in Book 3 of the *Politics*:

> One problem concerning the citizen remains: is it really the case that the citizen is he who has the right to take part in the government (*arkhe*) or should we call the *banausoi* citizens? If we are to include these persons also, who have no part in *arkhai*, such

goodness cannot belong to every citizen, this man being a citizen. But if such a person is not a citizen, in what class are we to put him? He is not a metic nor a *xenos*. Can we say that there is no absurdity here? He is in the same position as slaves and freedmen. It is certain that we must not call citizens all those without whom there would be no city. Even children are not citizens in the same way as adults. Adults are citizens simply; but children are only hypothetically so. They are citizens, but imperfect ones. In ancient times the labouring population was slave and foreign in some places, which is why most of them are so today; and the best city will not make labourers citizens. If, however, he too is a citizen then we must say that the goodness we spoke of does not belong to every citizen, nor to every free man, but only to those who are released from necessary services. Those who provide necessary services for one man are slaves. Those who do it for the community are labourers (*banausoi*) and workmen (*thetes*).[45]

It is clear that for Aristotle the problem of the *banausos* as citizen is only a marginal, almost academic, problem. That the problem could be so marginal depended, at Athens at least, on the way in which the permanent labour force in craft production is dominated by slaves. Were this not the case Aristotle's question about the citizenship rights of the *banausos* would become a very serious one indeed.

The ideology of Athenian democracy depended upon the equality of the citizen body. Only if all citizens could reasonably be considered to be in certain senses equal could democratic mechanisms of government, and in particular popular courts, assembly and selection of magistrates by lot, be sustained. One sense in which it was important to be able to consider citizens equal, was in the ability to make political decisions: it is in the area that Protagoras' epistemology is so important for democracy, for it stressed that man was the measure and that while there could be better and worse judgements it was not a matter of some men being right and others wrong.[46] But there is also a practical sense in which citizens must be observed not to be grossly unequal, and that is in their access to the organs of democratic government: one side of this comes in the stress on the rule of law, but another side concerns physical access. This practical side is very much at issue in Pericles' Funeral Speech in Thucydides 2:

> The law secures equal justice for all in their private disputes, and according to a man's worth, as each enjoys a reputation for doing certain things well, he gets particular respect in public affairs not on a basis of rotation but according to his merit, and if a man has some good to contribute to the city he is not prevented because poverty makes his distinction less apparent. In matters of communal interest we respect the freedom of citizens, and in areas of mutual suspicion in our day-to-day manner of living, we neither get angry with our neighbour if he enjoys something, nor do we give him those black looks which do no immediate harm but put a burden on relations. We associate in a relaxed manner as regards private affairs, and in public matters fear, especially, keeps us from disobeying both those who are holding some office at any one time and the laws, and particularly those laws that work for the benefit of those who are wronged and all that are unwritten but are agreed to carry a burden of shame with them. (2.37.1–3)

It is vital for the plausibility of Pericles' claims in this passage that there should not be observable in Athens any significant number of free-born Athenians who were not "released from necessary services".[47]

Athens can be seen to have protected her democracy against the threat posed by those poor citizens, whose rights were, all too clearly, only hypothetical, in other ways too. Most notable here is the claim in Demosthenes 57 that: "Euboulides' slander of us is not only against the decree, it is contrary to the laws which command that the man who abuses one of the citizens, male or female, for working in the agora should be liable to prosecution for slander (*kakegoria*)." But in the same category should be seen the inviolability of the citizen's body, in direct contradistinction to the body of a slave. Demosthenes, again, puts this most clearly: "If you really want to know what difference it makes whether one is slave or free, you would find the greatest difference is this: for slaves it is the body that is liable for punishment for all misdemeanours, but free men, however great their misfortune, can at least keep their bodies safe."[48] This is a distinction which is constantly played up in Old Comedy, and although there is no doubt that this is in part because there is something curiously humorous about physical violence, the political importance of thus keeping slaves in their place, and so emphasizing the very different place of the citizen, is not to be ignored.[49]

I began this chapter with a tendentious hypothetical reaction to the story of Socrates and Aristarkhos, in which I suggested that Athenian use of slaves was both economically irrational and contrary to democratic principles. In the course of the chapter I have endeavoured to show that this is the very reverse of the truth. There was a high degree of economic rationality to Athenian behaviour with regard to the employment of slaves: many of the jobs which slaves were employed to do were jobs which were either only worth having performed if they cost no more than minimal maintenance (as with domestic labour for most of the population) or else yielded insufficient clear profit to enable a citizen family to survive, let alone to achieve upward social mobility. Aristotle's discussion of the slave as a "living tool" (*organon empsukhon*)[50] is helpful here: slaves were employed precisely in those circumstances where what was required was merely an instrument, and where the only human labour that could be justified economically was the labour of humans who approximated to tools. But there were compelling political reasons for using slaves too: slave labour in occupations where the labourer approximated to a tool was vital to the prospect of maintaining democratic principles. Only if citizens could be exempted from the obvious subservience to others involved in domestic labour and from the degradation of performing physically constricting and scarcely tolerable tasks such as working in the mines was it possible for them to maintain that they all were equal and all equally had an active role to play in sustaining democracy.

It has often been maintained that it was only the presence of slaves that gave citizens the leisure to devote to politics,[51] and it is in this sense that Finley maintained that the growth of freedom and the growth of slavery went hand in hand.[52] There is a sense in which this seems to be a dubious claim: the agricultural basis of the citizen economy was itself enough to ensure that for much of the year time was not at a premium for the Athenian citizen, and slaves were not required to free the citizen to engage in political activity. But there is another sense in which Finley's claim seems correct: it was, arguably, only the presence of slaves that enabled the fiction of citizen equality to be maintained. Slaves ensured that citizens were not obliged to perform domestic tasks for others or work in craft workshops or the mines where they would both have been deprived of leisure and have been quite apparently subject to, rather than on a par with, other citizens. The prejudice so frequently found against having to spend one's life working indoors, in a situation of dependence on others, was part of a strategy which, by so strongly stressing the degradation of roles other than those of the citizen farmer, served to suggest that all who were not compelled to produce for or work for others were of course equal. Such prejudice was the prejudice of those who liked to regard themselves as an élite, and it was a prejudice shared with and taken over from the aristocracy. But similarly the whole ideology of democracy in Athens was élitist (and framed the aristocracy's terms) as it separated off Athenians as superior to all others, Greeks and barbarians alike.

Was this dependence of Athenian democracy on an underclass of slaves (and similarly on an underclass of women, but that is another story)[53] a unique product of the pressures of direct democracy? We might imagine that once one is dealing with a "representative" democracy the respects in which citizens must be seen to be equal are much reduced – that they need to have equally unhindered access to the ballot box but little else. But to take that view is to assume that shared voting privileges are all that membership of a modern democratic community is about. Clearly, whether they are formally defined or not, civic rights are a bundle in which the ability to cast a vote is only one part. The greater the number of respects in which citizens can expect to be equal, the more difficult it is to achieve a situation where even a fiction of such equality can be maintained. It was not *democracy* as such which slavery enabled in Athens, but a particular conception of the citizen body as made up of an essentially homogeneous body of men, none of whom were subject to constraints imposed by other individuals. This is a conception which modern Western democracy certainly shares with classical Athens.

If we ask why Athens came to depend on slaves, our answer must have both economic and political elements. For dependence on slavery could only occur when there was a society which both consciously identified itself as sharing at least some basic political and social rights and privileges on essentially equal conditions, and came to regard it as necessary or desirable to engage in enterprises which would have been impossible without using others in such a way as to make the pretence that they shared those basic rights and privileges impossible to sustain. Although in Athens the circumstance in which the impossibility of employing citizen labour can be most easily illustrated is the silver mines, it is arguable that it is the scale of the economic unit which is really crucial: large agricultural estates were in the end as incompatible with wholly citizen labour as were industrial enterprises, as the case of Sparta (for all the additional complicating factors involved) might be held to demonstrate. Both democracy and oligarchy might be dependent on slaves: the maintenance of an aristocracy in the face of pressure to acknowledge the effective dependence of the city on a wider body of citizens, and the undertaking of economic activities on any large scale within a city with a citizen body with established privileges, both demanded an underclass who were excluded from the citizen body. Given the combination of a certain conception of citizenship with economic units larger than the household it is difficult to see how some form or another of slavery was to be avoided.

The graphic exploitation of slaves, in enabling the visible exploitation of citizens to be avoided, upheld an ideology rather than simply a body of practices. If we observe the way in which American democracy was built on the back of negro slavery, the way in which British democratic practice has developed through the exclusion of women, and the way in which both America and western Europe currently exploit certain sections of immigrant labour,[54] we might note that modern representative democracy's more restricted citizen freedoms are equally built on the effective denial of those freedoms to those whose citizenship links are conveniently tenuous.[55]

# NOTES

1   Such is, I think, the implication of Jones 1957: 25.
2   Hypereides frg. 33 Blass, 29 Kenyon, *Souda* s.v. 'Ἀπεψηφίσατο. The word "slaves" actually has to be restored in the *Souda*'s text, but that restoration, and the context, seem safely to be inferred from frs 31 and 32 Blass (27 and 28 Kenyon).
3   Athenaios, *Deipnosophistai* 272c; Thucydides 7.27.5 with de Ste. Croix 1957: 56 for the interpretation of *kheirotekhnai*. On questions of Athenian demography in the fourth century see Hansen 1985 (especially pp. 28–36 on Ktesikles). Paul Cartledge has pointed out to me that it is just possible that Thucydides had reliable information about the number of slaves fleeing during the Peloponnesian War from the tithing of the money raised from selling them on.
4   Lysias 12.19; Demosthenes 27.9; Aeschines 1.97; Demosthenes 37.4; Demosthenes 36.11 with Davies 1971: 433–4.
5   Lysias 5.5.
6   Demosthenes 45.86.
7   One can compare the expectation of the disabled man defending his right to a state pension that it was reasonable for him to expect to have a slave: Lysias 24.6.
8   The Attic stelai are *IG* i$^3$ 421–30. Excerpts with commentary are to be found in *ML* 79 with translations in Fornara (1977/83) 147D. Full discussion is to be found in Pritchett 1953, 1956; the list of sailors is *IG* i$^3$ 1032.
9   See Lewis 1966.
10  On Axiokhos see Davies 1971 no. 600 VI (B).
11  These groups of slaves can be compared with those attested in the wills of philosophers given by Diogenes Laertius: Aristotle's will (D.L. 5.11–16) mentions at least 12 slaves, for 4 of whom freedom is arranged; Theophrastos' will (5.51–7) mentions 8 slaves and arranges to free 5; Straton's will (5.61–4) mentions 7, arranging freedom for 4; Lykon's will (5.69–74) mentions 13, arranging freedom for 11.
12  *IG* ii$^2$ 1951. See the discussion in Garlan 1988b: 166.
13  Compare Finley 1980: 82.
14  *IG* i$^3$ 476.183ff (408/7). On this see Randall 1953.
15  *IG* ii$^2$ 1672.190.
16  With the possible exception of the maverick claim at [Demosthenes] 42.20.
17  Xenophon, *Poroi* 4.15–16.
18  Conophagos 1980:341ff. for a figure of 11,000, Kalcyk 1982 for a figure of 22,100. Lauffer 1979 suggests that at the fourth-century peak over 30,000 slaves may have been working in the mines.
19  Compare Xenophon, *Memorabilia* 3.6.12.
20  See Lewis 1959: 231.
21  Demosthenes 57.35, 42.
22  Cf. Theophrastos, *Characters* 16.12.

23  Theophrastos, *Characters* 22.10; Lysias 1.8, 16, 37; [Demosthenes] 47.55–60; Menander, *Georgos* 56ff.
24  So [Demosthenes] 47.56, Menander, *Samia* 236ff.
25  Compare also the use of *doulos* and *oiketes* together in *Laws* 763a and 853d where it is similarly clear that the *oiketai* are a subset of *douloi*. I do not find any clear evidence for thinking that in the classical period *oiketes* (or *therapon*) could be used of a free man (contrast Wood 1988: 49).
26  The case for large-scale use of slaves was made by Jameson 1977, and from another angle by de Ste. Croix 1981. The case against is strongly put by Wood 1988.
27  Xenophon, *Oikonomikos* 13, and see especially Garlan 1988a.
28  Osborne 1985: 41 n.82.
29  Garnsey 1985; cf. Osborne 1987: 46 "about 40 per cent of which was probably exploited for agriculture of some sort".
30  Garnsey 1988 suggests 17.5 per cent as "likely" area cultivated with cereals each year.
31  Osborne 1992.
32  Halstead and Jones 1989; compare also Davis 1977: chapter 2, part 4 (for modern Metaponto). The harvesting of olives can also be extremely labour intensive (see Wagstaff and Augustson 1982: 113–20, table 10.12 and fig. 10.7), but unfortunately we have no way of assessing the area of olives in classical Attica nor how the olives were distributed between estates of rich and of poor.
33  Halstead and Jones give a figure of 30 days for the harvest period, but that is allowing for harvest of wheat, which ripens slightly later, as well as barley. Since it is generally thought that barley predominated in the Attic harvest I have accordingly calculated with that in mind.
34  Early modern English figures for reaping and binding are considerably lower than even the lowest of Halstead and Jones' figures: compare L. Meagre *The Mystery of Husbandry* (London, 1697) 66 and J. Mortimer *The Whole Art of Husbandry* (1707), both reckoning that a reaper and binder can manage 1 acre a day (i.e. 5 man-days a hectare for reaping and binding). Columella gives 1 ½ days per *iugerum* for reaping wheat, 1 day per *iugerum* for barley (2.12.1). Halstead and Jones note that their highest figures are a product of having a high proportion of elderly women in the labour force, and that faster rates were expected of hired labour.
35  Compare the conclusions of Halstead and Jones (1989: 47) on how tight the harvest period is even for those who are farming the minimum area necessary for subsistence. Halstead reports (paper to Laurence Seminar in Cambridge, 25 May 1992) that Greek farmers themselves reckon that about 3 ha. of cereals is as much as the normal family labour unit can harvest.
36  Note that it is hired bands of harvesters who dominate the ancient evidence for hired agricultural labour: Xenophon, *Hiero* 6.10; Demosthenes 18.51. Cf. Euripides' satyr play *The Reapers*, put on at the same time as *Medea*.
37  Compare Osborne 1991 on Phainippos' strategy.
38  Osborne 1987: 13–16.
39  Gallant 1991: 11–33, 60–112.
40  Aristotle, *Politics* 1252b12 apropos of what is, interestingly, a misreading of Hesiod, *Works and Days* 405.
41  Halstead reports that elderly modern Greek farmers suggest that you need a farm of 5 ha. or more to make it worthwhile keeping a yoke of oxen (although some sharing of oxen between households does occur) (Laurence Seminar, Cambridge, 25 May 1992).
42  Todd 1990: 168.
43  Aristotle, *Politics* 1334a20–1 quotes the adage "no leisure for slaves". See on this de Ste. Croix 1981: 184.

44 Xenophon, *Oikonomikos* 4.2–4.
45 Aristotle, *Politics* (1277b33–1278a13).
46 Plato, *Theaetetus* (especially 166e–167b), and the myth in the *Protagoras* (320c–328c). See especially Farrar 1988.
47 It is worth noting that Aristotle goes on to discuss limitation of citizenship rights in some democracies to those born from two citizen parents. Has he changed tack here, or is he observing an unduly high proportion of those of mixed parentage among those performing banausic tasks? If he does associate those of mixed parentage with those performing such tasks, it might be the case that we should see Pericles' Citizenship Law as staving off a crisis resulting from citizens of mixed birth obviously lacking full citizen rights. Pericles' law would have solved this by redefining the citizen in such a way as to exclude these *banausoi*.
48 Demosthenes 22.55; compare also Xenophon, *Oikonomikos* 13.9 where treating slaves as simply body is part of treating them as animals, and so making the same assumption which lies behind Aristotle's "natural" slaves.
49 For a marvellous illustration of this see Herodotus 4.1–4 (with the discussion by Finley 1980: 118).
50 Aristotle, *Politics* 1253b23–1254a13. On the question of the relationship between slavery and technological underdevelopment see Finley 1965. It will be clear from what I go on to say that the presence of a substantial subservient work-force is in my view more important than the presence of slaves as such, in the juridical sense.
51 So Sinclair 1988: 196–200.
52 Finley 1959: 164 (=1968: 72 and 1981: 115). Finley 1980: 89–90 comes much closer to stressing the ideological side (although with a curious emphasis on "psychology").
53 Cf. Hansen 1991: 318. Compare also Vidal-Naquet 1970.
54 This chapter has eschewed the explicit employment of comparative data from other societies. For a demonstration of just how illuminating such comparison can be, see Cartledge 1985.
55 Readers may find it instructive to compare what I have said with the account of Athenian slavery in Orlando Patterson's *Freedom* (London, 1991), which I read after completing my paper. Patterson perceives the political importance of slavery at Athens, but stimulatingly views it in a rather different perspective, as the following quotation from p. 78 will suffice to indicate: "The slave's alienness enhanced the value of the freeman's nativeness. And the master class, in turn, paid for its desecration of the community with the intrusion of slaves and other foreigners by making a special value of what it shared with all who were neither slaves nor aliens." I am grateful to Paul Cartledge, Willem Jongman, Anton Powell, Guy Rogers, Stephen Todd, and students and staff in the Ancient History department at Leiden for comments on an earlier version of this chapter.

## BIBLIOGRAPHY

Cartledge, P. A. (1985) "Rebels and *sambos* in classical Greece: a comparative view", in Cartledge and Harvey 1985, 16–46.
Cartledge, P. A. and Harvey, F. D. (eds) (1985) *Crux. Essays Presented to G. E. M. de Ste Croix on his 75th Birthday*, Exeter and London: Imprint Academic and Duckworth.
Conophagos, C. (1980) *Le Laurium antique*, Athens: Athena.
Davies, J. K. (1971) *Athenian Propertied Families 600–300 BC*, Oxford: Clarendon Press.
Davis, J. H. R. (1977) *People of the Mediterranean*, London: Routledge & Kegan Paul.

Farrar, C. (1988) *The Origins of Democratic Thinking. The Invention of Politics in Classical Athens*, Cambridge: Cambridge University Press.

Finley, M. I. (1959) "Was Greek civilisation based on slave labour?", *Historia* 8: 145–64, reprinted in Finley (1968) and (1981).

—— (1965) "Technological innovation and economic progress in the ancient world", *Economic History Review* 18: 29–45, reprinted in Finley (1981) 176–95.

—— (ed.) (1968) *Slavery in Classical Antiquity*, 2nd edn, Cambridge: Heffers.

—— (1980) *Ancient Slavery and Modern Ideology*, London: Chatto and Windus.

—— (1981) *Economy and Society of Ancient Greece*, ed. B. D. Shaw and R. P. Saller, London: Chatto and Windus.

Fornara, C. W. (ed.) (1977/83) *Translated Documents of Greece and Rome*, Vol. 1: *Archaic Times to the end of the Peloponnesian War*, Johns Hopkins University Press, 1977; 2nd edn, Cambridge: Cambridge University Press, 1983.

Gallant, T. W. (1991) *Risk and Survival in Ancient Greece. Reconstructing the Rural Domestic Economy*, Cambridge: Polity Press.

Garlan, Y. (1988a) "A propos des esclaves dans *l'Économique* de Xénophon", in M. Mactoux, E. Geny (eds) *Mélanges P. Lévêque*, Paris: Les Belles Lettres, 237–43.

—— (1988b) *Slavery in Ancient Greece*, translated by J. Lloyd, Ithaca and London: Cornell University Press.

Garnsey, P. D. A. (1985) "Grain for Athens", in Cartledge and Harvey (1985) 62–75.

—— (1988) *Famine and Food Supply in the Graeco-Roman World. Responses to Risk and Crisis*, Cambridge: Cambridge University Press.

Gordon, R. L. (ed.) (1981) *Myth, Religion and Society. Structuralist Essays by M. Detienne, L. Gernet, J.-P. Vernant and P. Vidal-Naquet*, Cambridge: Cambridge University Press.

Halstead, P. L. J. and Jones, G. (1989) "Agrarian ecology in the Greek Islands: time stress, scale and risk", *JHS* 109: 41–56.

Hansen, M. H. (1985) *Demography and Democracy. The Number of Athenian Citizens in the Fourth Century* BC, Herning: Systime.

—— (1991) *The Athenian Democracy in the Age of Demosthenes*, Oxford: Blackwell.

Jameson, M. H. (1977) "Agriculture and slavery in classical Athens", *CJ* 73: 122–41.

Jones, A. H. M. (1957) *Athenian Democracy*, Oxford: Blackwell.

Kalcyk, H. (1982) *Untersuchungen zum attischen Silberbergbau. Gebietstruktur, Geschichte und Technik*, Frankfurt.

Lauffer, S. (1979) *Die Bergwerkssklaven von Laureion*, 2nd edn, Forsch. ant. Sklav. 2.

Lewis, D. M. (1959) "Attic manumissions", *Hesperia* 28: 208–38.

—— (1966) "After the profanation of the Mysteries", in E. Badian (ed.), *Ancient Society and Institutions: Studies Presented to Victor Ehrenberg*, Oxford: Blackwell, 177–91.

Osborne, R. G. (1985) *Demos. The Discovery of Classical Attika*, Cambridge: Cambridge University Press.

—— (1987) *Classical Landscape with Figures. The Ancient Greek City and its Countryside*, London: George Philip.

—— (1991) "Pride and prejudice, sense and subsistence: exchange and society in the Greek city", in J. Rich and A. Wallace-Hadrill (eds), *City and Country in the Ancient World*, London: Routledge.

—— (1992) " 'Is it a farm?' The definition of agricultural sites and settlements in ancient Greece", in B. Wells (ed.), *Agriculture in Ancient Greece. Proceedings of the Seventh International Symposium at the Swedish Institute at Athens, 16–17 May, 1990*, Acta Instituti Atheniensis Regni Suediae, Series in 4°, XLII, 21–5.

Pritchett, W. K. (1953) "The Attic Stelai. Part 1", *Hesperia* 22: 225–99.

—— (1956) "The Attic Stelai. Part 2", *Hesperia* 25: 178–317.

Randall, R. H. (1953) "The Erechtheum workmen", *AJA* 57: 199–210.

Sinclair, R. K. (1988) *Democracy and Participation in Athens*, Cambridge: Cambridge University Press.

Ste. Croix, G. E. M. de (1957) "Slavery", *CR* 7: 54–9.

——(1981) *The Class Struggle in the Ancient Greek World*, London: Duckworth.

Todd, S. C. (1990) "*Lady Chatterley's Lover* and the Attic orators: the social composition of the Athenian jury", *JHS* 110: 146–73.

Vidal-Naquet, P. (1970) "Esclavage et gynécocratie dans la tradition, le mythe et l'utopie", in C. Nicolet (ed.), *Recherches sur les structures sociales dans l'antiquité classique*, Colloques nationaux du CNRS, Paris: CNRS, 63–80, translated in Gordon (1981) 187–200 and in Vidal-Naquet (1986) 205–23.

——(1986) *The Black Hunter. Forms of Thought and Forms of Society in the Greek World*, Baltimore and London: Johns Hopkins University Press.

Wagstaff, J. M. and Augustson, S. (1982) "Traditional land use", in A. C. Renfrew and J. M. Wagstaff (eds), *An Island Polity. The Archaeology of Exploitation in Melos*, Cambridge: Cambridge University Press, 106–33.

Wood, E. M. (1988) *Peasant-citizen and Slave. The Foundations of Athenian Democracy*, London: Verso.

# Women and Democracy in Fourth-century Athens

## *Michael H. Jameson*

Michael Jameson discusses ancient criticisms of democracy for its supposed tendency to grant undue freedom to women and slaves.

The exploitation of persons of subordinate status took two contrasting forms in Greece, as we have come to understand especially from Moses Finley and Yvon Garlan.[1] The older and perhaps at one time universal type consisted of a series of gradations socially, juridically, politically, from persons with the most complete power and privilege to those with the least. Instead of clearly defined categories, the result was a continuous spectrum ranging from full, adult male members of the community (among whom there were further distinctions of property and genealogy) through serf-like statuses to chattel slaves. Sparta and the Cretan cities are the clearest examples. Some degree of movement between the grades is observable. By contrast, democratic Athens is the best example of societies with a few, sharply delineated statuses – adult male citizens, resident foreigners (metics, among whom are included freedmen), and chattel slaves. Women are a further category but also divided threefold, between those whose guardians (*kurioi*) are citizens or foreigners and those who are themselves slaves.

Michael Jameson, "Women and Democracy in Fourth-century Athens," in P. Brulé and J. Oulhen (eds.) *Esclavage, guerre, économie en Grèce ancienne. Hommages à Yvon Garlan* (Rennes: Presses Universitaires de Rennes, 1997), pp. 95–107.

It has been pointed out that in societies such as Athens where adult males of citizen birth enjoyed the greatest political rights without property qualifications, the exclusion of the unfree and of women was most thorough. Spartan women were notoriously free in their behavior and influential (e.g., Arist. *Pol.* 1269b–1270a). Athenian women were ideally silent, anonymous and invisible, except in certain cult contexts. They were to confine themselves to the house, not even answering a knock on the door and certainly not running out to the street (Menander Fr. 592 Koerte). They were not to associate with unrelated male visitors who came to the house. Their ownership of property was severely limited. The same sharpening of distinctions is found between slaves, a single category, and the free, and again between foreigners and natives with, by the mid-fifth century, strict prohibitions on intermarriage. The more valuable the rights of membership in the community became, the higher the barriers between the citizens and the excluded.

But at the same time there were proportionately far more foreigners permanently resident in Athens, and vital to the economy, than in most Greek cities, although grants to them of citizenship were very rare. Chattel slaves too were unusually numerous and played a large and varied rôle in social and economic life. Alongside the inverse relationship between the freedom of citizens and the rights of all other inhabitants there needs to be set a Greek view of the situation which has attracted less attention. This is the claim that in Athens foreigners, slaves and especially women were, in fact, exceptionally and dangerously free and equal in the encounters of daily life, whatever custom and law laid down, and that this was directly attributable to the extreme form of democracy. It is particularly this alleged freedom of women under democracy that I wish to address in this essay.

Plato's surprising recommendation in the *Republic* that in the ideal state women be given the same training as men and that qualified women serve as guardians (451–457) has tended to obscure the more conventional conceptions of women to be found in his writings. He has no doubt that women as a whole are inferior to men (455; *Laws* 781b). They are subject to emotions more than are men and certain soothing forms of music are appropriate for them (*Laws* 909e–910b). With children, they share a fondness for bright, variegated colors (*Republic* 557c). Most remarkable is his insistence that democracy fosters the freedom of women, a dangerous development that both he and Aristotle link to that posed by the freedom of slaves. Democracy, by promoting the concept of liberty, subverts all hierarchical relationships in society and thus opens up the possibility of liberty for both women and slaves and hence their equality with male citizens.

> "[The desire for liberty] necessarily penetrates...into private houses and finally to the implantating of anarchy even in the animals.... So the father must practice becoming like his child, and being afraid of his sons, while the son acts like the father and shows no respect or fear for the parents, all for the sake of his freedom. Metic and citizen and citizen and metic, all must be equal, and the same goes for the visiting foreigner."

Teachers and older men in general ingratiate themselves with their young charges while the young do not take them seriously but act as if they were on the same level.

"The liberty of the masses reaches its very limit in such a city [a democracy] when the purchased slaves, male and female, are no less free than those who paid for them. And the degree to which equal rights (*isonomia*) and liberty apply to the relations of women to men and of men to women, is something I nearly forgot to mention." (Plato *Rep.* 562e–563b)[2]

Compare with this a passage in the oligarchic pamphlet written in the last decades of the fifth century and included in the manuscripts of Xenophon's writings (*Ath. Pol.*1.10–12):

"At Athens extreme lack of discipline (*akolasia*) prevails among slaves and metics. There one cannot strike them and a slave will not get out of one's way. Let me explain the reason for this local custom: if it were customary for a free man to beat a slave, or (for that matter) a metic or a freedman, one would often strike an Athenian (citizen) thinking he was a slave. The people there are no better dressed than the slaves and the metics, and they look no better. If anyone is surprised that the Athenians allow slaves to live so well there, and some even to live extravagantly, they can be shown to do this too quite deliberately. For wherever a city's power is maritime, for financial reasons it is absolutely necessary to be subservient to the slaves in order to profit from their earnings and the same applies to setting them free [i.e., their owners take a cut from their wages and profits, and they are freed on condition of payments to their former owners]. Where slaves are well-to-do, it is no longer to my advantage for my slave to be afraid of you. At Sparta my slave fears you (which may seem right and proper) but if your slave fears me, there is the danger that he will give me the money he has earned (and to which you are entitled as his master) so as not be in danger himself. This is why we have granted freedom of speech (*isegoria*, literally "equality of speech") both to slaves when they face free men and to metics when they face citizens because the city needs the metics on account of the many crafts they practice and our maritime way of life. That is why it is quite reasonable that we have also granted metics freedom of speech."

One need not suppose that the upper classes were, in fact, inhibited as they made their way through the streets of Athens. The hyperbole itself is revealing.

Plato, further on in the passage we were considering, gives a comic twist to the Old Oligarch's splenetic version of what was evidently a topos:

"No one who had not experienced it would believe how much more liberty the beasts have (in a democracy) than anywhere else. The dogs absolutely act out the old saying, 'Like mistress, like maid,' and the horses and donkeys are accustomed to making their way with complete freedom and dignity, bumping into anyone they meet on the street who does not get out of their way" –

A familiar experience, we are told, when one leaves Athens for the countryside (*Rep.* 563c–d; cf. *Laws* 942c–d: military training removes *anarchia* entirely from beasts as well as the men they serve). A complaint levelled against slaves and foreigners by Pseudo-Xenophon is now shown to be an example of a universal break-down of relationships brought about by extreme democracy.[3] In well-ordered, traditional societies the élite were identified unambiguously. Both custom (dress, ornaments, hair-style,) and natural condition (health and stature, for instance) marked off classes and statuses. Even in more moderate democracies, the free poor might not differ greatly in appearance from the slaves but they knew their place in the social hierarchy. The élite, for their part, were united on the necessity of keeping all others in their respective places.

In such societies, no slave had an opportunity to engage in more than the most menial work or to be entrusted with responsibilities and to be rewarded accordingly (the farm bailiff is an exception but that was a job dealing with other slaves, largely out of sight of citizens). In Athens, however, slaves and citizens performed the same tasks, sometimes side by side, as the records for the construction of the Erechtheion show, and if the slave was to earn enough to be profitable to his owner his conditions of work and life needed to approach those of the free workman.[4] Whereas in the New World slavery and race were inseparable, in antiquity everyone was at risk of enslavement. In practice, the Greeks derived the bulk of their slaves from non-Greek peoples. But although these included the grey-eyed, red-haired Thracians of the poet Xenophanes and a great many Anatolians, the racial affiliations of most slaves would not have revealed their status. On the other hand, the free poor, whether citizen, metic or freedman, with little or no land or other property to their name, would often have had to work for others, a subservience that could seem incompatible with the status of a citizen. Meanwhile talented slaves were earning good wages for their owners and being given the responsibility of running businesses as well as farms. From a traditional point of view, things were turned upside down.

The free ways of metics and slaves at Athens are the subject of Pseudo-Xenophon's explanation. Aristotle builds on Plato's equation of democracy and license to focus on women. He sees democracy, in which artisans and wage-earners (*banausoi* and *mistharnountes*) predominate, in contrast to the democracy of farmers (*Pol.* 1296b), as equivalent to tyranny, with the *demos* as tyrant.

> "Also the things that occur in the final form of democracy are all favorable to tyranny – dominance by women (*gunokratia*) in the homes, in order that they may carry abroad reports against the men, and lack of discipline (*akolasia*) among the slaves, for the same reason; for slaves and women do not plot against tyrants, and also, if they prosper under tyrannies, must feel well-disposed to them, and to democracies as well (for the common people also wishes to be sole ruler). Hence also the flatterer is in honor with both." (*Pol.* 1313b–1314a)

Aristotle employs for solemn political theory what in the theater was a comic theme – a man is happy in the *agora* "but when the poor wretch opens the door of his house, woman controls everything (*gunê kratei pantôn*), orders him about, fights him at every turn" (Menander *Fr.* 251, 5–7). Women and slaves are not feared by the tyrant because they are not rivals to his power as free citizens must be. So he treats them with tolerance and they him with flattery. (The flatterer of the *demos* is the *demagogue*.) Aristotle speaks of "dominance by women in the home." They are not merely equal but superior in power in the household and this is said to be granted to them (presumably by the tyrant or the tyrannical regime) *in order that* they may report abroad, outside the house, against the men. There is relaxation of controls (*anesis*) over slaves for the same reason. Again, the tyrant's enemy is the free male citizen who, in a household where women rule and slaves are relatively free, cannot be sure of the confidentiality of his speech and associations. Women, as well as slaves, are able to go outside the house to report what has gone on inside. The possibility of discontent or conspiracy being divulged is as advantageous to a democracy as it is to a tyranny. (The notion of women as secret agents or provocatrices is anticipated at *Pol.* 1313b 11–17 in a reference to Hieron's *potagôgides* at Syracuse.) Freedom of movement as well as of speech for women and slaves is seen as characteristic of democracies and tyrannies. Needless to say, for Aristotle *gunokratia* anywhere is contrary to nature, the male being naturally superior to the female (*Pol.* 1254b), the one ruling, the other being ruled (1260a). Aristotle encapsulates anxiety over the freedom of women and slaves in a vision of espionage and offers it as the explanation for a much broader phenomenon.

The passages we have been examining all seem to reflect a common anti-democratic theme which persisted in one form or another for at least a century. Full democracy in the eyes of its detractors threatened by its very nature three distinctions vital to the existence of the *polis*: (1) between free men and slaves; (2) between citizens and foreigners; (3) between men and women, who ideally participated only in the life of the family and, indispensably, in religious activities. The erosion of boundaries between these statuses would have been regarded by all Greek *politai* (i.e. free male *polis* members) as tantamount to anarchy. The anti-democratic argument claimed that full democracy without property qualifications led inevitably to this anarchy. Meanwhile, despite the looming shadow of Macedon, internally the Athenian democracy survived and in some respects flourished.

It requires no serious demonstration to show that, for all the alarmist talk of our sources, there was not the slightest possibility of an overthrow of male, citizen rule by slaves, resident foreigners or women. Slaves were no threat and there were no slave revolts at Athens until the second century BC.[5] Their procurement from many different sources, as recommended by the philosophers (cf. Arist. *Pol.* 1330a), is just what happened at Athens. In daily life they were isolated from other slaves or worked in small groups and were closely involved with individual households, the great exception, of course, being those in the mines, but even there they did not work in large gangs. That this alarm on the part of the privileged is also directed against resident foreigners and women shows that the anxiety takes the form of fantasy.

The real concerns of the citizen body are not likely to have been uniform throughout. Comparison with modern societies suggests that the attitude of the lower classes to others excluded from their civic privileges, both those richer and socially more acceptable than themselves and their economic equals and inferiors, is likely to have been ambivalent. We do not, however, hear of the inflammatory issue of today, citizens' deprivation of employment by foreign immigrants or slaves, in part perhaps because of the reluctance to admit to the need of working for someone else.

The perspective of the upper classes is, as always, a good deal clearer. Pseudo-Xenophon offered a plausible description of the relations between men of different status in the streets of Athens. All the poor are lumped together – citizens, foreigners and slaves – but the equal rights of one element indistinguishable to the eye in the mass of the poor, the poor citizens, puts all the poor beyond the reach of discipline. One could not strike a man who looked poor, nor a woman. How easy it was for citizen men to strike women they took to be slaves can be seen from incidents reported in the Demosthenic corpus ([Dem.] 59.9–10, [Dem.] 47.55–67; in the latter case men claiming property had to be dissuaded from carrying off a son of the citizen family whom they had taken to be a slave (61). No doubt, all small boys playing around farm yards looked much alike).

Two reports illustrate the upper classes' assumption that all the excluded statuses were aligned with the *demos* against their betters. In 404 BC Theramenes assures the Thirty Tyrants that he had always fought against the view that there could be no good democracy without the participation of "slaves and those who, from poverty, would sell the city for a drachma (i.e., the free, native poor)" (Xen. *Hell.* 2.3.48), as if the enfranchisement of slaves was ever the goal of the radical democracy.[6] From 318 BC we have an account from Plutarch (*Phocion* 34) of the condemnation of the anti-democratic general Phocion and his associates. It claims that slaves, foreigners, and disfranchised citizens were among the judges while women as well as men (*pasi kai pasais*) were allowed into the theater where the trial took place. What is of interest here is the linking of all three excluded categories (slaves, foreigners and women) as having had a hand in the humiliation of the conservative hero, not in the factuality of the claim.[7] The point of view of Plutarch's source is fully in accord with Plato's, that the principles of democracy inevitably lead to the breakdown of essential status distinctions, and with Aristotle's, that women and slaves conspire against the free (upper-class) males. The metic philosopher is silent about his own category.

When it comes to women in the democracy, a category with no direct impact on politics, one must ask what accounts for the philosophers' tirades whose tone, when not simply comic, verges on the hysterical. There was, to be sure, a long tradition of Greek misogyny, often dressed in comic guise, beginning for us with Hesiod and Semonides of Amorgos. In Greek culture as a whole the largest, most conspicuous and most permanent source of possible subversion to the state and to the established social order was none other than "woman." The irrationality of women, and there-fore their innate opposition to the well-ordered society managed by rational men is recognized as a characteristic tenet of Greek male ideology. "[...] male attitudes to women [...] are marked by tension, anxiety and fear. Women are not part of [...] the male ordered world of the 'civilised' community; [...] they threaten continually to overturn its stability and to subvert its continuinity [...]", to quote John Gould. Or, in the words of Claude Mossé: "Dans la cité des hommes, la femme est du côté de tout ce qui menace l'ordre: le sauvage, le cru, l'humide, le barbare, l'esclave, le tyran."[8]

But whereas it is evident that male writers of all types and at all times could easily tap the rich vein of the misogynist tradition, this does not explain why the alarm is sounded at this time and linked precisely with democracy. It may be chance that Pseudo-Xenophon, writing in the last third of the fifth century, speaks only of foreigners and slaves and has nothing to say of (3), the equality and freedom of women. Or it may be that it was not until the fourth century that anxiety on this score, genuine or feigned, was joined to the other two. In Aristophanes' *Lysistrata* (411) and *Ecclesiazousae* (392) women make use of the institutions of contemporary Athens but an excess of democracy is not specified as the cause of their insurrection. Nor does it seem to me that these plays show that philosophical discussion of the ideal rôle of women was a subject of current debate. Their plots are examples of the topsy-turvy world of Aristophanic fantasy. At a deeper level, however, they may express the permanent anxiety of the Greek masculine world over its imperfect control over the female other half.[9]

Plato and Aristotle's fantasies of imminent or present *gunokratia* are no less unrealistic but their true target is not women's liberation but democracy against which they employ the clichés of misogyny. And yet, I suggest, the realities of everyday life in democratic Athens offered the toehold of verisimilitude without which satire cannot be effective. One of the few interpreters of Plato to consider *Republic* 563a critically finds Plato's comments so absurd in view of the lack of liberty for intellectuals as well as women that she cannot believe Plato has Athens in mind when describing the tolerance of the extreme democratic state.[10] But Plato uses the *topos* of Pseudo-Xenophon which is explicitly applied to Athens, and one of the interlocutors in the *Republic* confirms that it is, indeed, a specifically Athenian traffic jam Plato has described. In any case, what other democracy could either Plato or Aristotle be referring to?

In fact, after the flurry of genuine, threatened, or alleged prosecutions for impiety directed against intellectuals at Athens in the late fifth century and after the single certain case of a death penalty and execution, that of Socrates, we hear of no action against philosophers for seventy-five years, until 323 BC when Aristotle prudently withdraws from Athens on the death of Alexander. But in this same period we know of three cases of prosecutions of women for impiety, and at least three other cases in which, though not charged, or not charged with impiety, their dangerous behavior plays a prominent part. They are all, as far as we can see, foreigners, and there are charges or implications of servile origin, sexual and social promiscuity, orgiastic cults and affronts to the vital mysteries of citizen women, of drugs and magic, and of alien penetration of the citizen body. The citizen's wife is the particular and vulnerable target – foolish women may see the acquittal of the wicked foreigners as permission to do as they like ([Dem.] 59.11). The contagion that is feared – lack of self-control or discipline (*akolasia*) – is characteristic of women and the young. Solon's law restricting women at funerals and festivals was to prevent *to atakton kai to akolaston* (Plut. *Solon.* 21, the same two qualities that characterize the Thessaly to which Sokrates declines to escape, Plato *Crito* 53d).[11]

Foreign women, most of them purported to be ex-slaves, introducing new private cults, dealing in vulgar and hostile but trivial forms of ritual action, participating illegitimately in ceremonies of citizen women – these seem very marginal figures to bulk so large in Athenian rhetoric and legal action in defense of piety and purity. An explanation may be proposed for the concern over them, and over the allegedly free, equal and power-hungry women of the philosophers. While the public, political sphere remained impregnable so long as the democracy survived, in the area of social relations the discrepancy between ideal and the real had reached a point that it served to fuel anxiety over status relations in general. The economic ties between citizens and metics, the attachment of the slave as *oiketes* to an *oikos*, no doubt affected in practice the boundaries between the statuses. It was, for instance, the act of a Boorish Man to discuss important matters with his slaves rather than friends or family but no doubt it happened (Theoph. *Characters* 4.6).

The discrepancy was most evident, constant and intimate in the case of Athenian women. The standards of respectable women staying at home, leaving the house neither for shopping nor work, and appearing in public only at festivals and funerals and then only properly attended, were articles of ideology, not necessarily a description of current practice. To be sure, Plato in the *Laws* (781b), all fear of liberated women forgotten, raises the problem of inducing women to eat at public messes when they are "accustomed to living withdrawn and darkly." An élite should have been able to keep its women at home with the help of slaves, but the example of non-élite women and the lack of sharp demarcation *within* the citizen body may have made this difficult. The farther down the economic scale the less feasible it became. Poorer women of any status had to shop, work in the fields, and help in the family's business as needed or run their own business, or even hire out to others, though this may be described as "slavish" (*doulika*, Dem. 57.45). "How is it possible to prevent the women of the poor (*aporoi*) from going out?" (Aristot. *Pol.* 1300a, cf. 1323a, "The poor have to use their women and children as servants because they lack slaves.")[12] In a society where political power was in the hands of "the many" the majority of the majority was inevitably poor, however poverty was defined. Just how the Athenian citizen population was divided economically is a complex problem. It seems likely that most Athenians were neither wealthy nor close to destitution and that there was, in effect, a large "middling" population. We do not know where the line was drawn in respect to working women any more than we do for the ownership of slaves.[13]

There was a comparable contradiction in the attitude to work in general. The orators freely cite the vulgar occupations of their opponents while it is evident that many in the audience were similarly employed. K. J. Dover has suggested as a possible explanation that the listeners may have adopted the values of the well-to-do. This could apply equally to the attitude towards the seclusion of women. In the modern world one might compare the prized respectability of the lower middle class as it seeks to distance itself from a lower class.[14]

The freedom of movement of women in the democracy is taken by Aristotle to exemplify the general freedom they enjoy under a radical regime, but it is not to be separated from the freedom of foreigners, slaves, and, we must not forget, beasts. In the philosophers' parables, democracy through tolerance of these liberties under-mines the *polis*, with no distinction being made between social and political relations. For Pseudo-Xenophon this stemmed from the distinctive maritime character of Athenian democracy, both militarily and economically. It benefitted from the free economic activity of foreigners and the relative independence of many slaves, in both cases of both sexes, we might add. The radical democracy, with the poorest citizens supplying the bulk of the fleet's rowers, ensured the dignity of the poor and, practically, of their women who because of their poverty violated by their activity outside the house the standards of behavior to which rich and poor paid lip service. Even within the house all women, but especially those who were not rich, bore responsibility for running the household as an economic unit (cf. Xenophon's *Oeconomicus*, with allowance for the wealth involved). Their bossiness in the house, which Aristotle's *gunokratia* implies, was also something expected of them.

Formally the three categories of exclusion endured within the larger, traditional structure into the Hellenistic and Roman periods. But the society of the *poleis* as understood by the most privileged members was changing in important respects, most obviously in democratic Athens, in the direction of the significantly different Hellenistic world. In addition to the shift of most political power from individual or hegemonic cities to much larger monarchies, there were social and economic changes underway, which had not waited for the conquests of Alexander to make their appearance. The economy of the fourth century differed markedly from that of earlier centuries and social relations could not remain unaffected.[15] The large proportion of the Attic population that consisted of resident aliens and slaves, came to be matched in many Greek cities (cf. Arist. *Pol.* 1326a). Without significant political power and the opportunities as well as the risks offered by city-state bellicosity, the attractions of citizenship may have faded for all but the wealthy. While democracy in Athens had protected all the non-élite thanks, in part, to the difficulty of distinguishing among them, and this had allowed them to engage effectively in the economic life of the city, the continuing growth of pragmatic economic and social relationships did not depend on political democracy but on that tolerance against which the critics of democracy had inveighed.

The condition of women in the Hellenistic world also changed in various ways, though our evidence outside Egypt is largely limited to the upper classes among whom wealthy women became prominent, and much remains speculative. Marriage came to be more of an equal contract between two persons, supported in Stoic ethics by the concept of the mutually supportive couple. Legal and economic rights increased with the greater mobility of men and the *de facto* self-reliance of their women. But it is generally agreed that the fundamental subordination of women to men hardly changed.[16] More important for women may have been the decline for most men of the public sphere and of the structures supporting it and consequently the greater importance of the family and other social ties, such as the cult associations of individuals and families.[17] In Athens, which now in some respects lagged behind the new foundations, the city's religious life was dominated by an élite to a greater degree than under the democracy in its prime (though then too the rôle of families with religious prerogatives had been recognized). The imposition of sumptuary laws and of the office of *gunaikonomos* to control women was an internal measure directed at the upper classes, but at Athens that office may not have outlived the philosophical tyranny of Demetrius of Phaleron. Neither were relevant to the poor.[18]

None of this is revolutionary. The most stubborn boundary, that between slave and free, endured, unaffected in practice by new philosophies, but the form it took universally in Old Greece was that of chattel slavery.[19] Slaves continued to be economic agents for individual families. While government was, in the hands of the wealthy, and economic disparities and class tensions had greatly increased,[20] most of the free poor were still citizens and internal social relations do not seem to have abandoned the restraint established by Athenian democracy. The conditions for women were a long way from the philosophers' nightmares of liberty and equality but, aside from the attempts at regulation of élite expenditure and display, there is no indication of any increase in repression. One suspects, though one cannot prove, that what had suited the needs of democratic Athens in practice was found now to be advantageous for the rest of a non-democratic Greek world. The Attic language was, then, not the only Athenian creation that become a *koine* [common language].[21]

## NOTES

1   Moses Finley, *Economy and Society in Ancient Greece*, ed. B. Shaw and R. Saller, New York, Viking Press, 1982, ch. 8; Yvon Garlan, *Les Esclaves en Grèce ancienne*, 1982 (references are to the revised edition translated by Janet Lloyd, *Slavery in Ancient Greece*, Ithaca and London, Cornell University Press, 1988).

2   This passage is discussed by Jaqueline de Romilly, *Problèmes de la démocratie grecque*, Paris, Hermann, 1975, p. 113–16, who stops short of *Rep.* 563b.

3   " 'The regulation of traffic,' remarks Bosanquet, perhaps a little sententiously, 'is in some degree a real test of social order.' [...] No doubt this is what Plato means" (James Adam, in *The Republic of Plato*, Cambridge, Cambridge University Press, 1900, on 563c). Rather, the relations of the components of a society unlike any Greece had known before are the issue. Plato, for all his amusement with the beast in the road, saw what we might call the sociological implications of democracy.

4   R. H. Randall, Jr. "The Erechtheum Workmen," *AJA* 57 (1953), p. 199–210; Michel Austin and Pierre Vidal-Naquet, *Économies et sociétés en Grèce ancienne*, Paris, Armand Colin, 1972, p. 300–307.

5   Revolts by the Laurion miners, the first probably stimulated by reports of the Sicilian slave revolts, Diod. 34.2.19, Athen. 6.272e–f; Garlan, *op.cit.*, p. 183–184.

6   Aristotle (*Pol.* 1319b) assumes that radical democracies will be lax in their standards, admitting illegitimate sons and those with only one citizen parent in order to give the *demos* a majority.

7   Claude Mossé, *Athens in Decline 404–86 BC*, London and Boston, Routledge and Kegan Paul, 1973, p. 103–104, hesitates to accept the report but seems to draw a conclusion from it: "We shall have to admit that if Plutarch's assertion is well founded, the Athenian *demos* must have countenanced the presence in its ranks of slaves, aliens and even women. This reveals the extent to which the traditional ideal of the *polis* had altered in a few years." Only the admission of the disfranchised seems to me plausible, but the exaggeration is of a piece with earlier expressions of alarm.

8   J.-P. Gould, "Law, Custom and Myth: Aspects of the Social Position of Women in Classical Athens," *JHS* 100 (1980), p. 57; Claude Mossé, *La Femme dans la Grèce antique*, Paris, Albin Michel, 1983, p. 139–140. Cf. also the very balanced study of Roger Just, *Women in Athenian Law and Life*, London and New York, Routledge, 1989, ch. 9 and 10. For an influential essay by an anthropologist, see Sherry Ortner, "Is Female to Male as Nature is to Culture?" in Michelle Zimbalist Rosaldo and Louise Lamphere, editors, *Woman, Culture and Society*, Stanford University Press, Stanford, 1974, p. 67–87. Cf. also the collected essays of Carole Pateman, *The Disorder of Women. Democracy, Feminism and Political Theory*, Cambridge, Polity Press, 1989. For exploration of a number of these themes in myth, see Pierre Vidal-Naquet, "Esclavage et gynécocratie dans la tradition, le mythe, l'utopie," *Le chasseur noir*, Paris, 1981, p. 267–88 (translated and edited as "Slavery and the Rule of Women in Tradition, Myth and Utopia," by R. L. Gordon in *Myth, Religion and Society*, Cambridge, Cambridge University Press, 1981, p. 187–200).

9   Claude Vatin, "Recherches sur le mariage et la condition de la femme mariée à l'époque hellénistique," BEFAR 216; Paris, Boccard, p. 11: "le poète conjure par le rire une angoisse diffuse."

10  Julia Annas, *Introduction to Plato's Republic*, Oxford, Clarendon Press, 1981, p. 300.

11  *Akolasia* was characteristic of democracy in the eyes of another of its critics, cf. Isoc. 7.20, 121.131. I hope to offer a study of these "dangerous women" elsewhere and here only

call attention to them as a further example of heightened anxiety over women in the fourth century: Ninos (Dem. 19.281); Theoris ([Dem.] 25.79–80); Phryne (Athen. 13.590e); Sinope ([Dem.] 59.116–117); Alke (Isaeus 6.48–50); Neaira ([Dem.] 59). A number of these cases are reviewed from a different perspective by H. S. Versnel, *Inconsistencies in Greek Religion I. Ter Unus*, Leiden, E. J. Brill, 1990, p. 127–131. I know of only one prosecution for impiety in this period that does *not* involve a "dangerous woman," that of a group of Delian men for *asebeia* in expelling Athenian administrators from the island, *IG* II² 1635, 134–40.

12 The fact that women of the lower class worked and left the house has been recognized in recent years but there has been less interest in its implications. Cf., e.g., Sarah B. Pomeroy, *Goddesses, Whores, Wives, and Slaves. Women in Classical Antiquity*, New York, Schocken Books, 1975, p. 73; Mossé, *La Femme*, p. 58–59; Orlando Patterson, *Freedom in the Making of Western Culture*, Basic Books, 1991, p. 106–108; David Cohen, *Law, Sexuality and Society. The Enforcement of Morals in Classical Athens*, Cambridge, Cambridge University Press, 1991, p. 150–154; Virginia J. Hunter, *Policing Athens. Social Control in the Attic Lawsuits, 420–320 BC*, Princeton, Princeton University Press, 1994, p. 20, 29, in a study which also explores the informal powers of Athenian women; Elaine Fantham et al., *Women in the Classical World. Image and Text*, New York, Oxford University Press, 1994, p. 106–109.

13 See, most recently, Victor Davis Hanson, *The Other Greeks*, New York, Free Press, 1995, especially p. 478–479. Victor Ehrenberg wrote that "only very poor people of Athenian origin" would have allowed their women to work outside the house (*The People of Aristophanes*, New York, Schocken, 1962, p. 205). I do not see the justification for "very." For women beyond the age of child-bearing the restrictions probably were not strongly felt. "The woman who goes out of the house should be of such an age that on meeting her one asks not whose wife (*gune*) she is but whose mother" (Hyperides *ap.* Stob. 74.33).

14 K. J. Dover, *Greek Popular Morality in the Time of Plato and Aristotle*, Berkeley and Los Angeles, University of California Press, 1974, p. 34–35, who, however, is more inclined to suppose that jurors were in fact "fairly prosperous." Josiah Ober, *Mass and Elite in Democratic Athens. Rhetoric, Ideology, and the Power of the People*, Princeton, Princeton University Press, 1989, p. 272–277, cites examples of public respect or at least tolerance for hard and even menial work, but grants that simultaneously "popular ideology reflected an aristocratic ethos which regarded all manual labor as inherently slavish [...]" (277). For the hoplite as the ideal Athenian, cf. Hanson, *op. cit.*, p. 384–385.

15 See, e.g., Mossé, *Athens in Decline*, p. 91; John K. Davies, *Wealth and the Power of Wealth in Classical Athens*, New York, Arno Press, 1981, p. 38–87; Paul McKechnie, *Outsiders in the Greek City in the Fourth Century BC*, London and New York, Routledge, 1989; Edward E. Cohen, *Athenian Economy and Society. A Banking Perspective*, Princeton, Princeton University Press, 1992, p. 3–8.

16 Cf. William S. Ferguson, *Hellenistic Athens. An Historical Essay*, London, Macmillan, 1911, p. 85–87; Vatin, *op. cit.*; Pomeroy, *op. cit.*, ch. 7; Riet Van Bremen, "Women and Wealth," in Averil Cameron and Amélie Kuhrt, editors, *Images of Women in Antiquity*, London and Canberra, Croom Helm, p. 223–242; Fantham et al., *op. cit.*, p. 155–162.

17 Cf. W. S. Ferguson, "The Attic *Orgeones*," Harvard Theological Review 3 (1944), p. 69–140.

18 Vatin, *op. cit.*, p. 254–261. Ferguson, *Hellenistic Athens*, p. 38–47, still valuable for details, shows himself a convinced follower of the anti-democratic critics: "[...] an *élegant* like Demetrius could not but be disgusted at the licence of the Athenian rabble – the lack of the respect of the young for the old, of the common for those in authority; the impertinence of the slaves and the offensive displays of the parvenus and vain women; in

a word, at the results of the democratic theory which had sought, so far, as possible, to permit men *zen hos tis bouletai* [to live as they wish] (41)". Élite anxiety would seem to have been in full flood at the beginning of the twentieth century.

19  Patterson, *op. cit.*, ch. 11. The various earlier forms of dependency were generally assimilated to the free poor. The rural peasantry of the newly conquered regions of the east are another matter. See Garlan, *op. cit.*, p. 106–112.

20  See, e.g., Frank W. Walbank, *The Hellenistic World*, London, Fontana, 1981, p. 167–175.

21  The issues discussed in this essay were included in a paper on "Dangerous Women – the Subversion of the Polis" presented to the workshop on "Reason and Religion in Fifth-century Greece" at the University of Texas at Austin in September 1996. I am grateful for the comments of the other participants.

# Women and Democracy in Ancient Greece
## *Marilyn Katz*

Marilyn Katz seeks to explain why it might be that the subject of women in ancient democracy has received only cursory schol- arly attention and suggests avenues for future research.

Women were excluded from political rights in ancient Athens. Women of citizen birth did not participate in assembly deliberations, hold political office, or serve as jurymen in the courts. This much is clear, undisputed and frequently acknowledged. The meaning of women's exclusion from political rights for our understanding of Athenian democracy, however, is much less clear. But this issue is rarely addressed – indeed, it is widely believed to require little or no explanation. Why is this?

In the first part of this essay I identify three areas of scholarship in which the question of women's exclusion from political rights has been elided from the study of both women and democracy in ancient Athens. In the second section, I suggest that the evasion of this question is tied to a specific historiographical paradigm. And in the final section I discuss some new approaches to Athenian democracy and offer some suggestions for a new approach to the study of women and democracy in ancient Athens. My overall aim is to establish that women's exclusion from political rights in ancient Athens is a topic that requires analysis and explanation, and that our collective failure to have engaged this issue has important historical and historiographical roots.

## Eliding the Question

Speaking generally, the question of women's exclusion from political rights in ancient Athens comes up in the works of three groups of scholars: (1) older scholars con-

Marilyn Katz, "Women and Democracy in Ancient Greece," in Thomas M. Falkner, Nancy Felson, and David Konstan (eds.), *Contextualizing Classics: Ideology, Performance, Dialogue* (Lanham, MD: Rowman & Littlefield, 1999), 41–68, pp. 41–8, 50–68.

cerned with "Women, Position of," to cite from the heading of the entries in the first and second editions of the *Oxford Classical Dictionary*, (2) contemporary scholars of Athenian democracy; and (3) contemporary scholars of women's studies in Classical Antiquity. And, again speaking generally, this is what is said about it: "Athenian women's political rights? That's easy. They didn't have any." Or: "They didn't have any political rights, but so what? Neither did any other women until the twentieth century." Or, finally: "Yes, it's true that Athenian women didn't have any political rights. But neither did any other free Athenians except for male citizens. And they were a minority. So it wasn't important."

I begin with "Women, Position Of," and an abbreviated citation of the entries in the 1949 and 1970 editions of the *Oxford Classical Dictionary* (emphases mine):

**WOMEN, POSITION OF.** In the course of ancient history the social and economic position of women passed through many phases.... The changes were sometimes due to the difference between European and Asiatic ideas of women, sometimes to the effect on family life of long-continued foreign wars, sometimes to the influence of an ascetic religion....

2. In the society pictured in the Homeric poems, and especially in the *Odyssey*, women held an honoured place.... [But] in Ionia during the seventh century BC an idea became prevalent, perhaps due to Asiatic influence, that women were inferior beings....

3. *After 500 BC the Athenians adopted Ionian ideas of womanhood, and the whole structure of Athenian social life was arranged for men's sole benefit. No education was thought necessary for girls, a marriage was arranged for them as soon as possible, and after that the less that was heard or seen of them the better. The Athenian house was small, dark, and uncomfortable; but women spent most of their time indoors, for nearly all forms of outdoor recreation were closed against them.*

4. The conquests of Alexander swept away many Greek prejudices and enlarged the social as well as the political horizon. The ideas that all men but Greeks were barbarians and that all females were inferior to males were both seen to be false.... (Wright 1949: 960)

**WOMEN, POSITION OF.** GREECE. (a) Upper-class women as pictured by Homer and the tragedians enjoyed a moderately free social life within their own circle....

(b) Middle- and lower-middle-class women are known mainly from democratic Athens. *Their lives were much more restricted, since they were married very early in life...and stayed almost entirely in their homes, being regarded as responsible for the three duties of raising children, producing clothes, with their maidservants' help, [and] protecting the house.... Some women received elementary education, knew something of civic affairs, and had a considerable influence on their husbands; all took part in the family's religious life, and shared in that of the State. They suffered from the middle-class snobbery which ordains that gentlewomen should not work.... Women had no political rights* and could not act in law except to divorce their husbands...and give evidence under oath; they could not own property, but the State took elaborate precautions to protect them from being left

destitute, and to secure the marriage of orphans and *epiklêroi* ("heiresses") and to ensure
that the elderly were protected.... Older women, especially widows, had more freedom
and independence. (Lacey 1970: 1139–40)

Wright in 1949 does not address the matter of political rights at all. Lacey in 1970
does, but he falls into my first category of answers ("they didn't have any; end of
discussion"). In the third edition of the *OCD* (1996), the category "Women,
Position Of," has, mercifully, disappeared. But even so, Helen King's discussion of
women's rights is brief. Here is what she says s.v. "women": "Ancient women lacked
political rights: they could not attend, speak at, or vote in political assemblies, nor
could they hold political office. However, they could exert influence through men"
(King 1996: 1623). (I leave to one side the question whether these remarks represent
an improvement over Lacey's.)

Let me turn now to contemporary scholarship, and to remarks on the topic
by scholars of Athenian democracy and women's studies. In *Democracy Ancient
and Modern*, M. I. Finley states: "Women were excluded [from the assembly];
so were the fairly numerous non-citizens who were free men...and so were the
far more numerous slaves" (Finley 1985:51). And Josiah Ober, in *Mass and
Elite in Democratic Athens* notes likewise that "a majority of the total adult population were excluded from participation in political life" (Ober 1989: 5). These
are representative and unexceptional statements – they could be multiplied many
times over.

But whereas Finley, Ober, and others go on to discuss the implications of the fact of
slavery for an analysis of democracy in ancient Athens, and to take note at various
points of the part played by resident aliens in the communal life of the polis, the
exclusion of women is either regarded as unproblematic or left unanalyzed.[1] And this
is true generally in discussions of ancient Athenian political life.[2]

What about women's studies scholars? Sue Blundell devotes about a page of her
recent book, *Women in Ancient Greece*, to the topic "Political Status," and she
concludes: "since democracy created a growing dichotomy between activities which
were public and collective, and those which were private and individual, it [demo-
cracy] accentuated the disparity between males and females" (Blundell 1995: 129).
The multiply-authored recent Oxford volume on *Women in the Ancient World*,
however, comes to an opposite conclusion: "since most of the [Athenian] population
had no political rights, the possession of such rights did not pointedly distinguish
men from women" (Fantham et al. 1994: 75). For, the authors go on to add, all free
Athenians other than male citizens "were increasingly relegated to the private
sphere." Who is right, if either is? Or, more importantly, what is wrong with the
picture we find in both works on Athenian democracy and on women in Ancient
Greece?

At one level, of course, the answer seems obvious. As Christian Meier argues in *The
Greek Discovery of Politics*: "We may be tempted, on grounds of mere numbers, to
call the extreme democracy of Athens an oligarchy, since the free and equal who
enjoyed full political rights were a small minority beside metics, slaves and women.
But this is to apply modern criteria" (Meier 1990: 154). And Ober remarks likewise:
"The limitation of the franchise to freeborn males is certainly undemocratic by
current standards, but to deny the name democracy to Athens' government, on the

grounds that the Athenians did not recognize rights that most western nations have granted only quite recently, is ahistorical" (Ober 1989: 6).

As a fact of the matter this is certainly correct – the extension of full political rights to women and all men in western democracies is a phenomenon of the twentieth century and, principally, of the 1920s. But the ancient Greeks did not themselves regard the exclusion of women from political rights as unproblematic; Plato offered an alternative to it in the *Republic*, and Aristotle was concerned in the *Politics* and elsewhere to justify it. And *we*, clearly, do not regard slavery as irrelevant to an understanding of the nature of democracy in the ancient world, although the conviction that slavery is incompatible with democracy is not only a "modern" viewpoint, but also a relatively recent one.

"Ahistoricity" and the importation of "modern viewpoints" into historical analysis are, to be sure, historiographic errors. But it is clear that concern to avoid anachronism does not by itself explain the historiographic inattention to women's lack of political rights in discussions of both Athenian democracy and women's status. Rather, there are other factors which, in my view, have led us collectively to regard Athenian democracy as largely irrelevant to the study of women, and women as largely irrelevant to the study of Athenian democracy.

Principal among these is the influence of the ideology of "separate spheres" and the sharp distinction between private life and the public sphere which was inherited from the public discourse and political struggles of the eighteenth century. The importance of this heritage becomes clear when we examine some of its specifics and consider some recent challenges by feminist political scientists and others to democratic theory.

## "Separate Spheres" and Civil Society

Older scholars, represented especially by Wright, did not even address the matter of women's political rights in ancient Athens. Why was this? A clue appears in Gomme's famous 1925 essay, which Wright references. There, Gomme noted that three aspects of the evaluation of women's status needed to be kept distinct: what he called "the legal, the social, and that of general estimation" (Gomme 1937: 90). But, he went on to claim, "the women of France . . . in the matter of property and political rights are in an inferior position to those of England, but no one would suggest that they are socially less free or held in less high honour."[3] The conclusion – implied but not stated explicitly – followed that the matter of women's "position" or "status" was defined best by social role and "general estimation," and that it was unrelated to legal and political rights.[4]

Gomme's 1925 article was the last major scholarly statement on the issue before it was brought forward again for discussion under the influence of 1970s feminism. But it is relevant to note that Gomme's article was published only a few years after the institution of universal suffrage in Britain in 1918, and during the time when the struggle was still being fought for women's political equality, which was not achieved until 1928.[5]

For Gomme's discussion of the subject was exemplary, not exceptional. He had set out to contest the "orthodox" or "commonplace" view that "whereas in the Aegean age and in Homer the position of women was a noble one, in Athens of the classical period it was ignoble" (Gomme 1937: 89). The particulars of Gomme's viewpoint – the "heterodox" one – were not new, and can in fact be traced back in the scholarly literature to 1830.[6] But neither argument – orthodox or heterodox – took into account the issue of women's political status in either the ancient or the modern world.

Why did women's political and legal rights not figure in the scholarly discussions on status? My answer to this question is a short one, but the demonstration of its cogency will be rather longer. The answer, in brief, is that the particulars of women's status in ancient Athens were investigated in a very specific way – with reference to a model of domesticity that was developed in the eighteenth century to rationalize women's exclusion from civil society then.

Let me explain. Up until the eighteenth century, other societies were studied, as they were by the ancient Greeks themselves, as "collections of customs" (Hodgen 1954: 162–206). The "customs" which were investigated by the anthropologists of the sixteenth and seventeenth centuries had included the religious, sexual, marital, funerary, vestimentary, alimentary, *and* political practices of the "other" peoples of the globe. And among these "other" peoples the ancient Greeks and Romans were often arrayed alongside the natives of the Hudson Bay, for example, or the Japanese or Mexicans or other "exotic" peoples.

But in the course of the eighteenth century, in the public debates carried on in meetings, clubs, newspapers, journals, and pamphlets, and in the private ones conducted in salons, both the political organization of the ancient Greeks and Romans and the question of women's place in civil society were subjected to a renewed and different kind of scrutiny. From the eighteenth-century perspective and under the influence of the revival of Hellenism, the customs and practices of the ancient Greeks were no longer items in a cabinet of curiosities, but potential models for new and invigorated forms of anti-monarchical political organization. And the status and social role of women in ancient Greece were, likewise, invoked as reference-points for the development of an ideology of women's place in the new social orders of the eighteenth and nineteenth centuries.

This development occurred against the background of a specific set of socio-political conditions – namely, the French Revolution, the Declaration of the Rights of Man, and proposals for the civil emancipation of women which were brought forward in the 1790s in France, Germany, England, Holland, and elsewhere.[7] And despite improvements in women's legal rights over the course of the next decade, the Napoleonic Civil Code of 1804 reinstitutionalized the dependent status and legal incompetence of married women. This Code influenced the legal status of women throughout Napoleonic Europe (Käppeli 1993: 485), and although it incorporated large parts of prerevolutionary customary law (Arnaud-Duc 1993: 97), it retained also *both* a recognition that women were free and independent subjects before the law *and* an insistence that married women were economically, legally, and personally subordinate to their husbands' patriarchal authority. As one scholar has remarked about this situation, "it was an important subtlety of the law that women had rights that they were nevertheless incompetent to exercise."[8]

Married women's legal subordination to their husbands was challenged and modified in a variety of ways in the course of the nineteenth century, under the influence primarily of the feminist groups and movements of the second half of the century. But contemporaneously with the incorporation of wives' legal subordination into the laws and civil codes of the late eighteenth and early nineteenth century, there developed also an ideological model which both supported and rationalized this subordination – the model of bourgeois domesticity or the ideology of separate spheres.

Herbert Marcuse summarized the resulting changes in family structure as follows: "Running parallel to the liberation of man as a 'citizen' whose whole existence and energies are devoted to 'society' and its daily economic, political, and social struggles, is the commitment of the woman and her whole being to her house and family, and the utilization of the family as a 'refuge' from daily struggles" (Mohrmann 1984: 108). The supporting ideology for this structure, like the civil codes which gave it legal force, did not represent simply a regression to traditionalism, despite the claims of an article in an 1838 issue of a feminist newspaper that "women are [now] more deprived of all rights than under the Ancien Régime" (Perrot 1993: 481). Rather, the ideology of separate spheres redefined women's traditional role in ways, as a great deal of evidence makes clear, that women themselves found satisfying and rewarding. [...]

[Katz goes on to elaborate on the develop-    domesticity in the eighteenth and nine-
ment and appeal of the model of feminine    teenth centuries.]

[...] This new model of women's place influenced, in its turn, the study of women in ancient Athens. For, if we ignore the well-known particulars of the debate on women's status in ancient Athens, and focus instead on isolating the *topics* around which the question was argued, we find that they resolve easily into four: (1) domesticity, (2) education, (3) arranged marriages, and (4) social life. These four topics appear over and over and with remarkable regularity in the vast majority of scholarly studies of women's status in ancient Athens, and were codified as the parameters of the issue in the 1949 edition of the *OCD*.[13] Most of these studies advance the orthodox or negative judgement of the matter: that Athenian women (1) were household drudges, (2) uneducated, (3) forced into loveless arranged marriages, and (4) excluded from a meaningful social role. These same topics turn up, however, in A. W. Gomme's 1925 article, which contested the orthodox position and advocated a more moderate view, arguing (4) that the women of tragedy enjoyed freedom of movement, (3) that those of comedy married for love, (2) that women generally were "educated enough to be corrupted by the sophists and poets," and (1) that Athenian women were no more "confined to their homes and domestic occupations" than those of the nineteenth century (Gomme 1937: 102, 97). These four topics correspond closely with the principal issues around which the ideology of separate spheres was originally formulated, and it is clear that the parameters governing the discussion of women's status in the scholarly literature were derived directly from this model. In the light of this relationship, then, we need to reconfigure our understanding of the debate on the status of women in ancient Athens.

For it was not ever a debate about women's status as properly understood – that is, about their legal, social, and political rights and disabilities. (Status is, after all, in the first place a legal term.) But it did have a specific and historically conditioned reference-point, and this was the model of bourgeois domesticity, the ideology of separate spheres. The study of Athenian women's status was accommodated to this model and evaluated according to its parameters. Thus, Athenian women's status was found "low" because, for example, they were not educated and did not dine with their husbands; or it was found "high" because their roles as housewives and educators of the young were valued.

In neither case, however, did the analysis take into account that the standard itself, the ideology of separate spheres, was a contested domain of political and sociological meaning. Consequently, the "debate" was more apparent than real, for the heterodox and orthodox positions represented the two sides of a single conservative and traditional viewpoint – namely, one which took the division between public and private for granted and regarded women's exclusion from political life as incidental. From this perspective, it remained only to be decided whether ancient Athenian women were household prisoners or whether their confinement to domesticity was of a piece with its modern, more "enlightened" version.

Furthermore, it is not surprising that the question whether Athenian women were "regarded with contempt" or not by Athenian men figured so prominently in the debate on status. For the ideology of separate spheres was just that – an ideology, a new way of conceptualizing the persistence of women's traditional roles in the context of the emergence of civil society for men. In other words, women's status had not changed, but the way of looking at it had. The eighteenth- and nineteenth-century middle-class housewife was now seen as man's "helpmeet, not his handmaid." In the light of such formulations, it became important for scholars defending the dignity (or condemning the indignity) of women's status in ancient Athens to focus, likewise, on how ancient Greek women were viewed by men.

Contemporary studies of women and society in ancient Athens no longer concern themselves with women's status or "Women, Position Of." But, like the older studies, they do elide the question of women's relationship to the political domain. To be sure, they do not do so by ignoring it altogether. Instead, the standard of reference has shifted in one of two directions: (1) toward comparisons with contemporary Mediterranean peasant societies or (2) toward a redefinition of the relationship between *oikos* [household] and *polis* [city-state].

I leave to one side the adequacy of the peasant model: it is illuminating when applied to the politics of reputation, the interaction of honor and shame, and the complementarity between male and female social roles.[14] But it is largely irrelevant to a consideration of women's exclusion from political rights.[15] The new emphasis on the *oikos* as a specifically political unit, on the other hand, implicitly challenges traditional conceptions of the relationship between the public and private spheres in ancient Athens (e.g., Foxhall 1989; Jameson 1990; Patterson 1994; cf. also Cohen 1991: 70–97).

For a sharp distinction between private life and the public sphere is one of our chief legacies from the political theory of the seventeeth and eighteenth centuries and from the political practices of the eighteenth and nineteenth centuries. Under the influence of this division Athenian democracy was studied almost exclusively as the ancient form of public life. By the same token, the investigation of women's relation to the *polis* was consigned to the domain of ancient Greek "private life." Our investigations of democracy and women's place in ancient Athens are still very much influenced by this heritage.

Classical liberal political theory, as is well known, distinguishes between public and private, and constructs civil society as a universal realm of freedom divided between a private realm in which citizens pursue individual social and economic interests and a public domain in which they express their political rights. But as feminist political theorists like Carole Pateman have pointed out, "because liberalism conceptualizes civil society in abstraction from ascriptive domestic life, the latter remains 'forgotten' in theoretical discussion. The separation between public and private is...re-established as a division *within* civil society itself, within the world of men."[16]

Recent studies which emphasize the public or political aspects of the *oikos* implicitly recognize the political dimension of the most irreducibly private unit within the social order. They do not, however, go so far as to systematically interrogate the public/private dichotomy itself. Nor do they incorporate aspects of the dispute over whether there was, in fact, a clearly articulated private sphere in Athenian democracy (e.g., Hansen 1996 and Ober 1996). At the same time, scholars concerned with the issue of a private sphere in political life have largely ignored the question whether the distinction between *to idion* [private] and *to dêmosion* [public] might have applied to women, even when it is acknowledged (as it frequently is) that women had a public role to play in the *polis*. Rather, just as in classical liberal theory, the concept of *to idion* is constituted in male terms, and the *oikos*, together with the women in it, are construed as an aspect of an Athenian man's private sphere.[17]

But it makes a difference whether women's confinement to domesticity is or is not theorized and practiced against the background of a political order based on the principle of the natural rights of the individual to "liberty, property, security, and resistance to oppression," to cite from the second article of "The Declaration of the Rights of Man." As a Montagnard deputy was able to argue in 1793, the exclusion of women from political life *then* amounted to a negation of democracy, and was tantamount to their conversion into the "helots of the Republic." "Call them *wives* or *daughters of citoyens*," he said, "but not *citoyennes*." "Either get rid of the word or grant [it] its substance."[18]

Against the background of the theory of natural law, then, and of states organized on the principle of individual rights, women's confinement to the domestic sphere and wives' legal subordination to their husbands represented theoretical and practical contradictions within the system. And accordingly, the historical resolution of these contradictions for women, for propertyless men and, in the United States, for slaves, has required the reinterpretation of liberal democratic theory, the translation of its rhetoric into reality, and the incorporation into the body politic of all previously excluded groups.

No such considerations, however, would apply to the exclusion of women from the political sphere in ancient Athens, where, as Aristotle makes clear, the first principle of *polis* organization was community (*koinônia*), not the rights of the individual.[19] Nevertheless, we do encounter in our fifth- and early fourth-century sources a series of reflections on the lot of women, including the claim that "the nature of men and women is the same"[20] or that "the virtue of a man and of a woman is the same."[21] And some scholars have even argued that "at the end of the fifth century, the woman question was the order of the day."[22]

Furthermore, Greek tradition preserved the memory of a mythical time when women had the vote, but lost it, along with their own names, after electing Athena over Poseidon as tutelary deity of the acropolis.[23] Aristophanes' *Ecclesiazusae* retains a veiled reference to that tradition, and Plato's *Republic* enisions its translation into practice. But, as Plato and others saw, the inclusion of women in the body politic was not simply a matter of drawing the same circle a little larger. Rather, it meant substantive changes in the nature of the political domain itself, and in its relation to other dimensions in society. If political rights were extended to women, then not only the household but the nature of the state as such was altered. Plato drew this conclusion himself, of course, but he also beat a fast retreat from the radicalism of the *Republic*, such as it was.

Nevertheless, we would probably not be far wrong in arguing that the contemporary reluctance to interrogate Athenian women's exclusion from political rights is influenced, at least in part, by the continuing persistence of the traditional family and the division it installs between men's and women's roles. In other words, slavery has disappeared in Western democracies, and the extent of its deformation of the ancient democratic ideal is consequently readily open to investigation. But the exclusion of women performed by the Athenian political sphere is still operative in our own society, despite women's suffrage. And this is particularly the case if we adopt the views of Carole Pateman, who argues that, in the contemporary world, full citizenship is constituted by the individual's capacity to earn a wage.[24]

## Toward a New Approach

Most major studies of Athenian democracy of the last twenty-five years adopt the program, in some part, of examining "democracy ancient and modern." But none addresses the question of women's rights, either ancient or modern, other than to acknowledge that they did not exist in the ancient *polis*. How might we assess the topic of "democracy ancient and modern" so as to take women's exclusion from citizenship into account?

The ancient Greeks, as we have noted, did not take women's exclusion from political rights for granted. Neither, however, were they able to explain it, aside from Aristotle's famous remarks in the *Politics* on the female deliberative faculty (1260a12–14).[25] And this consideration was relevant to only the most narrow definition of the citizen – namely, those members of the community who possessed, by reason of status, gender, or age the capacity to exercise the rights entailed in self-government (*kai archein kai archesthai*; 1277b14–15).[26]

Sealey has claimed that women's political disabilities in ancient Greece resulted from their incapacity to bear arms (1990: 151–53). And this argument has a long history: it figured prominently, for example, in nineteenth-century anti-suffragist arguments (Harrison 1978: 77–78). Sealey adduces no evidence for his thesis, however, and appeals instead to what he says "Greeks thought about women in relation to armed fighting" – that "a woman who wielded a weapon was a creature of nightmare." But in the literary and historical record, from the shield of Achilles in the *Iliad* to the battle of Chaeronea in 338 BCE, women take up arms readily enough when the city is under seige, and there is no particular indication that this disturbed their husbands' sleep.

Nevertheless, the view that "war is men's business" is a familiar topos in Greek thought, from Homer onward. And Philo of Alexandria, who often reflects a traditional Greek perspective about social values, probably does so also when he reconstructs Moses' reasoning on the matter of inheritance by females: "men should divide inheritances among themselves, to be taken as the reward for military service and the wars of which they have borne the brunt; while nature, who grants to women exemption from such conflicts, clearly also refuses them a share in the prizes assigned thereto."[27]

In the *Lysistrata*, however, the dispute between the official and the heroine pits men's part in war against women's childbearing services to the *polis*, and this comic exchange may reflect popular political rhetoric of the period. For in the second half of the fifth century reflections on female equality appear in the literature (Flacelière 1971; cf. Wright 1923) and, as Hanson has argued recently, the ideology of the citizen as hoplite was developed during the same period (Hanson 1996). Medea drew on the same cultural logic as Lysistrata when she claimed priority for child-bearing over battle, and we are all familiar with the Spartan equivalence between "*le lit* [the bed]" and "*la guerre* [war]" (Loraux 1995).

In the early modern period, wives and children often accompanied men to the battlefield, and the support services provided by women "camp followers" were an essential part of the military enterprise (Hacker 1981). Similarly, when Plataea was under Spartan siege in 429 BCE, 110 women remained behind in the city to cook and provision a garrison 480 strong.[28] Documented cases of women soldiers (disguised as men) appear in the seventeenth and eighteenth centuries (Hacker 1981: 658–59), and some women who fought in the French army during the revolution were awarded state honors.[29] Among the ancient Greeks, Telesilla was famous for leading the women of Argos in a successful defensive action against Cleomenes in the early fifth century, and the city erected a monument in her honor.[30]

Women's traditional exemption from military obligation ultimately explains as little about their exclusion from political rights in ancient Athens as it did in the nineteenth century. In the ancient world, women did not ever serve as hoplites, but other non-citizens did. This service did not, however, entitle them to the privileges of citizenship. In the modern world, as we all know, military service for women has emerged as a consequence of citizenship instead of a condition for it. Sealey's chapter epigraph cites from the Fundamental Law of the Federal Republic of Germany, to the effect that women cannot be obligated for military service or for combat duty if enrolled in the armed services. He does not, however, go on to observe that a provision of this same document entitled women to the franchise.[31]

We saw earlier that, in discussions of political rights, Athenian women are often grouped together as "outsiders" with metics (resident aliens) and slaves. And Charles Hedrick has argued recently that these groups, taken together, in fact defined the (otherwise hollow) category of citizenship in ancient Athens by virtue of their exclusion from its privileges.[32] But these groups were not all excluded from citizenship in the same manner, either in theory or in practice. Let me turn to a brief consideration of barriers to full political rights in the ancient and modern worlds.

The people of Athens were divided into three principal groups according to status: citizens, metics or resident aliens, and slaves. Of Athenians who resided in Athens[33] in the fourth century – the only period for which we can generate a reasonable demographic picture – roughly 31 percent were citizens, 24 percent were metics, and 45 percent were slaves. But full political rights were the province of male citizens only. That is, both status and gender were barriers to political rights. Consequently, male citizens constituted approximately ten percent of the total population and about twenty percent of the adult population (Hansen 1991: 94).

How does this compare with the modern situation? In the modern world, gender and status have also operated as barriers to full political rights, but so have race, religion, ethnicity, and, most commonly, property. After the passage of the Reform Act of 1832 in England, for example, about 4 percent of the adult male population possessed the franchise, and this increased to only 8 percent following the reforms of 1867 (Bowles & Gintess 1986: 43). The group excluded by these property-restrictions was primarily the working-class population, whose numbers had increased dramatically in the course of the nineteenth century as a result of widespread industrialization.

In Britain by 1911, less than 30 percent of the total adult population (Bowles & Gintess 1986: 43), and only 58 percent of the adult male population, was enfranchised (Jacoby 1976: 144). Thus, if we compare Britain in 1911 with Athens in the fourth century, access to full political rights was open to less than 60 percent of the adult male population in Britain, and to 20 percent of the adult male population in Athens. But if slaves were excluded from the comparison, then the figures for Britain and Athens would be comparable: about 60 percent of the free adult males in both populations.[34] Athenian democracy in its most developed form was distinctive as compared with the modern world, then, in that *only* gender and status, and *not* property, were barriers to full political rights. But now let us consider our excluded groups further. These included, we recall, metics, slaves, and women, which we shall take up in that order.

First, resident aliens: they do not enjoy full political rights even in modern democracies, though they may become citizens through naturalization. The same was true in ancient Athens, where the privileges of citizenship might be extended to metics individually, on the basis of their services to the *polis*,[35] or as a group, for the same reasons.[36] And it is worth noting incidentally that the status of metic disappears from the historical record in the Hellenistic period, when the *polis* was still very much alive and well over a large part of the Mediterranean world.

What about slaves? In Athens, if slaves were freed, they assumed the status of metics and thus became eligible for citizenship[37] – something which, to be sure, few ever attained; the vast majority of slaves retained their status throughout their lives. Nevertheless, just as with metics, some proposals were brought forward for mass enfranchisement of slaves (in connection with the battle of Arginousae in 406,[38] for example, or after the battle of Chaeronaea in 338[39]).

In ancient Athens, then, neither slavery nor metic status was *in principle* an insurmountable barrier to citizenship in ancient Athens: the exclusion of metics and slaves from political rights was not a principle of Athenian democracy but rather a fact of Athenian life, and it is worth keeping these two categories distinct.

We are down to women, then. Both in principle and in actuality there was only one barrier to full political rights in ancient Athens, and that was the barrier of gender. No woman ever acquired full political rights in ancient Athens, and thus, in the Athenian democracy, women were the only group excluded both on principle and in practice from political rights.

It is not quite right, then, to claim, as the Oxford volume does, that "the possession of [political] rights did not pointedly distinguish men from women" (Fantham et al. 1994: 75). For all men could potentially acquire such rights, but no woman could. But it is not quite right either to argue, as Blundell does, that "democracy...accentuated the disparity between males and females" (Blundell 1995: 129). For all native Athenian women had specific entitlements within the *polis* which no non-citizen men (or women) enjoyed.[40]

These did not, to be sure, include rights within the specifically political domain, but, as in the modern world up until women's suffrage, they were also real enough. The women of Plataea, for example, must have been included in the decree of 431 which granted citizenship to the Plataeans.[41] And the concept of women's naturalization was as familiar to Athenians as it was to the hundreds of thousands of immigrant women who came to the United States before 1920. When Apollodorus is discussing the case of Neaera in the late 340s BCE, for example, he insists that she was neither "born an *astê* townsperson nor made a *politis* female citizen."[42]

In the modern world, arguments for female suffrage often appealed to the distinction between "citizen" women and others, which was regarded as self-evident. An anonymous Frenchwoman writing in 1793, for example, and referencing an article in the penal code which assigned one penalty to men and another to women and foreigners, claimed: "No doubt without wanting to, you [Frenchmen] have assimilated French women and girls to men who are strangers to the *patrie*. What! Are women not citizens?" (Proctor 1990: 117). And if, as is often claimed, the citizen men of Athens were conscious daily of the distinctions that marked them off from non-citizens (e.g., Hansen 1991: 62), the same must have been true for the citizen women of Athens.[43]

The term "citizen woman" is usually regarded as an oxymoron and "passive citizen" is sometimes suggested as an alternative. But this term has a specific historical meaning which does not coincide with that of *politês* [(male) citizen] in late fifth- and fourth-century Athens. It arose to describe the status of those citizens who were excluded from political rights in the French National Assembly's decree of 22 December 1789. This decree limited the franchise to those approximately four million men (out of a total population of approximately twenty-eight million) whose property was sufficient to pay in direct taxes the equivalent of three days' work (Lewis 1993: 3, 31; cf. Proctor 1990: 186, n.8).

Are native Athenian women better understood, then, as privileged outsiders within the Athenian *polis*? Or, perhaps, as underprivileged citizens of it?[44] The first term would conflate them erroneously with *xenoi* ("foreigners"), who possessed no entitlements in Athens but who, unlike women, might be granted the right to appear before the assembly. And the second is not, to my mind, an improvement over "citizen women," if this is understood as Patterson explains it: "Athenian women should be understood as standing within the citizen class as participants in the *polis* in ways marking them off in law and in public consciousness from the non-Athenian and the non-free" (1994: 202).

Patterson's essay appeared in a volume which contests a perspective on Athenian democracy characterized generally as "constitutionalist."[45] This approach focuses on institutions, abstracts the political domain from the rest of society, and subordinates other aspects of sociocultural life to it. The competing approach is centered on the *polis* as a community of its citizens, and privileges the socio-economic and cultural aspects of the *polis*, arguing that it was through the citizens' regular involvement in these aspects of *polis* life, along with their participation in the strictly political sphere, that a sense of civic identity was engendered and fostered. This perspective is oriented toward the *polis* community as a lived reality, and toward *politeia* as the city's "way of life" – a definition also found in Aristotle's *Politics* (1295a: 40–b1). It aims at an inclusive rather than exclusive understanding of the nature of the political community, and does not limit itself either to public life or to those arenas of public life that were the exclusive province of fully enfranchised citizens.

This approach opens new avenues for understanding women's role in Athenian democracy, and this is especially true if we focus on how the Athenian *politeia* constituted itself as such on a day-to-day basis, and on how its constituent groups regularly came into contact with each other. For example, let us consider how the Athenian population was distributed with respect to wealth and daily activities.

As Aristotle explained in the *Politics*, "the real difference between democracy and oligarchy is poverty and wealth. And thus, whenever political power is restricted to the wealthy – be they many or few – this is an oligarchy, and whenever the poor rule, it is a democracy" (1279b40–1280a3). Rule by the poor, then, is the defining characteristic of democracy. But "poor" in this context, as the Greek word for it makes clear, does not mean "impoverished,"[46] but rather something more like "without independent means" (*aporoi*), by contrast with the group called *euporoi* or "well-off." Aristotle's definition of democracy, then, is derived from the facts that, as he says, the masses are always and by definition *aporoi*, and that in the democratic *polis* access to rule or political rights was open to all citizens regardless of their property-status.

Recent studies have shown that only about 1.4 percent of citizens were sufficiently wealthy to live on income alone; the rest, of whom another 5.6 percent were well enough off to be called upon to bear public expenses, worked for a living (see Casson 1984; Davies 1981: 34–37; Hansen 1991: 112–15; Jones 1957: 79–91). Among citizens, then, a small percentage was reasonably well-off, and the same was probably true with respect to metics.

Furthermore, a calculation of "working days" (Sinclair 1988: 225–27) which includes the days on which the Council, Assembly, and jury courts met, and includes also the number of citizens involved, yields the following: about 3200 citizens (the Councilmen, members of the jury courts, and 700 magistrates), or roughly 10 percent of the citizen body in the fourth century, were directly engaged in political life for between half and three-quarters of the year.[47] Six thousand citizens (some of whom were identical with the first group), or about 20 percent of the citizen body, attended the forty annual meetings of the assembly, some of which lasted only part of the day.

Religious festivals, which occupied the whole day, and which were either annual or monthly, occurred on one hundred and fifty days of the year, and there were also about fifteen days of the year regularly constituted as "impure." The Council and jury courts did not meet on annual festival or impure days, and the assembly did not meet on any religious holiday. Festivals were celebrated by the community as a whole: some of them were open to slaves and metics, and citizen women participated in most of them, although not necessarily in all events. But there were other festivals for women only, many local festivals in which women participated, and many cults established by groups of metics for their own members.

Political rights in ancient Athens, then, were an important privilege, but as a practical matter we are very far from the conventional portrait of the average Athenian male as a leisured individual who spent the majority of his time debating questions of justice and deliberating on matters of national policy while his wife remained at home. In terms of social practice, a great many more citizens spent a great deal more of their time either celebrating religious rituals or working for a living than they did occupied with the affairs of state. And the same, in all likelihood, held true for the majority of women and metics.

We have become used to thinking of women like Ischomachus' wife in Xenophon's *Oeconomicus* as the ideal type of ancient Athenian womanhood. Like most of the women we encounter in fourth-century orations, however, she belonged to that small percentage of Athenians who were well-off (see Pomeroy 1994), and she embodied that ideology of woman's place which we encounter everywhere in our ancient sources, from tragedy and New Comedy to philosophy and rhetoric. But ideology was not social reality, either in ancient Athens or in eighteenth- and nineteenth-century Europe and North America. A better candidate for the typical Athenian woman, I suggest, is the bread-seller of Aristophanes' *Wasps* or the women who appear in the curse-tablets.[48] These women work alongside their husbands, and while some of them were certainly metics, others belonged to the citizen class.

The citizen *artopólis* [bread-woman] of the *Wasps*, for example, does not hesitate to avail herself directly of certain legal procedures: she readily summons Philocleon before the *agoranomos* [market supervisor] on a charge of "damage to goods" and brings along a witness to the summons (Aristophanes, *Wasps* 1406–8). This *agoranomos*, like the "Forty"[49] and like other *polis* officials, could act independently when the sum at stake was less than ten drachmae; when more was involved, the matter was passed on to the "arbitrators." Only if arbitration failed was the case sent on to the jury courts. Seen from this perspective, women's exclusion from the jury courts takes on a different cast. In the areas which probably mattered most to most of them, they had the same access to legal remedies as men did.

The curse-tablets suggest that the women of the *agora* [market], who are often denounced in groups – along with other women and men, and their husbands and wives – formed a lively society. Thus, when severe poverty was not a factor, the lives of these women may well have been more varied and interesting than those of "middle-class" women. In 1920, Helen MacClees, a working women herself, one presumes, wrote about the women of the Attic inscriptions that they appeared to have enjoyed "the freedom which the necessities of common life, as earning part of the family income, marketing, washing in the streams or at the fountains, or working in the fields," gave to them; this was a privilege, she continued, which prosperity denied to middle-class women (MacClees 1920:5).

An approach to "democracy ancient and modern" which takes women like these into account would begin by abandoning the traditional focus on Aristotle's definition of the citizen (*politês*) in Book III of the *Politics*. This definition is constructed around a specific philosophical goal – the delimitation of the category of citizen in the "strict," "pure and simple," or "absolute" sense (*ton haplôs politên* 1275a19). It does not pretend to encompass the multiplicity of even the adult male citizen's *koinóniai* ("associations," "communities") which, in the *Ethics*, are described as part of the political realm (1160a8–9, a21, a28–29), and to a number of which Aristotle alludes in the *Politics* (e.g., 1280b36–38; cf. 1325b26–27). And it omits reference also to the important area of military service, which Aristotle takes up in a later section of the *Politics* (1279b3–5).

A better starting-point would be Aristotle's definition of the *polis* in Book III of the *Politics*. There, Aristotle argues that the *polis* is "a community of families and villages in a perfect and self-sufficing life, by which I mean a happy and honorable life," and that a common locality, intermarriage among citizens, and a variety of clubs and associations operate as the means for achieving that end (1280b33–35). This more inclusive definition of the ancient *polis* highlights the function of the family in Athenian democracy rather than relegating it to an artificially constructed and ana-chronistic private sphere. Such a perspective requires also that we study the political sphere itself, not by abstracting it from the *polis*, but in relation to other domains of communal life and with reference to forms of collective representation like civic ideology.

## Conclusion

It has been almost a quarter of a century since the first *Arethusa* special issue on "Women in the Ancient World" inaugurated a new approach to the study of women in ancient Greece. We have learned a great deal since that time about many of the particulars of women's lives, and many of the older assumptions have been denatural-ized. We have a more sophisticated understanding about forms of representation and about the role of the female in the realm of the ancient Greek imaginary. But the topic of women's exclusion from political rights remains inadequately theorized – trapped still by the contradictions of a liberal democratic theory and practice inherited from the eighteenth century.

Analyses of "democracy ancient and modern" which omit women and women's rights are necessarily incomplete. Dismissing sexual difference as irrelevant or periph-eral precludes a critical understanding of important and, indeed, constitutive aspects of democratic theory. In order to interrogate these dimensions of democracy, we would need to incorporate aspects of the feminist critique of political theory and practice. For, as Pateman has remarked, "feminism does not...merely add some-thing to existing theory and modes of argument. Rather, feminism challenges the patriarchal construction of modern political theory" (Pateman 1989: 14).

Contemporary studies of "democracy ancient and modern" take for granted both women's exclusion from political rights in antiquity and their accession to rights in the modern period. The specific meaning of women's exclusion or inclusion, how-ever, falls out of the analysis, along with the issue of what is entailed in women's "citizenship." The latter remains a vexed question in the modern world, but it was no less so in antiquity. For, as Aristotle observed about the ancient *polis*, "women are half of the free population." And the political education of women, consequently, had necessarily to be carried on with a view toward their incorporation in the *politeia* [citizen body] – if, that is, "it makes any difference for the goodness of the *polis* for the women to be good" (*Politics* 1260b15–20).

With reference to that particular consideration, Aristotle concluded, simply and concisely: "it necessarily makes a difference" (*anagkaion de diapherein*). The burden of my essay overall has been to argue that, for us, too – for our understanding of both the ancient *polis* and modern democracy – women's exclusion from political rights "necessarily makes a difference."

## NOTES

1   Ober, for example, argues that the "exclusion of 'others' [including women] from the political sphere was . . . a very important factor in the coalescence of the political society of the Greek polis" (Ober 1989: 6). But when he takes up discussion of "the ramifications of exclusivity for the Athenian citizen" body's definition of itself (p. 6; the subject is discussed on pp. 261–66), citizen women disappear from the analysis except as their role is implied in the term "parents."
2   Ste Croix questions whether women, by virtue of their exclusion from political rights, should be defined as a class (Ste Croix 1981: 98–103). But he comes to no conclusion on the matter.
3   Gomme 1937: 90. French women were enfranchised first by the preliminary constitution of 1944 issued by the provisional government of the French Committee of National Liberation in Algiers. After the liberation of 1945, the constitution adopted in 1946 (which brought into being the Fourth Republic) included the enfranchisement of women.
4   Cf. the remarks of John Gould, who draws attention to "the striking lack of interest in discussions of the social position of women in their juridical status" (Gould 1980: 43).
5   The 1918 bill enfranchised all men over the age of twenty-one and all women over the age of thirty.
6   Jacobs 1830; see my summary of Jacobs's argument in Katz 1992: 73–75.
7   The first was the Marquis de Condorcet's "Essay on the Admission of Women to Civil Rights" of 1790, followed by Olympe de Gouges's "Declaration of the Rights of Woman and Female Citizens" in 1791. Mary Wollstonecraft's *A Vindication of the Rights of Women* and Theodor von Hippel's *The Civil Advancement of Women* were both published in 1792, and both were inspired directly by the events in France and the public discussions and proclamations accompanying them. For Holland, see Vega 1996.
8   Ibid.
[. . .]
13   For example, "It is a great blot on Athenian civilisation that the position of woman had retrograded since the days of Homer. Her business now is simply to be the housewife and housemother, to apportion to the slaves their domestic work, to regulate the stores, to weave and superintend the weaving of garments, and to bring up the girls and little boys. She has received no particular education beyond these domestic accomplishments. Her place is inside the house. She may go abroad at festivals or on other recognised occasions, if properly attended, but the best woman, according to the Athenian definition, is she of whom 'least is said for either good or harm'" (Tucker 1906: 81–82).
14   For example, Cohen 1991: 133–70, with references to earlier scholarship.
15   For, regardless of how traditional and sex-segregated their social lives may be, the women of modern Greece have the right to vote and to equal pay for equal work (Articles 4 and 22 of the Greek Constitution).
16   Pateman 1989: 122; cf. Ibid.: 123: "the fact that patriarchalism is an essential, indeed constitutive, part of the theory and practice of liberalism remains obscured by the

apparently impersonal, universal dichotomy between private and public within civil society itself."

17   For example, "The *politês* did not forget his role as an *oikos*-member when he entered the public realm; certain accepted techniques of self-representation allowed, encouraged, or even required him to make that membership explicit" (Ober 1996: 180).

18   Sledziewski 1993: 47. Compare the contemporary debate over the appropriate designation for Athenian "citizen" women, discussed below.

19   On which see Ober 1996 and Ostwald 1996.

20   Attributed to Socrates by Xenophon in *Symposium* 2.9.

21   Attributed to Antisthenes the Cynic, the student of Socrates, by Diogenes Laertius, *Lives of the Greek Philosophers* VI.12.

22   Flacelière 1971: 701. It is worth noting here that as recently as 1991 Hall observed that current work in the field of women in ancient Greece has failed adequately to address "the problem represented by a certain number of late fifth and early fourth century sources which express discontent with the lot of women and articulate arguments for their greater freedom" (1991: 362).

23   Augustine, *City of God* 18.9, referencing Varro.

24   "Today, despite a large measure of civil equality, it appears natural that wives are subordinate just because they are dependent on their husbands for subsistence" (Pateman 1989: 123; cf. 142–43 and 221).

25   I cannot make sense of Swanson's claim that "Aristotle is reluctant to propose that women be eligible for citizenship for prudential and philosophical reasons," because "by including such a provision . . . he might risk not having its other provisions taken seriously" and because "making his proposal explicit might give the appearance of contradicting the claim that women should perform domestic duties" (Swanson 1992: 60).

26   That is, excluding male citizens who were either under thirty or over sixty years of age (1275a17–18).

27   *Life of Moses* 2.236; trans. Colson. Readers familiar with the biblical passage in question (*Numbers* 27: 1–11) will remember that Moses, if he reasoned as Philo did, was overruled by God. In the ultimate disposition of the matter of female inheritance (*Numbers* 36: 1–12), biblical law adopted a practice equivalent to that of the Greek epiclerate.

28   Thucydides 2.78. The ratio of women to men at Plataea is close to that allowed by an 1801 English regulation restricting women in a Rifle Corps regiment to six per one hundred men (Hacker 1981: 660).

29   Proctor 1990: 155–56, 169. A decree of 1793, however, excluded women from the military and also attempted to reduce the number of camp followers (pp. 170, 185 n.2).

30   Plutarch, *Moralia* 245c–f; Pausanias 2.20.8; cf. Herodotus 6.77–83.

31   Women in Germany were first enfranchised under Article 109 of the 1919 Constitution of the German Republic, which was suspended by presidential decree in 1930; following the war, Article Three of the 1949 Basic Law (*Grundgesetz*) of the Federal Republic of Germany guaranteed equal rights for men and women.

32   Hedrick 1994; cf. also Roberts 1996, esp. 198–99.

33   That is, excluding *klêrouchoi*: Hansen 1991: 53.

34   In the United States, after the emancipation proclamation of 1865, male suffrage was made universal by the fourteenth amendment to the Constitution and extended specifically to blacks by the fifteenth amendment of 1868. This represented at the time an historically unprecedented enfranchisement of propertyless workers, which included the 20 percent of free men and 30 percent of former slaves who, together, made up then 50 percent of the economically active male population (Bowles & Gintess 1986: 49). Blacks, however, were rapidly disenfranchised after the Compromise of 1877 and the end of

Reconstruction in the South, and did not acquire full access to political rights until the passage of the Civil Rights Laws of the 1960s.

35  For example, Dionysius I, tyrant of Syracuse, and his sons were made citizens by a decree of 368 BCE (IG II$^2$ 103).

36  For example, a decree of 431 BCE granted Athenian citizenship to the Plataeans, who had been the Athenians' allies in the war with Persia (Demosthenes 59.104–6), and another of 405 incorporated Samians, who had been allies in the Peloponnesian War, into the citizen body (IG I$^3$ 127 [= II$^2$ 1]).

37  The slave Pasion is the best known example.

38  Scholiast to Aristophanes, *Frogs* 694.

39  Hyperides, frr. 32–33. For discussion see Whitehead 1977: 162, 170 n.73, 173 n.117, and Hansen 1991: 88.

40  See Patterson 1986. And for an argument that the citizenship law of 451/0 BCE led to a new importance for women in citizen identity, see Osborne 1997.

41  Plataean women, along with old men and children, had been evacuated to Athens at the beginning of the Spartan siege (Thucydides 2.6; cf. 2.72, 78, 3.68).

42  Demosthenes 59.107. On the terminology, see Patterson 1986.

43  Such, at any rate, was the claim of Apollodorus (himself the son of a former slave) in Demosthenes 59.111; see Patterson 1994: 210; cf. 202.

44  Cf. Whitehead (1977: 90, referencing Harrison) on whether the metic should be regarded as "a privileged foreigner [or] an underprivileged citizen."

45  See especially Boegehold and Scafuro 1994; see also Ostwald 1996 and Ober 1996.

46  The "poor" in the sense of "impoverished" were *penêtes*.

47  Between 200 and 260 days of a 354-day year.

48  As David Cohen observes: "bits and pieces of evidence from Aristophanes offer better evidence for the lives of ordinary women than do the set-piece speeches of a Medea or Andromache" (1991: 165).

49  Before 403/2, "deme judges."

# REFERENCES

Arnaud-Duc, N. 1993. "The Law's Contradictions." In G. Fraisse and M. Perrot, eds., *Emerging Feminism from Revolution to World War*, Vol. IV of G. Duby and P. Schmitt Pantel, eds., *A History of Women in the West*, pp. 80–113. trans. A. Goldhammer. Cambridge, Mass.

Blundell, S. 1995. *Women in Ancient Greece*. Cambridge, Mass.

Boegehold, A., and A. Scafuro, eds. 1994. *Athenian Identity and Civic Ideology*. Baltimore.

Bowles, S., and H. Gintess. 1986. *Democracy and Capitalism: Property, Community, and the Contradictions of Modern Social Thought*. London.

Casson, L. 1984. "The Athenian Upper Class and New Comedy." In *Ancient Trade and Society*, pp. 35–69. Detroit.

Cohen, D. 1991. *Law, Sexuality and Society: The Enforcement of Morals in Classical Athens*. Cambridge.

Davies, J. K. 1981. *Wealth and the Power of Wealth*. New York.

Dawson, R. 1986. " 'And This Shield is Called – Self-Reliance': Emerging Feminist Consciousness in the Late Eighteenth Century." In R.-E. B. Joeres and M. J. Maynes, eds., *German Women in the Eighteenth and Nineteenth Centuries*, 157–74. Bloomington.

de Ste Croix, G. E. M. 1981. *The Class Struggle in the Ancient Greek World*. Ithaca, N.Y.

Fairchilds, C. 1984. "Women and Education." In S. I. Spencer, ed., *French Women and the Age of Enlightenment*, pp. 97–110. Bloomington.

Fantham, E., H. P. Foley, N. B. Kampen, S. B. Pomeroy, and H. A. Shapiro. 1994. *Women in the Classical World*. New York.

Finley, M. I. 1985. *Democracy Ancient and Modern*. 2nd edition. London.

Flacelière, R. 1971. "Le Féminisme dans l'ancienne Athènes." *CRAI*: 698–706.

Foley, H. 1981. "The Conception of Women in Athenian Drama." In H. Foley, ed., *Reflections on Women in Antiquity*. New York.

Foxhall, L. 1989. "Household, Gender, and Property in Classical Athens." *CQ* n.s. 39: 22–44.

Gomme, A. W. 1937. "The Position of Women in Athens in the Fifth and Fourth Centuries B. C." In *Essays in Greek History and Literature*, pp. 89–115. Oxford.

Gould, J. 1980. "Law, Custom and Myth: Aspects of the Social Position of Women in Classical Athens." *JHS* 100: 38–59.

Hacker, B. C. 1981. "Women and Military Institutions in Early Modern Europe: A Reconnaissance." *Signs* 6: 643–71.

Hall, E. 1991. "Reconstructing the Ancient Greek Woman." *Gender & History* 3: 359–65.

Hansen, M. H. 1991. *The Athenian Democracy in the Age of Demosthenes*. Oxford.

——. 1996. "The Ancient Athenian and the Modern Liberal View of Liberty as a Democratic Ideal." In J. Ober and C. Hedrick, eds., *Dêmokratia: A Conversation on Democracies, Ancient and Modern*, pp. 91–104. Princeton.

Hanson, V. D. 1996. "Hoplites into Democrats: The Changing Ideology of Athenian Infantry." In J. Ober and C. Hedrick, eds., *Dêmokratia: A Conversation on Democracies, Ancient and Modern*, pp. 289–312. Princeton.

Harrison, B. 1978. *Separate Spheres: The Opposition to Women's Suffrage in Britain*. New York.

Hedrick, C. 1994. "The Zero Degree of Society: Aristotle and the Athenian Citizen." In J. P. Euben, J. R. Wallach, and J. Ober, eds., *Athenian Political Thought and the Reconstruction of American Democracy*, pp. 289–318. Ithaca, N.Y.

Hodgen, M. T. 1954. *Early Anthropology in the Sixteenth and Seventeenth Centuries*. Philadelphia.

Jacobs, F. 1830. "Beiträge zur Geschichte der weiblichen Geschlechtes." In *Abhandlungen über Gegenstände des Alterthums*, Vol. IV of *Vermischte Schriften*, pp. 157–554. Leipzig.

Jacoby, R. M. 1976. "The British and American Women's Trade Union Leagues." In B. Carroll, ed., *Liberating Women's History: Theoretical and Critical Essays*, pp. 137–60. Urbana.

Jameson, M. H. 1990. "Private Space and the Greek City." In O. Murray and S. Price, eds., *The Greek City from Homer to Alexander*, pp. 171–95. Oxford.

Jones, A. H. M. 1957. *Athenian Democracy*. Oxford.

Katz, M. A. 1992. "Ideology and 'The Status of Women' in Ancient Greece." *History and Theory* Beiheft 31: 70–97.

Käppeli, A. -M. 1993. "Feminist Scenes." In G. Fraisse and M. Perrot, eds., *Emerging Feminism from Revolution to World War*, Vol. IV of G. Duby and P. Schmitt Pantel, *A History of Women in the West*, pp. 482–514. trans A. Goldhammer. Cambridge, Mass.

King, H. 1996. "Women." In S. Hornblower and A. Spawforth, eds., *The Oxford Classical Dictionary*. 3rd edition, pp. 1623–24. Oxford.

Lacey, W. K. 1970. "Women, Position of." In N. G. L. Hammond and H. H. Scullard, eds., *The Oxford Classical Dictionary*. 2nd edition, pp. 1139–40. Oxford.

Lewis, G. 1993. *The French Revolution: Rethinking the Debate*. London.

Loraux, N. 1995. "Bed and War." In *The Experiences of Teiresias: The Feminine and the Greek Man*, pp. 23–43. trans P. Wissing. Princeton.

McClees, H. 1920. *A Study of Women in Attic Inscriptions*. New York.

Meier, C. 1990. *The Greek Discovery of Politics*. trans D. McLintock. Cambridge, Mass.

Möhrmann, R. 1984. "The Reading Habits of Women in the Vormärz." In J. C. Fout, ed., *German Women in the Nineteenth Century: A Social History*, pp. 104–17. New York and London.

Ober, J. 1989. *Mass and Elite in Democratic Athens.* Princeton.

——. 1996. "The Polis as a Society: Aristotle, John Rawls, and the Athenian Social Contract." In *The Athenian Revolution. Essays on Ancient Greek Democracy and Political Theory*, pp. 161–87. Princeton.

Osborne, R. 1997. "Law, the Democratic Citizen and the Representation of Women in Classical Athens." *Past and Present* 155: 3–33.

Ostwald, M. 1996. "Shares and Rights: 'Citizenship' Greek Style and American Style." In J. Ober and C. Hedrick, eds., *Démokratia: A Conversation on Democracies, Ancient and Modern*, pp. 49–61. Princeton.

Pateman, C. 1989. *The Disorder of Women: Democracy, Feminism and Political Theory.* Stanford.

Patterson, C. 1986. "Hai Attikai: The Other Athenians." *Helios* 13: 49–67.

——. 1994. "The Case Against Neaera and the Public Ideology of the Athenian Family." In A. Boegehold and A. Scafuro, eds., *Athenian Identity and Civic Ideology*, pp. 199–216. Baltimore.

Perrot, M. 1993. "Stepping Out." In G. Fraisse and M. Perrot, eds., *Emerging Feminism from Revolution to World War*, pp. 449–81. Vol. IV of G. Duby and P. Schmitt Pantel, eds., *A History of Women in the West.* trans. A. Goldhammer: Cambridge, Mass.

Pomeroy, S. B. 1994. *Xenophon, Oeconomicus: A Social and Historical Commentary.* Oxford.

Proctor, C. E. 1990. *Women, Equality, and the French Revolution.* Westport, Conn.

Roberts, J. T. 1996. "Athenian Equality: A Constant Surrounded by Flux." In J. Ober and C. Hedrick, eds., *Démokratia: A Conversation on Democracies, Ancient and Modern*, pp. 187–202. Princeton.

Rousseau, J. -J. 1911. *Émile or Education.* trans B. Foxley. London and Toronto.

——. 1960. *Politics and the Arts: Letter to M. d'Alembert on the Theatre.* trans A. Bloom. Glencoe, Ill.

Sealey, R. 1990. "Women and the Unity of Greek Law." In *Women and Law in Classical Greece*, pp. 151–60. Chapel Hill, N.C.

Sinclair, R. K. 1988. *Democracy and Participation in Athens.* Cambridge.

Sledziewski, E. 1993. "The French Revolution as the Turning Point." In G. Fraisse and M. Perrot, eds., *Emerging Feminism from Revolution to World War*, pp. 33–47. Vol. IV of G. Duby and P. Schmitt Pantel, eds., *A History of Women in the West.* trans A. Goldhammer. Cambridge, Mass.

Swanson, J. A. 1992. *The Public and the Private in Aristotle's Political Philosophy.* Ithaca, N.Y.

Tucker, T. G. 1906. *Life in Ancient Athens.* London.

Vega, J. 1996. "Feminist Discourses in the Dutch Republic at the End of the Eighteenth Century." *Journal of Women's History* 8: 130–51.

Whitehead, D. 1977. *The Ideology of the Athenian Metic.* Cambridge.

Wollstonecraft, M. 1995. *A Vindication of the Rights of Women.* Cambridge.

Wright, F. A. 1923. *Feminism in Greek Literature from Homer to Aristotle.* London.

——. 1949. "Women, Position of." In M. Cary, J. D. Denniston, J. Wight Duff et al., eds., *The Oxford Classical Dictionary.* 1st edition, p. 960. Oxford.

Zucker, S. 1984. "Female Political Opposition in Pre-1848 Germany: The Role of Kathinka Zitz-Halein." In J. C. Fout, ed., *German Women in the Nineteenth Century: A Social History*, pp. 133–50. New York and London.

# Further reading

Cohen, David, *Law, Sexuality, and Society* (Cambridge, 1991).

Cohen, Edward E., *The Athenian Nation* (Princeton, 2000).

Garlan, Yvon, *Slavery in Ancient Greece*, trans. J. Lloyd (Ithaca, NY, 1988).

Hedrick, Charles, "The Zero Degree of Society: Aristotle and the Athenian Citizen," in *Athenian Political Thought and the Reconstruction of American Democracy*, eds. P. Euben, J. R. Wallach, and J. Ober (Ithaca, NY, 1994), 289–318.

Hunter, Virginia J., *Policing Athens. Social Control in the Attic Lawsuits, 420–320 BC* (Princeton, 1994).

Just, Roger, *Women in Athenian Law and Life* (London, 1989).

Kallet-Marx, Lisa, "Thucydides 2.45.2 and the Status of War Widows in Periclean Athens," in *Nomodeiktes*, eds. R. Rosen and J. Farrell (Ann Arbor, 1993), 133–43.

Osborne, Robin, "Athenian Democracy: Something to Celebrate?" *Dialogos: Hellenic Studies Review* 1 (1994), 48–58.

—— "Law, the Democratic Citizen and the Representation of Women in Classical Athens," *Past and Present* 155 (1997), 3–33.

Patterson, Cynthia, "The Case against Neaira and the Public Ideology of the Athenian Family," in *Athenian Identity and Civic Ideology*, eds. A. L. Boegehold and A. C. Scafuro (Baltimore, 1994), 199–216.

—— "Athenian Justice: The Metic in Court," in *Law and Social Status in Classical Athens*, eds. V. Hunter and J. Edmonson (Oxford, 2000), 93–112.

Zeitlin, Froma, "Aristophanes: The Performance of Utopia in the *Ecclesiazousae*," in *Performance Culture and Athenian Democracy*, eds. S. Goldhill and R. Osborne (Cambridge, 1999), 167–97.

# Glossary of Greek Names and Terms

---

**agora**: civic center and marketplace.

**Alcmaeonids** (also **Alcmaeonidae, Alkmaeonidai**): an old and prominent Athenian family.

**archon**: generally, a magistrate; at Athens, one of the highest offices.

**Areopagus**: a hill in Athens; the term also commonly refers to the council of former magistrates that convened there.

**Aristophanes**: Athenian comic playwright of the fifth and early fourth centuries BC.

**Aristotle**: Greek philosopher of the fourth century BC and author of many works, including *The Politics* and possibly *The Constitution of the Athenians* (= *Athenaion Politeia*).

**Attica** (also **Attika**): an area on the southeastern Greek mainland that comprised the territory of the Athenian state.

**basileus** (plural **basilees/basileis**): king or prince.

**boule**: a council. At Athens, the *boule* usually refers to the Council of 500 established by Cleisthenes.

**choregos**: producer of a chorus at Athens.

**Cleisthenes** (also **Clisthenes, Kleisthenes**): Athenian politician and reformer who is often credited with bringing democracy to Athens ca. 508/7 BC.

**demes**: local villages in Attica that, after the reforms of Cleisthenes, registered citizens and formed the basis for the new Athenian tribal system.

**demos**: the people. In different contexts the term can mean either the whole citizen body of the state or the relatively poor majority of citizens.

**Demosthenes**: Athenian politician and orator of the fourth century BC.

**dikasteria**: jury courts.

**dike**: justice. Also lawsuit; judicial punishment.

**Diodorus of Sicily**: Greek writer of a universal history who lived in the first century BC.

**Dorians**: one of the major Greek ethnic groups.

**ecclesia** (also **ekklesia**): public assembly.

**Euripides**: Athenian tragedian of the fifth century BC.

**Herodotus**: fifth-century Greek historian; author of the *Histories*.

**Hesiod**: epic poet; author of *Theogony* and *Works and Days*.

**Homer**: legendary creator of the epic poems *The Iliad* and *The Odyssey.*

**Ionians**: one of the major Greek ethnic groups.

**Lacedaemonians**: another term for Spartans.

**liturgies**: services on behalf of the Athenian state, to be performed by the wealthy; included such duties as producing a tragic chorus or outfitting and maintaining a warship (see *choregos, trierarch*).

**Medes**: a people who lived southwest of the Caspian Sea and once held a great empire; the term is often used by Greek authors as a synonym for the Persians.

**metic**: a resident alien.

**metrioi**: "middling" men; see article by Ian Morris, chapter 1.

**oikos**: household.

**oligarchy**: literally meaning "rule by a few," the term typically refers to constitutional orders in which political power is restricted to particular families or classes of citizens.

**ostracism**: practice at Athens (and reportedly in other democracies) enabling citizens to vote unpopular or dangerous political leaders into exile.

**Peisistratids** (also **Pisistratids, Pisistratidae**): the family of the Athenian tyrant Peisistratus; typically used to refer to his sons Hippias and Hipparchus who ruled after his death.

**Peisistratus** (also **Pisistratus**): Athenian tyrant of the third quarter of the sixth century.

**petalism**: a Syracusan law similar to ostracism by which citizens could vote unpopular or dangerous political leaders into exile for five years.

**Phalerum** (also **Phaleron**): the old harbor at Athens.

**Piraeus**: the main harbor at Athens.

**polis**: a Greek city or city-state.

**politeia**: constitutional order of a state; also, in Aristotle's *Politics,* a term for a constitution that mixed oligarchic and democratic elements.

**prytaneis**: the fifty-man standing committee of the Athenian Council of 500.

**Pseudo-Xenophon**: unknown author of a treatise on the Athenian constitution dating to the last third of the fifth century.

**seisachtheia**: measure sponsored by Solon in the early sixth century to release Athenians from burdens of debt.

**Solon**: Athenian statesman, lawgiver, and poet; initiated significant political and social reforms in early sixth-century Athens.

**stasis**: factional conflict, often violent.

**strategos** (plural **strategoi**): general.

**Thucydides**: Athenian historian of the Peloponnesian War; lived in the second half of the fifth century BC.

**trierarch**: generally, the captain of a trireme (the preeminent warship of the day); in Classical Athens, one who undertook to outfit and maintain a trireme for a year's service with the fleet. This was the most expensive of the liturgies at Athens, and in time often came to be shared by more than one person in a given year.

**trittues** (also **trittyes**): thirds; used to describe one of the elements of Cleisthenes' new tribal system at Athens.

**tyranny**: autocratic government in which the lone ruler (by himself or through a member of his immediate family before him) gained power by non-constitutional means. Sometimes, but not always, a pejorative term in Greek usage.

# Index

Achilles 9, 10–12, 13, 14–15, 28–9, 42, 43, 44
Achradina 128, 129, 131, 133, 136
Acrae 132
Acragas 131, 134, 135
administrative officials *see* public office
advice-poetry 52
Aeschines 176, 177, 266
Aeschylus, *Persians* 60
Aetna (Aitna) 129, 132
Agamemnon 10, 11, 12, 14, 15–16, 17–18, 28, 29, 42, 43, 44, 54
Agatharchus 197
agriculture
  cereal harvesting 271, 278n 32–6
  economics of 271–3
  land ownership 270–1
  slave labour 270, 271
Aigospotamoi 267
Aischines 204, 217
Ajax 83
Alcaeus 50, 55, 57
Alcibiades 146, 151n 28, 196, 197, 202, 205, 206, 207, 209n 17, 217, 220, 221–2
  *hubris* 196, 221, 222
Alcmaeonids 81–2, 84, 90, 93, 97, 100, 101, 115, 118, 119, 196
Alcman 51, 56, 57
*alethea* 50, 52, 60
Alexander the Great 2
aliens 282

citizenship 3, 92, 128, 162, 173, 263–4, 282, 302
  naturalization 143, 162, 303
  women 287
Ambracia 2
Amphipolis 145
amphoras 56
Anacreon 50, 57, 89
Anaxilas 129
Anchimolos 82, 90
Androtion 176–7
Antileon 126
Antiochus of Syracuse 134
  *History of Sicily* 134
  *On Italy* 134
Antiphon 176
Apelles 133
Aphrodite 55
Apollo 8, 9, 61
Apollodorus 303
*aporos* 173
Archaic period 7, 35, 46, 47, 57, 95
Archedice 88
Archilochus 50, 57, 58
archons 78, 79, 91, 93, 105, 177, 185
Areopagus 79, 126
Arginusae Islands 145, 302
Argives 2
Argos 2, 5, 48, 49, 56, 99, 126
Aristagoras 83
Aristarkhos 273
Aristeas 56

aristocracy
aristocratic birth 223, 224
athletic contests 35, 57, 196, 205
clubs 98, 107, 206
decline of 36
dissatisfaction with and criticism of 33, 34,
35, 36, 43, 44
early attitudes towards 30, 31, 33
elite behaviour 238
epic criticism of 33, 36, 43
*hubris* 52, 54, 58, 214, 215, 241
inter-polis aristocracy 46
juridical role 33
luxury culture 55, 60, 61–2, 198,
223
middling aristocrats 51, 53
Orientalizing movement 56
power struggles 33, 34, 97
primacy of honor 240, 241
proto-aristocratic class 35
self-promotion 35
supra-polis elite 62
Syracuse 130, 137, 138
violation of norms 31, 33, 34
warrior-aristocracy 41
*see also* elite leadership
Aristogeiton 76, 86, 87, 88, 89, 93–5, 94
(figure), 217
Aristophanes
*Acharnians* 95
*The Assemblywomen* 251–61
*Ecclesiazousae* 286, 300
*Lysistrata* 97, 103, 286, 301
*Wasps* 305
Aristotle 55, 77, 101, 271, 287
on citizenship 165, 263–4, 279n 47,
305–6
*Constitution of the Athenians* 45, 77–81,
88–92, 96, 100, 101, 103, 106, 118,
145, 177, 250–1
on democracy 77–81, 158–9, 172, 264–5,
284, 304
on freedom and equality 163, 164, 175,
234
on household management 262–3
on *hubris* 217
on kingship 162
*Nicomachean Ethics* 143
on oligarchy 158, 159
on the *polis* 306
on *politeia* 125–6, 136, 143, 149n 15

*Politics* 46, 92, 125–6, 141–3, 145, 158–9,
160, 162, 163, 164, 171, 175, 234,
262–5, 273–4, 295, 300, 304, 305–6
on public office holding 159, 164
*Rhetoric* 217
on sacrifice 49
on slaves 262–3, 275
on Syracuse 136, 137, 141–3, 148n 5
on women 263
Artaphernes 84
artisans 273–4, 284
*see also* craft activities
Ascra 52
Asheri, David 131–5
Athenagoras 124–5, 146
Athenian democracy 2, 4, 59, 76–122, 147,
172, 176, 177
Aristotle's account of 77–81, 92
Cleisthenes' reforms 76, 91, 92, 113,
117–22, 159, 264
ideology 156–8, 172–3
introduction 76, 96
Solon's reforms 76, 77–81, 91, 98, 166,
204
*see also* Athenian revolution; *boule*;
citizenship; elite leadership
Athenian revolution (508/7 BC) 95–111
Acropolis siege 84, 97, 99, 101, 102,
103–4, 110n 19
attempt to overthrow the *boule* 84, 90, 99,
101, 102, 104, 106, 116
Cleisthenes and 84, 90, 96, 97–9, 100,
107–8, 108n 3, 114, 115–16, 117
contest for political influence 97–8
*demos*, role of 96, 98, 100, 102, 106, 107,
108, 115, 116
Spartan intervention 76, 82, 83–4, 85, 89,
99–100, 101
Spartan surrender and expulsion 90, 99,
100, 101–2, 104, 116
Athens 47, 49, 56, 63
burial rituals 49, 55
calendar year 93
demographic picture 301–2
late-archaic Athens 98
"middling" ideology 47, 48, 55
Peisistratid tyranny 76, 81, 82, 83, 86–8,
90, 93, 97
re-democratization 2
*atimia* 239, 240, 243
*autonomia* 173

Bacchylides 60, 61
*basileis* 8, 52, 54
begging 57
Berger, Shlomo 135–9
Boeotians 85
Boiotos 191, 215, 216, 239
Bolkon 144
*boule* 63, 76, 79, 90, 91, 96, 103, 105, 106, 118, 250
  addressing 203
  appointments 203–4
  attempt to overthrow 84, 90, 99, 101, 102, 104, 116
  pre-assembly discussions 3, 202–3

Cadmus 59
Camarina 131, 132, 136
Cambyses 152
carpenters 58
Casmenae 132
Catana 129, 131, 132
cavalry service 166
Chaeronaea (Khaironeia) 266, 302
Chalcideans 85
Chalcis 126
Charilaus 126
Charon 58
children
  and citizenship 162, 248, 264, 274
  exclusion from elite rituals 48
  illegitimacy 92, 264
Chios 1
citizen-dignity 240, 241
  collective defence of 241, 244
citizenship 160–7
  American 159–65
  Aristotle on 165, 263–4, 279n 47, 305–6
  children and 162, 248, 264, 274
  communal values 160, 165, 166, 167, 299
  and equality 162, 163, 274, 275
  excluded classes 3, 224, 302
  formal status, creation of 98
  individualistic values 160
  material and psychic value of 240
  naturalization 143, 162, 303
  old men and 162, 264
  residence qualification 115
  and rights 3, 79, 160, 161–2, 163, 165, 166, 176, 223, 276
  women and 3, 162, 248, 282, 292–3, 294–5, 299–300, 302–3, 306, 307

civic rights and responsibilities 3, 79, 160, 161–2, 163, 165, 166, 176, 223, 276
class
  relations 32–3
  visible distinctions 283–4
  *see also* aristocracy; the poor
Classical era 2
Cleisthenes 36, 59, 76–7, 83, 84, 88, 90–2, 92, 93, 96, 97–9, 99, 100, 101, 107
  Alcmeonid heritage 90, 114, 115
  expulsion 99
  and foundation of Athenian democracy 84, 90, 96, 97–9, 100, 107–8, 108n 3, 114, 115–16, 117
  realist and idealist views of 100, 109n 14
  reforms 76, 91, 92, 114, 115, 117–19, 159, 264
  relationship with the *demos* 107–8, 109n 10, 115
Cleomenes 82, 83–4, 85, 89, 90, 96, 97, 99, 101, 102, 103, 104, 106, 109n 17
Codrus 82, 85
coinage
  Athenian 79
  Sicilian 131–2, 134
colonization 35, 36
Colophon 57, 58
communal and individual interests 30, 31, 32, 34, 36
conflict resolution 36, 52, 213
Congress of Gela (424/3 BC) 134
Constant, Benjamin 175–6
constitutional reform
  Cleisthenes 76, 91, 92, 114, 115, 117–19, 159, 264
  Solon 76, 77–81, 91, 98, 119, 166, 204
  Syracuse 128, 133, 139n 22, 141
contract theory 244n 2
Corax 134, 146–7
Corcyra (Kerkyra) 2, 207, 208, 209
Corinth 48, 49, 55, 56, 85, 209
Corsica 133
Cos 59
Council of 500 *see boule*
courts 3
  juries 3, 141, 197, 199, 200, 207, 220, 235, 236, 237, 264
  right of appeal 79
  witnesses 192–3, 213–14

courts (*continued*)
  women's use of 305
  *see also* lawsuits
craft activities
  economics of 272, 273
  free labour 268
  silver mining 268–9
  slave labor 265–6, 268, 269, 272–3, 274
Crete 49, 53, 55, 56
Croesus of Lydia 61
cults 54, 119, 305
  mystery cults 60–1
  orgiastic cults 287
  political cults 172
curse-tablets 305
Cylon 84, 101, 110n 19
Cyrene 2, 59, 92, 264

Dahl, Robert 46, 47
damage, laws concerning 189
Darius 84, 88, 153–4
Dark Ages 35, 48, 55
debt cancellation 77–8, 79, 80, 119
decision-making 1, 46, 185, 234, 274
  early Greek attitudes 8
  Principle of Equal Consideration of Interests 47, 53, 62
  Strong Principle of Equality 46, 47, 59, 62, 63
  *see also* public assemblies
Delphi 36, 53, 61, 82, 90
demagoguery 4, 92, 130, 140, 145, 146, 147
Demaratus 85
demes 91, 100, 115, 119, 204, 207
Demetrius of Phaleron 289
democracy
  archaic origins 7–68
  Aristotle on 77–81, 158–9, 172, 264–5, 284, 304
  basic premise 1
  criticisms of 3–4
  definition 3, 140
  democracy-liberty-equality triad 171–2, 178
  evolution and growth 1–3, 45–63
  geographic spread 2, 123
  ideological models 113
  impetus for 2, 63
  institutions 3

middling ideology 51–4, 57, 58, 59, 62, 63
modern democracy 3, 4, 171, 172, 179, 185
modern scholarship 4–5
poverty–democracy link 145, 158, 173, 250, 286, 304
  as set of political ideals 171
  as set of political institutions 3, 171
  *see also* Athenian democracy; equality; freedom
democratic abuse 213, 220–5
Democritus 173
*demokratia* 1, 95, 116, 117, 121nn 15, 19, 152, 172–3
  *see also* democracy
Demonax of Mantineia 59
*demos* 118, 119, 145
  direct government by 1, 3, 59, 140, 147
  dissatisfaction among 30
  and foundation of Athenian democracy 96, 98, 100, 102, 106, 107, 108, 115, 116
  Homeric epic and 44
  homogeneity 218, 219
  power 30, 185, 232, 241, 244
Demosthenes 176, 177, 187, 204, 266, 267, 269, 272, 275
  *Against Meidias* 120n 6, 187–201, 211–31, 235–44
  exposition of the law 189–90, 214
  on *hubris* 187, 193, 196, 198, 199, 212, 213, 223, 225, 235, 238, 240
  on slavery 275
*dikasteria* 78, 79
  *see also* courts; juries
Diocles 137, 143, 146, 147
Diodorus of Sicily 126–30, 132, 134, 136, 137, 144, 145, 146, 148n 3
  *Bibliotheke* 141
Dionysius of Syracuse 309n 35
dithyrambic competitions 205
domestic work 269–70, 273
Draco's code 78
drinking groups 56
drinking songs 90, 91, 93–5
Ducetius 129, 132, 133, 136, 144
*dynesteia* 118

Edmunds, Lowell 41–5
*ekklesia see* public assemblies

Elba 133
elegy 51, 53
Eleusis 85
*eleutheria* 164, 165, 171, 240
    democratic ideal 177–8
    dual nature 175
    and modern democratic liberty
        compared 171, 172, 174, 175, 176,
        177, 178–9
    political cult 172–3
    self-determination 174, 177, 178, 180n
        43
    slavery and 178
    social sense 177
    uses and senses of 173–4
    *see also* freedom
Elis 2
elite leadership 1, 3, 4, 119, 185
    friends and agents 206, 208
    influence and patronage 204–6, 207, 208
    liturgies and 205
    models of good leadership 34
    Pericles 186, 201, 202
    *see also* generals
elitist ideology 46, 47, 48, 51, 54–9, 59, 62,
    113, 276
Empedocles 134
Enki 34
*epheboi* 205–6
Ephialtes 76, 117
Epicharmus 134
epics
    historicity 28, 41
    social aspects 28, 41
    *see also* Homer
epinician poetry 59–60
equality 1, 3, 158, 160, 171, 172
    American citizenship and 162, 163
    Aristotle on 163, 164
    citizenship and 162, 163, 274, 275
    communal entity 165
    and decision-making 234, 274
    exercising 163
    freedom as precondition for 163
    *isonomia* 59, 114, 117, 152, 153, 172,
        173
    and liberty 160, 172
    natural equality 163
    political equality 240
    Principle of Equal Consideration of
        Interests 47, 53, 62

public and private spheres 234
    of rights 163
    Strong Principle of Equality 46, 47, 48,
        59, 62, 63
Erekhtheion 268, 284
eroticism 58
Euaion 191, 215–16, 217, 239, 240, 242
Euboea 136
Euboulos 204
Eumaeus 33
*eunomia* 54
Eupatrids 101, 120n 9
Euripides, *Suppliant Women* 154–5, 172
Euthynos 191, 215, 217, 238–9
evil
    Hesiod on 34–5
    Sumerian thought 35
execution 176

families
    female domesticity 297, 298, 299
    patriarchy 263, 296
    phratries 115, 119, 204, 207
    role and function 249, 306
    *see also* children; marriage; women
farming class 35, 36, 158, 270, 272–3
festival performances 205, 304–5
France 104–5
    Declaration of the Rights of Man 159,
        299
    franchise 303, 307n 3
    revolution 104–5, 106, 116, 178
    siege of the Bastille 106, 110n 27
    women's legal status 296
franchise
    Athens 302
    England 302
    France 303, 307n3
    Germany 301, 308n 31
    United States 308n 34
fraud 189–90
freedom 1, 3, 141, 156, 158, 160, 162, 163,
        167n 3, 171
    in American thought 164
    communal entity 165
    and equality 160, 172
    in Greek thought 164–5, 165
    individual liberty 175–6, 240
    and liberty 167n 3
    political freedom 174, 175, 178, 180nn
        43, 44

freedom (*continued*)
  positive and negative freedom 174, 175, 178
  and power problematic 233
  private and public spheres 174, 175, 178
  of speech 172, 177, 178, 251
  *see also eleutheria*
funerals
  ancestral rites 55
  cemeteries 48, 49
  elite funerals 48, 49, 55
  grave goods 49, 56
  intramural burial 48
  of the lower orders 48
  spending on 61

*geitones* 52
Gela 131
Gelon 61, 126, 127, 128, 131, 141, 143
generals 201–2
  arbitrary and/or harsh punishment
    of 144–5, 147, 207
  constitutional power 202
  election 201–2, 207
  military powers 202
  tribal candidates 91, 201–2
Glaukos 29
gods
  epic gods 58
  and justice 34
  *see also* individual deities; religion; sacrifice
Gorgias 134
*graphe paranomon* 98
grave goods 49, 56
Great Man approach to history 96, 114
greed 77
Grote, George 4, 176, 178
  *History of Greece* 4
*gunaikonomos* 289
*gymnasion* 206

Hansen, Mogens Herman 171–82
Harmodius 76, 86, 87, 88, 89, 93–5,
    94 (figure), 217
Hector 29
*hektemoroi* 204
Helen 54
Hellenistic era 2
Hera 18, 55, 56
Heraclea Pontica 2
Hermocrates 124, 137, 138, 145, 146

Herodotus 59, 61, 81, 97, 98, 101, 164
  on Athenian liberation from tyranny 81–6,
    99, 100, 103, 105–6, 107, 114, 115,
    116
  and *demokratia* 117, 121n 15
  *Histories* 81–6, 152–4
  on kingship 153
heroes
  dependence of the community on 54
  obligations 29
heroic code 29
Hesiod 7, 25–7, 33–4, 50, 51, 54, 57, 62,
    286
  egalitarianism 53
  on kingship 26
  *Theogony* 25–6, 34, 43, 52
  *Works and Days* 25–7, 33, 41, 43, 44,
    51–2
*hetaireiai* 98, 107, 206
Hieron of Syracuse 61, 126, 127, 131, 132,
    135, 285
Himera 61, 131
Hipparchus 81, 86–7, 88, 89, 91
*hippeis* 78
Hippias 59, 81, 86, 87, 88, 89, 90, 97, 102,
    115
Hippocrates 83
Hipponax 58
home, protection of the 176–7, 192
Homer 41, 50, 51, 54
  historicity 28, 41
  *Iliad* 7–21, 28–30
  *Odyssey* 7, 21–5, 30–3, 52, 54
  Panhellenization of 54
  political thought 41–2, 43, 44
homicide 78, 189, 191, 215
*homonoia* 48
honor 29, 42, 47, 57, 214, 216, 240
  and hubris 213, 243
hoplite army 32, 35, 36, 166, 206
  arms and armor 56, 166
  non-aristocratic segment 32
household management
  Aristotle on 262–3
  slave labor 269–70
houses 61
*hubris* 211–25
  Alcibiades 196, 221, 222
  aristocratic 52, 54, 58, 214, 215, 241
  Aristotle on 217
  and attacks upon citizens 241

democratization of 215
Demosthenes on 187, 193, 196, 198,
    199, 212, 213, 223, 225, 235, 238, 240
destructive *hubris* 54
and dishonor 240
epic treatment of 54
and honor 213, 243
hubristic assault 239
ideology of 212, 213, 217
legal function 213
prosecutions for 212, 215, 235
pursuance of pleasure 217
rhetoric of 212–14
and wealth 54, 198, 237, 268
Hyperbolos 204, 206
Hypereides 266

Ibycus 57
*Iliad* 7–21, 54
    anti-aristocratic tendency 29–30, 41–2
    battle scenes and parades 32
    political thought 41–2, 43, 44
impiety, acts of 197, 267, 287
Inessa 129, 132
*Instructions of Amenemopet* 53
Isagoras 59, 83, 84, 85, 90, 97, 98, 99, 100,
    103, 106, 107, 109n 7, 115
*isonomia* 59, 114, 117, 152, 153, 172,
    173

Jameson, Michael H. 281–92
juries 3, 141, 197, 199, 200, 207, 220, 235,
    236, 237, 264
    social composition 236
justice 33
    class-based 145
    and communal wellbeing 33
    divine 33, 34
    enforcing 34
    human injustice 33, 34
    *see also* courts; law; lawsuits

Katz, Marilyn 292–309
Kedon 90–1
Kerkyra *see* Corcyra
Khaironeia *see* Chaeronaea
Kimon 204, 205
Kineas 90
kingship 35, 43, 44, 153, 154, 155
    Aristotle on 162
    decline of 35

expansionist kingships 61
    Herodotus on 153
    Hesiod on 26
    Homeric epic and 43, 44
    idealized 26
    irresponsible 27, 30, 34
    king–community relationship 32
    tribal kingship 35
Kleon 203, 204
Knossos 56
Kokalos 134
kraters 56

Lakedaimonios 207
land ownership
    agricultural land 270–1
    aristocratic 36
    redistribution 80, 129, 131
    smaller landholders 35, 36
law
    citizen protection the hallmark of
        democracy 177
    civic control of 53, 55
    Demosthenes' exposition of 189–90, 214
    *isonomia* 59, 114, 117, 152, 153, 172,
        173
    legal penalties 189–90, 214
    *nomos* 53, 164, 167
    and slaves 190, 214, 251, 275, 283
    Solon's reforms 77–8
    *thesmos* 53
lawsuits 206–7
    *Against Meidias* (Demosthenes) 120n 6,
        187–201, 211–31, 235–44
    dispute-settlement 213
    individual vs. community conflicts 232
    narrative strategies of lawtexts 218
    opportunities for self-promotion 206, 207
    political motives 207
    prosecution for *hubris* 212, 215, 235
    witnesses 192–3, 213–14
Leipsudrion 89–90
Leontini 131, 132
Lesbos 57
liberty *see* freedom
liturgies 197–8, 205, 216
Locri 131
lot, selection by 78–9, 91, 234
luxury 55, 60, 61–2, 198, 223
Lydia 60, 61
Lysias 205, 266, 269

magistracies 78–9, 118, 173
  accountability 140
  appointment 78–9, 159, 164
  Aristotle on 159
  property qualifications 119
  prosecution of 177
  Solon's reforms 79
  Syracuse 128, 133
Maiandrios 59
Mantinea 2, 126
Marathon 91
maritime character of Athenian
    democracy 172, 205, 288
marriage 289, 293, 297
Megabyzus 153
Megacles 91
*megaloprepeia* 49, 55, 60
Megara 1–2, 48, 85
Melanthus 82
Menander, *Georgos* 269
Mentor (*Odyssey*) 25, 31, 32
*mesoi* 48, 62
Messana 131, 137
metalwork 49, 56
*methexis* 166
metics 92, 178, 248, 251, 266, 268, 284,
    287, 302, 305
Metiochos 206
*metrioi* 48
middling ideology 46, 47, 48, 51–4, 57,
    58–9, 60, 62, 63
military and patriotic training 205–6
Mimnermus 55, 57
minority rights 164
misogyny 52, 53, 286, 287
mixed constitutions 4
  *see also politeia*
modern democracy 3, 4, 171, 172, 179, 185
monarchy *see* kingship
Morris, Ian 45–68
multiculturalism 159–60
Myron 126
mystery cults 60–1
Mytilene 204

*naukrariai* 79, 91, 101
Naxos 59
Naxus (in Sicily) 131, 132
neighbors 52
Nicias (Nikias) 145, 203, 205, 206, 207,
    209n 17

Ninmah 35
*nomos* 53, 164, 167

Ober, Josiah 95–111, 113, 114–15, 116,
    143, 232–47, 294
Odysseus 19, 20–1, 29, 30, 33, 43, 44
*oikos* 28, 30, 35, 37n 8
  management 262–3, 269–70
  relationship between *polis* and 298
oligarchy 5, 63, 115, 125, 126, 153, 154,
    177
  Aristotle on 158, 159
  collapse of 47
  Sparta 2, 5–6, 177
Olympia 61
oratory 146–7, 232–44
  *Against Meidias* (Demosthenes) 120n 6,
    187–201, 211–31, 235–44
  dialectical give and take 234
  negotiation of democracy through 234–5
  oratory–power relation 232, 234–5, 243,
    244
  *see also* rhetoric
Orientalizing movement 56–7, 60, 66n 67,
    68n 89, 223
Ortygia 131, 133, 135, 136
Osborne, Robin 265–79
ostracism 3, 76, 91–2, 98, 140, 206
  Syracuse 130, 133, 137, 141, 143, 144,
    145
Ostwald, Martin 159–70
Otanes 59, 153, 175

Pandora 34
Paros 56
patriarchy 263, 296, 307n 16
Peisistratid tyranny 76, 81, 82, 83, 85, 86–8,
    90, 93, 118, 121n 20
Peisistratus 76, 81, 91, 101, 110n 19, 117
Peloponnesian War (431–404 BC) 2, 76, 202
Penelope 22, 23, 24, 31–2
Pericles 76, 119, 120n 5, 150n 20, 156–8,
    185–6, 201, 202, 203, 206, 207, 208
  funeral oration 156–8, 172, 249–50, 274
periodization 95, 96
Persia 60, 115
personal outrage, laws concerning 190
petalism 130, 133, 137, 141, 143, 144, 145
phalanx 56, 57
Phalerum 82
Phayllus 133, 144

*philia* 42, 48
Philip of Macedon 204
Philo of Alexandria 301
*philotimia* 240
Phleious 2
Phocion 286
Phocylides 51, 53, 55, 58, 62
phratries 115, 119, 204, 207
Pindar 60, 133
pious deeds 60, 61
Pittacus 67n 77
Plataea 61, 301, 303, 308n 28
Plato
   *Laws* 270, 282, 287
   *Republic* 43, 267, 282, 287, 295, 300
   on women 282, 287, 300
pleasure, pursuance of 217
Plutarch 145, 202, 207, 209, 286
poetry
   advice-poetry 52
   *ainos* poetry 53, 61
   Archaic period 47, 49–51
   elegy and iambus 51, 53
   elite sympotic poetry 54, 57
   elitist tradition 51, 54–5, 57, 58
   emergence of individual poets 50
   epinician tradition 59–60, 61
   heroic model 54–5, 57
   hexameter poetry 51, 53
   lyric poetry 51
   middling poetry 51, 55, 57, 58
   oral poetry 49
   source problems 47, 49–51
   *topoi* 50–1, 52
   Ur-poets 50
   *see also* epics
*polis* 35, 36, 43, 58, 175
   Aristotle on 306
   community of defense 37n 8
   in Homer 30
   relationship between *oikos* and 298
   socio-economic and cultural aspects 304
*politeia* 125, 136, 142, 143, 149n 15, 162,
   164, 166, 304
   Aristotle on 125–6, 136, 143, 149n 15
   Syracuse 125–6, 136, 142
political thought, emergence and
   development of 7–68
Polyaenus 137
Polycrates 44
*polykoiranie* 30

Polyzalos 131
the poor 158, 283–4, 285
   attitudes towards 52, 53–4, 58
   communal responsibility for 34
   free poor 285, 289, 293–4
   in the *Odyssey* 32–3
   political participation 3, 220, 250–1
   poor women 288
   poverty–democracy link 145, 158, 173,
      250, 286, 304
population growth 35
pottery 49, 56–7
power
   coercion paradigm 232–3, 235, 244n 2
   collective resistance to 241
   definition 232
   discourse paradigm 233–4
   early Greek attitudes towards 8, 26
   individual vs. social power 235, 240, 241,
      243, 244
   of the masses 30, 185, 232, 241, 244
   oratory–power relation 232, 234–5, 243,
      244
   state as primary locus of 233
Praxiteles of Mantinea 134n 1
priests 60–1
*Prolegomena* 146
Prometheus 34–5
property, redistribution of 177
property classes 78, 166
property qualifications 3, 78, 118, 119, 140,
   165, 185
Protagoras 274
protection of person, home, and
   property 176–7, 192
*Protests of the Eloquent Peasant* 53
Pseudo-Xenophon ("The Old
   Oligarch") 145, 250–1, 283, 284, 285,
   286, 287, 288
public assemblies 1, 3, 4, 78, 98, 140, 145,
   212, 250
   anarchic potential 208, 209
   attendance numbers 202
   policy making 208
   pre-assembly council discussions 3,
      202–3
   proposals and decrees 202, 203, 204,
      207–8
   punitive actions 145
   speech and authority in Homeric
      assemblies 7–25

public assemblies (*continued*)
  Syracuse 123–5
  witnessing function 32
public choruses 188–9, 197, 198, 200, 205,
    216, 217, 219, 220, 235
public office 1, 3, 158–9, 185, 264
  access to 164, 165, 274, 275
  accountability 3
  archons 78, 79, 91, 93, 105, 177, 185
  cavalry service 78, 166
  election to 3, 204
  eligibility for 163, 165
  liturgies 197–8, 205, 216
  payment for 3, 118, 141, 148n 7, 159,
    234, 273
  property qualification 3, 78, 119, 165,
    185
  treasurers 78, 79, 166
  working days occupied by 304, 305
  *see also* magistracies
public and private spheres 174, 175, 178,
    234, 298–9
Pylos 203
Pythoness 82

Raaflaub, Kurt A. 28–38, 41
religion
  American 167
  Eastern practices 56
  elite religion 56, 289
  festivals 205, 304–5
  liturgies 197–8, 205, 216
  part of civic order 167
  women's duties 248, 304–5
  *see also* sacrifice; votive offerings
revolutionary speech acts 104–5, 106
rhetoric 3, 130, 134, 146, 203
  abusive civic rhetoric 223–5
  barbarian vs. Greek opposition 223
  of the collective 219
  "everybody knows" topos 238, 246n 26
  hubristic 212–14
  self-presentation 236
  *see also* oratory
Rhodes 3
Rhodes, P. J. 201–10
rioting
  Athens (508/7 BC) 96, 102–4, 106, 107,
    116
  historical assessment of 106–7
Robinson, Eric W. 75, 121n 19, 140–51

Rome 3, 4

sacrifice 48
  Aristotle on 49
  expense of 49
  rituals in chiefs' houses 48, 49
  sacrificial space 49
  sanctuaries 49, 55
Salamis 61, 126
Samons, Loren J. 113–22
Samos 57, 59
sanctuaries 49, 55, 57
Sappho 55, 57, 60
Sardis 57
Sarpedon 29
scapegoat complex 196, 222
*seisachtheia* 78, 80, 177
self-determination 174, 175, 177, 178
self-restraint 174, 175
Selinus 131
Semonides of Amorgos 286
Seven Sages 36
Sicily 2, 59, 131–5
  Deinomenid epicracy, dissolution of 131
  enfranchisement of foreigners and
    mercenaries 128, 135, 141, 143
  land redistribution 129, 131
  republican city states 131–2
  revolution 135–8
  *see also* Syracuse
Sicyon 2
silver mining 268–9, 272, 276
Simonides 61, 89
Skamandrios 29
slaves 158, 173, 265–79, 282
  agricultural work 270, 271
  aristocratic preference for 265–6
  Aristotle on 262–3, 275
  Athenian slave population 266, 269
  chattel slavery 262–3, 267, 282, 289
  class of slave owners 267–8
  craft activity 265–6, 268, 269, 272–3, 274
  dependence on 275, 276
  domestic work 269–70
  economics and politics of 265–79
  and *eleutheria* 178
  enfranchisement 80–1, 248, 286, 302
  exclusion from political rights 3, 248
  extent of domestic ownership 266–7
  free ways of 283, 284
  the law and 190, 214, 251, 275, 283

procurement 284, 285
prosperous slaves 251, 284
revolts 137, 285
Sparta 251
United States 162, 276
women 269–70
social mobility 36
Socrates 44, 265, 273, 287
Sogenes of Aegina 60
Solon 36, 53, 54, 58, 62, 76, 77–81, 96,
    101, 114, 117, 287
  political poetry 77, 80–1
  reforms 76, 77–81, 91, 98, 119, 166, 204
Sophilos 191, 215, 238–9
Sophocles 216
Sophron 134
sovereignty 3, 105, 140, 233
Sparta 4, 59, 85, 176, 276
  age classes 205
  military intervention in Athens 76, 82,
    83–4, 85, 89, 90, 97, 99–100, 101
  oligarchy 2, 5–6, 177
  slaves 251
  women 282
speech-act theory 113, 114, 116, 117
sport and athletics 57, 58
  combat sports 216
  elite conflicts and expenditure 35, 57, 196,
    205
  outlet for competitive impulses 216
  victory odes 59–60
Straton of Phaleron 192–3, 220, 221, 239,
    240, 243, 246n 28
sumptuary laws 289
symposia 56, 57, 206, 213
Syracuse 2, 61, 123–51
  civil strife 128–30, 132–3, 136–7
  constitutional reforms 128, 133, 139n 22,
    141
  culture 134, 137
  demagoguery 140, 145, 146, 147
  democracy 132–4, 140–51
  demos 140, 142, 143, 144,
    145, 147
  Diodorus' account of 126–30
  "General Settlement" 137
  growth and importance 133, 137
  magistracies 128, 133
  mercenary-citizens 128, 135, 141, 143
  "old" and "new" citizens 131, 132–3,
    136–7

petalism (ostracism) 130, 133, 137, 141,
    143, 144, 145
pioneers of rhetorical theory 146–7
politea 125–6, 136, 142
popular assemblies 123–5
populist ideology 144, 145, 147
post-tyrannical polis 133–4, 136–7, 141,
    142
republican Syracuse 132–3
revolt against tyranny 127–8, 131, 135–6,
    141, 142
tabooed language 218, 239
taxation 198, 232, 238
Telemachos 21, 22–4, 25, 30–1, 32
Telesilla 301
Temenites 133
temples 49, 62, 81–2
Teos 57
Thebes 2
Themistocles 206
Theognis 50, 51, 53, 58, 62
Theophrastus 234, 269
Theramenes 286
Thersites 19–20, 29–30, 44
Theseus 154–5, 175
thesmos 53
Thessaly 49, 59, 82
Thettalos 89
Thrasybulus 126, 127–8, 131, 135, 136,
    141, 148n 2
Thucydides 86, 97, 123, 132, 133, 141,
    145, 175, 201, 204, 205, 207
  History of the Peloponnesian War 86–8,
    123–5, 156–8, 185–6, 201, 202, 249–50
  on the Peisistratid tyranny 86–8
  on Pericles 185–6, 201, 208–9
  on Syracuse 142, 144, 146, 150n 21
Timarkhos 266, 272
Tisias of Syracuse 134, 147
torture 176
trade 36
tradition, negotiation of 50
tragedy, Athenian 61
treasurers 78, 79
tribal assemblies 118
tribal system 78–9, 83, 91, 118–19
trierarchs 205
tripods 55–6
Trojan War 7
Tyche 127, 133

Tyndarides 129–30, 133, 137, 141, 148n 6
tyranny 58, 115, 118, 119, 155, 173, 177,
    222–3
  Aristotle on 126
  characteristic behavior 223
  Peisistratid tyranny 76, 81, 82, 83, 86–8,
    90, 93, 97, 118, 121n 20
  Syracuse 127–8, 131, 135–6, 142
Tyrtaeus 57

United States 4
  citizenship 159–65
  Declaration of Independence 159, 160–1,
    163, 164, 165, 167n 3
  Fourteenth Amendment 161–2, 163–4,
    165
  franchise 308n 34
  revolution 178
utilitarianism 178

violence, coercive 233
voting practices 3, 78–9, 91, 234
votive offerings 49, 55–6, 62
  lavish offerings 55, 62
  Oriental 56, 57
  state offerings 62
  tripods 55–6

warfare
  archaic Athenian military actions 101
  aristocratic leaders 101
  heroic warfare 54–5
  neighborhood conflicts 35
  political and moral problems 34
  women and 300–1
warrior-aristocracy 41
wealth 3, 60
  and anti-democratic attitudes 237
  distribution 304
  and dominance 63, 237, 241
  and greed 77
  and *hubris* 54, 198, 237, 268
  individual vs. community conflicts 232
  liturgies, expenditure on 205, 220
  luxury culture 55, 60, 61–2, 198, 223
  political eminence, correlation with 220
  precondition for the middling life 53, 54
  and vulgar display 238
weights and measures 79
wet-nurses 269
Wilson, Peter J. 211–31

women 281–309
  access to legal remedies 305
  alleged freedom under democracy 282,
    288
  anxiety over freedom of 282–3, 284–5,
    286, 289
  Aristotle on 263
  *The Assemblywomen*
    (Aristophanes) 251–61
  and contagion 287
  domestic work 269–70, 273
  domesticity 297, 298, 299
  education 297
  exclusion from political rights 3, 162, 248,
    282, 292–3, 294–5, 299–300, 302–3,
    306, 307
  foreign women 287
  and inheritance 301
  legal and economic rights 289
  marriage 289, 293, 297
  misogyny 52, 53, 286, 287
  and patriarchal authority 263, 296
  Plato on 282, 287, 300
  poor women 288
  prosecutions for impiety 287
  relation to the *polis* 298
  religious duties 248, 304–5
  separate spheres ideology 293–4,
    295–300
  social life 297
  Spartan women 282
  standards of respectable women 249, 282,
    287–8, 307n
  status 297–8
  subordination 263, 282, 289, 296–7,
    299
  supposed dominance in the house 284,
    288
  US citizenship 162
  and warfare 300–1

Xanthippus 92
Xenophanes 58, 62
Xenophon 250, 269, 283
  *Memorabilia* 265
  *Oikonomikos* 269, 270, 273, 279n 48,
    288, 305

*zen hos bouletai tis* 173, 174, 175
Zeus 26, 27, 33, 34, 42, 43–4, 59, 128
Zeus Eleutherios 136, 141, 173